MW01038268

ROCK CLIMBING
WASHINGTON

Third Edition

Jeff Smoot

GUILFORD, CONNECTICUT

FALCONGUIDES®

An imprint of The Rowman & Littlefield Publishing Group, Inc.
4501 Forbes Blvd., Ste. 200
Lanham, MD 20706
www.rowman.com
Falcon and FalconGuides are registered trademarks and Make Adventure Your Story is a
trademark of The Rowman & Littlefield Publishing Group, Inc.

Distributed by NATIONAL BOOK NETWORK

Copyright © 2019 Jeff Smoot

Photos by Jeff Smoot unless otherwise noted.
Maps by The Rowman & Littlefield Publishing Group, Inc.

All rights reserved. No part of this book may be reproduced in any form or by any electronic
or mechanical means, including information storage and retrieval systems, without written
permission from the publisher, except by a reviewer who may quote passages in a review.

British Library Cataloguing in Publication Information available

Library of Congress Cataloging-in-Publication Data available

ISBN 978-1-4930-3941-8 (paperback)
ISBN 978-1-4930-3942-5 (e-book)

∞™ The paper used in this publication meets the minimum requirements of American
National Standard for Information Sciences—Permanence of Paper for Printed Library
Materials, ANSI/NISO Z39.48-1992.

Printed in the United States of America

The author and The Rowman & Littlefield Publishing Group, Inc., assume no liability for
accidents happening to, or injuries sustained by, readers who engage in the activities described
in this book.

WARNING:

**Climbing is a sport where you may be seriously injured or die.
Read this before you use this book.**

This guidebook is a compilation of unverified information gathered from many different climbers. The author cannot assure the accuracy of any of the information in this book, including the topos and route descriptions, the difficulty ratings, and the protection ratings. These may be incorrect or misleading, as ratings of climbing difficulty and danger are always subjective and depend on the physical characteristics (for example, height), experience, technical ability, confidence, and physical fitness of the climber who supplied the rating. Additionally, climbers who achieve first ascents sometimes underrate the difficulty or danger of the climbing route. Therefore, be warned that you must exercise your own judgment on where a climbing route goes, its difficulty, and your ability to safely protect yourself from the risks of rock climbing. Examples of some of these risks are: falling due to technical difficulty or due to natural hazards such as holds breaking, falling rock, climbing equipment dropped by other climbers, hazards of weather and lightning, your own equipment failure, and failure or absence of fixed protection.

You should not depend on any information gleaned from this book for your personal safety; your safety depends on your own good judgment, based on experience and a realistic assessment of your climbing ability. If you have any doubt as to your ability to safely climb a route described in this book, do not attempt it.

The following are some ways to make your use of this book safer:

1. Consultation: You should consult with other climbers about the difficulty and danger of a particular route prior to attempting it. Most local climbers are glad to give advice on routes in their area; we suggest that you contact locals to confirm ratings and safety of particular routes and to obtain first-hand information about a route chosen from this book.

2. Instruction: Most climbing areas have local climbing instructors and guides available. We recommend that you engage an instructor or guide to learn safety techniques and to become familiar with the routes and hazards of the areas described in this book. Even after you are proficient in climbing safely, occasional use of a guide is a safe way to raise your climbing standard and learn advanced techniques.

3. Fixed Protection: Some of the routes in this book may use bolts and pitons that are fixed in place in the rock. Because of variances in the manner of placement, weathering, metal fatigue, the quality of the metal used, and many other factors, these fixed protection pieces should always be considered suspect and should be backed up when possible by equipment that you place yourself. Never depend on a single piece of fixed protection for your safety, because you never can tell whether it will hold weight. In some cases, fixed protection may have been removed or is now missing. However, climbers should not add new pieces of fixed protection unless existing protection is faulty. Existing fixed protection can be tested by an experienced climber and its strength determined. Climbers should never add bolts or drilled pitons to an existing route. They should climb the route as equipped by the first ascent party or choose a route more within their ability—a route to which they do not have to add additional fixed anchors.

Be aware of the following specific potential hazards that could arise in using this book:

1. Incorrect Descriptions of Routes: If you climb a route and you have a doubt as to where it goes, you should not continue unless you are sure that you can go that way safely. Route descriptions and topos in this book could be inaccurate or misleading.

2. Incorrect Difficulty Rating: A route might be more difficult than the rating indicates. Do not be lulled into a false sense of security by the difficulty rating.

3. Incorrect Protection Rating: If you climb a route and you are unable to arrange adequate protection from the risk of falling through the use of fixed pitons or bolts and by placing your own protection devices, do not assume that there is adequate protection available higher just because the route protection rating indicates the route does not have an X or an R rating. Every route is potentially an X (a fall may be deadly), due to the inherent hazards of climbing—including, for example, failure or absence of fixed protection, your own equipment's failure, faulty protection placement, or improper use of climbing equipment.

4. Failure to Warn of a Particular Hazard: Although an effort has been made to warn of known hazards on particular routes, this guide does not warn of every hazard that exists on every route. Climb carefully and be watchful for potential hazards.

There are no warranties, whether expressed or implied, that this guidebook is accurate or that the information contained in it is reliable. There are no warranties of fitness for a particular purpose or that this guide is merchantable. Your use of this book indicates your assumption of the risk that it may contain errors and is an acknowledgment of your own sole responsibility for your climbing safety.

CONTENTS

Overview

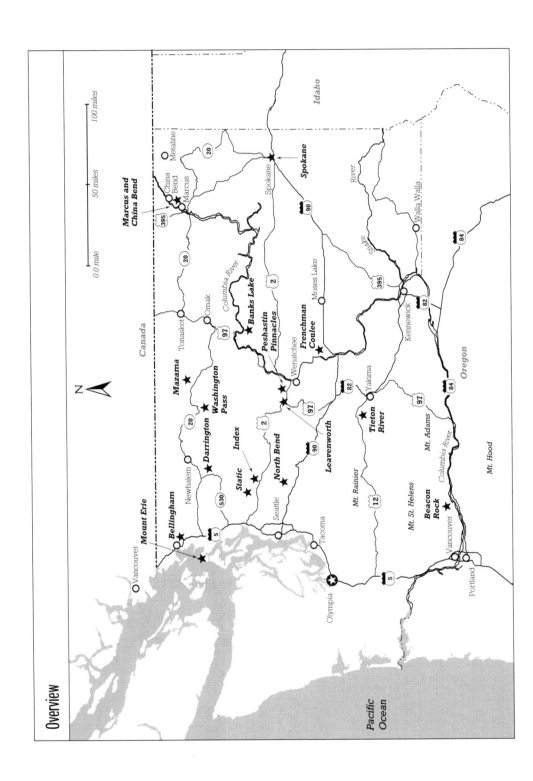

PREFACE

The variety of rock climbing opportunities in Washington is impressive, to say the least. The Index Town Walls are reminiscent of Yosemite's finest cliffs, only better, with a preponderance of thin, vertical crack routes and unlikely face and friction climbs. Leavenworth offers nearly every kind of climbing imaginable, from steep granite face and friction routes to sandstone slabs, and all manner of cracks, thin and wide, long and short, steep and overhanging. Darrington has knobby slabs galore, plus some long free routes and a few big wall–type aid climbs. Static Point has many long, runout friction routes on smooth granite slabs, reminiscent of Yosemite's Glacier Point Apron. Mount Erie offers a variety of easy, accessible face and crack climbs, while Little Si and Exit 38 offer sport climbing close to the urban and suburban sprawl of Puget Sound. Vantage and Tieton River Canyon have hundreds of crack and face routes on basalt and andesite rimrock. Washington Pass offers alpine rock at its finest, while nearby Mazama has a dozens of sport climbs, short and long, and promise of dozens more. The Spokane areas feature a variety of face and crack routes and some newly developed sport crags. New crags are being discovered and developed every year. There is something for everyone on Washington rock. Enjoy it all!

With so many new routes established on crags across the region each year, publishing a comprehensive guide including all of the routes in Washington state would be nearly impossible, and would cost so much to compile and print that nobody would be able to afford it. The point of publishing a complete catalog of all routes is lost on the majority of climbers when there are dozens of routes at every area that are rarely if ever climbed, whether because of dirt, moss, lichen, loose rock, access issues, approach difficulties, poor protection, or just plain unpleasant climbing, and where every area has its own guide. Take Index Town Walls, for example, where probably less than half of the existing routes have actually been climbed more than a few times in the past decade. Granted, it might be nice to have a guide point out the bad routes so you wouldn't waste your time or risk your life on them, but that's not traditionally what climbing guides are for—they're supposed to show you which routes are which and direct you to the routes you might actually want to climb.

In that spirit, this remains a "select" guide to the best and most popular routes in Washington state. Some will criticize this guide, whether for its selection of routes or because it isn't comprehensive. As for route selection, the guide is broad in scope, including as many good quality routes from as many areas as possible. And certainly, comprehensive guides will continue to be published for each area, and this guide is not intended to replace those guides. It is hoped that this guide, by providing a broad selection of routes throughout the state and weeding out the lesser quality and just plain awful routes, will be a lasting resource for climbers of all levels of experience and ability, and will help to spread climbers out and alleviate overcrowding at the more-popular areas.

The current update includes some new crags and areas (perhaps not new to all climbers in the state but new to this guidebook), in addition to "cleaning up" some areas and adding new routes or variations of others. Smaller local and regional guidebooks will continue to bridge the gap for those seeking every detail of every route at any given area.

ACKNOWLEDGMENTS

Writing a guidebook of this scope and breadth would be impossible without the help of others. It is impossible to name everyone who ever gave me route information, opined about ratings, drew me a topo, showed me a photo, belayed me up an obscure route, or criticized the business of guidebook writing as the reason for overcrowding or environmental destruction at their favorite crags. Everyone's comments and criticisms were helpful, if not always constructive, and I apologize to those not named here who assisted in their way with the compilation of this guide.

I extend my sincere appreciation to those who provided assistance in preparation of this guide and its predecessors, including Matt Arksey, Ken Beane, Don Brooks, Garth Bruce, Bryan Burdo, Bill Centinari, Sean Courage, Darryl Cramer, Greg Collum, Chandler Davis, Paul Fish, Andy Fitz, Cal Folsom, Marlene Ford, Ben Gilkison, Brittany Goris, Chris Greyell, Mark Gunlogson, Peter Gunstone, Beth Harman, Eli Helmuth, Jason Henrie, Mathias Holladay, Ryan Hoover, Mack Johnston, Tim Keigly, Jeff Kelly, Larry Kemp, Matt Kerns, Dallas Kloke, Mark Kroese, Cliff Leight, Dan Lepeska, Daniil Magdalin, Mike Massey, Brendan McMahan, Ron Miller, Ed Mosshart, Tim Nelson, Per Nesselquist, Nick O'Connell, Michael Orr, Matt Perkins, Eric Ponslet and Lucie Parietti, Nic Plemel, Bill Robins, Michael Rynkiewicz, Andrew Sell, Russ Schultz, Jim Speaker, Matt Stanley, Michael Stanton, Charlie Voorhis, David Whitelaw, Leland Windham, Forest Woodward, and Jim Yoder. Thanks to production editor Kristen Mellitt and cartographer Melissa Baker for their assistance with this edition. My apologies to competing guidebook authors for encroaching on "their" territory, and thanks to those who showed me around their crags or shared route information with me. Special thanks to all the climbers whose pioneering spirit and hard work has led to the establishment of and preservation of access to the many routes included in this guide. Keep up the good work! As always, thanks to my loved ones for their enduring patience, and to my parents for letting me run wild in the mountains during my youth.

Anyone with new route information, comments on routes and ratings, better topos or photos, or who wants to correct first ascent information or other misinformation or disinformation contained in this guide, is encouraged to pass it along to me to help improve future editions.

Kevon Shea on Poison Ivy Crack (5.9), Icicle Creek Canyon

INTRODUCTION

HOW TO USE THIS GUIDE

This guide is designed with two primary goals: first to get climbers to the crags, then to help them identify the routes. Access information is conveyed by written descriptions of trails, scrambles, etc., and by maps corresponding to the written descriptions. Hopefully access and approach information in this guide is detailed enough so that nobody will get lost on the approach or wonder how to get down off a route. A mix of photos and topos is used to show route location and details. In addition to photo overlays and topos, brief written route descriptions are provided for each route, hopefully providing enough detail to help you locate the routes and avoid nasty surprises where possible without completely spoiling your effort to onsight a given route.

The layout of this guide may occasionally seem confusing to newcomers to a given area. At some areas, routes are described in the traditional left-to-right format, but routes in other areas are described in the order they are encountered as you approach them. In some cases, this means routes may be described in one direction, then another, starting from where the access trail reaches the cliff. In other cases, a route that is approached via another route may be described immediately following the approach route, even though it is not the next route in order on the crag. The purpose of using this format is to merge route approaches and route descriptions in an intuitive manner so users of this guide can easily approach and locate the routes.

In this guide, directions given assume you are facing the rock, unless otherwise stated. Directions may seem confusing when you are approaching a cliff from above. Wherever this confusion may arise, a compass direction is provided. Most of the maps are oriented with north pointing up, but all maps include a directional arrow pointing more or less northward.

RATINGS

Most climbers will begin using pitons for protection at 5.0. An easy class 5 climb, for a competent rock climber, will be rated at 5.0 or 5.1. Difficulty increases to 5.9, which is a climb of exceptional severity, with 5.10 being the ultimate difficulty possible.

—Fred Beckey, 1965

The ubiquitous and venerable "Yosemite Decimal System" (actually the Tahquitz Decimal System, but nobody seems to care) is used in this guide. It should require no explanation for those with any rock climbing experience. Those who aren't familiar with this system probably should take a climbing instruction course and learn more about climbing techniques and dangers before heading for the crags.

To summarize, Class 1 and 2 are easy off-trail scrambling where risk of falling is low although a fall could still cause injury or death. Class 3 is exposed, rocky scrambling that is easy, but where a fall would probably be fatal. Class 4 is basically difficult Class 3, where a rope is used to belay. Class 5 is technical rock climbing where a leader places intermediate protection to reduce the length of possible and sometimes imminent falls. Class 5 ratings are subdivided into decimal subdivisions, where 5.0 is the easiest and 5.15 is presently the hardest. From

5.10 up, ratings have been further subdivided into letter grades "a" through "d," with a 5.10a being just harder than 5.9 and 5.10d being almost 5.11. In an effort to keep topos uncluttered, in this guide the initial Class 5 designation has been left out of the rating; thus, a 5.10d route will usually show up as ".10d" on topos and photos.

A word of caution is in order with respect to letter grades: They are not always absolutely accurate and are constantly the subject of debate among climbers. Ideally, routes are rated based upon a consensus among climbers who have done them, but personal bias often distorts the actual rating. Climbers usually agree about whether a given route is 5.10 or 5.11, but may argue forever over whether a route is 5.10b or 5.10c. Given that ratings are not absolute, think of a 5.10a or b as an easier 5.10 and a 5.10c or d as a harder 5.10 and so on. Just don't fall into the trap of thinking every rating in this guide is absolute, as it is simply impossible to give any route an exact rating when nearly every climber has a different opinion of how hard a given route seems.

This guide tries to rate routes based on what an on-sight leader would think rather than what someone might think after they had climbed the route a few times. This may sometimes increase the historical rating of a given route, but it is hoped this will provide a more accurate "what-to-expect" rating rather than an "I've-got-it-wired" rating. This guide also attempts to bring some conformity to ratings throughout the state.

Holds have been known to break off, changing ratings for better or for worse. Thus, be prepared for anything on every route. Just because a route is rated 5.10a in this guide doesn't mean it isn't harder because a key hold broke off, or easier because a thin flake pulled off to leave a good edge.

The Yosemite Roman numeral grading system is used for routes longer than one or two pitches. Under this system, a Grade I should take an hour or two at most; Grade II should take only a few hours; Grade III half a day; Grade IV most of a day; Grade V all day or overnight; and Grade VI two days or more for just the climbing, not counting approach and descent. On Grade IV and V routes, experienced parties may be able to finish the route and descend in a day (or even a few hours!), but most climbers should be prepared for the likelihood of a bivouac. Grade I climbs are not noted as such in this guide, only Grade II and above. Any route of one or two pitches is probably Grade I; routes of three or more pitches start moving into the Grade II area. Some climbers have managed two or three Grade IIIs in a day, while others have been observed having a Grade VI experience on a Grade III route, so be aware that this is a subjective system, and your actual climbing experience may vary depending upon several factors, usually weather, fitness, and experience.

Quality Ratings

The following quality ratings are included in this guide to let climbers know which routes are deservedly more popular than others:

⊖   Not recommended; worse than no stars
★   A good route; worth climbing
★★   A very good route; recommended
★★★   An excellent route; highly recommended
★★★★ A classic, must-do route

Keep in mind this is a subjective system of relative quality; just because a route does not have any stars doesn't necessarily mean it is not worth climbing. An attempt has been made to bring some conformity to quality ratings throughout the state, so a two-star route in the Tieton will seem as good as a two-star route at Mazama, Little Si, or Minnehaha. Routes with no stars aren't necessarily bad, but they aren't necessarily good, either. Only routes with a ⊖ are deemed unworthy, due to loose rock, dirt, vegetation, or simply due to unpleasant climbing. But if that's your thing, go for it!

Seriousness Ratings

Most routes have adequate protection, whether in the form of bolts and fixed pins, or cracks and pockets in which protection devices can be placed, which means there is enough available natural or fixed protection on most routes to keep you from hitting the ground if you fall off. However, there are some routes that have little or no protection, or have very poor protection or pass loose rock, where a fall would likely lead to injury or death. Routes with protection difficulties, serious runouts, or other unavoidable hazards will be designated using the system introduced by Jim Erickson in his *Boulder Climbing Guide* (1980), as follows:

PD Protection difficult: although adequate, protection may be difficult to place or a little too far apart for comfort.

R Difficult climbing is poorly protected: a fall from difficult climbing will likely result in injury.

X Difficult climbing is unprotected: a fall from difficult climbing will certainly result in serious injury or death.

In this guide, the "protection difficult" designation (PD in most guides, PG or PG-13 in others) is assumed on all routes. Placing reliable protection is inherently challenging, and failure to properly place protection can lead to an injurious or fatal fall on any route. If protection is so manky that it seems sure to pull out no matter how well you place it, or if it's so hard to place that some climbers opt for running it out, an R rating seems justified. A route with an R rating may have long runouts above good protection, short runouts above poor protection, unavoidable loose rock, or exposure to other objective hazards where you stand a better than average chance of being rushed to the hospital or possibly killed if you fall off at the crux or on a difficult move. A route with an X rating is likely to have no reliable protection or dangerously loose rock or other hazards, where a fall from the crux or a difficult move will almost certainly send you to the emergency room or worse. When you climb an X-rated route, you are literally taking your life in your hands. Such routes are best toproped or avoided.

Keep in mind that all routes have serious fall potential, particularly if you don't have the right gear, don't place it correctly, climb beyond your ability, or climb unroped. Even short falls with good protection can be fatal or result in serious injury if you hit something on the way down. Routes having an R or X rating are those that are known to have unavoidable dangers. Absence of an R or X does not mean a route is not serious, only that those who have climbed it have not reported any significantly unprotected or dangerous climbing. Every route should be considered serious, regardless of the protection. Be careful!

Lucie Parietti on the Bear Hug pitch (5.8), *Southwest Rib,* South Early Winters Spire, Washington Pass. ERIC PONSLET & LUCIE PARIETTI, WWW.ERICANDLUCIE.COM

A note on seriousness ratings: Some routes have well-protected crux moves, but have long runouts on easier ground. For example, on *Steel Pulse* at Index, the 5.10c crux is well protected, but the second pitch includes an 80-foot runout on easy Class 5. Thus the route is quite serious, since if you lose your balance or slip at the top of the easy section, you could fall 160 feet! But an R rating for that route seems heavy-handed, since the difficult climbing is well protected and as one climber callously opined, "Anybody who falls off the easy part deserves to die." Keep in mind the fact that many routes have long runouts on easy sections and those routes may not have an R or X rating. Also keep this in mind: Many a fatal fall has occurred on easy ground, so use great care when it's runout, even when it's easy.

Regardless of the seriousness ratings given in this guide, when climbing you must always proceed with due caution, a reasonable regard for your safety, and at your own risk. When in doubt about a route's safety or your ability to safely climb it, back off.

CLIMBING SAFETY

Inexperience is one of the leading contributing factors in serious climbing accidents. While this guide offers a few safety tips that may be of use to inexperienced and experienced climbers alike, be aware that this is not a climbing instruction book. Don't rely on these tips as a complete discourse on climbing safety. This guide does not tell you how to tie knots, place gear, belay, rappel, or do anything else other than how to locate and identify the routes. This is a guide to the rocks, not how to climb them. If you don't have climbing experience, seek professional help! Hire a climbing guide or instructor and learn the fundamentals before you injure or kill yourself or your climbing partner. Then practice, practice, practice, practice!

Most climbing dangers can be minimized by following some simple rules: climb within your limits; never lead too far above protection; make sure protection is well placed before climbing on; double-check knots, harnesses, gear, and rappel setups before and during your climb; back up questionable gear or anchors; stay away from loose rock; and wear a helmet. Of course, even if you exercise perfect judgment, you can still be injured or killed. Even short falls can be fatal, and even experienced climbers sometimes screw up.

Watch out for old bolts and poorly placed fixed pins. There are still numerous routes sporting rusty and bent 0.25-inch bolts and even more routes with rusty or loose fixed pins. Also watch out for bolts with loose hangers ("spinners") and mangled, broken fixed pins, which are difficult to clip and not entirely trustworthy. Also be aware that even relatively new bolts sometimes break or fail, and fixed pins become loose or damaged over time. Check fixed protection carefully before you rely on it. If you have any doubts, replace it or back it up.

Although a conscientious effort was made to accurately portray the number and location of bolts and fixed gear, there are so damn many of them now it's impossible to be completely accurate. Errors will no doubt occur, whether by showing a bolt that isn't really there or by not showing a bolt that is there. As a general rule, you should trust this guide only as far as you can throw it. If you can't see a bolt or fixed pin, don't assume it is there even if this guide shows it. Bolts and fixed pins shown in this guide may have been removed or relocated since publication, or someone may have sandbagged the author into believing a bolt or pin is there when in fact it isn't. Frost wedges pitons out of cracks, bolt hangers are sometimes stolen, and occasionally an offensive bolt is chopped. The latter hasn't been much of an issue here as it has been in other ethical hotbeds, but it still happens.

A great many climbing accidents occur on the way down, so take care where and how you descend. On most routes, descents are simple walk-offs, lower-offs, or one-pitch rappels, but on longer routes, where multiple rappels and rocky, brushy ledges and gullies are the norm, be extra cautious. On such descents, it may be foolish to descend after dark or during a storm. A forced bivouac may be uncomfortable, but it sure beats rappelling off the end of your rope or slipping on wet or loose rock in the dark. Be prepared for changes in weather and, at a minimum, carry extra food, water, rain gear, and a flashlight. An unplanned bivouac needn't be unpleasant, after all.

Many descents are via lowering or rappelling from trees or anchors; however, always know your descent route before attempting a climb, and check your rappel setup, harness, and anchors before committing to a rappel or lowering off.

Many avoidable deaths and injuries have resulted from poor communication and practice while descending. Some climbers have tried simultaneous rappels (two climbers rappelling on opposite ends of the same rope) to save time, with disastrous results. Some have tried to lower off routes using a rope that is too short, finding out the hard way that their belayer did not use an end knot. Others have been dropped when their belayers have taken them off belay, mistaking "lower me off" for "take me off." And, of course, some have rappelled off the ends of their ropes, having failed to tie a backup knot, assuming incorrectly the ropes would reach the ground or the next anchors.

Wear a helmet to protect against falling rock and dropped equipment, and to protect your head during a fall. Climbers have suffered fatal head injuries while rappelling from roadside crags, and spontaneous and climber-caused rockfall are not uncommon at most areas covered in this guide, and climbers frequently drop gear, which can be just as dangerous. Given the predominance of climbers taking selfies while climbing these days, you should wear a helmet whenever climbers are above you to avoid becoming the inevitable first selfie-inflicted climbing casualty.

There has been an increasing trend of climbers bringing their kids and dogs along to the crags, which has created safety issues. If you bring kids to the crags, keep them out from under climbers and away from the base of the cliff to protect them from getting hit by dropped gear or rock (or the occasional falling climber). Put helmets on them for the sake of safety. If you bring your dog to the crag, keep it leashed and tied out of the way of other climbers. Your dog may be friendly, but not everyone likes dogs, especially dogs running loose and sticking their noses in other people's business while they're trying to tie in or belay. If your dog bites or is not well behaved, leave it at home.

Reading *Accidents in North American Climbing* can give you a real insight into the causes of climbing accidents and help you avoid those situations. Above all, think about each climbing situation as though your life depends on it, because when you think about it, it really does.

OTHER HAZARDS

In addition to the dangers inherent to climbing, many other potential hazards await you both on and off of Washington's many crags. Each chapter briefly identifies known hazards particular to that area, which are discussed in detail here. This is not a complete listing of all potential hazards, only of those that are common. Other localized hazards are mentioned in the appropriate chapter of the guide.

In western Washington, there are relatively few hazards other than those directly related to climbing. During late summer, yellow jackets and other stinging insects can get nasty, and the dank woods are often infested with mosquitoes and biting flies. Bats and other critters can be found in cracks; territorial owls may swoop in on you from the trees. Bears and cougars, though rarely seen, may be encountered and might even attack; a recent fatal cougar encounter serves as a reminder that wild animals can be dangerous. More likely, you will encounter meth heads and petty criminals prowling the woods and parking lots, and drunken idiots randomly shooting up in the woods. You might also encounter hunters during hunting seasons, although they are rarer on the west side than the east side. Wooden infrastructure such as stairs, ramps, and bridges tends to rot. Boulders and trails may be slippery when wet. Slugs may slime up the holds.

In eastern Washington, you may encounter a plethora of non-climbing hazards. Ticks and rattlesnakes head the list of nasty critters, and yellow jackets are particularly vigorous at some crags. Bears, cougars, bats, and owls are present in most eastern Washington areas, and are more frequently encountered as climbers invade more of their territory. Mountain goats are often encountered on higher-elevation walls and alpine routes. Grizzly bears reside in the North Cascades and have supposedly been spotted as far south as Cle Elum and Mount Rainier, although they are very rarely encountered by climbers. Efforts to introduce more grizzlies into the Cascades could change this in the future. Less menacing but more common is poison ivy and oak, which can be found at many a crag near Leavenworth, in the Tieton, Banks Lake, and Spokane areas, and elsewhere. Also menacing are hunters during the autumn months; shotgun blasts echoing through the Leavenworth, Tieton, and Mazama areas are at best merely distracting. A hiker was once shot by a young bear hunter in the North Cascades, so it is not out of the realm of possibility. During hunting season, try to wear bright, unnatural-colored clothing so you don't become an accidental target, hike out before dusk, and wear a headlamp if you are out after sunset.

Forest fires have raged through several climbing areas over the past decades, leaving millions of charred trees behind, time bombs waiting to fall on unsuspecting climbers. In fire-scourged areas, beware of these "widow-makers," of holes left by subterranean fires that burned tree roots long after the surface fires went out, and of fire-heated blocks and boulders, which are often very unstable.

At all areas, untreated surface water is unsuitable for drinking. Bring your own water and plenty of it, particularly when climbing on hot summer days, to avoid dehydration.

Loose rock may be encountered at all areas throughout the state. Some areas have more loose rock than others; be particularly careful when climbing at Mount Erie, North Bend, Fossil Rock, Vantage, Mazama, Washington Pass, and Deep Creek. Specific areas subject to high rockfall danger are pointed out, but beware of loose rock at all areas. Also beware of dropped gear, which can be equally injurious. Wear a helmet!

Rattlesnakes are common in all central and eastern Washington areas. They tend to hide among the rocks and bushes, particularly on sunny exposures or near water during the summer and fall and in early morning and late afternoon, when they are most active. They generally don't like us and will slither away if allowed to do so, but if threatened or alarmed they may strike, sometimes even without warning. If you are bitten by a rattler, seek medical treatment immediately. If you encounter a rattler, please be biodiversity-friendly and don't kill it; it will slink off into the bushes or under a rock if you harass it sufficiently, but be careful not to get too close.

Ticks are at their worst during spring and early summer, but can be encountered any time of year in some areas. Ticks latch onto you and your dog while you are hiking and quickly set about their business of finding a nice place to burrow under your skin. If you keep an eye out, you can usually remove ticks before they do any damage. Ticks can transmit Lyme disease, which has been fatal to humans in some cases. If you find a tick has burrowed beneath your skin, consult a physician as soon as possible. If you perform an occasional tick check, you will probably avoid any problem. Remember to check your dog, too!

The bright green leaves of poison ivy and poison oak grow in threes. The plants are often found in gullies and shady areas along the bases of cliffs, particularly in Icicle Creek Canyon, the Tieton River Canyon, and at Banks Lake and Minnehaha. If you don't know what poison oak looks like, have someone point it out to you or look it up, and avoid it or you'll be sorry. Not only are the leaves poisonous, but so are the stems and roots. Also, though dogs may not suffer an allergic reaction, they can transmit the oil that causes the rash to you, so keep your dog out of the brush if you know what's good for you.

Stinging insects such as yellow jackets, bees, wasps, and hornets are likely to be encountered in nearly all areas. If you run into an aggressive species, get stung, or encounter a swarm, run like hell!

Overall, the biggest non-climbing-related hazard out there is other people, especially those dangerous characters—drug addicts, the mentally ill, zealous gun advocates—who sometimes live on the fringe of society, i.e., out in the woods around some popular climbing areas. Car prowling is on the rise, making it a bad idea to leave your rack or anything of value in your car or even on the ground while you're climbing. With homelessness and mental illness issues increasing, you're more likely now than in years past to encounter sketchy characters while out climbing—and everywhere else, really. It's a good idea to buddy up, report any suspicious activity, and be cautious when confronting suspicious characters.

EQUIPMENT

Again, this is not a climbing instruction book and won't tell you what equipment to use on any route. A suggested gear list will be included for most routes, but it is up to each individual climber to decide what gear to bring on a given route and where to place it.

A 9.5- to 10.5-millimeter by 70-meter rope is recommended, especially on sport crags to facilitate single-rope rappels or lowering off. Hardly anybody uses an 11-millimeter rope any more, and 50-meter ropes are all but useless on many modern pitches. Even 60-meter ropes are now too short for many routes; 70-meter ropes have become the new standard, and 80-meter ropes are recommended on some routes. On many routes, anchors are set to facilitate lowering or rappelling from a single 70-meter rope; if you have a 60-meter rope, you're going to have a tougher time getting down from some routes, and risk making the fatal mistake of lowering or rappelling off the end of your rope. So as not to have to repeat myself, assume you need a 70-meter rope on all modern sport routes that don't obviously end less than 80 feet up and even then, tie a knot in the end of your rope just in case it turns out to be not quite long enough. Store your rope properly, protect it from situations that cause damage (e.g., bleach, gasoline, motor oil, sand, prolonged exposure to sunlight, excessive heat or dampness) and keep it clean. If you have any reason to doubt your rope's strength, retire it!

This guide includes gear recommendations, usually a general recommendation to bring gear up to a certain size. As an example, if this guide recommends protection ("pro") to 2 inches, that means most climbers have found gear up to 2 inches in size is adequate to protect the route. In that case, bring a selection of gear from small wired nuts to chocks and spring-loaded camming devices ("active pro" such as Camalots, Super Cams, Power Cams, Friends, Technical Friends, TCUs, and so on, referred to generically as "cams" in this guide) up to 2 inches in width. Most parties have found adequate protection placements for gear up to the recommended size, but that does not mean larger gear cannot be placed. To be on the safe side, especially on longer routes, bring along a few pieces up to 1 inch larger than the largest recommended size, just in case.

On sport routes, it is usually sufficient to bring only quickdraws, although sometimes it is possible or desirable to place gear in between the bolts to minimize runouts. On bolt-protected leads with substantial runouts, bring some nuts, camming devices, and other small protection, just in case.

This guide uses the term "cams" to refer to spring-loaded camming devices of all sizes, "nuts" to refer generically to wired nuts and chocks ("passive pro"), and "gear" to refer generally to any climber-placed protection devices. Sometimes the term "standard rack" is used; this means a comprehensive rack including some wired nuts, a range of cam and/or chock sizes, and several quickdraws; the longer the pitch/route, the larger the rack. If a specific piece of gear is required or recommended to protect a route, such as a #3 Tech Friend or a #4 Camalot, it will be specified as such, although in general a more generic gear list is provided, leaving the subtleties of figuring out which piece to place where up to you. Occasionally this guide refers generically to "wired nuts," which should be taken to mean wired stoppers, RPs, and other similar small wired protection devices. Specific brand names may be used, such as RP, but unless a particular size is referenced that term may be taken to mean any wired brass stopper or similarly tapered wired nut. Where the guide says to bring a #5 RP, a #2 Camalot, a #4 Rock, or a #3 HB nut, bring exactly that piece, since previous climbers have reported that it is useful or necessary for protection on a given route.

On routes where specific gear is not recommended, bring a comprehensive rack, which should include several small wired nuts, some midsize chocks, and several small to midsize cams with at least one piece larger than the recommended size. Always bring slings, to reduce rope drag and to facilitate rappels from trees, or to replace worn out rappel slings, which are commonly encountered.

It is up to you to decide what protection is necessary on a given route and to rack accordingly. Knowing what kind of gear to bring and how to place it is learned only through experience. If you don't have experience placing equipment, practice before you start leading. Your first lead is no place to learn how to place gear. Gym climbers especially should learn the art of protection from a more-experienced partner, mentor, or guide before they try their first "trad" lead. Take the time to learn the craft of placing gear; your life depends on it.

WEATHER

Washington's weather is partly responsible for the influx of climbing gyms, particularly in western Washington, where it is too often raining or overcast to go "real" climbing. By contrast, Leavenworth boasts 300 days of sunshine a year, although it is suspected that this number was fabricated by the local chamber of commerce to boost tourism. Even so, when it's raining at North Bend or Index, it is often merely cloudy or overcast at Leavenworth, Mazama, or in the Tieton, and it may be sunny at Vantage and other points east.

Weather on the west side of the Cascade Range is often wet due to prevailing winds that blow moist Pacific Ocean air up against the mountains. Between November and June, it rains plenty at North Bend, Index, and Darrington, which accounts for the lush forests and, unfortunately, abundance of vegetation on the rocks. Summer and autumn months are usually sunny, but don't rely on it. Mount Erie has a microclimate all its own and is sometimes dry even when it is raining at Darrington and Index, but again, don't count on it.

By contrast, Leavenworth and other eastern Washington areas are usually sunny; at least, it is often not raining on the east side of the Cascades even when it is pouring buckets in Seattle. For western Washington residents, consider Leavenworth, Vantage, and the Tieton areas as hopefully dry alternatives on rainy days, but call ahead to be sure so you don't drive for two and a half hours only to have to turn back because it's raining there, too.

Western Washington areas are generally cooler than those in eastern Washington during the summer and more prone to rainstorms during the spring and fall. Eastern Washington areas can get quite hot during the summer months and quite cold during the winter and are subject to afternoon lightning storms, but offer usually pleasant spring and fall climbing.

During winter, it is usually either too cold or too wet to do much rock climbing, except at Vantage, where the south-facing cliffs are sometimes warm enough for climbing in December and January. When it's really cold, frozen waterfalls offer ice climbing opportunities near Leavenworth, Index, Banks Lake, and Vantage, for those who are into that sort of thing.

Whenever the weather is doubtful, call ahead and ask about current weather conditions. Phone numbers of ranger stations are included in the Appendix; an early morning phone call to a local restaurant or coffee shop, or even a social media shout-out, can give you helpful weather beta.

FIRST ASCENT INFORMATION

First ascent information is included in this guide, but sparingly. This information generally includes the names of the climbers who made the first ascent and the year of their ascent. Where this information is conflicting or in doubt or could not be confirmed, a best-guess is made. If you made a first ascent that is not reported in this guide, my apologies, but first ascent information is well chronicled in nearly every local guide available. If you are interested in finding out who developed a given route, refer to the local guidebook listed in each chapter.

In this guide, FA means first ascent; FFA means first free ascent (i.e., no aid or hangs), but not necessarily first redpoint ascent, especially on pre-1986 routes (before redpointing became widely adopted in this country); FFL means first free lead, commonly used when a toprope route was later led; and FKA means first known ascent or first reported ascent, where there is conflicting information about who first did a route or it seems obvious someone did the route prior to the first reported ascent. On post-1986 sport routes, FA generally means first redpoint ascent. FCA may mean either first clean ascent or first confirmed ascent, depending upon the context in which it is used (i.e., whether the route is an aid route or free climb).

STYLE AND ETHICS

Generally speaking, style is how you climb on the rock, ethics is what you do to the rock and how you feel about it. Hangdogging is a style; rappel bolting and hold gluing require ethical consideration. Washington climbers as a whole do not have a widely accepted climbing ethic. As at other areas, the few who are actively putting up new routes tend to dictate the local ethic. Most Washington climbers haven't widely adopted rappel bolting (that is, we aren't *all* out drilling holes in the rock), although it has become widely accepted and for the most part climbers are happy to climb sport routes developed by others. However, given the amount of overbolting, chipping, and gluing that has gone on, some discussion of style and ethics seems appropriate.

Stylistic trends (sometimes referred to as "social ethics") such as hangdogging, rappel inspection, rehearsing, toproping, pre-protecting, free soloing, etc., are relatively meaningless to everyone but you. Although some climbers may frown on rehearsal and hangdogging, if you 'dog your way up a route, it affects no one but you. For that matter, some climbers frown on the use of tape, preferring to climb cracks without it, but that shouldn't stop anyone from taping up for a crack route if that's what they want to do. And chalk may be unsightly and might actually lead to rock decomposition, but almost everyone uses chalk as they see fit. Whether chalk use is a stylistic or ethical consideration is arguable. It looks bad sometimes, and is a depleting mineral resource, but it seems pretty harmless and usually washes off all but overhanging routes, especially in rainy western Washington.

Really, the only troublesome issue with respect to hangdogging and pre-placing gear is how it affects rights in claiming first free ascents. In the old days, it hardly mattered as long as you did all the moves continuously free. Many a "first free ascent" was done yo-yo style, with climbers taking turns climbing higher than their partner, placing another piece of gear, falling off and lowering, until one of them actually finished the pitch without falling off. Even lowering to a no-hands stance was considered acceptable way back when. Nobody thought about hangdogging or "working" a route before redpointing it. Then in the mid-1980s, largely due to European influence, it all changed. Everybody started hangdogging and rappel bolting (except traditionalists who saw the trend as an artificial means of "free" climbing), and standards jumped.

By current standards, to claim a true free ascent, you are supposed to climb the route in the best possible style, from bottom to top, placing all gear during your ascent and not weighting any gear (i.e., redpoint). Preplacing gear or leaving it in place between attempts (i.e., pinkpointing) or leaving the rope clipped through the highest gear and essentially toproping what you or your partner have already climbed (i.e., yo-yoing) is now considered rehearsal even if you manage to do all the moves free. Hanging on the rope to rest or work, without lowering and starting over from the bottom (i.e., hangdogging) is considered aid, and an ascent done with hangs must have an A0 rating until redpointed. Modern climbers consider an ascent to be free no matter how much hangdogging, yo-yoing, toproping, pre-protecting, or other means of rehearsal, pre-inspection, and pre-protection are employed, so long as a redpoint ascent is ultimately achieved.

Tactics such as bolting, manufacturing or "improving" holds, scarring cracks, and "gardening" require serious ethical consideration, as they affect not only climbing but also the climbing environment itself (hence the occasional reference to "environmental ethics"). While lead-placed bolts are rarely criticized (except bolt ladders placed to facilitate free climbing), rappel bolting has generated no small amount of controversy. Many climbers from the old days, and even a few modern purists, feel rappel bolting is an illegitimate means of establishing new routes. Still, rap-bolted routes abound and the technique is considered by the vast majority as legitimate, even desirable, especially when bolts are well placed and installed in moderation to create quality sport routes. Adding new bolts to existing routes (retrobolting) is frowned upon, however, except if added by the first ascent party, with their permission, or by community consensus if the first ascent party is not around to give permission. Bolts added to existing routes are usually soon removed, especially on traditional routes that someone decides to turn into a sport route. Not every route needs to be a sport clip-up; if you can't lead a trad route on gear, toprope it or leave it alone for those who can. Rebolting of routes (that is, replacing old, questionable bolts) is a very good idea. By all means replace bad bolts; just don't drill new holes if you can avoid it, and please remove the old bolts and studs if you can.

Some rappel-bolted routes feature a long, difficult runout to the first bolt, which may be overcome by bold leading, or use of a cheat stick. This is often done to keep other climbers from stealing bolt hangers, but it creates a dangerous situation for climbers who don't know better. If the first bolt seems a little far off the ground and the climbing to get there seems a little too hard, leave the route alone, or use a cheat stick to make the clip.

Although one Washington guidebook said, "It is unusual to find a bolt next to a reasonable RP placement," there are several routes in this guide where reasonable protection is within arm's reach of a rappel-placed bolt. Of course, there are some rappel-bolted routes that don't have enough bolts. Whether a route is over bolted or under bolted depends upon who is doing the drilling. Those placing rappel bolts should at least be sure they are placing enough bolts to make a route safe, but take care not to place too many and take advantage of natural protection as much as possible. New route pioneers should also be careful not to squeeze too many bolt lines in on a given crag. Every square foot of rock does not need a bolted climbing route!

As for placing bolts, power drills are standard equipment in most areas. Keep in mind that power drilling is illegal in all state parks, wilderness areas, and national parks, unless there is a climbing management plan in place that allows it, so if you are planning on placing bolts in such an area, you must do it the old-fashioned way or risk getting cited or arrested. For that matter, you might still get cited for any drilling in designated wilderness areas, particularly if the US Forest Service ban on use of fixed anchors remains in effect.

Fixed quickdraws are commonly left in place on bolts at popular sport crags, especially on hard, overhanging routes. Fixed draws are unsightly at best, and can be dangerous due to weakening over time due to wear. It's unwise to trust fixed draws entirely, as they may be damaged from aging, weather, or overuse. It's preferable from an ethical standpoint not to leave fixed gear in place, but it isn't much of a problem at most areas. Some fixed draws and chains

Dan Lepeska on the first ascent of *No Such Thing as a Free Lunge* (5.11d R/X), Castle Rock, Tumwater Canyon

actually make routes safer by minimizing the possibility of a rope or draw being cut over a sharp edge, but some of them sure are ugly.

More serious ethical issues are chipping and gluing. Chipping—that is, purposely manufacturing holds with a chisel, drill, or otherwise—is, in this author's opinion, absolute desecration of the rock, which is completely unnecessary and a shameful insult to all climbers. Unfortunately, it continues to happen. But aside from blatantly carved holds and drilled pockets, climbers occasionally "improve" a pin scar so it accepts fingertips or RPs, or lever off thin flakes to leave bigger edges. Amazingly, holds are sometimes removed or made smaller to make a route more difficult! While the occasional improvement of a bad hold might seem acceptable, the line is difficult to draw between what is acceptable and what is not. Once you begin justifying any hold improvement, what won't you do? Climbers in some areas have bolted and glued on rocks and plastic holds and cut cracks with masonry saws. If it's okay to purposely widen a pin scar so an old aid crack goes free, why not just cut your own crack, or drill finger pockets up a blank wall? If it's acceptable to reinforce a creaky hold with glue, why not just glue on some rocks?

A bright line is easily drawn. If you're altering the route to affect its difficulty rather than its safety, it's wrong. It's one thing to lever off a loose flake or block so it doesn't pull off and kill someone, and quite another to drill out a finger pocket or glue on a hold because a move "won't go" without it. If a route is too hard for you to climb in its natural condition, adding a hold is no different than pulling up on a bolt—it's aid climbing. Sometimes it's damn hard, but using glued and chipped holds is still aid climbing. If a route is too hard (or too easy) for you, please leave it for later climbers rather than desecrating the rock to bring the route down (or up) to your level. If you want to manufacture routes, become a route setter at your local climbing gym.

As for reinforcing holds with glue, if a hold is so loose it needs glue to stay on, it seems best just to clean it off. Better yet, just leave it alone. Reinforcing holds with glue doesn't magically turn a chosspile into a world-class sport crag. A chosspile is a chosspile, no matter how much glue you use.

As for removing loose rock, by all means make routes safer, but be careful not to trundle stones down on unsuspecting hikers and climbers below. Big rocks can get rolling and can (and have) hit cars and people. Don't be the guy (or gal) who causes that!

Many old aid climbs have been led clean, using only gear and hand-placed pitons. Once an aid climb has been led clean, it should not be nailed ever again. Repeated nailing damages the rock and changes the character of the route. Still, even easy, clean aid climbs occasionally get nailed by ignorant or arrogant climbers. Sometimes clean routes (and even free routes) are nailed as a protest to the selfishness of free climbers who have bolted and freed several former aid lines.

Please don't steal fixed pins, quickdraws, or bolt hangers. There is nothing worse than arriving at a bolt during a gripping lead and finding nothing to clip in to—unless it is going to clip a fixed pin during a gripping lead and finding it gone. And those quickdraws you find on hard sport routes have not been abandoned; they belong to somebody and taking them is theft. Stealing fixed gear puts other climbers in danger, and besides, it isn't very nice.

As for gardening, many Washington routes were once veritable gardens of ferns, moss, and lichen. Routes such as *Botany 101* and *Japanese Gardens* weren't named for their sparkling clean rock, after all. Unearthing new routes is a long-standing tradition in Washington. Unfortunately, in their zeal to climb "new" routes, sometimes the cleaning crews unwittingly scrub and bolt routes that were pioneered by earlier climbers. They also scrub off endangered plant species, leaving behind an unsightly swath of sparkling clean rock. This certainly improves those routes, making them pretty and accessible to the masses, but modern pioneers should be careful not to carelessly erase other life forms or the legacy left behind by earlier generations in the process.

There is no last word on climbing style and ethics. Overbolting, pin-scarring, and sculpting and gluing holds are a dangerous legacy to leave for future generations of climbers. But basically, around here anyway, if you aren't trashing the rock or other climbers, or threatening access to a climbing area, by all means go for it and enjoy yourself. Just try to set a good example for other climbers, and non-climbers as well.

THE ACCESS FUND

The Access Fund is a national nonprofit organization dedicated to keeping climbing areas open and preserving the climbing environment. In Washington the Access Fund has coordinated land purchases to save climbing areas from development, sponsored trail projects at Castle Rock, Little Si, and Frenchman Coulee, and worked with land managers to address climbing and access issues at nearly every area in Washington. For more information, call (303) 545-6772 or visit their website: www.accessfund.org.

WASHINGTON CLIMBERS COALITION

The Washington Climbers Coalition (WCC) is affiliated with the Access Fund and dedicated to addressing issues of specific concern to Washington climbers, principally promoting and preserving access to Washington's crags. The WCC is composed of climbers working together for Washington climbers. The WCC's mission is to get climbers involved in discussion of issues related to climbing area management and access, encourage active involvement in coordinated efforts to take care of Washington's crags, and maintain good relations with other recreational users, land managers, and landowners. The WCC publishes a periodic newsletter and maintains a message board exclusively for Washington climbing access issues. And the WCC's website provides information about each climbing area in the state, including a summary of each area's climbing, history, and current access situation, with contact information for all land managers. For more information, visit www.washingtonclimbers.org.

WASHINGTON ANCHOR REPLACEMENT PROJECT

The Washington Anchor Replacement Project (WARP) is a nonprofit organization with the core mission of replacing aging and unsafe climbing anchors throughout the state. In 2016, WARP became part of the WCC. WARP raises funds to buy bolts and anchors, which are installed by volunteers. For more information, visit WARP's website at https://washington anchors.org.

Karl Kaiyala on the first pitch of *Sisu* (5.11c), Upper Town Wall, Index LARRY KEMP COLLECTION

PRESERVATION AND ACCESS

by Andy Fitz, Former Access Fund Regional Coordinator

This guide will point you to some wonderful climbing. Whether we can continue to enjoy the same climbing ten years from now depends largely upon how you act. At nearly every climbing area in the state, climber impacts have drawn scrutiny from land managers and, in some cases, the broader public. We must come together, now, to change the direction of our sport.

The sheer number of people climbing means that climbing ethics can no longer afford to dwell on arcane questions such as whether a bolt should be placed on lead or rappel. Instead, climbing ethics must focus on limiting environmental impacts so our sport can be sustainable. A certain level of impact is inevitable with climbing. Unless those impacts are limited, however, climbers will be faced with one of two prospects: 1) land managers will step in to limit or close climbing; or 2) climbing areas themselves will be destroyed. Neither outcome is acceptable.

The solution cannot come through a set of rules. Instead, the solution must come through climbers adopting an attitude of always looking to minimize their impacts. What follows are suggestions to help you toward that attitude.

On the Ground. Climbers have a far more serious impact on the ground than on the cliffs. Soil erosion, in particular, is a problem at many Washington crags. Most of our climbing areas have become popular without a well-thought-out trail system to deliver people to the cliffs. Where there are no established trails, look for the least destructive way to get to the wall. For example, walk on rock instead of soil. In the mountains, stay on the perimeter of a meadow rather than walking directly through it. Avoid hiking directly up a steep slope; instead, cut across the slope, changing direction frequently. You'll save energy and save the hillside.

Where repeated traffic has established several paths, choose the path that provides the most durable option rather than based upon whether it is the quickest way to get to the crag. In open areas such as Frenchman Coulee, choose the most heavily traveled path until a better trail is built.

Once at the wall, unload your gear and take breaks on large, flat rocks or other durable surfaces to avoid damaging vegetation. Set your belay so that it's close to the climb. This will allow others to pass around you without disturbing more ground at the base of the cliff.

If you are camping, use established sites where the ground is already barren. Respect fire closures: At Frenchman Coulee (Vantage), open fires are restricted from April 15 to October 15, and restrictions are common in the Leavenworth and Tieton River areas.

Climbers at most Washington crags do not have access to an outhouse. Urinate on bare ground away from vegetation, climbing routes, and trails. Dispose of solid waste at least 200 feet away from trails, the base of climbs, water sources, or campsites. Avoid small depressions that may be drainages and dark, cool environments such as under rocks. Dig into the top, organic layer of soil, deliver your package, and stir soil into the hole until it is filled. Disguise the area and pack out your toilet paper in a ziplock bag.

Finally, don't leave behind used tape, old slings, or cigarette butts. Bring along a small bag for your litter and whatever other trash you may find.

The choice is ours. We can preserve the natural feel of our crags or let incremental change lead to an ugly maze of erosion, trash, and filth. If we don't choose to preserve our crags, a land manager will choose preservation for us by banning us from the cliffs.

On the Cliffs. Bolts have opened many wonderful new avenues of climbing in the last decade. They have also served as a lightning rod for access issues.

If bolts are to remain a part of climbing, climbers must place them responsibly. At Frenchman Coulee, four routes are squeezed onto three sides of Satan's Tower. Two more are squeezed onto one face of the Medicine Man pillar. At many sport crags, it is necessary to resort to a guidebook to determine which bolts belong to which climb. For many climbers, the net effect of excess bolting is to rob each line of its individual appeal and character. For land managers, the net effect is to leave them asking whether every square inch of rock will eventually be bolted.

Climbers can reduce bolting conflicts by critically evaluating each climb. Does a new line add diversity to the area, or simply add more of the same? Does it follow a compelling natural line instead of simply filling up unbolted space? Does it stand alone without impacting the aesthetics of existing routes? Is it located in an area that can withstand the impact of the people who will climb it? Is it located where it will not offend the sensibilities of non-climbers? If the answers to these questions are no, the line should not be bolted.

Climbers can also reduce bolting conflicts by taking every measure to reduce the visual impact of bolts and anchors. Use discreet anchors at the top of climbs. If chains are used, use short lengths and camouflage them to match the rock. If slings are used, choose natural-toned webbing over brightly colored slings.

As for the bolts themselves, use commercially painted hangers that match the rock, or camouflage hangers yourself before installing them. A paint store can mix a flat-toned paint that will match the rock. It is also possible to retro-paint already installed hangers by using a carefully cut cardboard stencil to keep paint off the rock.

Avoid disturbances to animals. Do not feed them or leave food within easy reach. Avoid nesting sites at or near a cliff in the spring and early summer. Watch birds as they circle and land to learn where they are nesting.

Finally, although cleaning loose and friable rock is sometimes necessary for safety, do not alter the rock to create (or remove) holds. Manufacturing a hold may open up a route, but it also may close a climbing area.

Social Courtesy. While many climbers may not think about it, climbers' social behavior is an access concern. At Little Si, a popular hiking trail passes within a few yards of the crags. The cliffs amplify climbers' shouts and conversations; boom boxes and screams let out after a failed redpoint attempt come through loud and clear to hikers looking to commune with the woods.

At Exit 38, many climbs begin directly off a designated cross-state trail. Many climbers look upon the wide, level tread as a belay supercamp, spreading out ropes, packs, and Crazy Creek chairs directly in the path of oncoming hikers and bikers. This could lead to a serious conflict for equestrians and hikers using the Hall Creek trestle.

Jessica Campbell on *Thin Fingers* (5.11a), Index Lower Town Wall FOREST WOODWARD

Problems such as these can only hurt climbers. Use your head and be sensitive to other users. Take the time to educate them about climbing. We will all reap the benefits.

Respecting Restrictions. The degree of freedom land managers grant us depends on how well we abide by the rules they establish.

Washington State Parks areas: Much of Index, Peshastin Pinnacles, Exit 38 (Iron Horse State Park), Beacon Rock, Deep Creek, portions of the Banks Lake area, Larrabee/Chuckanut Mountain (near Bellingham), and Horsethief Butte are all managed by Washington State Parks. State Parks has a statewide climbing regulation (WAC 352-32-085) that allows climbing in these areas, but prohibits activities such as bolting and route cleaning unless allowed under a park-specific management plan. As of 2018, such plans exist for almost all these areas, but climbers should review the specific restrictions in each plan before cleaning and establishing any new routes at these areas.

OTHER CONSIDERATIONS

Everything you do in the wilderness—your route, your gear, choosing your campsite—should reflect a commitment to the idea of minimum impact. Looking closely and thinking carefully will allow you to assess potential human impact in any given situation and to adjust your behavior accordingly. The right attitude will do more to preserve the wilderness than any number of rules and regulations. When you leave the wilderness, there should be no trace that you have been there.

—National Park Service

While most of us won't be as conscientious as the park service would like, climbers should do what they can to minimize their impact on the environment. In the absence of established trails to crags, don't blaze your own. Multitudes of paths cause increased erosion—as happened at Peshastin Pinnacles, Vantage, and Smith Rock before trail relocation efforts were undertaken. Use chalk sparingly and opt for muted rappel slings over brightly colored ones. Discard trash appropriately—this includes cigarette butts! Finally, do your best to respect wildlife (look but don't touch) and comply with the closure of some cliffs due to nesting peregrine falcons, notably Beacon Rock, Midnight Rock, the Upper Town Wall.

Most of the climbing areas included in this guide are located in state parks, wilderness areas, nature reserves, and other designated areas covered by various regulations and laws designed to protect the environment and wildlife from human impacts. These rules and regulations are intended to preserve and protect, not to restrict or annoy climbers. The following are not rules but common-sense suggestions that, if followed, will keep climbers on the good side in the eyes of land managers:

- If you pack it in, pack it out. And if you find litter lying about, be a good sport and pack that out, too.
- Stay on established trails and don't cut switchbacks or blaze new shortcuts if possible. If there is no established trail, consider establishing a trail (except in wilderness areas and parks, where trail construction would be illegal). Where there is no established trail, step lightly and do your best to avoid causing unnecessary erosion and plant damage.

- Use dark-colored slings and camouflage bolts and chains so they blend in with the rock. White, red, and day-glo runners are obnoxious and unsightly. When removing old slings, don't just chuck them down the cliff; pack them out.
- Keep chalk use to a necessary minimum. Don't leave a dotted line up the crag if you don't need to do so. Colored chalk never quite caught on, but if you can, use chalk matching the color of the rock you are climbing, or none at all.
- When placing bolts, use only as many bolts as are necessary to adequately protect a route. But don't leave dangerous runouts, either. Check local regulations before drilling!
- Keep gardening to a necessary minimum. You needn't defoliate an entire crag just to climb one route. And don't cut down trees for any reason. Sure, logging a crag may expose it to the sun, allowing it to dry out faster and make for better photos, but it's a selfish thing to do.
- Plan your actions so as to make the least impact on the environment, and try to leave the area in better shape than you found it.

HUMAN WASTE DISPOSAL

Some of the climbing areas in this guide have toilets; most do not. Human waste disposal is a major environmental problem in high-use areas without pit toilets. Ideally, everyone would pack it out, but in reality few take the time or effort to do so. Let's face it—it's gross! So, if you're not inclined to pack it out, here are some ideas:

- Use toilets where provided and go before you start climbing, which may save you some discomfort and embarrassment in addition to being environmentally conscientious.
- Where toilets aren't available, don't go anywhere near streams, rivers, lakes, or any other surface water. The general rule is 200 feet from the nearest surface water, but the farther the better.
- In lowland forests and desert areas, dig a 6-inch-deep cathole in the surface soil, disturbing the soil as little as possible, and bury it. Don't just hide it under a rock.
- In higher-elevation areas, digging holes can cause severe damage to plant life. Above timberline and in alpine areas, it is always recommended that you pack it out or use acceptable surface disposal methods.
- Surface disposal is acceptable in low-use alpine and subalpine areas and remote desert areas, but by all means do so well away from water sources, campsites, and trails. When using surface disposal methods, the recommended practice is to scatter and smear feces with a stick to maximize exposure to air and sun and thus speed up decomposition. It sounds gross, but it is environmentally sound.
- Don't burn toilet paper. Burning trash has caused many wilderness fires. Buried toilet paper often returns to the surface due to erosion or when animals dig it up. Pack it out if you can.
- Whenever you have to go in the wilderness, you should try to "go where no man has gone before."

- If you're rich, consider donating a solar-powered composting toilet to the cause. They're only a few thousand bucks, and I'm sure you can find a way to write it off.

If you bring your dog with you, be a responsible dog owner and carry a supply of poo bags—and use them. Don't let your dog run loose pooping all over the trail and the base of the cliff. Really, climbers should all be using doggie bags to pack out their own poop, but at the very least dog owners should take care of their dogs.

TRAILHEAD PARKING PASSES

Parking passes are now required at nearly every climbing area in Washington state. US Forest Service trailheads require a Forest Pass purchased in advance. A National Forest Day Pass is presently $5, and an annual Northwest Forest Pass is $30. A Washington State Parks day pass is presently $10, and an annual Discover Pass is $30. Parking passes are available from many outdoor retailers, US Forest Service offices, the Department of Licensing, and at some parks, campgrounds, and trailheads.

VANDALISM AND THEFT

Don't leave valuables in your car, visible or otherwise, as ripoffs occur frequently at many areas. Thieves will take just about anything—climbing gear, cameras, sleeping bags, CDs—even your Bosch! Don't tempt would-be thieves—keep your stuff in the trunk or take it with you. It's a good idea to bring only what you really need and only what you can carry with you, so you don't end up leaving something valuable in the car for someone to steal.

Car theft from climbing areas and trailheads is much more common than it used to be. It's not unusual to have your stuff stolen then find it for sale on Craigslist or eBay. Even if nothing is stolen, would-be thieves might still break your windows. Parking in a high-use, high-visibility area is a good idea to avoid theft and vandalism, although determined thieves will break into a car no matter how visible and high-use a parking area is. Whatever you do, don't leave notes saying where you've gone or when you'll be back, or you'll surely be victimized. And be careful if you catch somebody prowling or breaking into cars; they might run off, or they might attack you.

If your rack is stolen, check for it on Craigslist in a few days. If you see an add advertising gear that the seller obviously doesn't have any familiarity with (one such ad offered "crampsons" and "camlocks" for sale), that's a sure sign it's stolen. Through social media, climbers can alert each other to potential stolen gear for sale, and sometimes recover the gear from the bad guys.

IN CASE OF EMERGENCY

In most areas of Washington state, dial 911 in case of an emergency. In areas without 911 service, you are probably best off dialing the operator for assistance. Otherwise, look up the local sheriff's office, fire department, or police department in the blue pages of the telephone directory. In remote areas, carrying a cellular phone or two-way radio is a good idea. Several hikers and climbers have used phones and radios to summon their own rescues. However, don't be lulled into a false sense of security just because you have a cell phone, as there are many "dead zones" where cell coverage is spotty or nonexistent. It is still best to let someone know where you will be climbing, so they know where to start looking for you if you are overdue.

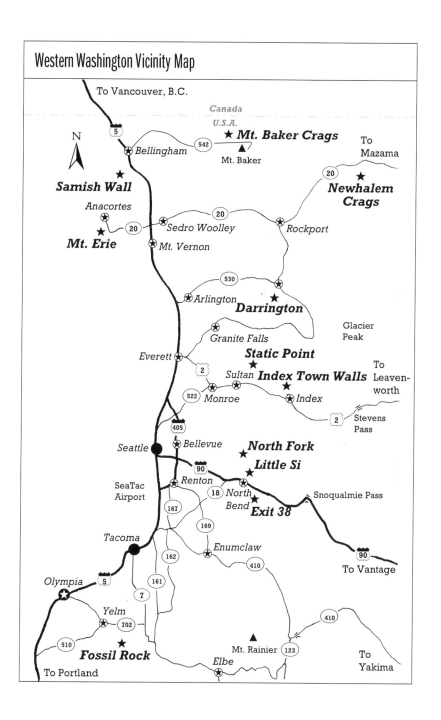

Western Washington Vicinity Map

To Vancouver, B.C.

Canada
U.S.A.

N

5

Bellingham 542 ★ **Mt. Baker Crags**

▲
Mt. Baker

To
Mazama

Samish Wall

20

Anacortes

20

★
Mt. Erie

Sedro Woolley

Mt. Vernon

Rockport

20

★ Newhalem
Crags

530

Arlington

★
Darrington

Glacier
Peak

Granite Falls

Everett

2

Sultan

Static Point
★

★ **Index Town Walls**

To
Leaven-
worth

522 Monroe

Index

2

Stevens
Pass

405

Bellevue

Seattle ●

★ **North Fork**

90

★
Little Si

Renton

SeaTac
Airport

18 North
Bend

Exit 38
★

Snoqualmie Pass

167

169

Tacoma ●

Enumclaw

162

410

90

To Vantage

Olympia

5

161

7

410

Yelm

702

510

★
Fossil Rock

▲
Mt. Rainier 123

To Portland

Elbe

To
Yakima

The Index Town Walls comprise one of this state's finest granite climbing areas. The area is composed of two major cliffs—the Upper and Lower Town Walls—and countless smaller walls, crags, slabs, and buttresses hidden in the dense second (third? fourth?)-growth alder, maple, and fir forest above the small town of Index, Washington. The area's Yosemite-like climbing in close proximity to the urban sprawl of Seattle makes it one of the most popular climbing areas in Washington state.

Type of climbing: Index Town Walls combine easy accessibility; a homey, low-key, rural ambience; and steep, mostly clean granite with hundreds of routes, many in the 5.10 to 5.13 range, plus a few remaining big-wall-type aid climbs and long, hard free routes. Composed of highly textured granite, the rock on the main cliffs is consistently steep, with lots of pumping cracks and some unlikely face climbs. Incidental cliffs feature long face climbs and friction, short cracks, and sport climbs of varying degrees of difficulty, from 5.6 to 5.13. There are still a few classic aid routes on the Upper Wall, although most of the aid has been eliminated at this point. Clean aid ascents are still acceptable after a wall route has gone free. Although Index has some excellent sport climbs, it is still primarily considered a "trad" climbing area, with abundant steep cracks of all sizes.

Brief history of area: The industrial past of Index Town Walls is well evidenced by the scars left by turn-of-the-twentieth-century quarrying, which served to remove much of the Lower Wall before eventually halting. Granite removed from the area may be seen in building foundations throughout the Northwest, including the capitol steps in Olympia. Luckily, much rock was spared the drills and dynamite.

Climbing at Index no doubt began during the quarrying era, but the first reported routes were established during the 1960s. These were aid climbs, following obvious natural lines on the Upper and Lower Walls. The big wall pioneers of the 1960s and early 1970s included Fred Beckey, Ron Burgner, Pat Timson, Jim Langdon, Roger Johnson, Mark Weigelt, Jim Madsen, and others. Eventually climbers focused their attention on less obvious routes, and by the late 1970s there were many long, difficult aid climbs and several free climbs as well. Many aid cracks, suffering scars from repeated nailing, were climbed clean during this period, and the clean-climbing ethic was widely adopted by local climbers. Climbers active during this period included Don Brooks, Dave Anderson, Rich Carlstad, Julie Brugger, Carla Firey, Ron Burgner, Thom Nephew, Pat Timson, Cal Folsom, and others.

New attitudes about cleaning and protecting, combined with a learned intuition about what was possible on Index's

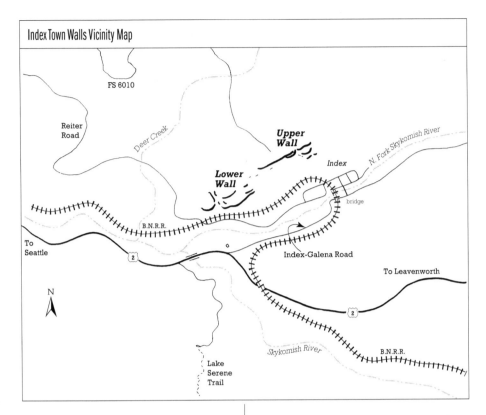

FS 6010

Reiter
Road

Deer Creek

Upper
Wall

Index

N. Fork Skykomish River

Lower
Wall

bridge

B.N.R.R.

To
Seattle

2

Index-Galena Road

To Leavenworth

2

N

Skykomish River

B.N.R.R.

Lake
Serene
Trail

varied granite, resulted in the establishment of many new routes during the early 1980s. By 1990 nearly every aid route on the Lower Wall had been climbed free. Particularly active in freeing the aid lines were Jon Nelson, Terry Lien, Darryl Cramer, and Greg Olsen. The legacy of aid climbing was largely responsible for the freeing of many routes: Pin scars left by countless aid ascents have served the new age of free climbers well, as best evidenced by Todd Skinner's free ascent of *City Park* (5.13d) in 1986. With the advent and wide acceptance of rappel bolting, many unlikely free climbs were pioneered during the late 1980s and early 1990s, including many sport routes and some amazing Grade IV free routes on the Upper Wall. Index sport route pioneers of this period include Greg Child, Greg Collum, Max Dufford, Andy deKlerk, Matt

Kerns, and many others. Development has continued to the present day: Many of the last aid lines on both the Upper and Lower Walls have been freed in recent years, many with traditional gear and sporting runouts, and several more long, hard free climbs have been established on the Upper Wall.

Although Index has been declared "climbed out" several times in the past, new route development continues to this day, with many new routes established on the Upper Wall, Diamond, and adjacent cliffs since the newest guidebook to the area was released in 2017. There does not seem to be an end in sight for new route development at Index.

Seasons and climate: Weather at Index is typically wet, particularly from late fall through spring. Convergence of moist marine air with cooler mountain air seems

Chris Gentry aiding *Snow White* (5.7 A2), Index Lower Town Wall CHRIS GENTRY COLLECTION

to wring all the rain down on the western slopes of the Cascade Range. Thus, Index gets soaked while Leavenworth stays comparatively dry. As a general rule, if it's raining in Seattle or Leavenworth, it's raining at Index. From late June through early September, the weather is usually fair. At any other time, if it isn't raining, be thankful. Some of the routes dry out quickly, and climbers are often on the walls even on "rainy" days. Check current weather information before you head out, and make friends with an Index local who can give you up-to-the-minute weather beta.

Precautions and regulations: Many climbers feel Index's routes are underrated, particularly routes rated 5.11b and 5.11d. Some locals feel this is because the ratings in other areas are wrong, but a 5.11d at Index sure feels harder than a comparable 5.11d elsewhere, particularly the thin cracks. If you haven't climbed here before, try a couple of easier routes to get a feel for the rock and the ratings before trying something at or near your limit.

Although Index's rock is generally sound, there are loose blocks and flakes here and there. Expanding flakes have been known to spit out gear—and climbers—but cams have reduced if not eliminated that problem. Rockfall is infrequent, except in the Quarry Area and occasionally in the Great Northern Slab. Given the expanding nature of the rock (mass wasting has occurred within recorded history—that's how the big talus field below the quarry wall got there), there have been remarkably few accidents and fatalities at Index. Dropped gear is more of a problem in crowded areas; helmets are recommended.

Another local hazard is stuff being thrown off the Upper Town Wall. A road leads to the top of the wall, where visitors have been known to toss rocks, tree limbs,

beer bottles, car parts, and even entire cars. The main fall zone is toward the left side of the wall, but climbers visiting the Upper Wall should be alert for trundling activity above, and take appropriate precautions.

Despite rebolting developments, there are still a few rusty old bolts on Index's walls. These old bolts have been known to break. Although most bolts on free routes have been upgraded, many old aid routes still feature rusty ladders. You should back these up where possible, and feel free to replace them, but contact the Washington Anchor Replacement Project first to make sure someone isn't already on the job. Bolt hanger and fixed pin theft used to be rampant at Index. Even though a fixed pin or bolt may be shown in this guide, don't believe it's there unless you see it. Please don't steal hangers or fixed pins! It's not only selfish, but it can create a dangerous situation for other climbers.

Since most of Index's long-established aid routes have been climbed free in whole or in part, it is important to limit hammered placements on these routes. Continued pitoning will further disfigure the rock and alter the character of these climbs for future climbers. Even on routes requiring hammered placements, nailing can and should be kept to a necessary minimum. Hammerless nut, hook, and piton placements are abundant, so please use nailing only as a last resort.

Many of the less-popular Index routes have become overgrown with moss and ferns and should not be climbed in their present condition. As a general rule, popular routes get cleaned each spring, so if the route stays dirty into summer or is overgrown, it probably isn't worth the effort. This being a select guide, if a route is so unpopular that it has grown over, it probably isn't included.

As at other areas, Index Town Walls are often affected by seasonal raptor nesting restrictions or closures. A notice will usually be posted at the trailhead, but climbers should check applicable websites and social media for current restrictions.

Ownership of the Index Town Walls is complicated. The Lower Town Wall was acquired by the Washington Climbers Coalition in 2010, although the WCC plans to donate its parcel to Washington State Parks. The Lower Town Wall parcel is officially known as the Stimson Bullitt Climbing Reserve in honor of Stim Bullitt, a noted climber and philanthropist who died in 2009. The rest of the area lies on Washington State Parks, US Forest Service, and private land. Ownership and access information changes; for current information, go to www.washington climbers.org.

Gear and other considerations: A standard rack at Index should consist of an assortment of wired nuts, some mid-range stoppers and hexes, and several cams or large nuts with duplicates in the 1- to 3-inch range. Because of typically parallel-sided, slightly flaring cracks and expanding flakes, cams are highly recommended. RPs and similar wired nuts seem to work well in pin scars. A typical Index route may require protection as small as a #2 RP and as large as a #4 Camalot all in the same pitch. Slings are crucial if you want to avoid rope drag on long pitches, especially those that aren't straight up cracks. Double ropes (at least 60 meters) are recommended for most rappels, although some sport routes are set up for single-rope descents using 60- or 70-meter ropes. In general, a 70-meter rope is recommended on many routes to avoid uncertainty and potential problems descending on a rope that is too short.

Camping and accommodations: The town of Index offers a few amenities. There is a general store, a pub, and public restrooms, but little else. There are several restaurants and motels in towns along US 2 (Sultan, Gold Bar, Skykomish), but the nearest town with all accommodations is Monroe, 20 miles west on US 2.

There are a few unofficial campsites beside the river near the Lower Wall, including the "Wagonwheel" area just upriver from the Lower Wall parking area, but these sites are usually occupied. There are some other unofficial bivouac sites along Index-Galena Road and at various other spots in the vicinity. Ask around; somebody probably has a favorite spot. As a last resort, Troublesome Creek or San Juan campgrounds can be found about 10 miles up Index-Galena Road, and Money Creek, Beckler River, and Miller Creek campgrounds are located near Skykomish, about 12 miles east of the Index turnoff on US 2. These campgrounds are closed much of the year. The long-awaited toilet at the Lower Town Wall was installed in late 2018. Please use it!

Emergency services: In case of emergency, dial 911. The nearest hospital is in Monroe, 20 miles west on US 2.

Other guidebooks: Chris Kalman and Matty Van Biene's *The Index Town Walls* (2017) is the current comprehensive guide to Index climbing. Mountain Project covers many of the classic Index routes as well. Clint Cummins's topo guide, *Index Town Wall Climbing Guide* (1993), is available online and covers most of the old classics (and then some).

Finding the crags: Index is located just north of US 2, about 40 miles east of Everett, and only about one hour northeast of Seattle when there isn't traffic, or one and a half hours west of Leavenworth. Exit US 2 at the Mount Index Cafe and follow Index-Galena Road into town; from there the walls are immediately obvious. If you're heading up the Lookout Point Trail, park near the schoolhouse (across the street from the Bush House Inn) if you can find parking; you may have to park across the river. If you're climbing at the Upper or Lower Wall Areas, park at the Lower Town Wall, about 1.25 miles west from the Bush House Inn, again, if you can find parking. Climbing at Index has become much more popular in recent years, leading to overcrowding in some areas and difficulty in finding parking some days. Because of the frequency of car prowling thefts these days, do not leave anything of value in your vehicle here or, really, anywhere else.

LOWER WALL

Index's Lower Wall surely ranks as one of Washington's finest crags, with perhaps the greatest concentration of clean, steep cracks of any cliff in the state, even rivaling Yosemite's Cookie Cliff in number and quality of climbs. The cliff is located on the lower left side of the Index Town Walls and is identifiable from town by a large white scar. Reach the wall by driving southwest from town. Take a left at the Bush House Inn and follow the county road to the graded parking lot across the railroad tracks from the wall. You can't miss it!

The Lower Wall is about 0.25 mile in width and rises to a height of about 500 feet at its highest point. The main portion of this wall is an obvious, clean, weathered cliff, vertical at its base and tapering back to a steep slab near its top, which is strafed with vertical crack systems intersected by abundant ledges. The Lower Wall is bordered on the left by a steep dihedral known as Roger's Corner. Immediately left of Roger's Corner is the Great Northern Slab, a block, slabby section of rock that features some of the area's best "easy" routes and some steep slab test pieces. Directly above Roger's Corner is a small, dihedral-infested cliff that is fittingly known

Lower Wall Area Approach Map

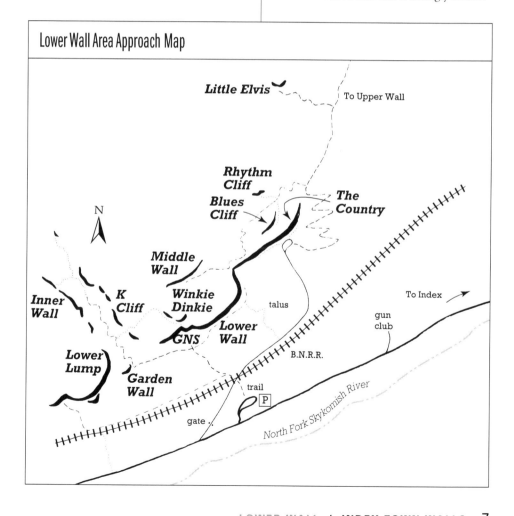

as the Dihedral Wall. Just right of the Dihedral Wall is The Shield, a crackless, rounded slab on the upper left side of the Lower Wall proper. About 50 yards up and left from the Dihedral Wall is the diminutive Winkie Dinkie Cliff. All of these areas are fairly obvious from the railroad tracks directly above the parking area. Not immediately obvious are the Lower Lump, a blocky, forested dome located about 0.25 mile southwest of the Lower Wall; the Garden Wall, a small, slabby cliff situated about 100 meters southwest of the Great Northern Slab; and the Inner Wall, a hidden canyon dividing the Lower Lump and Lower Wall area. Immediately right of the Lower Wall is an immense scar left by turn-of-the-century quarrying. The rightmost section of the Lower Wall cliff band, beyond the Quarry Scar, is known as The Country. Directly above The Country and barely visible from below are Blues Cliff and Rhythm Cliff, which are reached via a spur trail off the Upper Wall Trail, which continues along the top of the quarry scar to the reclusive Middle Wall. There are myriad routes on the small cliffs in between the Lower and Upper Walls, which are not included in this guide. For information about old, obscure routes not included in the current Index guide, refer to the Cummins guide, which is available online.

As elsewhere in this guide, all descents are via lowering or rappelling from trees or anchors, except as otherwise noted. Most Index routes now have two-bolt anchors atop each pitch.

Great Northern Slab

Heading north from the parking lot and across the railroad tracks, a trail leads you straight to the Great Northern Slab (GNS), which has many of the easiest routes at Index

and is often crowded. A dark, dirty wall flanks the slab on the left. The left side of the slab has several 5.6 crack routes while the right side is steeper with climbs rated 5.10 and up. Rappel from various anchors and trees.

Great Northern Slab– Left Side

1. Great Northern Slab (5.6) ★ This route climbs the thin twin cracks on the upper left side of the slab. Begin with the low-angled ramp on the left (5.2) or the easy flake/corner below *Libra Crack* (5.0) to reach the rusty old iron bolts, then climb directly up (5.7) or traverse around from the left to reach the slab. A second pitch leads to the top (5.6 or 5.7, depending on which variation you take). Pro: to 2 inches.

2. Pisces (5.6 or 5.10a) ★★★ The obvious hand crack on the right side of the slab. The initial section of the crack is an excellent 5.10a jam crack popularly known as *Libra Crack*, which can be avoided via a ramp on the right. Pro: to 2.5 inches. (FA: Mark Weigelt, Mike Berman 1969)

3. Taurus (5.7) ★ From atop the big pillar just right of *Libra Crack*, climb right up a slabby corner and traverse under the *Aries* roof to a step-across move below a small triangular roof. From there, continue up either of two flakes to the top of the slab, or up a 5.10a corner crack another 10 feet right of the triangular roof. Pro: to 2 inches.

4. The Lizard (aka Aries) (5.8+) ★★ This popular route begins from the base of the wall, climbing a short, exfoliated fist crack to the initial ledge, then up a superb thin corner crack to a flaring chimney. Grunt up the crux chimney (or bypass it like everyone else does), then undercling out the left side of the big

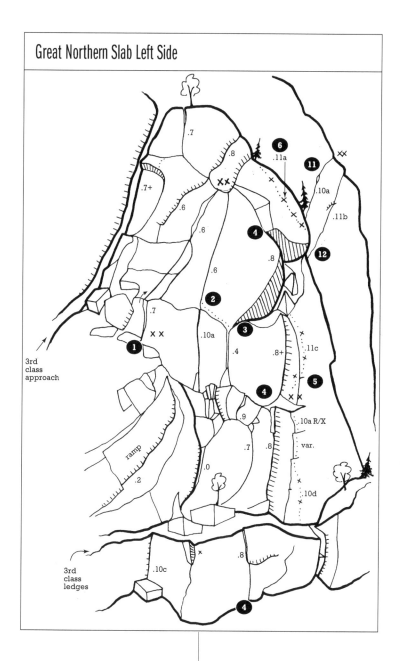

Great Northern Slab Left Side

.7

.8

.11a

6

11

.7+

xx

.10a

.6

x

.11b

.6

4

xx

.8

12

.6

2

.7

3

xx

.10a

1

.4

.8+

.11c

3rd
class
approach

x

5

4

x

.9

.10a R/X

.7

.8

var.

ramp

.0

.2

x

.10d

3rd
class
ledges

.10c

x

.8

4

roof to the *Pisces* anchors. Pro: to 3 inches. (FA: Ron Burgner, Thom Nephew 1970)

5. On the Verge (5.11c) ★★ Palm up the bolted arête immediately right of the *Aries* chimney. Can be combined with *Voyage to the Bottom of the Verge* (the 5.10d arête right

of the *Aries* dihedral) in a single pitch. Pro: quickdraws; gear to 2 inches.

6. Air Over Aries (5.11a) ★ A variation that climbs the slab above the roof. Make sure the bolts have hangers before you commit yourself. Pro: quickdraws; slings.

Great Northern Slab– Right Side

The following routes are located on the broad slab between the *Aries* dihedral and Roger's Corner (the obvious big, blocky dihedral dividing the Great Northern Slab and Lower Wall). The routes are reached via a short scramble up and right from the base of the *Aries* dihedral, or via a trail of sorts leading leftward and up from the start of *Princely Ambitions.*

7. Sonic Reducer (5.12a) ★★★ One of Index's early slab test pieces, following the line of

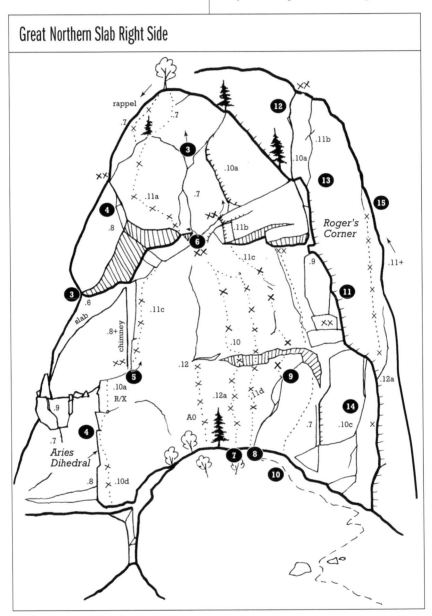

Great Northern Slab Right Side

closely spaced bolts on the left side of the smooth slab. Pro: quickdraws. (FA: Jon Nelson, Greg Olsen, Russell Erickson 1984)

8. Pretty Vacant (5.11d) ★ This squeezed-in sport route ends high on the slab, sans anchors; traverse left to finish on *Sonic Reducer* or right to *Terminal Preppie*. Would get more stars if it was an independent line. Pro: quickdraws.

9. Terminal Preppie (5.11c) ★★★★ A popular test piece combining face, slab, and crack climbing in one pitch, with a couple of roofs thrown in for fun. Pro: quickdraws, gear to 0.5 inch, including small wired nuts; "Long Dong" piton and #3 Friend helpful to supplement protection. (FA: Greg Olsen, Jon Nelson 1983)

10. Strength Through Bowling (5.10d) ★ Used to be a dirty, loose pitch through the roof right of *Terminal Preppie*, but it has been cleaned up. Pro: quickdraws, a few cams to 3 inches.

11. Roger's Corner (5.9+) The big dihedral dividing the Great Northern Slab and the Lower Wall. Start via a short, wide crack, then up the corner. Variations possible, most are dirty. Pro: to 4 inches.

12. Breakfast of Champions (5.10a) ★★★ The steep, airy hand crack above *Roger's Corner*. Approach via that route (5.9+), or from *Taurus* via the step-across move and ramp. A 60-meter rappel from this route's anchors reaches the ground. Friable rock. Pro: to 3 inches. (FFA: Julie Brugger, Carla Firey 1974)

13. Marginal Karma (aka Windmills) (5.11b) ★ The thin crack right of *Breakfast of Champions*. Usually toproped from the *Breakfast of Champions* anchors. Friable rock. Pro: to 2 inches.

14. Sugar Bear (5.10c) ★ Variation start of *Roger's Corner,* via dirty cracks. Fun when cleaned up. Pro: to 1 inch.

15. Virgin on the Ridiculous (5.12a) ★ The prominent arête right of *Roger's Corner.* Begin just right of *Sugar Bear,* climbing cracks and face on or just left of the arête. An excellent route if it has been retrobolted, otherwise some questionable fixed pins and scary runouts (R/X). Friable rock. Pro: quickdraws if retrobolted; RPs, small cams, and gear to 2 inches if not.

Dihedral Wall

Just above and right of the Great Northern Slab is this small wall featuring several dihedrals and a large roof. It has several popular one-pitch routes, most of which are 5.11. Dihedral Wall is best approached from the top of the Great Northern Slab via an exposed traverse (belay across if any doubts). To descend from the Dihedral Wall and The Terrace area, most parties rappel *Breakfast of Champions* and *Roger's Corner*.

16. Terminator (5.10b) ★ A bolted knobby slab and cracks on the left side, passing a roof low down. Height dependent; 5.10d if you can't reach the knob over the roof. Pro: quickdraws, gear to 2 inches.

17. Cup & Saucer (5.11d) ★★ A dihedral leading to the big roof. This stemming test piece is a direct and better start to *Julie's Roof.* Pro: quickdraws.

18. Julie's Roof (5.11a) ★★ The dihedral directly below the big roof. The route passes the roof on the right to enter a steep corner, or on the left. Pro: to 2 inches.

19. Gogum (5.11a) ★ The rightmost dihedral on Dihedral Wall. Pro: to 2 inches.

Dihedral Wall Area

Winkie Dinkie Cliff

Just up and left from the top of the Great Northern Slab and left of Dihedral Wall is the diminutive Winkie Dinkie Cliff, which has a few routes in the 5.8 to 5.12 range, only one of which is really popular. This cliff is usually approached by climbing Great Northern Slab, although a hard-to-find trail supposedly leads here from the Inner Wall Trail. Rappel from anchors.

20. Gorilla My Dreams (5.10a) ★★ A sport route climbing the big, right-facing flake (the one with all the bolts). It's a strenuous layback, pumpy but not technical. Pro: quickdraws; long slings to reduce rope drag.

21. Timberjack (5.8) ★ A flake and crack line left of *Gorilla My Dreams*. Pretty good for the grade. Pro: to 4-5 inches.

The Shield

The Terrace is the grassy slope below and right of the Dihedral Wall. Approach and descend as for the Dihedral Wall—exposed! Above on the right is The Shield, a broad, rounded slab, with the following routes.

22. Lamar's Trust (5.10a) ★ A friction climb up a slab between Dihedral Wall and The Shield. Pro: quickdraws, gear to 2 inches.

23. Newest Industry (5.11a) ★★★ An airy friction route that begins just right of the obvious curving flake and follows bolts up the exposed slab, finishing through roofs. Runout on easy ground. Save some gear to back up the belay anchors. Pro: quickdraws; gear to 2 inches. (FA: Darryl Cramer, Greg Olsen, Terry Lien 1986)

Lower Wall

Lower Wall–Left Side

The left side of the Lower Wall has numerous steep cracks, flakes, corners, and arches and features some of Index's most popular free climbs. A trail leads right along the base of the wall, passing an obvious clean arête and slab, which has a few popular boulder problems.

24. Dwarf Tossing (5.12b) ★ A free version of the old *Snow White* aid route, crossing that route, almost joining *Princely Ambitions*, with a wild lunge. Pro: quickdraws, gear to 1 inch.

25. Nobody Tosses a Dwarf (5.12) ★ This one follows the approximate line of the second pitch of *Snow White*. Start up *Princely Ambitions* to anchors on the right, then head straight up to the horizontal roof, traverse right under the roof, then finish straight up. Get on it. Pro: quickdraws, gear to 1 inch. (FA: Ben Gilkison)

26. Princely Ambitions (5.10a) ★★ A popular two-pitch route on the left side of the wall. Begin via flakes leading right, then back left into the easier upper crack system. The first pitch is harder now that a big flake came off. The second pitch climbs a wide corner to the terrace at the base of *Newest Industry*. Pro: to 2 inches, long runners.

27. Doctor Sniff and the Tuna Boaters (5.11a) ★ A right-curving flake right of *Princely Ambitions*' second pitch leads to a thin crack that turns into a flaring slot. May require cleaning. Pro: to 1 inch, including wired nuts and TCUs.

28. Model Worker (5.11c) ★★★ An early sport route climbing to the flake of *Frog Pond*. Most parties stop at the chain anchors above the cedar stump (5.11b to here), but

Lower Wall–Left Side

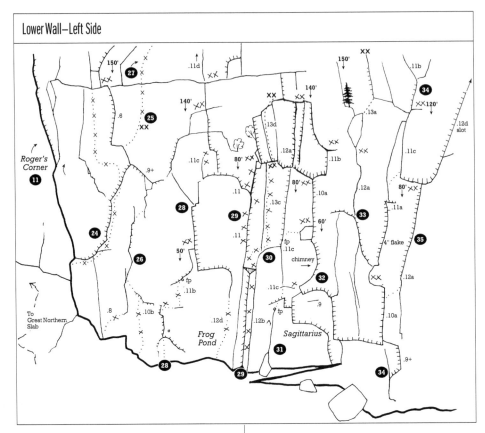

the best part of the route is higher up. Can be linked with *Newest Industry* by climbing a 5.11d thin corner crack above the upper anchors. Pro: quickdraws, #2.5 Friend to first anchors, to 2.5 inches to finish. (FA: Greg Olsen, Jon Nelson 1982)

29. Numbah Ten (5.12b) ★★★ The obvious dihedral 10 feet left of *Iron Horse*. It used to be an infrequently climbed aid route (A3), but through the miracle of rappel bolting it is now a very difficult sport route. Pro: quickdraws. (FFA: Larry Kemp, Max Dufford 1988)

30. Amandala (5.13c/d) ★★★ A challenging sport route climbing the obvious bolted arête above and right of the *Numbah Ten* dihedral. Begin as for *Numbah Ten*. A continuation turns the roof and continues to the *Iron Horse*

ledge (5.13d). Pro: quickdraws only to first anchors, include wireds for full pitch. (FA: Andy deKlerk 1991; Ben Gilkison complete 2007)

31. Iron Horse (5.11d) ★★★★ A popular test piece climbing a pin-scarred crack left of *Sagittarius*. A crux face section foils most on-sight attempts. Exit via the hollow flake on the right, or go for broke through the roofs. An enjoyable, popular clean aid pitch (C2) as well. Pro: to 1 inch. (FFA: Peter Croft to flake 1981; Dick Cilley complete 1984)

32. Sagittarius (5.10a or 5.11b) ★★★★ The obvious big, arching flake right of *Iron Horse*. Climb the arch and an intimidating flaring chimney to reach the hollow flake anchors (5.9 to here); keep going up a steep corner crack to anchors at the roofs (80 feet,

Flyura Zhirnova on *Model Worker* (5.11c), Index Lower Town Wall LARRY KEMP COLLECTION

Lower Wall Area

The Shield

Narrow Arrow

Lower Wall
Right Side

Lower Wall
Left Side

5.10a) or continue up the thin crack above to higher anchors (5.11b). Pro: to 4 inches. (FA: Pat Timson to hollow flake 1974; Mark Moore to roof 1982)

33. Ten Percent Meteorological Vinculation (5.13a) ★★★
A free version of the old aid route between *Sagittarius* and *Japanese Gardens*. From atop the 5.10a flake of *Japanese Gardens,* go left up the superb thin crack (5.12a) to anchors below Chopper Flake. Descend from the anchors if you've had enough, or continue for the full first pitch to the Park Benches (150 feet, 5.13a crux, runout with difficult protection). Continue up the final pitches, which ascend the right side of The Shield via steep, exposed friction (5.11d). Pro: quickdraws; gear to 2 inches; #5 BD microstopper sideways below the crux. (FFA: Ben Gilkison 2007)

34. Japanese Gardens (5.11d) ★★★★
A classic four-pitch free climb following the line of the Lower Town Wall's original aid route directly up the middle of the wall. Climb the obvious big flake system right of *Sagittarius* through a small roof, where a crux thin crack/face move reaches a small ledge 120 feet up. A thin corner crack or right-hand variation (*Trout Farm Massacre,* 5.11c) continues up to the Park Benches to join an arching flake system that continues two pitches to the top. The steepness, quality of rock, and continuous difficulty combine to make this one of the finest multipitch free climbs in Washington. Pro: to 4 inches; bring at least one 4-inch cam for the first pitch, plus wired nuts, RPs, and TCUs. (FFA: Jon Nelson, Terry Lien 1984)

35. Stern Farmer (5.12b) ★★★
The shallow dihedral immediately right of the first pitch of *Japanese Gardens*. Start up *Japanese Gardens,* then traverse right into the corner and ascend to anchors below the roof. *Stern*

Farmer Complete (5.12d) continues up the formerly A3 flare above the roof to a higher roof, joining the upper pitches of *Bat Skins*. Pro: to 3 inches, including multiple wired nuts and TCUs, slings to reduce rope drag. (FFA: Terry Lien, Tom Michael 1984; Mike Schaefer complete 2005)

Lower Wall–Right Side

Just right of the lowest point of the Lower Wall is an obvious vertical pin-scar crack; this is *City Park,* perhaps the most unmistakable route at the Lower Wall, unless it's the flake and dihedral of *Godzilla* just right.

36. Bat Skins (5.12a) ★★
A right-leaning arch just left of the *City Park* bolt ladder leads to a tricky face (5.11a) and the first anchors. If you do the full first pitch, it's 5.12a stemming and face climbing up knobs. The route continues to the Park Benches (5.11b or 5.11d, depending on which crack you take). Pro: to 1.5 inches to first anchors, with TCUs and long slings; quickdraws and to 2.5 inches if you continue.

37. City Park (5.13d or 5.10b C1) ★★★★
The first pitch of this old four-pitch aid route is without a doubt the best easy aid crack in the state, but it's also a very difficult free climb. Start via the obvious bolt ladder (5.10b), then climb the even more-obvious thin crack to an exposed ledge 120 feet up (C1 or 5.13d). Pro: to 2 inches, with many small wired nuts for the first pitch. The original route continues to the Park Benches (5.10b), then gets lost in obscurity. (FA: Roger Johnson, Richard Mathies 1966; FFA: Todd Skinner 1986)

38. Godzilla (5.9) ★★★★
A steep, airy flake and corner system just right of the *City Park* thin crack, one of the best pitches of its grade in Washington. Begin either via a

Lower Wall—City Park Area

short dihedral on the right or the 5.10b bolt ladder, then up the flake and corner, with a final thin crack to get to the ledge. Continue via the second pitch of *City Park* (5.10b) to the Park Benches. Pro: to 3 inches; cams recommended. (FA: Don Harder, Donn Heller 1972)

39. Park Ranger (5.10a/b) ★★ A moderate free route to the top of the Lower Town Wall connecting *Godzilla* and the second pitch of *City Park* (or the *Leapin' Lizards* continuation of *Godzilla*) to the Park Benches, then moving right to thin corner crack that starts a two-pitch finish following the approximate line of the old *City Park* aid route. Gets dirty; if you are cleaning it, be sure to warn people below as the fall line is right on the start of *City Park/Godzilla*. Pro: to 3 inches; small cams and nuts.

40. Slow Children (5.10d) ★★★★ A superb thin, flaring corner crack high on the wall. Start via *Godzilla,* then climb the second pitch of *City Park* (5.10b) to reach the Park Benches, from where this obvious slot continues skyward. Rappel from anchors, or continue up *Tommy's Sandbox,* a 5.11a pitch that continues to near the top of the wall. Pro: to 1 inch, including many wired nuts. (FA: John Carpenter, Terry Lien, Jon Nelson, et al. 1980)

41. Natural Log Cabin (5.11d) ★★★ Cracks, corners, and flakes lead up to the stem box cutting through the big blocky overhang left of the *Narrow Arrow Overhang*. Descend from anchors or continue on a 5.11c pitch up the corner left of the *Narrow Arrow* summit pillar. Pro: to 2 inches; cams. (FA: Terry Lien, Jon Nelson, Nicola Masciandaro)

42. Narrow Arrow Overhang (5.13a) ★★★★ Climb up to and over the obvious roof below the *Narrow Arrow*. Funky climbing up

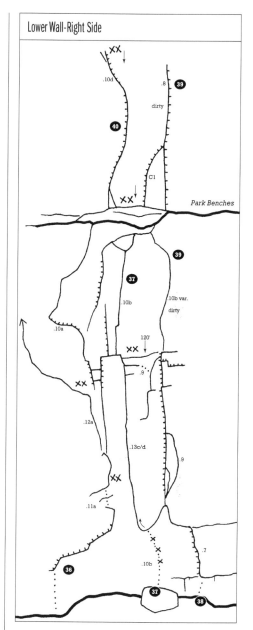

Lower Wall-Right Side

Park Benches

box corners and arêtes, with a tenuous crux right below the roof. The route has multiple chain anchors, so you can do shorter, easier versions if you aren't up to the full pitch. Pro: quickdraws; slings for rope drag; gear to 2 inches, small wired nuts. (FFA: Ben Gilkison 2008)

Lower Wall—Narrow Arrow Area

43. The Cleft (aka Narrow Arrow Direct)

(5.12c or 5.11 C2) ★★ A four-pitch route up cracks and corners right of the *Narrow Arrow* overhang to the summit of the Narrow Arrow. The first pitch ascends shallow cracks and corners directly to the ledge just right of the *Narrow Arrow Overhang* (free at 5.12c or aid at C2). Most bypass this pitch by climbing *Shirley* or rappelling in from above. From the ledge, ascend a stellar dihedral (5.10a) to ledges, then a short, thin crack (5.11a) gains a chimney that leads up to an alcove/roof, from where a burly offwidth (5.10) continues to a ledge just below the Narrow Arrow summit. A 5.11b thin crack traverse on the right offers an escape variation if offwidths aren't your idea of fun. Pro: to 2 inches, many smaller pieces, then big stuff for the offwidth. (FFA: pitch 1 Dave Moroles, pitches 2-3 John Stoddard)

44. Shirley

(5.11c) ★★★ This steep dihedral left of *Thin Fingers* features strenuous stemming and thin, flaring jams. Start via an obvious white right-leaning arch to the left side of the *Thin Fingers* ledge (5.10b, a good pitch in its own right) and continue straight up the corner. From the upper ledge, traverse left to *The Cleft* dihedral or finish via one of several 5.10d cracks along the way. May be dirty, but worth cleaning. Pro: to 2 inches; cams.

45. Thin Fingers

(5.11a) ★★★★ An Index classic, climbing the very obvious vertical cracks splitting the white wall right of the Narrow Arrow overhang. To get there, climb the white arch start as for *Shirley;* a dirty, direct 5.10a crack; or the 5.9 chimney start of *Tatoosh* to a ledge. From there it's all crack to the anchors. Pro: to 2.5 inches, including several finger to hand-size cams. (FFA: Paul Boving 1976)

46. Tatoosh/Free at Last

(III, 5.9 or 5.10b) ★ A pair of intertwined routes on the right side of the Narrow Arrow. Begin from the base of the wall or traverse in to a half chimney (5.9) on the right side of the wall, then climb a corner crack/ramp or right-facing flake to a ledge. Step left to a steep corner crack (5.10a) or right to a scruffy offwidth (5.8+). This much can be done in one long pitch (with attendant rope drag) or two pitches. From the blocky ledge, join the *Narrow Arrow* route for one pitch (an easy, dirty ramp), then continue straight up the corner system above for two more pitches. The original route exited left at the top (5.10b), but the old A2 variation on the right goes free at 5.10d. If that's not hard enough, there's a 5.12 face pitch up the headwall right, without a doubt the airiest pitch on the Lower Town Wall. Pro: to 3 inches will suffice, although a larger piece for the offwidth may help.

47. Death to Zeke

(5.11d) ★ A prominent right-curving arch just down and right of the Narrow Arrow summit. To get there, climb *Tatoosh* and traverse Class 4 ledges, or take any of the other routes leading to the ledges. Pro: to 2.5 inches, mostly small, including RPs and TCUs.

Quarry Area

The far right side of the wall, left of the huge talus slope, is the Quarry Area, with many steep, angular cracks. The rock deteriorates as you move right, with menacing loose blocks aplenty. Rappel anchors abound, making descents possible from several places, although a few rappel anchors are kind of scary.

48. With Apologies to Walter B.

(5.11c) ★★★ A thin crack splitting the prominent Bonatti

Pillar right of *Tatoosh*. A short, crux face traverse gains the crack. Gets dirty. Pro: to 1 inch, including wired nuts and small cams.

49. Quarry Crack (5.9) An intimidating overhanging offwidth that isn't as hard as it looks. Pro: to 2 inches, including cams.

50. Narrow Arrow Route (5.7 R/X) Ascend the pile of amazingly loose blocks just right of the Bonatti Pillar (if you dare!) to gain the upper ledges, from where a dirty Class 5 ramp and Class 4 traversing on blocky ledges gains the esteemed Narrow Arrow summit. It's the easiest way to get there, but why bother? Pro: to 3 inches.

51. Let's Barbecue (5.11c) ★ A steep crack in a shallow corner. Quality climbing but usually needs cleaning. Starts on the prow of the pillar to the right of the Narrow Arrow. Select your choice of approach pitches, none of which is highly recommended (except *Thin Fingers*). May be dirty. Pro: to 1 inch.

52. Bob and Doris (5.10c) ★ The steep corner crack continuation of *Let's Barbecue.* May be dirty. Lousy rappel anchors unless they've been upgraded. Pro: to 2 inches.

Garden Wall

No topo. The Garden Wall is a small cliff located at the start of the Inner Wall Trail, about 100 meters left from the base of *The Slab*. It has a recognizable diagonal flake running from the lower left to upper right (*A Touch Too Much*, 5.11b R/X), a mossy slab (*Weed B Gon* 5.10c), and a short, steep, bolted knobby face on its upper right side (*Knob Job,* 5.10d ★★★, the best and probably the cleanest route on the wall). The cliff is growing back over with moss and ferns, and the routes are usually dirty and infrequently climbed.

Inner Wall

Most of the routes at the Inner Wall are on the steep, mossy walls at the highest point of the gap, although a few routes have been done on walls on either side as one approaches this secluded area and farther into the canyon. As one climber sagely noted, "Only *Toxic Shock* and *Even Steven* are worth climbing" at the Inner Wall. It's almost true, but there are a few other routes worth doing. How to tell which ones they are? They're the ones not grown over with moss and ferns. Inner Wall routes are often wet and aren't the best choice during spring or after a rainy day. Bolts and hangers have been stolen from many sport routes here, making it unlikely you will be able to climb them unless you go to the trouble of replacing bolts and hangers. (Several of these sport routes are shown on the topo but should not be climbed unless hangers are in place.) The routes are obvious once you get there. Most descents are by rappel.

Inner Wall Trail

The Inner Wall (also known as the "Inner Walls") is a narrow canyon located between the Lower Wall and Lower Lump formations, reached via a trail that forks left just below the Great Northern Slab. As you hike in from the parking lot, just as you reach the talus at the base of Great Northern Slab, take the left fork and hike along a shelf to Garden Wall; from here the trail switchbacks up into the woods, reaching the Inner Wall in about twenty minutes. There are dozens of routes in this area, many of which are intermittently obscured by moss and ferns before being rediscovered by the cleaning crews. Refer to the current Index guide or the old Cummins guide for details.

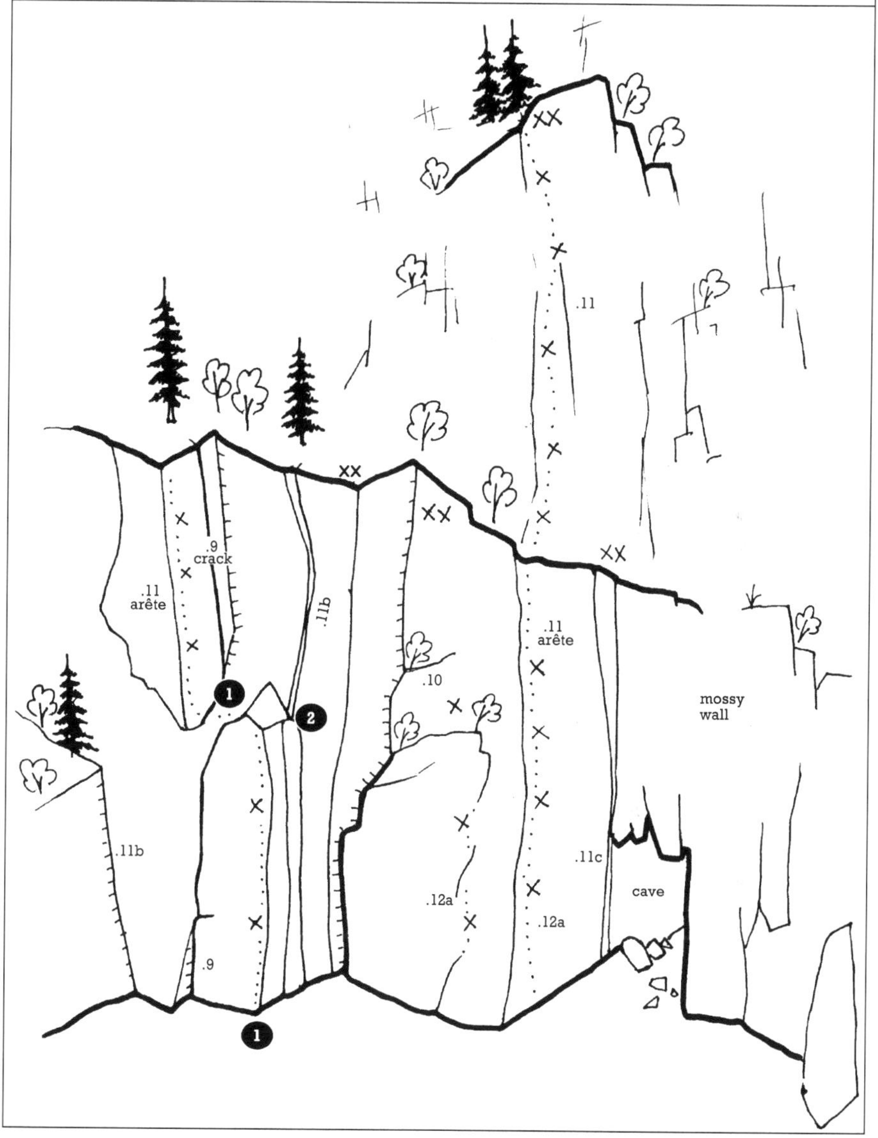

Inner Wall–Left Side

1. Toxic Shock (5.9) ★★★ The striking steep hand crack on the left wall of the upper dihedral begins with a short layback. Can be led in one pitch or two. Rappel from the big fir tree. Pro: to 3 inches. (FA: Steve Strong, Greg White 1981)

2. Even Steven (5.11b) ★★ The obvious twin thin cracks above the pillar. Begin via the wide cracks on the right side of the arête or via the first part of *Toxic Shock*. May need cleaning. Rappel from a tree. Pro: to 1 inch, including RPs and TCUs.

Inner Wall–Right Side

Directly across the canyon from *Toxic Shock* is Grandeur Buttress, a mossy wall with a few dirty routes in the 5.7 to 5.11 range. In the gully up and right of Grandeur Buttress is Trap Balls Buttress, which has several routes in the 5.9 to 5.10 range. Many of the routes on this side of the canyon were cleaned up in 2018, but will probably creep back into mossy obscurity unless they are kept clean. Expect to do some scrubbing if you plan on climbing here.

3. Corner Flash (5.7) ★ No topo. The obvious crack directly across the canyon from *Toxic Shock*. Pro: to 3 inches.

4. Agent Orange (5.11c R) ★★ No topo. Lead the thin, scantly protected face just left of *Corner Flash*. Two variation starts, both 5.11, both with adequate protection if you place it well, but still tenuous. Pro: wired nuts; small cams.

5. Delusions of Adequacy (5.11a) ★★ No topo. Traverse over to, then ascend the blocky corner system about 30 feet left of *Corner Flash*, a cleaned-up version of an old variation start to *Agent Orange*. Pro: wired nuts; small cams; quickdraws.

Lower Lump

The Lower Lump is the dark, blocky, forested dome on the far left side of the Lower Wall formation. There are several routes on the Lower Lump, but an abundance of vegetation and some scary-looking rock has made this area decidedly unpopular. There are a few good, slabby routes on the

"shield" on the far left side of the Lower Lump that have retained some popularity. Approach via a trail about 50 feet beyond the obvious big boulder beside the railroad tracks, about 0.25 mile west from the Lower Wall crossing.

1. Beetle Bailey Arch (5.11a) ★★ Begin via the obvious flake at the base of the shield, with two bolts (5.11a) leading to the flake's top. Most climb only the first pitch and rappel, as the remaining pitches tend to be dirty and runout. Nasty when wet. Pro: to 2 inches; lots of quickdraws.

2. Metal (5.11c) ★ Climb the *Beetle Bailey* flake to the ledge, then climb the bolted slab leading just left at first, then straight up the slab to anchors below the upper arch. Pro: quickdraws.

3. Racer X (5.10b) ★★ Climb the *Beetle Bailey* flake to the ledge, then traverse left and follow bolts and fixed pins up the slab to anchors. A scary runout at the crux may give you pause. Pro: mostly quickdraws, but include a #3 Friend.

Quarry Scar

To the right of the Lower Wall is the immense scar left by turn-of-the-century quarrying, looming above a huge talus slope. The wall here is mostly dirty and shattered, with many loose blocks. There was once a scary aid route up the middle of this face through some huge overhangs, but during the winter of 1980 the overhangs came crashing down, depositing the many large boulders in the talus below. (The talus provides a few practice climbs and scary boulder problems, but the area has been principally used as a toilet over the years—beware!). Much loose rock on the Quarry Scar remains

Lower Lump-Left Side

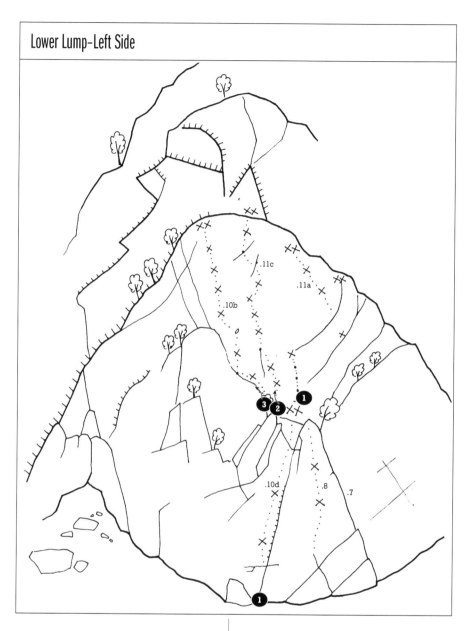

poised and ready to fly; what's solid is dirty, so climbing here is not very popular—nor is it recommended. A few aid routes have been done on the Scar, but they receive very few ascents.

Orc Tower

Orc Tower is the prominent pillar right of the Quarry Scar. Several routes lead to the base of this esteemed formation, and two routes reach the rubble-strewn summit. There are several sport routes in the vicinity of *Patrick's Flake,* the obvious crack on the

be careful when climbing in this area. If there are climbers above you, get out of there quick! Double-rope rappels are the norm for routes in this area. Don't just lower off unless you are certain your rope is long enough!

1. Patrick's Flake (5.10+) The obvious crack/flake below Orc Tower. Pro: to 2 inches.

2. Savage Garden (5.11d) ★★ A retro-classic climbing the steep wall about 50 feet right of *Patrick's Flake,* starting from an anchor bolt on an exposed ledge. A cleaner and easier version (5.11b) goes left to chain anchors at the top. Pro: quickdraws.

3. Elvis-Nixon (5.11a) ★★ A popular approach for *Wipe* and *Kite Flying Blind.* A bolt in a clean white dihedral marks the usual start. Traverse in from the corner to get to the first bolt. The initial moves are exposed and should be protected. Continue up the bolted face to cracks just right of a blocky flake/corner to reach the anchors below *Wipe.* Pro: to 1 inch, including wired nuts, #1 Tech Friend.

4. Frank-Presley (5.11a) ★★ A better approach pitch for *Kite Flying Blind,* connecting the bolts up the face just right of *Elvis-Nixon.* Pro: quickdraws.

5. Mourning Star (5.8) ★ No topo. An easier route a little down and right from *Frank-Presley.* Angles right to anchors just left of *Zoom.* Pro: quickdraws; gear to 3 inches.

shelf directly below Orc Tower that provides the dividing line between the loose, potentially dangerous rock of the Quarry Scar and the more solid rock of The Country. Some of the routes in this area are dirty and have friable rock, but retrobolting and cleaning has made several of these more worthy of attention.

To reach these routes, approach as for The Country to the cave door, then hike up a trail leading left along the base of the cliff, rather than traversing across the talus below the Quarry Scar. Orc Tower and the Quarry Scar are notorious for loose rock, so

6. Wipe (5.11a) ★★ An obvious crack system climbing a clean buttress visible about 100 yards up and left from the cave door. Usually approached via *Elvis-Nixon*. Pro: to 1 inch, including RPs.

7. Kite Flying Blind (5.11c) ★★ Another fine route climbing cracks nearer the arête immediately right of *Wipe*. Usually approached via *Elvis-Nixon*. Retrobolted. Pro: quickdraws.

8. Over-Orcsposed (5.12a) ★★ A sport line climbing the outside face of Orc Tower. Link via *Frank-Presley* and *Kite Flying Blind* (four pitches: 5.11a, 5.11c, 5.11a, 5.12a). Pro: quickdraws.

The Country

The Country is the farthest right flank of the Lower Wall, above and to the right of the cave door. The rock is blocky, with many flakes, roofs, dihedrals, and ledges and abundant vegetation. The routes are concentrated in sections of clean rock and are mostly obvious when you look closely. Approach via the road leading along the railroad tracks and in to the cave door. Rappel from various anchors.

9. Zoom (II, 5.10d) ★★★ A popular three-pitch route climbing the steep wall about 100 feet left of the cave door. The first pitch starts directly above a stump, passing a few bolts to reach a left-facing corner, then up a knobby wall with thin protection to the

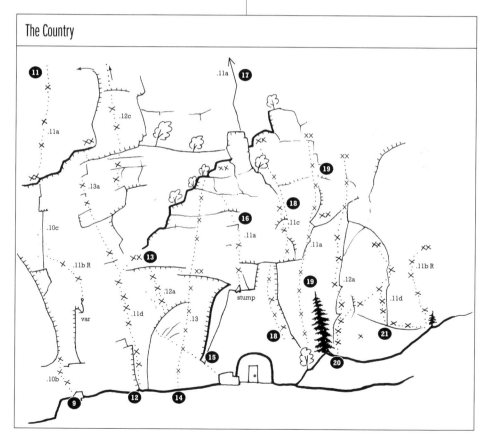

The Country

initial ledge. The second pitch is a brushy ledge traverse up and right to the base of the obvious flake/chimney system above, which completes the route. Most parties rappel after the first pitch, but the third pitch is worthy. Pro: to 3 inches, including RPs and Friends (a #2 RP is highly recommended). (FA: Jon Nelson, Steve Strong 1983)

10. Leave My Face Alone (5.11a) ★★ A popular second-pitch variation of *Zoom.* Climb the first pitch of *Zoom,* then go left and up a dirty right-facing flake and cracks (5.9) to reach a bolted face just right of the *Kite Flying Blind* arête. Retrobolted and ready. Pro: lots of quickdraws.

11. Hairway to Stephan (5.11a) ★★ Another second-pitch alternative to *Zoom,* this one continues up the bolted face directly above the anchors. One long pitch of enjoyable face climbing leads to anchors. Retrobolted. Pro: lots of quickdraws.

12. Little Jupiter (5.11d or 5.13a) ★ A short face pitch about 50 feet left of the cave door. Start in an obvious short dihedral and climb the knobby face to the *Big Science* anchors. If you do the complete pitch, it's 5.13a (one very hard move). Pro: quickdraws, plus a #2 TCU recommended for the first pitch; gear to 1 inch for the rest, including RPs and TCUs.

13. Big Science (5.12a) ★ A short, knobby face pitch immediately left of the cave door. Traverse in from the right or climb directly up the knobby face (5.11a) to reach the crux bulge. Pro: to 0.5 inch, quickdraws.

14. Indextasy (5.13-) ★★ A sport climb up knobs finishing right of *Big Science.* A second pitch has been completed. Pro: quickdraws. (FA: Mike Massey 2017).

15. S.S. Ultrabrutal (5.7) A right-leaning crack just left of the cave door, best climbed to set up a toprope on *Big Science* or to approach *Tunnel Vision.* Pro: to 2 inches.

16. Tunnel Vision (5.11a) ★ From the stump at the top of *Ultrabrutal's* initial corner, directly above the cave door, climb a steep, blocky face to anchors. Pro: quickdraws, wired nuts, TCUs.

17. Angora Grotto (5.11a) ★★ Climb *Tunnel Vision,* then continue right to this long, right-facing corner crack that passes a roof and continues up a bolted headwall. The crack gets dirty, making this route less popular than it deserves to be. Pro: to 2 inches.

18. Climax Control (5.11c) ★★★ The leftmost of two bolted routes just up and right from the cave door. Originally led on gear, it's been retrobolted for your convenience. Pro: quickdraws. (FA: Greg Collum, Larissa Collum, Cal Folsom)

19. Cunning Stunt (5.10c) ★★★ The next bolted route to the right, joining *Climax Control* briefly halfway up before angling right to its own anchors. Pro: all quickdraws. (FA: Greg Child, Greg Collum)

20. Fifth Force (5.12b) ★★★ An excellent, steep sport route climbing thin flakes and edges right of the cave, starting behind a large cedar. Pro: quickdraws suffice, although RPs may be helpful to minimize runouts. (FA: Greg Collum, Greg Child, Greg Olsen 1987)

21. Spooner (5.11d) ★ A tricky route right of *Fifth Force,* beginning with an overhanging hand traverse leading to a bolted seam/corner. A variation (*Force Fed,* 5.11d) links *Fifth Force* and *Spooner* via a traverse. A continuation pitch (*G is for Giners,* 5.12a) continues up the steep headwall. Pro: quickdraws.

22. Heart of the Country

(5.11b R) ★★ An excellent route on the right side of The Country, featuring one of the best crack pitches at Index. An unprotected slab (5.10b R) starts off the first pitch, which hardly anybody ever climbs, opting instead for the first bit of *G.M.* to get to the beautiful, clean crack higher up (5.11a). Rappel *G.M.;* double ropes recommended. Pro: to 2.5 inches. (FA: John Stoddard, Randy Stout 1980)

23. G.M. (5.9) ★★ A popular, moderate line up the far right flank of The Country. A brushy corner leads to a ledge, above which steep, wide cracks pass an overhang. Continue up cracks to the top of the wall and rappel the route. Pro: to 4 inches suffices, but bring bigger stuff if you've got it. (FA: Ed Gibson, Greg Markov 1973)

24. Phone Calls from the Dead

(5.11b) ★★ A face climb up the knobby wall right of the second pitch of *G.M.,* ending at anchors. Pro: quickdraws; RPs.

The Country

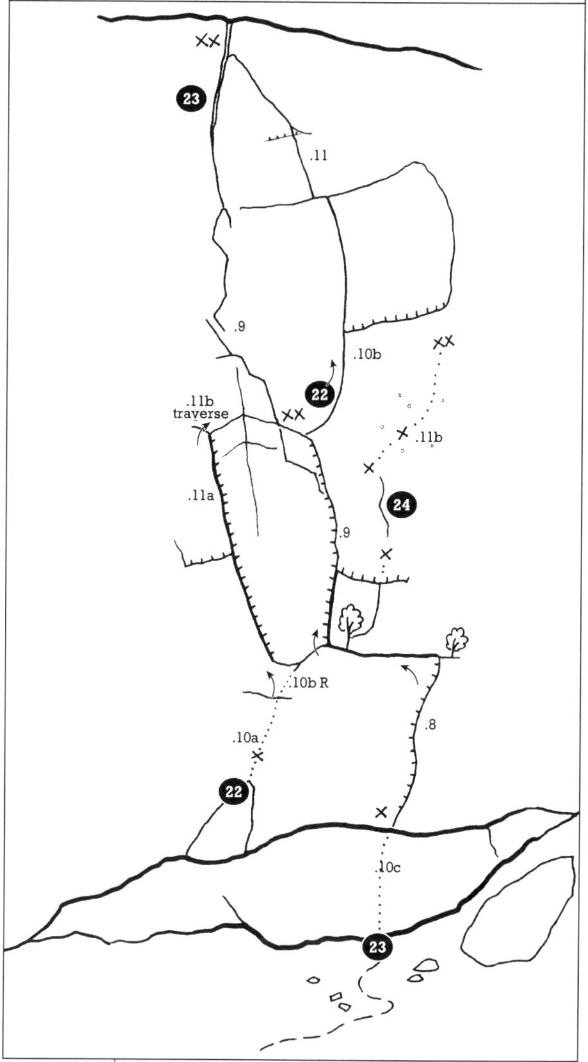

Upper Wall Trail

The Upper Wall Trail begins from The Country, just right of the cave door. It is a marvel of trail engineering, developed over a span of years through the vision and effort of Cal Folsom, leading more or less directly from the Lower Wall to the Upper Wall in about forty-five minutes, a vast improvement over the old "trail" that led up from the railroad crossing in town. There are several small walls and cliffs along the approach, with numerous short, often dirty, and neglected routes. Refer to the new Index Town Walls guide (Van Biene/Kalman 2017) for route details.

Blues Cliff

Blues Cliff is a small cliff perched just up and right of Orc Tower, almost invisible from below. It's small by Index standards, but bigger than most sport crags at other areas included in this guide. To get there, hike up the Upper Wall Trail about fifteen minutes to the first fork (the Middle Wall trail). Go left and continue uphill until the trail flattens out and Rhythm Cliff becomes visible uphill to the right. Three trails diverge at a boulder, one up and right to Rhythm Cliff, one straight ahead to the Middle Wall, and an easily missed spur trail down and left to Blues Cliff. The routes are described from right to left as you encounter them on the approach.

1. Rhythm and Bolts (5.11b) ★★ A steep slab pitch on the right side. Bolts lead left to anchors below the blocky roof. Pro: quickdraws.

2. Blues Riff (5.11b) ★★ About 30 feet left of *Rhythm and Bolts* are these facing corners leading to anchors at the left end of the roof. Difficult stemming. Sometimes brushy and dirty, but popular enough that it gets cleaned occasionally. Pro: quickdraws.

3. BB Cling (5.12a) ★★ A continuation of *Blues Riff,* climbing up briefly, then traversing right across a horizontal thin crack above the roof, then connecting the bolts up the neat headwall. Double-rope rappel, or two single-rope raps for the descent. Pro: quickdraws.

4. Etch-a-Sketch (5.11b) ★ An edgy slab leads to a left-leaning flake/arch. A short (crux) left traverse joins *Written in Stone,* from where the route traverses right to the *Blues Riff* anchors. A variation continues up *Written in Stone* to add a second crux. Pro: quickdraws.

5. Written in Stone (5.11b) ★★ A distinct slab/dike leads right, but at the sixth bolt head straight up to anchors in a mossy corner. The lower slab is neat; the upper crux can be dirty. A variation continues right up the slab to the *Blues Riff* anchors. Pro: quickdraws.

6. Blue in the Face (5.12c) ★★★ About 20 feet left of the start of *Written in Stone* is this steep sport route, climbing a broad, rounded, flaky corner system up to and over a distinct roof. Lots of bolts make this route easy to find, but it's no walk in the park. A 60-meter rope is helpful. Pro: quickdraws. (FA: Greg Collum, Matt Kerns 1992)

7. Cry Baby (5.11c) ★ A left-leading dike leads to anchors about 50 feet up the prominent steep arête on the left side of the cliff. A four-bolt extension increases the grade to 5.12a. Pro: quickdraws.

8. Black Cat Bone (5.11d) ★ On the left side of the cliff is an obvious thin flake below a steep corner system. Climb this flake, pass the initial bulge, then head right and up the thin crack to anchors atop the *Cry Baby* arête. The original start is via a dirty thin crack on the right. Pro: quickdraws, gear to 1 inch.

9. 12-Gauge IQ (5.12c) ★★★ Start as for *Black Cat Bone,* but traverse left after the initial bulge and up the obvious right-facing corner, passing a roof and finishing up the headwall. Sustained. A 60-meter rope is helpful. Pro: quickdraws. (FA: Greg Collum, Matt Kerns 1994)

10. Accidental Discharge (5.11b) ★★ At the far end of the cliff is this popular, slabby route climbing up to and along a sloping arête. Double ropes for the rappel. Single-bolt anchor. Pro: quickdraws.

Blues Cliff

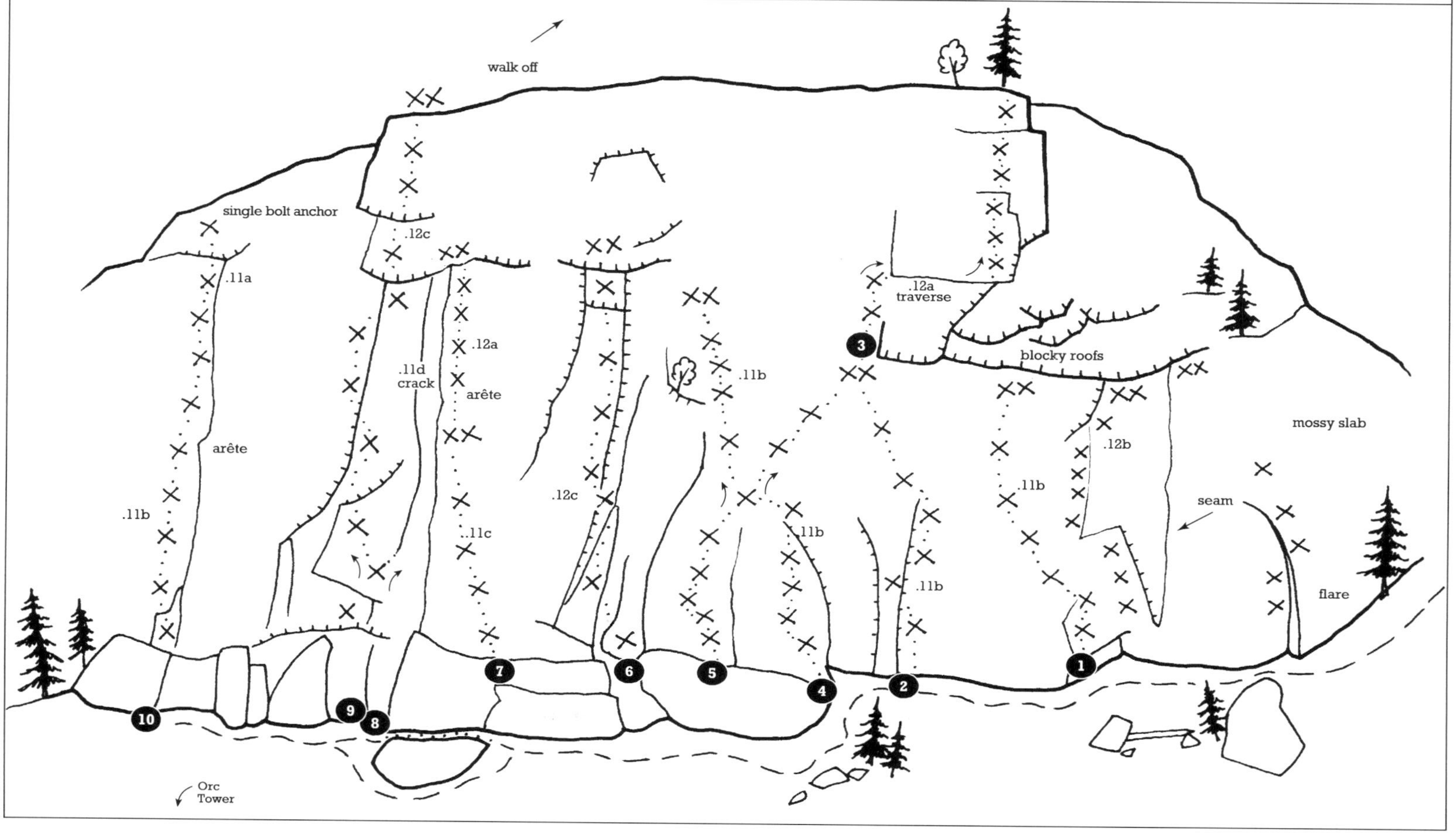

mossy slab

flare

seam

.12b

blocky roofs

.11b

.12a traverse

.11b

.11b

.11b

walk off

.12c

.12a arête

.11d crack

.12c

.11c

single bolt anchor

.11a

arête

.11b

Orc Tower

1
2
3
4
5
6
7
8
9
10

Rhythm Cliff

Hidden in the dank, mossy, mosquito-infested woods, just uphill from Blues Cliff, is Rhythm Cliff—a big, blocky wall with two improbable-looking sport climbs that are better and easier than they look. Approach as for Blues Cliff, but head uphill from the Middle Wall trail until you can see the cliff (barely) through the trees. Scramble up mossy rock to the routes.

1. Unnatural Act (5.11b) ★★★ A monstrosity climbing up to and through the incredibly blocky roofs on the right side of the cliff. Climb under the arch, then traverse right along the wall below the big roofs, then up around the corner to anchors. Considered one of the best sport routes at Index. Beware of sharp edges. Pro: quickdraws. (FA: Greg Collum, Matt Kerns 1992)

2. Stud Farm (5.11c) ★★ Start as for *Unnatural Act,* but follow the bolts left across an arête to anchors below the big roof. A popular variation (*Horseplay*) links this route with *Unnatural Act* by traversing right at the roof. Pro: quickdraws.

Rhythm Cliff

UPPER WALL

The Upper Wall is so obvious from town that it needs no real description. It is Washington's most accessible big wall, hosting several difficult aid routes. In recent years, with the advent of large-scale rappel bolting and cleaning, some improbably long, moderately hard free climbs have been established on the Upper Wall.

In addition to the Upper Wall proper, there are several incidental cliffs in the vicinity, most notably The Diamond, a steep, angular wall just right of the Upper Wall; Lookout Point, a slabby buttress on the far right; and several smaller cliffs hidden here and there among the trees.

For most of the Upper Wall aid routes, a big wall rack is necessary, although most can be climbed hammerless, and a few have been free climbed. While most of the aid routes are Grade IV, don't count out the possibility

of a bivouac. The same is true of some of the longer free routes; if you aren't climbing fast enough, you may find yourself high on the wall at nightfall. If you aren't prepared for a bivouac, it's bound to be unpleasant at best. Be prepared for bad weather. The long, free routes on the Upper Wall mostly require comprehensive racks supplemented by lots of quickdraws, since most of the free climbs are predominately bolt protected. Route-finding on the modern free climbs usually isn't difficult; just follow the bolts, but bring some gear to fit in here and there. In the fine tradition of modern sport climbing, a few of these routes end short of the top.

For the most part, approaches to the Upper Wall and incidental cliffs follow good trails from town or from the Lower Town Wall (described where appropriate in the text). The Upper Wall may be reached from above, but it takes just as long or longer than approaching from below. Also, it's not a good

Upper Wall

The Cheeks

The Diamond

Davis-Holland Area

Dana's Arch Area

Madsen's Ledge Area

Rattletale Wall

Upper Wall Area Approach Map

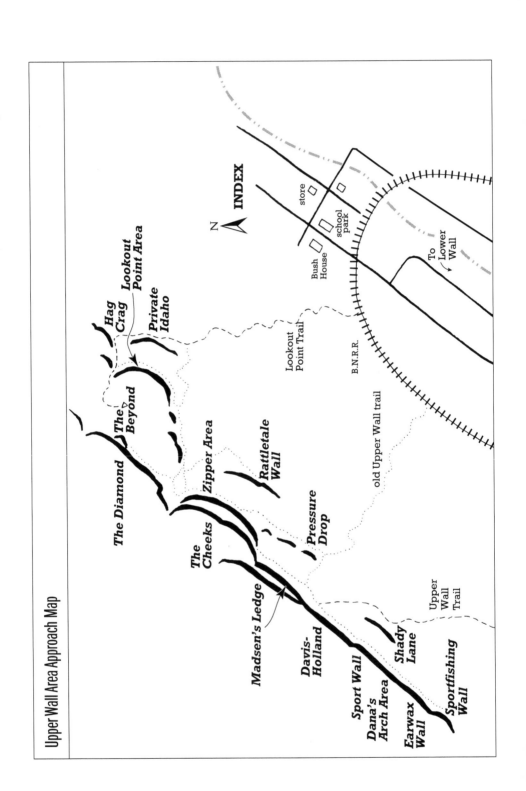

INDEX

N

The Diamond

Hag Crag   *Lookout Point Area*

The Beyond

Private Idaho

Zipper Area

The Cheeks

Rattletale Wall

Madsen's Ledge

Pressure Drop

Davis-Holland

Sport Wall

Dana's Arch Area

Shady Lane

Earwax Wall

Sportfishing Wall

Upper Wall Trail

Lookout Point Trail

old Upper Wall trail

B.N.R.R.

Bush House

school
park

store

To Lower Wall

idea to leave your car parked unattended for any extended period of time at the Upper Wall parking area. Because the top of the Upper Wall is accessible by road, yahoos sometimes throw things off the wall, including rocks, logs, bottles, car parts, and so on, as evidenced by debris sometimes found at the base of the wall, particularly in the area of *Backroad* and *Dana's Arch.*

Descents are either by rappel, long walk-offs, or combinations of the two. The standard descent route is via rappel down the gully left of *Backroad,* where one long or two shorter rappels from a tree reach the base of the cliff. It is also possible to outflank the cliff on the left. And you can always rappel straight down the cliff via one of the new sport climbs, which have fairly reliable anchors, much less manky than the old rappel anchors on *Davis-Holland.*

Sportfishing Wall

At the far left margin of the Upper Wall, about 50 yards left of the more obvious Earwax Wall, is Sportfishing Wall, named for the first route climbed here. Its most obvious route is the bolted arête of *Everest Without Lycra.* Approach via the Upper Wall Trail, which ends at the base of *Davis-Holland.* Traverse left along the base of the Upper Wall past *Backroad,* where a steep scramble up a gully, aided by a knotted rope, reaches the base of Earwax Wall. If the rope isn't there, fight your way through the brush to the left of the gully or take your chances with the gully. Continue briefly along the base of the wall to Sportfishing Wall.

1. Sportfishing (II, 5.10c) ★ Left of the prominent gully on the far left side of the Upper Wall is this three-pitch route, climbing a steep flake to a crack in a bubbly white wall, passing several ledges to reach the top of the wall. A reasonable through route, although not often climbed. May be dirty. Pro: to 2 inches.

2. Vanessa Del Rio (5.12d) ★ A sporty route just right of the start of *Sportfishing,* passing a few bolts up the steep, angular face, past a roof, then up the obvious steep hand crack to anchors. May need cleaning. Pro: quickdraws; gear to 2.5 inches.

3. Everest Without Lycra (5.11b) ★★★ The obvious bolted arête marking the right-hand edge of the Sportfishing Wall. Begin in the corner just left of *Squeeze It* and finish at anchors above a roof. A 60-meter rope is helpful. Pro: lots of quickdraws. (FA: Greg Child, Greg Collum 1988)

4. Squeeze It (5.11b) ★ A short, blocky, bolted arête and face route just right of the *Everest* arête. Pro: quickdraws; #2.5 Friend recommended.

Earwax Wall

Earwax Wall is a flat, steep, golden-colored wall on the left side of the Upper Wall, with an obvious traversing overhang at about midheight. The wall is split by three prominent thin cracks and has a plenitude of bolts marking the wall's various 5.12 and 5.13 sport climbs. Earwax Wall has some of Index's best sport routes and perhaps the greatest concentration of hard climbing in the area.

5. Friends in Holy Places (5.11a) ★ An obvious flaky crack and corner on the left side of Earwax Wall (just right of the *Squeeze It* arête) leads to a horizontal crack and flake. Pro: to 2 inches, including cams.

Sportfishing Wall and Earwax Wall

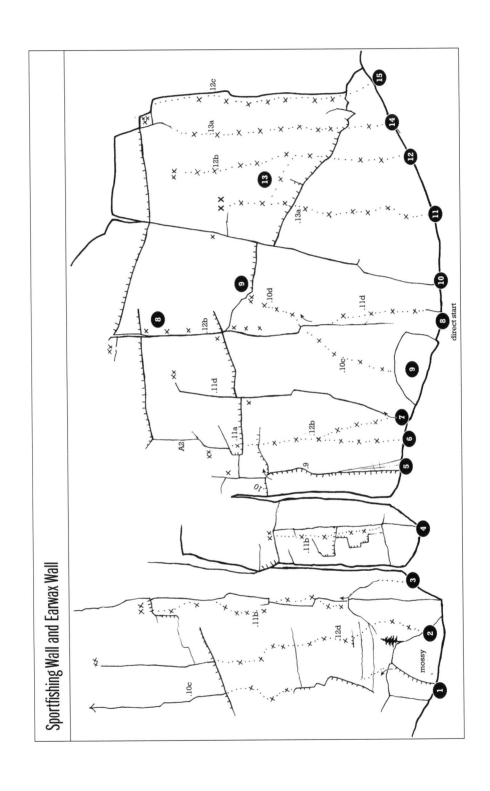

6. Sweatshop (5.12b) ★ The leftmost sport route on Earwax Wall, following a line of bolts directly to the first belay of *Friends*. A retrobolted variation start begins just left of *Domestic Violence*. Pro: quickdraws; thin nuts.

7. Domestic Violence (5.11d) ★★ The left-most crack route on Earwax Wall. Ascend the right-slanting crack through the roofs to a ledge above. Gets dirty. Pro: to 2 inches, including RPs and TCUs.

8. Killslug (5.12b) ★★ Earwax Wall's middle crack line, which is crisscrossed with several variations. The original version starts via the bolted face on the left (as for *Sideshow*). A 5.11d direct start variation raises the overall grade a notch. Pro: quickdraws.

9. Sideshow (5.10d) ★★★ The easiest and most popular pitch on Earwax Wall. Start as for *Killslug,* but continue across the crack and right to chain anchors just below the roof. A direct start variation is 5.11d. Pro: quickdraws. (FA: Greg Collum, Matt Kerns, Larissa Collum 1989)

10. Earwax (5.11c) ★★★ The rightmost crack, a striking, right-leaning thin crack splitting its namesake wall right of *Domestic Violence*. Pro: triplicate sets of RPs and TCUs. (FFA: Terry Lien, Jon Nelson 1983)

11. Young Cynics (5.13a) ★★ The first sport route right of *Earwax*. It's 5.11d to the ring bolt, 5.12b A0 if you pull up on the ring bolt, 5.13a if you don't. Pro: quickdraws.

12. Soul on Ice (5.12b) ★ A sport route just right of *Young Cynics,* leading past the roof to a bolt anchor in the middle of nowhere. Pro: quickdraws; #2.5 Friend recommended.

13. Raggedy Andy (5.12b) ★★ **and Raggedy Ann Variations** (5.12a) ★★ Traverse left from the third and fourth bolts, respectively, of *Soul on Ice* to the *Young Cynics* anchors.

14. The Antidote (5.13a) ★★ A bolted face just left of the *Biology* arête, with a crux high up. Pro: quickdraws.

15. The Biology of Small Appliances (5.12c) ★★ An obvious sport route climbing the bolted arête on the right edge of Earwax Wall. Pro: quickdraws.

Dana's Arch Area

Between *Davis-Holland* and Earwax Wall is a broad section of the Upper Wall with only a few distinctive features. The most obvious feature here is Dana's Arch, a short, clean, arching flake. There are several old aid routes here and some newer multipitch sport routes reaching the veritable heights of the Upper Wall. Be wary of yahoos throwing stuff off the top of the wall in this area, a potential hazard judging by the debris occasionally found at the base of the wall here.

16. Jungle Fun (5.11c) ★★ A two-pitch sport route on the wall between *Dana's Arch* and *Backroad*. The 5.10c first pitch is the popular approach for *Beat Box* and *Tempituous*. Pro: quickdraws.

17. Beat Box (5.11d) ★★ A two-pitch continuation of *Jungle Fun*, angling left up cracks and overhangs along the approximate line of the prominent black watermarks. Pro: quickdraws.

18. Tempituous (5.11d) ★★★ A popular line climbing three pitches, including the first pitch of *Jungle Fun*. Knobby, overhanging face climbing connects the bolts to anchors just short of the top of the Upper Wall. Pro: quickdraws.

19. Imperial Fun (5.12a) ★★★ An airy sport finish to the *Dana's Arch* route, best approached via rappel from the top of the

Dana's Arch Area, Sport Wall, and Davis-Holland Area

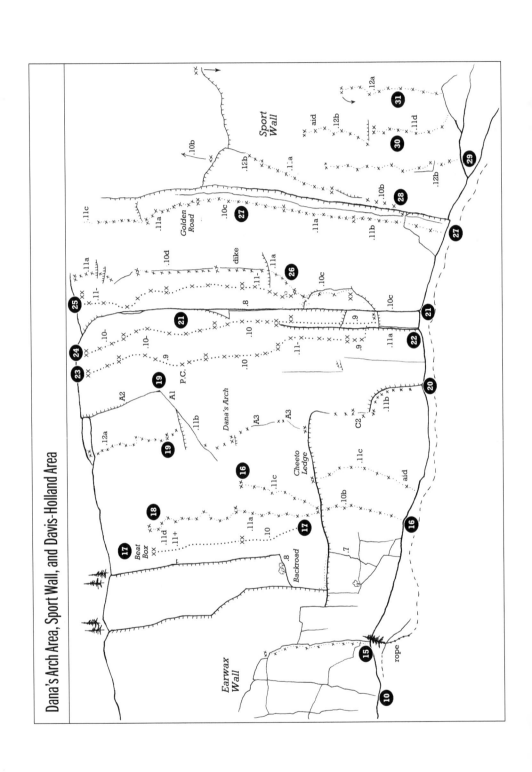

wall to the anchors. Pro: quickdraws; fixed rope or second rope recommended to help ensure a successful escape if the route proves too difficult.

20. Dana's Arch (5.11b) ★★ A short sport route climbing the obvious bolted, left-arching flake about midway between Earwax Wall and Sport Wall. The flake was first led free on gear but retrobolted to avoid further pin scarring by aid climbers. The original aid route continues to the top of the wall (III, A3). Pro: quickdraws for the arch, aid rack for the rest.

21. Lamplighter (III, 5.10c A3) ★ An old aid route starting with a clean, blocky offwidth/chimney. The first pitch is free at 5.10c. The remainder of the route is dirty, blocky aid climbing up chimneys and cracks (III, A3). Pro: gear to 3 inches for the first pitch; aid rack for the rest.

22. Another Man's Car (5.11c) ★★ A first pitch variation to *Lamplighter* taking the off-width just left. Pro: big cams.

23. Psilocybe Cyanescens (5.11a) ★★★ A recent addition climbing the wall left of *Lamplighter*. Climb *Another Man's Car's* first pitch until you can undercling out a flake left to the arête. Pitch two climbs a snaking dike then goes hard left to anchors. Bolts and cracks lead three more pitches to the top of the wall. Pro: same rack as *Another Man's Car* plus quickdraws and more thin to middling gear. (FA: Michal Rynkiewicz, Logan Fusso, Chandler Davis 2018)

24. The Brett Thompson and Scott Fuller Memorial (5.10c) ★★★ A five-pitch route climbing corners, cracks, and thin face directly above the first pitch of *Lamplighter*. Pro: quickdraws; mostly smaller gear to 3-4 inches will suffice. (FA: Michal Rynkiewicz, Chandler Davis, Ryan Hoover 2016)

25. The Crimson Eye (5.11a) ★★★ A five-pitch route up the wall right of *Lamplighter*, climbing a series of flakes, cracks, and crimpy faces. Start via the first pitch of *Lamplighter*, but continue right at the top to a set of higher anchors, then continue upward. Pro: quickdraws; mostly small gear up to 3 inches for the first pitch. (FA: Michal Rynkiewicz, Chandler Davis, Ryan Hoover 2016)

26. Heaven's Gate (III, 5.11a) ★★★ A superb four-pitch line right of *Lamplighter*, following bolts pretty much straight up once you get past the initial offwidth/chimney. Start as for *Crimson Eye*, then follow the bolts. Pro: many quickdraws plus gear to 3 inches for the first pitch. (FA: David Gunstone, Darryl Cramer)

27. Golden Road (III, 5.11c) ★★★ This route climbs the arête and face just left of the big corner system left of the Sport Wall. Surmount the big flake at the base of the wall, then follow bolts up the prow, which isn't as hard as it used to be due to rockfall damage. The fifth pitch is now the crux, climbing a knobby face through the big roof. Pro: quickdraws; some gear. (FA: Benjit Hull 2007)

28. Wildest Dreams (II, 5.12b) ★★★ A four-pitch route beginning from the start of *Golden Road*, then striking up the left edge of the Sport Wall and crossing the ledge traverse of *Davis-Holland*. Pitches of 5.10, 5.11a, 5.12b, and 5.10. Rappel from the pitch four anchors unless you want to grovel to the top. Pro: quickdraws; wireds; TCUs. (FA: Chris Henson 2007)

Sport Wall

The Sport Wall is the portion of the Upper Wall bounded by *Davis-Holland* on the right

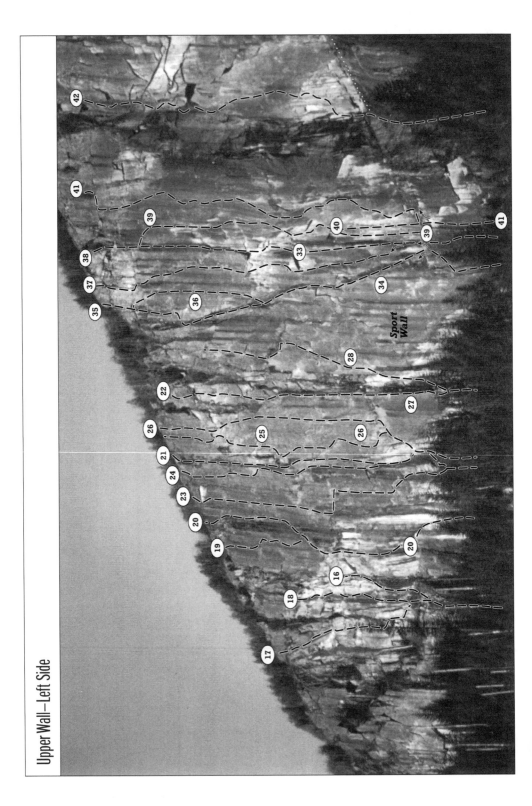

and a big, mossy corner on the left. Originally, this wall was used only as the descent route for *Davis-Holland,* with two bad bolts for anchors. After the anchors were replaced, climbers noticed the lower half of the wall's potential. Now there is a plethora of bolts protecting several 5.12 sport climbs.

29. Scatterlings (5.12c) ★ The leftmost sport route on the Sport Wall, beginning about 20 feet right of the flake where *Golden Road* and *Wildest Dreams* begin. The route starts from a ledge that is often wet. Pro: quickdraws.

30. Quiet Lands (5.12a) ★★★ A short, left bolted traverse leads to steep, edgy face climbing, with anchors above a short arch. The first pitch is excellent and very popular. A second pitch is 5.12b with an aid move. Pro: quickdraws.

31. Heart's Desire (5.12a) ★★★ A direct and popular sport route following bolts just right of *Quiet Lands.* Pro: quickdraws. (FA: Keith Lenard, Jeff Walker 1992)

32. Calling Wolfgang (5.12b) ★★ A sparsely bolted sport route right of *Heart's Desire.* A second pitch (*Straight to Voicemail,* 5.12c) continues upward. Pro: quickdraws; midsize nuts; #1.5 to #2.0 Friends recommended.

33. Child Abuse (5.12d) ★★ Just left of the first pitch of *Davis-Holland* is this bolted arête; at the arête's end, move left and follow a left-meandering line of bolts past a small roof. *Child's Play variation* (5.11d) starts as for *Child Abuse,* but continues straight up and then right to join *Davis-Holland* at the ledge. Pro: quickdraws, #4 Rock.

Davis-Holland Area

The *Davis-Holland* route is one of the most prominent routes on the left side of the Upper Wall, climbing the distinct, clean, right-facing dihedral system. Several routes climb the wall just right of *Davis-Holland.*

34. Davis-Holland (III, 5.10c) ★★★★ The obvious clean dihedral system just up and left from the talus slope reached at the end of the trail. An obvious short corner crack (5.9) reaches a ledge. From the ledge, traverse left and climb the clean corner crack to anchors 100 feet up. A third pitch up the dihedral (some face moves) reaches a pillar 300 feet up the wall. Most parties rappel from here, either down the route or to one of the Sport Wall anchors. Everyone else continues up *Lovin' Arms* to the top. Pro: to 3 inches, including small cams. (FA: Dan Davis, John Holland 1964; FFA: Unknown)

35. Lovin' Arms (III, 5.10c or 5.11c) ★★★★ A popular finish to *Davis-Holland,* adding three 5.10 pitches (or a 5.11c variation) to reach the top of the Upper Wall. From the pillar at the end of the third pitch of *Davis-Holland,* continue up the crack and chimney above to a bolt belay, then traverse right to a bolt (5.11c or A0 move), or traverse higher up (5.10c version). Exposed cracks and face continue to the top. May be dirty. Pro: to 3 inches. (FFA: Dan Lepska, Larry Kemp via 5.10c variation 1983; Pat Timson via 5.11c variation 1984)

36. Senseless Thoughts of Paranoia (III, 5.11a) ★★ A direct line up the wall right of *Lovin' Arms.* From the *Davis-Holland* pillar, angle right to a ledge, then up the steep face to a thin corner crack. From the end of the crack, face and cracks lead up and left to join *Lovin' Arms* or another variation to the top. Pro: Gear to 2 inches; wireds and cams, quickdraws. (FA: Dave Gunstone, Roger Brown)

Sport Wall and Davis-Holland Area

37. Rise and Fall (IV, 5.12b) ★★★ A long, hard free route up the steep wall right of *Davis-Holland*. Start via *Davis-Holland*'s first pitch, then climb *Green Dragon*'s initial corner until the bolts head left up the steep wall. Follow the bolts up the wall, if you can. Pro: quickdraws and thin gear for occasional cracks. (FA: Greg Child, Andy deKlerk 1991)

38. Green Dragon (IV, 5.13a or 5.11a A3) ★★★ A semi-popular aid route climbing the corner system immediately right of *Davis-Holland*. The first pitch is a nice 5.11a thin crack alternative to reach the *Davis-Holland* ledge. The route has been climbed entirely free and is highly recommended as a "five star" free route. Pro: quickdraws and gear to 3 inches, many Lost Arrows, knifeblades, skyhooks if aiding, although now that it's a free route please don't nail. (FFA: Justen Sjong, Ben Gilkison 2007)

39. Town Crier (V, 5.12d or 5.9 C3) ★★★ Index's most popular aid route (the first pitch of *City Park* notwithstanding), which now goes free, climbing a line immediately right of *Green Dragon,* starting with an obvious chimney (5.9) to reach a big ledge (Big Honker Ledge). Continue up face cracks and left past a large roof, then up a crack system, passing several more roofs. Pro: quickdraws; gear to 3 inches. (FA: Fred Beckey, Dave Becksted 1966; FFA: Justen Sjong, Ben Gilkison 2007)

40. Twelve Angry Bees (5.11c) ★★ A sport route climbing the bolted face just right of the *Town Crier* chimney, directly to Big Honker Ledge. Pro: quickdraws.

41. Swim (IV, 5.11d A0) ★★★ Another long, improbable, mostly free route up the wall right of *Town Crier*. Begin from the base of the wall and climb the obvious bolted face past a roof (5.11d). The second pitch (5.11d) starts just right of *Twelve Angry Bees,* up a rightward-leaning bolted face to reach anchors at the base of a left-facing arch. Sport climbers usually rappel from here. Those who continue climb the arch, then aid up a short bolt ladder to get to the headwall. Three more pitches of surprisingly moderate, highly exposed climbing (up to 5.11c) follow the bolts to the top. Pro: lots of quickdraws; gear to 3.5 inches. (FA: Darryl Cramer, Greg Olsen, Larry Kemp 1991)

Madsen's Ledge Area

Directly above the talus slope at the base of the waterfall are several routes, the most prominent of which is the *Golden Arch*. One pitch up is Madsen's Ledge, a long ledge system reached via any of several routes, including a via ferrata that starts on the far-right end of the cliff, following a few hand lines to the first rungs (use at your own risk). The ledge may be traversed from end to end; most of the traverse is Class 3, but there are some Class 5 sections. Most of the routes in the path of the waterfall are wet until late summer.

42. Technicians of the Sacred (IV, 5.12b) ★★★ A long free route up the highest point of the Upper Wall. The first pitch to Madsen's Ledge climbs a bolted, rounded corner just right of the waterfall. From Madsen's Ledge, continue up a left-facing corner to a ledge, then traverse right to anchors, then up the steep headwall to the lip of *Golden Arch*. The next pitch climbs the bolted arête above the arch (5.12b) or an easier traverse in from above (5.11b), then continues up the headwall to the top. Mostly fixed, cruxes can be aided on fixed gear. Pro: lots

Davis-Holland and Madsen's Ledge Areas

of quickdraws; plus gear to 1.5 inches. (FA: Andy deKlerk 1991)

43. Beat to Quarters (5.12a) ★★★ A recent sport pitch starting on the left end of Madsen's Ledge, just left of the second pitch of *Technicians of the Sacred*. Pro: quickdraws. (FA: Tom Ramier)

44. Bang! (5.13b) ★★★ The leftmost of a cluster of sport pitches starting just right of the second pitch of *Technicians*. Pro: quickdraws. (FA: Tom Ramier)

45. Whimper (5.11c) ★★★ The middle sport right of *Technicians*. Pro: quickdraws. (FA: Tom Ramier)

46. The Method of Reconciling Disparate Parts (5.12b) ★★ The rightmost of the three sport routes right of *Technicians*. Pro: quickdraws. (FA: Tom Ramier)

47. The Golden Arch (IV, 5.11c A3) ★★ The obvious left-facing corner/arch system slicing up the right flank of the Upper Wall. The first pitch goes free (5.11c), but is not the best of the free routes leading up to Madsen's Ledge. The arch itself is still an aid route, but is highly recommended if you're into aid climbing. Pro: gear to 3 inches; Lost Arrows, knifeblades, sky hooks. (FA: Jim Madsen, Ron Burgner 1967)

48. Starfish Enterprise (5.11d) ★★★ A semi-independent free climb up the headwall right of *Golden Arch*. Start up the bolted face just right of the *Golden Arch* route straight to anchors, then angle right to join *Good Girls* for two pitches. Below the roof, go left and pretty

much straight up the wall to the top. Call it "A0" if you use the bolted-on brass starfish as a hold. Pro: quickdraws plus a few small cams (.3 to .5 Black Diamond cams recommended) for the first and last pitches. (FA: Tom Ramier 2016)

49. The Call of Cthulhu (III, 5.13a) ★★★★ Climb the first pitch of *Starfish Enterprise*, then go left, up beside the arête of *Golden Arch* for one pitch to anchors. Continue through the roofs and up to the top of the

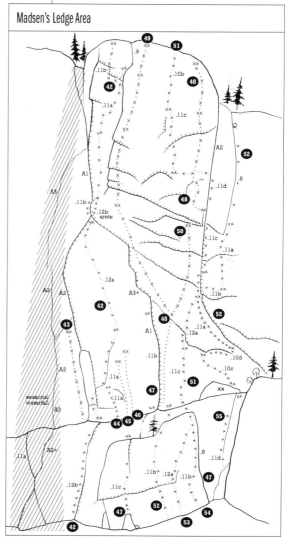

Madsen's Ledge Area

Madsen's Ledge

wall, paralleling *Technicians of the Sacred* on the right. Six pitches in all including the first pitch of *Starfish*. Mostly bolted. Pro: quick-draws plus small cams as for *Starfish*. (FA: Tom Ramier 2018)

50. Seven Sermons to the Dead (5.12c) ★★ Connect the bolts straight up from the first anchor of *Starfish* through a roof. Pro: same as for *Starfish*. (FA: Tom Ramier 2018)

51. Good Girls Like Bad Boys (5.12a) ★★★ A popular six-pitch sport route that climbs the headwall between *Starfish* and *Sisu*. Try any of the variations up to Madsen's Ledge (the via ferrata is the most popular) to a direct bolted face just right of the start of the arch. One pitch up takes you to the lip of the big arch on the right. Continue up the steep corner, then exit left, crossing *Starfish*, then following bolts all the way to the top. Pro: lots of quickdraws. (FA: Karl Kaiyala, Darryl Cramer 1991)

52. Sisu (III, 5.11c) ★★★ Another long free route up the headwall right of *Golden Arch*, this one zigzagging up the wall to the big arch of *The Ave* (an old aid route) before striking out right up the headwall. Most parties forego the initial 5.11b pitch, opting instead for the easier chimney or via ferrata to reach Madsen's Ledge. Most also skip the "summit" and rappel off from anchors at the base of the final crack pitch. Pro: lots of quickdraws. (FA: Karl Kaiyala and party 1991)

53. Geritol (5.12a) ★ A slabby sport route just right of the first pitch of *Sisu*. Pro: quickdraws.

54. Over Forty (5.11c) ★ The slabby sport route immediately left of *The Ave* chimney. Pro: quickdraws.

55. Electromatic Mark IV (5.11d) ★ Climb a thin layback flake with several bolts just right of *The Ave* chimney. Pro: to 2 inches, including many small cams.

The Cheeks

The Cheeks is the streaky, blocky cliff on the right side of the Upper Wall, best identified by the dark chimney splitting the formation vertically. The Cheeks features a variety of routes from one to five pitches in length. Its best routes are one- and two-pitch affairs beginning from the base of the formation, although several routes have been established on the ledge bisecting the formation at mid-height. A grungy Class 5 traverse (the Perverse Traverse) reaches the ledge (called the Prance Platform or the Beach, depending on whom you talk to). Descend by rappel from anchors or trees.

1. Wilmon's Walkabout (II, 5.11c) ★★ A three-pitch route on the left side of The Cheeks, the first two pitches of which go free. The route begins in a left-facing corner with a bolt at the start. Pro: gear mostly to 1 inch, plus a few larger pieces.

2. Sedan Delivery (5.11d) ★★★ A thin crack up a knobby, concave wall left of the second pitch of *Wilmon's Walkabout*. Pro: to 1 inch. *Direct Delivery* (5.12a) is a direct first pitch to *Sedan Delivery,* starting just left of the initial corner of *Wilmon's Walkabout*. Pro: multiple pieces from wireds to 1 inch.

3. The Black Sea (5.11d) ★★★ Two pitches of steep, stellar cracks, corners, and knobs ascending the black-streaked wall on the left side of The Cheeks, starting from a boulder at the far-left edge of the Perverse Traverse. There are several variation second pitches, each in the 5.11+ range. Pro: quickdraws;

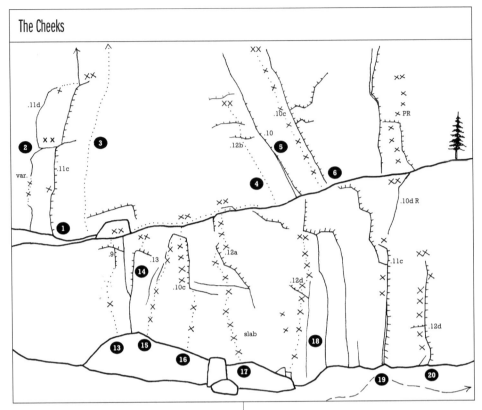

gear to 3 inches. (FA: Tom Ramier, Derek Pearson, Jon Nelson)

4. Normandy (5.12d) ★★ A sport route climbing the white wall through overhangs just left of *Heaven's Rear-Entry Vehicle*. It's either a good route or a sandbag, depending on who you ask. Pro: quickdraws. (FA: Tom Ramier)

5. Heaven's Rear-Entry Vehicle (5.10) ★ The full name of this route is *Heaven's Rear Entry Vehicle Parked Out Back, Tow-Away Zone*. Whatever you call it, it is the left-leaning chimney system just above the end of the Perverse Traverse. Three pitches. May need some cleaning up from time to time. Pro: to 4 inches, mostly in the 2- to 3-inch range.

6. Between the Cheeks (5.10c) ★★ A sport route between the two prominent chimney

systems splitting The Cheeks. Pro: lots of quickdraws.

7. The Sea Cucumber (5.11a) ★★ A new three-pitch route climbing the wall just right of *Between the Cheeks*. Start by climbing a tree until you can clip the bolts, then continue (5.7) to a ledge on the left. Continue up the beautiful 5.10d corner, then continue straight up (5.11a) to a rightward traverse on "rad holds," where "some trickery" awaits. A steep two-pitch variation start via *The Barnicle* (5.11+) avoids the tree, starting on *Between the Cheeks* and trending rightward to join *The Sea Cucumber*. Pro: quickdraws, gear to 1 inch. (FA: Michal Rynkiewicz, Chandler Davis, Ryan Hoover)

8. Albinestone (5.11d) ★★ A sport route on the white wall just left of the start of *Stock Options*. Pro: quickdraws.

9. Stock Options (aka Apes and Ballerinas)

(5.10d) ★★ A two-pitch route right of *The Zipper*'s upper pitches, following a crack system left of the prominent overhangs. Start via a fist crack to gain the upper corner pitch. Rappel the route. Pro: to 4 inches, including duplicate sets of everything from RPs to 4 inches.

10. Crack in the Cosmic Egg (5.12c) ★★ The

obvious steep, thin, bolted flake just right of the start of *Stock Options*. A second pitch is an open project. Pro: quickdraws; small stuff. (FA: Tom Ramier)

11. A Wisdom That Is Woe (5.13a) ★★

Another sport route climbing the overhang right of *Cosmic Egg*. The route to the right of this is *Hasselhoff* (5.11dc) and ends on the anchors for *Wisdom*, in case you want to set up a toprope. Pro: quickdraws.

12. Lien-Michael (aka The Terry Michael Route) (5.11d) ★★ A route through the over-

hangs above the right end of the Beach. Pro: to 2 inches, including TCUs. (FA: Terry Lien, Tom Michael)

The Zipper Area (Lower Cheeks)

The lower half of the Cheeks is a steep, white-streaked wall. The routes are described from left to right.

13. Black Planet (5.9) ★ A knobby face

climb on the far left side of the lower wall of The Cheeks, about 150 feet left of *Clay*. A single bolt protects the face moves; the crux moves are higher up. Pro: quickdraws, gear to 1.5 inches.

14. The Gerberding Route (5.9) ★ The cor-

ner crack immediately right of *Black Planet* leads to a short roof. There are a couple of toprope routes (5.11c, 5.12a) in between

Gerberding and *Infinite Jest* that have been led but can be easily toproped. Pro: gear to 2.5 inches.

15. Infinite Jest (5.13b/c) ★★ A sport route

up the water-streaked wall just left and around the corner from *Friendly Fire*. Pro: quickdraws. (FA: Tom Ramier)

16. Friendly Fire (5.10c) ★ A bolted corner

about 20 feet right of *Black Planet* leads up to anchors on the Perverse Traverse. A good alternative to the traverse for those headed for the Beach. Pro: quickdraws.

17. Engines of Archimedes (5.12a) ★ A

devious sport route just right of *Friendly Fire*. Pro: quickdraws.

18. The Boneyard (5.12b) ★ The bolted

route on the left edge of the *Clay* amphitheater. Pro: quickdraws.

19. Clay (5.11d R) ★★★ The striking corner

crack in the middle of The Cheeks' lower wall. The first pitch overhangs in its entirety, starting with a 4-inch crack and narrowing to the strenuous crux. A sparsely protected slab crack (5.10d R) continues to the Beach. Pro: to 3 inches, including RPs. (FA: Terry Lien, Jon Nelson 1984)

20. All Dogs Go to Heaven (5.12d) ★ A

sport route just right of *Clay*, climbing a steep, bolted dihedral to chain anchors.

21. Fiction (5.11b R) ★ A sparsely bolted

friction route climbing the left side of The Zipper slab. The crux is protected well enough, but a fall from easier moves high on the slab could be trouble. Deadly when wet. Pro: quickdraws.

22. The Zipper (5.10b) ★★ A free start to the

old aid route leading up to and through the obvious Ice Cream Scoop roof. It's A2 if you continue through the roof to the Beach.

The final three pitches go free at 5.11b. Pro: to 1.5 inches for first pitch; numerous to 4 inches, including knifeblades, for the complete route.

23. Attractive Nuisance (5.12c) The first of the overhanging sport routes right of *The Zipper,* climbing a very overhanging, bolted corner to anchors. If you do the *Extended Play* finish, it's 5.13a. The route is always dry and is thus more popular than it deserves to be. Pro: quickdraws.

24. La Bomba Roof (5.12b) Follow a steep corner crack past a roof and up to anchors. Almost always dry. Pro: quickdraws.

25. Bent (5.11d) ★ A sport route round the corner from *La Bomba Roof,* climbing up a semi-chimney, then traversing between roof tiers, crossing *Pedal to the Metal,* and finishing up to anchors farther right. A shorter version, *Half Bent,* starts up *Pedal to the Metal.* Pro: quickdraws.

26. Danny Boy (5.12a) Connect the bolts up the tiered roofs to anchors just over the lip.

27. Pedal to the Metal (5.12b) ★ A sport route passing the roofs on the far right side. Pro: quickdraws.

28. Faeries Wear Boots (5.11a) ★★ A varied pitch climbing cracks, corners, and knobs just right of the *Bent* roof to the *Less Than Zero* anchors. Pro: quickdraws, gear to 1.5 inches. (FA: Michal Rynkiewicz, Chandler Davis, Ryan Hoover)

29. Less Than Zero (5.11c) ★★ Arching thin cracks and corners. A fine line when clean. Pro: to 3 inches.

30. The Wizard (5.10c) ★ Climb the blocky arête right of the first pitch of *Less Than Zero.* Pro: quickdraws.

31. Bravo, Jean Marc (5.11a) ★★ A left-leaning thin crack about 50 feet right of a prominent bolted arête on the far right side of The Cheeks' lower wall. Often wet. Pro: to 1 inch.

32. Pressure Drop (5.11a) ★★ An obvious straight-in finger crack on the small wall directly downhill from the left edge of The Cheeks formation. Hike down from the base of the Upper Wall or left from the *Clay* area. Gets dirty, but worth cleaning. Pro: to 2 inches.

33. Rattletale (5.10a) ★★★ A series of right-facing dihedrals on the left side of the low cliff band directly below *The Zipper* area. The first pitch is dirty, but the second climbs a clean, wide corner crack. The final chimney is not anybody's favorite pitch, but there it is. Pro: to 3 inches. There are several other worthwhile routes on the Rattletale Wall; refer to the current Index guide for details.

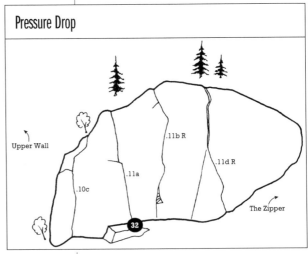

Pressure Drop

The Cheeks and The Zipper Area, Rattletale Wall

The Zipper Area

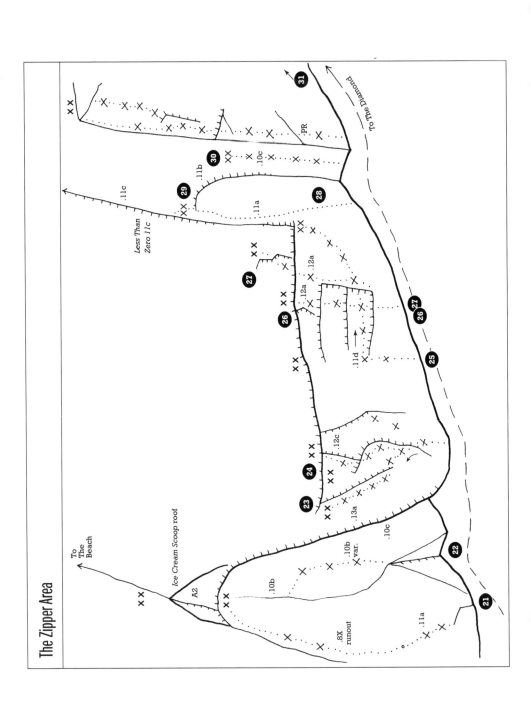

To The Beach

Ice Cream Scoop roof

A2

.8X runout

.10b

.10b var.

.11a

.10c

.13a

.12c

.11d

.12a

.12a

.11a

.11b

.10c

.11c

Less Than Zero 11c

PR

To The Diamond

21 22 23 24 25 26 27 27 28 29 30 31 26

The Diamond

The Diamond is the broad, angular cliff right of The Cheeks. A huge left-facing dihedral is the wall's most obvious feature. An enormous boulder lies at its base. The Diamond is easily reached from the base of The Cheeks, or via the gully leading to *The Dihedral* (a once-repeated A4 route in case you're interested). A few long free climbs have been established on The Diamond, including the delectable *Centerfold*. Descents from The Diamond are usually made by rappelling down *Centerfold*. All of the recent routes on The Diamond are equipped to be descended using a single 70-meter rope except *A National Acrobat*, which requires an 80-meter rope or double ropes.

1. The Dark Crystal (II, 5.11b) ★ A three-pitch route climbing a wild arch and successive leaning corners just left of the massive *Dihedral* corner. A bolted 5.9 slab pitch from the cave behind the big boulder offers an alternate start. Often wet, probably dirty. Pro: to 3 inches, including Friends and small cams.

2. Nativity in Black (III, 5.11d) ★★★ Start via the bolted chimney out of the cave (5.9) then continue up pitch one of *The Dark Crystal* and pull the roof straight above rather than traversing left. Climb the arête then go left up the obvious rail and continue upward to the top of The Diamond. Nine pitches in all. Pro: quickdraws; double rack to 3 inches

The Diamond and Duck Wall

plus 4- and 5-inch cams if you have them. (FA: Michal Rynkiewicz, Ryan Hoover)

3. A National Acrobat (III, 5.12-) ★★★ A "modern classic" according to the latest Index guide, this route has a little of everything. Start the same as *Nativity in Black* through the *Dark Crystal* arête, then go right into *The Dihedral* and continue pretty much straight up from there. Nine pitches in all. Pro: same rack as *Nativity in Black.* (FA: Michal Rynkiewicz, Ryan Hoover)

4. Centerfold (II, 5.11a) ★★★ A popular route climbing a crack system leading straight up the center of The Diamond's main wall. Begin about 50 meters right and uphill from The Diamond gully via a short, easy ramp and corner system, or by a bolted face just left. Bolt-protected face moves lead left and up to the first anchors. A short, bolted face section gains the crack system, which leads upward two more pitches to anchors. A final crack pitch reaches the top of a pillar. Rappel the route. Pro: to 2 inches, including wired nuts and TCUs. (FA: Cal Folsom, Andy Tuthill 1988)

5. Sliding into First (5.11c) ★★ The preferred start to *Centerfold,* climbing the bolted face just left of the initial corner of *Centerfold,* which continues directly to the first anchors instead of traversing. Pro: quickdraws.

6. Jack O' Diamonds (II, 5.11a) ★★ Climb the first two pitches of *Centerfold,* then traverse left from the anchors and continue up the obvious crack system splitting the headwall. Descend via *Centerfold.* Pro: to 2 inches.

7. Megalomania (II, 5.11b) ★★ A five pitch sport route that leaves *Centerfold* on the second pitch, veering left after the third bolt

and rejoining Centerfold at its second pitch anchor. The next pitch break right, eventually leading back to climbing the Centerfold arête. Exposed! (FA: Ryan Hoover, Michal Rynkiewicz, Stamati Anagnostou 2018)

8. Sabbra Cadabra (III, 5.11a) ★★★ An eight-pitch venture up the wall just right of *Centerfold,* touted as "a climb for the ages" on Mountain Project. Shares a start with *Hell Bent for Glory,* then break left 15 feet up the second pitch and face climb up to a long finger crack on pitch four. Continue up and around the *Eyelid* roof on the left. Pro: quickdraws; gear to 1.5 inches. (FA: Michal Rynkiewicz, Chandler Davis, Ryan Hoover, 2018)

9. Hell Bent for Glory (III, 5.10d) ★★ A seven-pitch route up the crack and corner system on the right side of The Diamond. The first two pitches follow cracks and corners to the base of the prominent left-facing corner of pitch three. Face, cracks, and corners continue to an exposed roof finish. Pro: quickdraws; gear to 4 inches. (FA: Jim Yoder, Fred Grafton; FFA: Michal Rynkiewicz, Chandler Davis, Ryan Hoover, Derek Pearson)

10. The Black Raddish (III, 5.11c) ★★ Climb the first two pitches of *Hell Bent,* then start up the corner immediately left. The next pitch starts up a sloper rail then cuts left via thin, technical face climbing. Continue stemming upward, then break right up a vertical triple seam to face climbing. The next pitch (dubbed the "Sucker Fish" pitch, 5.11c) starts by passing an overhang, with exposed, athletic face climbing above. Pro: lots of quickdraws, singles to 1 inch. (FA: Michal Rynkiewicz, Chandler Davis, Ryan Hoover 2018)

The Beyond

Up and right along the base of the cliff from the start of *Centerfold* is a small buttress and arête known as The Beyond, with several routes in the 5.10 to 5.12 range.

11. Pork Chop Torpedo (5.11a) ★ A dihedral crack on the left that widens from bottom to top. Pro: to 4 inches.

12. Just Give 'em Whiskey (5.11d) ★★ A thin crack near the center of the wall leads to a bolted face and crux dyno for the top. Pro: to 1 inch, quickdraws.

13. Nearly Naked Now (5.10d) ★ The obvious bolted arête on the right. Pro: quickdraws.

Duck Wall

The Duck Wall is a blocky formation located directly below The Diamond. It has several routes, most of which are okay when cleaned up but otherwise are not popular. The routes below are the current Duck Wall "classics." Approach as for The Diamond, turning right at the gully right before reaching Rattletale Wall. The approach trail has been improved and is in good shape as of fall 2018. If you top out on Duck Wall you can scramble up to the base of The Diamond and keep climbing.

14. Man in the Box (5.11a) ★★ A nice-looking addition that stands out for its radical hanging stembox. Traverse right along the base of the wall up a short hill and

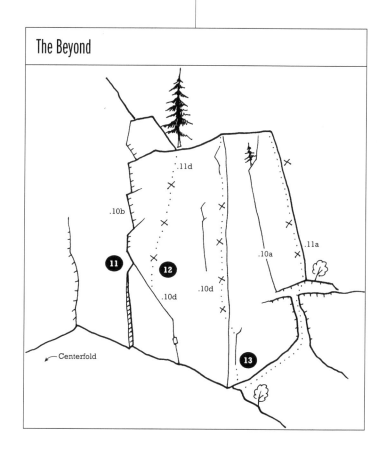

The Beyond

.11d

.10b

11

12

.10d

.10d

.10a

.11a

Centerfold

13

granite stepping-stones to reach the base of the climb. Face climb past three bolts and traverse right into a corner. Continue up the obvious stembox (5.10a), then continue traversing left on the slab (5.11a) then up through the final overhangs. Pro: lots of quickdraws. (FA: Derek Pearson, Michal Rynkiewicz, Ryan Hoover, Ried Hurtig, Marc Bow 2018)

15. Little Fire (II, 5.10c) ★★ The longest route on Duck Wall. From the end of the second fixed line, easy climbing leads to a steep corner. Traverse right on easier terrain to below a roof, then cut back left beneath the roof and up a thin crack to the top. Pro: a few quickdraws; rack to 4 inches. (FA: Derek Pearson, Brian Ebert 2013)

16. Planet Caravan (II, 5.10d) ★★ Another recent addition on the far left (uphill) side of Duck Wall, consisting of three short pitches that pack in a lot of variety, including textbook stemming corners and a rare squeeze chimney, finishing through a roof. Pro: rack to 3 inches; small wired nuts; quickdraws; slings for rope drag. (FA: Michal Rynkiewicz, Stamati Anagnostou, Ryan Hoover, Jon Nelson 2017)

17. Endless Skies (5.12a) ★★★ An airy variation fourth-pitch finish to *Planet Caravan* climbing out the overhanging wall 30 feet right of that route. Pro: same rack as *Planet Caravan* to get there, then quickdraws. (FA: Michal Rynkiewicz, Stamati Anagnostou 2017)

18. Message of Love (5.11b) ★ No topo. A new addition on the far left side of Duck Wall, a compression route that packs a punch. Pro: quickdraws. (FA: Michal Rynkiewicz 2018)

Stamati Anagnostou on *Endless Skies* (5.12a), Duck Wall, Index Town Walls
Ryan Hoover

Lookout Point Area

Directly above the town of Index, Lookout Point is the collective term used to describe the group of slabby cliffs below and to the right of The Diamond. A good trail to Lookout Point starts just before the Upper Wall Trail. Find it by crossing the bridge about 100 meters beyond the railroad crossing near the Bush House. The trail splits after some distance, heading right to Private Idaho and left to The Diamond gully and Lookout Point. (See Upper Wall Area Approach Map on page 34.) Routes and cliffs are listed as you approach on the trail.

Private Idaho

Private Idaho is the small cliff band located at the base of Lookout Point proper. The Lookout Point trail forks right and passes directly below this cliff. There are some fun routes here and many obscure ones hidden among the trees and moss (which are best left to revegetate). Descend by walking off the right side, or by rappelling from trees or anchors.

1. I Am in Top a Shader (5.11c) ★★ A clean slab pitch on the far left end of Private Idaho. Tricky slab climbing leads to tricky crack climbing. Pro: tricky finger-size gear; quickdraws. (FA: Jon Nelson, Darryl Cramer)

2. 900 Oil-Stricken Waterfowl Taken to Ocean Shores (5.10c) ★ A bolted slab leads to a corner and crack. Pro: quickdraws; small nuts; a midsize cam. (FA: Greg Olsen, Jon Nelson)

3. Eraserhead (5.11c) ★ A very short, knobby slab pitch on the left side of the cliff. Pro: quickdraws.

4. Wet Dream (5.9) ★ The obvious left-leaning dihedral. Usually wet and dirty. Pro: to 2.5 inches.

5. Curious Poses (5.11a) ★ A very short, clean dihedral with one hard move. From the ledge above the corner, finish via the right-hand crack. Pro: to 1 inch.

6. Magic Fern (5.8) An off-hand crack just right of the aforementioned dihedral. Finish via the left-hand crack. Pro: to 3 inches.

7. I Can See Your House From Here (5.12+) ★ The bolted buttress left of *Senior Citizens*. Pro: quickdraws. (FFA: Brent Kertzmann)

8. Senior Citizens in Space (5.7) ★★ The dihedral immediately left of the obvious bolted arête of *Spineless*. Pro: to 2 inches.

9. Spineless (5.11b) ★★ The blunt, bolted arête on the far right side of the cliff. The slabby crux is supposedly "easy" once you figure it out. Pro: quickdraws. (FA: Greg Collum, Greg Olsen 1988)

Hag Crag

No topo. Just right from Private Idaho is this slabby buttress, featuring a prominent dihedral and several knobby friction routes in the 5.7 to 5.11+ range. Several easier routes on the right side are often used for instruction.

Lookout Point

The following routes climb on the cliffs of Lookout Point proper, located just above Private Idaho. A trail up a steep gully on the right climbs to the top of Lookout Point. Another trail traverses the ledge above Private Idaho from Lookout Point to The Diamond gully. One route is reported on the right side of the gully. Several routes begin from the ledge. Descents are problematic

Private Idaho and Lookout Point

Lookout
Point

Lookout
Point
Gully

The
Diamond
Gully

trail

Private
Idaho

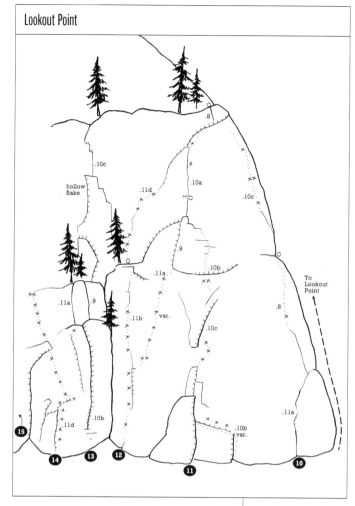

Lookout Point

hollow
flake

.10c

.11d

.10a

.10c

.8

.9

.11a

.10b

.9

.11a

.11b   var.

.10c

.8

To
Lookout
Point

.11a

.11a

.10b

.11d   .10b

.10b
var.

15

14   **13**   **12**   **11**   **10**

A very easy but completely unprotected section on the second pitch mars this otherwise excellent route. Two double-rope rappels down the central gully. Pro: to 1.5 inches. (FA: Jeff Kelly, Jeff Boucher, Matt Arksey 1987)

12. The Dukes of Stratosphere (5.11d) ★★★ A two-pitch route left of *Steel Pulse* climbs discontinuous cracks linked by bolted slabs and eventually joins *Steel Pulse* just under the final roof. Rappel as for *Steel Pulse*. Pro: to 1 inch. (FA: Matt Arksey, Jeff Kelly 1991)

13. Law and Order (5.10c R) ★ An obvious two-pitch route climbing the prominent dihedral system left of the gully and *Dukes of Stratosphere*. The initial shallow corner is often dirty and is difficult to protect even when clean, but the remainder of the route is enjoyable. A good cleaning might renew this route's former popularity. Rappel the route; 60-meter ropes are recommended. Pro: to 2 inches.

on the longer routes, involving long rappels from trees, or short rappels combined with brushy scrambling to reach the Lookout Point gully.

10. Bad Reputation (5.11a) ★★ Cracks and slabs up the right edge of the Lookout Point wall. Pro: to 2 inches.

11. Steel Pulse (5.10c) ★★ An enjoyable three-pitch route up the slabby buttress on the right side of Lookout Point. The route begins via any of three variations; most parties climb the short corner in the middle, although a bolted 5.10b traverse is an option.

14. Spit (5.11d) ★ A line of bolts left of the first pitch of *Law and Order* mark the start of this long pitch. Climb a sloping arête to a slabby finish. Like its neighbor, it gets dirty and is not often climbed. Pro: quickdraws.

15. Act of a Strange Boar (5.10c) ★★ About 60 feet left of the start of *Law and Order* is this clean, thin corner crack. The cracks on either side of the dihedral are 5.10b and 5.10d respectively. Pro: gear to 1 inch. (FA: Derek Pearson, Carolyn Marquardt, Eric Hirst, Jon Nelson 2012)

16. Lookout Point Direct (5.11a) ★ Three long pitches climb more or less directly up the middle of the formation to its summit. After some first-pitch grubbing, layback, jam, and face climb upward. Pro: quickdraws; gear to 4 inches.

17. Solitude (II, 5.11d) ★★ A five-pitch route on the left side of Lookout Point. Start up *Peanuts to Serve You*, the 5.9 pitch just below *Bobcat Cringe*, then keep going up cracks, corners, slabs, and chimneys, with a dyno for a jug at the top. Said to be good; may need cleaning. Pro: comprehensive rack to 4 inches.

18. Bobcat Cringe (5.12b) ★★★ An overhanging thin crack on the left side, about 100 meters left from the start of *Law and Order*. Considered by some to be the best hard, thin crack in Washington. Pro: quickdraws, gear to 1 inch. (FFA: Terry Lien, Darryl Cramer 1992)

19. And Say (II, 5.11b) ★★★ A five-pitch line connecting all the best rock on the far left side of Lookout Point. Approach via a fixed line on the left side of the wall, then climb a corner crack that gets wide at the top. Continue up a slab to a thin crack (5.11a). More slabby crack and face follows. Finish up a vertical thin crack and short, vertical knobby wall. Pro: quickdraws; gear to 3 inches. (FA: Derek Pearson, Michal Rykiewicz, Ryan Hoover, Chandler Davis 2018.)

STATIC POINT

Static Point is a large, slabby granite buttress stuck way out in the woods north of Sultan, so remote that it was discovered by airplane. Logging road access originally made it possible to drive to within about an hour's walk of the cliff. Further logging activity shortened the walk to about thirty minutes, in addition to worsening the ambience of the area with nearby clear-cutting. Still, the area has seen an increase in popularity over the years, and you will sometimes even encounter other climbers here, most of whom will be climbing *On Line,* the area's most popular route.

Type of climbing: Climbing at Static Point is friction at its finest, and the routes rarely vary, mostly involving moderately angled slab climbing on fairly smooth, slightly knobby granite with widely spaced protection, usually in the form of 0.5-inch bolts and gear behind flakes and in discontinuous cracks. A few routes follow crack systems, but the best routes are on the slabs.

Brief history of area: As legend has it, Static Point was first spotted by climbers during an airplane flight over the Cascades during the early 1980s. A small group of climbers, including David Whitelaw, Don Brooks, Chris Greyell, and Duane Constantino, established most of the routes during the next few years, keeping the area relatively secret. Most of the routes were established on the lead, but with the aid of battery-powered drills to facilitate quicker bolt placement—a controversial tactic at the time, although nobody knew it was happening since only a small group of climbers was active.

The area was first publicized in Whitelaw's *Private Dancer,* a novel, artsy guidebook published in 1985. The area became briefly popular, but since the late 1980s there has been very little new route activity. Most climbers visiting Static Point are content to repeat the classic lines, which is well enough.

Seasons and climate: Climbing season is generally from May through October, from approximately when the snow melts to when it starts falling again, although summer and early fall are the best seasons to visit Static Point. Weather at Static Point is typically similar to the weather at Index and Darrington (i.e., predominately wet in spring and fall), although its southern exposure generally means faster drying time. In spring, snow lingers late and temperatures are generally cooler. Intermittent hot and cold, calm and windy, and rainy and sunny periods should be expected year-round, so have a shirt, sweater, and rain gear handy even if it's a warm, sunny day.

Precautions and regulations: At Static Point, runouts of 30 or 40 feet are not uncommon, and there are a few full-pitch runouts on easy ground. Thus, these routes are fairly serious, although in the same sense as Glacier Point Apron (Yosemite) routes:

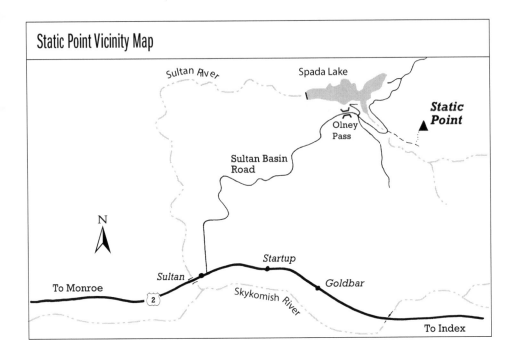

Static Point Vicinity Map

Sultan River

Spada Lake

Static Point

Olney Pass

Sultan Basin Road

N

Startup

Sultan

Goldbar

To Monroe

2

Skykomish River

To Index

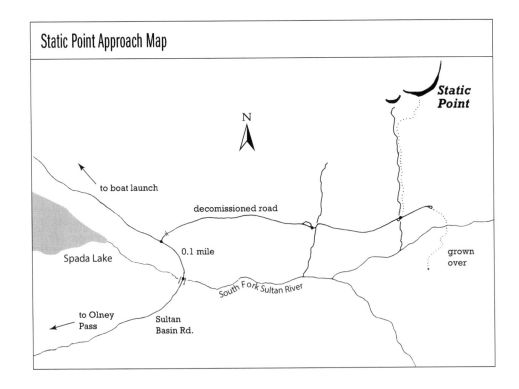

Static Point Approach Map

Static Point

N

to boat launch

decomissioned road

Spada Lake

0.1 mile

grown over

South Fork Sultan River

to Olney Pass

Sultan Basin Rd.

The cliff is rarely considered too steep, and falls are most often grating slides (wear long pants). Yes, they can hurt and result in injury, but so far no one has reported being too seriously injured here, and there are no fatalities on record. However, if a bolt fails, you're history. According to some reports, a few of the original bolts could be removed by hand! All in all, the bolts seem pretty secure now, so don't think they're all booby trapped. Just exercise caution, and don't climb beyond your ability. If you find a questionable bolt, don't trust it farther than you'd be willing to fall onto it.

Because most of the routes involve several pitches of climbing at an area miles distant from anything, with poor cell-phone coverage, commitment is a factor to consider. A rescue could be long in coming, so plan ahead, and let someone know where you plan to be so they'll know where to start looking.

Static Point lies within the Sultan Basin Recreation Area, a protected area because Spada Reservoir is the city of Everett's primary water supply. Upon entering the area, you are supposed to register, although nobody seems to bother. It is interesting to note that, among other things, it is illegal to litter in the watershed, which includes human waste. It is uncertain what one is supposed to do when nature calls, but if you want to adhere to the rules, you should hike out and drive back to the toilets at Olney Pass to do your business. Instead, try taking care of business before you enter the watershed, so it isn't a problem. Either that or bag it and carry it out.

This area is subject to closure, and several roads in the area have been or may be decommissioned, which have already or will add considerably to the approach hike.

Gear and other considerations: Although most Static Point routes are bolted slabs, gear is a necessity on almost all routes. Bring quickdraws, plus a selection of wired nuts and cams to place in cracks and behind the many flakes you will encounter on most routes. Even with gear, most of the routes are runout in places. A 50-meter rope is adequate for some pitches, but you'll end up simul-climbing a few unless you bring a 60-meter rope or longer. Double ropes are necessary for most rappels.

Camping and accommodations: The towns of Sultan and Monroe have all the necessary accommodations, including gas, food, and lodging. Most climbers visit for the day and head back to town at night. You could bivy at the parking lot, but overnight camping is not permitted in the Spada Lake watershed, so if you camp here don't be surprised if you are asked to leave or possibly cited. There are bivouac sites along the road before Olney Pass, outside the watershed, although this isn't the best area for camping out.

Emergency services: In case of emergency, dial 911. The nearest hospital is in Monroe.

Other guidebooks: Whitelaw, David. *Weekend Rock*; Cramer, Darryl. *Sky Valley Rock*.

Finding the crags: Follow US 2 to Sultan, located about 30 miles northeast of Seattle. At the east edge of town, turn north onto Sultan Basin Road and follow it about 13 miles, first on pavement, then gravel, to Olney Pass, where a registration booth and sign mark the entrance to Spada Lake Basin. Assuming the gate is open, from the pass continue straight ahead on the main road (the middle or right fork, not the overgrown far right fork that is almost always gated), which leads down and right, soon crossing the South Fork Sultan River. Just beyond the bridge, on the right, is a narrow road, decommissioned years ago and easy to miss. Park here and walk the old roadbed. If the access road is closed, you'll have to park at Olney Pass and hike or bike in. Check the signs at Olney Pass for current access restrictions.

Either way, hike in from the main road. About a mile from the main road is a rocky stream gully, above which you can see a prominent granite slab. Cross the stream and take a left at the rusty culvert pipe lying on the road, then hike up the stream gully. A trail materializes soon enough.

The approach trail strays right after several hundred meters of scrambling up the gully, reaching Static Point's left side just below Tombstone Ledge, very near the start of *On Line*. A path meanders right along the base of the slabs. Routes are described from left to right as you traverse along the base of the slab.

Tombstone Ledge Area

Tombstone Ledge is one of the more obvious features of Static Point, as it is the only ledge on the entire left side of the wall. The ledge is named after a small block of granite perched there. Four routes begin from the ledge. Tombstone Ledge is best reached by climbing *On Line* and rappelling down to the *American Pie* anchors, or by climbing *Wrong Line,* which follows fairly clean Class 5 cracks to the ledge. A Class 3 scramble on the left side is hard to locate and not recommended. Don't try scrambling straight up the obvious corner from trail's end; it is tricky finding the easiest route and involves Class 4 and 5 climbing on dirty, rotten rock.

If getting onto Tombstone Ledge is problematic, getting off the ledge is more so. The best way to get off the ledge is probably to climb *American Pie* and then rappel over to the *On Line* anchors and down that route. This can be a problem if another party is on that route, so either be patient or try another way. The standard rappel route begins at the obvious small tree on the right side of the ledge. Be careful not to knock rocks onto people below, as there are many loose blocks on this rappel line, which also involves some loose scrambling. It is supposedly possible to traverse left off the ledge into the woods, but this seems unreasonably risky. The Class 3 route is difficult to spot from above, so if you don't know where it is, be careful. Another option is to rappel from trees on the left side of the ledge (two long rappels), which is fairly straightforward but brushy.

1. The Corner (5.8) ★ The only dihedral in sight. Unprotected but easy friction leads rightward near the top. Pro: to 2 inches.

2. Cashman (5.10c R) ★ The sparsely bolted slab immediately right of *The Corner*. Very runout. Pro: quickdraws.

3. Black Fly (5.8 R) ★ A runout slab left of *American Pie*. Pro: quickdraws, gear to 0.5 inch, with small wireds.

4. American Pie (5.10a R) ★★★ An excellent friction pitch leading up from the rotten pillar at the right end of Tombstone Ledge, passing a roof with a runout crux finish. Pro: quickdraws, #2.5 Friend. (FA: David Whitelaw, Duane Constantino 1983)

The following routes begin from the base of the slab, about where the approach trail meets the rock. None is obvious from below, unless you have good eyesight and can spot the belay anchors—or the other climbers already on the route.

5. Wrong Line

(5.8) A direct route to Tombstone Ledge, climbing more or less straight up corners and cracks from where the trail meets the slabs. Aim for the double dihedral flake visible from the ground; stay out of the dirty corner system to the left. Three pitches, no bolts. Many variations possible. Kind of fun if you follow the path of most resistance. Pro: all gear to 2.5 inches.

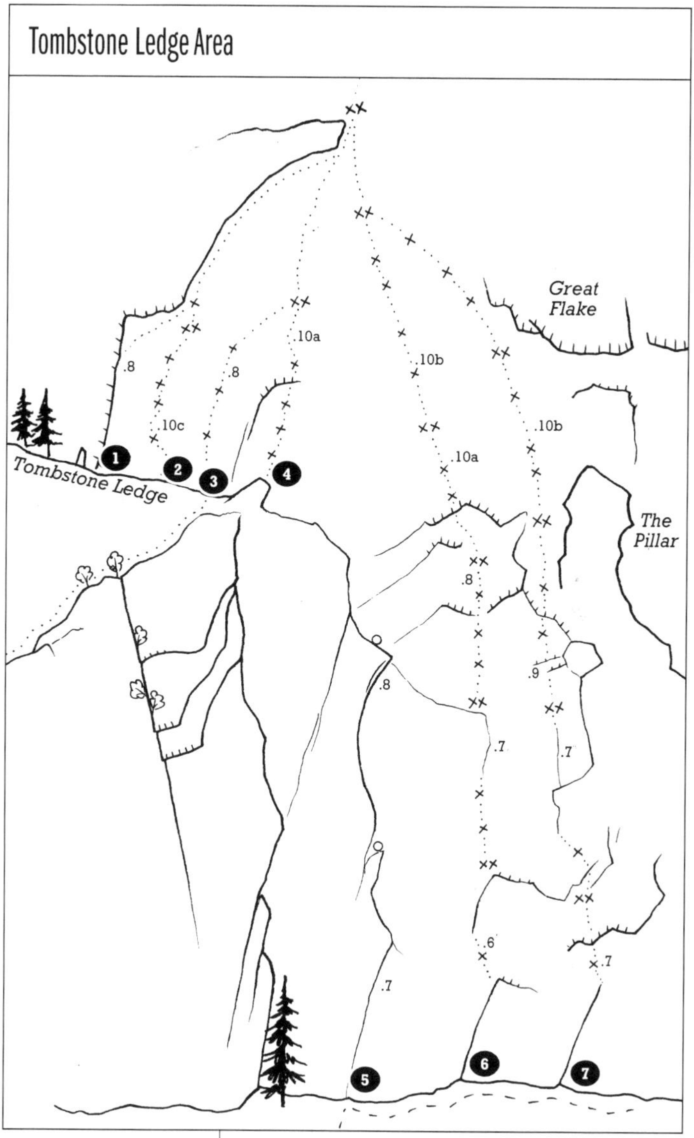

6. On Line (III,

5.10b R) ★★★ This direct Static Point classic is the area's most popular route, for good reason. Begin about 50 feet right of where the trail meets the slabs. Look for the first bolt (10 meters up) and a short corner/roof to identify the route—or just start climbing and hope you end up on route. For the remainder of the route's six pitches, link flakes, slabs, and ledges, following bolts that are few and far between. Sporting runouts, with relatively well-protected cruxes. A 60-meter rope is recommended. Pro: quickdraws, plus some thin gear and a #1.5 Friend. (FA: Don Brooks, Dave Whitelaw 1983)

Tombstone Ledge Area

Great Flake

The Pillar

Tombstone Ledge

7. Off Line (III, 5.10a R) ★ Another long, slightly less direct route just right of *On Line*. The route eventually traverses left to join *On Line* at the top. Some sporting runouts. This route is usually climbed only when *On Line* is too crowded. Pro: to 1 inch, with many small wireds.

Tombstone Ledge and the Pillar

The Pillar

Some distance right of Tombstone Ledge is The Pillar, a 40-meter-high detached flake situated some two pitches up, directly above the Lost Charms Tree. Routes in this area tend to follow natural features of the rock (i.e., cracks), and thus have fewer bolts. There are several routes in this area that are not included in this guide; they are generally 5.9 to 5.10 and involve substantial runouts just like all the other Static Point routes. If you're game, pick a line and see where it goes.

It should be noted that approaching along the base of the slabs is somewhat complicated here. The true base of Static Point drops off just beyond *Off Line.* To stay with the routes, traverse straight across the exfoliation, which involves some exposed but easy Class 5 moves.

Descent routes are discussed where appropriate. Generally, routes left of The Pillar rappel down *On Line* or from Tombstone Ledge; routes right of The Pillar usually are descended by rappelling the route of ascent.

8. Lost Charms (III, 5.10b) ★★
From the Lost Charms Tree, climb up and right, then back left into a corner system to the Pillar Ledge. Climb up just right of The Pillar, then cross the aptly named Bridge Flake and belay at its far side. Continue up a finger crack to ledges, then left up flakes to the Great Flake. From there, it is possible to head left to reach the Mohawk, from where it is possible to rappel to

Tombstone Ledge. A direct finish continues from the top of the Great Flake directly up the slab to reach the left side of a prominent arch, which is traversed to the *Shock Treatment* rappel. Pro: to 3 inches.

Spencer's Spaceport

Right of the Lost Charms Tree and up half a pitch is Spencer's Spaceport, a ledge system

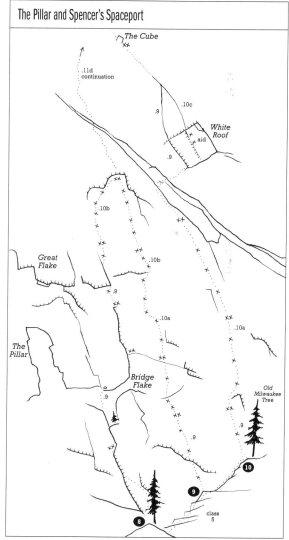

The Pillar and Spencer's Spaceport

The Pillar and Spencer's Spaceport

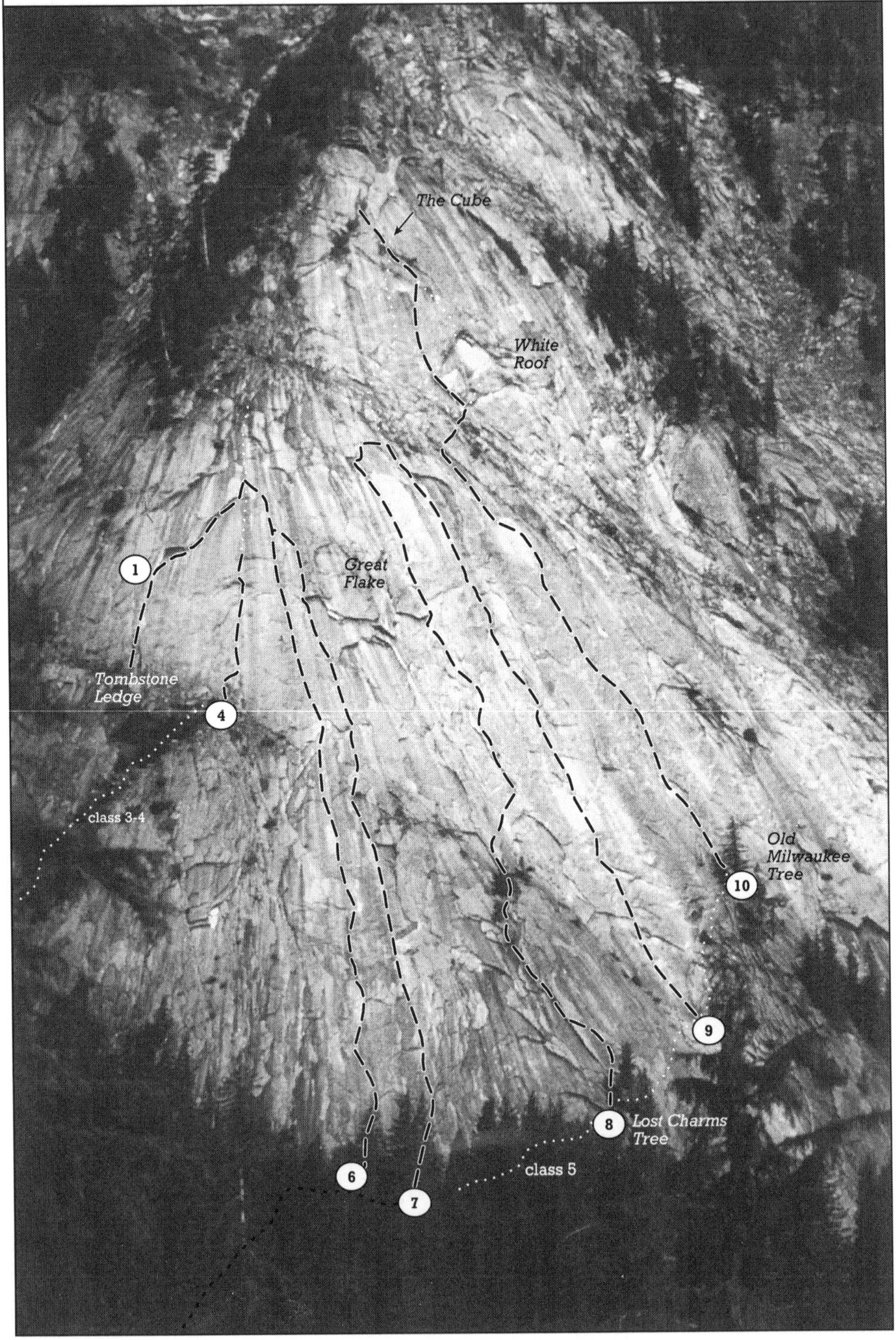

The Cube

White Roof

1

Great Flake

Tombstone Ledge

4

class 3-4

Old Milwaukee Tree

10

9

8 Lost Charms Tree

6

7

class 5

from which several Static Point classics begin. The easiest way to reach the Spaceport is to traverse a ledge rightward from the first pitch of *Lost Charms*. Many parties do not rope up for the scramble to the Spaceport, but it is recommended here because there is some moderate, exposed Class 5 climbing. At the far, upper right end of the ledge is the Old Milwaukee Tree, visible from below as the highest tree on the upper right side of Static Point.

9. Shock Treatment (III, 5.10c R) ★★★
Another Static Point classic, but less traveled because it is not as easy to get to as *On Line*. Begin at the lowest point of the Spaceport, climbing past a bolt to a roof, then up runout slabs to a stance. Continue left and up, passing bolts and flakes. The crux third pitch ends at a sling belay known as the Offshore Belay Rig. A final pitch leads to the Broken Band. Rappel the route. Several long runouts. Pro: to 3 inches. (FA: Chris Greyell, Dave Tower, Dave Whitelaw 1984)

10. Static Cling (II, 5.10a R) ★★
Another of Static Point's better outings. From the Old Milwaukee Tree, climb directly up a dihedral to a pedestal belay. Continue straight up poorly protected friction to a small overlap and a short crux slab to a ledge. Climb a left-facing arch to more runout friction to reach the ledge system that diagonals across the slabs. Pro: quickdraws, RPs.

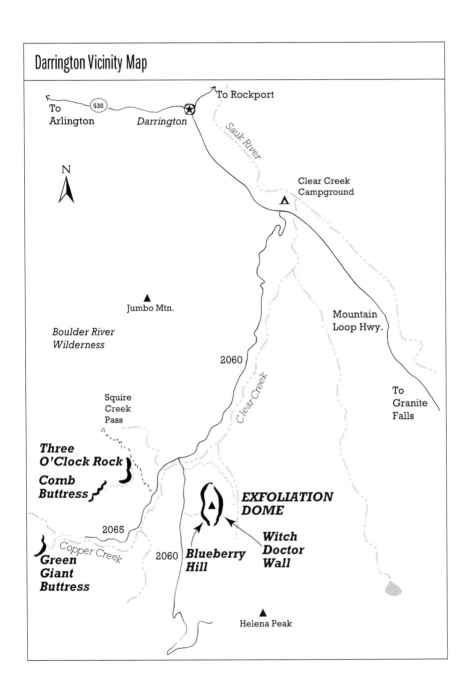

Darrington Vicinity Map

To Rockport

To Arlington · 530 · Darrington

Sauk River

N

Clear Creek Campground

Jumbo Mtn.

Boulder River Wilderness

Mountain Loop Hwy.

2060

Squire Creek Pass

Clear Creek

To Granite Falls

Three O'Clock Rock

Comb Buttress

EXFOLIATION DOME

2065

Green Giant Buttress

Copper Creek

2060

Blueberry Hill

Witch Doctor Wall

Helena Peak

Darrington may be the most underrated rock climbing area in Washington. By all accounts, Darrington has excellent rock, interesting and varied climbing, and is close enough to the Puget Sound sprawl to make it a popular area. Still, Darrington goes begging for climbers. Perhaps it is the moss, dirt, and rainy weather that keep climbers away; either that or the endless slabs. Whatever the reason, nobody seems to climb here. But someone must, as there are many excellent routes on Darrington's slabs and buttresses, even several new routes established during the past few years.

Type of climbing: Most of Darrington's routes involve friction slabs linked by discontinuous crack systems. At its best, Darrington climbing consists of knobby, multipitch friction routes up clean granite slabs. At its worst, it involves mossy, brushy crack systems and long, committing descents. The most popular of Darrington's crags, Three O'Clock Rock, has many excellent slab routes from 5.6 to 5.11 in difficulty, and a few decent crack lines. Three O'Clock Rock's routes range from single-pitch test pieces to multi-pitch classics. Darrington also has some long, moderate free climbs, especially on Green Giant Buttress and Blueberry Hill, and several long aid routes on Witch Doctor Wall.

Brief history of area: The first climbers to visit this area concentrated their efforts on Exfoliation Dome; not surprisingly, Fred Beckey was instrumental in the first ascent of *Witch Doctor Wall,* a Grade V aid route up the steepest, highest part of the wall, first climbed in 1969.

During the 1970s, a few intrepid explorers ventured onto Darrington's other walls, pushing routes up most of the more obvious slabs and cracks. Active in Darrington's climbing development during this era were Don Brooks, Duane Constantino, Chris Greyell, Brent Hoffman, and David Whitelaw, who together or with others put up many of the area's classics. Routes of this era were established in traditional style, with bolts placed where necessary, on lead. Not surprisingly, a few routes feature thought-provoking runouts from dubious 0.25-inch bolts.

Since the 1980s, relatively few new routes have been established, although recent pioneers have managed to find several worthwhile routes here and there, mostly short rappel-bolted slabs, but also several longer routes, particularly on Green Giant Buttress and Blueberry Hill. Matt Perkins has been most active in recent years and is the official steward of Darrington climbing; his website (www.mattsea.com/darr) includes current access information and topos to many of the area's best routes.

Seasons and climate: Weather at Darrington is typically wet, varying from perfect to overcast to soggy, particularly from late fall through spring. Convergence of moist marine air with cooler, higher elevations of the Cascade Range seems to wring all the rain down on the western slopes of the mountains. Thus, Darrington has a reputation for being wet. From late June through early September, the weather is usually fair. At any other time, if it isn't raining, be thankful.

For weather information, call the Darrington Ranger District office at (360) 436-1155.

Precautions and regulations: Most of Darrington's routes were established in traditional style, with bolts drilled from stances on lead, meaning route-finding is not always easy and runouts are the norm. Even following the bolts can be difficult, as they are often far apart. Many routes feature long runouts from old 0.25-inch bolts, not a pleasant prospect for someone climbing at or near their limit. Generally, crux moves are well protected, but easier sections may be sparsely protected, if at all. Climbers have been actively replacing old bolts, but it's a big job, so don't expect shiny new bolts on every route.

Those planning on establishing new routes should be mindful that most if not all of the cliffs lie within the Boulder River Wilderness Area, where installing fixed anchors is illegal. Also, as the rocks mostly lie within a designated wilderness area, do your best to avoid adverse impacts.

Weather can pose problems for unprepared climbers at Darrington, especially on the bigger walls. Darrington is one of the wettest rock climbing areas in Washington, if moss is a valid indicator. If there's any chance of rain, it is a good idea to carry rain gear on any multipitch route, or at least have it in your pack for the hike out. It is a bad idea to climb Witch Doctor Wall, Blueberry Hill, or Green Giant Buttress during questionable weather, as already risky descents can become deadly during storms. Also, on some of the

big walls, allow plenty of time to climb and descend before dark. If you get caught on a route or atop a wall after dark, it is probably best to stay put until morning, as descents can be deadly after dark. Be prepared for an unplanned bivouac, which is not an uncommon occurrence.

Because of approach and descent difficulties, many of Darrington's walls are infrequently visited. In the event of a climbing accident, a rescue may be long in coming, particularly on the more remote walls. It is a good idea to let someone know where you will be climbing, so they know where to look for you if you get stuck for any reason.

Restrictions: The Darrington crags are managed by the Mt. Baker/Snoqualmie National Forest. Power drills are prohibited within wilderness area boundaries, so bolts may only be placed (and replaced) by hand.

Gear and other considerations: A typical Darrington rack consists of many quickdraws and several small nuts and cams up to 2 or 3 inches. On most routes, you will find good protection at or near the crux, but may find sporting runouts on easier sections in between. However, on many unprotected sections you will be able to place gear, so even on bolt-protected routes it is a good idea to bring a small rack in addition to quickdraws. Bring slings for rappel anchors and to tie off trees, shrubs, and even the occasional knob, to take advantage of all possible natural protection.

Double ropes are required for nearly all rappels, and a 60-meter rope is recommended. If you encounter old, tattered rappel slings, replace them, and pack the old slings out instead of littering them at the base of the slabs.

Camping and accommodations: Most climbers visit Darrington for the day and

Lucie Parietti on *Dreamer Direct* (5.10a), Green Giant Buttress, Darrington ERIC PONSLET &
LUCIE PARIETTI, WWW.ERICANDLUCIE.COM

head home at night. Those who stay over-night bivouac at or near their cars at various places along the approach roads. There's a neat spot at the base of the Granite Side-walk below Blueberry Hill, with a fire pit and great views across the valley to Three O'Clock Rock and Green Giant Buttress. Technically, camping here isn't allowed, but it's still a preferred spot. Alternatively, drive past the Squire Creek Pass trailhead to road's end and bivouac at the Green Giant Buttress turnaround. Again, this is not an approved bivouac spot but is often used, particularly by climbers wanting an early start up Green Giant Buttress, and by hunters. Those want-ing to avoid illegal bivouacs should consider camping at Clear Creek Campground or other nearby Forest Service campgrounds. Contact the Darrington Ranger District office for information (see Appendix).

Darrington features some ameni-ties, including a grocery store, gas station, bank (with an ATM), liquor store, and laundromat.

Emergency services: In case of emergency, dial 911. The nearest hospitals are in Mount Vernon and Everett.

Guide services/local equipment suppliers: There are no local guide services or equip-ment suppliers, unless you need a chainsaw or power drill (both of which are illegal to use in this area).

Other guidebooks: The Darrington Rock Climbing website (www.mattsea.com/darr) has topos of many of the most popular routes in the area and current access information.
Whitelaw, David. *Weekend Rock*.

Finding the crags: From I-5, take exit 208 and follow WA 530 east 31 miles to Dar-rington (about one and a half hours northeast of Seattle). Alternatively, take Mountain Loop Highway north from Granite Falls, or WA 17A south from WA 20 from Concrete.

From Darrington, head south on Moun-tain Loop Highway at the four-way stop (where WA 530 heads north). Follow the highway almost 2.5 miles, then take a right turn onto FR 2060, which is well marked on the right just before the entrance to Clear Creek Campground. Follow this unpaved road to a fork at about 5.5 miles. Take the right fork to reach Three O'Clock Rock, Comb Buttress, and Green Giant Buttress; the left fork leads to Witch Doctor Wall and Blueberry Hill. Approach hikes are described in detail in the introduction to each wall.

The forest service has tried to close the road in the past, usually citing lack of funds to maintain the many roads and trails in the Darrington Ranger District damaged by winter flooding. Apparently the decisions to close the road were made without consider-ation of climbers using the road for access, and lobbying efforts have kept the road open so far. The best thing climbers can do to keep the road open is to climb at Darrington regularly and let the forest service know the area is being used. It is a good idea to call the Darrington Ranger District office first to find out if the road is open and passable. If the road happens to be closed to vehicles, it is passable on foot and mountain bike, albeit a longer approach than your average sport crag.

Check the Darrington Rock Climbing website for current access. It is usually the most up-to-date source.

THREE O'CLOCK ROCK

Three O'Clock Rock is the most popular of Darrington's walls. It has many mossy, brushy, overgrown cracks and corners, but the majority of routes climb the cleaner slabs in between. These knobby slabs provide enjoyable, sporting climbing. Most of the routes were established on lead, meaning the climbing tends to be somewhat runout on all but the newest rappel-bolted routes. A few routes climb all the way to the top of Three O'Clock Rock, but the best climbing is on the lower half of the rock, which is cleaner.

Three O'Clock Rock needs no real description, since it is plainly visible from the road as you approach. About 6 miles from Mountain Loop Highway on FR 2060 is the Squire Creek Pass Trail (number 654). Park in the turnout and hike up the trail for about thirty minutes. The trail eventually reaches the base of the North Buttress, on the far right-hand side of the rock, directly below *Silent Running.* From here, a trail leads left along the base of the slabs. A more direct scramble up talus and through Douglas maple branches leads directly from the trail to the base of the Big Tree routes.

The Big Tree/Kone area, on the right flank of the South Buttress, has the best and most popular routes on Three O' Clock Rock. Many parties climb and rappel their way from right to left across *Big Tree One, Cornucopia, The Kone,* and *Tidbits,* an excellent day's climbing that unfortunately clogs up the routes when more than one party arrives with the same agenda. If these routes are packed, spread out. There's plenty of room.

All descents are by rappel unless otherwise noted. Most rappels are from

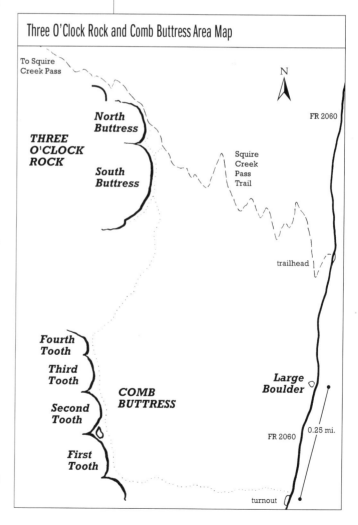

Three O'Clock Rock and Comb Buttress Area Map

To Squire Creek Pass

N

FR 2060

THREE O'CLOCK ROCK

North Buttress

South Buttress

Squire Creek Pass Trail

trailhead

Fourth Tooth

Third Tooth

Second Tooth

First Tooth

COMB BUTTRESS

Large Boulder

FR 2060

0.25 mi.

turnout

Three O'Clock Rock

double-bolt anchors, although you may find yourself rappelling from a tree here and there. If you plan on climbing any multi-pitch routes, bring some extra slings in case you need to tie off a tree or bush for a rappel anchor. If you replace worn slings, please pack the old ones out instead of littering them.

North Buttress

The North Buttress of Three O'Clock Rock is the broad, brushy slab on the far right side of the rock. It has four routes, all involving multiple pitches of slab climbing. The dike of *Total Soul* and the dihedral of *Bushy Galore* are the most prominent features here. The Squire Creek Pass Trail leads directly to the toe of the North Buttress, just below the start of *Silent Running*. The routes are described from right to left as you encounter them when traversing along the base of Three O'Clock Rock from where the trail meets the rock.

1. Mystery Tour (III, 5.9+) ★★ A five-pitch route up the slabs right of *Silent Running*. Start up two pitches of easy bolted slab climbing to anchors (*Road to Nowhere*, 5.3); can be combined in one pitch. Angle right, then up two straightforward bolted slab pitches. A final short pitch joins *Silent Running*, but most forego this pitch and rappel. Pro: quickdraws; gear to 2 inches.

2. Silent Running (III, 5.9 or 5.10b) ★★★ An excellent line up the slabby right side of

Three O'Clock Rock North Buttress

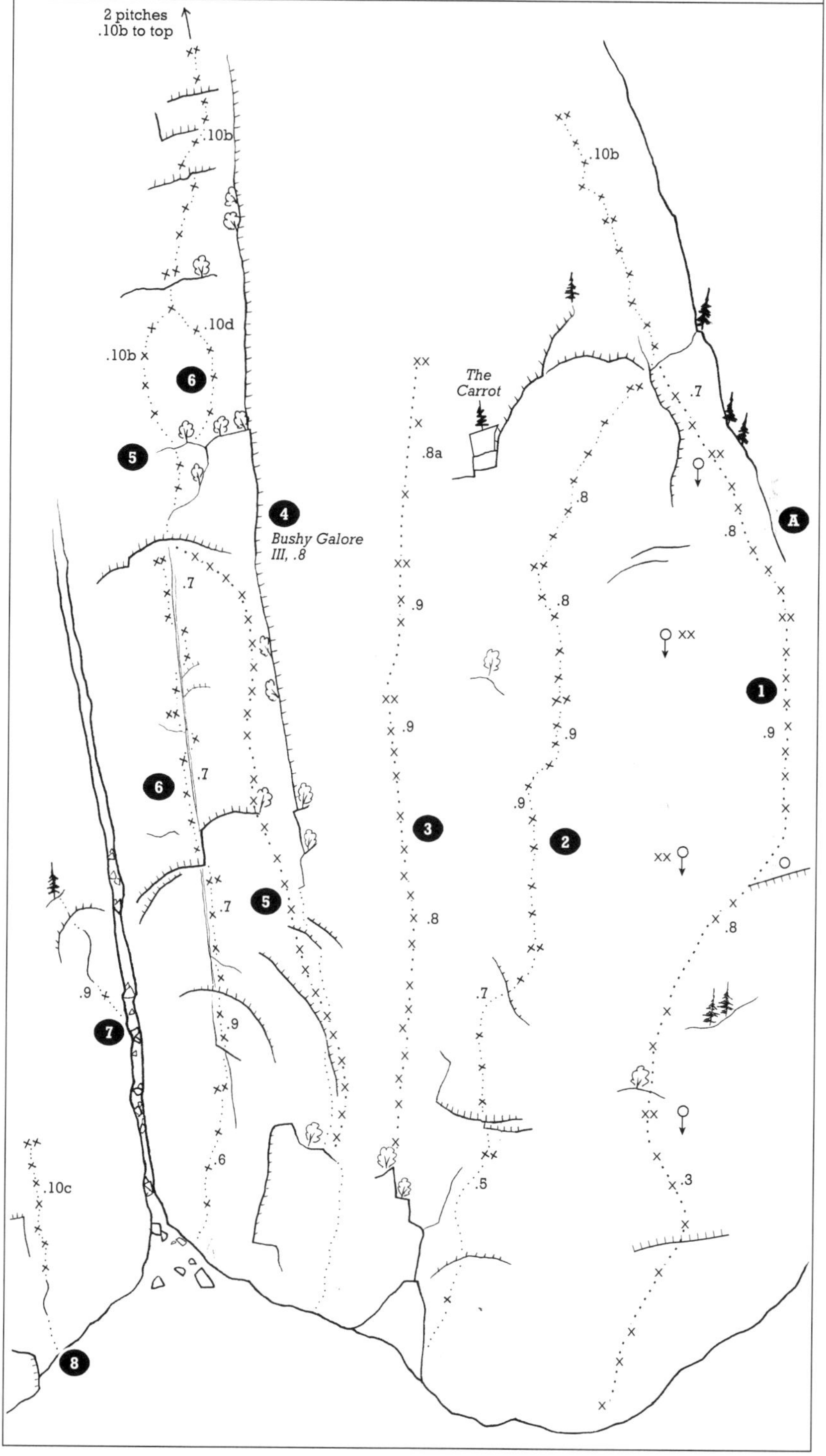

2 pitches
.10b to top

.10b

.10d

.10b

.8a

The Carrot

.7

.8

.8

.9

.8

.9

.9

Bushy Galore
III, .8

.7

.7

.9

.9

.8

.9

.7

.7

.9

.5

.6

.5

.3

.10c

6

5

4

6

5

3

1

2

A

7

8

the North Buttress. The old line has been cleaned up and straightened out, with additional bolts, better anchors, and a new finish with a bonus 5.10b pitch. The first pitch is still long and runout but easy up to the roofs. Connect the bolts up the slab, trending right under the arch. Rappel the route or the rappel line between *Silent Running* and *Mystery Tour*. Pro: quickdraws; gear to 2 inches.

3. Revolver (III, 5.10a) ★★ Another multi-pitch route up the North Buttress, starting and finishing left of *Silent Running*. Stays wet later than its neighbors, and rockfall has damaged some bolts. If it's dry and the bolts are repaired, it is a worthwhile route. Pro: quickdraws; gear to 2 inches.

4. Bushy Galore (III, 5.8) An obvious route up the dihedral system on the upper left side of the North Buttress slab, included more for posterity than to persuade anyone to actually climb it. Getting to the dihedral involves some route-finding skill on runout terrain. Once there, fight your way up the bushes as far as you are inclined to go. Rappel the route or *Total Soul*. Pro: to 2.5 inches; slings.

5. Penny Lane (II, 5.10c) ★★ A four-pitch variation start to *Total Soul*, starting pretty much as for *Bushy Galore* then connecting bolts up the slabs left of the dihedral system, eventually joining *Total Soul* at its fourth-pitch anchors. Pro: quickdraws; gear to 2 inches.

6. Total Soul (III, 5.10b or 5.10d) ★★★ Basically the old *Rubber Soul* route, conveniently retrobolted for your protection. The first four pitches follow the white dike up through the roofs; after that, successive 5.10 pitches left of the dike continue to the top of the North Buttress. Pro: quickdraws; gear to 2 inches.

South Buttress

The South Buttress is a broad, slabby cliff, with many mossy corners, cedar trees, and knobs, and features most of the popular routes at Darrington. It is divided from the North Buttress by a blocky gully. The routes are described from right to left as you encounter them while traversing along the base of the cliff from the gully.

7. The Jinx (5.9) Scramble up the blocky gully that divides the buttresses. Here—hopefully—you'll find a bolted slab leading to a roof. Cleaned and rebolted; said to be better than it looks. Pro: quickdraws and gear to 2 inches.

8. Pucker Up (5.10b) ★★ Just down and left from the gully is a line of bolts leading up a rounded slab, just right of an arête/roof. Pro: quickdraws.

9. Northwest Passage (5.10a) ★★ Shallow, flaring cracks lead to a bolted slab. Find a passage through the trees to a second bolted slab. Can be continued via the old *Big Tree II* variation. Pro: quickdraws; gear to 2 inches.

10. Stance or Dance (5.10a) ★★ Curving cracks lead up the slab; a crux face section links the cracks. Can be continued to join the *Big Tree II* variation. Pro: to 2 inches; quickdraws.

11. Big Tree (II, 5.7) ★ One of the original routes on Three O'Clock Rock. Begin via a prominent, jagged 4-inch crack on the left side of a flake about 30 feet above the ground, and climb the thin crack above to a ledge with several cedars. Traverse right a bit, into a left-facing corner system, then head up the corner until you can traverse left across a big, horizontal crack. The traverse gets you to a big, left-facing dihedral, which

Three O'Clock Rock-South Buttress

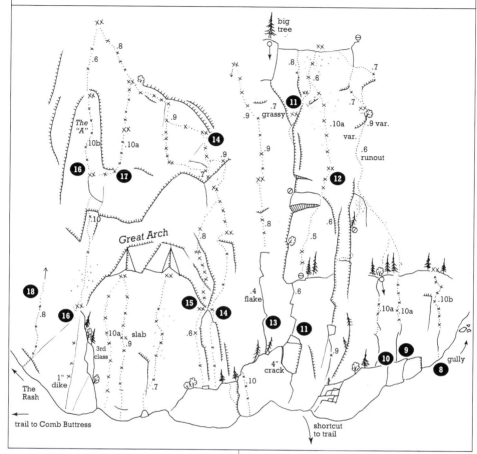

leads up to anchors at the convergence of two slabby corners. The best finish is via a knobby slab above and right (runout 5.6); the corner leading straight up is kind of dirty (5.8); and the corner leading left is grassy (5.7). Assuming you climb the 5.6 slab, a narrow ledge traverse leads to the namesake Big Tree. Continue a few pitches above the Big Tree if you like; most parties rappel from the Big Tree, down the line of *Cornucopia*. The *Big Tree II* (5.7 R) variation climbs a corner and runout slab farther right, then traverses left to the Big Tree. Pro: to 3 inches will suffice; slings to reduce rope drag.

12. Big Tree 2000 (II, 5.10a) ★★★ A direct variation of the Big Tree routes. Start up the cracks to the ledge, then climb the easy slab to the roof. Pass the roof on the right side and continue up the knobby slab, connecting the bolts to anchors at the upper ledge. Pro: same as *Big Tree* route, plus quickdraws.

13. Cornucopia (II, 5.9) ★★ A three-pitch route climbing slabs more or less directly to the Big Tree. The route begins atop a small ledge left of the *Big Tree* start. Scramble up rocks and roots to the ledge, then up and right to the base of a long flake. Ascend the flake (5.4), then climb a short pitch to

anchors (5.8). Continue straight and left up the final slab pitch to anchors. Some runouts, but the cruxes are adequately protected.

Rappel down *The Kone*. Pro: quickdraws; gear to 3 inches.

14. The Quin Konehead Pre-Memorial Route (aka The Kone) (II, 5.9) ★★★ One of Darrington's best routes, offering five pitches of excellent, sparsely bolt-protected friction climbing. The route begins from the ledge just left of the *Cornucopia* flake, climbing a slab between two left-facing corners, then rightward and up and over a prominent small roof (5.9). The route continues, traversing left above a small roof then up a knobby slab, crossing a thin crack and up slabs to the left edge of a long roof. A final, easier pitch leads left to anchors atop *Tidbits*. Rappel that route. Pro: to 1 inch; quickdraws, TCUs, and wireds. (FA: Duane Constantino, David Whitelaw 1979)

15. Till Broad Daylight (5.8+) ★★★ A direct variation of *The Kone,* climbing slabs around the right edge of the Great Arch, connecting with *The Kone* after three pitches. Pro: quickdraws, TCUs, wireds, slings for rope drag.

16. Tidbits (II, 5.10b) ★★ A popular route, usually done immediately after rappelling off *The Kone.* About 50 feet left from the base of the roof slab is a thin dike running straight up a slab; climb this dike (retrobolted) or scramble up brushy ledges on the right to a ledge. Continue up a knobby slab, connecting the bolts past a roof to a thin crescent crack. Continue up the "A" (an apex formed by facing dihedrals, visible from below). Easier climbing above the "A" leads to the rappel anchors. Somewhat runout in places, like everything else at Darrington. Pro: to 1 inch; quickdraws.

17. Gastroblast (5.10a) ★★ A two-pitch linkup of *Tidbits* and *The Kone.* From the base of the "A," traverse right, connecting the bolts across then up the knobby slab to join *The Kone* at its third belay. Two pitches, somewhat runout. Pro: to 1 inch.

18. Magic Bus (III, 5.8) ★ A long route that is rarely climbed, except for the first two pitches. The route begins about 30 feet left of the dike-start to *Tidbits,* where a line of bolts begins about 10 feet above a small roof (a solution pocket just above the roof may help you identify the route). Pro: to 3 inches.

19. Rashionalization (5.7) ★★ About 50 yards up the trail from the *Tidbits* dike, the trail peaks. Just above and right is a left-leaning corner. The route begins via the corner and slabs above, although most parties begin via *Butterflies.* From bolt anchors, climb left up The Rash, an obvious, knob-studded slab (easy Class 5 but totally unprotected!). Continue left around loose blocks to a ledge. Rappel the route. Pro: to 3 inches, slings to tie off knobs.

20. When Butterflies Kiss Bumblebees (5.8) ★★ Where the trail peaks (about 50 yards up the trail from the *Tidbits* dike), a ledge traverses left to an obvious thin, clean flake. Climb the flake and short slab above to bolt anchors, then up and right, following well-spaced bolts up a knobby slab. Pro: to 1 inch; quickdraws.

21. Luke 9:25 (5.10b) ★★ Just left of and downhill from the first pitch of *Butterflies* is an obvious bolt line climbing a knobby slab. The first pitch (5.8) begins on the left and crosses an older bolt line; the second pitch climbs straight up the knobby slab to a small ledge with anchors. Rappel the route. Pro: quickdraws; #0 TCU recommended.

22. Mistress Jane's Chains (5.9) ★ About 100 feet up the trail from the start of *Luke 9:25* is this obvious, short route, climbing a bolted slab to chain anchors 60 feet up. Pro: quickdraws.

23. Please Mr. Custer (5.11c) ★ A two-pitch route climbing a prominent 10-inch

Three O'Clock Rock South Buttress

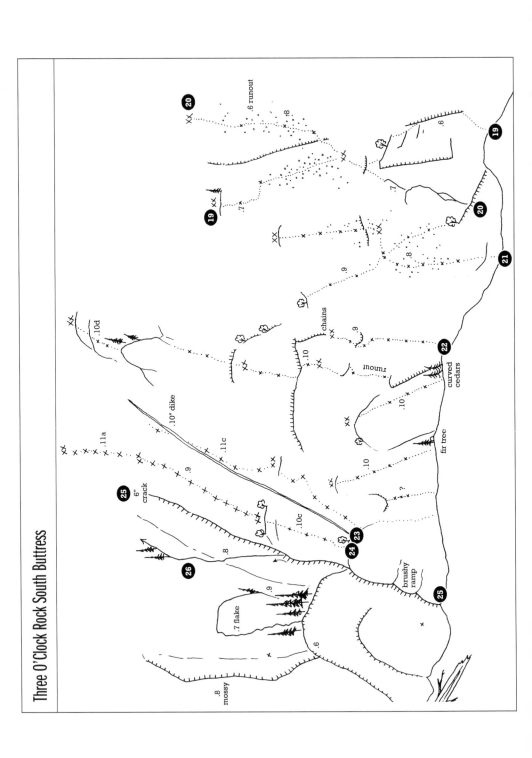

dike leading up the slab immediately right of *Masters of the Universe*. The first pitch (5.11b) follows bolts below and right of the dike to anchors. The second pitch follows the dike the rest of the way. Pro: quickdraws. (FA: Ron Miller, Dave Hutchinson 1994)

24. Masters of the Universe (5.11a) ★★★
A three-pitch route up the clean, slabby buttress immediately right of *Conan's Crack*. Pitches of 5.10c, 5.9, and 5.11a lead upwards, following bolts. Rappel the route. Pro: quickdraws. (FA: Rich Folsom; Dan Waters, Ron Miller complete 1993)

25. Conan's Crack (II, 5.8) The obvious big crack system on the far left side of Three O'Clock Rock. Climb up to four pitches up the dihedral, then rappel the route. Rarely climbed, but useful for reference purposes. Pro: to 6 inches. (FA: Don Brooks, Brent Hoffman 1973)

26. The Plan (II, 5.8) ★ From start of *Conan's Crack* proper (about 80 feet up), climb the obvious hand crack on the left, then find your way up the forested buttress. Rappel down *Conan's,* or from trees as soon as possible after the good quality climbing ends. Pro: to 2.5 inches.

COMB BUTTRESS

Comb Buttress, or The Comb, is the large, many-buttressed slab located up and left from Three O'Clock Rock. The comb's "teeth" stand out as clean, slabby granite buttresses divided by forested gullies. There are several routes, from one to seven pitches in length, ranging from 5.8 to 5.10, and much more potential. It is not often visited.

The first edition of this guide (1999) describes and illustrates a dozen or so routes on Comb Buttress. The route descriptions and topos may be out of date. The Darrington Rock Climbing website does not currently provide any information about Comb Buttress. If you're into adventure climbing, go for it.

GREEN GIANT BUTTRESS

Hidden at the head of Copper Creek Canyon is Green Giant Buttress, which would be one of Washington's most popular crags except for the difficult approach and the abundance of moss, dirt, and foliage on some of the routes. There are several good multi-pitch slab routes, ranging from 5.8 to 5.11c in difficulty. *Dreamer* gets most of the traffic, although there are half a dozen routes that are worthy of attention.

Despite popular opinion, the approach to Green Giant Buttress isn't really that bad. Continue on FR 2060 beyond the Squire Creek Pass trailhead. At 7.25 miles the road forks; stay right, following the main road. The road gets rough at about 7.75 miles and ends just short of 8 miles. Either hike or drive the final 0.25 mile to road's end. Continue up the canyon toward Green Giant Buttress,

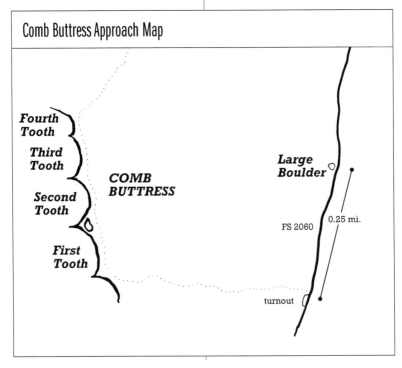

Comb Buttress Approach Map

Fourth Tooth

Third Tooth

COMB BUTTRESS

Second Tooth

First Tooth

Large Boulder

FS 2060

0.25 mi.

turnout

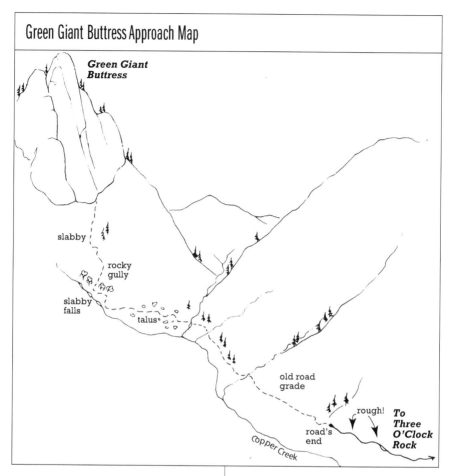

Green Giant Buttress Approach Map

Green Giant
Buttress

slabby

rocky
gully

slabby
falls

talus

old road
grade

rough!

**To
Three
O'Clock
Rock**

road's
end

Copper Creek

first following an old road now overgrown by alders. In about ten minutes the trail drops down through a hemlock grove and crosses a stream via a small foot log. The trail continues through hemlock forest another ten minutes or so before crossing a rocky streambed. Shortly beyond, the trail reaches Copper Creek. Cross the creek and continue up a talus slope on the other side until you reach the base of a slabby waterfall, where the trail skirts up the right stream bank then enters a narrow, rocky gully that leads through slide maple up to the base of Green Giant Buttress.

Descents from the top of Green Giant Buttress are best made down *Dreamer*, where anchors have been installed to facilitate rappels—lots of rappels! The alternative is an insidious mix of downclimbing and rappelling down the gully right (east) of *Botany 101* (the main gully/corner splitting Green Giant Buttress). It is unwise to climb Green Giant Buttress during questionable weather, as a descent from this wall is difficult already, and quite dangerous during a rainstorm. It would be foolish to attempt a descent from Green Giant Buttress after dark, although a few fools have managed it.

1. Dreamer (IV, 5.9) ★★★ A ten-pitch route up Green Giant Buttress, one of the finest long free climbs in Washington. Start at the base of *Botany 101,* climbing left up easy

Green Giant Buttress

Green Giant Buttress

slabs and a long crack ending at a big bush. From there, continue up the slabs, trending leftward. Good route-finding skills are a big plus on this route, since you can't always see the next bolt. Rappel the route. A direct start is 5.10a. Pro: to 3 inches. (FA: Duane Constantino, Chris Greyell 1979)

2. Safe Sex (5.8+) ★★★ A slightly easier, more direct, and better protected variation of *Dreamer,* climbing slabs and cracks in between *Dreamer* and the old *Botany 101* route (which followed the brushy corner system directly). Pro: to 2 inches; quickdraws. (FA: Matt Perkins and partners)

3. Urban Bypass (5.10b) ★★★ A bolted slab variation third pitch of *Dreamer.* On the second pitch of *Dreamer,* traverse left to anchors at a tree, then connect the bolts until you rejoin *Dreamer* higher up. Pro: Lots of quickdraws.

4. Giant's Tears (II, 5.11c or 5.10c A0) ★★ A direct start to *Dreamer,* climbing the broad slab left of *Botany 101.* The route starts about 100 yards left of the start of *Dreamer,* at first climbing easy ramps to a ledge below a bolt ladder. Either climb the bolt ladder (free at 5.11c, or A0) or the curving crack on the left (5.7), then continue up the slab to a ledge with bolt anchors. Continue past a small roof and up cracks and corners, eventually joining *Dreamer.* Pro: quickdraws; gear to 2 inches. (FA: Duane Constantino and party 1980)

5. Boomerang (III, 5.11a) ★★★ A two-pitch linkup of *Botany 101* and *The Fast Lane,* climbing the obvious boomerang-shaped section of rock several hundred feet up and on the right side of *Botany 101.* Thrash your way up the first three pitches of *Botany 101,*

then head up the obvious knobby, bolted slab. An alternative start is to climb *Dreamer* or *Safe Sex* to the point where they diverge on the third pitch, and traverse right across the slab (relatively easy but unprotected) into *Botany 101* and the base of the route. The route ends below the Great Roof. Rappel the route or continue up *The Fast Lane.* Pro: quickdraws; gear to 1 inch. (FA: Ron Miller, Dan Waters 1995)

6. Lost in Space (II, 5.10a) ★★ Another two-pitch linkup of *Botany 101* and *The Fast Lane.* Either mow your way up the first three pitches of *Botany 101* or traverse in from *Dreamer* or *Safe Sex* (as for *Boomerang*). The route follows an obvious flake/crack system just right of *Boomerang,* and ends below the Great Roof. Continue up *The Fast Lane* or rappel.

7. The Fast Lane (IV, 5.11c R) ★ A long free climb up the striking prow right of *Botany 101.* The route begins just right of the start of *Botany* at a blocky flake. Follow the bolts right up the slabby face to discontinuous cracks and slabs left of and on the prow. Three pitches of enjoyable climbing up to 5.10c lead to the Great Roof, where most parties choose to rappel (down *Boomerang* or *Lost in Space,* which you might as well climb while you're here). If you continue, pass the roof on the right side, from where face climbing leads slightly rightward then back to the rib (one aid move or 5.11b free). The crux pitch leads over a roof to thin, dirty cracks, from where two easy pitches and some Class 4 climbing reach the top. Runout and dirty in places. Pro: to 2 inches, including TCUs. (FFA: Bryan Burdo, Andy Cairns 1986)

EXFOLIATION DOME

Exfoliation Dome is the massive rock spur of Helena Peak that looms up on the left as you drive up FR 2060. The dome is an "isolated peak," according to Fred Beckey, and is the most arduous and serious climbing objective in Darrington, although it has routes that are more accessible than those at Green Giant Buttress. As is the case with Waterfall Column and Jupiter Tower in Leavenworth, Exfoliation Dome has some long, complex approaches and difficult descents, but also has some very approachable multipitch routes with reasonable descents. There is plenty of rock here, and potential for many new routes, both free and aid. Still, some of the routes on Exfoliation Dome have been climbed only once, and for some reason nobody really wonders why.

To approach the eastern wall (Witch Doctor Wall), drive up the left fork of FR 2060 about 0.5 mile to a spur road heading back the other way. There is a turnout on the right, big enough for two cars. The spur road is overgrown by alder and is easy to miss. At last check a cairn was in place, making the road easier to identify. Hike up the road for about ten minutes and continue straight ahead toward the stream. Where the road forks, continue straight to the stream. Alternatively, turn right up the road, which dead-ends shortly, then continue through the woods, trending leftward. Most parties follow the stream. If you do so, hike upstream for an hour or more, staying right at stream junctions, until you can scramble up to the base of Witch Doctor Wall. There is no trail, but as others have noted, one would be most welcome.

Approaches to the western slab (Blueberry Hill) are not as time consuming, and are more direct. Both approaches follow rocky stream beds and low-angled granite slabs leading up directly from FR 2060. The approach to the *North Buttress* follows

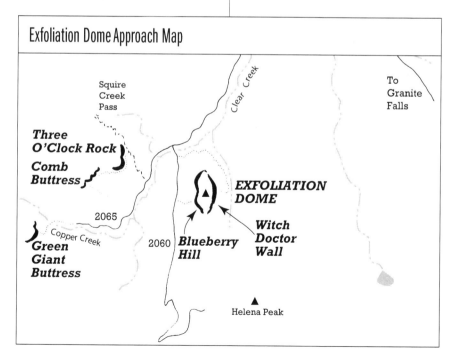

Exfoliation Dome Approach Map

a stream gully 1 mile up the road. The approach to the West Slab area goes up a rocky stream bed just past the 1.25-mile mark and climbs the Granite Sidewalk, a prominent low-angled slab reached in about 200 yards. None of these approaches are recommended when wet or icy, as the slabs can become quite slippery, and a slip in some places from the Granite Sidewalk could easily be fatal.

Descents from Exfoliation Dome range from merely unpleasant to downright dangerous. Numerous descent routes have been pioneered, although two are considered standard. Descents are most commonly made down the *West Slabs* rappel route, which is said to be unpleasant. Alternatively, the *23rd Psalm* rappel (down the route) is said to be better, although it is difficult to find from above. The *North Buttress* route and the woods north of *23rd Psalm* can be rappelled, although they are unpleasant and time consuming. In reality, none of the descent routes is particularly fast or enjoyable. Just as a trail to Witch Doctor Wall would be welcome, so would a reliable, fast, easy-to-find rappel route off the top of Exfoliation Dome. Bring a bolt kit, just in case your chosen rappel route doesn't work out.

If you get caught on top of Exfoliation Dome during bad weather, the fastest way off is via the Southeast Buttress, on the Witch Doctor Wall side, where three rappels lead to the trees. Of course, once down, a long walk awaits you. This descent route is best reserved for occasions when a fast way off the dome is needed, unless you enjoy bushwhacking.

If you get caught after dark atop Exfoliation Dome, it is best to stay put until daylight. Be prepared to wait out bad weather or darkness, as it would be foolish to attempt to descend the dome in either condition. Not that fools haven't succeeded, mind you.

It's just better to wait unless you absolutely can't.

Be aware that rock on Exfoliation Dome is active, meaning that large rockfalls have and will no doubt continue to occur. As the name implies, rock here is exfoliating, and big flakes peel off from time to time. Rock scars on Blueberry Hill and slabs left of Witch Doctor Wall provide ample testimony. When climbing in the vicinity of new rock scars, beware that surrounding rock is probably still quite loose.

Blueberry Hill

Blueberry Hill is the broad slabby face on the back side of Exfoliation Dome, as seen from Three O'Clock Rock. The vividly exfoliated rock is strafed with odd corners, roofs, and ledges. It would appear that many routes could be pioneered here, both free and aid, even after the many new routes climbed in the past decade. It also appears that large sections of rock could peel off with little provocation.

1. Ancient Melodies (5.11a) ★★ No topo. A seven-pitch route up the Proxima Wall just right of the Western Slabs. The route follows the prominent clean slabs to the top of the wall. Approach via the Granite Sidewalk, then scramble across a ledge and up a gully to the base of the route. The route is predominately bolted, with some gear supplementing protection. Rappel the route; two 60-meter ropes will work. A detailed topo is available on Mountain Project. Pro: quickdraws; gear to 3 inches. (FA: Danny Coltrane, Mark Hannah, Stephen Packard, J. R. Storms 2012)

2. Blueberry Route (aka West Buttress) (III, 5.9) ★★ This route climbs slabs and corners to the upper ledge (Blueberry Terrace),

traverses left, then finishes to the top via one of several possible variations. To approach, stroll up the Granite Sidewalk to the base of the buttress. A fairly easy pitch leads up to a stump, from where the real climbing begins. From the top, rappel the *West Slabs*. Pro: to 2 inches.

3. West Slabs (aka Westward Ho!) (II, 5.9) ★★ A four-pitch bolted slab route up the slabs just right of the *West Buttress*. Rappel the route. Pro: quickdraws.

4. Dark Rhythm (III, 5.10c) ★★ An eight-pitch line up the slabs left of *Blueberry Route*. Route-finding should not be a problem, as there are plenty of bolts to follow. Getting to the start of the route involves finding a 15-foot stump, then traversing brushy slabs leftward 100 feet. From the terrace, rappel the route or continue to the summit and down the *West Slabs* rappel line. Pro: lots of quickdraws; slings to reduce rope drag.

5. Rainman (III, 5.10c) ★★ Another long route up the slabs left of the *Blueberry Route*. To approach, traverse the base of the slabs about 300 feet left of the start of *Blueberry Route*. Each of the first five pitches is 5.10. Descend as for *Dark Rhythm*. Pro: quickdraws; gear to 2 inches.

6. Jacob's Ladder (III, 5.11c) ★★ An eight-pitch route climbing up through the roof system left of *Rainman*. Approach by traversing the base of the slabs about 800 feet left of the *Blueberry Route*. The first two pitches are moderately angled and relatively easy; the second pitch is 185 feet long. From here, the angle kicks up to provide pitches of 5.10b, 5.11c, 5.10b, 5.10b, and 5.9, then a final 5.8 pitch to reach the left end of Blueberry

Blueberry Hill

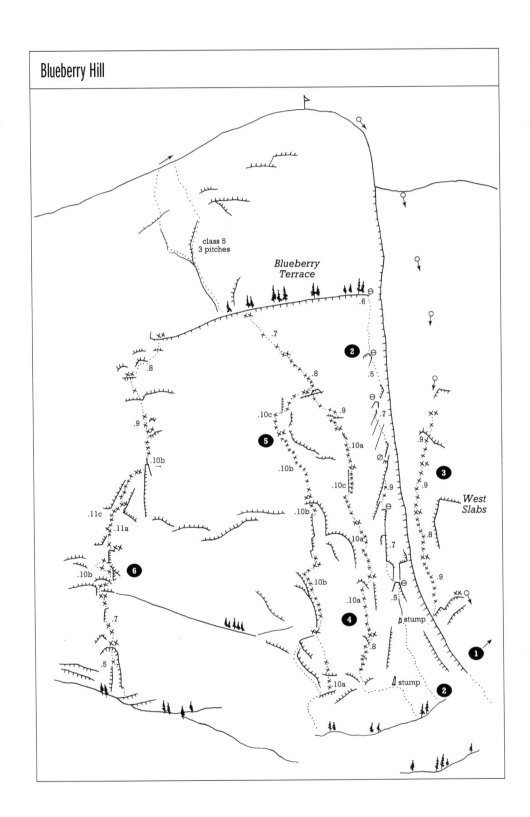

class 5
3 pitches

Blueberry Terrace

West Slabs

stump

stump

Terrace. Those not up to the 5.11 moves can aid past them, making the route 5.10c A0. Rappel the route, or finish via one of the *Blueberry Route* variations to the top and rappel the *West Slabs*. Pro: quickdraws; gear to 2 inches; long slings.

7. 23rd Psalm (IV, 5.9 A3) ★★ Slabby aid climbing at its finest. Begin up slabs and corners below the prominent arch, then nail your way over the arch. Four consecutive aid pitches (A3, A3, A1, A2), then free climbing to the top. Pro: cams, nuts and pins to 2.5 inches; bat hooks.

8. North Buttress (II, 5.10d) ★ The shortest technical route to the summit of Exfoliation Dome, but at the cost of a long approach and ridge traverse. Getting to the route takes longer than climbing it. You can rappel the route, but it isn't highly recommended. Pro: to 1.5 inches, including small wireds and a few pins.

Witch Doctor Wall

Witch Doctor Wall is the most impressive of Darrington's walls, and one of the most difficult to approach. So far there are only four routes reported on Witch Doctor Wall proper, but given the number of difficult free climbs on Index's Upper Town Wall, there appears to be much potential for long, hard free and aid routes here and on adjacent slabs.

Witch Doctor Wall is about as close to a big wall as Washington rock climbers get. As with other big wall climbs, be prepared for anything, including bad weather, bivouacking, and retreat. Bring a comprehensive rack, a bolt kit, rain gear, and extra provisions in case you get stuck in bad weather or darkness. Retreat could be difficult from some of the routes, particularly in bad weather. Large

rockfalls have occurred on this side of Exfoliation Dome in the not-so-distant past.

9. Thunder Road (IV, 5.6 A3) ★ A long aid route up the right side of Witch Doctor Wall. A detailed topo can be found in the old Brooks/Whitelaw guide (see Bibliography).

10. The Checkered Demon (V, 5.7 A3) An obvious aid line climbing the great right-leaning arch in the middle of the wall. Easy climbing reaches the base of the arch. Three aid pitches under the arch and some mixed climbing continue above. At the top, angle left to the top. Refer to the Brooks/Whitelaw guide for details (see Bibliography).

11. Sunday Cruise (III, 5.9) ★ A surprisingly moderate free climb up the center of Witch Doctor Wall. Climb to the base of the unmistakable arch of *Checkered Demon* (easy scrambling to 5.6), then traverse left to a corner/ramp and belay in some bushes. Continue up an easy pitch to a big ledge, then up another pitch, passing a short, difficult crack and easier arch. Two easier pitches lead to the top. If it were more accessible, had a better descent line, and received enough traffic to keep it clean, this route might become popular. Pro: to 3 inches, many small pieces. (FA: Dave Tower, Duane Constantino, Chris Greyell 1979)

12. The Witch Doctor (V, 5.7 A3) ★ An inobvious aid line up the left side of the wall. A detailed topo can be found in the old Beckey guide or the Brooks/Whitelaw guide (see Bibliography).

13. Snake Charmer (III, 5.11-) ★★ A six-pitch venture up the far left side of Witch Doctor Wall, one of the rare all-free routes up the wall that would be massively popular but for the approach. Approach until you are directly below the prominent buttress, the

last feature before the big gully on the left. The first two pitches follow a left-trending crack system to just left of a cluster of trees. Continue up a flake to a ledge, then traverse right (crux) to more flakes and cracks that lead upward. Some bolted sections but mostly gear. Rappel the route except the final rappel anchor is left of the route; a single 70-meter rope should suffice. Pro: double rack to 3 inches; quickdraws; slings. (FA: Dave Burdick, Ralph Bodenner, Austin Siadak, Fritz Cahall, Elliott Waldon, Zac West)

Of the lowland rock climbing areas in the Puget Sound region, Mount Erie is unique. Located less than a two-hour drive north from Seattle, Mount Erie offers abundant climbing opportunities, including several challenging sport routes. While most of the early routes are moderately rated, there are several recent additions up to 5.12 in difficulty. The climbing is uncharacteristic for western Washington, especially the modern sport routes, featuring steep, thin, bolt-protected face climbing up slabby to vertical blocky walls that are fully exposed to sunlight and "ocean" views. Mount Erie's dioritic rock is fairly solid despite its sometimes dubious appearance, but it is crumbly in places just the same. Although Mount Erie will never achieve the popularity of Index, Leavenworth, or the North Bend area sport crags, it offers a pleasant diversion, not only for climbing but also for just hanging out, with commanding views of Puget Sound and Whidbey and the San Juan Islands, Mount Baker and the North Cascades, and hiking trails leading off in all directions.

Type of climbing: Mount Erie's climbing varies from easy, old classics to hard, modern sport routes, on rock ranging from slabby to vertical, and from good to bad to simply awful. The area's bolted face routes are the best, as the cracks tend to be discontinuous and shallow, making protection somewhat dubious on some otherwise decent routes. Aside from the sport routes, Mount Erie has

some fun traditional climbing and a wealth of relatively poor routes up brushy, mossy, flaky buttresses, ramps, and gullies.

Brief history of area: Mount Erie's climbing potential was tapped early on by a group of local climbers, headed by Dallas Kloke, who wrote the area's first guide in 1971. Kloke, along with various other regulars, established dozens of routes during the late 1960s through the 1970s. Many of their aid routes were climbed free in the 1980s, and by the late '80s sport climbers began discovering Mount Erie's steep unclimbed faces. Two climbers in particular, Ken Beane and Tim Nelson, were responsible for many of the modern routes established at Mount Erie, although Kloke remained active in developing routes up until his death in 2010, and several others have been and continue to be active here.

Seasons and climate: Climbing is possible year-round at Mount Erie, as its westerly location, low elevation, and southern exposure make it warmer and drier than many other areas. The best climbing conditions are usually encountered from March through October. Midsummer afternoons can be insufferably hot. Due to a rain shadow effect from the Olympic Mountains, Mount Erie is sometimes dry even when it's raining elsewhere.

Precautions and regulations: As this is the only rock climbing area in Washington

Mike Massey on *Intimidator* (5.10a), Powerline Wall, Mount Erie MIKE MASSEY COLLECTION

with a paved road to the summit, it has the dubious honor of being the only area in the state where a helmet should be considered mandatory, particularly on the Summit Wall. Even on weekdays, it is unwise to climb without a helmet here. Broken glass along the trail leading along the base of the Summit Wall should give a clue as to what the tourists and high-school truants do with their trash. On weekends, some of the dozens of tourists and their children regularly toss fir cones, rocks, pop cans, even beer and wine bottles off the cliffs. Even the occasional tourist comes plummeting down! It is recommended that you post a lookout atop the cliff to see that nobody bombards you. Otherwise, wear a helmet, and watch out below!

Also, beware of large groups on training missions here. Several clubs and groups use Mount Erie for beginning rock courses and rescue practice. On such days, and on sunny weekends year-round, the mountain is pretty much tied up, although it may be possible to climb on some of the lower cliffs without hindrance—if you can find a parking spot, that is.

Permits for large groups and organizations are no longer required, but it is best to call ahead to schedule mass use of the mountain and to make sure no other group has the mountain tied up that day. For that matter, it's a good idea to call ahead so you can avoid the disappointment of driving 90 miles to find out there's no place to park within miles

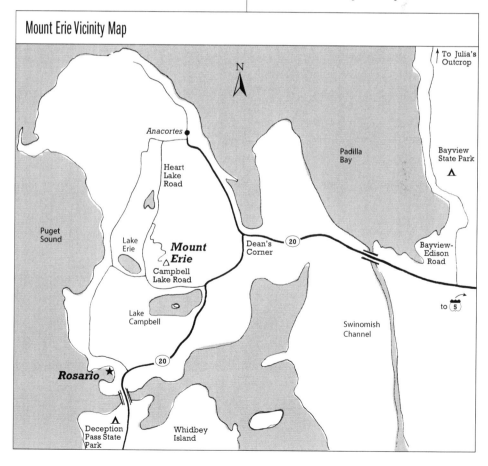

Mount Erie Vicinity Map

Mount Erie Approach Map

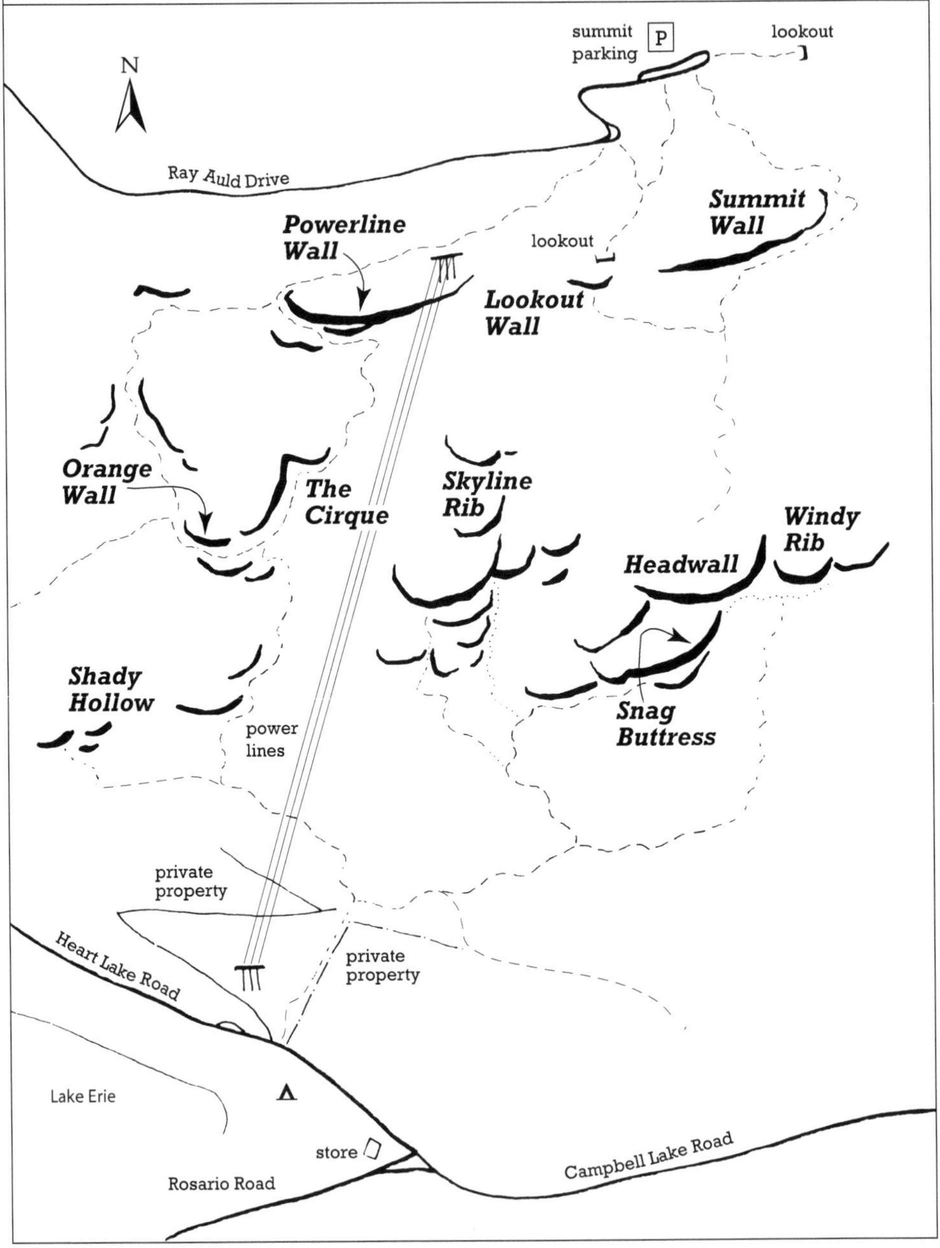

N

summit parking [P] lookout

lookout

Summit Wall

Powerline Wall

Lookout Wall

Ray Auld Drive

Orange Wall

The Cirque

Skyline Rib

Windy Rib

Headwall

Shady Hollow

Snag Buttress

power lines

private property

private property

Heart Lake Road

Lake Erie

store

Rosario Road

Campbell Lake Road

of the mountain. Call the City of Anacortes Parks and Recreation Department at (360) 293-1900 for information.

The park opens at 6:00 a.m. and closes at 10 p.m., so don't leave late or you'll be locked in. No alcoholic beverages, fires, firearms, or fireworks are allowed inside the park, and dogs must be on leashes at all times. As elsewhere, please pick up after yourself.

Certain cliffs are occasionally closed to climbing during raptor nesting season. Check current restrictions before you climb. Also, watch out for ticks.

Gear and other considerations: A standard Mount Erie rack should consist of several wired nuts, some midsize chocks, and cams, plus slings to reduce rope drag, especially on longer routes. For sport routes, a rack of quickdraws will almost always suffice, although a few wired nuts and TCUs should be carried to supplement bolt protection.

Camping and accommodations: Overnight camping in the park is not allowed. There are several nearby campgrounds, which tend to be crowded on weekends. Most do not take reservations, so you'll have to take your chances. Deception Pass State Park is just a few miles south of Mount Erie on WA 20; it has 251 campsites; call (360) 675-2417 for information. Bayview State Park is located several miles north of WA 20; it has 108 campsites; call (360) 757-0227 for information. The closest campground is Lake Erie Trailer Park, located at the intersection of Campbell Lake Road and Heart Lake Road, about 0.25 mile south of the lower trail parking area, behind Lake Erie Grocery; it has twenty campsites; call (360) 293-1900 for information.

There are currently no restrooms in the park; the one toilet they had was vandalized and may be out of service at any time due to recurring vandalism. The nearest restrooms are at Lake Erie Grocery; they are private, but open for customers (so buy something, will ya?). The city of Anacortes is only ten minutes north of the park and has all accommodations, including ATMs, restaurants, grocery stores, and motels.

Emergency services: In case of emergency, dial 911.

Other guidebooks: Dallas Kloke's guide, *Rockin' on the Rock!: A Guide to Mount Erie Rock Climbing*, updated in 2013 by Jim Thompson and Aaron Bryant. There are a lot more routes here than are included in this guide, so if you enjoy climbing at Mount Erie it is worth picking up the current guide.

Finding the crags: To reach Mount Erie from I-5, drive west from Mount Vernon on WA 536 toward Anacortes, or via WA 20 from Burlington. Both routes converge into WA 20 after about 5 miles. At Dean's Corner, take a left (staying on WA 20 toward Deception Pass), then a right onto Campbell Lake Road, where Mount Erie's cliffs are finally seen rising above on the right. Take the next right (Lake Erie Grocery) and go about 1 mile north to the park entrance.

Alternatively, from Anacortes, head west at the first traffic signal as you enter town from Mount Vernon, then after several blocks, where the road jogs uphill and left, turn left toward Heart Lake on 11th Avenue to reach the park entrance in about 3 miles. Signs point the way from both directions, so finding your way isn't a problem.

From the entrance gate, a steep, winding road (Ray Auld Drive) reaches the summit. A trail also reaches the cliffs from below, although you need to look hard to find it (it starts from the power lines about 0.25 mile north of Lake Erie Grocery).

Mount Erie Overview

Trails lead to all of the major cliffs, both from above and below. However, many obvious trails lead only to the brink of a cliff or gully, where downclimbing seems an unlikely prospect. Many cliffs may be reached by traversing grassy ledges and descending gullies, but be careful to stay on the more well-established paths.

The lower trail crosses private property, and there is limited parking, so be respectful of property owners' rights and avoid creating a nuisance. No Trespassing signs are posted, so you could be subject to arrest and prosecution by using the lower trail approach. The lower trail is discussed in more detail where relevant.

To check on current access restrictions, contact the City of Anacortes or refer to Mountain Project, which should have the most up-to-date information.

UPPER CLIFFS

The upper cliffs of Mount Erie include the Summit Wall, Genesis Wall, Powerline Wall, and The Cirque. All may be reached via trails beginning at or near the summit parking area. Most approaches involve scrambling down ledges. If you reach a dead end, try a different way.

Summit Wall

The uppermost of Mount Erie's cliffs is the Summit Wall, which is sometimes referred to as the "Practice Cliff" or "Mounties' Wall." It is a steep, blocky face with several easy to moderate leads. From the summit parking area, head east through the trees to reach the top of this cliff. The easiest descent route is via ledges on the right side as you face the cliff (on the left as you approach the rim from the summit parking area).

Climbers here should beware of "falling" objects, which are regularly hurled off the top of the cliff by unthinking tourists and their children, who sometimes fall off themselves. Helmets are highly recommended. On weekends, posting a guard atop the cliff might be a good idea.

1. Sidewalk (5.3) ★ The ramp system leading up and left from the start of *The Apex*. Pro: to 2 inches.

2. The Apex (5.0) The obvious wide chimney splitting the cliff. Pro: to 3 inches.

3. The Open Book (5.6) ★★ A prominent dihedral crack just left of *The Nose* overhang. Pro: to 2 inches.

4. The Nose (5.8 R) Not recommended. Climb up and around *The Nose* overhang on its right side. Loose rock, poor protection. Pro: to 2 inches.

Summit Wall

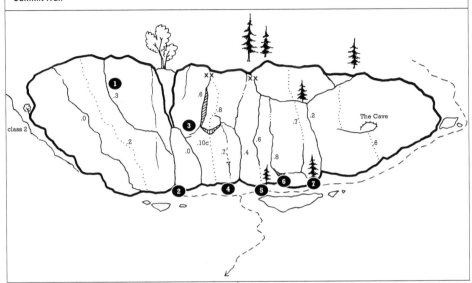

class 2

The Cave

Nosedive ("Nose Direct") variation (5.10c TR) ★ Climb up to and directly over the roof.

5. Jack of Diamonds (5.6) ★ A crack system starting with face moves past a short overhang. Pro: to 2 inches.

6. Queen of Diamonds (5.8 R) ★ A shallow crack system just right of *Jack of Diamonds,* with difficult overhanging face moves at the start and a blocky finish. Usually toproped. Pro: to 1 inch; RPs. (FA: Dallas Kloke, Scott Masonholder 1970)

7. King of Diamonds (5.7) About 20 feet right of *Queen of Diamonds,* climb a short overhang to a shallow seam and thin face. Pro: to 2 inches.

Lookout Wall

Lookout Wall is the small cliff located about 50 meters left of Summit Wall. It is easily reached from Summit Wall via a low trail traversing grassy benches and some talus. It

has two obvious crack lines (5.4 on the right, 5.7 R on the left), and a sport route climbing the steep upper face of the wall (5.11d) after suffering through the poorly protected 5.7 moves below.

Powerline Wall

Powerline Wall is the leftmost of the upper cliffs on Mount Erie. It has several routes, accessible from a trail leading down from the road turnout on the right (just where Ray Auld Drive makes its final curve left before reaching the summit). Most of the routes are easy to moderate (up to 5.8) cracks and slabby faces, but there are several popular sport routes now.

Once you arrive at the wall, scramble down ledges on the left side of the rock (facing the cliff, on the right as you hike down from the parking area). Alternatively, you can traverse grassy ledges left from the Summit Wall. The routes are listed from left to right as you descend along the base of the cliff. Rappel from anchors or scramble over the top.

Powerline Wall

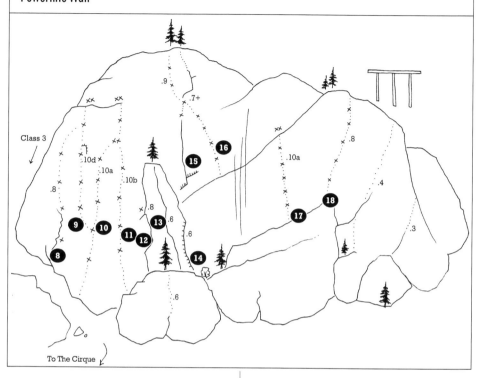

Class 3

To The Cirque

8. False Impressions (5.8) ★ The bolted line on the left, starting from a prominent flake. Retrobolted. Pro: quickdraws.

9. Beam Reach (aka Intimidator) (5.10d) ★ The first route right of the *False Impressions* flake. Start via *Intimidator,* traversing left from the second bolt. A bit contrived, but entertaining. Pro: quickdraws.

10. Intimidator (5.10a) ★★ The middle bolt line, and the best of the Powerline Wall sport routes. Pro: quickdraws.

11. Sushi Eatin' Mermaids (aka Terminator) (5.10b) ★★ The rightmost sport route on Powerline Wall, beginning at the toe of the blocky ledges leading up to Treeshadow Ledge. Pro: quickdraws.

12. Treeshadow (5.8) ★ Scramble up blocky ledges right of the sport routes, then climb up the thin, right-angling dogleg crack starting just left of the prominent fir tree. The route ends at a fir tree on a ledge about 60 feet higher. Continue up easier slabs to the top. A direct variation (5.10b) climbs directly up to a bolt before traversing right to rejoin the normal route. Pro: to 2 inches.

13. Psycho (5.6) ★ This is the left-leaning, blocky crack system beginning just right of the fir tree on Treeshadow Ledge. From the upper fir tree ledge, continue up easier slabs to the top of the cliff. Pro: to 2 inches.

14. Leaning Crack (5.6) Near the middle of Treeshadow Ledge is this blocky, left-leaning crack, choked with salal, which leads to the upper fir tree of *Psycho*. Pro: to 2 inches.

15. Tindall's Terror (5.7+) ★★ Start as for *Leaning Crack,* but traverse right about 30 feet up onto a big ledge, then climb the obvious crack up to a slab with two old bolts. Pro: to 2 inches.

16. Scarface (5.9) ★ A bolted route just right of *Tindall's Terror,* crossing that route near the top. Pro: quickdraws.

17. Dirtyface Direct (aka No Holds Barred) (5.9+) ★ The first bolted route right of the dirty water streak on the right side of Powerline Wall, approached via the grassy ramp right of *Tindall's Terror.* Pro: quickdraws.

18. Finishing Touch (5.8) ★ A bolted slab on the right edge of Powerline Wall. Pro: quickdraws.

The Cirque

Directly below the Powerline Wall is The Cirque, a steep, blocky cliff that has several old, obscure routes and some new sport climbs of the overhanging, pumping variety. Although technically part of the lower cliffs, The Cirque is conveniently reached from above via a trail leading downward from the base of Powerline Wall, scrambling down a short chimney then staying right (facing down) until you come to an overhanging

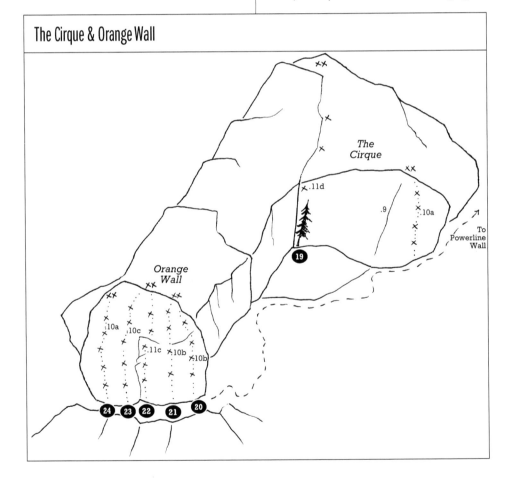

The Cirque & Orange Wall

wall. Around the corner is The Cirque, an amphitheater of blocky, overhanging rock. Continue downward and to the right on exposed grassy ledges to reach the Orange Wall.

19. Tree Route (5.11d) ★ A popular route climbing the steep corner system in the center of The Cirque amphitheater. Scramble up the chossy slab to the apex of the amphitheater, then climb a tree to gain the steep headwall. Continue to anchors on the ledge above. Pro: quickdraws; sling for tree; gear?

Orange Wall

The Orange Wall is a short, orange and black streaked buttress at the toe of The Cirque formation, with several sport routes. To get there, descend from The Cirque, following an indistinct trail across grassy ledges. An easier trail leads back up via a gully on the left side of Orange Wall. If coming from below, Class 3 scrambling and bushwhacking up the gully on the right or an eroded trail skirting cliffs on the left side will get you there. Descend from anchors atop the routes.

20. Clockwork Orange (5.10b) ★ The rightmost route on Orange Wall. Bouldery at start, but eases up. Pro: quickdraws.

21. Green Tangerine (5.10b) ★ The second sport route from the right, following bolts up and right of a black water streak. Pro: quickdraws.

22. Karnage (5.11c) ★★ The middle sport route, climbing the steep wall just left of the water streak and past a bulge. Pro: quickdraws.

23. Sunkist (5.10c) ★★★ The best of Orange Wall's routes, climbing a streak of orange rock. Pro: quickdraws.

24. Gator (5.10a) ★★ The leftmost route on the Orange Wall (unless something else has been squeezed in). Bouldery at the start. Pro: quickdraws.

Sunset Slabs

On the lower west shoulder of Mount Erie are Sunset Slabs, two small slabs that offer a few short, easy routes, making them a suitable area for practice, but not much else. The slabs are best approached from Powerline Wall, descending westward along a fairly well-defined trail. There are several routes in this area, in the 5.4 to 5.10 range, but few that are very popular.

Sunshine Slabs

This small cliff band is located on the lower left side of Mount Erie, just left of the trail ascending from below. It has several unpopular routes in the 5.2 to 5.6 range. Before trying the approach, view Mount Erie from the Lake Erie Grocery so you know what you're aiming for.

LOWER CLIFFS

The lower cliffs of Mount Erie dwarf the upper cliffs for pure bulk, although the upper cliffs have a greater concentration of quality routes. The lower cliffs look impressive, but upon close inspection are revealed to be mostly small buttresses and gullies with few distinct route opportunities. Snag Buttress and The Headwall are the exceptions, offering a dozen or so routes on steep, solid rock.

The lower cliffs are most easily reached via the lower trail, although they can also be reached from above by traversing across from The Cirque, or via two rappels down The Headwall/Snag Buttress. The lower trail begins at the power lines, about 0.25 mile north of the Lake Erie Grocery on Heart Lake Road. There is room for about four cars to pull off alongside the road. Don't overcrowd this parking area; if you are parked on the road, you could be ticketed, towed, or hit. If the parking area is full, find another place to pull off the road and hoof it to the trailhead. Hike the 248 trail up into the woods for about 10 minutes to a junction with the 247 trail. Go right on 247 briefly then up an unmarked side trail to reach Snag Buttress and the Headwall or left to reach a brushy trail that leads to Powerline Wall. Or stay left to reach the Shady Hollow area.

There have been access issues with the lower trail, which crosses private property. As of this revision, lower trail access issues have been resolved, however you should be alert to updates and respect any closures reinstated to preserve good relations with the landowners. Hopefully climbers and hikers will continue to enjoy unrestricted access via the lower trail. If the lower trail is closed, use one of the upper approach options.

Skyline Rib

Skyline Rib is the nondescript wall left of Snag Buttress, which is more of a slabby, heavily vegetated buttress than a wall or rib. It has several routes, but few that are more than glorified scrambles up brushy gullies. To get there, head left from the first grassy slope below Snag Buttress and follow a trail through a madrona grove. Eventually the trail ends at a chimney, where Class 4 climbing regains the trail, which eventually reaches a broad ledge directly below Black Lichen Slab, an obvious dark streak about halfway up the cliff.

25. Convulsions (5.8) ★ Scramble up to the ledge and climb the slabby crack just left of the black streak, then up grassy ledges to the big slab above. Climb the slab (old 0.25-inch bolts) and continue up grassy ledges to the top of the wall. A variation finish up the right side of the slab is 5.7. Pro: quickdraws, plus gear to 1.5 inches. (See the Mount Erie overview photo at the start of this chapter.)

Snag Buttress

One of the most easily identifiable of Mount Erie's cliffs is Snag Buttress, distinguished from surrounding rock by the gnarly snag perched on a ledge midway up the lower cliffs, and the impressive headwall above. Snag Buttress and environs have several of Mount Erie's best hard sport climbs, and a few moderate traditional routes.

To get there, hike the lower trail to the fence's end, then take the right-hand fork, staying left at junctions, and finally climb through brushy woods to reach grassy, terraced slopes. The trail angles right and ultimately reaches Snag Buttress at the base of

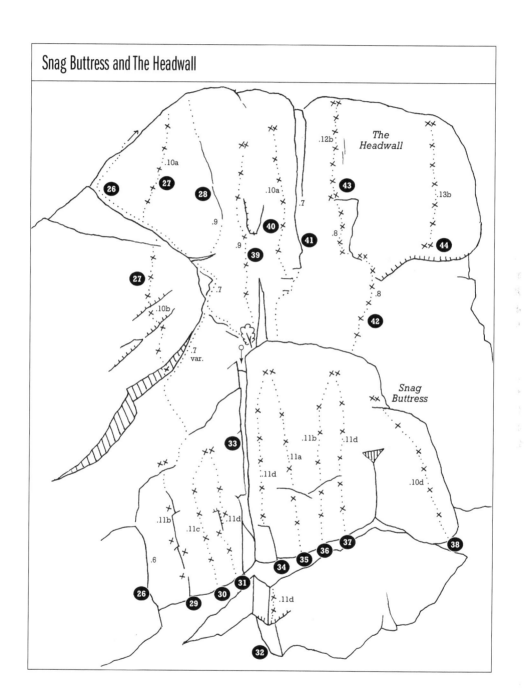

Snag Buttress and The Headwall

Sean Courage starts up *Zig Zag* (5.6), Mount Erie.

a prominent right-facing dihedral (the start of *Zig Zag*). The routes are listed from left to right as you approach on the trail. Most of the routes begin from a narrowing ledge. The ledge is exposed in places, so stick clips are recommended unless your belayer can anchor in (which is recommended anyway). Traversing the entire ledge involves some exposed Class 3 climbing, which can be very awkward when carrying a pack or rope, so be careful or hike around via a lower trail. Rappel from anchors atop each route, or continue to the top and hike down.

26. Zig Zag (II, 5.7) ★ An old favorite climbing the left side of Snag Buttress. Start via the obvious right-facing corner crack, then climb a short slab to anchors. Continue traversing up and right (runout but easy) to a gully, then up to the Snag ledge. Climb left and up a flake to reach a left-leading ramp. Easier climbing leads to the top. Pro: to 2.5 inches.

27. On Eagle's Wings (5.10b) ★★ From the anchors atop *Harrison's*, climb straight up the slab to the roofs, then connect the bolts through the roofs and headwall to join *Zig Zag* at the ramp. A final 5.10a pitch follows bolts to the top. Pro: Same as for *Zig Zag*, plus quickdraws and slings.

28. Diving Board (aka Springboard) (5.9 R) ★★ Once you gain the upper ramp of *Zig Zag,* teeter out on the obvious snag and climb the steep slab above directly to the top of the wall. Some sporting runouts. Pro: to 3 inches.

29. Harrison's Diretissima (aka Frogs in Space) (5.11b) ★★ The obvious left-angling seam immediately right of the opening dihedral of *Zig Zag*. Originally led free without the bolts. Pro: quickdraws; wired nuts; cams.

30. Ground Zero (5.11c) ★★ The first bolted face route right of the seam. Pro: quickdraws; TCUs to 1 inch.

31. Pinhead (5.11d) ★★ The bolted line through the bulging face about 20 feet right of the seam, beginning just left of a small fir tree. Pro: quickdraws; TCUs to 1 inch.

32. Down Under (5.11d) ★ A short problem climbing the overhanging wall below the ledge, starting directly beneath and finishing at the fir tree. Pro: quickdraws, plus a sling for the belay.

33. Snag Buttress Direct (5.10d) The blocky crack system splitting Snag Buttress. Pro: to 2.5 inches.

34. Cat Fud (5.11d) ★★ A steep, difficult face pitch beginning just right of the blocky crack system, immediately left of a shrubby cedar tree. Surmount a large, Oregon grape-choked flake and continue up the bulging face, connecting the bolts to anchors. Pro: quickdraws.

35. Crimp the Bucket (5.11a) ★★ Just right of the shrubby cedar, pass two bolts to gain a rounded ledge, then continue up the bulging headwall above. Pro: quickdraws.

36. Visions of Doom (5.11b) ★★ About 10 feet right of the cedar, pass two bolts right of a right-facing flake to gain the sloping ledge, then continue up the difficult headwall to anchors. Pro: quickdraws.

37. Hydrophobia (5.11d) ★★ At the right margin of the ledge is a large, multilimbed cedar tree. This route begins just left of the tree, connecting the bolts up the bulging wall. Pro: quickdraws.

38. Razorblade Suitcase (5.10d) A thin face route on the far right side of Snag Buttress. To get there, traverse across the ledge

(exposed Class 3, be careful!). Friable rock. Pro: quickdraws and a midsize TCU.

The Headwall (Wall of Voodoo)

Above Snag Buttress proper is a steep orange headwall, known variously as The Headwall, Middle Wall, and Wall of Voodoo, which has a couple of hard, airy sport climbs and some more moderate fare. To get there, either climb up from below via one of the Snag Buttress routes, or rappel in over the top, assuming you can find the right trail to get you there without walking off a cliff. For those arriving from below, *Zig Zag*'s final pitch offers an easy escape if you end up bailing from one of the other routes. For those arriving from above, look for anchors and gear placements hidden near the rim.

39. Redemption (5.9) ★ Follow bolts leading directly up from the snag to anchors. Pro: quickdraws.

40. Freedom Fighter (5.10a) ★★ The sport route immediately left of *Ray Auld Memorial*. Pro: quickdraws.

41. Ray Auld Memorial Route (5.7) The shallow corner/chimney system splitting The Headwall. Pro: quickdraws; gear to 3 inches.

42. Touching the Sky (5.8) ★★ A bolted route starting from the far right edge of the Snag ledge, leading to the base of *Cat's Away*. Two pitches, or one long pitch with rope drag. Pro: quickdraws; slings.

43. When the Cat's Away, the Mice Will Play (5.12b) ★★★ A sport route leading up the impressive headwall. Thin, technical climbing with awesome exposure make this the best sport route at Mount Erie. Originally a bolt-free project, but . . . Approach via *Ray Auld* or *Touching the Sky*, or rappel

in to anchors. Pro: quickdraws. (FA: Ken Beane 1989)

44. Project (5.13b) ★★★ Probably completed by now. Looks awesome!

Shady Hollow Area

A hidden wall way down and left of the lower cliffs, which has several short sport routes. There are several other short routes and projects (5.6 to 5.12) on the small walls and slabs in this area, but the best routes are on Shady Hollow Wall proper. To get there, follow the Sunset Trail down from the top or find a trail leading in from the road grade and up to the cliffs. The trail forks at a log; head left to reach Shady Hollow Wall, passing a very short 5.11 route with two bolts. The right fork leads to a cluster of cliffs with several very short, bolted routes.

45. Bone Traverse (5.10b) ★ Start from the first bolt of *Eager Beaver*, then traverse right and climb past three more bolts to anchors. Pro: quickdraws.

46. Eager Beaver (5.9) ★ The third sport route from the left, climbing directly up the wall to anchors shared with *F.U.M.R.* Pro: quickdraws.

47. First United Methodist Route (aka F.U.M.R.) (5.10b) ★ Another four-bolt extravaganza. Pro: quickdraws.

48. Spyders (5.10b) ★ The leftmost of Shady Hollow Wall's sport routes, with—you guessed it!—four bolts. Pro: quickdraws.

49. Allen Henshaw Pre-Memorial Route (5.6) ★ A corner crack on the left side of the formation across the Death Gully from Shady Hollow Wall. To get there, take the right-fork trail from the log and scramble up to the base of the wall, using a fixed line.

Shady Hollow Approach Map

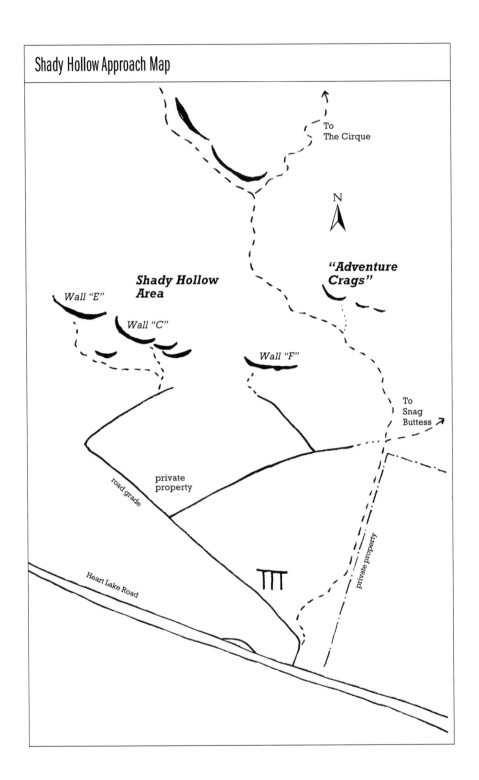

To
The Cirque

N

"Adventure Crags"

Shady Hollow Area

Wall "E"

Wall "C"

Wall "F"

To
Snag
Buttess

road grade

private property

private property

Heart Lake Road

Shady Hollow Area

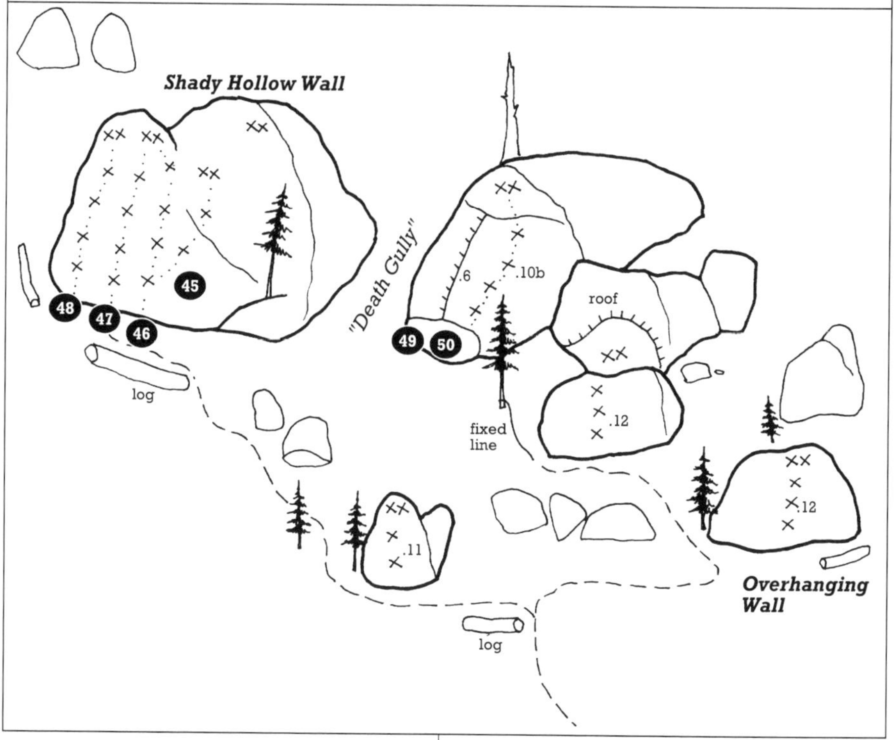

Shady Hollow Wall

"Death Gully"

.6   .10b

roof

48 47 46   45

49 50

log

fixed line

.12

.12

.11

Overhanging Wall

log

Rappel from anchors, not the dead tree. Pro: to 2 inches.

50. Finger Lickin' Good (5.10b) ** Follow a line of five bolts up the right side of the steep slab. Descend from anchors, not the dead tree.

Wall "F"

The next two routes are located on the farthest right of the Shady Hollow walls

Wall "F"

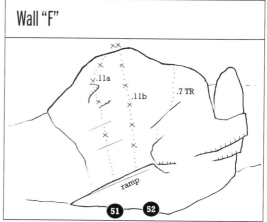

.11a

.11b   .7 TR

ramp

51   52

("Wall F" in the Kloke guidebook), which is approached via the next spur up the road grade. From the road grade's end, crash through the bushes to the left side of the wall, then up a ramp to the start of the routes.

51. The Full Monty (5.11a) ★ The leftmost of the two sport routes ascending from the ramp through roofs on the left side of the crag. Runout above the last roof, unless retrobolted. Angle right at the top to the anchors unless new anchors are in place.

52. Flying Circus (5.11b) ★★ The next sport route right from *Full Monty,* climbing the steep slab to the anchors. Thin, edgy friction.

ROSARIO

Near Rosario Beach, only a few miles southwest of Mount Erie, is a small sport crag featuring half a dozen routes in the 5.10 to 5.13 range. It is a small, shady crag dubbed the "Refrigerator Wall" by devotees because it stays cool even on hot days, and is quite cold and clammy during cooler weather. The crag was initially discovered by Tim Nelson and Stuart Ford, but was developed by Leif Johnson and Andrew Sell, with Johnson, Sell, Ford, Michael Orr, and Jitka Senkyrikova bagging first ascents during a relatively short time period.

The crag appears to lie within or on the boundary of Deception Pass State Park, and fear of violating park rules briefly delayed its development. The only stated objection to climbing here is to leaving gear on the wall. Accordingly, please remove all quickdraws, slings, and other gear from the wall before you leave, and make an effort to keep the area litter-free and quiet so that other climbers can enjoy access to this unique venue. Granted, other visitors are responsible for most of the litter here, but climbers can make a good impression by cleaning up after themselves and others.

To get there, follow Rosario Road west from the Mount Erie Grocery. In just over a mile the road forks; stay left, following Rosario Road southward another 2 miles. Where the road curves sharply to the left, Rosario Beach Road heads downhill on the right. Follow it, taking the right fork at the picnic area, to reach the park entrance. The wall is on the left, just outside the park entrance gate. The routes are listed from left to right. Descend from anchors atop each route.

The Refrigerator Wall

1. Green Giant (5.13a) ★★ A challenging sport route on the left. Pro: quickdraws.

Rosario Vicinity Map

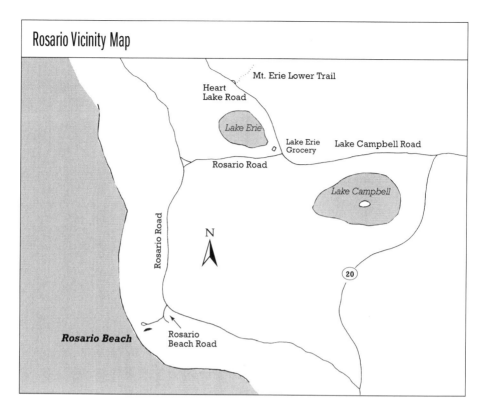

The Refrigerator Wall

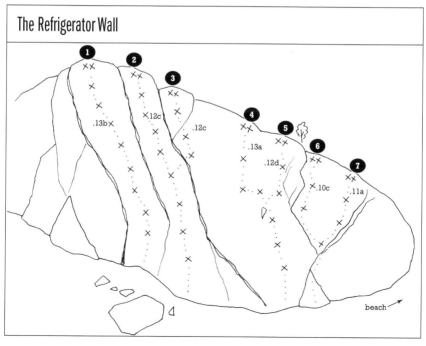

2. Power Anorexic (5.12c) ★★ The second route from the left, climbing a left-angling, severely overhanging, grooved face between two crack systems, finishing at anchors on the left.

3. Priapism (5.12c) ★★ A slightly harder finish variation of *Power Anorexic,* climbing to that route's fourth or fifth bolt before traversing right and up a headwall to another set of anchors.

4. Total Eclipse (5.13a) ★★ The middle route, starting up a greenish wall. At midheight, go left and up the headwall to chain anchors. Being tall helps at the crux.

5. Sissy Boy (5.12d) ★★ A finish variation of *Total Eclipse,* going right at midheight and up to anchors just left of a small shrub.

6. S-Crack (5.10c) ★ A zigzagging route starting up a blocky flake, then angling left and up the obvious flaring crack/flake. A bit runout unless you place gear in the crack.

7. The Girlfriend Route (5.11a) ★ The rightmost route on the wall, starting as for *S-Crack,* then angling right up a big flake and finishing up the short headwall above. Used to be 5.9, but a hold broke.

BELLINGHAM AREA

Bellingham is the northernmost of western Washington's major cities, and for many years has been thought of by climbers merely as the town you pass through on your way to Squamish or Mount Baker. However, during the past decade, a small cadre of local activists developed several dozen sport routes on various cliffs and crags in the Bellingham area. Because Bellingham is about ninety minutes north of Seattle on Interstate 5, and Mount Baker Rocks are over two hours away, these areas will probably not lure many Seattle-area sport climbers away from North Bend anytime soon. But one of these areas, Samish Wall (aka the Bat Caves), is definitely worth a visit.

Type of climbing: Bellingham rock consists of two distinct areas, Mount Baker Rocks and Samish Wall. Mount Baker Rocks are located along Mount Baker Highway (WA 542), east of Bellingham, and consist primarily of short sport climbs with short approaches on the standard-issue metavolcanic rock found elsewhere in the state (such as North Bend and Mazama). There are about three dozen reported routes here, up to 5.12+, on rock ranging from steep to overhanging, including routes that reportedly stay dry all year.

Samish Wall, on the other hand, is an exposed metasedimentary dome located high on Chuckanut Mountain, which has some longer traditional routes as well as the ubiquitous sport routes. A long approach hike and tales of friable rock have kept many climbers away, but it is an interesting area with some worthy routes.

Bellingham also has a couple of decent bouldering areas: Larrabee State Park, located on the Chuckanut highway just southwest of town; and Sehome Hill, located on the Western Washington University campus.

Brief history of area: Climbers first visited the area in the 1960s and early 1970s, climbing the obvious crack lines at Samish Wall, and rumors abounded about the area's potential, although few actually visited. Most of the area's potential remained untapped until the mid-1990s, when rappel bolting allowed some routes to be developed on slabs and faces. Those same sport climbers developed a few dozen sport routes in the Mount Baker Rocks during the same time period. Local activist Jason Henrie is responsible for much of the sport route development at the Bat Caves and Mount Baker Rocks, along with Justin Sjong, Kris Taylor, Greg Heffron, Matt Diamond, Rob Knowles, and others.

Seasons and climate: Mount Baker Highway leads to one of the state's best ski areas and is on the shady side of Mount Baker, making it a poor prospect as a spring destination. Come in the summer and fall for the best climbing conditions. Due to its elevation and proximity to the Strait of Juan de Fuca, Samish Wall can be a wet, windy place to climb. The best season is late summer and

117

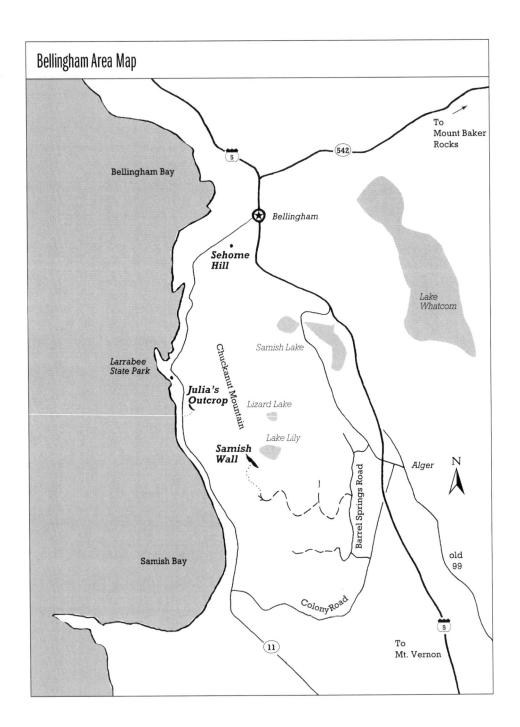

Bellingham Area Map

Bellingham Bay

To
Mount Baker
Rocks

5

542

Bellingham

Sehome
Hill

Larrabee
State Park

Julia's
Outcrop

Chuckanut Mountain

Samish Lake

Lizard Lake

Lake Lily

Lake Whatcom

Samish
Wall

Barrel Springs Road

Alger

N

old
99

Samish Bay

Colony Road

11

5

To
Mt. Vernon

fall, after the trails dry out and the hikers have moved to higher ground.

Precautions and regulations: The metasedimentary rock of Samish Wall is reportedly harder than the nearby Chuckanut sandstone but just as friable, meaning you should wear a helmet here, especially while belaying, in case someone pulls off a hold. Although caving is popular here, climbers lacking caving experience should stay out of the caves. The area is fairly remote, involving a 2.5-mile approach hike. There are usually a lot of hikers and mountain bikers on the trails here; watch out for mountain bikers racing down the trail. Hikers occasionally toss stuff off the top of the cliff, also warranting the wearing of a helmet. Because the rock is friable, check bolts before relying on them completely, and place gear with care to avoid having it pull or blow out.

Like all metavolcanic sport climbing areas, beware of loose and falling rock at Mount Baker Rocks. Refer to the *Bellingham Rock!* guide for additional precautions and regulations.

Gear and other considerations: For sport routes, a rack of a dozen quickdraws should suffice for nearly any route in the area. For traditional routes at Samish Wall, a rack up to 3 to 4 inches will be sufficient except for the *Samish Wall Crack* route, which will take the biggest gear you have and then some.

Helmets should be considered mandatory due to friable rock and falling objects.

Camping and accommodations: There are campgrounds in the area including at Birch Bay State Park on the Chuckanut highway. Bivouacking near the Samish Wall is possible, but most climbers make a day trip of it.

Emergency services: In case of emergency, dial 911. The nearest medical services are in Bellingham.

Other guidebooks: Henrie, Jason. *A Rock Climber's Guide to Bellingham Rock!* The second edition of this guide also included maps and topos for the Samish Wall and Julia's Outcrop. Mountain Project has information for about a dozen routes and boulder problems in the area.

Finding the crags: To reach Samish Wall, follow I-5 to the Alger exit (exit 240) and head west about 0.4 mile to Barrel Springs Road. Turn left and drive about 1 mile to a gravel road (Road B-1000) with a Blanchard Hill Trail sign. Turn right and follow the gravel road for 1.6 miles to the lower trailhead, then turn left on another gravel road for about 1.6 miles to the upper trailhead. Continue past the Blanchard Hill/Lily Lake trailhead another 0.6 mile and take the first spur road on the right. A trail begins here that leads about 2.5 miles to Samish Wall.

SAMISH WALL (BAT CAVES)

Samish Wall is a cluster of metasedimentary cliffs located high on Chuckanut Mountain. The area is popularly known as the Bat Caves, due to a rare species of bat that lives in talus caves at the base of the cliff. A popular destination for hikers (who call it Oyster Dome), it has only recently become better known as a climbing area. So far, the area has not become too popular, usually allowing a greater sense of isolation than your usual sport crag, except for the hikers who flock to the summit for the views.

There are currently about three dozen routes here, ranging from 5.4 to 5.12d in difficulty; only about half of the routes are described here. For information on the routes, consult the *Bellingham Rock!* guide or the second edition of *Rock Climbing Washington*.

JULIA'S OUTCROP (GOVERNOR LISTER CLIFF)

Julia's Outcrop is a small cliff of Chuckanut sandstone located just off of Chuckanut Drive, south of Larrabee State Park. There are eleven reported routes in the 5.7 to 5.11 range.

Approach via Chuckanut Drive (WA 11). If coming from the north, go about 1.5 miles past Larrabee State Park to a turnout just past mile marker 12. If coming from the south, go almost 1 mile past Oyster Creek Inn. Park in the wide turnout on the west side of the highway. A trail begins across the highway, leading past the Governor Lister memorial boulder and up a creek bed past and under logs. A fixed rope is in situ to help you past the steepest trail section.

For route information, refer to the second edition of *Rock Climbing Washington*.

NORTH BEND

North Bend, a rural community half an hour east of Seattle, is perhaps best known as the setting for the television series *Twin Peaks*. Nestled beneath the shoulders of Mount Si, this once small bedroom community for the logging industry had only two claims to fame: the only stoplight in the entire length of I-90, and tourist hotspot Snoqualmie Falls. But all good things come to pass. The freeway was rerouted during the 1970s, and during the late 1980s a strip mall went in. Soon after, housing developments sprang up and tourists flocked to the Mar-T Cafe for that damn good coffee and cherry pie. In one decade, North Bend was transformed from logging town to bedroom community to blatant tourist trap.

For climbers, North Bend's transformation was just as profound. North Bend used to be merely the place you turned off to get to the Mount Si Trail, which was—and still is—used for training by mountaineers with their sights set on Mount Rainier, big peaks in the Cascade Range, and beyond. During the early 1990s, however, a small group of climbers began exploring the many mossy cliffs visible on the slopes of Mount Si, long dismissed by area climbers as unworthy compared to Index and Leavenworth. What they found was a virtual gold mine of unclimbed rock. Sure, some of it was chossy, but with cleaning, these crags yielded many sport climbing gems.

The first area to be explored and developed was Little Si, a craggy little peak just across the Snoqualmie River from town, where dozens of routes were established. Later, as word got out about Little Si, the area became very crowded. And why not? Here was a sport climbing area just a half hour drive from a major metropolitan area, featuring many excellent routes on rock ranging from slabby to wildly overhanging, with ratings running the gamut from 5.6 to 5.14. As a result of overcrowding, more nearby crags—notably Deception Crags and the North Fork areas—were explored and developed, producing many more sport routes, from 5.5 to 5.14.

Type of climbing: Climbing at Little Si, Deception Crags, and North Fork is predominately sport climbing. There are a few exceptions, but most of the routes follow lines of rappel bolts up slabby to overhanging rock. The best rock, dubbed "rhino rock" by its devotees, is steep, juggy, and rough, providing pumpy, varied climbing with lots of long reaches and thin moves between buckets and good edges. The overhanging rock stays fairly clean and dry despite oceans of moss and ferns on surrounding rock.

The routes range from 40 feet to 200 feet in length, although most of the routes—being sport routes—are 80 feet or less to the anchors. There are a few routes easier than 5.9, but most of the better-quality routes are 5.10 or harder. Little Si has the greatest concentration of 5.12 and 5.13 sport routes in Washington, with a few 5.14 routes and one that is almost 5.15.

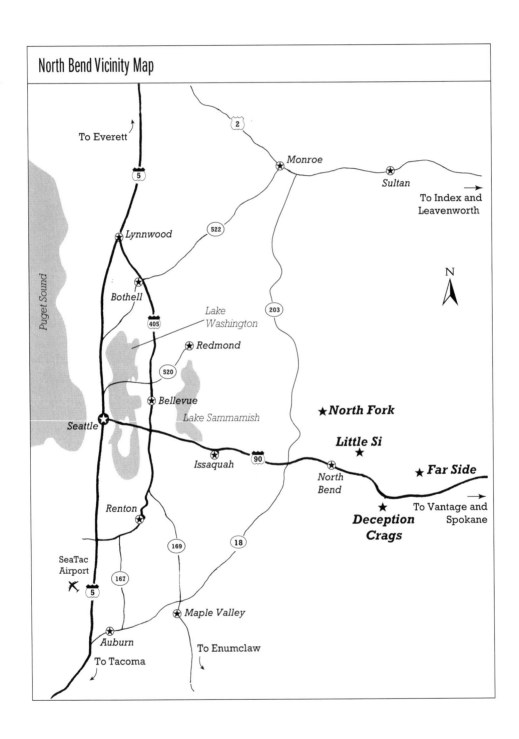

North Bend Vicinity Map

To Everett

2

Monroe

Sultan

To Index and
Leavenworth

5

Lynnwood

522

Bothell

405

Lake
Washington

203

N

Redmond

520

Puget Sound

Bellevue

Lake Sammamish

★North Fork

Seattle

Little Si
★

Issaquah

90

★ Far Side

North
Bend

Renton

To Vantage and
Spokane

★
Deception
Crags

169

18

SeaTac
Airport

167

5

Maple Valley

Auburn

To Enumclaw

To Tacoma

Brief history of area: In a nutshell, Seattle-area sport climbers owe a debt of gratitude to Bryan Burdo, one of the driving forces of new route production in western Washington. His tireless exploration of seemingly every rocky outcropping in the foothills east of Seattle led to the discovery of many better-than-expected crags (and some as-bad-as-expected crags) and ultimately to the establishment of hundreds of routes within an hour's drive of Washington's most heavily populated area. A profile of Bryan Burdo appeared in *Climbing,* Issue No. 159.

After release of Burdo's guide, *Exit 32: North Bend Rock,* in 1992, everybody "discovered" Little Si, and overcrowding forced the new-route crews to look elsewhere. Burdo and his crew moved on to Deception Crags, several obvious cliffs above the interstate just east of North Bend, which had been dismissed by most climbers as unworthy because of their "motley-looking" rock. Other climbers were also active in developing newly discovered crags, including the massive North Fork Crag. There's more rock awaiting discovery in the Cascade foothills, but driving times and approach hikes are sure to get longer and longer.

Precautions and regulations: The Little Si and Deception Crags climbing areas are located on Washington State Department of Natural Resources and Parks & Recreation land, and are subject to regulations. Little Si is part of a Natural Resource Conservation Area (NRCA), and only "low impact" activities are allowed. Under the NCRA's 1997 Public Use Plan, climbing at Little Si is restricted to five designated areas: Repo Rocks, the Woods, World Wall I, World Wall II, and Canopy Crag. To protect plant communities atop the cliffs, climbers are not permitted to top out, but must lower or rappel from anchors.

Loose rock is a problem, particularly at the tops of most of the crags. Even where allowed, it is best to lower or rappel from anchors instead of scrambling off. Some crags are prone to random rockfall, so helmets are recommended. The rock gets worse as you move eastward. Little Si's rock is the best of the North Bend areas; Exit 38 has more loose rock; and the Far Side has the worst rock of the bunch. North Fork's rock varies in quality, with some solid steep faces and some loose, overhanging walls.

Watch out for slugs, as they tend to slime up the holds. Also, there are bears in these woods, so don't leave food lying about unguarded. Actually, cougars are more of a threat than bears, although they tend to attack solitary hikers, children, and pets nearer to the suburban fringe, but one attacked two mountain bikers in 2018, killing one of them, so be alert and know how to respond if you encounter a cougar in the wild.

Camping and accommodations: North Bend lies on the fringe of the suburban sprawl of Seattle, and camping is limited. Denny Creek Campground, located about 5 miles west of Snoqualmie Pass and about fifteen minutes east from Exit 38, is probably the best nearby campground. If you don't already live nearby, camp out at a motel, or make some friends and crash at their place. Bivouacking in the woods is a possibility, if you don't mind the occasional stray bullet or serial killer, or a visit by your friendly local forest ranger or sheriff's deputy. If you're not averse to driving some distance, there are some roadside campsites about 15.5 miles up North Fork Road, just over 0.5 mile uproad from the North Fork Crag trailhead. North Bend has all accommodations, including motels, grocery stores, restaurants, gas stations, banks, and ATMs.

Emergency services: In case of emergency, dial 911.

Other guidebooks: Kurt Hicks's *Snoqualmie Rock* guide was released in 2018 and includes comprehensive route information for all North Bend climbing areas.

Finding the crags: North Bend is located 30 miles east of Seattle, along the I-90 corridor. Take exit 32 for Little Si and exit 38 for Deception Crags. North Fork climbing areas are about 20 miles north of town. Detailed approach descriptions for each area are provided where relevant.

LITTLE SI

Little Si is the most popular of the North Bend areas, due to its close proximity to the Seattle area and its comparatively good rock. It has dozens of popular sport climbs in the 5.9 to 5.14 range. World Wall I, the largest of Little Si's cliffs, is generally regarded as one of the best sport crags in the state.

To reach Little Si, take exit 32 from I-90, about thirty minutes east from Seattle, and head north on 436th Avenue Southeast (toward Mount Si). At Southeast North Bend Way, take a left and go about 0.2 mile to Mount Si Road; turn right and go just over 0.4 mile, crossing the Snoqualmie River and continuing on Mount Si Road a bit to the parking lot, on the left. Be aware that the gate is locked at the time posted, so don't stay too late or your car will be locked in. If the parking lot is full, park in the overflow lot back toward the bridge, or continue to the Mount Si trail parking lot and hike back to the Little Si trailhead, paying heed to traffic as you walk along the narrow, winding road.

From the trailhead, hike up the well-worn trail to where it levels out on an old roadbed, then proceed westward and downhill across a seasonal stream. Shortly past the streambed, the trail bends northward and enters the shady canyon separating Mount Si and Little Si, where the crags are first seen, on the left. Take the left fork to reach Blackstone, Repo, British Aisles, and The Woods; continue on the main trail a few minutes farther to reach World Wall I. Approaches to individual crags are described within the text.

Dogs are allowed in the Mount Si Conservation Area, but must be leashed; please clean up after them if you bring them along, even if no one else does. For that matter, please clean up after yourself, and use proper

Little Si Vicinity Map

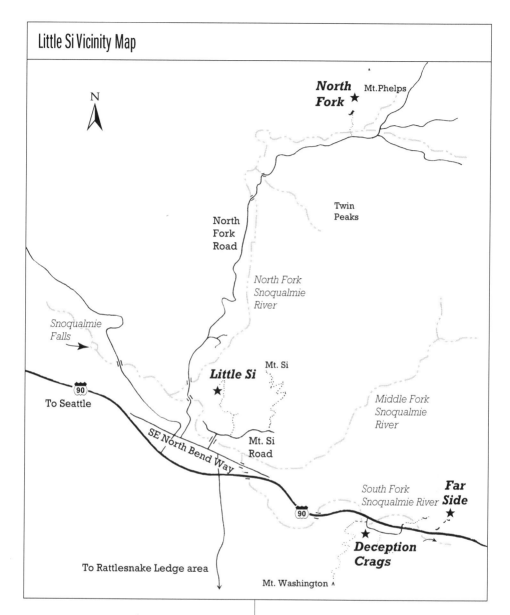

human waste disposal methods when you do your business. The nearest toilet is at the parking lot.

Climber-caused erosion is a major concern at Little Si. A network of trails has caused damage along the base of the various crags, particularly the approaches to Repo Walls and A.W.O.L. Mitigation efforts have been largely successful, but please do your best to avoid adding to the problem and stay on the most obvious path.

Under the area's management plan, climbing at Little Si is limited to only the areas included in this guide, and to Canopy Crag, a small cliff not described here. Climbing is not allowed on any of the other cliffs in the area.

Little Si Approach Map

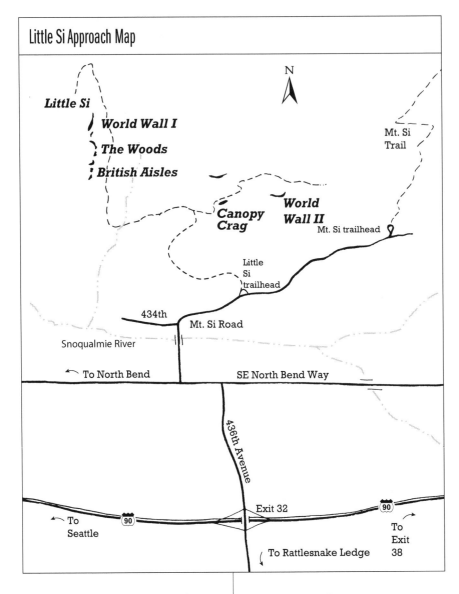

N

Little Si

World Wall I

The Woods

British Aisles

Mt. Si
Trail

Canopy
Crag

World
Wall II

Mt. Si trailhead

Little
Si
trailhead

434th

Mt. Si Road

Snoqualmie River

To North Bend

SE North Bend Way

436th Avenue

Exit 32

90

90

To
Seattle

To
Exit
38

To Rattlesnake Ledge

Finally, although the rock is mostly solid, there are some suspicious-looking flakes, loose blocks, and creaky handholds on a few routes, so test holds before committing to them. Helmets are recommended for everyone, but especially belayers, since rocks knocked off by climbers above are a common hazard.

The British Aisles

The several lesser crags of the Little Si group are collectively known as The British Aisles. They are approached via a side trail leading left from the climbers' kiosk. The British Aisles crags have some of Little Si's most popular routes, and as a consequence they are heavily used, making erosion a serious problem here. Trail work has mitigated some climber impacts, but please take care to avoid further erosion.

Blackstone Wall

Blackstone Wall, the leftmost of Little Si's crags, is a small, chossy-looking, blocky cliff with several routes and linkups that are better than they look and fairly popular. Lower or rappel from anchors atop each route. Make sure your rope is long enough before you commit to lowering or rappelling, as some of the anchors are high up.

1. Stumblesome Fridge (5.9) A bolted route on the far upper left side of the crag. Pro: quickdraws.

2. Winter's Coat of Armor (5.10a) Begin just right of the corner on the left side of the main wall. Pro: quickdraws and a small cam.

3. The Big Easy (5.9) ★ Presently the third bolted route from the left, starting just left of the fir tree and climbing past a small roof and up the headwall to anchors. Pro: quickdraws.

4. Stepping Stone (5.10a) ★ The middle route, beginning at a left-facing corner and climbing past a ledge then up the bulging face to anchors atop the wall. Pro: quickdraws.

5. Blackstone 5 (5.10b) ★ The next bolted line to the right, angling to anchors at the top of the crag. Pro: quickdraws.

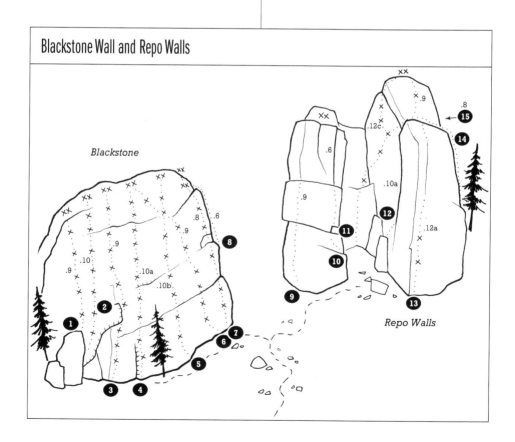

Blackstone Wall and Repo Walls

Blackstone

Repo Walls

6. Blackstone 6 (5.9) ★ Start at the base of the arête and connect the bolts angling left to the *Stepping Stone* anchors. Pro: quickdraws.

7. Human Foot (5.8) ★ The blocky arête on the far right end of the cliff. Pro: quickdraws.

8. Cranium Teaser (5.6) A short line up and around the arête, leading to anchors below the finish of *Human Foot*. Pro: quickdraws.

Repo Walls

The Repo Walls are the distinct twin buttresses immediately right of Blackstone Wall. These crags feature several short but entertaining routes. Rappel or lower from anchors. When setting up topropes, please climb one of the easier routes to avoid worsening erosion in the gullies on either side.

Repo I

Repo I is the slabby buttress on the left side, the first of the Repo crags reached as you approach from a mossy boulder alongside the trail. It has no sport routes, but a couple of short traditional routes that are often toproped.

9. On Second Thought (5.9) ★ The slabby face on the left, following thin cracks directly up the buttress. A 5.8 variation escaping to the hand crack is possible but not as fun. Pro: to 1 inch.

10. First Things Next (5.6) ★★ Climb the arête and short, perfect hand crack to the top. The blocky crack right of the arête is *First Things First* (5.6). There are also a couple of other short routes on the small wall around the corner to the right (5.5 to 5.7) that are easily toproped. Pro: to 2 inches.

Repo II

Repo II is the buttress on the right, with a golden-colored wall on its left side split by a distinctive, steep hand crack and a couple of other less-worthy routes. Again, if you're setting up a toprope, please climb an easier route to the anchors to avoid further erosion.

11. Whinosauras (5.12c) ★★ Up and left of *Mambo Jambo* is a golden wall with a curvy line of bolts. Find the anchor bolt in the gully, then follow the bolts, milking the short wall for all it's worth. A variation going straight up is easier (5.11c) but not as much work. Pro: quickdraws.

12. Mambo Jambo (5.10a) ★★ The obvious hand crack. Finish via the left-leading ramp and crack. Pro to 2.5 inches.

13. Little Big Man (5.12a) ★ The sharp arête just right of *Mambo Jambo*. It has bolts, but requires some thin gear unless you're willing to risk a ground fall (bad idea!). Clipping the second bolt is the crux unless you stick clip it.

14. Repo Man (5.9) The first route around the corner to the right, climbing a short corner. Pro: quickdraws.

15. Fixer Upper (5.8) The next route up to the right. Pro: quickdraws.

A.W.O.L.

Hidden among the trees just right of the Repo crags is A.W.O.L., a blobish, deformed buttress with several sport routes and a few traditional routes in the 5.9 to 5.11 range, of varying quality but mostly better than they look. The most obvious feature of A.W.O.L. is a big offwidth splitting the lower buttress (it's 5.10b if you're interested in that sort of thing). The routes

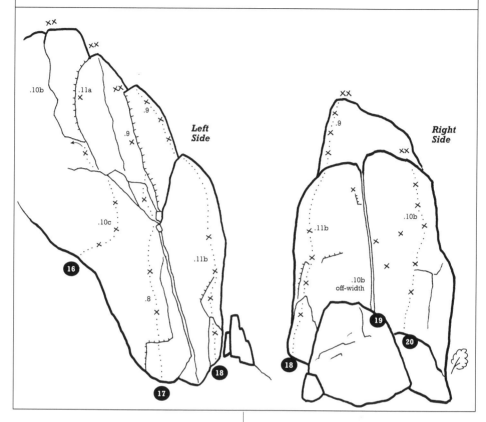

A.W.O.L.

Left Side

Right Side

are described from left to right. Descend by rappel from various anchors.

16. Collateral Damage (5.11b) About 40 feet left of the start of *Kinder, Gentler Nazis* is a blocky wall with three bolts. Continue up the short, bolted, right-facing corner that tops out at the anchors left of the *Kinder, Gentler Nazis* arête. Alternatively, finish via the 5.10b crack on the left (pro to 2 inches). Pro: quickdraws.

17. Kinder, Gentler Carpet Bombing (5.9) ★ A juggy face route starting up the steep, blocky face between two closely spaced fir trees and finishing via a dihedral crack to anchors. Pro: quickdraws, gear to 2 inches.

18. Little Hitlers (5.11b) ★ The bolted, flaky arête between *Kinder, Gentler Carpet Bombing* and the big offwidth. Clipping the third bolt is cruxy, and it's runout on easier ground to the upper arête, but otherwise this is a fun, challenging sport route.

19. You Asked for It (5.10b) ★ The obvious offwidth crack. Clean, but not pretty. Pro: to 4 inches. A 5.10b variation supposedly face climbs past the crack, utilizing three bolts to supplement natural protection. Any way you do it, you get what you deserve.

20. Goddess (5.10b) ★★★ The steep, juggy face on the far right side of the crag, about 15 feet right of the offwidth. One of the first routes at Little Si, and still one of the best.

To get there, scramble directly over a flaky ledge. Pro: quickdraws. (FA: Bryan Burdo, Pete Doorish 1991)

The Woods (Midland)

The Woods (lately known as Midland) are the several angular crags hidden among the fir trees on the left as you approach World Wall I beyond the mossy boulder. The most striking features here are two arêtes on the left side of the formation and a small, wide corner on the right. The central portion of the cliff looks like rubbish, but has some excellent hard face climbs. Descents are best accomplished by rappel unless you have long ropes.

The Woods–Left

The left flank of The Woods is marked by two unmistakable arêtes divided by a chossy dihedral. Although it is possible to traverse along the base of A.W.O.L. to reach this crag, please approach through the woods from the trail to avoid further erosion.

21. Lay of the Land (5.12a) ★★★ The striking arête on the far left side of The Woods, just down and right from *Goddess*. Steeper than it looks from below, with a crux finish that should send you flying. Pro: quickdraws.

22. The Nameless Tower (5.10d) ★★ The steep slab between the arêtes, with a short crack section. Pro: to 1 inch; quickdraws.

23. Sweet and Sticky (5.9) ★★ The blocky arête on the right, starting from a hollow, burned-out snag. Very runout to the second bolt unless you bring a few wired nuts. If you stop short at the *Violent Phlegms* anchors, it's 5.8. Pro: quickdraws.

24. Violent Phlegms (5.11a) ★ Just right of the *Sweet and Sticky* arête is this edgy slab route leading to anchors about 20 feet below the top of the arête. A little contrived, but the cruxes are entertaining. Pro: quickdraws.

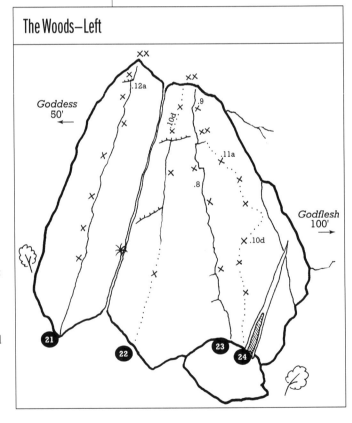

The Woods–Left

The Woods–Central

The central portion of The Woods has several difficult sport routes, all following obvious bolt lines. The routes are generally better than they look, but not always. They are described from left to right, beginning from the lowest point of the slab, at the base of a short, mossy dihedral crack.

25. Digitalis (5.12a) ★★ Just left of the dihedral is this flaky, bulging wall. Follow the bolts past a short roof and up the headwall. Consider stick clipping the second bolt; if you fell before the clip, you'd deck for sure. Pro: quickdraws; thin gear for the middle section unless you are very bold.

26. Exhume to Consume (5.7) The short corner crack. Kind of mossy. Pro: to 1.5 inches.

27. Human Glue (5.11d) ★ Several variations are possible from the *Exhume to Consume* anchors (5.10c to 5.11d). In the modern tradition, each short continuation has a name. This version continues up through the ugly roof to the *Godflesh* anchors. Can also be approached via *Street Cleaner* and its spawn. Scumming and lots of other fun stuff. Pro: quickdraws.

28. Street Cleaner (5.10a) ★ The slabby, bolted arête 15 feet right of *Exhume to Consume* leads to anchors below the roof. Beware of loose holds. Pro: quickdraws.

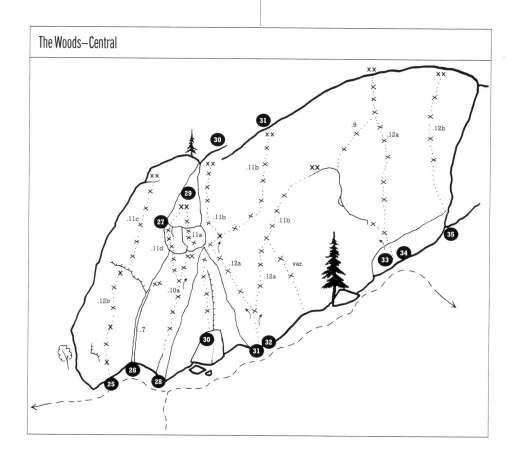

The Woods–Central

29. Godflesh (5.11a) ★★★ An excellent sport route through the blocky roof above the *Street Cleaner* arête. Not nearly as desperate as it looks. Pro: quickdraws; long slings recommended to reduce rope drag.

30. Gold Rush (5.11b) ★ Start up the short, bolted dihedral just right of the *Street Cleaner* arête, then skirt right around the roof and follow bolts up the slab to anchors (or traverse right to another set of anchors). Pro: quickdraws.

31. Yo Baby (5.11d) ★★ Just up and right from *Gold Rush* is a bulging face with two obvious bolt lines. This route climbs the left-hand variation, going directly up the thin, edgy face. Pro: quickdraws.

32. Moclips (5.12a) ★ The first bolt of this route and *Yo Baby* is shared. From there, follow the bolts right up the face to anchors atop the slab. Pro: quickdraws. The *Monkey Madness* variation (5.11c) avoids the crux of *Moclips* by climbing a flaky, indented face

farther right, passing two bolts to reach the fourth bolt of *Moclips*.

33. Bioclamatic Quandary (5.9) ★ A curving crack system just uphill from a prominent hemlock tree. Climb the crack and angle right up the slab. Pro: quickdraws; gear to 1.5 inches.

34. State of Perplexity (5.12a) ★ Connect the bolts up the grayish wall just right of *Bioclamatic Quandary*. Pro: quickdraws.

35. Double Take (5.12b) The rightmost route on the crag, climbing past several bolts up a usually mossy wall. When cleaned up, this is a decent route. Pro: quickdraws.

The Woods–Right

The rightmost portion of The Woods is a short, wide, overhanging amphitheater with a striking, leaning dihedral. There are a couple of short sport routes on the right. It is best reached by scrambling up the right side

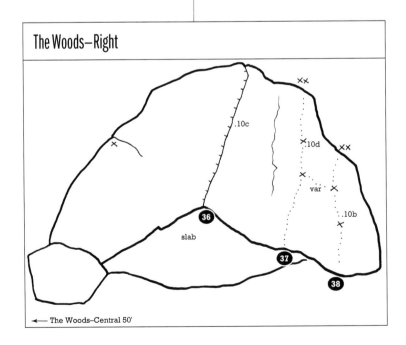

The Woods–Right

of The Woods–Central, about 50 feet right from the *Double Take* area.

36. Only In It for the Money (5.10c) ★ The obvious crack splitting the wall. Pro to 3 inches. The face just right of the crack is a 5.11a toprope problem.

37. Have You Told Your Husband Yet (5.10d) A short, bolted route on the right. Pro: quickdraws.

38. Gamonbozia (5.10b) A shorter bolted route on the far right. Can be linked with the route to the left (5.11b). Pro: quickdraws.

World Wall I

World Wall I is the major crag of the Little Si group, and is one of the best sport crags in Washington. It is visible as an overhanging white cliff just east of and below the summit of Little Si as you drive north on 436th Avenue Southeast. It is a steep, mostly overhanging wall of bulging, edgy rock, strafed with bolts. The Launch Ledge runs along its base about 30 feet above the woods. The ledge has some narrow spots and features some Class 2 scrambling. Dogs have fallen off the ledge, and reportedly two climbers who were roped together. Belayers should definitely clip in where possible, and stick clips are recommended if there is no anchor bolt.

The routes on World Wall I are described from right to left as you encounter them approaching along Launch Ledge. A lot of these "routes" are really only variations or extensions of other routes. Some of the hardest routes in Washington were created on this wall by linking up the hard parts of two or more other routes. Figuring out where the routes go can be confusing, especially since some holds and rests are disallowed on some routes. I'm sure someone will tell you if you're doing it wrong. Many of the routes have fixed quickdraws. Descend from anchors all over the place. A 60-meter rope will do for some routes, but a 70-meter rope is needed for others.

1. Jealous God (5.12a) On the far right side is a bulging buttress separated from the main wall by a chossy gully. This is the rightmost route up this buttress, climbing up and around the roof on the right. Pro: quickdraws.

2. False Idol (5.11c) ★ The middle line on the rightmost wall, climbing to anchors under the overhang. Pro: quickdraws.

3. Graven Image (5.12b) ★ A continuation of *False Idol,* climbing up and over the roof. Pro: quickdraws.

4. Disincarnate (5.11a) The leftmost and easiest route up the bulging buttress, avoiding the roof via a chossy-looking wall. Pro: quickdraws.

5. Opening Act (5.9) Climbs to anchors below the headwall. Pro: quickdraws.

6. End of the World (5.12a) ★ The steep arête right of *The Seam*. Approach via *Opening Act*. Pro: quickdraws.

7. Girls in the Gym (5.10c) ★ Climb to anchors below the headwall. A 5.12d pitch squeezed in between the seam and the arête continues up the headwall. Pro: quickdraws.

8. The Seam (5.13a) ★★ The obvious overhanging seam, also known as "the Crack," although if it was really a crack it probably would not have been bolted. Pro: quickdraws.

World Wall I—Right Side

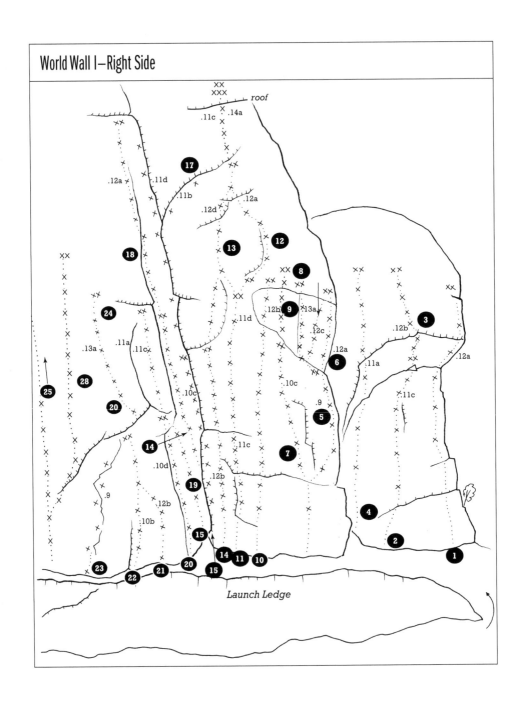

9. Judgment Day (5.12c) ★ Continue above the *Girls in the Gym* anchors. Pro: quickdraws.

10. Hang It Out to Dry (5.12b) ★★★ Presently the third bolted line right of the dihedral, climbing a steep, difficult wall to reach an even steeper, more difficult headwall to anchors. Technical and pumping. Pro: quickdraws. (FA: Matt Kerns 1995)

11. Rainy Day Women (5.11d) ★★★★ Just left of *Hang It Out to Dry* is this excellent, steep sport route, beginning in a short right-facing corner and passing a bulge in the first 30 feet. Lots of bolts lead up the wall to anchors 80 feet up. One of the most popular routes at Little Si, and not only because it's the easiest "5.12" in the area. Pro: quickdraws.

12. Deluge (5.12a) ★★ Continue above and beyond the *Rainy Day Women* anchors to anchors higher up. Bring lots of quickdraws.

13. Hydrophobia (5.12d) ★★★ Continue up and left after the crux of *Rainy Day Women* instead of going right to the anchors. Finishes at the *Deluge* anchors. The route has been extended past the roof to anchors at the top of the wall (*Skipping the Goods*, 5.14a).

14. Viagro (5.12b) ★ Yet another route squeezed in on this poor wall, this one climbing the narrow buttress between *Rainy Day Women* and *Son of Jesus*. A continuation to higher anchors is *Viagrophobia* (5.12c). Pro: quickdraws.

15. Son of Jesus (5.10c) ★ The dihedral, at least as far as the first anchors. From there, call it something else every time you reach a new set of anchors. Pro: quickdraws.

16. Vudu Guru (5.11d) ★ Continue above the first anchors, finishing to the left. Pro: More quickdraws.

17. Just One of the Boys (5.11b) ★ Continue above the first anchors, finishing to the right at the *Hydrophobia* anchors.

18. Spent (5.11d) ★ A squeeze job climbing a line of bolts just left of *Son of Jesus*. Continue to higher anchors to get *Totally Spent* (5.12a). Pro: quickdraws.

19. Devil's Advocate (5.9) ★ The face between the dihedral and arête. Pro: quickdraws; maybe a couple of wired nuts.

20. Dreaming of a Life of Ease (5.10d) ★ The blocky arête left of *Devil's Advocate*. Continue past the roof to higher anchors for the full treatment (5.11c). Pro: quickdraws. A variation of the second pitch (*Sinistral Purpose*) climbs a 5.11a crack. Pro: to 2 inches.

As you continue traversing the Launch Ledge left from the dihedral, the ledge narrows. Be careful—it's a ways down! There are anchor bolts in place here and there along the ledge; use them where they are available. Stick clip the first bolt to avoid the possibility of falling off and dragging your belayer with you (it's happened). Leave your dogs down below, so they don't fall off the ledge (it's happened).

21. Oedipal Complex (5.12c) A bulging, thin face route just right of *Jug or Not*. It's hard right from the start, more of a boulder problem than a route. Joins *Jug or Not* higher up. Pro: quickdraws.

22. Jug or Not (5.10b) ★ A left-facing dihedral marks the start of this popular route. Climb the corner, then follow the bolts to the *Reptiles and Amphetamines* anchors.

23. Reptiles and Amphetamines (5.9) ★★★ A juggy, overhanging face route following a flake to anchors 40 feet up. Easily the most often climbed pitch on World Wall I. Pro: quickdraws.

24. Oval Orifice (5.13a) ★★ Connect the fixed draws leading directly up the bulging headwall above the *Reptiles and Amphetamines* anchors.

25. Chronic (5.13b) ★★★★ A popular line up the bulging wall left of *Reptiles and Amphetamines*. Starts just left and independent of *Reptiles*. Connect the fixed draws, if you can get on the route. There's almost always someone on it. (FA: Bryan Burdo or Erik Kubiak)

26. Lizard King (5.13c) ★★★ Climb *Chronic* to its anchors, then continue directly up to the higher anchors shared with *Illness*.

27. Illness (5.13c) ★★★ Climb *Chronic* to its upper roof crux, then move right and continue up to an anchor above *Chronic*. *Extended Illness* (5.13c/d) continues to a higher anchor.

28. Dr. Evil (5.14a) ★★★ Start via *Chronic* to the third bolt, then bust out up the

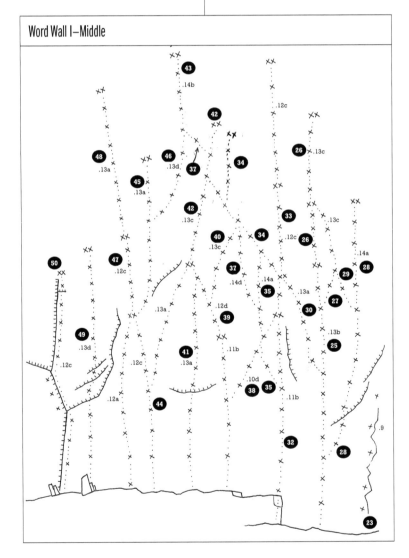

Word Wall I—Middle

sickeningly overhanging headwall above *Reptiles*. Pro: quickdraws.

29. Extended Evil (5.13c) ★★★ Link up *Dr. Evil* with *Illness/Extended Illness*. Good times.

30. Californicator (5.12d) ★★★ Start via *Chronic,* but head left at the sixth bolt and up to the *Aborigine* anchors. If you keep going to the *Technoriginie* anchors, that's *Californication* (5.13a).

31. Wide World of Fitness (5.14b) ★★★ A wide-ranging route linking *Californicator* with *Pornstar* to *Flatliner*, then up *Lost Horizons.* Basically if you want to take over half of the World Wall, this would be a good project for you. (FA: Ben Gilkison)

32. Aborigine (5.11b) ★★★ An overhanging, pumping, "easy" route climbing the over-hanging wall about 30 feet left of *Reptiles and Amphetamines*. The first bolt is 15 feet up, on a blocky wall just below a ledge. Continue up the bulging, flaky wall to anchors 70 feet up. Pro: quickdraws.

33. Technorigine (5.12c) ★★★ A Little Si classic, continuing *Aborigine* to higher anchors. For the full effect, climb *Extend-origine* to the highest set of anchors (5.12c). Pro: quickdraws.

34. Pornstar (5.13d) ★★★★ One of the most popular routes on the wall. Start up *Technorigine*, then go left and up a seam to anchors. Can also be started from *Chronic* via *Californicator*, which makes it *Pornification* (5.14a). Pro: quickdraws.

35. Whore of Babylon (5.14b) ★★ The bolted seam and headwall just left of *Aborigine*. Start up that route then head left and up to finish on *Pornstar*, Pro: quickdraws.

36. New World Order (5.14c) ★★★ Climb *Whore of Babylon* into *Pornstar*, then keep going up and left into *Lost Horizons*. (FA: Jonathan Siegrist)

37. Brave New World (5.14d) ★★★ Cur-rently the hardest sport route in Washington, a massive link-up sampling the cruxes of several hard routes. Climb *Whore of Babylon* just past its crux, then go left past four bolts to join *Pornstar* and *Flatliner* and finishing up *Lost Horizons*. (FA: Drew Ruana)

The next several routes begin from a blocky ledge system left of *Aborigine*. The most prominent feature of this section is a long black streak running down the wall. Sev-eral of the routes in this area are link-ups or extensions, offering a number of distinct problems. Be careful scrambling up to these routes, as there are several loose blocks, and it's quite a ways off the deck. Use anchor bolts where they are available, and for safe-ty's sake stick clip the first bolt if you doubt your ability to do the initial moves.

38. Slaborigine (5.10d) ★ The easiest route on this section of the wall. A traversing start to *Aborigine* that begins from the blocky ledge on the left, at the base of *Psychosomatic* (about 30 feet right of the black streak), and basically avoids the best part of *Aborigine*. Pro: quickdraws.

39. Psychosomatic (5.12c) ★★ The bolted face pitch starting just right of the *Gerbil Killer* roof. Steep, thin, and technical face climbing leads to anchors below a bulge 80 feet up. If you stop at the first anchors (5.11b to here), that's *Psycho Wussy*. Pro: quickdraws.

40. Chicxulbub (5.13d) ★★★ Climb *Psychoso-matic* to the first bolt past the *Psycho Wussy* anchor, then go right up a bolted overhang-ing wall. At the fifth bolt go right and finish up *Pornstar*. (FA: Drew Ruana)

41. Gerbil Killer (5.13a) ★★ Connect the bolts through a roof between *Psychosomatic* and *Propaganda*, finishing on the last few moves of *Psychosomatic*. Pro: quickdraws.

42. Hardliner/Flatliner (5.13a/5.13c) ★★★ *Hardliner* (5.13a) extends *Psychosomatic* to the next highest anchors. Continuing to the highest anchors is *Flatliner* (5.13b/c). Pro: quickdraws.

43. Lost Horizons (5.14a) ★★★ A 60-foot extension of *Flatliner*. Go slightly left of the last bolt (skip the anchor) of *Flatliner* to the top of the wall.

44. Propaganda (5.12c) ★★★ Climb the black streak more or less directly to anchors 80 feet up. One of the easiest routes to locate at World Wall I, but not so easy to climb. Pro: quickdraws. The *Hardliner* variation (5.13a) exits right to finish up *Psychosomatic*.

45. Black Ice (5.13b)★★★ A continuation of *Propaganda*, climbing the overhanging wall above the anchors. Perhaps a little runout? Potential for air time if you miss some key clips. Pro: quickdraws.

46. Event Horizon (5.13d) ★★★ Climb *Black Ice* to its last jug, rest, then cut right to finish up *Lost Horizons*.

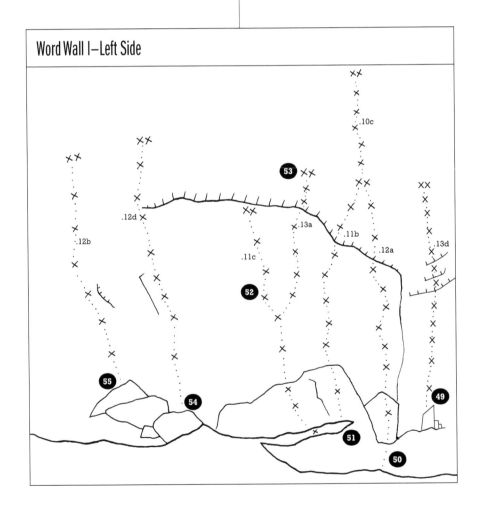

Word Wall I–Left Side

47. Bust the Rhythm (5.12c) ★★★ Follow the bolts up the face just left of the black streak, then up the overhanging corner on the left. A stemming test piece, assuming you can get past the face section below. Pro: quickdraws. The *Bust A Move* variation (5.12a) climbs the initial 80 feet of *Bust the Rhythm,* but exits right to *Propaganda*'s anchors.

48. Dreadlock ★★(5.12d) Climb *Bust the Rhythm* and just keep going. Bring every quickdraw you've got, and then some. Double ropes to rappel.

49. Enigma (5.13d) ★★ A line of bolts leads up the wall just left of *Bust the Rhythm* and directly over the obvious bulging overhang. Pro: quickdraws. (FA: Eric Kubiak)

50. Slug Lover (5.12c)★★ The obvious left-arching corner about 20 feet left of the black streak, passing the bulging overhang on the left and continuing to anchors 100 feet up. Pro: quickdraws.

On the far left side of World Wall I is a long, blackish roof. There are several more steep face routes in this area. Again, use anchor bolts where they are available, and be careful traversing the ledge, which is *very* exposed in a few spots.

51. Sweet Tooth (5.12a) The bulging face left of *Slug Lover,* angling left at the top to reach *Megatherion*'s anchors. Pro: quickdraws.

52. Megatherion (5.11b) ★★ Start just right of *The Bad Guy*'s anchor bolt, up a flake/arête, then up the steep, bolted face, passing the roof on the far right side. The big, glued-reinforced hold above the roof is popularly known as the "Horn of Plenty." A second pitch is 5.10c. Pro: quickdraws.

53. The Bad Guy (5.11c) ★★ Find an eye bolt on the gravelly ledge below the roof. From the anchor bolt, climb more or less straight up to anchors just below the roof. Pro: quickdraws.

54. Hadley's Roof (5.13a) ★ Start up *The Bad Guy* then stay right and turn the roof to anchors. Pro: quickdraws.

55. Black Is All We Feel (5.12d) ★ On the left margin of the roof is a thin black streak. This route climbs up to the streak and continues around the roof on the left. Pro: quickdraws.

56. Dairy Freeze (5.12b) ★ On the far left side of World Wall I, connect bolts up a blocky orange and brown wall. Pro: quickdraws.

There are a few more routes to the left, in the 5.10 range, said to be good. Who knows how many more routes might be squeezed in someday?

World Wall II

One of the most amazing crags in the area is World Wall II, an overhanging cliff with a few hard routes, some of which have what the local guidebook author refers to as "distinctive pockets" and "strategically positioned pockets" (i.e., manufactured holds). Basically, it's a big outdoor climbing gym with a lot of routes that suspiciously check in at hard 5.13 or 5.14. Whatever; it is what it is. Hike in as for the other Little Si areas to where you reach the fork in the road, where the trail levels out. Take a right, following the Boulder Garden Loop trail, which is an old roadbed. The trail levels off at a flat area and turns off to the left; stay on the old roadbed for about a rope length to a side trail on the right, which leads to a mossy boulder barely visible from the road. Follow the trail up to reach a carpet of moss leading to the brink of the cliff. Please stay off the moss to avoid further damage to this fragile ecosystem. To descend to the base of the

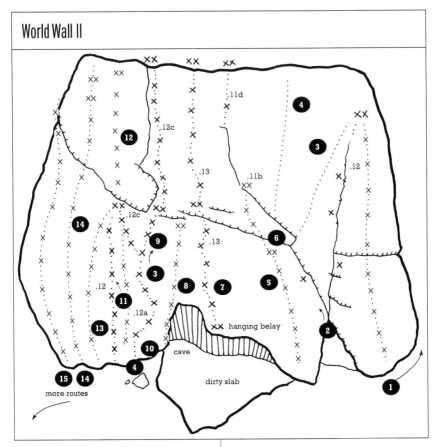

World Wall II

cliff, backtrack from the brink and scramble down the east side of the cliff (on the left as you approach from the road).

1. Pinching the Loaf (5.12c) The first route on the right side of the cliff, just right of the start of *Orgasmatron*. Pro: quickdraws.

2. Orgasmatron (5.12a) ★★★ The striking thin crack running diagonally across the wall from right to left, with a crux face finish. This route was once hyped as the "best hard crack" in Washington, but it's not exactly a crack climb. Pro: quickdraws; gear to 1 inch unless it's been fully bolted, which is likely. (FA: Bryan Burdo 1994)

3. Kung Fu Fighter (5.13c) Start up *Orgasmatron*, then follow the bolts leading up and

right to the anchors shared with *Pinching the Loaf* and the 5.12 crack route in between. Pro: quickdraws.

4. Don't Ask Don't Tell (5.14a) Climb up *Orgasmatron* a little farther, and then launch up the line of bolts and drilled holds. Pro: quickdraws.

5. Renaissance (5.12b) The first sport route left of *Orgasmatron*. Pro: quickdraws.

6. Reformation (5.12c) An extension of *Reinaissance* to the anchors midway up *Orgasmatron*. Pro: quickdraws.

7. The Sickness (5.14a) The steep sport route on the headwall left of *Orgasmatron*. It's 5.12d if you stop at the first anchors. Rappel in to the anchors above the cave, or batman up the rope if it's still there. Pro: quickdraws.

8. Hollow Hearted (5.13a) Start up the corner where the two sides of the wall converge, and keep going to anchors and beyond. Pro: quickdraws.

9. Paradise Lost (5.12c) The first sport route left of the cave, angling slightly right at the start, then proceeding directly up, skirting the blocky roof on the right and continuing to the top of the wall. Hardest when done in a continuous pitch. Many parties use a hanging belay midpitch, which makes it 5.12b with one point of aid unless you descend from the first anchors. Pro: quickdraws.

10. Gray People (5.12b) Start as for *Paradise Lost,* but follow the bolts diverging left to anchors under the blocky roof. Pro: quickdraws.

11. Project Clench (5.13d) A continuation of *Gray People* to the top of the wall. Pro: quickdraws.

12. Drill Sergeant (5.13b) A drill job squeezed in between *Paradise Lost/Gray People* and *Bones Brigade.* Pro: quickdraws.

13. Bones Brigade (5.13d) The middle of the bolted lines left of *Paradise Lost/Gray People.* Pro: quickdraws.

14. Fly Boys (5.13+) The third bolted line left of *Paradise Lost/Gray People*, which ends at the anchor shared with *Drill Sergeant* and *Bones Brigade.* Pro: quickdraws.

15. Unsung Heroes (5.13+) The first bolted line left of *Fly Boys*, which leads up through the roofs to its own anchor. Pro: quickdraws.

16. Le Misarête (5.14b) A difficult sport route up the arête on the left edge of the wall. Pro: quickdraws.

DECEPTION CRAGS (EXIT 38)

Deception Crags, popularly known as Exit 38 but also known as Mount Washington Crags, comprises the many small cliffs on the slopes of Mount Washington south of I-90 near exit 38 between North Bend and Snoqualmie Pass. Because of its close proximity to the Puget Sound sprawl, short approaches, ample parking, and mostly good climbing, Deception Crags has become popular with Seattle-area sport climbers. Part of the attraction of this area—aside from its easy accessibility—is its abundance of moderate sport climbs, from 5.5 to 5.11, with some 5.12s and 5.13s thrown in. Critics of the area complain about loose rock, of which there is much, and also the overall poor quality of many of the routes. Despite its shortcomings, Deception Crags has several worthwhile routes, and has remained popular even as newer areas have been developed.

To get to Deception Crags, take exit 38 off I-90, about 7 miles east of North Bend and 15 miles west of Snoqualmie Pass. Deception Crags is divided into two main areas, the Mount Washington Trail Area and the Trestle Area. Each area is discussed in detail below.

The initial routes in this area were developed by Bryan Burdo, but other local activists, notably Leland Windham and C. P. Little, established many Deception Crags routes, particularly on Amazonia, the Actual Cave, and Nevermind.

Most of the Deception Crags areas are on state parks land, and state parks land must be crossed to get to those not on state parks land, so be on your best behavior. Park off the road in designated areas. Don't litter, cut switchbacks, molest wildlife, or act like an idiot. In particular, when climbing routes directly above the old railroad grade, stay near the edge so you don't impede others' use of the trail. And please don't let your kids or dogs run loose or leave gear or ropes strewn across the trail grade, unless you want them to get run over by a cyclist or fall off the trestle.

Mount Washington Trail Area

To reach Mount Washington Trail, take the first right turn up a rough, rocky road that leads to the Twin Falls Trail parking lot (0.2 mile). Hike up the short trail until you meet the Cross-State Trail (an old railroad grade) and proceed westward to Mount Washington Trail. The trail is marked, but if the sign is missing, it's the first trail you come to, and it starts between two alder trees marked with green paint and the initials "MW" blazed into the tree on the left. All the crags are encountered as you hike up the trail. Side trails lead to the crags, but please try to stay on the main trail as much as possible to avoid adversely impacting this area, which is part of Iron Horse State Park. In particular,

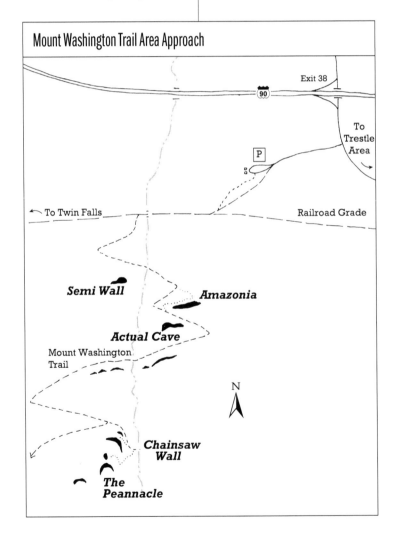

Mount Washington Trail Area Approach

Exit 38 Vicinity Map

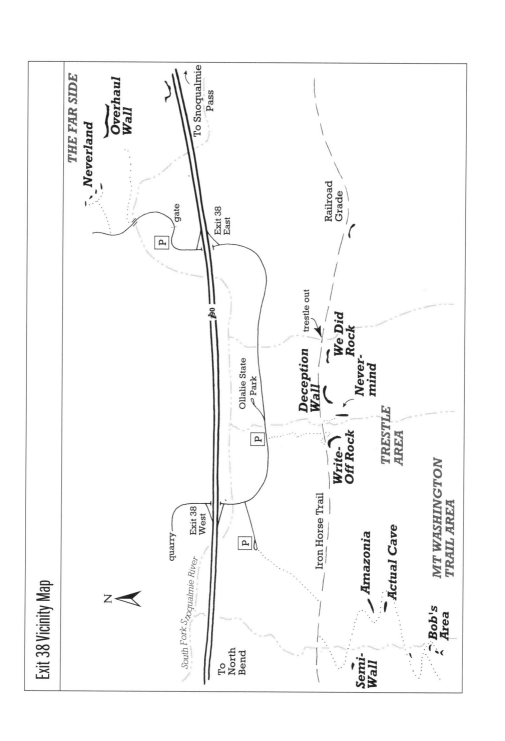

N

THE FAR SIDE

Neverland

Overhaul Wall

To Snoqualmie Pass

gate

P

Exit 38 East

Railroad Grade

trestle out

We Did Rock

Deception Wall

Never-mind

Ollalie State Park

P

Write-Off Rock

TRESTLE AREA

South Fork Snoqualmie River

quarry

Exit 38 West

P

Iron Horse Trail

Amazonia

Actual Cave

MT WASHINGTON TRAIL AREA

To North Bend

Semi-Wall

Bob's Area

don't use the climbers' trail between Amazonia and the Actual Cave, as it is eroding badly near the top. Definitely don't climb the gully directly to the Actual Cave, as further erosion will wipe out the trail.

Amazonia

About fifteen minutes up the trail is Amazonia, one of the best sport crags in the area, with several moderate routes. A climbers' trail leads left from the Mount Washington Trail where it switchbacks right shortly after crossing a culvert. The climbers' trail continues upward to the Actual Cave, but it is eroding badly and should not be used.

The routes are described from left to right as you encounter them on the approach. Descend from anchors atop each route.

1. Arboreality (5.10d) ★ A steep route on the far left side. Begin from a ledge with a large cedar tree, just up from the base of the wall. Follow the bolts up and left, passing a strenuous roof. Continuing to the *Tropicana* anchors is recommended; lowering from the first anchors drops you right into the cedar tree. Pro: quickdraws.

2. Tropicana (5.10c) ★★ A popular route climbing the steep, colorful face right of the cedar tree. Begin by turning the roof right of the tree to gain a ledge, then continue up the steep wall above to anchors. Pro: quickdraws.

3. Primus (5.11b) ★★ The first route right of *Tropicana,* marked by a bolt in a block below the roof and another bolt at the lip of a prominent roof. Turn the roof directly and climb the steep headwall to anchors. Pro: quickdraws.

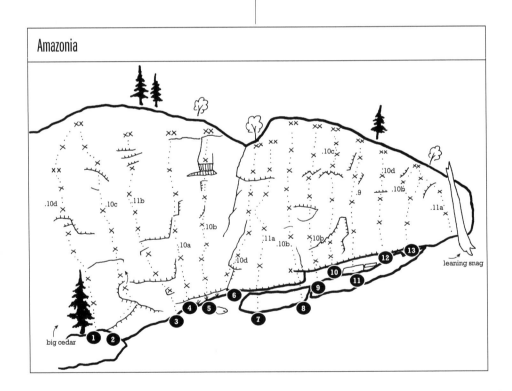

Amazonia

4. Iguanarama (5.10a) ★★★ Just right of the big roof is this steep, juggy face route, which is much easier than it looks. Pro: quickdraws.

5. Laceration of the Soul (5.10b) ★★ The next route to the right from *Iguanarama,* climbing the steep wall to a blocky roof finish. Pro: quickdraws.

6. Paste Human (5.10d) ★ A perennial drip falls down the center of the crag, forming a small pool at the base of the wall. Just right of the drip pool is a slabby arête. Connect the bolts up the arête, through a roof and up the steep headwall to the anchors just below a giant specimen of devil's club. Pro: quickdraws.

7. Drier Adhesive to the Corporal Abyss (5.11a) ★★ The sport route squeezed in between *Paste Human* and *Radioactive Decay.* One hard move at the start and it's over. Share a bolt with *Paste Human* unless you like long runouts. Pro: quickdraws.

8. Radioactive Decay (5.10b) ★ The next sport route to the right, starting only 3 feet right of *Drier Adhesive,* with a tenuous crux start. If you blow the clip, you might smack the ledge. Pro: quickdraws.

9. I Remember Drooling (5.10b) ★★ Turn the difficult roof about 10 feet right of *Radioactive Decay,* then easier climbing leads up and past a shallow cave to anchors. Pro: quickdraws.

10. Scrubbing Neon (5.10c) ★★ The first route left of the obvious corner/flake of *Sodflesh,* with a difficult move over the initial roof and more strenuous climbing on the headwall above. Pro: quickdraws.

11. Sodflesh (5.9) ★ About 50 feet right of the drip line is an obvious blocky, right-facing flake/corner. Surmount the flake, then climb the steep wall above. Pro: quickdraws.

12. Fire Walk on Me (5.10d) ★ About 10 feet right of the *Sodflesh* flake is this direct face route, with a difficult finish. Pro: quickdraws.

13. Ten-ish Ooze (5.10b) ★ On the far right side is this short route with two finish variations. The direct version climbs the short, right-leaning flake on the left. A 5.10a variation traverses right just below the final bolt. Pro: quickdraws.

Club Paradiso and the Actual Cave

Just above Amazonia is Club Paradiso, a blocky cliff with a small cave popularly known as the Actual Cave. It is easily reached via the Mount Washington Trail by taking about two steps south when you get there. (A climbers' trail leads up from Amazonia, but should not be used because it is badly eroded.) The routes on the right side range from 5.7 to 5.10, while the cave routes run the gamut from 5.11 to 5.13.

Club Paradiso

The right side of the Actual Cave formation is known as Club Paradiso. This big, chossy wall has yielded a couple of decent jug hauls in the 5.8 to 5.10 range, one of which is described below.

14. Trappline (5.10a) ★★ The sport route climbing the blocky, roofy wall 25 feet right of the cave. Pro: quickdraws.

The Actual Cave

The Actual Cave has several short but very difficult sport climbs. Most of the routes are really variations of each other, but they're all pretty damn hard. The Actual Cave is a

Club Paradiso and Actual Cave

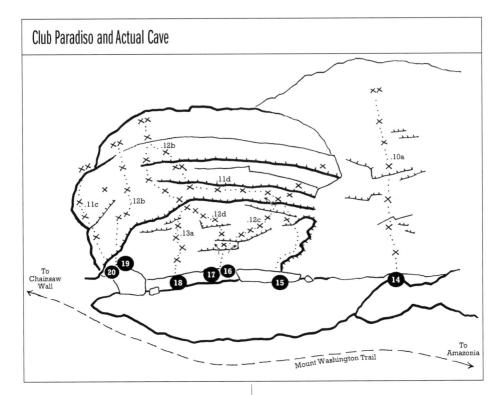

popular hangout on rainy days, as it usually stays completely dry all the way to the lip of the overhang.

15. Giant (5.11d) ★★★ An athletic route climbing out the right side of the cave, then traversing a horizontal crack left across the lip to anchors. Begin by climbing up the blocky right wall of the cave to clip the first bolt, then go for it. Pro: quickdraws. (FA: Bryan Burdo 1992)

Mr. Big variation (5.12b) ★★★ A continuation of *Giant,* passing another roof above the first anchors, adding a desperate crux to this already pumping route. Pro: quickdraws.

16. Cyanide (5.12c) ★ The rightmost of three improbable-looking routes climbing out from the back of the cave. If you manage the roof, join *Giant* to its anchors. Pro: quickdraws.

17. Spartacus (5.12d) ★ The middle route climbing out from the back of the cave, also joining *Giant* to its anchors. Pro: quickdraws.

18. Acid Rock (5.13a) ★ The leftmost and hardest of the cave routes, climbing up out of the cave, then left around the *Giant* roof to finish at the *Mr. Big* anchors. Pro: quickdraws.

19. Bikini Girls with Turbo Drills (5.12b) ★ A blocky face route climbing the far left wall of the cave. Overhanging, blocky, pumping climbing. The first two bolts are very close together, and stick clipping both bolts is recommended. Pro: quickdraws.

20. 100% Beef (5.11c) ★ The short sport route on the far left side, behind a tree. Pro: quickdraws.

Bob's Area

About 2 miles up the trail from the railroad grade is Bob's Area, a group of small crags set high above the valley. It takes about an hour to hike to Bob's Area, allowing an escape from the crowds at the lower, more easily accessible crags. Although the climbing here isn't anything to rave about, and the approach hike might dissuade many sport climbers, the views are magnificent, and there are actually quite a few fun routes.

Bob's Area features two cliffs, the Chainsaw Wall and the Peannacle, approached via a spur trail off the main Mount Washington Trail. Where the main trail switchbacks right (where several alder logs have been laid across the trail), continue left (straight) up a fainter path. If you're on the correct trail, in a few minutes you'll pass under a wall of incredibly shattered rock. About 50 meters beyond is a faint side trail leading up and right to Chainsaw Wall. In another 50 yards is a side trail leading up and right to the Peannacle. Both trails are suffering erosion and could use some rehabilitation before they get really out of hand.

Chainsaw Wall

Chainsaw Wall is a small cliff of solid rock located directly above the shattered rock band encountered on the spur trail. The rock here is unique to the area, featuring patches of very grainy, brownish rock on otherwise rounded, smooth gray stone. The crag has six routes, ranging from 5.7 to 5.12. None of these routes is particularly popular, but if you're looking for a little solitude on a crowded day, you might find it here.

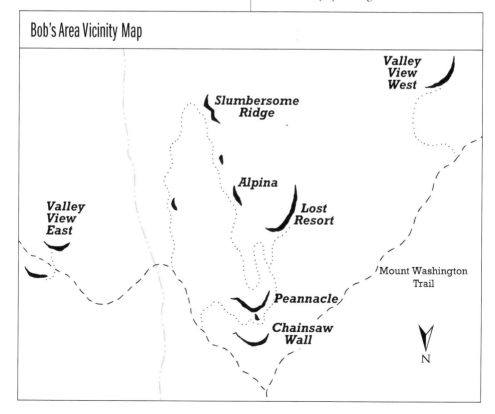

Bob's Area Vicinity Map

Chainsaw Wall and the Peannacle

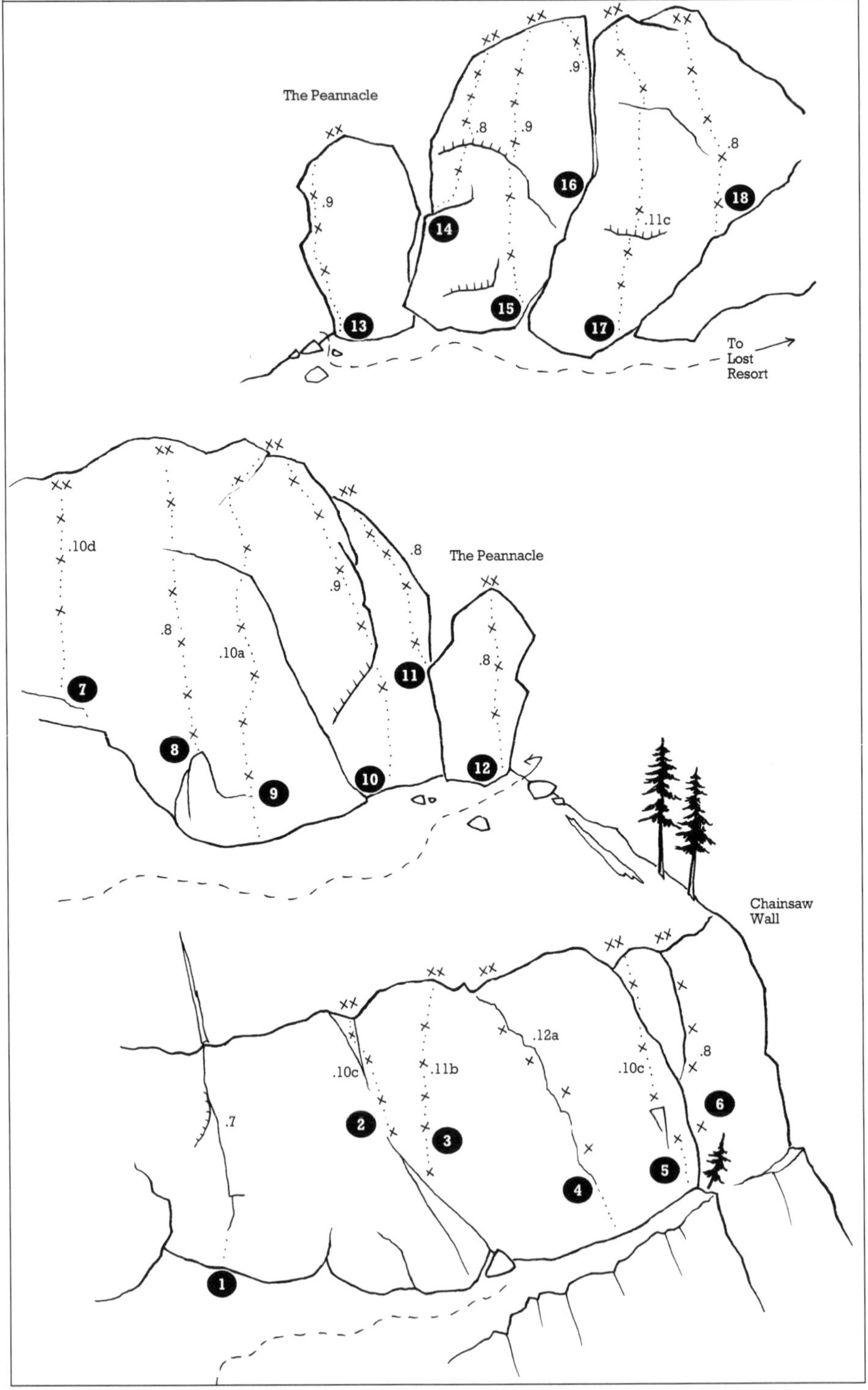

The Peannacle

.9

13

14

.8

.9

16

15

17

.11c

.8

18

To
Lost
Resort

.10d

.8

.10a

7

8

9

.9

.8

The Peannacle

11

10

.8

12

Chainsaw
Wall

.12a

.10c

.11b

.10c

.8

6

.7

2

3

4

5

1

1. Crack One with Me (5.7) ★ The short crack/corner on the far left side of the crag. Pro: to 1 inch.

2. Posthumous Joy and Elation (5.10c) ★★ Begin on the short ramp and stay left up the thin face to anchors in a corner. Pro: quickdraws.

3. My Evil Plans (5.11b) ★★ Start via the ramp, then right up the steep face. Pro: quickdraws.

4. Stihl Fingers (5.12a) ★★★ The thin, bolted seam splitting the steep wall in the middle of the cliff. Pro: quickdraws. (FA: Bryan Burdo 1996)

5. Texas Chainsaw Cheerleaders (5.10c) ★ A funky route starting at the right end of the ledge, climbing past a flaring slot to reach a left-leaning corner. Pro: quickdraws.

6. Chainsaw Chalupa (5.8) Start at the far right edge of the ledge into a corner system. Pro: quickdraws.

The Peannacle and Peannacle Wall

The Peannacle is a small pinnacle (more like a large boulder) perched on the mountainside just above Chainsaw Wall. It has two short routes, and the wall behind it has several more, all reached via a short trail leading up from the spur trail just beyond Chainsaw Wall. The routes aren't exactly classic, but the views make the Peannacle a recommended destination.

7. What Does Bob Want? (5.10d) ★ A short, steep bolted face on the far left edge of Peannacle Wall. Pro: quickdraws.

8. A Summer Known as Fall (5.8) ★ Pro: quickdraws.

9. Gallivant (5.10a) ★ A slabby face leads to a steep headwall; angle right to anchors. Pro: quickdraws.

10. Killer Bob (5.9) ★★★ A popular route climbing a steep corner and arête. Pro: quickdraws. (FA: Leland Windham, Erich Ellis 1996)

11. The Owl (5.8) ★ A slabby face leading up from the Peannacle notch. Pro: quickdraws.

12. Peanut Brittle (5.8) ★ A short sport route up the eastern face of the Peannacle. Pro: quickdraws.

13. Never Was a Cowgirl (5.9) ★ A short sport route up the western face of the Peannacle. Pro: quickdraws.

14. A Castle So Crystal Clear (5.8) ★ Climb up into an alcove and over a small roof to the slab above. Pro: quickdraws.

15. Awannaduya (5.9) ★★ A steep, blocky face leads past a roof to a slab finish. Pro: quickdraws.

16. One Chance Out Between Two Worlds (5.10b) ★ The ramp/crack system splitting the right side of Peannacle Wall, with a short face exit to anchors. Pro: to 3 inches, quickdraws.

17. The Magician Longs to See (5.11c) ★ A short, difficult face start, then easier climbing to the top. Pro: quickdraws.

18. Through the Darkness of Futures Past (5.8) A short, slabby wall on the far right side of Peannacle Wall. Pro: quickdraws.

Lost Resort

Lost Resort is a large sport crag located about 100 meters southwest of the Peannacle, reached via a good trail. It has a handful of good routes on steep, textured rock.

Lost Resort

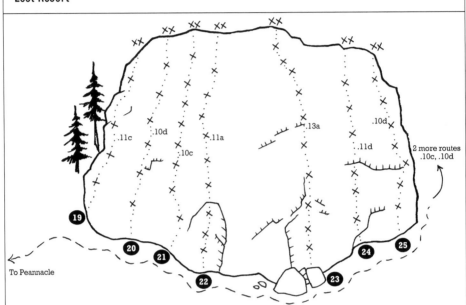

19. Give Yourself to Me (5.11c) ★★ Presently the leftmost route on the crag, climbing a steep face/arête to anchors. Pro: quickdraws.

20. Andante Faviori (5.10d) ★★ A steep, thin face. Pro: quickdraws.

21. Appassionata (5.10c) ★★ Another steep, thin face. Pro: quickdraws.

22. Crescendo . . . (5.11a) ★★ The route's full name is longer than this description. Pro: quickdraws.

23. Crawling from the Wreckage (5.13a) ★★★ A superb line up the steepest part of the crag. Pro: quickdraws.

24. Liberty Smack (5.11d) ★★ Pass the left end of the obvious roof and up the headwall to anchors. Pro: quickdraws.

25. Satoric Inclination (5.10d) ★★ Pass the right end of the roof. Pro: quickdraws.

Alpina

Alpina is a small, angular crag located just uphill on the ridge above Peannacle Wall. It has four short, popular routes. Approach via the trail forking off from the Lost Resort approach trail. The routes are described from right to left as you approach via the trail.

26. El Astronato (5.10b) ★ The rightmost route on the crag, climbing through blocky roofs to an alcove, then around a corner to a short headwall. Pro: quickdraws.

27. Green Buddha (5.11b) ★★ The next route to the left, climbing up to and ascending the short corner. Pro: quickdraws.

28. Inverted Rain Ascending (5.11c) ★★ The bolted line squeezed in between the corner and arête. Pro: quickdraws.

29. Aperture Ecstasy in a Nocturne Divine (5.11a) ★★★ The arête/face problem on the far left side. Pro: quickdraws.

Alpina

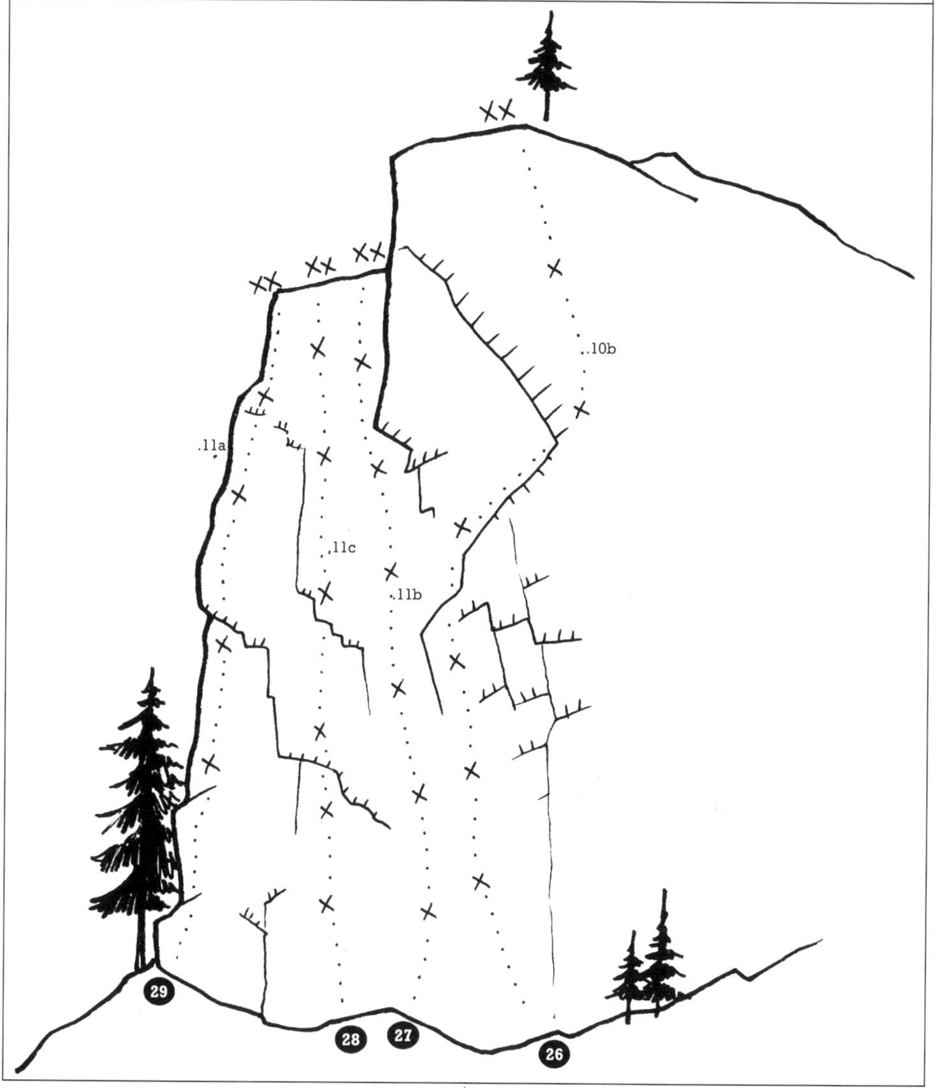

.10b

.11a

.11c

.11b

29

28 27

26

Slumbersome Ridge

Slumbersome Ridge is the highest of the major formations above Peannacle Wall. It is a blocky, angular crag, with a half-dozen east-facing routes that get morning sun and afternoon shade.

30. Ultra-Mega Slab (5.9) ★★ On the far right side of the crag is a square roof. Climb up a blocky corner to the roof, then exit to the right and ascend the slab above. Pro: quickdraws.

31. Ultra-Mega Crack (5.8) ★★ Exit the roof on the right and ascend the hand crack

Slumbersome Ridge

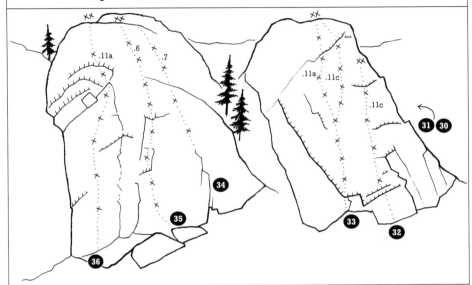

to the anchors. Pro: quickdraws, gear to 2 inches.

32. Imbibing Knowledge from a Mortal Furnace (5.11c) ★ Presently the first route around the arête to the left of *Ultra-Mega Crack,* ending at anchors halfway up the crag. Pro: quickdraws.

33. Stemming Out Beyond the Grey (5.11a) ★★ A direct line up the middle of the face left of *Ultra-Mega Crack.* A variation to the right is slightly harder (5.11c). Pro: quickdraws.

34. Autumnal Equinox (5.7) ★★ One of two routes up the slab across the gully from *Stemming Out,* this one following bolts on the right. Pro: quickdraws.

35. Slumbersome Ridge (5.6) ★★★ A clean, airy slab. Pro: quickdraws.

36. To Crest in Violent Slumber (5.11a) ★ A steep face and roof just left around the arête from *Slumbersome Ridge.* Pro: quickdraws.

Valley View East

Valley View East is located on the ridge about 200 meters east from the Bob's Area trail fork. Follow the road grade trail past the creek and around the bend. The cliffs are above and below the trail, all reached via short side trails. The half-dozen routes here range from 5.10 to 5.12, although none are quite as spectacular as the view up the South Fork Snoqualmie River valley.

Valley View West

Unlike its neighbor to the east, Valley View West has some spectacular climbing to complement its inspiring views. Located about a ten-minute hike beyond the Bob's Area fork up the Mount Washington Trail, Valley View West is a long cliff of compact rock, with unobstructed views. On a clear day, you can see Seattle and the Olympic Mountains. To get there, hike up the Mount Washington Trail about 0.3 mile from the Bob's Area turnoff. Pass an old stump on the

Valley View East and Valley View West

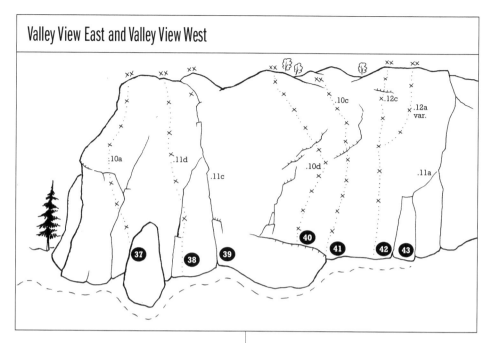

left, and in a few steps find a side trail leading up along the base of mossy rocks. Skirt around the little cliff bands and up the hillside about 200 meters to the cliff.

37. Stairway to Heavin' (5.10a) ★★★ Presently the leftmost route on the crag, beginning on the left side of a pillar. Climb a short, blocky wall and up the arête/face to anchors. Pro: quickdraws.

38. My Sorrow Bleeds with Such Delight (5.11d) ★★★ A steep, thin face line beginning just right of the pillar. Pro: quickdraws.

39. Ataxi Crack (5.11c) ★★★ The fine crack just right of *My Sorrow*. Pro: to 2.5 inches, quickdraws.

40. Traverse to the Hole (5.10d) ★ Start from a stumpy ledge near the middle of the crag and climb the steep wall, angling left up blocky rock to anchors. Pro: quickdraws.

41. Rock Party Vagabond (5.10c) A blocky line starting from a stump at the right end of the ledge. Not the best route on the crag. Pro: quickdraws.

42. And Empty It Remains (5.12c) ★★ A direct line up the steep face left of *Cascadian Crack*. An easier and more popular variation (5.12a) finishes at anchors just right. Pro: quickdraws.

43. Cascadian Crack (5.11a) ★★ A crack on the right edge of the crag. Pro: to 1.5 inches.

TRESTLE AREA

The Trestle Area is located directly above Ollalie State Park, and includes the several obvious cliffs visible from I-90, just above the old railroad grade and trestle. Because of its easy accessibility, this is the more popular of the Deception Crags areas, although much of the rock is just plain ugly. Helmets are recommended here, especially on Write-Off

Rock, Deception Wall, and We Did Rock, as handfuls of the stuff can be easily pulled off.

To get there, take exit 38 from I-90 and turn right. In about 0.5 mile is a large parking area just before the road crosses a bridge. The parking area is adjacent to the old highway, on the left as you drive in from the interstate. From the parking area, cross the road, step over the guardrail, and hike

Trestle Area Approach Map

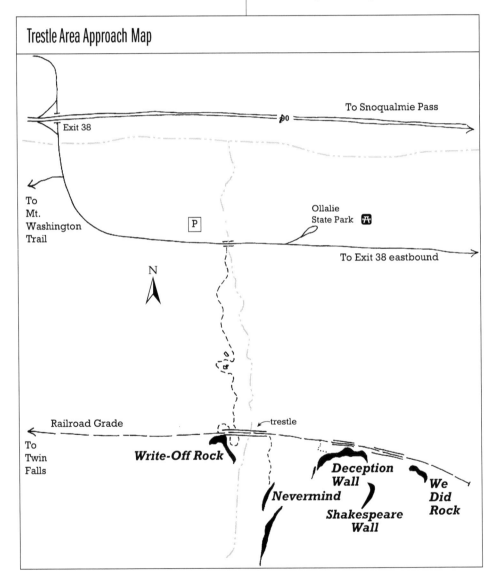

up to the trestle, first along the stream bank and then through the woods. The trail leads beneath the trestle, passing lower Write-Off Rock, continuing back underneath the trestle and up to the railroad grade and upper Write-Off Rock.

Some of the routes on Write-Off Rock, Deception Wall, and We Did Rock begin directly from the railroad grade. Because this is a heavy-use, multiuser trail, please keep the trail clear for other users. Also take extra care to avoid knocking off loose rock onto curious onlookers. Keep pets on a leash; dogs have fallen off the trestle. This is not a good area to bring small children.

Write-Off Rock

Write-Off Rock is the first crag you come to on the approach hike, just west of the trestle. A portion of the crag rises above the trestle, but the majority of routes are on the lower part of the wall known as The Substation, which is passed as you approach on the trail. This popular crag is usually crowded. The routes are described from left to right as you approach via the trail. Descend from various anchors.

Lower Write-Off Rock (aka The Substation) has several sport routes in the 5.9 to 5.12 range, which are mostly short, slabby, or grungy. Beware of loose rock, particularly atop the crag. Helmets are advised, since climber-caused rockfall is not an uncommon occurrence here.

1. Bwana Be Your Man (5.10b) Climb straight up the overhang on the far left side to anchors. Pro: quickdraws.

2. Stick Boy (5.12a) Turn the roof and climb the short headwall. Pro: quickdraws.

3. Slippery When Wet (5.10c) ★ Turn the roof and angle right to anchors. Pro: quickdraws.

4. You're Only Nice to Me When I Tie You Up (5.10d) ★ A steep, blocky face about 30 feet left of *Hangover Helper*. Finish at the anchors on the right; the left-hand finish is slightly easier, but not as popular. Pro: quickdraws.

5. Lovey Dovey (5.10b) ★ Ascend to anchors left of the pillar. A variation, *Namby Pamby* (5.10c), exits right and up the pillar's left edge. Pro: quickdraws.

6. Hangover Helper (5.11a) ★ Just left of the slab routes is a chossy gully. Just up and left of the gully is an obvious, bolted, over-hanging pillar. Climb up a blocky face and surmount the overhanging face on the right side. Pro: quickdraws.

7. Homo Erectus (aka No Running in the Halls!) (5.6) ★★ Climb more or less directly up the bubbly black slab. A fun route, but some loose rock at the top. Pro: quickdraws.

8. Rug Monkey (5.7) ★★ Angle right above the lip of an overhanging wall before heading up the slab. Pro: quickdraws.

Upper Write-Off Rock proper is the short, slabby wall encountered where the trail meets the railroad grade. It is a popular instruction crag, which is just as well, since none of its routes would otherwise see much traffic because they aren't that great, relatively speaking. The routes are listed from left to right. An easy Class 5 scramble up the ramp on the far left side can be used to set up a toprope. Beware of loose rock at the top; big chunks of it get knocked off regularly. Please try to keep the trail clear for other users.

Write-Off Rock

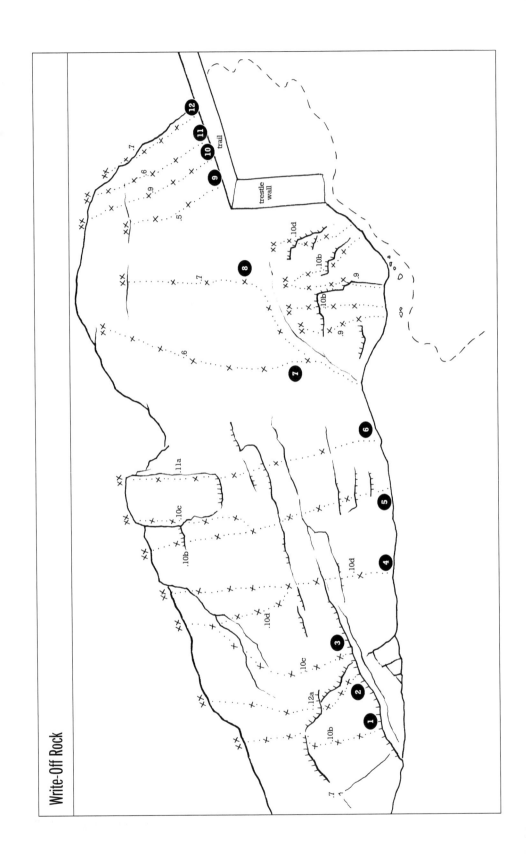

9. Flammable Pajamas (5.5) ★ The route on the left. Pro: quickdraws.

10. Knife in the Toaster (5.9) ★ The second route from the left. Pro: quickdraws.

11. Mom, There's Pink in My Burger (5.6) ★ The next route to the right. Pro: quickdraws.

12. Bottoms Up (5.7) ★ The route on the right. Pro: quickdraws.

Nevermind

Nevermind is a sport wall hidden in the trees across the creek from Write-Off Rock, with several steep, pumping routes. Nevermind is generally considered the best sport crag at Exit 38 (Amazonia notwithstanding), and is usually the most crowded. Although this wall has mostly solid rock, climbers should be aware of the risk of rockfall from the upper cliff, which has been reported. Helmets are recommended, especially for belayers, since some of the holds seem destined to pull off with little provocation.

To get there, cross the trestle from Write-Off Rock and immediately scramble up the rocky slope on the right, from where a trail leads to the base of the cliff. The routes are described from left to right as you encounter them on the approach. Because of the close proximity of the routes, route finding can be confusing. A few routes have several possible start and finish variations. When in doubt, just climb whatever route looks good to you or is unoccupied. Descend from anchors atop each route.

1. Rude Road (5.11c) The leftmost route on the Nevermind wall. Pro: quickdraws.

2. Steep Street (5.10d) ★ The next route to the right of *Rude Road*, passing a small roof and climbing the steep, juggy wall to anchors. Friable rock, so be careful not to pull too hard! Pro: quickdraws.

3. Under Arrest (5.12a) ★ Immediately right of *Steep Street*, pass a small roof and follow the bolts right up thin, slopey holds to anchors just left of a small fir tree. Pro: quickdraws.

4. Negatherion (5.11b) ★★ The next route to the right, passing a flake and small roof to reach a ledge just left of the shallow cave of *Corporeal Completion*, then continuing up the juggy headwall to anchors. Pro: quickdraws.

5. Corporeal Completion (5.11c) ★★ Slopey holds lead up the bulging wall to a shallow cave just right of *Negatherion;* continue up the pumpy headwall to anchors. Two finish variations are possible. Pro: quickdraws.

6. Powerless (5.10c) ★ The bolt line leading directly up from the left side of the shallow cave near the center of the wall. Pro: quickdraws.

7. Hangerville (5.11b) ★ Traverse jugs across the lip of the cave along an indistinct flake/ramp to reach the first bolt, then straight up the bolted face. Pro: quickdraws.

8. Neverigine (5.10a) ★★ Start as for *Hangerville* but continue traversing right, angling up the jugular face. Several finish options are possible; just connect the bolts to whichever anchors you choose. Pro: quickdraws.

9. Easily Amused (5.10c) ★★ The bolted face immediately right of the cave. Connect the bolts straight up to anchors. The *Constantly Amazed* variation (5.10d) goes left from the first bolt and crosses *Neverigine*. With bolts so close together, other variations are possible. Pro: quickdraws.

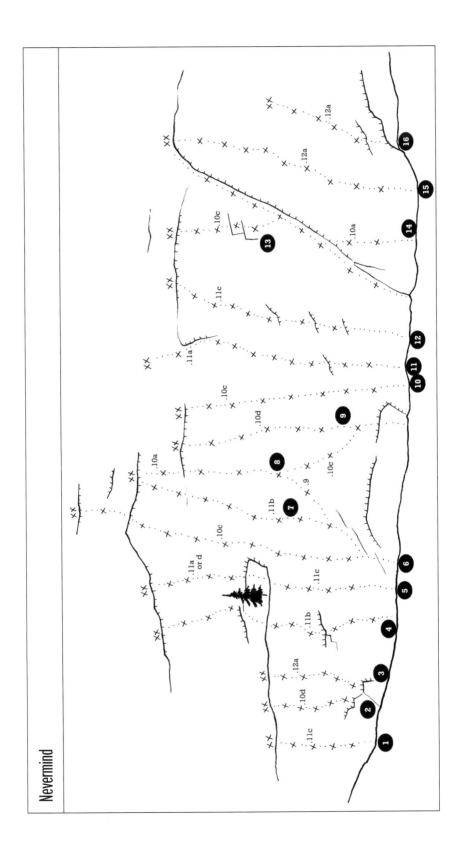

Nevermind

10. Love Bucket (5.10c) ★★ The bolted face immediately right of *Easily Amused*. Pro: quickdraws.

11. Architect Rally (5.11a) ★★ Connect the bolts up the steep, blocky wall immediately right of *Love Bucket*. Pro: quickdraws.

12. Canine Patrol (5.11c) ★★ The second sport route left of the *Strip Clip* ramp, immediately left of *Big Mama*. Pro: quickdraws.

13. Big Mama (5.10c) ★★ On the right side of the crag is an obvious right-leaning ramp starting with a flaky pillar. Climb up the pillar's left side and follow the ramp halfway, then finish up the steep, blocky face to anchors. Pro: quickdraws. (FA: C. P. Little 1994)

14. Strip Clip (5.10a) Climb the pillar's right side, passing two bolts, then head up the ramp all the way to the top. Usually climbed to set up a toprope on *Culture Shock*. Pro: quickdraws.

15. Culture Shock (5.12a) ★★★ On the far right side of the crag, just right of the *Strip Clip* ramp, is this overhanging sport route leading to anchors at the top of the ramp. Some say it's the best route at Exit 38. Pro: quickdraws. (FA: John Heiman 1995)

16. The Goblet (5.12a) ★★ About 10 feet right of *Culture Shock* is this shorter, slightly more difficult route leading to anchors halfway up the overhanging wall. Can be linked up with *Culture Shock* to make a longer but barely more difficult route (maybe 5.12b). Pro: quickdraws.

Deception Wall

Deception Wall is the most prominent of the Deception Crags when viewed from below, a long wall rising directly above the railroad grade, about 100 meters east from the trestle. It has several routes in the 5.8 to 5.13 range. Some of the routes begin from an exposed ledge on the upper right side of the crag, which are best approached via a short scramble on the right side. Most of the other routes start directly from the railroad grade. Please try to keep the trail clear for other users. Although the following routes are on relatively solid rock, Deception Wall has some very loose, shattered rock, so beware of random and climber-induced rockfall. Helmets are recommended, especially for belayers.

The routes are described from right to left as they are encountered as you approach along the railroad grade. Descend from anchors.

1. Won't Get Fooled Again (5.10a) ★★ Scramble up to a ledge 30 feet above the railroad grade. From the center of the ledge, climb a steep face, connecting the bolts to anchors. Pro: quickdraws.

2. The Underture (5.10c) ★ At the far left end of the ledge are chain anchors. From here, climb right and up a grayish face to anchors below the big roof. Stick clipping the first bolt is recommended because the ledge is narrow and exposed. Pro: quickdraws.

3. The Overture (5.11a) ★ From the ledge anchors, climb the steep, dark wall directly to the roof (5.10d to here), then up and over to anchors higher up. A stick clip is recommended here, too. Pro: quickdraws.

4. Underground Economy (5.8) A short, bolted route starting from the middle of the bridge. Pro: quickdraws.

5. Jiffy Pop (5.8) ★ A blocky face pitch starting from the left end of the bridge. Friable rock. The route can be continued via *Rat*

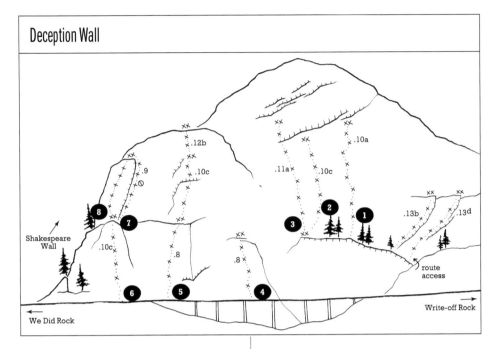

Deception Wall

Shakespeare Wall

.12b
.9
.10c
.10a
.11a
.10c
.10c
.8
.8
.13b
.13d

8 **7** **2** **3** **1**

6 **5** **4**

route access

We Did Rock

Write-off Rock

Face (5.10c), or all the way to the top via *I Can Fly* (5.12b). Pro: quickdraws.

6. Side Dish (5.10c) At the far left side of the bridge is this short, bolted face on a distinct buttress, which is best climbed as an approach to *Just Dessert.* Pro: quickdraws.

7. Just Dessert (5.9) ★★ A popular continuation of *Side Dish,* following the bolts up the right-facing, arching corner above. You can hike up and around the left side to get there, but it's steep and brushy going. One long rappel reaches the railroad grade. Pro: quickdraws.

8. Late for Dinner (5.11a) ★★ A bolted face alternative to *Just Dessert.* Pro: quickdraws.

We Did Rock

(See Trestle Area Approach Map on page 154.) We Did Rock is another 100 meters along the railroad grade beyond Deception Wall, across another trestle. This slabby crag

has several moderate slab routes in the 5.8 to 5.10a range, and one difficult sport route climbing the blocky, loose-looking buttress in the middle. The routes on the main slab are fun and fairly solid, but beware of loose rock higher up. We Did Rock has the distinction of being located directly above a gravel pit that is reportedly used for target shooting. Gunfire will certainly be distracting if you encounter it, but nobody's been shot—yet.

1. Easy Street (5.6) ★ The rightmost route on the crag, climbing a blocky slab. Pro: quickdraws.

2. Your Sister (5.7) The next route to the left. Very blocky. Pro: quickdraws.

3. My X Wife (5.10a) The next route to the left of *Your Sister.* Pro: quickdraws.

4. The Joker (5.10c) The next route to the left of *My X Wife.* Pro: quickdraws.

We Did Rock

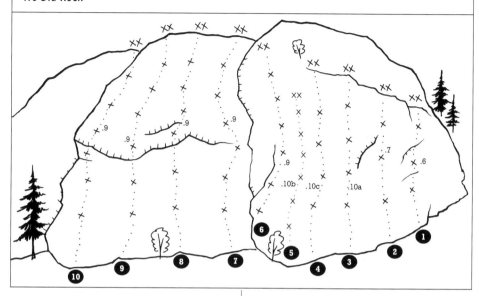

5. Bad Choo Choo (5.10b) Connect the bolts up the blocky overhanging buttress in the middle of the wall. Pro: quickdraws.

6. Blockhead (5.9) ★ Start up *Some Drugs*, then angle right up the blocky buttress right of the slab. Pro: quickdraws.

7. Some Drugs (5.9) ★ The rightmost route up the slab proper, staying left of the corner formed by the intersection of the slab and blocky buttress on the right. Pro: quickdraws.

8. Absolutely Nothing (5.9) ★★ The best route on We Did Rock. Pro: quickdraws.

9. Sobriety (5.9) ★ The next route to the left of *Absolutely Nothing*. You can make this 5.10-ish by climbing as directly as possible from bolt to bolt rather than zigzagging. Pro: quickdraws.

10. Black Caboose (5.9+) ★ The leftmost route up the blocky slab. Awkward and dirty in places but still fun. Pro: quickdraws.

THE FAR SIDE

The Far Side climbing area is located at the east end of Exit 38. It is a cluster of loose, blocky crags mostly hidden in the woods, which has mysteriously been transformed into a popular sport climbing area. There's no mystery why the area is so popular: An abundance of easy and moderate routes with reasonably short approaches allows climbers to spread out even farther. The Far Side was originally developed by Bryan Burdo, but latecomers filled in the blanks, developed new crags, and are still at it. There is still plenty of rock here to develop, although the best quality lines have already been done.

To get to the Far Side, take exit 38 off I-90 and follow the exit 38 road for about 2 miles, past the Deception Crags parking area, under the freeway overpass, and around a corner to the parking area. A new trail starts at the northwest end of the parking lot and parallels the road for a short distance; cross the river via the bridge, then find the trail on the right just across the bridge. The trail has been improved recently, with switchbacks added in places, and signposts have been installed at some side trails.

The Far Side Approach Map

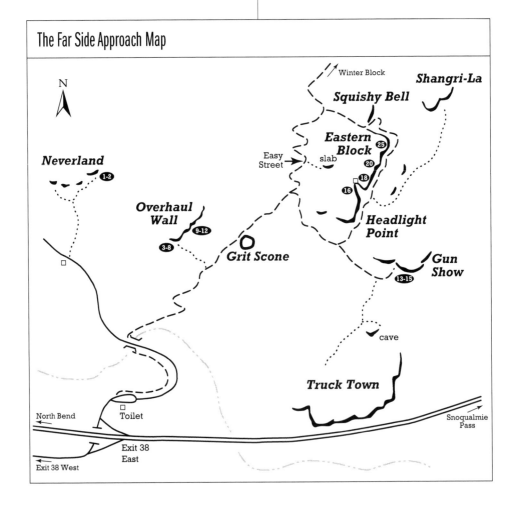

Climbers should be wary of loose rock at The Far Side. A lot of flaky, blocky rock may seem solid but end up falling on your head. Route ratings may change due to holds breaking. Significant rockfall has occurred here and will no doubt happen in the future. Wearing a helmet is highly recommended. Also, there are sharp-edged blocks and flakes on many of the routes, so bring several long slings to help prevent your rope from running over them.

The majority of routes are fully bolted, so you can climb all day with only quickdraws, but a few routes take gear, so it's a good idea to bring a handful of nuts and cams of various sizes, just in case.

Descriptions of and directions to the various crags are included here, but only a few Far Side routes are described in this guide. For details regarding other Far Side routes, buy the new *Snoqualmie Rock* guide or consult Mountain Project.

Neverland

Neverland is a cluster of small cliffs located west of the main Far Side climbing areas. It has four developed cliffs with a dozen or so reported routes in the 5.9 to 5.11 range (and a three-star "5.2+" route, apparently), mostly following a Peter Pan-esque naming convention. Only a few of the routes here are highly recommended. To approach, hike up the road across the bridge and continue a spell to a maintenance building (on the left). The trail to Neverland begins across the road from the building.

1. The Plank (5.10a) ★★ No topo. A three-pitch route on the Lost Boys formation, the largest of the Neverland crags, on the far right end of the group. Take the right fork trail to reach the wall. Start from a tree stump on the right side of the wall and climb up corners to anchors under a blocky roof. The next pitch goes left and up a short overhang to reach a nice, photogenic slab (crux). The final pitch climbs easier broken rock to higher anchors. The first two pitches can be combined in one, but rope drag can be a problem, and there are some sharp edges. It's easier to rappel straight down the cliff (using intermediate anchors on other routes) than to rappel the route. Pro: quickdraws.

2. I Can Fly! (5.11c) ★★ No topo. A short, overhanging headwall just left of and below the final pitch of The Plank. To get there, either climb the route leading directly to the base (Lost My Marbles, 5.10c) or climb The Plank as a warm-up and rappel in. Pro: quickdraws.

Overhaul

Overhaul is a broad, blocky cliff with some thirty routes in the 5.7 to 5.12 range, some of which are enjoyable despite their apparent defiance of gravity. It was the first Far Side wall to be developed, and is the last wall most visitors prefer to climb on. Frankly, I can't recommend it although it is reported to be not as bad as it looks. Some people apparently like climbing here.

To reach Overhaul, hike up the side trail heading up the hill just where the main trail levels out before reaching the Grit Scone. The side trail climbs steeply and reaches the far left side of the wall (at the area called Relief Camp), then traverses right to the other areas (Motherland and Slabbage Patch). On weekends, other parties may be climbing here, but on weekdays most people stick to the areas with good rock. In the interest of spreading people out, a few routes are included. No guarantee they are as

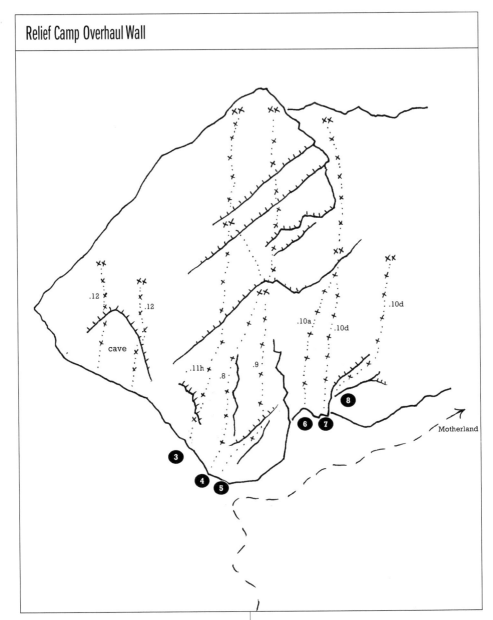

good (or bad) as they look. Don't judge too harshly, but do wear a helmet!

3. Complete Overhaul (5.11b) ★ Climb through the overhang low on the left side of the Relief Camp buttress, just a few feet up and left from where the trail meets the rock, easily identified by the single chain hanging

just above the gnarly overhang. Climb to the first anchor or keep going up and left to the top. Pro: quickdraws.

4. Chain Gain (5.8) ★ Climb sharp, broken rock up the nose of the buttress where the approach trail arrives at the wall. Continue up and right through the overhangs if you dare (*Chain Gang*, 5.11b). Pro: quickdraws.

5. Shelf Serve (5.9) ★ Traverse around to and then up the wall right of the nose of the buttress to the *Chain Gain* anchors. Pro: quickdraws.

6. Rhino Relief (5.10a) ★ The first bolted route up and right from *Shelf Serve*. Climb what looks like shattered rock left of some blocky roofs to anchors, then keep going if you dare. Pro: quickdraws.

Motherland-Overhaul Wall

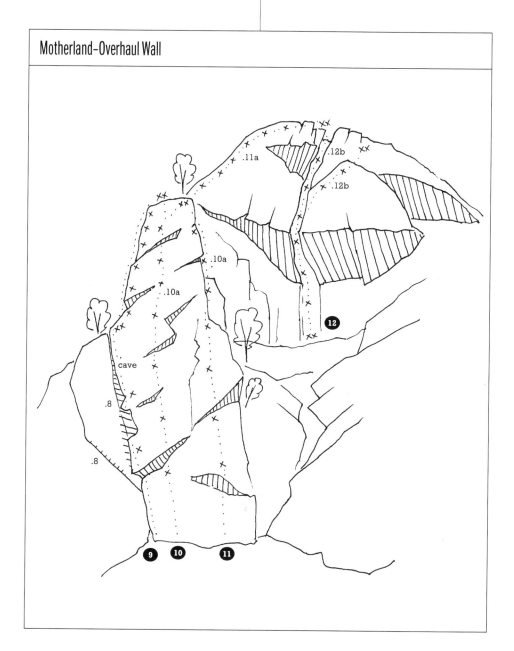

7. Give Until It Hurts (5.10d) ★ The next route right of *Rhino Relief*, tackling the blocky overhangs directly. Pro: quickdraws.

8. Jugular Vein (5.10d) ★ Traverse a ramp/slab above a cave, then haul blocky jugs to the anchors. Pro: quickdraws.

9. Corner's Inquest (5.7+) ★ The obvious blocky corner on the left side of Motherland, the blocky wall with the huge roof about 50 yards right from Relief Camp. A 5.10a finish (*Toying with My Affections*) goes right and up the arête at the top to higher anchors. Pro: quickdraws.

10. Toying with My Afflictions (5.10a) ★ Connect the bolts up the blocky white wall just right of the corner to finish at the anchors for Toying with My Affections. Keep going right across the lip of the roof if you dare (*Foreplay*, 5.11a). Pro: quickdraws.

11. Sheltered Upbringing (5.10b) ★ Climb the right side of the blocky white wall to the top. Pro: quickdraws.

12. Hovering Mother (5.12b) ★ Scramble up the grassy Class 3 gully to below the monster roof, then climb the ugly "birth canal" chimney through the roof. Must be better than it looks. A variation finish (*Offspring*, 5.12b) goes right to separate anchors. Pro: quickdraws.

The Grit Scone

The Grit Scone is a big hunk of slabby, mossy, hemlock needle-blanketed rock sticking up from the serene forest floor right next to the trail about a mile up from the parking area. You can't miss it. The rock isn't like the other rock in the area; it's conglomerate sandstone, deposited here by a receding ice age glacier. It has several short, popular climbs, all bolted (unless the bolts

were removed, as once reported, and not replaced). There are a dozen reported routes now, ranging from 5.4 to 5.11 in difficulty. The rock's small size and preponderance of easier routes makes this a popular beginners' crag, and it is often tied up with kids participating in climbing camps.

Sun Vista Slab (aka Easy Street)

Sun Vista Slab is a small, dark slab located on the upper south side of the Interstate Park formation. It has some of the best rock in the area—solid, compact, highly textured—with great views up the valley and several easy routes, making it a great place for your first sport lead. It is probably not a good instruction crag for groups of kids or for climbers with free-range dogs because the routes start from a ledge with a steep drop-off.

To get here, take the side trail leaving the loop trail just below the start of the first section of steep switchbacks. The routes are 5.4–5.5 in difficulty, all three-star routes, with a few sporting runouts on easy terrain. Lower or rappel from anchors.

Gun Show

Gun Show is the big, slabby buttress on the far east end of The Far Side crags. If you are driving east on I–90 toward exit 38, you can't miss it, especially if there are climbers on its most prominent route, the distinct long slab climb called *Endless Bliss*. It has a dozen or so routes in the 5.9–5.12 range, up to three pitches (unless you run pitches together), some of which are highly regarded, some not so much.

To reach Gun Show, hike up the main trail (just a few minutes past the Grit Scone) to an obvious side trail leading right. At last check an underground cable warning sign was still just before the trail. A few minutes of downhill hiking to the trail's lowest point is another side trail heading down the slope from a log, which leads directly to the base of the crag.

The chief complaint about climbing at Gun Show is the freeway noise, which makes it difficult to communicate. It's best to rappel rather than lower from anchors if you can't hear your belayer, to avoid accidentally being taken off belay. Get your signals straight before you climb and consider some visual signals here and at other Far Side areas beset by freeway noise.

The rock quality at Gun Show ranges from pretty good to poor. A significant rockfall occurred here recently, and there's no guarantee another won't happen in the future, here or at any of the North Bend areas. Some bolts were damaged but have been replaced. Check current conditions and climb carefully.

13. Endless Bliss (5.9) ★★ No topo. The long, clean slab in the middle of the formation with all the bolts and chipped holds. The route has two sets of anchors to facilitate descending with one rope, and it can be climbed in one longer pitch or two pitches. If you want to get really sporting, or feel the need to make a statement about over bolting and chipped holds, skip the best edges and a few bolts and see how it goes. Pro: quickdraws.

14. Super Squish (5.10d) ★ No topo. An alternate start to *Endless Bliss*, climbing the bolted corner just down and right. Pro: quickdraws.

15. Elation at the End of Eternity (5.9) ★★ No topo. A nice two-pitch line climbing the buttress left of *Eternal Bliss* more or less directly to the right edge of the rockfall scar

at the top of the cliff. Routes directly under the rockfall scar are understandably not as popular as they used to be. Pro: quickdraws.

Truck Town

Truck Town is the large cliff you drive by on I-90 as you head west from Snoqualmie Pass. It has several routes that don't overhang the freeway, on rock that is blocky and less fractured than the upper cliffs. The main Truck Town wall has some short, easier routes up to 5.9 in difficulty. The Truck Town Cave has some longer routes in the 5.11 to 5.13 range, pulling through big roofs. A trail leads downhill from the loop trail as you hike from the Grit Scone, before you get to the Gun Show trail. The original Far Side route, an overhanging hand crack called *Traffic Jam* (aka *Diamond in the Rough*) (5.11b), is located just off the freeway, and is hard to get to. Back in the day, we hiked in along the freeway shoulder, but you shouldn't do that. For route details, consult the *Snoqualmie Rock* guide.

Headlight Point

Headlight Point is a blocky crag at the lower end of the Interstate Park formation. It is the first formation reached while hiking up the loop trail from below (counterclockwise), and has several short, relatively easy routes on fairly solid rock on its southeast side that are popular when other areas are crowded.

To get to Headlight Point, follow the right fork of the loop trail down past the Gun Show side trail, and then up to where you encounter bolted rock. You'll first pass a short, compact, blocky wall with several short, bolted routes (mostly in the 5.6 to 5.7 range). Continuing up the trail you soon come to a side trail leading into the

Interstate Park Area

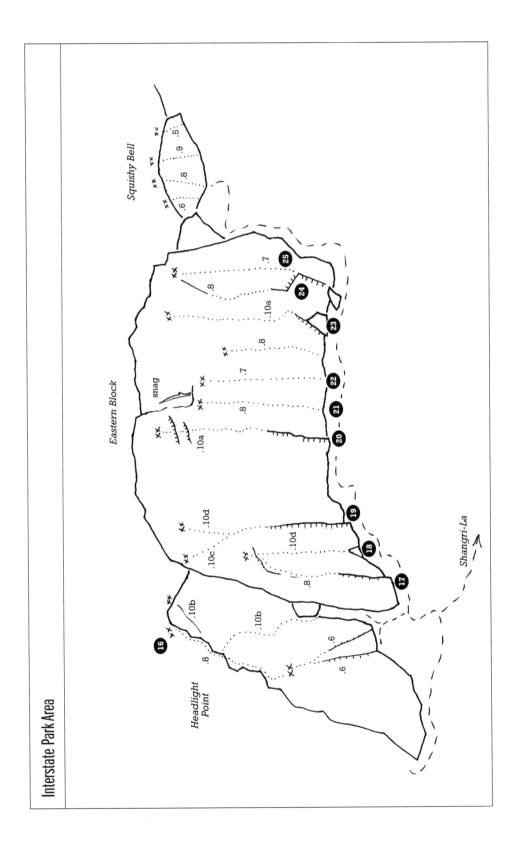

Block of Doom canyon, where a few more routes climb the left wall of the canyon to the upper reaches of Headlight Point. Alternatively, you can reach Headlight Point by descending the loop trail from Squishy Bell and past the Eastern Block.

Anchors on most routes allow for single-rope lowers/rappels, except those that go to the top of the wall. Always be sure your rope is long enough before you lower, of course. Freeway noise is a problem here, and there are some longer pitches where communication is difficult, if not impossible, other than by tugging on the rope.

16. Insomniac (5.8) ★★ Climb one of the two dirty 5.6 corners left of the Block of Doom gully to reach this fun, blocky arête that leads to the top of the cliff. A variation finish follows the crack on the right (*Bicycling to Bellingham*, 5.10c, gear to 3 inches). Pro: quickdraws; long slings to reduce rope drag.

Eastern Block

Eastern Block is the middle crag of the Interstate Park group, a long, steep cliff band with a fair number of routes that are quite popular and overall not too bad. The worst-looking route on the crag is one of the best, so don't let looks fool you. But do wear a helmet, especially when belaying, since your leader will no doubt knock a rock loose on you.

To get to Eastern Block, either hike up from below as for Headlight Point, or continue up the main trail another ten minutes from the Grit Scone and find the side trail (at the top of the first steep switchbacks) leading to the top of the cliffs at the head of a talus gully below Squishy Bell. If you take the wrong side trail, you may end up at the Sun Vista Slab instead. If you miss the turn, you'll end up at Winter Block eventually.

17. Impartial Eclipse (5.8) ★ Located around the corner to the right from the Block of Doom gully, climb the left edge of the obvious black slab to anchors shared with *Space Face*. Beware of rope drag. Pro: quickdraws.

18. Space Face (5.10c) ★★★ Start atop blocks and climb directly up the black slab to anchors. Pro: quickdraws.

19. Displacement (5.10d) ★ Around the corner to the right of the *Space Face* slab. Climb up a dark, right-facing corner and the wall above, staying right where another bolt line diverges to the left. A variation finish (*Strategic Displacement*, 5.10c) takes the left bolt line. Pro: quickdraws.

20. Ellie's Sweet Kiss (5.10a) ★★ There's a nice ledge near the middle of the wall from which several good routes begin. This route starts up a right-facing corner and continue up through blocky white roofs to anchors 10 feet left of a prominent white snag. May have a few loose holds, but otherwise good. Pro: quickdraws.

21. Ruins of War (5.8) ★ Connect the bolts to anchors just below and left of the white snag. Pro: quickdraws.

22. Ghosts of War (5.7) ★ Connect the bolts to anchors just below and right of the white snag. Pro: quickdraws.

23. Missing the Taco (5.10b) ★ About 30 feet left of *Kiss of the Crowbar* is this blocky route weaving through the overhangs. Pro: quickdraws; slings for rope drag.

24. Attack of the Butter Knives (5.8) ★ Starts just left of *Kiss of the Crowbar*, climbing left up a slabby corner then cutting back right up a crack to shared anchors. Pro: quickdraws.

25. Kiss of the Crowbar (5.7) ★★★ A Far Side favorite, climbing straight up what appears from below to be a vertical talus pile. The blocks have proven to be solid although there are a few friable-looking holds. Most parties skirt around the initial block on the left (bring a long sling to alleviate rope drag), but a direct start is more fun. Pro: quickdraws, plus a cam in the 1.5-inch range if you opt for the direct start, which you should).

Squishy Bell

Squishy Bell is a small wall at the head of the Interstate Park formation. It is a flat, vertical wall maybe 40 feet high, with just a few routes in the 5.5 to 5.9 range, all of which can be led or toproped, making it a popular instruction crag that is often clogged up with kids on climbing day camps. Lower or rappel from anchors.

Shangri La

According to the new *Snoqualmie Rock* guidebook, Shangri La is "home to some of the highest quality rock around" and is "graced with excellent climbs." If true, there is now a better reason to climb at the Far Side than "It's too crowded at Deception Crags." The guide reports a dozen routes or so in the 5.10 to 5.12 range that appear steep and blocky but not as fractured as some of the other Far Side crags. A trail leads down from the loop trail below Eastern Block. Refer to the *Snoqualmie Rock* guide for approach and route details.

Winter Block

Winter Block is the highest of the Far Side crags, and the least visited, probably because of the long hike, and also because it has only a handful of short, hard routes in the 5.10 to 5.12 range.

BEACON ROCK

Beacon Rock is a prominent basaltic formation rising above the Columbia River about 35 miles east of Vancouver, Washington, and some 40 miles west from Hood River, Oregon, near the town of Skamania. Standing 848 feet high, this volcanic plug is reputed to be the second-largest monolith in the world, after the Rock of Gibraltar. It is a popular tourist attraction; a trail leading to its summit offers panoramic views of the Columbia River Gorge. Due to its close proximity to the Portland area, Beacon Rock has long been considered an Oregon rock climbing area, although geographically it is located in Washington. As Jeff Thomas noted in his old *Oregon Rock* guide, "It's the best place to climb in Oregon, even if it is in Washington." Granted, Smith Rock has supplanted Beacon Rock as the "best place to climb in Oregon," but Beacon Rock is still a worthwhile climbing area.

Type of climbing: Beacon Rock offers mostly good quality, steep columnar basaltic andesite climbing, reminiscent of Devils Tower but more akin to Tieton River Canyon, running the gamut from thin-to-wide cracks, stemming test pieces, and a few bolted arêtes and faces. Although there are a number of one-pitch routes, most of Beacon Rock's routes are two to five pitches in length, up to about 400 feet on the highest portion of the south face. There are a number of routes in the 5.7 to 5.10 range, plus some 5.11 and 5.13 pitches. There's something for just about everyone at Beacon Rock.

Brief history of area: Beacon Rock has served as a landmark of the Columbia River Gorge for hundreds of years. Lewis and Clark camped at its base in November 1805, and gave it its name. It was renamed Castle Rock for a time, but the name Beacon Rock was officially restored in 1961. Henry J. Biddle purchased the rock in the early 1900s and constructed the summit trail, which was completed in 1918. The first ascent of Beacon Rock was claimed in 1901 by Frank J. Smith, Charles Church, and George Purser, via the northwest face. These climbers placed spikes and fixed ropes to facilitate their ascent, and iron spikes believed to have been used during that ascent are still in place. The first modern route done on Beacon Rock was the *Southeast Corner,* by John Ohrenschall and Gene Todd in 1952. This meandering line exploited the obvious weakness of the river face, following corners, ramps, and ledges up the right side of the south face proper, which was not climbed until 1961, when Eugene Dod, Bob Martin, and Earl Levin established the classic *Dod's Jam.* Route development continued through the 1960s and early 1970s, when most of Beacon Rock's classics were established or free climbed. Given the nature of the rock, only a few sport climbs have been developed here. Those that have been developed are bolted column arêtes and steep faces at the

Beacon Rock Vicinity Map

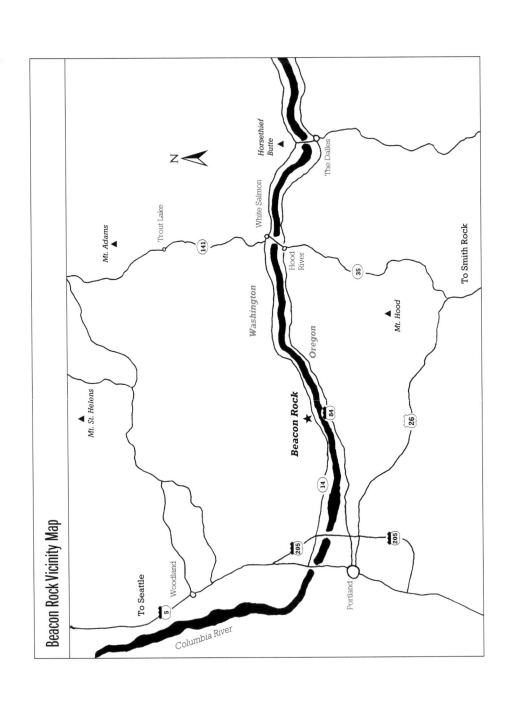

margins of the columns. There is limited potential for new route development at Beacon Rock, at least until the northwest face is opened to climbing, and while the enticing east face remains off-limits.

Seasons and climate: Climbing season at Beacon Rock begins after peregrine falcon nesting season, usually after July 15 each summer, sometimes sooner, sometimes later. Fall climbing at Beacon Rock is best, although summer climbing in the morning and evening is pleasant. Direct sun exposure makes the south face of Beacon Rock a virtual oven on many summer afternoons. But thankfully, if it's too hot for climbing, there's always windsurfing, hiking, and mountain biking. Winters are usually mild but often wet. Occasional deep freezes result in an abundance of frozen waterfalls in the Columbia River Gorge, but for the most part winter climbing here is unreliable.

Precautions and regulations: Beacon Rock is the centerpiece of one of Washington's most popular state parks, and as such is subject to various rules and regulations. Beacon Rock has a Climbing Management Plan in effect, which strictly regulates rock climbing. The most important rules and regulations are as follows:

- Climbing is restricted to the river face of Beacon Rock only. This rule is intended to preserve threatened plant species on the east face, and to prevent climber-caused rockfall onto the summit hiking trail on the west face. Consideration is being given to reopening a section of the northwest face to climbing, but at this time, the south face is the only area open to climbing.
- Beacon Rock is closed to climbing during peregrine falcon nesting season, usually from Feb 1 through July 15

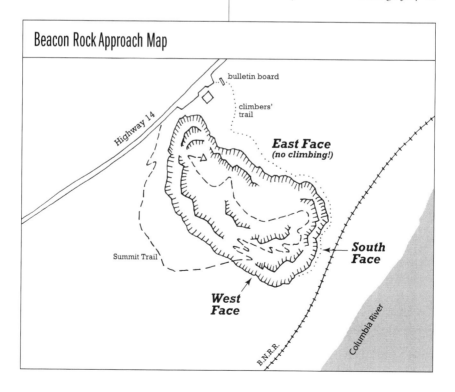

Beacon Rock Approach Map

bulletin board

climbers' trail

Highway 14

East Face
(no climbing!)

Summit Trail

South Face

West Face

B.N.R.R.

Columbia River

each year. In fact, a climbing hiatus was imposed at Beacon Rock for several years due to concerns over the falcons. The hiatus was lifted in 1997, but could be reimposed, especially if climbers ignore the climbing closure or tamper with the falcon's nest (presently at the right edge of Big Ledge). **The future of climbing at Beacon Rock depends on climbers respecting this closure and leaving the nest alone!**

- Climbers must use existing access trails to Beacon Rock. If climbers cause excessive erosion or negatively impact sensitive plant species, Beacon Rock may be closed to climbing. Also, the BNSF Railway tracks must not be used for access. Violators are subject to prosecution for trespass. Climber trespassing could lead to closure of BNSF land, which includes part of the climbers' access trail.

- Only earth-colored slings, webbing, and chains are permitted. Bolt hangers must be commercially manufactured for climbing use.

- Human waste must be contained and disposed of in appropriate park facilities. (The nearest toilet is at the parking lot; use it before you hike in, please!)

- Chalk is allowed. New routes using natural protection with rappel and belay anchors "necessary for safety" are permitted at the discretion of the first ascentionists. Power drills are permitted. However, new routes using fixed gear may be pioneered only with approval of the Climbing Advisory Committee.

- Organized groups and climbing classes of six or more persons must obtain a day-use permit prior to visiting the park.

Climbers should review the rules and regulations prior to climbing at Beacon Rock. They are posted on the bulletin board at the start of the climbers' trail. Any violation of the Climbing Management Plan is a criminal infraction under Washington state law and may result in restricted access or closure of Beacon Rock to climbing.

Rockfall is one of the primary hazards at Beacon Rock, and climbers are not very well protected from rockfall, especially below the trail, where rocks are sometimes accidentally dislodged and have even been purposely thrown down the river face by unthinking tourists and their children. Although the rock is mostly very solid, climbers should still be wary of rockfall and wear a helmet at all times. There is loose rock on ledges, so be careful not to rain rocks down on your fellow climbers. If you have a non-climber along, you can post a lookout at the end of the switchbacks on the trail. It's a nice place to sit and enjoy a sunny day—except for the steady stream of tourists, that is. A good way to avoid tourist-caused rockfall is to avoid the left side of Beacon Rock's south face on weekends.

Another hazard at Beacon Rock is poison oak. The stuff is relentless, growing back year after year on some routes despite gardening. Climbers used to organize annual route-cleaning days, where at the beginning of each season a number of routes would get scrubbed to remove poison oak, dirt, moss, etc. Since the area was closed for several years, this seems to have fallen out of practice, but the routes need regular cleaning to be climbed safely. Hopefully climbers will take up the challenge of keeping the routes clean so Beacon Rock can regain some of its former popularity. Cleaning of moss and small vegetation on existing routes is approved under the Climbing Management Plan. Just don't get overzealous and scrub off a sensitive plant species or remove any trees or shrubs, which is not allowed. Also, be prepared to replace rappel slings, fixed pins, and bolts, which can't be trusted until after careful inspection or replacement. But remember, install only earth-colored slings or chains, and only approved bolt hangers.

Climbers should be aware that some of the ratings are considered a little stiff. A 5.10c at Beacon Rock may seem harder to some, especially those not adept at climbing columnar cracks and corners. If you are new to this type of climbing, start well within your comfort zone before embarking on one of the harder routes.

Because the seasonal closure may be lifted early or remain in place later than July 15, call ahead if you plan on climbing at Beacon Rock to make sure the area isn't closed to climbing at the time you plan on visiting. Call Beacon Rock State Park at (509) 427-8265.

Gear and other considerations: As with other columnar rock, most routes at Beacon Rock require a comprehensive rack, including multiple sets of wired nuts, chocks, TCUs, and larger cams. The longer the route, the more comprehensive your rack should be. Some of the routes do some traversing, and require several long slings to reduce rope drag. Several routes feature fixed pins and bolts, so bring several quickdraws, especially on harder routes. Double ropes are recommended for rappel descents, although there are a few rappel lines that permit multiple single-rope rappels. Helmets are recommended, due to rockfall hazard. When replacing webbing and chains, remember that only earth-colored slings and chains are allowed, and bolt hangers must be commercially manufactured for climbing use.

Camping and accommodations: Fee camping is available at Beacon Rock State Park, which offers thirty-three tent sites plus several primitive and group sites. The park also features abundant picnic sites, kitchen shelters, "comfort stations," a dock and boat launch, and miles of roads and trails for hiking, mountain biking, and horseback riding. For more information, call Beacon Rock State Park at (509) 427-8265. All accommodations are available in Vancouver and Portland, which are about a forty-minute drive west on WA 14, and in White Salmon and Hood River, about a forty-five-minute drive to the east on WA 14. There are gas stations, grocery stores, convenience stores, and motels along the highway in both directions.

Emergency services: In case of emergency, dial 911 or find a park ranger. The Skamania County Sheriff is responsible for all search and rescue activity at Beacon Rock.

Other guidebooks: Olson, Tim. *Portland Rock Climbs*. 3rd ed.; Beacon Rock Topographic Resource Map; Thomas, Jeff. *Oregon Rock*.

Finding the crags: Beacon Rock is located about 35 miles east of Vancouver, Washington, on WA 14, the Evergreen Highway, running along the north bank of the Columbia River. For climbers coming from the west, simply follow WA 14 east from I-5 or I-205, just beyond the town of Skamania. If you are coming from the east, find your way to White Salmon (just across the Columbia River from Hood River, Oregon) and follow WA 14 west about 40 miles. Park in the parking area just off WA 14. A climbers' trail leads around the east side of Beacon Rock. Park rules are posted here. Sign in at the register before you climb, and sign out before you leave, if that is still required.

SOUTH FACE

The south face of Beacon Rock is an impressive 400-foot-high andesite colonnade. It is reached via a climbers' trail leading around the east side of the rock from the summit trail parking area. As the trail passes the southeast corner, it traverses up to the base of the rock near the *Cruisemaster* route. The routes are described from right to left, generally as encountered as you traverse along the base of the south face. Descend via rappel from various anchors, or continue climbing until you reach the summit trail, then descend via the trail. Descent routes will be discussed in the route descriptions,

where relevant. Although some rappel descents are possible with a single 50-meter rope, 70-meter ropes are now standard. Still, double rope rappels are necessary on some routes, and offer a faster means of descent.

Southeast Corner and Snag Ledge Area

The following several routes are located on the far right side of the river face of Beacon Rock, immediately left of the southeast corner. Most of the routes are one pitch in length, ending on a ledge system known as Snag Ledge. Descend via rappel from anchors on the ledges, or continue up one of the routes leading up from the ledges.

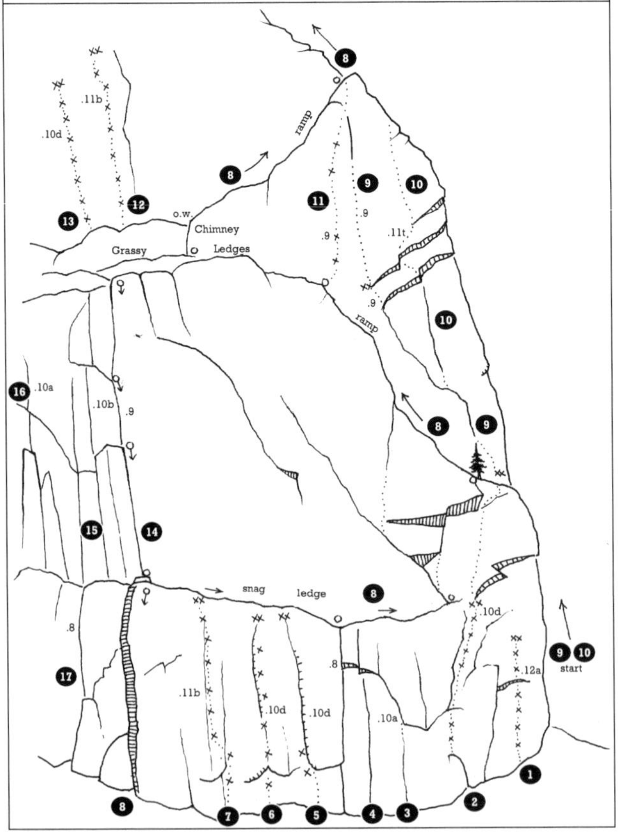

1. Stone Rodeo (5.12a) ★ An overhanging, bolted face pitch through a roof up and right from where the trail meets the rock. Requires some gear. Has a couple of loose blocks. Descend from anchors. Pro: quickdraws; cams to 3 inches.

2. Rock Police (5.10d) ★ A bolted face and corner/ramp left of *Stone Rodeo* leads to anchors left of the roofs. A second pitch joins *Southeast Corner* higher up. Pro: quickdraws; gear to 1 inch, including microcams.

3. Couchmaster (5.10a) ★ Start up the finger crack just right of *Cruisemaster*, pass a small roof, and continue up to join *Cruisin'*. Pro: gear to 3 inches, mostly smaller, plus

Beacon Rock–Southeast Corner

a #4 cam for the roof. (FA: Bill Coe, Gary Rall, Jim Opdycke 1985)

4. Cruisemaster (aka Cruisin') (5.8) ★★★
A popular thin crack pitch up the slabby wall below Snag Ledge, leading to an arching roof. Go left under the roof, pass it, and continue up a corner crack to the ledge. Variations up to and over the roof are possible (5.8 to 5.11c). Pro: to 3 inches, mostly smaller. (FA: Dennis Hemminger, Jim Opdycke 1985)

5. Icy Treats (5.10d) ★ One of several one-pitch routes on the wall between *Cruisemaster* and *Southeast Face*. This one starts up a bolted slab that leads into a white, left-facing corner. Pro: quickdraws; standard rack.

6. Blade Runner (5.10d) ★★ Climb up to and past a flaky apex roof into a shallow corner. Mostly bolted but requires some gear. Pro: quickdraws; gear to 2 inches.

7. Fire and Ice (5.11b) ★★★ A bolted arête about 50 feet left of *Cruisemaster*. Start up a bolted corner, then traverse left at the second bolt and connect the bolts and a thin seam to the anchors. Pro: quickdraws, thin gear. (FA: Tim Olson, Jim Yoder 1990)

8. Southeast Corner (aka Southeast Face)
(III, 5.7) ★★★ This meandering line was Beacon Rock's first technical rock climb, and remains one of the most popular routes on Beacon Rock. The route begins about 70 feet left of the bolted arête of *Fire and Ice,* climbing corners and cracks up to Snag Ledge. Traverse the ledge system right to its far right edge, then ascend slabby cracks up and right, skirting beneath the obvious overhangs, then climb a corner crack to a ledge with a big fir tree. Rappel from here, or continue left up the obvious ramps and corners to the Grassy Ledges. Scramble up to and ascend a short chimney, then follow the obvious ramp system right to the southeast corner of Beacon Rock. Easier climbing continues to the summit hiking trail. Several variations are possible along the way; refer to *Portland Rock Climbs* for details. Pro: to 3 inches. (FA: John Ohrenschall, Gene Todd 1954)

9. Young Warriors (5.9) ★★ A four-pitch venture up the right edge of the south face. A climbers' trail leads up to the southeast corner of the wall, where the bolted first pitch is obvious. Two pitches (5.8, 5.9) reach the tree ledge of the *Southeast Corner.* Continue up the arête and corners above, skirt the roofs on the left side, and wander up slabby rock to join the *Southeast Corner* route to the top. Enough bolts that route-finding shouldn't be a problem. Pro: quickdraws; gear to 2.5-3 inches.

10. Lost Warriors (5.11+ R) ★ A serious but appealing route paralleling *Young Warriors* on the right, tackling the roofs more straight on. Diverge from *Young Warriors* after one pitch, climbing inside and outside corners up the steepening wall, then weave your way through the roofs. Refer to Mountain Project for a blow-by-blow description and gear list. Pro: quickdraws; gear to 3 inches with some specific pieces recommended.

11. Cloud Nine (5.9) ★ Climb the *Southeast Corner* route to the Grassy Ledges, then head up the slabby wall above, rejoining the *Southeast Corner* higher up. Enough bolts now that route-finding shouldn't be a problem. A decent route when cleaned up. Pro: quickdraws; slings for rope drag; gear to 2 inches.

12. High and Mighty (5.11b) ★★ An exposed route on the slabby wall above and left of the short offwidth move above Grassy Ledges. Originally a trad route but may have

been retrobolted. Rappel from anchors or continue to the summit. Pro: quickdraws if bolted, otherwise thin gear to 1.5 inches.

13. Sacrilege (5.10d) ★★ One of the first fully bolted sport routes at Beacon Rock, climbing the steep wall left of *High and Mighty*. Pro: quickdraws.

South Face, First Tunnel Area

The following several routes climb the columns left of the first pitch of *Southeast Corner*, in the vicinity of the first of three man-made tunnels at the base of the rock. Descend via rappel or continue to the summit hiking trail.

14. Jill's Thrill (5.9) ★★ The corner system just up and right from the end of the first pitch of *Southeast Corner*, which is good when clean. Rappel the route without skipping rappel stations even if you think your rope is long enough. Pro: quickdraws; gear to 2.5 inches.

15. Fear of Flying (II, 5.10b) ★★★ A worthwhile route, climbing the first corner system left of the Snag Ledge anchors. Traverse briefly left and follow the corner cracks upward until necessary to traverse right to join *Jill's Thrill*. Rappel or continue up that route (5.9) to the Grassy Ledges. May be dirty. Pro: to 3 inches.

16. Right Gull (II, 5.10a) ★★★ An old classic 5.8 route with one 5.10 move. Climb the first pitch of *Southeast Corner*, then traverse ledges left and ascend the right side of a prominent pillar. Step across to the next pillar and belay. Two variations are possible here. Either climb straight up to a crack system, or step down and face climb left to a ledge, where your choice of 5.8 cracks lead upward. Continue to the Grassy Ledges.

Rappel or continue to the top via *Southeast Corner* or another route. Pro: to 3 inches. (FA: Dean Caldwell, Chuck Brown 1965; FFA: Dean Fry 1972)

17. Little Wing (5.8) ★★ The popular direct start to *Right Gull*, climbing the corners just left of the first pitch of *Southeast Face*. Pro: to 3 inches.

18. Old Warriors Never Die (5.12b) ★ A short, difficult bolted arête about 30 feet right of the first tunnel. Pro: quickdraws.

19. Seagull (5.10c) ★★ The corner crack immediately left of *Old Warriors*. Thin fingers, some stemming. Pro: to 2 inches; TCUs.

20. Ten-A-Cee Stemming (5.10c) ★★ The next corner to the left of *Seagull*, starting atop a boulder. A stemming test piece. Pro: to 2 inches; several small wireds. (FA: Avary Tichnor, Marlene Ford, John Haek 1983)

21. Av's Route (5.10d) ★★ The next corner left of *Ten-A-Cee Stemming*. Pro: to 2.5 inches. (FA: Avary Tichnor, Marlene Ford 1983)

22. Bluebird (II, 5.10b) ★★ A forgotten classic, climbing a corner system left of the *Right Gull* route, eventually joining that route. Traverse right up the brushy ledges above the second tunnel, as far right as possible, to anchors atop a pillar. There is a stiff 5.8 offwidth section below the pillar's top (pro to 6 inches or run it out). Continue up the steep right-hand corner crack (fist to hand, then narrows to finger), which gets progressively harder as you climb higher. The pitch ends on a ledge where *Right Gull* continues to the Grassy Ledges. May be dirty. Pro: to 3 inches.

23. Winter Delight (5.10b) ★★★ A popular pitch, climbing the first crack left of the first

Beacon Rock–South Face, First Tunnel Area

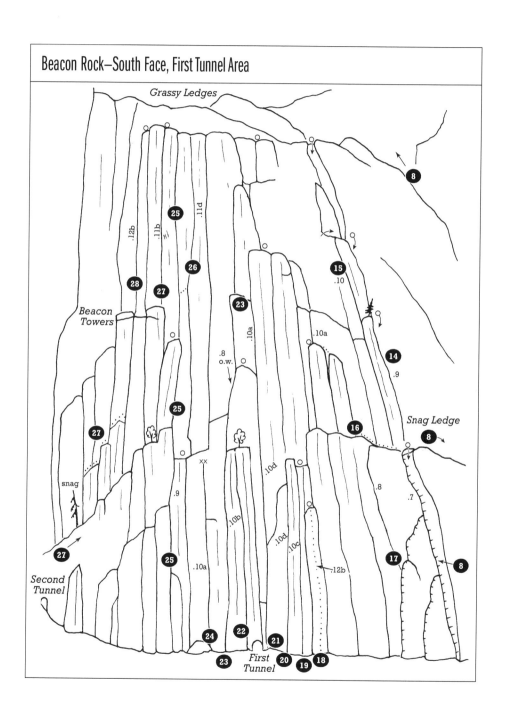

Grassy Ledges

Beacon Towers

Snag Ledge

snag

Second Tunnel

First Tunnel

.12b
.11b
25
.11d
26
28
27
23
15
.10
14
.9
.10a
.8 o.w.
.10a
25
16
8
27
.9
xx
.10d
.10b
.8
.7
.10d
.10c
27
25
.10a
.12b
17
8
24
22
21
23
20
19
18
8

tunnel. Pro: quickdraws; gear to 2 inches; #2 TCU recommended. (FFA: Ron Allen, Mike Jackson 1988)

24. Sufficiently Breathless (5.10a) ★★ A few feet left of Tunnel No. 1 is this corner crack that leads to anchors 60 feet up. Pro: gear to 1.5 inches.

South Face, Second Tunnel Area

The next several routes climb the columns near the center of the south face, above and to the left of the second of the tunnels. All of the routes on this portion of the cliff lead to the Grassy Ledges, although rappelling off after a pitch or two is a common practice, especially on the harder routes.

25. Blownout (II, 5.10a) ★★★ Another classic through route, ascending a steep corner system just right of the Beacon Towers ledges. Traverse right up the ledges above the second tunnel (or a 5.9 direct variation about midway between the first and second tunnels) to anchors, then continue up one of two steep cracks to the top of a pillar. The right-hand flake/finger crack (5.10a) is the original route; the left-hand crack is a 5.10a variation (*First Wind*). From the ledge, keep jamming up the corner crack above until you reach the Grassy Ledges. Pro: comprehensive rack to 3 inches; multiple to 2 inches. (FFA: Jeff Thomas, Ken Currens 1976)

26. Second Wind (5.11d) ★★★ A significant variation finish of *Blownout,* ascending the very thin crack that will "knock your socks off!" Climb 20 feet up *Blownout* until you can move right into a thin finger crack system that leads up through several small roofs. Good protection, clean rock, great exposure. Pro: to 2 inches; wireds and TCUs recommended.

27. Borderline (II, 5.11b) ★★★ An excellent two-pitch route starting from the ledges up and right of the second tunnel. Scramble up the ledges to a big, dead fir tree snag and belay. Ascend rightward up the left sides of several columns and the corner crack above to the Beacon Towers ledges. Continue up the steep corner leading skyward from the right edge of the ledge. Rappel the route or finish via *Sacrilege* or *Southeast Corner.* Pro: quickdraws; comprehensive rack to 2.5 inches. (FFA: Tim Olson, Wayne Wallace 1989)

28. Excalibur (5.12b) ★★★ The steep, thin corner crack directly above the left terrace of the Beacon Towers ledges. Start as for *Borderline* to the ledges. Without a doubt the best hard free route at Beacon Rock. Pro: quickdraws; comprehensive rack to 2.5 inches. (FA: Tim Olson, Wayne Wallace 1990)

29. Sky Fishermen (5.13a) ★★ A free version of the old *Grunge Book* route, climbing the corners and arête just left of *Borderline.* Climb the corner to a bolt, undercling left to a second bolt, face traverse (crux) left to an arête, then more face to a roof, and finish up the corner, which has been touted as "the most spectacular dihedral Oregon or Washington has to offer." Four bolts supplement tenuous gear placements. Pro: quickdraws; small stoppers and cams. (FFA: Matt Spohn 2013)

30. Flying Dutchman (5.10b) ★★ A lesser classic, climbing a long, continuous corner system just left of Beacon Towers. Pro: to 3 inches.

31. Ground Zero (III, 5.11d) ★★★ The direct corner system ascending the middle of the south face. The route starts about 50 feet left of the second tunnel, between two trees. Ascend the steepening crack system into the

Beacon Rock—South Face, Second Tunnel Area

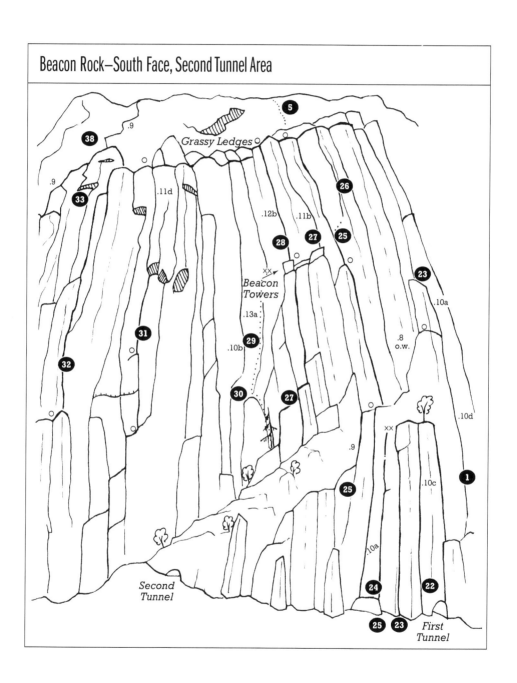

corner proper, then continue up the corner to the final roofs, which are passed on the left. Finish as for *Dod's Jam,* or rappel. Most parties bail after the first couple of pitches. Pro: comprehensive rack to 3 inches. (FFA: Darryl Nakihara, Mark Cartier 1985)

South Face, Third Tunnel Area

Note: Topo based on wide-angle photo. Routes are much steeper than they appear.

The following routes ascend the columns on the left side of the south face, in the vicinity of the third of the man-made tunnels at the base of the rock. Many parties climb the first two or three pitches to Big Ledge, then rappel. The peregrine falcon nest on Big Ledge should not be disturbed. The future of climbing at Beacon Rock depends on it!

32. Flying Swallow (III, 5.10d R) ★★★ The steep corner system starting at the far right end of a ledge system just up and right of the third tunnel. Approach via *Dod's Jam,* climbing halfway up the first pitch, then traversing right to reach the ledge system. Ascend a steep thin crack to a ledge on the left, then continue up the corner crack to a higher ledge. A short corner reaches the Grassy Ledges. Finish as for *Dod's Jam* or another nearby option, or rappel off. Runout, difficult to protect if fixed pins are not in place. Pro: comprehensive rack to 3 inches; duplicate to 2 inches recommended. (FA: Kim Schmitz, Earl Levin, Dean Caldwell 1965; FFA: Jeff Thomas, Del Young 1977)

33. Flight Time (5.11c) ★★★ The corner system just left of *Flying Swallow.* Approach as for *Flying Swallow* or via *Reasonable Richard.* Ascend the steep corner (many fixed pins) and the corner crack above to anchors. Continue past roofs to join *Dod's Jam.* Continue

or rappel. Difficult to protect in places. Pro: quickdraws; gear to 2 inches.

34. Blood, Sweat and Smears (II, 5.10c) ★★★ The long, steep corner system directly above the third tunnel. Start as for *Dod's Jam,* but halfway up the first pitch traverse right via friction moves linking discontinuous cracks (5.9) to a ledge system, then ascend the first corner, which passes a roof. From Big Ledge, finish as for *Dod's Jam* or your choice of alternatives. Might be dirty. Pro: comprehensive rack to 3 inches, including duplicate wireds and TCUs. (FA: Jeff Thomas, Bob McGown 1977)

35. Local Access Only (5.9) ★ A more direct start to *Blood, Sweat and Smears, Flight Time,* or *Flying Swallow.* Start just right of Tunnel No. 3 and ascend slabs and cracks right and up to the previously mentioned ledge system. Pro: quickdraws for bolts and fixed pins; gear to 1.5 inches.

36. Reasonable Richard (5.9) ★ Another direct start to the ledge. Start just right of the third tunnel and ascend slabs and a short corner fairly straight up to the ledge. Pro: to 2 inches.

37. Steppenwolf (III, 5.10d or IV, 5.11+ A0) ★★★ One of Beacon Rock's finest routes, at least to Big Ledge. Start as for *Dod's Jam* to just below the top of the pillar, where a short traverse (5.8) reaches a ledge at the base of the corner system, just below a large roof. Pass the roof and ascend the long, steep finger crack up the corner to Big Ledge (★★★ 5.10d). The complete route continues up the headwall above (first pitch free at 5.11d/5.12a), but most will finish via *Dod's Jam* or *Dastardly Crack,* or rappel off. Pro: comprehensive rack to 2 inches, including duplicate wireds and TCUs. (FFA: Bob McGown, Levi Grey to ledge 1977)

Note: Topo derived from wide-angle photo.
Routes are steeper than they appear.

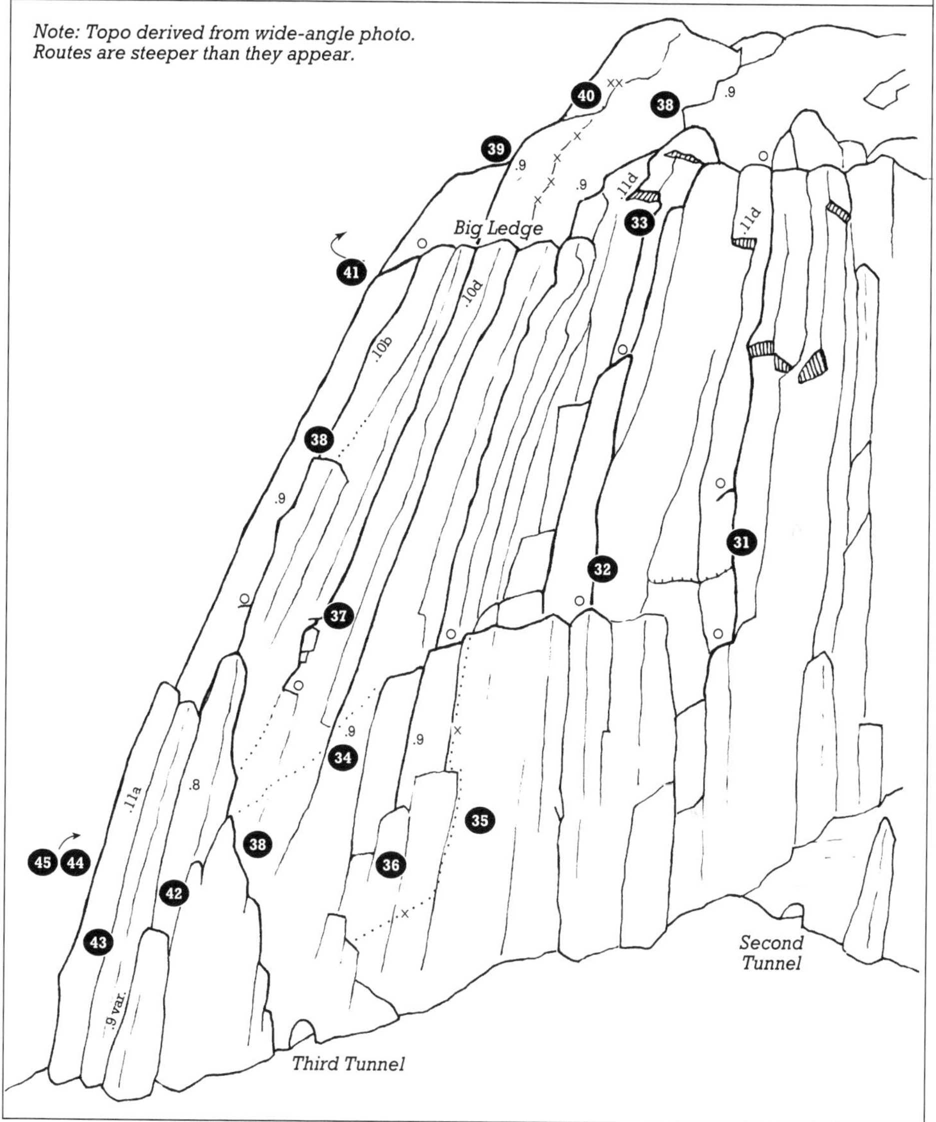

38. Dod's Jam (III, 5.10c) ★★★★ One of Beacon Rock's most popular classics. Start immediately left of the third tunnel and climb left up the right side of a slabby pillar (or start via *Free for All* like everyone else). From the pillar's top, continue up the corner a few feet and belay at a small stance. Continue up a steep layback to an exposed ledge, then up the crux hand crack above to Big Ledge. Rappel off or traverse right on the ledge (leaving the falcon nest alone) and continue around the big buttress via a steep crack, past an overhang, with some face climbing up the ramp leading right to a ledge. Thin cracks and corners lead up the headwall to the summit hiking trail. Beware of an easily avoided loose block on the upper part of the route, and of tourist-caused rockfall, especially on weekends. Pro: comprehensive rack to 3 inches. (FA: Eugene Dod, Bob Martin, Earl Levin 1961; FFA: Wayne Arrington, Jack Barrar 1972)

39. Dastardly Crack (5.9) ★★ A convenient and popular variation finish to *Dod's Jam,* climbing the corner crack directly above where *Dod's Jam* reaches Big Ledge. Said to be better than the final pitches of *Dod's Jam,* and the fastest way off from Big Ledge. Descend via the trail. Beware of tourist-caused rockfall. Pro: to 3 inches.

40. The Norseman (5.12b) ★★ Another variation finish to *Dod's Jam*, climbing the bolted arête on the right side of *Big Ledge.* Pro: quickdraws.

41. Squeeze Box (5.10b) ★★ Another variation finish to *Dod's Jam,* this one traversing down and left from Big Ledge and ascending a "bottomless" chimney and overhanging fist crack. Highly recommended, if you like that sort of thing. Pro: to 3 inches.

42. Free for All (5.8 or 5.9) ★★★ A classic corner crack on the left side of the *Dod's Jam* pillar, starting about 50 feet left of the third tunnel. This is a good first-pitch alternative to *Dod's Jam.* Surmount an initial short pillar (5.8 up the flake face or 5.9 layback up the left side), then cruise up the corner. Continue up *Dod's Jam* or rappel. Pro: to 2 inches.

43. Free for Some (5.11a) ★★★ The thinner crack just left of *Free for All.* Commonly done as two pitches, although one long pitch is feasible. Pro: to 2 inches. (FA: Bob McGown, Mike Smelsar 1987?)

44. Windsurfer (5.10a) ★★ The first corner crack left of *Free for Some.* Pro: to 4 inches.

45. Pipeline (5.11b) ★★★ No topo. On the right edge of the big, scary cave on the far left flank of the wall (the Arena of Terror), traverse right across an arête and ascend a thin corner crack to anchors. A second pitch (*Pipedream,* 5.11+ ★★, sustained) continues up the corner from the belay stance and is highly recommended if clean. Pro: to 2 inches.

West Face

The west face of Beacon Rock has a few popular routes. Hike the main Beacon Rock summit trail to just before it starts up the cliffs, then take a climbers' trail down and right to the base of the wall. Some of the routes are still dirty and have a few loose blocks and flakes, but will clean up with continued use. Although all of the routes have mostly fixed gear, bring a few cams and nuts along for intermittent gear placements that help alleviate some runouts. Descend via rappel from bolt anchors instead of scrambling off, to avoid knocking rocks down on hikers and other climbers. Refer to Mountain Project for additional route and approach details.

46. Time Bandits (5.10b) ★ A bolted face leads to anchors shared with *Kingpin* on the upper ledge, where several variations continue another pitch to the top. Pro: quickdraws.

47. Kingpin (5.9) ★★ Right of the start of *Time Bandits,* climb flakes and corners to a ledge, then up the slab above to anchors shared with *Time Bandits.* Pro: quickdraws; a few cams.

48. Garden Party (5.9+) ★ From the anchors of *Time Bandits / Kingpin,* move left and climb the slabs to the top of the wall.

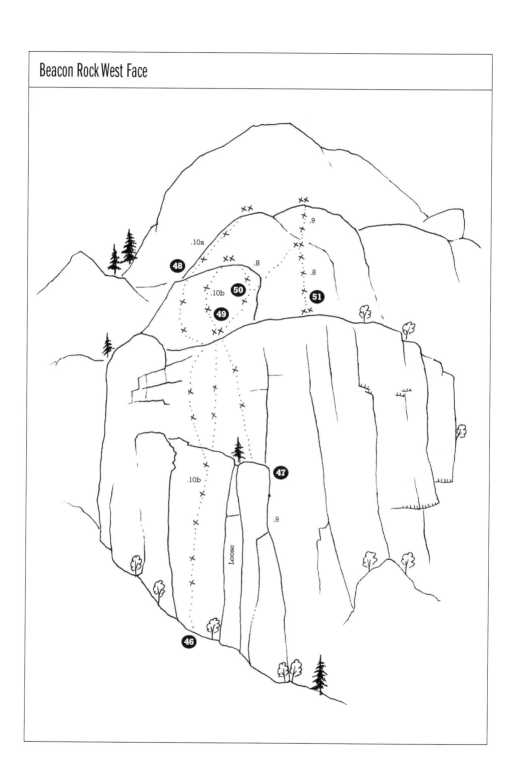

Beacon Rock West Face

49. Separation Anxiety (5.10a) ★ From the anchors, climb straight up the slab above.

50. Hazy Days (5.8) ★ From the anchors, go right and up the slab to anchors shared with *Separation Anxiety*.

51. Slow Train (5.8) ★ Traverse the ledge right from the *Kingpin* anchors to another set of bolt anchors, then climb the slab above to either of two sets of anchors. It's 5.8 to the first anchors, 5.9+ if you continue to the top. Pro: quickdraws; a small cam or two.

LEAVENWORTH

Leavenworth, Washington, the self-styled "Bavarian Village," is the hub of Washington rock climbing. This is mostly due to Leavenworth's central location, but also the fact that the town itself, not only the rock, provides a convenient place for climbers to meet, eat, and hang out. Leavenworth is blatantly and unashamedly a tourist town, with Tyrolean-style facades, umpteen gift shops, and countless dubious festivals enlivening what would otherwise be nothing more than a small town on the eastern flank of the Cascade Range. Unfortunately, the town has grown in popularity over the past several years, and is now often so crowded that, to steal a line from Yogi Berra, nobody goes there anymore.

There are three major climbing areas included in this chapter: Tumwater Canyon, Icicle Creek Canyon, and Snow Creek Wall. Peshastin Pinnacles, although traditionally a Leavenworth climbing area, is included in a separate chapter.

Type of climbing: Leavenworth climbing runs the gamut, from easy to hard, trad to sport, crack to face, short to long, with something for everyone to enjoy. The main Leavenworth areas—Tumwater and Icicle Creek Canyons—feature excellent, mostly solid granite and gneiss, with crack, face, and slab routes generally ranging from 5.4 to 5.12. Castle Rock, a 600-foot-high roadside cliff, is the most popular crag in the area, with a variety of excellent, airy routes mostly in the 5.6 to 5.10 range. Midnight Rock has many steep, pumping cracks, ranging from overhanging finger cracks to offwidths, mostly 5.9 and harder. Icicle Creek Canyon has a wide variety of excellent short crack, face, and friction routes on its many domes and buttresses, and is without a doubt the best all-around cragging area in the state. Nearby is Snow Creek Wall, a slabby 900-foot cliff visible from town, with several long, moderate free routes in the 5.7 to 5.11 range, including what is considered the area's most classic route, *Outer Space* (III, 5.9). Peshastin Pinnacles is a sandstone area about 10 miles east of Leavenworth, featuring many short friction routes and a few sandy cracks in the 5.4 to 5.11 range on its various slabs and towers. There are many other isolated sandstone slabs and pinnacles here and there in the Leavenworth area. The Enchantment Plateau, Lost World Plateau, and Stuart Range have some amazing rock climbing, which, due to its relative inaccessibility, is beyond the scope of this guide. For information about these areas, consult Fred Beckey's *Cascade Alpine Guide* or Jim Nelson and Peter Potterfield's *Selected Climbs of the Cascade Range*.

Brief history of area: Leavenworth is where Washington rock climbing began. The area's many crags were overlooked by climbers in the 1930s and early 1940s, whose sights were rightly set on the lofty granite peaks of the Stuart Range and the many

Sean Courage on *Givler's Crack* (5.8), Givler's Dome, Icicle Creek Canyon

unclimbed pinnacles, spires, and needles of the Enchantments. By the late 1940s, climbers were occasionally using a few crags for practice, which was all rock climbing was considered good for back then. You can still find an occasional rusty ring-angle piton left behind by the early era pioneers on an "unclimbed" route in Tumwater and Icicle Creek Canyons.

In 1948 the indefatigable Fred Beckey teamed up with Wes Grande and Jack Schwabland to climb the most obvious line up Castle Rock; their route, *Midway* (II, 5.5), is still one of the most popular routes in the area. Most of the early climbers' attention was focused on Castle Rock, although Beckey sought out and made the first ascent of nearly every major cliff in the area, along with anything having a summit, big or small, good or bad. As more climbers discovered rock climbing as a pursuit unto itself, more crags were "discovered" and more routes were established. During the 1950s and early 1960s, climbers gravitated to Midnight Rock, Rattlesnake Rock, Snow Creek Wall, and Peshastin Pinnacles, establishing a majority of the best routes in existence today. These pioneers included Ed Cooper, T. M. Herbert, Tom Hornbein, Don Gordon, Pat Callis, Pete Schoening, Eric Bjornstad, Fred Stanley, and a host of others, in addition to the ubiquitous Fred Beckey.

Most of the early ascents were done in the prevailing style of mountain ascents. That is, free climbing stuck pretty much to the easier cracks and faces; steep cracks were aided, sometimes using wooden blocks as pitons, and blank slabs and faces were bolted. There are still many old bolt ladders left over from these ascents; some of these bolts, more than forty years old, are still used for protection by today's free climbers. By the late 1960s and early 1970s, most of the aid lines

had been climbed free at fairly moderate grades. Most active during this period were Jim Madsen, Kim Schmidtz, Ron Burgner, Pat Timson, Mead and Tom Hargis, and Al Givler. After the aid lines were freed, climbers began exploring new crags, particularly in Icicle Creek Canyon. During the 1980s, dozens of new crags were developed, and many new lines on the major cliffs were climbed by the likes of Jim Yoder, Lee Cunningham, Doug Klewin, Dan Lepeska, Pat and Dan McNerthney, Tim Wilson, Dan Cauthorn, Gordon Briody, Kjell Swedin, Bob McDougal, and others. Particularly active in Icicle Creek Canyon in the late 1980s and 1990s were guidebook author Viktor Kramar, Geoff Scherer, Dave Lenz, Dave Bale, and a host of others seemingly willing to spend more time scrubbing lichen, trundling loose rock, and drilling bolt holes than actually climbing. Between 1992 and 1996, dozens of new routes were established throughout the Leavenworth area, and route development continues unabated.

Seasons and climate: Weather in Leavenworth is usually always good enough for climbing. The locals boast 300 days of sunshine per year, although that figure is suspect and was probably invented by the town chamber of commerce to boost tourism. From March to October, the weather is usually good. Leavenworth is protected by a rain shadow created by the nearby Stuart Range, making it a dryer alternative to Index on rainy days. Even when it is raining in Seattle, it is usually fair enough for climbing in Leavenworth. When it is raining in Leavenworth, Peshastin Pinnacles are usually dry enough for climbing. If it's raining there, Vantage is only an hour's drive away.

Temperatures regularly rise into the 90s and 100s during July and August, making it too hot to climb some days, but overall the weather is good, sometimes even in winter. The best climbing seasons are spring and autumn.

For weather information, call the US Forest Service at (509) 782-1413, or the local outdoor shop, Der Sportsmann, at (509) 548-5623.

Precautions and regulations: Beware of afternoon thunderstorms, which regularly roll through during the summer months. During such storms, it's a good idea to get down off the cliffs and wait until the storm passes before continuing climbing. Lightning strikes are rare, but quite possible. More threatening are sudden rainstorms, which can soak climbers and the rock, making climbing and retreating hazardous. During questionable weather, be ready to retreat, and have rain gear at the ready

Watch out for rattlesnakes, particularly in Icicle Creek Canyon. Ticks abound in Icicle Creek Canyon and at Snow Creek Wall, particularly in the spring but through summer months as well. Another potentially dangerous critter is the bat, a known rabies transmitter, which can be found in abundance at Peshastin Pinnacles and sometimes at other Leavenworth areas. Yellow jackets and stinging insects are a nuisance at many Leavenworth crags.

The big forest fires of 1994 weakened many trees, which have since come crashing down here and there. Salvage logging removed most of these trees. Still, climbers visiting Tumwater Tower, Goat Dome, Snow Creek Wall, and other areas in Tumwater and Icicle Creek Canyons should be wary. A tree falling in the forest does make a sound—a big one!

During hunting season, wear bright-colored clothing, or just avoid the more remote areas of Icicle Creek and Tumwater Canyons, popular deer hunting areas.

Nobody's been shot at yet in this area, but it's a realistic possibility.

Don't drink untreated surface water. Water is available in town, or from pumps at Eightmile and Bridge Creek Campgrounds. If you must drink stream or river water, it should be boiled or treated, to avoid *Giardia* and other bacterial and microbial contamination.

Gear and other considerations: Most routes require a comprehensive rack consisting of thin nuts and an assortment of cams, from 0.5 inch to 3 inches on most routes. The longer the route, the bigger the rack you'll need. On many sport routes, bring a few small cams and nuts, which can often be placed in pockets and behind flakes to reduce runouts between bolts. Slings are useful for reducing rope drag and tying off occasional trees and knobs. A 60-meter rope is recommended, and double ropes are required for many rappels.

Restrictions: Most Leavenworth crags are on land administered by the Wenatchee National Forest. There are no official restrictions for crags outside of wilderness area boundaries, although climbers are discouraged from removing vegetation from cracks. Within designated wilderness areas (such as at Snow Creek Wall), power drills are prohibited and entry permits are required. Bolts may be prohibited if the forest service's proposed ban on fixed anchors in wilderness is not reversed.

Falcons have been nesting in the vicinity of Midnight and Noontime Rocks, so these crags are closed to climbers May through July of most years. Notices are posted at the Castle Rock trailhead and local climbing shops and gyms, as well as on the Leavenworth Forest Service office website. To avoid any problems, plan your trip to

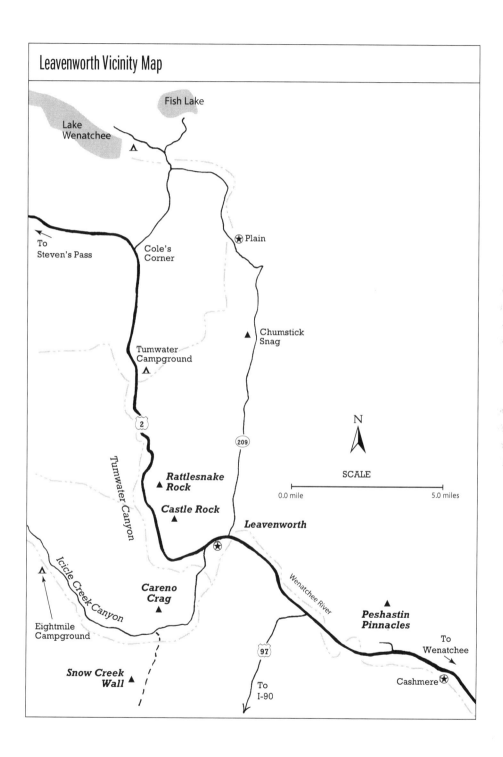

Leavenworth Vicinity Map

Fish Lake

Lake
Wenatchee

To
Steven's Pass

Cole's
Corner

⭐ Plain

Chumstick
Snag

Tumwater
Campground

Tumwater Canyon

2

209

N

SCALE

0.0 mile   5.0 miles

Rattlesnake
Rock

Castle Rock

Leavenworth

⭐

Icicle Creek Canyon

Careno
Crag

Wenatchee River

Peshastin
Pinnacles

To
Wenatchee

Eightmile
Campground

97

Snow Creek
Wall

To
I-90

Cashmere ⭐

Midnight Rock for the fall. Contact the Leavenworth ranger station at (509) 548-2550 or 2551 for current restrictions.

Camping and accommodations: Leavenworth has grocery stores, gas stations, hotels, motels, restaurants, showers, bars, banks, and ATMs, plus a golf course, miniature golf, and a train ride for those so inclined. You can find nearly every amenity necessary for modern climbers here, and a lot more. All too frequently, however, the town is beset by plagues of tourists. During the various festivals, and on most summer weekends, motel rooms and campgrounds are usually full.

The most popular campgrounds are Eightmile and Bridge Creek Campgrounds in Icicle Creek Canyon. There are more campgrounds farther up Icicle Road, and several others within a half-hour drive or so. Roadside bivouacking in Icicle Creek and Tumwater Canyons is no longer permitted, and you may be cited if caught. There are some sites where low-profile bivouacking is tolerated, but there aren't many left. For information on campground availability, contact the US Forest Service office at (509) 548-2550 or 2551.

Emergency services: In case of emergency, dial 911. The nearest hospital is in Leavenworth.

Other guidebooks: Kramar, Viktor. *Leavenworth Rock.* 4th ed. is the current comprehensive guide to the area.

Finding the crags: Leavenworth is no more than a two- or three-hour drive from about any point in Washington. To get there from Seattle, take I-90 east over Snoqualmie Pass, then north over Swauk Pass via US 97, then a few miles west on US 2. Alternatively, take US 2 east from Everett over Stevens Pass, which leads directly to Leavenworth. Likewise, from Spokane you can either take US 2 directly west through Wenatchee (shorter distance but longer driving time), or I-90 west to George, then north to Quincy via WA 281 and northwesterly to Wenatchee via WA 28 to join US 2.

TUMWATER CANYON

Tumwater Canyon, the deep gorge northwest of Leavenworth, has some of the best, most accessible rock climbing in Washington. The airy climbs of Castle Rock and Midnight Rock have been popular for decades, and the addition of dozens of traditional and sport routes on many nearby cliffs has merely added to the attraction.

Castle Rock, rising 600 feet directly beside the highway, is the most obvious of the Tumwater Canyon crags, and the most popular. It has many steep routes ranging from 5.4 to 5.12, with several classic lines. Above Castle Rock loom Midnight and Noontime Rocks, with Punk Rock at the rim. Midnight Rock, sometimes favorably compared with Yosemite's Cookie Cliff, has many excellent crack routes, mostly wide cracks, but some classic thin cracks and face climbs, including the amazing *R.O.T.C.* (5.11c), free climbed by Paul Boving in 1977. Just upcanyon from Castle Rock are Rattlesnake Rock and Piton Tower, with several enjoyable routes, including some of the area's best sport routes.

The massive walls of Jupiter Tower and Waterfall Column are impressive, but due to access problems, their obvious wealth of climbing routes has gone largely untapped. Many long routes await hardy pioneers willing to go to the trouble of crossing the river and hauling gear up the canyon walls to reach these big cliffs. There are numerous smaller and obscure cliffs and towers in Tumwater Canyon. Climbers of the Beckey generation went to great lengths to climb anything with a summit, no matter how difficult the approach or obscure the tower. Moss Tower and Hidden Tower, mentioned in Fred Beckey's 1965 guide, remain "hidden in the trees," and even by Beckey's estimation they were not worthy of repeat ascent.

There are many hidden slabs and walls on both sides of the canyon that appear to offer much potential for new routes. By far the most potential is across the river, but access problems mean only a few climbers have explored these areas, and until better access is afforded, few will repeat the established climbs, let alone pioneer new ones. For those up to the challenge, reference to *Leavenworth Rock* is appropriate,.

Tumwater Canyon Mileage Chart

The following chart lists mileages from the intersection of US 2 and Icicle Road in Leavenworth, and mileages between points of interest in Tumwater Canyon. Contrary to popular belief, Tumwater Canyon runs mostly north-south. US 2 traverses the canyon on its way from Stevens Pass to Wenatchee, providing convenient access to most of the crags.

Point of Interest	From Icicle Jct.	Between Points
Every Inch Is Hard	0.4	–
Clem's Holler	0.6	0.2
Tumwater Tower	1.0	0.4
Picnic Rock	1.6	0.6
Castle Rock	2.6	1.0
Rattlesnake Rock	3.3	0.7
Drip Wall	3.6	0.3
The Alps	4.4	0.8
Raft Rock	4.9	0.5
Waterfall Column	5.3	0.4
Swift Water	6.8	1.5
Tumwater Campground	8.5	1.7

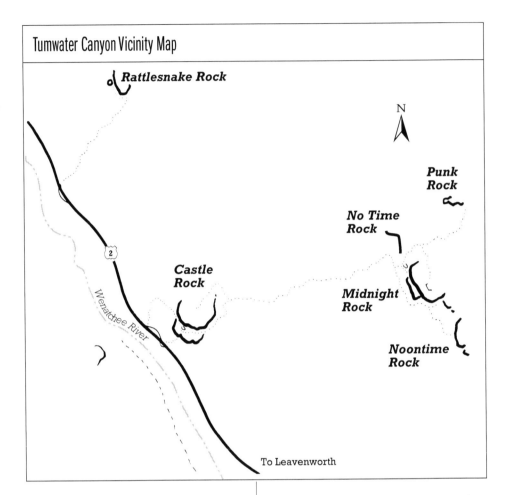

Tumwater Canyon Vicinity Map

Rattlesnake Rock

N

Punk Rock

No Time Rock

Castle Rock

Midnight Rock

Noontime Rock

Wenatchee River

To Leavenworth

Every Inch Is Hard

About 0.4 mile up US 2 from Icicle Junction is *Every Inch is Hard* (5.12b), a conspicuous zigzag crack toprope problem overhanging the highway. It is more of a landmark than a climbing route; very few have tried it, fewer have succeeded.

Clem's Holler

Clem's Holler is the collective name given to a group of slabs and crags located on the north canyon wall just inside Tumwater Canyon. The area is one of the more recently developed in the canyon, composed

of a half-dozen individual formations with about three dozen reported routes, primarily in the 5.8 to 5.11 range, and yet another place to get away from the crowds in Leavenworth, if that is still possible. A few of the routes are highly visible from the highway due to the usual aggressive style of lichen scrubbing practiced in this area, and this area has more than its share of the usual 5.10 bolted slabs, but there is some variety here and several very good lines. The approach trail begins just up the highway from the first turnout past *Every Inch is Hard,* on the left (river) side of the road as you approach from town. Pick a route; it is probably 5.10 unless it looks harder. For route details, refer to the current edition of *Leavenworth Rock*.

Castle Rock

Castle Rock is the obvious roadside cliff located about 3 miles northwest of Leavenworth via US 2. Rising some 600 feet directly above the highway, with a high concentration of routes varying in difficulty from 5.4 to 5.12, and with awesome exposure, Castle Rock is indisputably the most popular crag in the Leavenworth area, and rightly so.

Castle Rock is split into upper and lower sections by Logger's Ledge, a broad shelf that provides a convenient means of access to and descent from nearly all of Castle Rock's routes. The approach trail begins from the parking area at the base of the cliff, on the left, and leads across Logger's Ledge and eventually to the summit. To reach the base of Castle Rock, find a short trail leading up from the right edge of the parking area.

Castle Rock's popularity means it is often crowded, especially on weekends, although on some summer weekends the rock is inexplicably vacant. Crowded climbing conditions can lead to problems, although usually climbers can spread out and thus avoid traffic jams on all but the most popular routes. Rocks are frequently knocked off from Logger's Ledge onto climbers on the lower half of the cliff, making helmets a very wise accessory. The number of easier routes means that inexperienced climbers are often present on Castle Rock. They are prone to dropping the occasional carabiner or chock onto inattentive belayers and innocent bystanders. Use caution when beneath other climbers, and take care not to kick rocks off Logger's Ledge. Although rattlesnakes were once common at Castle Rock, they are rarely if ever seen anymore.

Several of Castle Rock's longer routes are Grade II. A complete ascent of Castle Rock from base to summit is Grade III by whatever combination of routes you choose.

Upper Castle Rock

Logger's Ledge splits Castle Rock into upper and lower halves. The more popular upper half is described first. A trail leads upward from the left side of the parking area, and takes about fifteen minutes to Logger's Ledge. The routes are described from left to right as you encounter them on the approach. Be careful not to knock off rocks from Logger's Ledge, as they are the major hazard to climbers below.

1. Rainshadow (5.12a) ★ Start up the ramp just left of the big boulder encountered just as you reach Logger's Ledge. A blocky wall above the ramp reaches an obvious right-slanting thin flake (5.11d). Continue up the overhanging face above (crux) to sling anchors. Pro: to 2 inches, including wired nuts.

2. Das Musak (5.11d) ★ From atop the big boulder, climb left past blocky roofs to the *Rainshadow* anchors. Athletic, technical, pumping—the works. Pro: to 2 inches; quickdraws for fixed pins.

3. Rainbow Connection (5.11b) ★ From the top of the big boulder, climb right and up past roofs to a thin crack. Pro: to 1 inch.

4. Saints (5.8) ★★ This three-pitch pseudo-classic begins via the obvious dihedral left of the *Angel* crack. Once past the initial corner, traverse blocky ledges left and up to a ledge with a large fir tree. Continue up a steep, shallow corner and short, difficult face, then easier cracks to the top. Pro: to 2 inches.

Upper Castle Rock

5. Angel (5.10b) ★★★ This popular route begins with the obvious thin crack just left of Jell-O Tower. The crack is the crux; the rest of the route is 5.7 or 5.8, depending on which way you go. Once past a short corner on pitch two, easier cracks and slabs lead to the top. Pro: to 2 inches. (FFA: Fred Beckey, Don Gordon 1962)

Short 'n Sassy variation (5.10a) ★ Link the *Saints* corner with *Angel*'s first belay ledge via a short, thin crack. Pro: to 1 inch.

Jell-O Tower

The following eight routes are located on Jell-O Tower (traditionally misspelled "Jello" Tower), the squat, blocky tower located on the left side of Logger's Ledge. You can rappel from anchors atop Jell-O Tower or continue to the top of Castle Rock.

6. Damnation Crack (5.8) ★★ The wide corner crack just right of *Angel,* with layback, jam, face, and stemming moves. A good test of your all-around climbing skills. You'll either love it or hate it. Pro: to 3 or 4 inches. (FFA: T. M. Herbert, Ed Cooper 1960)

7. No Such Thing as a Free Lunge (5.11d R/X) ★ A poorly protected route climbing the face between *Damnation* and *M.F. Direct,* joining *M.F. Direct* at the upper roof. "The longest possible fall is 20 feet, if protection

holds . . ." Best toproped. Pro: to 1 inch, including RPs and TCUs.

8. M.F. Overhang (5.10c) ★★★ A classic route up the arête and overhanging thin crack right of *Damnation*. Traditionally rated 5.10c, but some think it's 5.11a. Pro: to 1 inch. (FFA: Al Givler 1972)

M.F. Direct variation (5.11b) ★★ Stay left after the crux thin crack and continue up the left-leaning dihedral to an apex roof. Pro: to 1 inch; with small RPs and TCUs recommended. (FA: Peter Croft 1983)

9. The Nose (5.10d) ★★ An exposed pitch up the outside face of Jell-O Tower, climbing

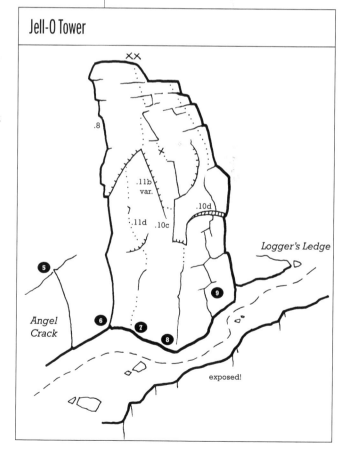

Jell-O Tower

Upper Castle Rock

thin, shallow cracks through a roof. Pro: to 1 inch. (FFA: Mead Hargis 1972)

10. South Face (5.8) ★★ A popular Jell-O Tower route, climbing a corner crack and face through a blocky roof, just down and left from the *Midway* chimney. Pro: to 2 inches.

11. Midway Route (5.5) ★★ Castle Rock's original route, and most popular, owing largely to its easy climbing, prominent position, awesome exposure, and fabled classic status. Begin via the wide chimney on the right side of Jell-O Tower. From the tower's summit, step across to the main cliff and traverse ledges right to reach the obvious wide crack system leading to the top. The original ascent reportedly climbed the dihedral as for *Midway Direct* before traversing over to the crack, but most parties since have traversed to the crack sooner following the current standard route. Pro: to 3 inches. (FA: Fred Beckey, Wes Grande, Jack Schwabland 1948)

12. Midway Direct (5.6) ★★★ An airy finish variation of *Midway*. Do the step-across move, then climb straight up a corner, step left, and climb exposed face moves to a broad ledge, from where many variations to the top are possible. Pro: to 2 inches. (FA: T. M. Herbert, Eric Bjornstad, R. Neufer 1960)

13. Midway Direct Direct (5.9) ★★ Traverse slightly left from the top of Jell-O Tower and climb a thin, bolted face, joining *Midway Direct* at the upper ledge. A good continuation of *Damnation Crack*. Pro: to 2 inches.

14. Winter Solstice (5.6) ★★ An exposed route paralleling *Midway* on the right. Climb the ramp right of the *Midway* chimney, angling left under the blocky overhangs, then directly up steep face and cracks above.

Pro: to 2 inches. (FA: Eric Bjornstad, B. Hooper 1960)

15. Devil's Fright (5.10c) ★★ A blocky roof above the *Winter Solstice* ramp. Continue up steep rock to the top. Pro: to 1.5 inches. (FFA: Jim Madsen, Ron Burgner 1966)

16. Devil's Delight (5.10c) ★★ The white, blocky wall and roofs right of *Devil's Fright*. Pro: to 1 inch. (FFA: Jim Madsen, Tom Hargis 1966)

17. Crack of Doom (5.10a) ★★★ An excellent, steep route climbing the obvious crack splitting the blocky wall at the right edge of the ramp. Continue up exposed face and cracks to the top. Pro: to 2.5 inches. (FFA: Jim Madsen, Tom Hargis 1966)

18. Old Gray Mare (5.8) ★★ A fun face pitch leading up the arête directly below *Crack of Doom*. Pro: to 1 inch.

19. Canary (5.8) ★★★ This airy, scary three-pitch outing up the steepest portion of upper Castle Rock is one of Leavenworth's best routes. Start via an obvious shallow corner, traverse right and climb a dihedral to a roof, where a short rightward traverse gains Saber Ledge. Alternatively, traverse farther right and climb a vertical crack, then mantle onto the ledge. From Saber Ledge, a scary leftward traverse leads to the lip of the overhang, where exposed, continuous face moves continue up the headwall. Not a good choice for your first 5.8 lead. Pro: to 2 inches; quickdraws; a #4.0 Friend to protect the roof traverse. (FFA: Hank Mather, John Rupley 1960)

20. Cat Burglar (5.6) ★★ A bouldering move gains an obvious ramp just right of the start of *Canary*. Continue up the ramp and shallow cracks to reach Saber Ledge, from where the route continues up the face and cracks right of the chimney. Pro: to 2 inches.

21. Diretissima (5.7) ★★ Discontinuous, shallow face cracks left of the start of *Saber* lead to Saber Ledge and beyond. Enjoyable, exposed climbing. Pro: to 1 inch. (FA: Eric Bjornstad, Ed Cooper 1960)

22. Saber (5.5) ★★★ Another old classic, climbing the obvious dihedral and chimney on the right side of upper Castle Rock. At the right end of Logger's Ledge, at the base of *Century,* climb left over a short buttress into the obvious big, slabby dihedral, which is followed to Saber Ledge. From the ledge, climb the obvious big chimney directly to easier face and cracks leading to the top. Pro: to 2 inches. (FA: Pete Schoening, Dick Widrig 1949)

23. Century (5.8) ★★ A continuous face climb up the buttress right of the *Saber* dihedral. Some old, mangled fixed pins and bolts protect the first pitch, which is continuously difficult. Not the best choice for your first 5.8 lead. Pro: to 2 inches. (FFA: Eric Bjornstad, Ed Cooper 1960)

Lower Castle Rock

Approach these routes from the right side of the parking area via a short trail leading to the lowest point of the wall. Beware of rockfall from Logger's Ledge; helmets are recommended. With many intersecting ledges, combinations of different routes are easily possible. The routes are described from left to right along the base of the rock, then again from left to right as you traverse along the lower ledge system.

The following several routes begin at the base of lower Castle Rock. The chimney of *The Fault* is the most obvious feature here.

24. Mr. Clean (5.10c) ★ The face route farthest left of *The Fault* chimney. After 20 feet of thin climbing it eases up. Pro: to 1 inch.

25. Smut (5.10a) ★ A thin face route up the middle of the wall left of the chimney, marked by a bolt at the start. Pro: to 0.5 inch; wired nuts.

26. The Fault (5.6) A long, meandering route climbing the line of least resistance from the base of Castle Rock to Logger's Ledge. A good route to combine with *Saber* for a Grade III, 5.6 outing from the bottom to the top of Castle Rock. Begin in the obvious big chimney in the middle of the lower wall, then follow rightward-wandering ramps up to and around the big roofs on the upper right side, eventually reaching Logger's Ledge just below the start of *Saber.* Either traverse off under *Bird's Nest Overhang* or climb a 5.6 dihedral directly to Logger's Ledge. Pro: to 3 inches. (FA: Eric Bjornstad, Ed Cooper 1960)

27. Blood Transfusion (5.10d) The route immediately right of *The Fault* chimney. Pro: quickdraws; gear to #1.5 Friend.

28. Clean Love (5.10b) ★ Face cracks just right of *Transfusion.* Pro: to 2 inches. (FA: Doug and Karen Klewin 1980)

29. AIDS Victim (5.10c) ★ A bolted face climb just right of *Clean Love.* Pro: quickdraws; a few pieces to 1.5 inches. (FA: Jim Yoder 1988)

30. Parental Discretion Advised (5.10b) ★ Another bolted face just right of *AIDS Victim.* Pro: quickdraws; a few pieces to 1.5 inches. (FA: Jim Yoder, Geoff Scherer 1988)

The following routes climb above the ledge system splitting the lower wall about 100 feet above its base. This portion of the wall is blocky, with many roofs and cracks. Most

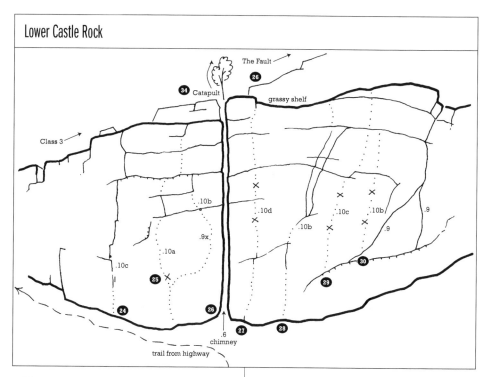

Lower Castle Rock

The Fault

(26)

(34) Catapult

grassy shelf

Class 3

.10b

.10d

.10c

.10b

.9

.10b

.9x

.10b

.9

.10a

(30)

.10c

(25)

(29)

(24)

(26)

(27)

(28)

.6
chimney

trail from highway

of these routes lead to Logger's Ledge, eventually.

31. Monkey Lip (5.11d) ★ An athletic route just left of the start of *Brass Balls,* traversing left under the roof, then turning the lip. Pro: to 1 inch, quickdraws for fixed pins.

32. Brass Balls (5.10b) ★★★ An improbable-looking route climbing past two big roofs on the left side of lower Castle Rock. Athletic moves past the first roof lead to a thin crack crux above the second roof. Save a few nuts and cams for the belay. Pro: to 3 inches, long slings to reduce rope drag. (FA: Jim Yoder, Paul Christiansen 1980)

33. Shriek of the Mutilated (5.12a) ★ The obvious thin crack splitting the big roof right of *Brass Balls.* Pro: to 2 inches, including TCUs.

34. Catapult (5.8) ★★★ A very enjoyable route climbing a crack and corner system

through the roofs directly above *The Fault* chimney. After passing the initial roof, continue up an exposed dihedral to easier ground, or hang out on Stoner's Ledge and dig the scene. Pro: to 2.5 inches. (FA: Jim Stuart, B. D. Nelson 1960)

35. The Vertebrae (5.10b) ★ From the big, flat ledge midway up *Catapult* (Stoner's Ledge is on the right), climb a thin crack directly through a blocky roof. Pro: to 1 inch.

36. The Bone (aka Penstemon) (5.9) ★★ The wide flake just right of the flat ledge. Surmount the horizontal pillar (The Spike) via a gymnastic heel hook and continue up easier ground to Logger's Ledge. Pro: to 3 inches.

37. Idiot's Delight (5.9) ★ Face climb left from the left end of the upper ledge of *The Fault,* then pass the roofs and continue up to Logger's Ledge. Fairly obvious when

Lower Castle Rock

you get there; it's the only way past the big roofs without getting horizontal. Pro: to 2 inches.

38. Bird's Nest Overhang (5.8) ★ An obvious thin roof crack at the far right end of *The Fault* ledges. Pro: to 2 inches.

Midnight Rock

Midnight Rock is the large formation perched atop the ridge above Castle Rock. This massive block of granite has been called "the Cookie Cliff of Leavenworth," although that comparison is only partly apt. While Midnight Rock has some of the finest crack routes in Washington, they are mostly wide cracks, which are intimidating for most climbers used to the thin crack and face climbs of Castle Rock and other areas in Leavenworth.

The long approach to Midnight Rock begins from Castle Rock, climbing a steep, sandy trail for about forty-five minutes. It is easy to get lost near the top; when faced with a box canyon, traverse right below a rocky buttress into the bushes to find the trail. The South Ramp area and Noontime Rock can be reached via a lower trail. Routes are described from left to right as you approach along the base of the wall. Descents from Midnight Rock can be made by walking off to the left side, down a rough trail. Rappel anchors are installed on many of the major ledges.

Note: Midnight and Noontime Rocks are subject to seasonal closure due to nesting raptors. Peregrine falcons nest in this area, which means no climbing from May through July most years. The forest service posts a notice at the trailhead when the closure is in effect, but check before climbing here during nesting season.

1. Curtains (5.10a) ★★ No topo. The obvious crack on the upper left side of Midnight Rock, well up around the corner from *Yellow Bird*. Pro: to 4 inches.

2. Nightingale (5.11d) ★ The thin crack immediately left of *Yellow Bird*. If you're not up to leading it, toprope it from anchors at the left end of V.W. Ledge. Pro: to 1 inch.

3. Yellow Bird (5.10a) ★★ One of the more popular routes at Midnight Rock, no doubt because it is one of the first routes encountered when you get there. A short roof with a prominent flake sticking up marks the start. Pass the roof and climb up the bolted face to a higher roof; traverse right and climb an exposed thin crack to V.W. Ledge. Continue up your choice of wide cracks to the top (5.6 or 5.9, depending on which crack you choose), or rappel from anchors on the left side of V.W. Ledge like everyone else does. Pro: to 3 inches (to V.W. Ledge). (FFA: Don McPherson, Tom Hargis 1972)

The following routes begin from Dead End Ledge, reached via an exposed Class 3 traverse. Most parties scramble across, although roping up isn't a bad idea—it's a long way down.

4. Twilight Zone (5.11c R) ★ The bolted face right of *Yellow Bird,* leading through a roof and up wide cracks to V.W. Ledge. The crux is well protected, but it gets scary higher up. Pro: to 4 inches, several large cams, double ropes recommended.

5. Wild Traverse (III, 5.9) ★ The longest route at Midnight Rock, traversing from the left end of Dead End Ledge to the upper right edge of the wall. Begin via the obvious corner, then traverse ledges right, around a corner and up a ramp to the base of *Twin*

Midnight Rock

Cracks, then across exposed ledges to finish via easier cracks and ramps up The Apron. Pro: to 2 inches. (FA: Fred Beckey, Tom Hornbein 1957)

6. Sometimes a Great Notion (5.10d) ★★★

A thin crack leading left from the dihedral start of *Wild Traverse* to reach V.W. Ledge. Pro: to 1 inch. (FA: Kjell Swedin, Bob McDougall 1980)

7. Black Widow (5.10c) ★ Above Dead End

Ledge is a big roof with two obvious offwidth cracks. This is the offwidth on the left, which widens to a narrow chimney as it passes the roof. Pro: to 5 inches, quickdraws for the old bolts.

8. Easter Overhang (5.10a) ★★★ The obvi-

ous wide crack splitting the roof above Dead End Ledge. One of the best offwidths in Washington. Pro: to 4 inches will suffice; a #11 hexcentric works well if you've got one; bring small stuff, too. Save some #2.0 to #3.5 Friends for belay anchors. (FFA: Jim Madsen, Ron Burgner 1967)

9. In Search of the Perfect Pump (5.11c)

★ An athletic climb through this obvious arching roof crack reaches the base of *Easter Overhang.* Pro: to 2 inches.

10. Stevens Pass Motel (5.12a) ★★★ A

superb pitch up the right-leaning dihedral crack above the far end of Dead End Ledge. Bolt-protected thin face moves gain the crack; wild, pumping laybacking and jamming continue up the overhanging, exposed corner. Once past the hard part, climb directly up a dicey seam (5.12a) to the base of *Twin Cracks* or escape left to *Wild Traverse* (5.9) and up. Pro: to 1.5 inches. (FA: Peter Croft 1984)

11. Twin Cracks (5.10c) ★ Double offwidths

directly above *Stevens Pass Motel,* just left of *R.O.T.C.* Pro: to 5 inches.

12. R.O.T.C. (5.11c) ★★★★ This rather over-

hanging thin crack right of *Twin Cracks* is widely considered to be the best crack route in Washington. Approach via *Wild Traverse* or *Sting,* or combine with *Stevens Pass Motel* for the best hard two-pitch linkup in the state. Pro: to 2 inches; lots of nuts and TCUs from 0.5 inch to 1 inch. (FA: Paul Boving 1977)

13. The Dagoba System (5.12c) ★★★ A

bolted face pitch up the steep wall immediately right of and around the corner from *R.O.T.C.* A stunning, improbable line, thin but very doable except for the crux, which resisted free attempts for years. Pro: quickdraws; a few TCUs and wireds to 0.75 inch for the lower and upper crack sections. (FFA: Andy deKlerk, Greg Child 1995)

14. Sting (5.10b) ★★ The leftmost of two

cracks leading from the ledges just up and right from Dead End Ledge. A good approach pitch for *R.O.T.C.* Pro: to 4 inches; two #4.0 Friends recommended. (FFA: Jim Madsen, Kim Schmitz 1968)

15. Wasp (5.10a) ★ The wider crack

right of *Sting.* Not as popular, but a little easier. Pro: to 4 inches; two #4.0 Friends recommended.

16. The Flame (5.8) ★★ Traverse 50 feet

right from Dead End Ledge to an obvious hand crack, which leads to an intimidating, exposed traverse rightward into a higher corner crack before joining *Wild Traverse* at The Apron. Pro: to 3 inches.

17. Rollercoaster Chimney (5.9) ★ The

wavy chimney above *The Flame.* It

Midnight Rock

reportedly has a 5.7 escape variation near the top, in case you chicken out. Pro: to 2 inches.

18. Plumbline (5.11d) ★★★ The steep, thin crack right of *Rollercoaster Chimney,* leading directly to the big block perched atop Midnight Rock. Approach via *The Flame* or *Frog Suicide,* and up a 5.10 flake to the base of the thin crack. Pro: to 1 inch. (FFA: Peter Croft 1983)

19. J.A.M. Session (5.10c) ★★ Start as for *Plumbline,* then traverse right up a long, right-trending flake. A thin slab leads to a left traverse under the big summit block. The route's name is an acronym derived from the first ascent party's first names; you will find very few jams here. Pro: to 1 inch. (FFA: Jay Ossiander, Al Givler, Mead Hargis 1972)

20. Frog Suicide (5.10a) ★★ A hand crack leading through a short roof right of *The Flame.* Finish via *Wild Traverse* or your choice of routes on this side of the wall. Pro: to 2 inches.

21. Diamond in the Rough (5.11a) ★★ A widening crack through a bigger roof a bit farther right from *Frog Suicide.* Pro: to 4 inches.

22. Supercrack (5.12) ★★★ A striking, widening crack splitting the headwall of *South Ramp.* Fingers, hands, fists, then offwidth through the overhanging finish. Washington's first 5.12 lead, it was unrepeated for decades. Approach via the lower pitches of *South Ramp* or traverse in to anchors and rappel to the base of the crack. Pro: to 5 inches. (FA: Pat Timson 1979)

23. South Ramp (5.10a) ★ The obvious long ramp on the far right side of Midnight Rock. Munge up chossy rock to the base of the

ramp, climb the ramp, then finish via *Wild Traverse.* Pro: to 2 inches.

24. Spellbound (5.11c) ★★★ A thin, overhanging crack on the far right side of Midnight Rock, up and around the corner from *Supercrack.* Approach via a scramble up from the base of Midnight Rock. Pro: to 1 inch. (FA: Matt Christensen 1970s)

Noontime Rock

Noontime Rock is the large wall visible shortly right from Midnight Rock. It is most easily reached by traversing below Midnight Rock. This wall is less fractured than Midnight Rock, and thus has fewer routes. There are two routes climbing Noontime Rock from base to top, with two one-pitch routes beginning from the upper ledges. Descents are usually made by walking off the right side.

1. Gulliver's Travels (5.12a) ★★ A multipitch free route climbing the obvious crack system up the middle of the wall, below the overhangs. Rarely climbed, probably due to the route's difficulty and long approach. Pro: to 3 inches. (FFA: Peter Croft, Dan Lepeska 1982)

2. Lilliputian Roof (5.11a) ★ The roof just right of the last pitch of *Gulliver's Travels,* a fitting finish variation to that route. You can rappel in if you want to avoid the 5.12 "approach." Pro: to 2 inches.

3. Shootout at High Noon (5.11a) ★ An overhanging flake/crack left of the last pitch of *Gulliver's Travels,* usually reached via rappel. Pro: to 2 inches.

4. Wall Street (5.11a) ★★ The first pitch of this old aid route goes free, and if you've

Noontime Rock

suffered the approach hike, you deserve it. Pro: to 3 inches.

No Time Rock

No Time Rock is a cluster of slabby walls located off to the left where the approach trail to Midnight Rock breaks off to the right at the rocky buttress. The dozen or so reported routes are in the 5.6 to 5.11 range, and none are highly recommended compared to the many more classic lines so close by on Midnight Rock. For details, refer to the current edition of *Leavenworth Rock*.

Punk Rock

Hidden at the ridge crest above Midnight Rock is this small crag with several routes. It is most easily reached via a jeep road leading up from Leavenworth, or via a long hike up from Castle Rock and past Midnight Rock to the ridge crest. Punk Rock has several crack routes, almost all of which are named after AC/DC songs, in the 5.8 to 5.11 range, and a few short aid pitches. This cliff is rarely visited, as none of the routes are quite worth the approach difficulties.

Rattlesnake Rock

Rattlesnake Rock is located on the east side of Tumwater Canyon, about 0.5 mile up US 2 from Castle Rock. It is easily seen from Castle Rock, and can be glimpsed from various points along US 2.

Park in the big, paved turnout on the river side of the highway just over 0.6 mile

upcanyon from Castle Rock. A sandy trail begins from the small turnout 50 yards up and across the highway. The trail, such as it is, is heavily eroded, so tread carefully to avoid further damage. After about fifteen minutes, the trail arrives at the base of the obvious *Viper Crack*. The majority of routes are around to the left, on the steep northwest face. Farther left is Piton Tower, the obvious free-standing pillar.

The routes are listed from right to left as they are encountered on the approach. Descend by rappel from various anchors.

1. Viper Crack (5.8) ★ The obvious crack on the downhill buttress, the first route you see

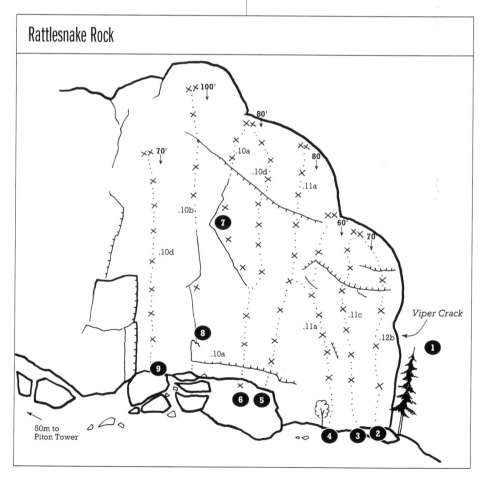

Rattlesnake Rock

as you approach via the climbers' trail. Two pitches to the top. Walk off or rappel. Pro: to 3 inches. (FA: Don Gordon, Ed Cooper 1959)

2. Zweibles (5.12b) ★★ The rightmost route on the sport wall, climbing yellow-streaked rock just left around the corner from *Viper Crack.* Retrobolted, but still a little runout for most. Pro: quickdraws; small cams.

3. Rock 'n Rattle (5.11c) ★★★★ The middle sport route on the lower right side, climbing a steep, yellow-streaked wall through an overhang. One of the best sport routes in Leavenworth, even better since it was retrobolted. Pro: quickdraws. (FA: Dean Hart, Randy Atkinson 1987)

4. Tubbing at the Ritterhoff (5.11a) ★★ The leftmost sport route on the lower right side of the sport wall, beginning directly above a small tree and passing the overhang on the left side. *Tubbing with Der Drillmeister* variation (5.11b, ★★) starts up *Tubbing* and joins *Drillmeister* for a long pitch. Pro: quickdraws.

5. Drillmeister (5.11a) ★★ Up and left from the *Zweibles* wall is a blocky ledge. This route begins from the right end of the ledge, passing a short overhang directly off the ledge, then connecting the bolts up the steep wall above. Pro: quickdraws.

6. Forearm Confusion (5.10d) ★★ Another sport route following the line of bolts leading directly above the anchor bolt on the right side of the blocky ledge. Steep, enjoyable face climbing all the way to the anchors. Pro: quickdraws.

7. Early Archeologist (5.10a) ★ Start as for *Forearm Confusion,* then angle left, following a diagonal crack, and finish via flaky face moves to anchors shared with *Forearm Confusion.* Pro: quickdraws.

8. Monty Python (5.10b) Discontinuous cracks on the left side of the sport wall, with a few bolts and fixed pins. If it was clean, it might get a couple of stars. Pro: to 0.25 inch, include TCUs and wired nuts.

9. Flying Circus (5.10d) ★★ A new sport route on the far left side of the wall, starting at the leftmost end of the ledge. Pro: quickdraws.

Piton Tower

Piton Tower is the small pillar just up and left from Rattlesnake Rock's sport wall. It has four routes (one on each face), but only the *Notch Route* is often climbed. Class 3 scrambling leads left from the sport wall to the notch. Descend by rappel back to the notch.

1. Notch Route (5.10a) ★ No topo. Awkward climbing up double cracks in a half chimney directly from the notch. Originally rated 5.8, but the rating keeps going up as the years go by. The big chockstone/flake seems solid, but don't crank on it too hard. Pro: to 1.5 inches. (FFA: Eric Bjornstad, Dan Davis 1961)

Jupiter Rock and Waterfall Column

Two of the most inaccessible walls in the Leavenworth area, Jupiter Rock and Waterfall Column are also two of the largest, with obvious potential for many long, classic routes. Jupiter Rock is the large pyramid-shaped cliff; Waterfall Column is obvious because of Drury Falls, a 600-foot waterfall that occasionally freezes. Unfortunately, approaching either of these walls is a horrendous undertaking, taking three hours or more to climb the steep, rocky gullies leading up to the cliffs. The river crossing alone deters most climbers from visiting these walls. Rafting across Jolanda Lake is the usual method, although during late summer, fording the river is possible in a few places, but not at all recommended. Hiking down from Tumwater Campground is possible, but is so time-consuming it is not a realistic option.

So far, only exploratory ascents have been made, climbing obvious lines. Few who have climbed here ever came back, and only a few routes done on Jupiter Rock and Waterfall Column have been repeated. The routes done on these walls, so far, are not worth the hassle of approach and descent. If you plan on climbing here, consider a multiday trip, with a base camp and plenty of supplies, so you can climb all you want and never feel the need to repeat the river crossing or approach hike ever again in this lifetime.

Climbing on Jupiter Rock and Waterfall Column is very adventuresome, and should be approached in the spirit of exploration. Pick a line in the hope it's a good one.

Tumwater Tower

Tumwater Tower is the large, isolated pillar located across the river from US 2 about 0.75 mile south of Picnic Rock (the obvious boulder just down from the highway about halfway between Castle Rock and Leavenworth. It has eight routes, four leading to the summit, but only one route worth climbing. Even then, because of an arduous approach, Tumwater Tower is not often visited.

The approach begins from Picnic Rock, a popular picnic and sunbathing spot about 1.5 miles upcanyon from Leavenworth. Cross the rusty old bridge and find the faint trail immediately on the left, through the bushes. Follow the trail, such as it is, as far as possible, staying as close to the river as you can (or fight through the underbrush and soot if you prefer). If you lose the trail, continue bushwhacking just above the river until you reach a rusty cable crossing the river. Continue

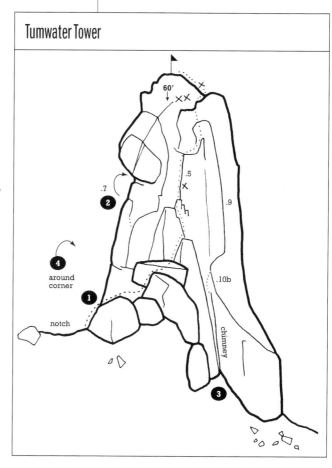

Tumwater Tower

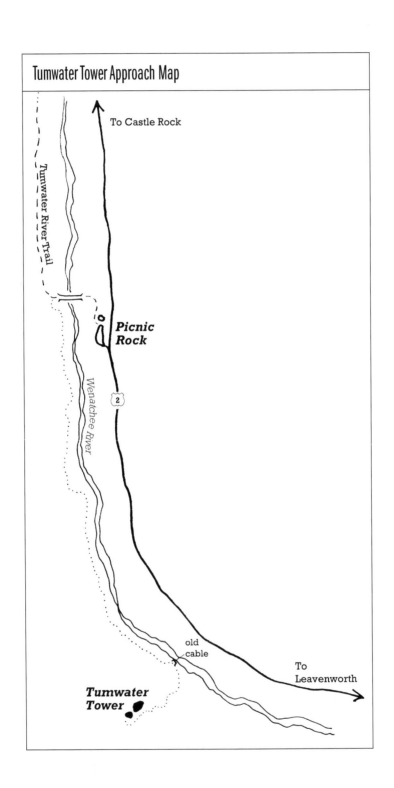

Tumwater Tower Approach Map

To Castle Rock

Tumwater River Trail

Picnic Rock

Wenatchee River

2

old cable

To Leavenworth

Tumwater Tower

downriver another 100 yards or so, then start climbing toward the tower.

Approaching the tower via the gully on the left is recommended, as the right-hand gully is steeper and has much loose rock. Once you reach the toe of the lower buttress, climb the steep, dirty gully on the left to reach the notch. Come early, before the day's heat makes the approach really miserable.

1. Regular Route (5.5) ★ The original route up Tumwater Tower is the most obvious line, climbing cracks and flakes from the notch to the summit ridge. Several variations are possible, up to 5.7. From the rappel bolts, a short, easy, exposed traverse leads to the summit. Pro: to 3 inches. (FA: Fred Beckey and party 1957)

2. Upper Notch Route (5.7) Climb up a corner crack to a flake and exit left around the arête to reach the top from the highway side. Pro: to 2 inches, slings.

3. Southeast Face (5.10b) ★ Start lower down and right from the notch, climbing a chimney to a crux face traverse to gain a straight-in crack. Might be better with a little cleaning. Pro: to 2 inches.

4. Highway Route (5.9) No topo. A dirty crack and slab on the outside face of the tower leads to the summit block. Another route that would improve with a little cleaning. Pro: to 1 inch; quickdraws.

Swift Water

The Swift Water picnic area, located about 6 miles upcanyon from Leavenworth, has several large boulders with some excellent problems. Most of the problems are obvious, but exploring will lead to more hidden among the trees across the highway, including the area's classic boulder problem, *Royal Flush,* a 5.10+ roof crack hidden across the highway from the parking lot.

For more about bouldering at Swift Water and other Leavenworth areas, refer to Kelly Sheridan's Leavenworth Bouldering guide (2015).

ICICLE CREEK CANYON

Icicle Creek Canyon is the deep gorge located south and west of Leavenworth. The Icicle, as it is commonly known, has some of the best cragging in Washington state, including several large walls and moderately large domes and buttresses, but mostly smaller cliffs, slabs, and boulders. A decade ago, the Icicle was regarded as a nice detour from the usual Leavenworth destinations, Castle Rock and Peshastin Pinnacles. The first guidebooks to the Icicle were published in 1989, and since then—largely due to the popularization of rappel bolting and a new-found willingness to spend hours or even days cleaning off lichen and dirt—climbers have transformed the Icicle into one of the state's most popular rock climbing areas. But it wasn't the bolts or the guidebooks that made the area popular; it was the routes, which vary from easy slabs to difficult overhanging cracks, thin and wide, long and short, 5.0 to 5.13. There's bouldering, toproping, friction, jamming, and face climbing, near the road and far above the canyon floor—something for everyone of any ability or ambition.

Access to the canyon is via Icicle Road, leaving US 2 at Icicle Junction on the western edge of town. The road enters the canyon proper about 3 miles from town. As soon as you enter the canyon, rocks start appearing right and left. Some of the crags are obvious; others are hidden among the trees and gullies above the road.

The Icicle has several campgrounds, including Eightmile and Bridge Creek, the two most popular, and others farther up the canyon. However, on weekends in particular, these campgrounds are often full. Bivouacking outside of designated campgrounds is strongly discouraged by the forest service. Signs saying No Overnight Camping, Private Property, and No Trespassing abound in the Icicle these days, a harsh reality for climbers of an earlier era who remember no such restrictions, when they could pretty much camp and climb wherever they liked. Sadly, the popularity of climbing and the privatization of the Icicle have led to many restrictions. Accordingly, if you intend to bivouac outside of an established campground, keep a very low profile, and don't be surprised if you are cited and ordered to leave by a ranger or sheriff's deputy.

According to posted signs, you can be fined up to $1,000 and jailed for up to ninety days for trespassing in the Icicle, so beware of and respect private property. If a sign says No Trespassing, don't trespass. Unfortunately, there is much unmarked private property in the Icicle, making it likely that you will unwittingly trespass either while climbing or while approaching or descending. If you know a climbing area to be on restricted private property, but still wish to cross the land or climb there, obtain advance permission from the landowner. Some owners will allow access to the rocks, so long as climbers stay out of sight. Others don't want climbers—or anyone else—on their land for any purpose, even to ask permission to pass. If in doubt, ask first or skirt around the property boundary. This guide will try to steer you clear of private property, but for the most part, the signs speak for themselves. Although this guide may indicate access across private property is permitted, any such permission may be revoked by the owners at any time without notice. Nothing in this guide should be construed as permission to climb on or pass over private property.

The Icicle is adequately developed, and barring the discovery of yet another

Icicle Creek Canyon Vicinity Map

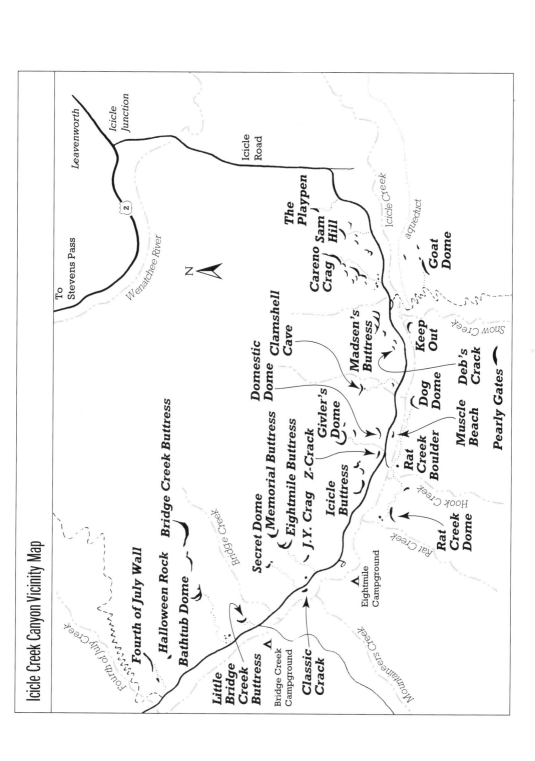

lichen-encrusted slab (which I have no doubt will happen), there seems to be quite enough routes here to keep climbers busy for years. Given the increasing encroachment of private ownership into several beloved climbing and bouldering areas, one might hope climbers would turn their attention away from scrubbing lichen and dirt and toward preserving access to the established areas threatened by privatization. Recent efforts at Sam Hill, Trundle Dome, and Careno Crag are encouraging, but there is much work to be done.

As for climbing dangers, aside from a few nasty runouts and some loose rock here and there, most of the climbing is fairly free of objective hazards. There have been fatalities here, but most were caused by climber error rather than objective causes. Still, flakes do break, pillars do topple, boulders obviously do crash down from time to time, and there are still old bolts and manky fixed pins on many of the older routes, so proceed with due caution.

Beware of rattlesnakes, poison ivy (particularly in the vicinity of Sam Hill, Careno Crag, and Madsen's Buttress), and ticks. Drinking water is available from pumps at Eightmile and Bridge Creek Campgrounds if you run dry. Be wary of hunters during autumn months. Finally, beware of falling trees, loose rock, and of stepping through a hole left by burned tree roots (the aftermath of the 1994 firestorm). There are still many fire-blackened pines ready to topple at the slightest provocation, and the fire left loose rock and lots of other nasty surprises for the unwary.

Icicle Creek Canyon Mileage Chart

The following chart provides mileages as calculated beginning from the intersection of US 2 and Icicle Road in Leavenworth, and mileages between points.

Point of Interest	From US 2	Between Points
The Playpen	2.8	–
Sam Hill	3.4	0.6
Gibson's Crack	3.6	0.2
Mountaineers' Buttress	3.7	0.1
Bolt Rock	4.1	0.4
Snow Creek Parking Lot	4.3	0.2
Air Roof	4.4	0.1
Deb's Crack	4.7	0.3
Cable Rock	4.8	0.1
Hammerhead Rock	5.2	0.4
Bruce's Boulder	5.6	0.4
Domestic Dome	5.7	0.1
Roto Wall	5.8	0.1
Z-Crack	6.0	0.2
Duty Dome	6.2	0.2
Icicle Buttress	6.4	0.2
Eightmile Campground	7.1	0.7
Classic Crack	7.5	0.4
Bridge Creek	8.5	1.0
The Sword	8.9	0.4
The Egg	9.1	0.2
Halloween Rock	9.4	0.5
Fourth of July Trail	9.6	0.2

The Playpen

The Playpen is the largest of a group of small rock outcroppings located near the canyon's entrance. It has four routes in the 5.10d to 5.11d range, all climbing cracks through roofs, but none that is really worth the approach, which crosses private property.

Sam Hill

Sam Hill is a small dome near the entrance to the canyon that features several short, high-quality slab routes. The dome is easily visible from the road at 3.4 miles, just before Gibson's Crack. Look for the dome with the obvious white streaks, far up on the right. (You may also see Trundle Dome farther to the left, which has obvious white streaks, too.) Park in a turnout near the pumphouse, about 3.3 miles from Icicle Junction. The approach trail is across the road; it's easy to find and follow, even if you start the wrong way; just head uphill toward the dome and you'll meet the trail eventually.

The following four routes are located on cliffs below Sam Hill. There are several other routes in this vicinity, particularly along The Underhill, a short, blocky cliff band directly below Sam Hill.

1. Ski Tracks Crack (5.9) ★★ The obvious slanting, parallel thin cracks on a rounded buttress just left of where the trail begins climbing toward Sam Hill. A thin flake could cut your rope if you fell above it, so put some gear in near the flake to keep the rope clear. Pro: to 2 inches.

2. Don't Forget Arête (5.9) ★★ About 200 meters right from *Ski Tracks Crack* is this obvious short, bolted arête. Pro: quickdraws.

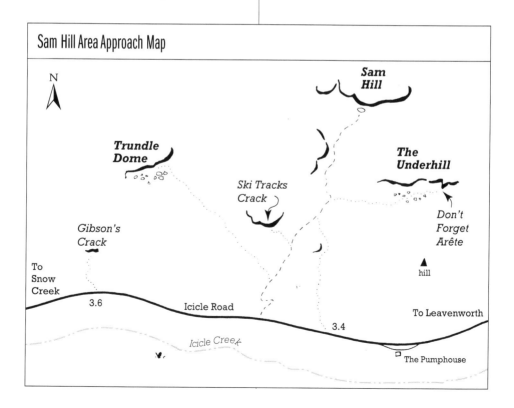

Sam Hill Area Approach Map

N

Sam Hill

Trundle Dome

The Underhill

Ski Tracks Crack

Don't Forget Arête

Gibson's Crack

hill

To Snow Creek

3.6

Icicle Road

To Leavenworth

3.4

Icicle Creek

The Pumphouse

Ski Tracks Cracks and Sam Hill

Sam Hill and The Underhill

3. Woof Woof Roof (5.10b) ★ Just left of *Don't Forget Arête,* climb slabby rock past a pine tree to a blocky headwall right of an overhang. Pro: to 2 inches.

4. Lunging for Lazarus (5.10b) ★ Start left of the pine tree and finish up cracks left of the roof. Pro: to 2 inches.

The following routes are on Sam Hill proper, and are described from left to right as they are encountered on the approach. Descend by rappel from anchors, or walk off to the right. Beware of poison ivy, which is plentiful, especially on the left side of Sam Hill.

5. Exhuming MacCarthys (5.8) ★ Scrubbed-off cracks on the far left side. Pro: to 2 inches.

6. Updraft (5.10c) ★★ A long pitch up the leftmost buttress of Sam Hill. Slabby, with a problematic crux. Pro: quickdraws, plus a few stoppers and TCUs; 60-meter rope recommended. (FA: Jim Phillips, Roger Johnson 1990)

7. Can Blue Men Sing the Whites? (5.10a) ★ A friction pitch squeezed in just left of *Groping for Oprah's Navel.* A fixed pin marks the start; join *Oprah's Navel* below that route's last bolt or try a direct finish. Pro: quickdraws.

8. Groping for Oprah's Navel (5.10c) ★★★ The middle and best of three obvious bolted slab pitches just above the flat boulder at the base of Sam Hill. Rappel from anchors. Pro: quickdraws. (FA: Ron Powell, Viktor Kramar 1991)

9. Box Spring Booty (5.10d) ★ The friction pitch immediately right of *Groping for Oprah's Navel.* Shares *Sam 'n Cams'* belay anchors. Pro: quickdraws, plus a wired nut at the start.

10. Sam 'n Cams' (5.6) ★ A thin, curvy flake just left of the fallen pine tree. Kind of grungy at the top. Pro: to 2 inches.

11. Fuzzy Packs a Lunch (5.9) ★ The intermittent crack system immediately left of *Contemplating Dog.* A tricky face move gains the crack. Pro: to 2 inches, including wired nuts and TCUs.

12. Contemplating Dog (5.10b) ★★ The rounded arête on the far right side of Sam Hill. Thin, edgy friction. Pro: quickdraws; wired nuts and cams to 1 inch.

Trundle Dome

This slabby wall, which features several good crack and face routes in the 5.9 to 5.11 range, is about 150 yards left of *Ski Tracks Crack.* Trundle Dome is visible from the road as a small, white-streaked cliff and is often mistaken for Sam Hill. Sighting the dome from the road makes it easier to find on the approach. Hike in via the Sam Hill trail, but angle left early on and scramble up slabs and over talus to the base of the wall. Trundle Dome gets good sun exposure in the morning, becomes a veritable furnace by midmorning on summer afternoons, but then gets afternoon shade.

The routes are described from right to left. Descend from anchors atop each route, or walk off to the right. Watch for poison ivy.

13. Bulkhead Blues (5.11c) ★★★ An excellent friction pitch up the right side of Trundle Dome. Pass an initial bulkhead to gain a sloping ledge, then friction up the steep slab. Pro: quickdraws; tiny wired nuts at the top. (FA: Ben and Tom Stanton 1995)

14. April Mayhem (5.9) ★★ The next route left of *Bulkhead Blues,* climbing up the right

Trundle Dome

side of the cowboy boot–shaped flake and up the bolted slab above. Pro: quickdraws; gear to 2 inches.

15. Boot Top Fracture (5.11a) ★ Start up a blocky corner near the middle of the dome, then exit right past a bolt and up the left side of the cowboy boot–shaped flake and crux slab above. Pro: to 2.5 inches; quickdraws.

16. Hundred Dollar Dash (5.10a) ★ Start as for *Boot Top Fracture*, but stay left to reach a left-facing corner system midway up the slab. Exit right, following bolts up the slab and over an arch to the anchors. Pro: quickdraws; gear to 2 inches.

17. Sonic Boom (5.10d) ★★ A crack and flakes lead past a small roof. Pro: quickdraws; gear to 2 inches.

18. Sonic Fest (5.11b) ★ Climb the flake left of *Sonic Boom*, then up difficult face moves. A toprope problem unless retrobolted.

19. Flake Fest (5.9) ★ A short corner crack leads to face climbing. Pro: to 1 inch; quickdraws.

Mountaineers' Buttress

One of the most popular crags in the Icicle is this heavily fractured series of stepped domes known by various factions of climbers as "Mounties' Buttress," "Mountaineers' Dome," and "Waddell's Buttress." Call it what you like; in this guide it is referred to as Mountaineers' Buttress. The crag is 3.7 miles up the road, and can be spotted on the right just before you reach the first of the cabins near Bolt Rock. This is a popular instruction crag and is heavily used on weekends.

The lower portion of the buttress has a number of short crack pitches ranging from 5.0 to 5.7, and some loose blocks. The middle flake buttress has two enjoyable crack climbs (5.6 and 5.4) on clean, white granite. The upper portion of the buttress has an obvious short, 4-inch roof crack (5.9). There are many other short, moderate-to-difficult toprope climbs and boulder problems on and in the vicinity of Mountaineers' Buttress, too many to include in this guide. It's a fun area to explore.

20. Gibson's Crack (5.5) ** About 100 meters downroad from Mountaineers'

Gibson's Crack

Buttress (at the 3.6-mile mark) is a small crag with this good, short hand crack. Pro: to 3 inches.

Careno Crags

Careno Crag is the large buttress visible as you round the corner just uproad from Mountaineers' Buttress. There are several cliffs in this area, which in this guide are referred to collectively as Careno Crags, although each cliff has its own name. Careno Crag, the largest of the group, has several excellent face and crack routes.

Access to Careno Crags may present a problem. The climbers' trail beginning from behind the big boulders just down the road from the Snow Creek Trail parking lot is on private property, and is posted no trespassing.

For those not willing to blatantly trespass, the approach options now appear to be traversing across the hillside from Mountaineers' Buttress, staying above the forest service boundary markers; or hiking up from the Snow Creek Trail parking lot to Madsen's Buttress, then scrambling over to Poison Ivy Crack to gain the old trail. One presumes a new access trail will be established, if one is not already in use, but until then climbers must be creative or bold in approaching Careno Crags.

There are several excellent boulder and toprope problems alongside the road in the vicinity of Bolt Rock. Unfortunately, all are now on private property and may soon be bulldozed to level the way for cabins. If you want to climb on them, be sure to obtain permission from the property owners.

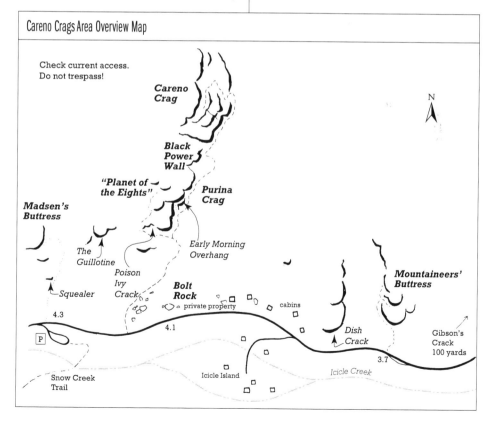

Careno Crags Area Overview Map

Check current access. Do not trespass!

Careno Crag

Black Power Wall

"Planet of the Eights"

Purina Crag

Madsen's Buttress

The Guillotine

Early Morning Overhang

Poison Ivy Crack

Squealer

Bolt Rock

private property

cabins

Mountaineers' Buttress

4.3

4.1

P

Dish Crack

Gibson's Crack 100 yards

3.7

Snow Creek Trail

Icicle Island

Icicle Creek

21. The Prow (5.11c TR) ** Just up the road from the last of the cabins below Careno Crags is Bolt Rock, a huge roadside boulder with this obvious steep prow. A little harder since some holds broke off. On private land; ask permission. (FFA: Erik Thixton 1976)

Purina Crag and Vicinity

Purina Crag is the lowest of the Careno Crags. The most obvious feature of Purina Crag is the huge roof of *Early Morning Overhang* (5.12a), easily visible from the road. Most of the crag is chossy, but there are some good routes on Purina Crag proper and on the smaller walls and the buttress left of and above the crag.

The Prow

Purina Crag

The following routes are located on Purina Crag proper, in the vicinity of *Early Morning Overhang*. To reach the routes, stay on the higher trail ascending toward the roof. The routes are listed left to right, in the order you encounter them as you ascend from below. Beware of poison ivy and loose rock.

22. Chow Time (5.9) The corner crack up and left from the start of *Crude Buddha*. Pro: to 4 inches.

23. Crude Buddha (5.11b) ★ A bolted face route climbing a short ramp past a roof and up the right side of a slabby arête. Easy to spot because of all the bolts. Rappel from anchors or scramble down the gully behind *Poison Ivy Crack*. Pro: quickdraws.

24. Existential Exit (5.10a) ★ A thin crack and face traverse lead into a hand crack just right of the *Crude Buddha* arête. Rappel from anchors or scramble off. Pro: to 2 inches, including TCUs.

25. Early Morning Overhang (aka Ride of the Valkyries) (5.12a) The obvious thin crack splitting the big roof. A blocky 5.7 pitch gets you to the roof. Some loose rock below the roof. If you can't do it free, aid it (C2). Pro: to 3 inches; cams. (FFA: Hugh Herr 1986)

Orange Speckled Buttress

Just right of and below *Early Morning Overhang* is the so-called Orange Speckled Buttress, a steep, angular wall liberally splashed with orange lichen. There are several routes climbing a close cluster of cracks and corners; one is 5.8, the rest 5.10b. The trail to Careno Crag passes directly below the routes, so if you have some spare time, give them a try. Refer to the *Leavenworth Rock* guide for route names and details.

Black Power Wall

About 100 meters uphill from Orange Speckled Buttress is this obvious black-and-white-streaked wall with two prominent corners, one white and one black. The corners are both middling 5.10, but neither is highly recommended.

26. Black Power (5.12a R) ★ A bold, technical lead up the obvious black prow. Pro: to 2.5 inches, including RPs and quickdraws.

Careno Crag

Careno Crag proper is the large, slabby, multidihedraled dome at the upper end of the group of crags above *Early Morning Overhang,* visible directly above the cabins near Bolt Rock. It has several good, multipitch lines, and is one of the best all-around crags in the Icicle. The routes are described from left to right as encountered on the approach. Descents are best made by rappelling where anchors are available, or by walking off to the right from the upper ledge, which involves traversing exposed ledges and scrambling down gullies, with some loose rock.

27. Bale-Kramar (5.10b) ★★ A long route up the left side of Careno Crag, the first bolted route you encounter on the approach trail. Climb a short, slabby arête, then easier rock to anchors 40 feet up and even easier climbing to higher anchors. From there, follow bolts up a slabby buttress to a grassy shelf at the base of a steep crack; climb the crack, then follow the bolts straight to the upper ledge. Three to five pitches, depending on where and how often you belay. Pro: to 2 inches; lots of quickdraws. (FA: Dave Bale, Viktor Kramar 1995)

28. Regular Route (5.10b) ★★ This is the central dihedral system of Careno Crag, one of the most popular multipitch routes in the Icicle. The first pitch climbs a slabby thin crack and bolted face to a ledge at the base of the corner. Continue up cracks to a broad, grassy ledge with a large pine tree. A final pitch climbs face and thin cracks just behind the pine tree. To descend, rappel back to the ledge and walk off to the right. Pro: to 3 inches, including cams and wired nuts.

29. Passing Lane (5.10a) ★ A variation of the first pitch of *Regular Route*, climbing a short crack and bolted slab about 30 feet right of the initial crack. Pro: quickdraws; gear to 2 inches.

Careno Crag

Careno Crag Proper

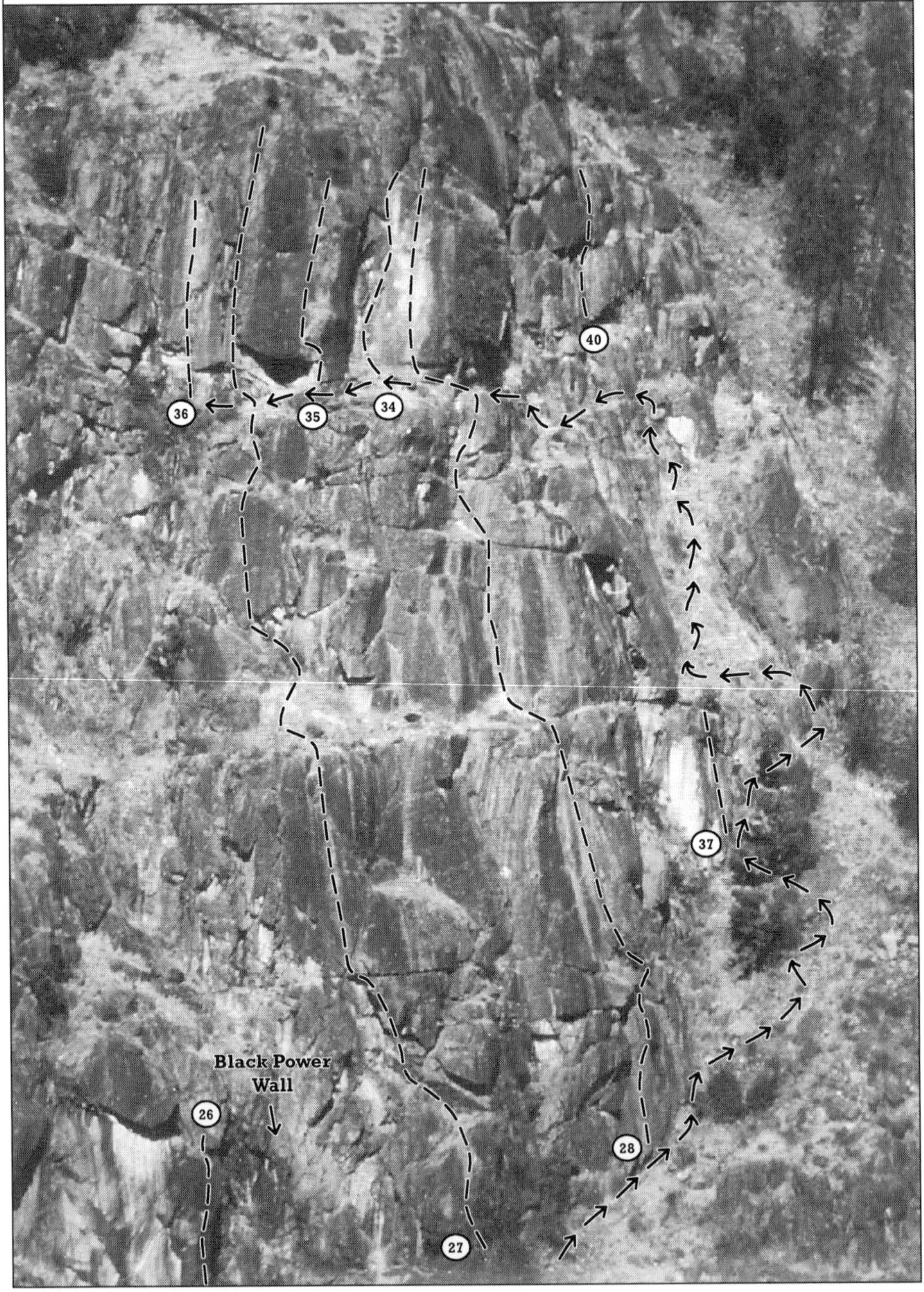

40
36
35
34
37
Black Power Wall
26
28
27

30. Nubbin Grubbin' (5.11c) ★★ The first bolted slab pitch left of the second pitch of *Regular Route*. Harder since a hold broke off. Pro: quickdraws.

31. Cool Struttin' (5.10a) ★★★ A fun, bolted friction pitch left of *Nubbin Grubbin'*. Pro: quickdraws. (FA: Dave Bale, Viktor Kramar 1995)

32. Lone Soldier (5.11b) ★ The slabby arête immediately right of the third pitch of *Regular Route*. Pro: quickdraws; gear to 1 inch including TCUs.

33. Killer Bs (5.10c) ★★ The bolted slab right of *Lone Soldier*. Mostly 5.8, with a thin move at the top. If a crucial flake breaks off, the rating will go up. Pro: lots of quickdraws.

34. Heave Ho (5.10a) ★★ A bolted slab immediately left of the final pitch of *Regular Route* leads to a crack finish, or joins that route. Pro: quickdraws; gear to 1.5 inches.

35. Giant Steps (5.11b) ★★ A difficult traverse across the lip of the obvious roof just left of the pine tree leads to an engaging finish up a slabby buttress. Pro: quickdraws, plus a couple of long slings and a couple of TCUs to 0.25 inch.

36. Pocketmeister (5.10a) ★★★ An enjoyable face pitch about 40 yards left of *Giant Steps*. Lots of quartz pockets. Pro: quickdraws. (FA: Dave Bale, Viktor Kramar 1994?)

The following routes are located farther up the base of Careno Crag, continuing right up the trail from the start of *Regular Route*.

37. Pumpline (5.11a) ★★ A short thin crack up the center of the short wall about 100 feet up and right from the start of *Regular Route*, passing a block/roof at the top. Pro: to 2 inches, including wired nuts and TCUs. Bring a sling and some small gear for the

belay. Scramble off to the right, or continue up *Finders Keepers*.

38. Free Floyd (5.10b) ★ The thin crack just right of *Pumpline*. The reachy face crux is harder if you're short. Pro: to 1 inch.

39. Finders Keepers (5.9) ★ A bolted slab just right of the ledge above *Pumpline*. Pro: quickdraws.

40. Condo Corner (5.10b) ★ The obvious corner crack about 50 yards up and right from the top of *Pumpline*. Chossy scrambling gets you to the base of the corner, which could use some more cleaning. Rappel from slings; the walk-off sucks. Pro: to 2 inches.

Poison Ivy Crags

As you ascend from Bolt Rock, just before you reach the rock, the trail forks left and uphill. Follow this fork to reach *Poison Ivy Crack* and several other nearby crags located above and left of Purina Crag. These crags feature several popular routes, mostly in the 5.8 to 5.9 range. The routes are described in the order encountered on the approach. (See Careno Crags Area Overview photo.)

41. Poison Ivy Crack (5.9) ★★ A fun, short corner crack. As the name implies, watch out for poison ivy. Difficult to see from below, but easy to identify when you get there. Scramble down the gully behind the crack. Pro: to 2 inches, mostly smaller; bring a couple of cams in the 2- to 3-inch range for the belay.

42. Staring at the Sun (5.11b) ★ No topo. The steep, thin slab just left of *Poison Ivy Crack,* with three bolts. Pro: quickdraws, plus 2- to 3-inch cams for the belay.

43. Just Another Sucker on the Vine (5.8) ★ A bolted face route uphill and right from *Poison Ivy Crack*. Chimney up behind a scary-looking flake, then up a short crack and the slab above. Walk off to the left. Pro: quickdraws.

44. Small Change (5.8) ★★ The leftmost of three routes on a small cliff (dubbed "Planet of the Eights" in *Leavenworth Rock*) above *Just Another Sucker on the Vine*. A single bolt protects face moves leading to a right-leaning crack. Rappel from anchors, or scramble off to the left. Pro: to 2 inches; quickdraws.

45. Surveillance of the Assailants (5.8) ★★ The route squeezed in between *Small Change* and *Make Mine a Bold One*. Pro: quickdraws; gear to 2 inches.

46. Make Mine a Bold One (5.9) ★★ Face climb past three bolts on the right to the *Small Change* anchors. Scramble off to the left, or rappel. Pro: quickdraws; TCUs to 1 inch.

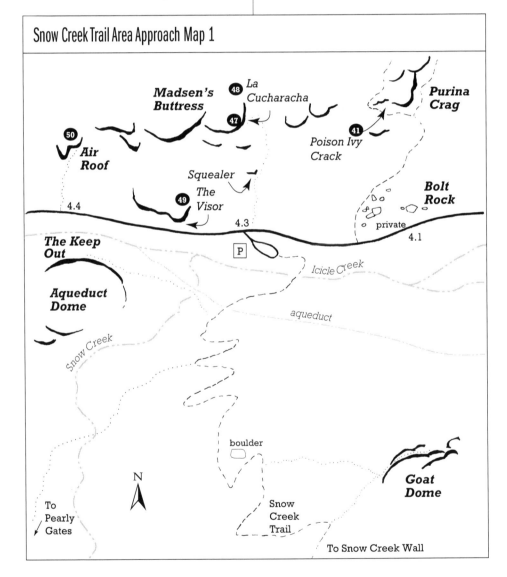

Snow Creek Trail Area Approach Map 1

Snow Creek Trail Area

The Snow Creek Trail parking lot is located 4.3 miles up Icicle Road from US 2, shortly beyond Bolt Rock. There are a number of boulders, cliffs, and buttresses across the road from the parking area, most visibly The Visor, a curving overhang rising directly above the road. These several formations are collectively known as Madsen's Buttress, and offer numerous toprope and lead problems of varying quality, generally in the 5.9 to 5.11 range, mostly not worth the trouble. Numerous routes here are not included in this guide, so by all means, feel free to explore.

Madsen's Buttress

Atop the rightmost buttress of Madsen's Buttress is an obvious pine tree. Just below and right of this, almost out of sight from the parking lot, is *La Cucharacha*. The approach trail begins directly across the road from the parking lot.

47. La Cucharacha (5.10d) ★★ No topo. See map on page 230. Thin cracks left of the

Madsen's Buttress—Left Side

obvious wide chimney. A pumping lead, but usually toproped. Pro: to 2.5 inches.

48. Madsen's Chimney (5.10a) See map on page 230. The wide chimney right of *La Cucharacha*. Best toproped. Pro: Big!

The Visor Area

Just up and across the road from the entrance to the parking lot is a prominent arching roof of The Visor (A3+). Several roadside routes in the 5.7 to 5.10 range are in the vicinity of this roof, mostly of dubious quality with adequate to poor protection, none of which is highly recommended. Up the road about 100 meters from The Visor, somewhat hidden about 50 meters up a gully on the right (presently just above a speed limit sign), is Air Roof, a large roof on a small, slabby buttress. There are several more routes here and on adjacent cliffs, but only *Air Roof* is popular.

49. The Visor (aka The Fairy Tale) (5.13d) The obvious arching roof directly above the road across from the entrance to Snow Creek Trail parking lot. An old aid-practice crack, it has been bolted and climbed free. It's a chossfest getting to the bolts, with loose, scary rock. Pro: quickdraws.

50. Air Roof (5.11b) ★ The obvious thin crack through the roof. Gets dirty and has some flaky rock. Pro: to 1.5 inches. If toproping, beware of getting your rope stuck in the crack and of rope cutting on the lip if you pendulum during a fall.

A bit farther up the road from *Air Roof,* on the right, are these obvious crack routes on the big boulders facing the road.

51. Williams' Five-Twelve (5.12a) ★ The obvious right-leaning, diagonal thin crack

Williams Five-Twelve

Deb's Crack

on the boulder just above the road. Usually toproped, but can be led. Pro: to 0.75 inch; include several small TCUs and wired nuts.

52. Deb's Crack (5.10d) ★★ On the boulder up and left from *Williams' Five-Twelve* is this striking overhanging, left-slanting crack. A brutal, pumping lead for such a short crack.

No wonder it's usually toproped. Pro: to 2 inches; cams.

53. Zig-Zag (5.11b TR) ★ The short corner, ramp, and thin face problem just left of *Deb's Crack.*

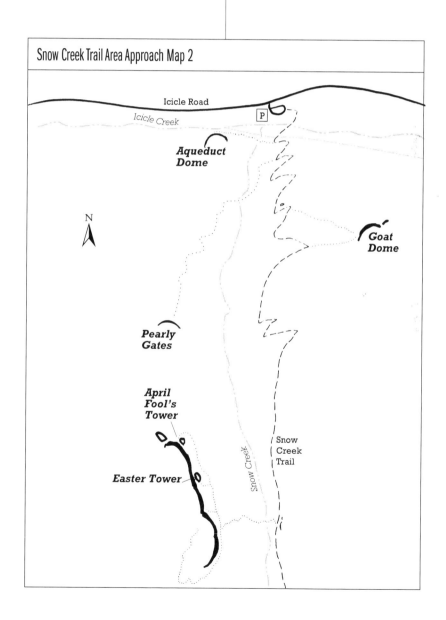

Snow Creek Trail Area Approach Map 2

Icicle Road

Icicle Creek

P

Aqueduct Dome

N

Goat Dome

Pearly Gates

April Fool's Tower

Easter Tower

Snow Creek

Snow Creek Trail

Aqueduct Dome (The Keep Out)

Aqueduct Dome is the true dome located just upstream and across from the Snow Creek Trail parking lot. This dome is also known as The Keep Out because of Keep Out signs posted in its vicinity. It has half a dozen routes in the 5.8 to 5.11 range, none of which is particularly worthwhile. The original route, *Crystal Crack* (5.8), climbs a unique crack formed by a vertical, 2-inch quartz dike that can be seen from Icicle Road.

While it used to be common to approach these routes by climbing around the fence and crossing the bridge, climbers should be aware that this is trespassing and could result in trouble (i.e., a big fine and possibly jail time). A longer approach can be made from Snow Creek Trail, leaving the trail just beyond the aqueduct crossing (at the DANGER, KEEP OUT sign) and crossing Snow Creek to reach the dome. Given the access issues and difficulties, you should probably do what the signs say.

Goat Dome

Goat Dome is the slabby buttress visible directly up and left from the Snow Creek Trail parking lot. It has several slab routes, mostly involving friction and thin edging, and a few cracks to round things out. Approach via Snow Creek Trail. About 0.75 mile from the trailhead, the trail switchbacks below and then above a large boulder, from which Goat Dome is easily visible. A trail of sorts begins about 50 feet up the trail from the boulder, crossing the salvage logging slash to reach the dome on the upper right side. Alternatively, continue up the trail a few hundred yards to where it switchbacks

closer to the dome, and traverse grassy ledges to the dome.

The routes are described from right to left, the order in which they are encountered as you approach from the trail. Descents are commonly made by rappel, although it is possible to walk off on the right side if you climb all the way to the top. The following routes begin from a flaky ledge about 50 feet above the base of the slabs on the far right side.

54. Fiendish Flake (5.8) The obvious flake on the upper right side, about 50 feet above where the trail meets the dome. Not popular because it requires big pro and has crappy belay anchors. The best descent is to traverse left and rappel *Jet Lag Jeopardy*. Pro: to 5 inches.

55. Walnuts and Wingtips (5.10a) ★ The first route left of *Fiendish Flake*. A fixed pin in a seam marks the start; angle left to the crux friction finish. Pro: to 1 inch, including small TCUs.

56. Jet Lag Jeopardy (5.10c) ★★ A thin seam left of *Wingtips* leads to a bolted slab. Pro: quickdraws, plus a couple of wireds and TCUs.

57. The Great Outdoors (5.10d) ★★★ The leftmost route beginning from the blocky ledge that includes *Wingtips* and *Jet Lag*. Thin edging and friction. Pro: quickdraws. (FA: Dave Lenz, Viktor Kramar, Mike Marriott 1989)

58. Fact or Friction (5.10b) A short, bolted slab just up from the anchors of *Walnuts and Wingtips*. A skinny tree makes a dubious rappel anchor. Pro: quickdraws.

The following routes begin just down and left from *The Great Outdoors,* above a flaky ledge system traversing the slabs.

59. Gladiator (5.11c) ⋆ Just right of *Shitz on a Ritz* is this bolted slab route passing the right edge of a large roof and up a slight dish. Double ropes for the rappel. Pro: quickdraws.

60. Shitz on a Ritz (5.11a) ⋆⋆⋆ The route immediately right of *Sunrise Crack,* passing the roof and continuing up thin edging and friction. Highly recommended despite the name. Double ropes for the rappel. Pro: quickdraws. (FA: Geoff Scherer 1989)

61. Sunrise Crack (5.10c) ⋆ One of the original routes on Goat Dome, this very thin crack splits the roof at its apex on the left and continues up the slab above. Double ropes for the rappel. Tricky. Pro: to 1 inch, including TCUs. (FA: Tobin Kelly, Frank Stern 1979)

62. Shin Splints (5.11c) ⋆ A bolted slab pitch starting just left of *Sunrise Crack* and crossing that route about 15 feet below the upper ledge. Double ropes for the rappel. Pro: quickdraws.

63. Friction Addiction (5.10b) Above the anchors atop *Sunrise Crack* is this short, bolted slab starting with a shallow crack. Pro: quickdraws, plus gear to 1 inch.

Goat Dome

64. Jitterbug Boy (5.10a) Left of *Friction Addiction* is another bolted slab. A little run-out. Pro: quickdraws.

65. Black Sheets of Rain (5.9) ★★ Yet another bolted slab, this one just left of *Jitterbug Boy*. Pro: quickdraws.

66. Unknown Entity (5.9) About 50 feet left of the *Sunrise Crack* roof is this very obvious thin crack in a corner. Kind of mossy higher up. Pro: to 2 inches.

67. Quarks in Question (5.10a) ★ From the top of *Unknown Entity,* continue up a bolted slab to anchors. Pro: quickdraws.

68. Knobs of Shame (5.10a) ★★ Just left of *Unknown Entity* is this popular route, climbing a bolted slab to a ledge below an obvious flaky roof. Continue up the short crack, passing the roof on the left, then finish up the middle bolted slab on the upper buttress. Rappel the route; double ropes helpful. Pro: to 2 inches, mostly quickdraws.

Pearly Gates

69. Dick Is Dead (5.10d) ★ Immediately left of the start of *Knobs of Shame* is another bolted slab pitch leading to the roof. Pro: quickdraws.

70. Manic Mechanic (5.10a) ★ From Guano Ledge, climb the second pitch of *Knobs of Shame* (5.8 crack left of roof), then finish via the left-hand bolt line up the upper slab. Pro: to 2 inches, mostly quickdraws.

Pearly Gates

Pearly Gates is one of the most popular crags in Icicle Creek Canyon. This cliff of sparkling white granite jutting out from the canyon wall below the northern end of the Snow Creek Wall formation was exposed by the 1994 firestorm, but was not fully explored until 2001, when a majority of the routes were first climbed. The routes are predominately crack lines, including several stellar thin cracks on rock that has been favorably compared to the alpine granite faces of the Enchantments and Stuart Range.

Climbers favor the crag due to its northwesterly attitude, which keeps it shady until late afternoon.

The cliff is approached via a climbers' trail that leaves the Snow Creek Trail just after the aqueduct crossing, angling right and crossing Snow Creek via foot logs, then climbing the canyonside to the base of the formation. The approach takes about thirty minutes. The foot logs are bound to wash out one of these springs, which could complicate the approach. Climbers are cautioned to stay on the path and not take shortcuts to avoid erosion on this popular trail. Beware of hungry goats.

71. Poison Balance (5.11d) ★★★ The left-leaning flake just left of *Celestial Groove.* Pro: to 1.5 inches.

72. Celestial Groove (5.9+) ★★★ An obvious line up a crack in a wide corner on the far left side of the crag. Pro: to 2 inches.

73. Pearly Gates (5.10c) ★★ Thin cracks over the roof just right of *Celestial Groove.* Pro: to 1.5 inches; quickdraws.

74. Purgatory (5.10d) ★ Climb a crack, then traverse left along a seam to join *Pearly Gates* above the roof. Pro: to 2 inches; small wireds.

75. On Parole (5.10d) Start in the crack as for *Purgatory,* but continue straight up. Pro: to 2 inches.

76. Leap of Faith (5.10d) ★★★ A thin crack with a difficult start leads to face climbing. Pro: to 1.5 inches; quickdraws.

77. Cloud Nine (5.9) ★★★ A two-pitch line up the middle of the left side of the crag, beginning with a long, clean crack and finishing up a bolted corner. Pro: to 3 inches; quickdraws.

78. Cloudburst (5.10a) ★ A second-pitch variation to *Cloud Nine,* angling left from the belay, then back right up the clean face to the upper anchors. Pro: to 2 inches.

79. Easy Pickings (5.10a) ★ A variation start to *Cloud Nine,* starting with a bolt-protected crux, then a thin crack and more face moves. Pro: to 2 inches; quickdraws.

80. No Room for Squares (5.8) ★ The first of four distinct crack pitches right of the first pitch of *Cloud Nine.* Pro: to 2 inches.

81. Lost Souls (5.9) ★ The next crack to the right of *No Room For Squares.* Pro: to 2 inches.

82. Last Rites (5.10a) ★ The next crack, with a dogleg right midway up. Pro: to 3 inches.

83. Angelic Curses (5.10b) ★ The fourth crack, thinner than the others. Pro: to 2 inches.

84. Golden Delicious (5.8+) ★★ Another two-pitch line climbing up the middle of the crag. Scramble up the ledges from the right side to gain the start, then up you go. Pro: to 2 inches; quickdraws.

85. Divine Line (5.11c) ★★ A thin crack angling left through a roof. Pro: to 1 inch. This and the next three routes can be finished via *Tool Time.*

86. Solar Power (5.11b) ★ Another thin crack just right of *Divine Line.* Pro: to 1 inch.

87. Heaven's Sake (5.10a) ★ Climb cracks in a corner system. Pro: to 2 inches.

88. Loaves of Fun (5.8) ★★ Best described as double cracks with unusual knobs sticking out between them. Pro: to 2.5 inches; slings to tie off knobs.

89. Hepped Up on Goofballs (5.11a) ★★
Most easily located as the route left of *Veins of Glory,* climbing a flake to a good crack. Pro: to 2 inches.

90. Veins of Glory (5.10b) ★ A bolted line following a quartz vein, with a crux roof thrown in for fun. Pro: quickdraws.

91. Tool Time (5.9) ★★★ A bolted slab pitch leading to the top of the crag. Getting there is the hard part unless you climb *Loaves of Fun.* Pro: quickdraws.

92. Milky Way (5.10a) ★★★ A two-pitch line up the highest part of the crag, with a convenient ledge halfway up. Pro: to 1 inch; quickdraws.

93. Speak No Evil (5.10d) ★ A bolted line up the water-streaked slab leading to the grassy ledge. Pro: quickdraws.

94. Dog Ate My Topo (5.7) ★★ A bolted line up the far right edge of the dark slab. Pro: quickdraws.

95. The Reflector (5.8) ★★ One of two pitches leading up the bright white slab from the grassy ledge. This is the one without bolts. Pro: to 1 inch.

96. The Scene Is Clean (5.9) ★★ The other pitch, on the right edge of the white slab, with bolts. Pro: quickdraws.

Hammerhead Rock

On the right side of the road, just up from *Deb's Crack* and directly across the creek from Dog Dome, is Hammerhead Rock, a small, slabby buttress with a couple of cracks and face routes in the 5.6 to 5.10 range. The prominent boulder on the right, just off the road, is The Hand. A trail begins just right of The Hand and leads to Clamshell Cave.

Clamshell Cave

Clamshell Cave is a hidden crag with several routes in the 5.5 to 5.10 range. No single route justifies the hike, but combined there are enough decent routes to make the trek worthwhile. The Cube, a 20-foot-high boulder at the base of the crag, has some excellent boulder problems, including a classic 5.7 jam crack. A trail leads around The Hand on the right and up behind Hammerhead Rock, crossing a creek and climbing briefly to the crag in about ten minutes from the road.

97. Clamshell Crack (5.5) ★ The obvious big crack. Pro: to 5 inches.

98. Forty-Four Fifty (5.9) ★★ The first route right of *Clamshell Crack,* passing a roof and climbing slabby cracks to the top. Pro: quickdraws; gear to 3 inches.

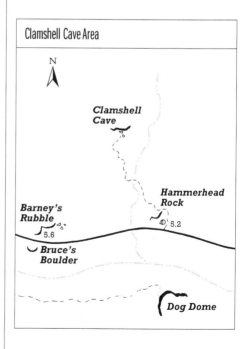

Clamshell Cave Area

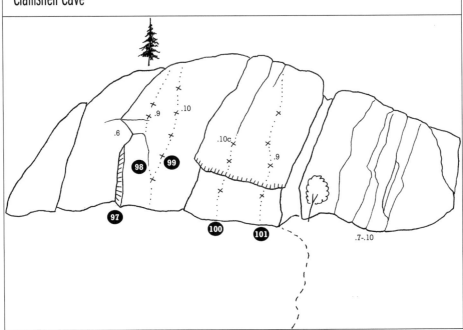

Clamshell Cave

99. Stolen Thunder (5.10c) ★★ The second route right of *Clamshell Crack,* sharing a first bolt with *Forty-Four Fifty* but passing the roof on the right side and climbing the slab above. Pro: quickdraws; gear to 1 inch.

100. Eagle's Wings (5.10c) ★★ The leftmost of two routes passing the roof in the middle of the crag. Pro: gear to 2 inches; quickdraws.

101. Eagle's Prey (5.9) ★★ The rightmost of two routes passing the roof. Pro: quickdraws; gear to 2 inches.

Bruce's Boulder

Bruce's Boulder is the small roadside dome located at about the 5.6-mile mark, on the left as you drive upcanyon. It is a heavily used practice area, with handlebar bolt anchors on top. There are many short friction and crack toprope routes in the 5.0 to 5.11 range.

Across the road from Bruce's Boulder is a slabby buttress known as Barney's Rubble, with several cracks and friction problems. Nobody seems to know where the name came from; it used to be referred to simply as "the rocks across the road from Bruce's Boulder." Anyway, this formation has a variety of toprope and lead problems up to 50 feet high in the 5.4 to 5.11 range. There are also several good boulder problems in the vicinity.

Both Bruce's Boulder and Barney's Rubble are excellent instruction crags, offering a great variety of climbing situations of varying difficulties, with opportunities for leading practice on sound rock. As such, they are usually crowded on weekends.

Muscle Beach

Muscle Beach is a small dome perched above several deep pools in Icicle Creek. Once a locals-only crag, it is now a very popular hangout, with four toprope problems in the 5.10 to 5.11 range, and an opportunity to prove yourself by leaping off the ledge into the icy-cold waters of Icicle Creek (not recommended for obvious reasons, but it is still done). The trail used to be hidden in the trees, but forest fires burned out the brush, making the crag easily visible on the left, just as Domestic Dome becomes visible as you drive up the canyon road shortly beyond Bruce's Boulder. Also, a cabin has been built across the creek from this crag, making it far from secluded, another fine example of "progress."

Domestic Dome
(Flake Buttress)

Domestic Dome is located on the right as you near Z-Crack Buttress, and is most easily identified by the dead tree reclining just below the obvious flake on the upper left side, as viewed from the road. There are a few routes on the road face, but the best routes climb the big slab on the far right side of the formation. Walk off to either side, or rappel from anchors.

102. Connie's Crack (5.2) A short crack on the upper left side, about 40 feet left of the flake. To get there, scramble up to the ledge left of the snag, or climb a 5.6 slab pitch directly. Walk off, or rappel from the tree. Pro: to 3 inches.

103. Underachiever (5.8) ★★ A bolted slab pitch just left of the obvious flake visible

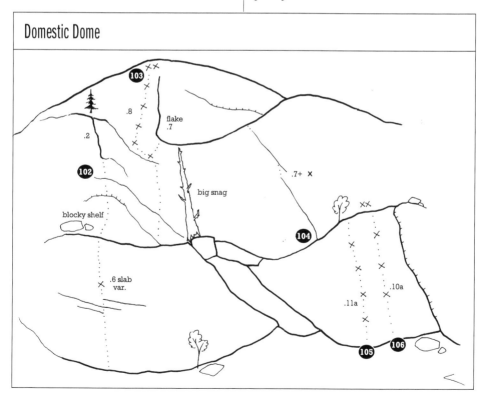

Domestic Dome

from the road. Approach as for *Connie's Crack*. A 5.7 variation gains the lichen-riddled flake. Pro: quickdraws.

104. Not to My Lichen (5.7 X) Disconnected seams lead to the ledge right of the flake; finish up the flake. Climbed prior to the first reported route on the crag, with one lousy stopper protecting the first pitch. Has been scrubbed, probably retrobolted. If not, don't bother.

105. No Boom Boom Tonight (5.11a) ★★ The leftmost of two bolted slab pitches located about 100 feet right and down from the flake. Pro: quickdraws, plus some small gear.

106. White Streak (5.10a) ★★ The rightmost of the two short, bolted slab pitches. Pro: quickdraws.

On the far right side of Domestic Dome is a large, steep slab with several bolted routes. Approach via the recently graded road, then directly to the slab. Rappel from anchors atop each route, or walk off to the right.

107. Domestic Friction (5.10d) ★ A slab route on the left, starting just right of a big pine tree and climbing a direct slab to anchors. Pro: quickdraws.

108. Domestic Principles (5.11a) ★★ A direct bolt line up the upper slab, starting with a dogleg bolt line lower down. Pro: lots of quickdraws. (FA: Doug Klewin, Gordon Briody 1988)

109. Domestic Bliss (5.10b) ★ Climb the slab on the far right, then up the arête on the right side of the upper slab. A difficult clip mars this otherwise fine route. Pro: quickdraws.

110. Dry Clean Only (5.10a) ★ Start as for *Domestic Bliss*, then go right and up an easy slab to a short crack finish. Pro: to 2 inches.

Roto Wall

Between Domestic Dome and Alphabet Wall is this short, slabby wall distinguished by several vertical and horizontal cracks and grooves. It is a popular practice wall, with several short cracks and slabs ranging from 5.3 to 5.8 in difficulty.

Alphabet Wall (Z-Crack)

Alphabet Wall is located on the right, directly across from the Rat Creek Boulder access road. It has three obvious crack routes and two less obvious routes on the left. The trail to Givler's Dome begins on the right. Scramble or walk off to the right.

111. Return to the Womb (5.10c) No topo. Around the corner left of *Z-Crack* is an alcove. This route climbs the big huecos out the back side of the alcove and up the short, reachy face above. Pro: quickdraws.

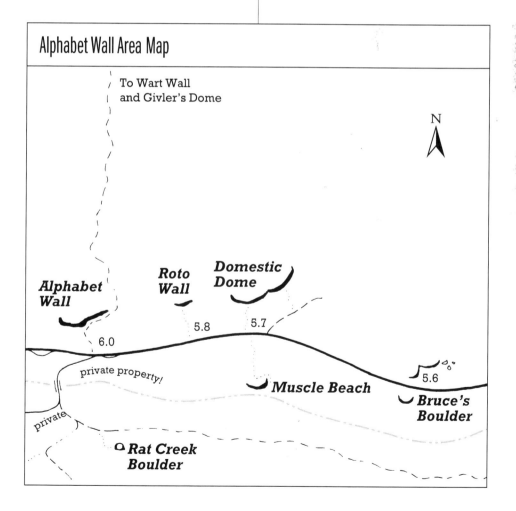

Alphabet Wall Area Map

To Wart Wall and Givler's Dome

N

Alphabet Wall

Roto Wall

Domestic Dome

5.8

5.7

6.0

private property!

Muscle Beach

5.6

Bruce's Boulder

private

To Rat Creek Boulder

112. Jaws of Life (5.11b) ★ No topo. Climb the arête left of *Z-Crack* and up the short slab to the top. Pro: quickdraws.

113. Z-Crack (5.10d) ★★★ The obvious Z-shaped crack on the left side of the wall, beginning with a difficult move over a roof. Pro: to 2.5 inches, including TCUs and wireds.

114. Meat Grinder (aka Alcove Crack) (5.10a) ★★★ The middle crack system, climbing wide cracks through a small roof. A variation start via the crack on the left is more difficult (5.10c). Pro: to 3 inches.

115. Dogleg Crack (5.8+) ★★★ The thin hand crack on the recessed wall right of *Alcove Crack*. A face variation just right may be toproped (5.10a). Pro: to 2 inches.

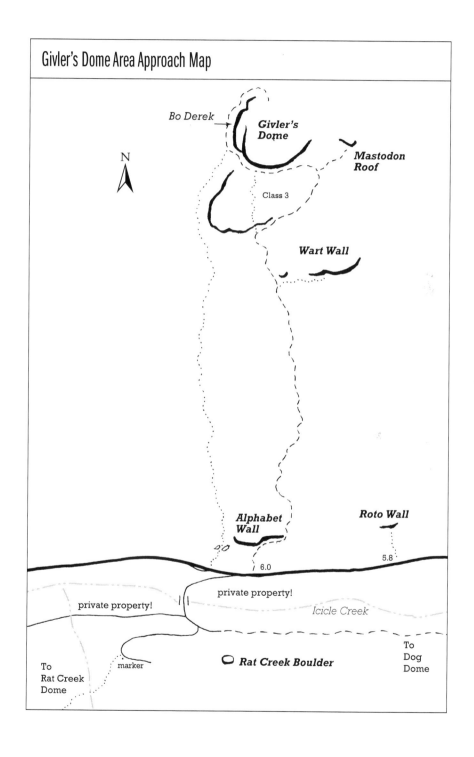

Givler's Dome Area Approach Map

Bo Derek →

Givler's Dome

Mastodon Roof

N

Class 3

Wart Wall

Alphabet Wall

Roto Wall

6.0

5.8

private property!

private property!

Icicle Creek

To Dog Dome

marker

◯ **Rat Creek Boulder**

To Rat Creek Dome

Givler's Dome Area

Givler's Dome is the large, rounded buttress situated high above Alphabet Wall. Its main route is easily visible from the road as a white streak up the center of the dome, which is usually occupied by climbers en route. A trail leads around the right side of Alphabet Wall and up to the base of the dome. There are many small formations located to either side of the trail, with a variety of climbs including steep cracks, roofs, and knobby slabs. These formations are listed in order as you ascend toward Givler's Dome.

Wart Wall

The Wart Wall is a small, slabby cliff with a preponderance of knobs and a few cracks. The wall is approached from the Givler's Dome path, by striking out right from just above the White Spot outcropping. It has a dozen or so slab and crack routes, but only a few are really worth climbing. Some are perilously runout.

116. Liquid Nitrogen (5.12a) ★★ The corner left of *The Edge,* leading to a line of bolts that protect the hardest moves. Pro: to 1 inch; quickdraws.

Wart Wall

117. The Edge (5.10b R) ★ The knobby slab just right of the obvious sloping arête near the center of the wall, beginning about 20 feet left of a large pine tree. A ground fall is possible from the crux, just below the second bolt. Pro: quickdraws.

118. Wicked Warts (5.11c) ★★ The bolted slab just right of *The Edge*. Once you get past the crux bulge, it's much easier. Pro: quickdraws.

119. Warts in My Shorts (5.10b) ★ Presently the first bolted slab route right of the big crack splitting the slab. Pro: quickdraws.

120. Five Gray Knobs (5.9) ★ The next bolted slab route to the right of *Warts in My Shorts*. Pro: quickdraws.

121. Power Drain (5.10d) ★ The rightmost bolted slab. Steep at the start, and a bit run-out. Pro: quickdraws.

Givler's Dome

Givler's Dome is the broad dome located high up on the hillside above *Z-Crack*, and is one of the most popular climbing areas in the Icicle, with many of the finest routes and, alas, a fairly long approach. The dome is situated about a half-hour walk directly uphill from Alphabet Wall, and is easily

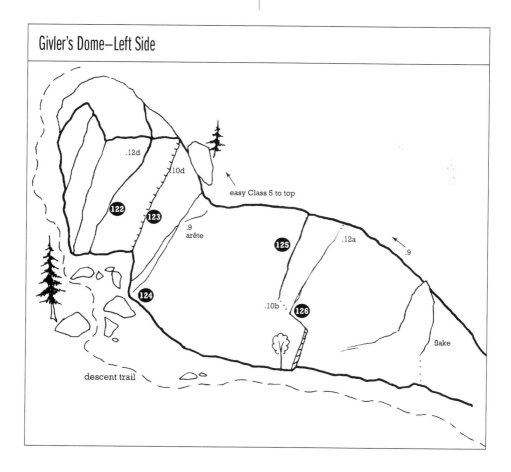

Givler's Dome—Left Side

Givler's Dome

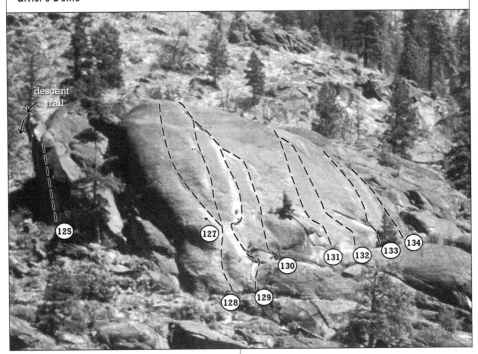

descent trail

125 127 130 128 129 131 132 133 134

identified by the crack splitting the dome approximately down the middle. The trail leads right at a rocky buttress, then back left across a shelf to the base of the crack route; alternatively, many parties scramble directly up ledges and gullies (Class 2 or 3). Another trail leads up a gully on the left, beginning just left of Alphabet Wall.

There are many fine friction and face routes on the south face of the dome, mostly with Tuolumne-style runouts. On the left flank of the dome are a few good crack climbs. The central crack system is the easiest and most popular route, and is usually crowded. The routes are listed from left to right, beginning at the top of the descent trail and continuing down the left side of the dome.

122. Never-Never (5.13a) ★★ This is the striking, very overhanging, grainy

finger-to-hand crack in the left wall of the uppermost dihedral. Cannot be mistaken for anything else. Pro: to 2.5 inches. (FFA: Todd Skinner 1983)

123. Bondage (5.10d) ★ The dihedral crack just right of *Never-Never,* with an incredibly leaning left wall. Pro: to 3 inches.

124. The Enema (5.9+ R) The arête right of *Bondage.* May be dirty. Marginal protection. Pro: unknown.

125. Bo Derek (5.10b) ★★★ The striking thin flake on the left side of Givler's Dome, considered by the first ascent party to be "the perfect 10." One of the better crack routes in the Icicle, even if the crux is face climbing. Pro: to #3.0 Friend. (FA: Bob Plumb or Pat McNerthney, Doug Klewin 1980)

126. Dudley Moore (5.12a) ★ The overhanging thin crack right of *Bo Derek*. Pro: mostly small, plus #3.0 Friend or equivalent.

127. The Barfing Hoof (5.9 X) A scary route up the leftmost portion of the main face of Givler's Dome. Climb the crack route to the flake, then climb left up a dished slab, following bolts if you can find them. Horror stories of bent bolts and long runouts have kept traffic on this route to a deserved minimum. Pro: quickdraws. (FA: Doug Klewin, Pat McNerthney 1980)

128. Wilson-McNerthney (5.10c) ★★★ A popular friction route up the slab left of *Givler's Crack*. From the base of the wall, climb the edgy slab to the flake (5.10a); you can exit here and finish up the crack route if you've had enough. A bit runout, especially after the crux moves. Pro: quickdraws, plus a couple of cams in the 1- to 3-inch range for the belay. (FA: Tim Wilson, Pat McNerthney 1989)

129. Givler's Crack (5.8) ★★★★ An Icicle classic, climbing the obvious crack splitting Givler's Dome. This was one of the state's most popular routes long before a guide was published. The initial 5.8 corner crack can be avoided by hiking right and around via a ledge. A couple of exposed face moves gain the crack, which is well protected. Pro: to 2 inches. (FA: John Marts and party 1960s)

130. Neat Route (5.10b) ★ The bolted face route just right of the crack. Climb to anchors, then exit via the crack. Pro: quickdraws.

131. It Doesn't Get Any Neater Than This (5.10a) ★★ The bolted slab route just left of *Timson's Face*. It gets neater, but this route is still pretty neat. Pro: quickdraws.

132. Timson's Face (5.10d) ★★ The first of Givler's Dome's face routes, and still the best—except for the runout to the first bolt, that is. Pro: quickdraws. (FA: Pat Timson 1972)

133. Quaaludes and Red Wine (5.10b) ★ Right of *Timson's Face* is yet another bolted face climb, which is a bit more runout than the others. Pro: quickdraws and TCUs; #2.5 Friend said to be helpful.

134. Just for the Bolt of It (5.10a) ★ The rightmost—and hopefully the last—of the bolted slab routes on Givler's Dome's main slab. They could probably squeeze a couple more in, but really! Pro: quickdraws.

135. Mastodon Roof (5.11c) ★ No topo. The wide crack through the roof about 100 yards right of Givler's Dome. Pro: to 4 inches.

Rat Creek Boulder

Across the creek from *Z-Crack* is a huge boulder that has several fun boulder and toprope routes in the 5.8 to 5.13 range. The name is a misnomer, as the boulder is closer to Hook Creek, as recognized by the latest guidebook to the area, but it was always called Rat Creek Boulder until recently, so Rat Creek Boulder it will remain, at least in this guidebook. Whatever you call it, the boulder is located on private property, and the only access at present—short of hiking in from the Lost World Plateau or fording the creek and hiking up from Dog Dome—is across a private road and bridge. Access to the boulder was permitted at last check, but not to the other domes and boulders farther upstream. Please respect the owner's rights and limit your use to the Rat Creek Boulder only. Of course, property owners change, and so do their minds, so it may be that in the future Rat Creek Boulder will be off-limits. If current signs say No Trespassing, ignore them at your peril.

Slug Rock

As you hike downstream from Rat Creek Boulder, on the right, directly across the creek from Bruce's Boulder, is an unmistakable rounded buttress called Slug Rock, a misnomer as there are no slugs anywhere near here (but it can get slimy when wet). There are three reported routes, rated 5.8, 5.9, and 5.10, respectively. Refer to *Leavenworth Rock* for route details.

Dog Dome

Downstream from Rat Creek Boulder, and directly across Icicle Creek from Hammerhead Rock, is Dog Dome, which is not very well hidden among the trees but is hard to get to. Dog Dome has several popular bolted slab routes in the 5.8 to 5.10c range on the right side, and a couple of routes around to the left that are not as popular. The customary approach to Dog Dome is to hike downstream from Rat Creek Boulder (private property must be crossed, but access is presently allowed). The following routes, listed from left to right, are well worth the hike, but are looking a little shaggy. Rappel from anchors; double ropes necessary on the longer routes.

136. Canine Capers (5.10a) ★★ The leftmost of the bolted slab routes on the right side of Dog Dome. Pro: quickdraws.

137. Spayed in the Shade (5.10b) ★★ The next route to the right, starting atop some boulders. Pro: quickdraws.

138. Hyperhound (5.10c) ★★ The original slab route on Dog Dome, near the center of the slab. Pro: quickdraws.

139. Pitch in Heat (5.8) ★★ A crack on the far right leads to a crux friction move at the top. Pro: to 2 inches; quickdraws.

140. See Spot Run (5.9) ★★ A short, bolted slab leads up to a small roof. Pass the roof to reach anchors shortly above. Pro: quickdraws.

141. Hot Koko (5.8) ★★ The rightmost bolted slab, ending at anchors below a tree. Pro: quickdraws.

Dog Dome

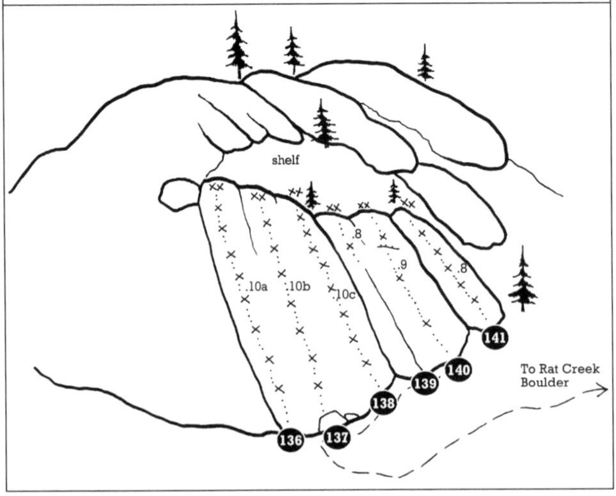

Hook Creek Dome

Uphill and right from Rat Creek Boulder is this distinctive, blocky crag, which has seen some exploratory ventures but has only one notable route. Take the spur road immediately right of Rat Creek Boulder to a marker, then head into the bushes, cross Rat Creek, and hike up the slope to the dome. The only worthy route is a 5.11 face climb just right of the prominent chimney facing downhill; it's rarely climbed and probably dirty.

Rat Creek Dome

Rat Creek Dome is the rounded buttress visible across the creek from Icicle Buttress. The dome has a number of striking cracks and roofs, and has several established routes including some recent additions in the 5.10 and 5.11 range. However, access to Rat Creek Dome is problematic, and as a result few visit this crag. The road along the creek is now a private driveway and **cannot** be used. It is possible to traverse the steep, grassy slopes well above the road, but this is arduous and time-consuming, and not quite worth the effort given the few quality routes at Rat Creek Dome. Probably the most popular route here is *Atlas Shrugged* (5.11c), a toprope problem on the "real" Rat Creek Boulder, but even it is barely worth the trouble of getting there. Refer to *Leavenworth Rock* for approach and route details.

Duty Dome

Among the jumble of buttresses and towers located between Givler's Dome and Icicle Buttress is Duty Dome, located just left of and below Eagle Rock (now known as Warrior Wall). It can be identified by the large Gumball Roof on the upper right side, and has several one- to three-pitch routes of varying worthiness.

To approach Duty Dome and Warrior Wall, hike up the gully directly toward Eagle Rock. Side trails leading to the various cliffs are self-evident. The routes are described as you encounter them on your approach.

The following several routes are located on a short, slabby wall below and right of the main buttress, directly below the distinctive Gumball Roof, which is unofficially known as "Fish Face" because of the names bestowed upon the routes by those who pioneered them.

142. Looney Tuna (5.10a) ★ Presently the lowest route on Fish Face, climbing a steepening slab to a tree. Pro: to 2 inches; quickdraws.

143. Virgin Sturgeon (5.9) ★★ Up and left from *Tuna* is this short pitch passing a small roof at the start. A short crux face section links cracks higher up. Pro: to 2 inches; quickdraws.

144. Bohemian Blowfish (5.8) Cracks and friction in between *Sturgeon* and *Sardine*. Pro: to 2 inches.

145. Sardine Routine (5.9) ★ The leftmost route on Fish Face, marked by a bolt at the start. Pro: quickdraws; gear to 2 inches.

146. Off Duty (5.10a) ★★★ One of the Icicle's better face routes, climbing a knobby slab on the upper right side of Duty Dome. To get there, scramble up to the grassy bench above Fish Face. Most parties rappel after the first pitch, which is easier than descending the gully after doing the second pitch. Pro: quickdraws; plus a #2.0 or #2.5 Friend. (FA: Dave Lenz, Viktor and Alicia Kramar, John Halley 1988)

147. Straight Street (5.9) ★★★ The bolted arête pitch left of *Off Duty* leads to corner cracks and an undercling left to avoid the big roof. Pro: quickdraws; gear to 2 inches.

148. Jazzy Document (5.9) ★★ A short route at the base of the wall about 50 meters left of Fish Face. Connect the bolts up this colorful

Duty Dome

wall, which graces the cover of *Leavenworth Rock's* first edition. Pro: quickdraws.

149. Heart of Gold (II, 5.10a) ★★★ A recent four-pitch line on the left side of Duty Dome, on the next buttress left from *Jazzy Document*. Continue up *Prime Rib* if four pitches is not enough. Pro: Quickdraws.

150. Prime Rib (5.10b) ★★ A three-pitch continuation of *Heart of Gold,* finishing

up the left side of Warrior Wall. Pro: quickdraws.

151. Urban Nomads (5.10a) ★★ On the far left side of Duty Dome, climb up and behind a large detached flake (easy Class 5) to bolt anchors, then climb the crack directly above through a crux roof. Pro: to 2 inches.

152. 300 Motivational Tapes (5.10c) ★ The blocky dihedral crack just right of *Nomads*. Pro: to 2 inches.

Warrior Wall

Warrior Wall is the bulbous cliff located behind Duty Dome, and is the most prominent crag in this area of the Icicle. It can be readily identified by its dihedrals, and because from some vantages it resembles a bird skull. It has several decent routes, although the approach and descent leave much to be desired. Approach via a gully right of Duty Dome. If you find yourself scrambling up scary choss, you're in the wrong gully. Alternatively, climb *Off Duty* to the top, which leaves you directly opposite Warrior Wall.

153. East Face (5.10d) ★ The rightmost of two bolted slab routes to the right of the prominent arête forming the "beak" of the formation. Two pitches following bolts. May be dirty. Pro: quickdraws, gear to 2 inches.

154. Duke of Ballet (5.11b) ★ The bolted slab right of the prominent arête forming the "beak" of the formation. The initial slab is the crux, and most parties rappel from the first anchors, although the route continues to the top. Pro:

quickdraws for first pitch; gear to 3 inches if you go all the way.

155. The Warrior (5.10d) ★★★ The striking, left-leaning dihedral immediately left of the arête. Hardest at the top. Pro: to 2 inches. (FA: Pat Timson, Rick LeDuc 1970s)

Duty Dome and Warrior Wall

156. Weekend Warrior (5.10c) ★ Just a bit farther left of the arête, climb a bolted face to this left-slanting crack. Easiest if you stay in the lower crack; the thinner crack just above the main route is a harder variation (5.11b). Pro: to 2 inches; TCUs for harder variation.

157. Peaceful Warrior (5.10b) ★ A corner crack leads to a single bolt protecting moves up a knobby slab to reach *Weekend Warrior's* anchors. Pro: to 1.5 inches; quickdraws.

158. Potato Chip Flake (5.10c R) No topo. The very thin, expanding flake on the left side of Warrior Wall. Pro: to 2 inches.

Hidden Tower

Hidden Tower (also known as Peek-a-Boo Tower) is the short, stubby pinnacle located just up and right from the base of Warrior Wall. The standard route up the tower is presently rated 5.9, and there are a handful of routes up to 5.10 here for those inclined to climb obscure pinnacles and slabs. Refer to the current edition of *Leavenworth Rock* for more route details.

159. West Face (5.9) ★ No topo. A slab traverse angles to the left arête, then up wide cracks to the top. Pro: to 4 inches; quickdraws.

Icicle Buttress

Icicle Buttress is the large, slabby formation rising directly above the road about 0.25 mile up the road from *Z-Crack*. It has an assortment of short, steep crack climbs, complemented by several short and long slab pitches. Routes are described from left to right, approximately as they are encountered when approached via the standard approach for each area of the cliff. Descents from routes on Icicle Buttress can be troublesome, and on some routes you must climb up and out to escape unless you are willing to downclimb or leave gear behind. Once on top, you may walk off to either side, although it's easiest to descend to the left.

The following several routes are on the left side of Icicle Buttress. The upper tier routes are usually approached via *R & D* or *Cocaine Connection*. Be careful when scrambling along the shelves and ledges, as there are occasional Class 5 moves.

160. R & D (5.6) ★★ From a snag near the base of the cliff on the far left side, climb two fairly easy pitches more-or-less directly to the base of *Cocaine Crack*, then up the chimney just right, finishing via the steep buttress directly above the crack or via a straight-in crack just right. Follow the widening crack to the top. A 5.10a variation passes the prominent roof low on the route. Pro: to 3 inches.

161. Cocaine Crack (5.10a) ★★ The obvious curving crack on the left side of the formation. Approach via *R & D* or *Cocaine Connection*. Rappel from anchors, continue up *R & D,* or scramble off left. Pro: to 3 inches, mostly 1 inch and below. (FA: Del Young, Catherine Freer 1980)

162. Cocaine Connection (5.7) ★ A long, bolt-protected slab right of the start of *R & D.* As the name implies, this is a customary approach route for *Cocaine Crack.* Pro: quickdraws.

163. Big Bertha (5.11d) ★ The big crack through the huge roof high up on Icicle Buttress. Pro: to 6 inches.

The following several routes are on the bottom tier of Icicle Buttress, and are somewhat hidden from view by maple trees along the base of the cliff. These routes are easily approached from the road.

Icicle Buttress

164. Spaghetti Sauce (5.8) ★ Climb either of two obvious curvy flakes in the left-hand corner. Two variation starts and finishes. Pro: to 2 inches.

165. The Arch (5.8) ★ The prominent right-leaning arch traversing across the slab below *Forking Crack*. Pro: to 2 inches.

166. Forking Crack (5.9) ★ The obvious forking crack. Pro: to 4 inches.

167. Chicken Gully (5.4) The gully right of *The Arch*. Usually climbed to approach *John Henry* and kin. Pro to 3 inches.

The following routes are located on a small, blocky cliff band above the sloping shelf at the center of Icicle Buttress, more or less directly above *Forking Crack* and below *The Cave Route*. The routes may be reached most directly from the slabs above *Forking Crack* by climbing *Chicken Gully* or any other nearby route.

168. John Henry (5.11a) ★★ A straight-in thin crack on the left. Pro: to 2 inches.

169. Dark Shadows (5.10d) The obvious chimney. Pro: to 3 inches.

170. Vise Grip (5.11a) ★★ A face climb right of *Dark Shadows*, passing just left of a small roof. Pro: to 1 inch.

171. 'Tober (5.10a) ★★★ A face climb on the far right, around the corner from *Vise Grip*, with a short crack at the end. Pro: to 1 inch.

The following routes are located directly above the *Vise Grip* wall, and are most easily reached by climbing *Chicken Gully* and scrambling right around the *Vise*

Grip wall or by traversing in from *Cocaine Connection*.

172. The Cave Route (5.4) ★ An easy pitch leads to the obvious alcove high on the upper right side of Icicle Buttress, from where ramps and cracks lead right. Pro: to 2 inches.

173. 'Vember (5.10c) ★ A right-angling crack system just right of and below *The Cave*. The popular continuation of *'Tober*. Pro: to 2 inches.

The following several routes are visible along the base of the cliff, on the right side, directly above the road. Climb these and you'll no doubt catch the attention of passing "tourons."

174. Ions (aka Eye-ons) (5.11b) ★ The bolted slab on the left. Runout but relatively easy to the first bolt. Pro: quickdraws.

175. Tourons (5.10b) ★ Another bolted slab just right of *Ions*. Pro: quickdraws.

Eightmile Rock (Classic Crack Buttress)

Eightmile Rock (also known as Classic Crack Buttress) is a short wall located

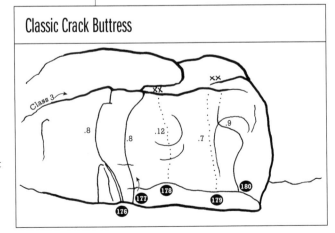

Classic Crack Buttress

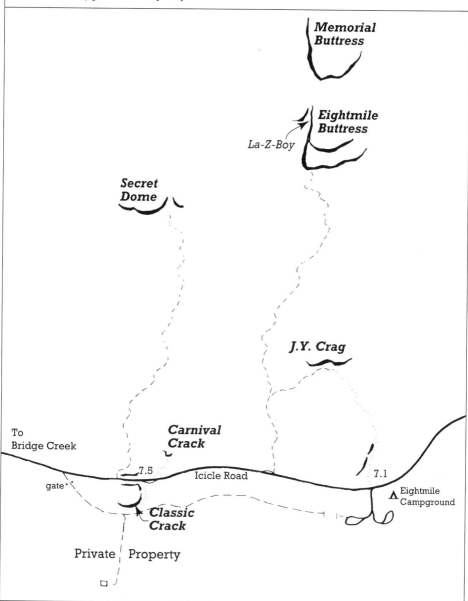

just upriver from Eightmile Campground. It can be reached either by descending directly from the road or by hiking in from the campground. It has several short crack and face problems in the 5.8 to 5.11 range, which are usually toproped. Classic Crack

Buttress is located on private property. Behave yourself so the privilege of climbing here is not revoked.

176. Left Crack (aka Twin Cracks) (5.8) ★
The shallow, flaring cracks just left of *Classic*

Carnival Crack

Crack. A direct start up the wide, flaring slot on the right is 5.9+. Pro: to 2 inches will suffice; cams recommended.

177. Classic Crack (5.8+) ★★ The obvious wide hand crack splitting the wall. Traditionally rated 5.8, but many think it's harder. Usually toproped, but a sporting lead for the aspiring 5.8 crack climber. Pro: to 3 inches.

178. Doin' the Dishes (5.12b TR) Thin face climbing up the dirty, concave wall just right

of *Classic Crack.* Reportedly harder since holds broke off.

179. Mickey Mantle (5.7 R) Face climb up the blunt arête just left of *Deception.* Best toproped. Pro: wired nut.

180. Deception (5.9) ★ This shallow, left-leaning crack on the far right side is harder than it looks. Pro: to 1 inch.

181. Carnival Crack (5.10c) ★ Across the road and about 100 meters down from

Classic Crack Buttress is this obvious off-width splitting an angular, flat-topped buttress. Usually toproped, since nobody seems to be able to afford enough big pro to safely lead it. Pro: to 8 inches.

182. Trapeze (5.12a TR) ★★ The thin seam immediately left of *Carnival Crack*.

Secret Dome

A hidden slab located uphill from *Carnival Crack*. A hidden trail starts just across the road from Classic Crack Buttress, going left

of *Carnival Crack* and up the hillside fifteen minutes to the dome. Rappel from anchors.

183. Anorexic Edges (5.10b) ★★★ The best route at Secret Dome, and the most obvious. Climb up a short crack to a ledge, then up the prow and easier slab to the top. Pro: quickdraws; gear to 3 inches for the initial crack. (FA: Geoff Scherer, Viktor Kramar 1990)

184. Balance of Power (5.10a) ★★ Just down and left from the initial crack of *Anorexic Edges,* climb past bolts up a black streak, then up shallow cracks and the easier upper slab

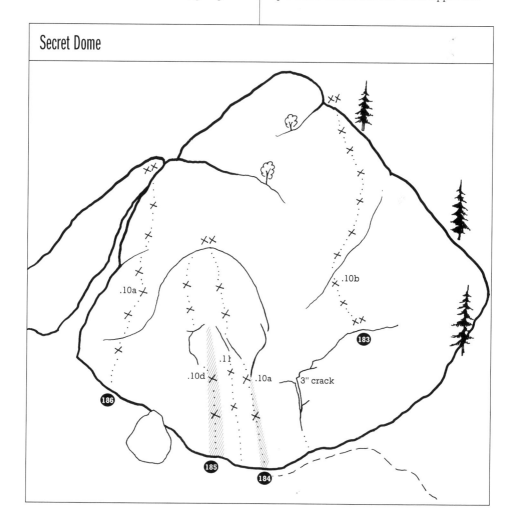

Secret Dome

.10a
.10b
.11
.10d .10a 3" crack
186
185 184

to anchors. A 5.11 direct start passes two bolts just left; stick clip the first bolt if you know what's good for you. Pro: quickdraws; cams to 3 inches.

185. Stolen Moments (5.10d) ★★ Climb the steep, thin face on the left, following another black streak to shallow cracks and up the easier upper slab. Pro: quickdraws; small to midsize cams.

186. Bulimic Bulges (5.10a) ★ A sloping ramp on the far left side leads past a crux bulge and up easier friction to anchors way up on the left. Pro: quickdraws.

J.Y. Crag

J.Y. Crag is a hidden cliff located directly across the road from Eightmile Campground. The crag has several obvious crack, roof, and

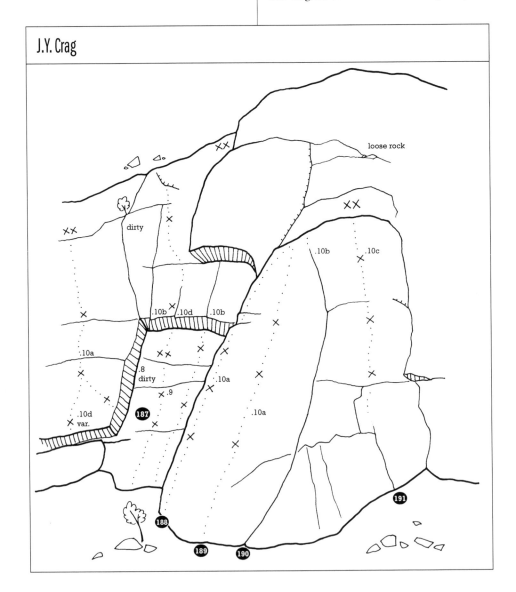

J.Y. Crag

slab routes in the 5.9 to 5.10 range, most of which are dirty and mossy, but a few of which are clean and popular. To get there, take the right spur trail from the Eightmile Buttress trail about 200 yards up from the road, or find your way up through the woods directly across from the campground entrance.

The following several routes climb a clean slab on the right side of J.Y. Crag, and share anchors about 60 feet up. Several toprope variations are possible. Beware of loose rock above the anchors.

187. Secret Cragsman (5.8) A dirty corner and crack through the left end of the roofs. A direct finish (*Janet's Diary,* 5.10a) climbs the thin crack over the roof above. Probably dirty, but fun when cleaned up. Pro: to 2 inches.

188. J.Y. Arête (5.10a) ★★ The leftmost route on the clean slab on the right side of the crag, connecting the bolts up the left-hand arête. Pro: quickdraws.

189. Ragweed (5.10a) ★★ The next bolted slab route right of the arête, just left of the crack. Pro: to 1 inch, including small cams, quickdraws.

190. Armed Forces (5.10b) ★★ The obvious shallow crack splitting the slab, with a crux face exit. Pro: to 1.5 inches.

191. Six Digits in the Hole (5.10c) ★★ The right-hand bolted slab route. Pro: quickdraws.

Eightmile Buttress

Eightmile Buttress is the large, semi-forested buttress visible high above Classic Crack Buttress. There are a few multi-pitch routes and a couple of one-pitch

cracks on the steep left side of the buttress. To get there, find the trail about 100 yards up the road from the campground entrance, and start hiking. Approach as for J.Y. Crag, continuing around to the left and up. Please do your best to stay on the established trail, to avoid further erosion. Descend by walking off or rappelling, depending on which route you are on and how high you climb.

192. Tree Route (II, 5.6 or 5.7) ★★ This route is very popular despite the long approach and descent. Begin on the left margin of the buttress, climbing a poorly protected chimney (5.6) or an angling crack on the right (5.7) to a ledge. A scrambling pitch leads to a roof and a 6-inch-wide white crack (5.4), which ends on a broad shelf. Either traverse off rightward and descend from here, or continue up through trees on the right to a ramp system that leads to the top via one of several variations (up to 5.9). From the top, descend right and down a broad gully. Pro: to 4 inches.

193. Ms. Tremendous (5.10b R) The left-hand of two routes climbing the slabby buttress about 50 meters right from the start of *Tree Route.* Scary runouts. Pro: to 3 inches; quickdraws.

194. Mr. Tremendous (5.10b) ★★ The right-hand route, which is justifiably more popular than its mate. The route is easy to follow, as it ascends a well-scrubbed, bolted swath just right of the "arête" of the buttress. The first pitch ends on a grassy ledge; the second pitch ends on a broad shelf, from where you can walk off or rappel. Pro: to 2 inches; quickdraws.

195. La-Z-Boy (5.11b) ★ No topo. Way up the gully left of the start of *Tree Route,* hidden behind a grove of slide maple, is this

Eightmile Buttress

steep, blocky route. Fight your way through the maple, then climb a flaky crack to an obvious protruding flake (the Recliner). Sit a spell, then power up the thin crack to the top. Pro: to 2 inches.

Little Bridge Creek Buttress

Across the road from the entrance to Bridge Creek Campground, and just left through the trees, is this small, steep-walled cliff (also known as Bridge Creek Rock) with a number of excellent climbs. A trail leads up from the left side of the private road directly across from the campground entrance. Beware of private property on the right, and don't park in the driveway. There are endangered plant species here, so no more scrubbing off lichen, please. The routes are listed from right to left as you approach from the road.

196. Gutbuster (5.12d TR) No topo. The very short, very difficult overhanging seam just above where the trail meets the cliff.

197. Arms Control (5.10b) ★★ The obvious arch, flake, and face route on the left side of the dirty dihedral. A good all-around test of climbing technique. Walk off to the left. Pro: to 2 inches, including small to midsize cams. (FA: Brent Hoffman, Gary Jones 1982)

198. Conscientious Objector (5.10a R) ★ Just left of the arête left of *Arms Control* is this slanting groove. Iffy protection for the first 30 feet. A direct face/seam start on the left has been toproped (5.11b). Pro: to 1.5 inches.

199. Dishonorable Discharge (5.10c) ★ An overhanging thin crack leads through a nasty flaring slot. You'll either love it or hate it—or both! Pro: to 2 inches.

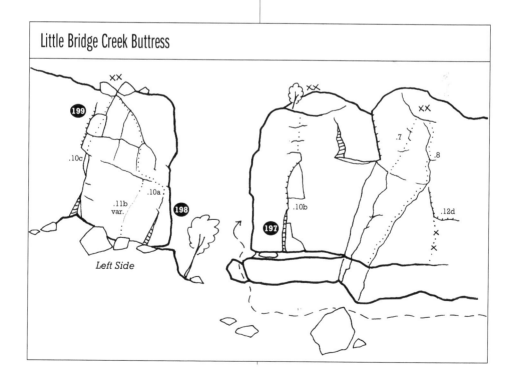

Little Bridge Creek Buttress

The Sword

About 0.25 mile up from Bridge Creek Campground is this humongous, cubic boulder that has several difficult toprope problems in the 5.11 to 5.13 range. The Sword is not visible from the road; a short trail leads there, passing other boulders along the way. There are several good problems in this area. The trail to Bathtub Dome begins here, angling left as you pass Underwear Rock, the first bouldering wall encountered (about 50 feet off the road).

Bathtub Dome

Bathtub Dome is a comparatively small buttress plainly visible above Little Bridge Creek Buttress, the lowest of the cliffs descending from Icicle Buttress. Bathtub Dome has several easy and moderate routes in the 5.5 to 5.10 range, a few of which must be worth the long approach hike, judging by the number of climbers who visit this crag. The approach discourages most climbers from climbing here, but this intriguing crag has become increasingly popular. If you climb everything while you're here, you may never need to suffer the approach hike again.

Bathtub Dome

Approach via a trail leading up from Underwear Rock, about 0.3 mile up from Little Bridge Creek Buttress, on the right (near The Sword boulder). It's hot and sweaty by afternoon; definitely an early morning approach if you know what's good for you. The routes are listed from bottom to top, left to right. Descend by rappel off the top buttress, then hike off to the right.

Many new routes have been done in this area in recent years, on Bathtub Dome proper and satellite crags. Refer to *Leavenworth Rock* for details.

200. The Ring (5.10d) ★ A good approach pitch for the upper routes, climbing a steep face and cracks on the far left side of the lower wall. Pro: to 2 inches.

201. Toilet Trouble (5.6) The easiest route up Bathtub Dome, but not its best. Pro: Not much.

202. New Fixtures (5.7 R) ★ This route climbs the lower buttresses leading up to Bathtub Dome proper. The first pitch follows an obvious, poorly protected dike to a ledge; the second pitch climbs cracks above a large block to the main ledge below the next three routes. Pro: to 4 inches.

203. Just Ducky (5.9) ★★★ A long, entertaining pitch up the left side of Bathtub Dome. Pro: to 2 inches. (FA: Gordon Briody, Fred Rose 1996)

204. The Drain (5.9) ★★ Slabby face climbing leads directly up the middle of the main face to an easier crack. Pro: to 2 inches, including small cams.

205. Shower Stall (5.10a) ★★★ The blocky face on the right edge of Bathtub Dome's main face, visible from the road as a white streak. Fun, airy climbing. Pro: to 2 inches, including small cams. (FA: Gordon Briody, Viktor Kramar 1989)

The Condor (Condor Buttress)

Just up from Bathtub Dome is The Condor, a large, rounded, slabby buttress that has four reported routes, including the fairly recent sport magnet, *Condorphamine Addiction*. Approach as for Bathtub Dome and keep going another twenty minutes up the slope. *Condorphamine Addiction* is the most popular route on Condor Buttress, but probably not for long if the other routes are cleaned up and retrobolted, or if someone decides to scrub and bolt another line for which there appears to be potential. If you want more information about the other routes here, refer to *Leavenworth Rock* for details.

206. Condorphamine Addiction (5.10b) ★★★ A seven-pitch bolted line climbing to the top of Condor Buttress. Great fun, but can get crowded with more than one party trying to climb or rappel at the same time. Some pitches are short enough to link together. The bolts are close enough in several places that some climbers skip clips to avoid running out of quickdraws, especially when linking pitches. Easier variation first pitches on either side. Pro: twelve to fifteen quickdraws; double ropes for rappels recommended.

Bridge Creek Buttress

Bridge Creek Buttress is the mammoth wall visible above Bridge Creek Campground. It has several established routes, and appears to have potential for more long free and aid climbs. If Bridge Creek Buttress was closer to the road, it would have dozens of classic, multipitch routes. But the approach is long and arduous, which discourages most climbers from visiting this impressive wall. Refer to *Leavenworth Rock* for approach and route details.

Condor Buttress

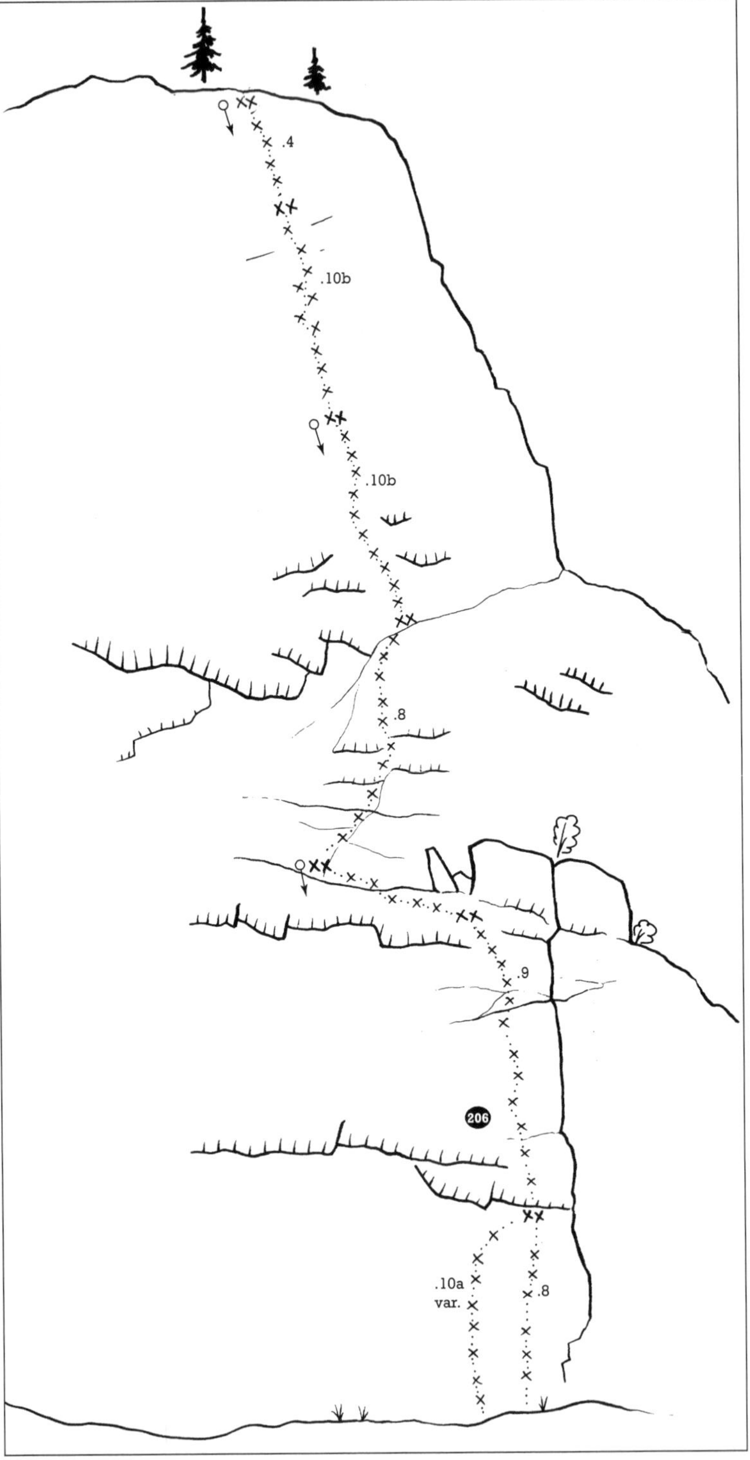

.4

.10b

.10b

.8

.9

206

.10a
var.

.8

The Egg

Another 0.2 mile uproad from Bridge Creek Campground from Underwear Rock and The Sword is The Egg, a small, rounded boulder on the right, hidden in the trees. There are several entertaining boulder problems near here, and a couple of lead routes on the blocky cliffs just up the road.

Halloween Rock

About 0.25 mile downroad from the Fourth-of-July trailhead is a small crag, barely visible from the road, with one decent 5.9 slab on the left and a couple of toprope routes on the right.

Fourth-of-July Buttress

This popular crag is located just downroad from the Fourth-of-July Trail. It features about a dozen routes in the 5.7 to 5.11 range, including the Icicle's best steep face climbing. Park at the trailhead, and be sure to lock your car, keeping valuables out of sight or taking them with you. The trail begins about 20 meters downroad from the

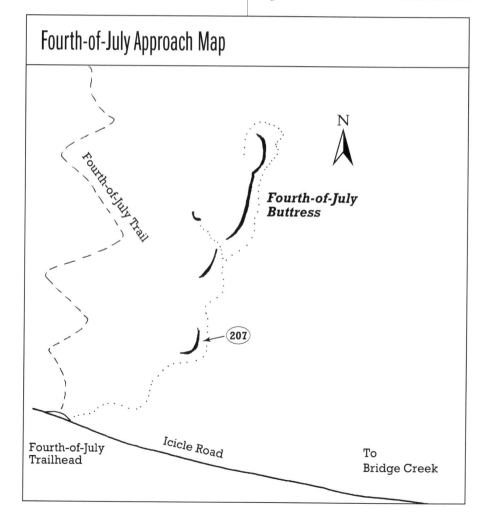

Fourth-of-July Approach Map

Fourth-of-July Buttress

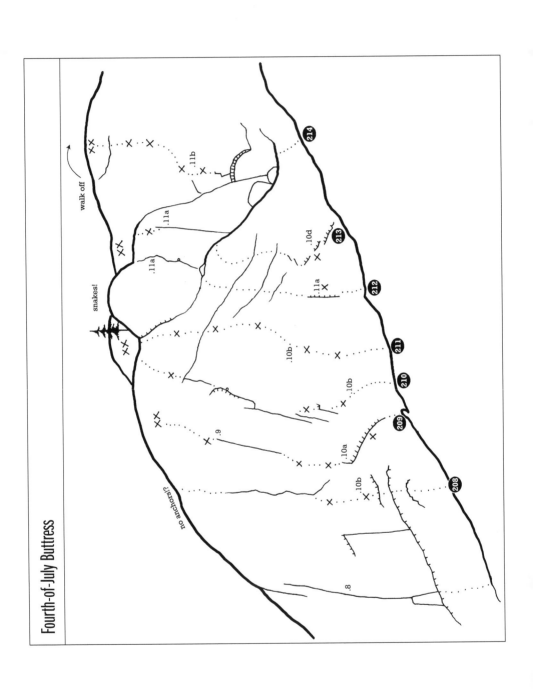

trailhead, and skirts around a lower buttress and up sandy slabs to the wall.

207. Silhouettes (5.7) ★★ No topo. The bolted slab on the left about 100 yards up the trail from the road. Pretty decent for a short 5.7 slab. A direct variation is harder (5.9) and unprotected. Pro: quickdraws.

208. Lunging for the Rafters (5.10b) ★
Climb a short, blocky, overhanging face just down from *Bolt Fairy* and up the bolted headwall past a crack. If you can't find the anchors, you won't be the first. Pro: quickdraws; TCUs.

209. Return of the Bolt Fairy (5.10a) ★★
Traverse left up a short ramp under an overhang, then face climb up to and past a shallow crack. Pro: to 1 inch; quickdraws.

210. Beer & Loafing in Leavenworth
(5.10b) ★★ Just right of the start of *Bolt Fairy,* climb straight up to a bolt about 15 feet off the ground (crux), then up cracks and a flake (5.9) to the anchors. Pro: to 1 inch; quickdraws.

211. Facelift (5.10b) ★★★ The obvious steep, bolt-protected face, easily the best route on the crag. Reachy at the crux. Pro: quickdraws. (FA: Doug Klewin, Dave Lenz, Viktor Kramar 1988)

212. Just the Facts, Ma'am (5.11a) ★ Right of *Facelift* is a single bolt beside a small left-facing corner. Climb past the bolt and up to the left of two obvious cracks on the upper headwall, then up and over to the belay. The first crux is more technical, the final overhanging face moves more pumping. Pro: to 2 inches, including a variety of cams.

213. All My Friends Are Assholes (5.11a) A bolt in a fractured white wall marks the start of this route. Climb up grungy rock to the right-hand crack in the headwall, then up that crack to the top. You can skip the lower part of the route by traversing up the ramp from *Blue Moon.* Pro: to 2 inches, including a variety of cams.

214. Blue Moon (5.11b) ★★ The rightmost route on the wall, climbing past an overhang then up a steep, clean, bolted face. Grungy start, funky bolt spacing, but otherwise enjoyable. Pro: to 1.5 inches; quickdraws.

Snow Creek Wall Detail Map

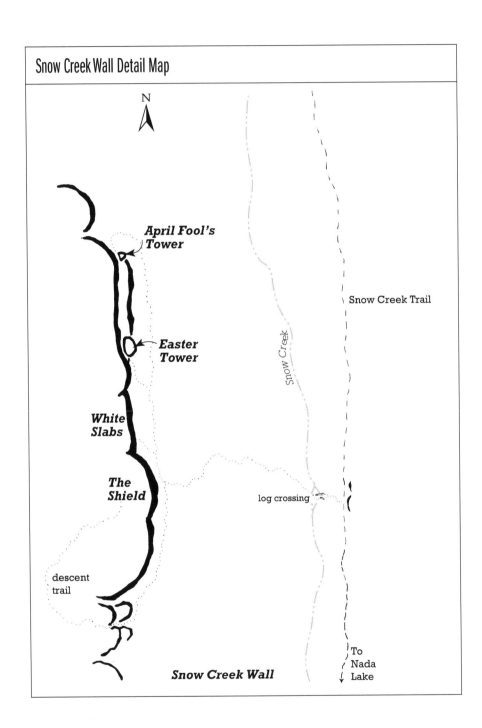

N

April Fool's Tower

Snow Creek Trail

Snow Creek

Easter Tower

White Slabs

The Shield

log crossing

descent trail

To Nada Lake

Snow Creek Wall

SNOW CREEK WALL

Snow Creek Wall is the largest singular cliff included in this guide. It rises some 900 feet from base to summit, and extends in width more than 0.25 mile above Snow Creek, just above where the creek begins its cascade down into Icicle Creek Canyon. Snow Creek Wall offers numerous multi-pitch routes on its slabby, weathered granite, ranging from one to eight pitches in length, mostly climbing crack systems linked by knobby slabs, from 5.6 to 5.12 in difficulty. Some routes are very serious in nature, with little or no protection or long runouts between bolts, but most of the area's routes are relatively safe and enjoyable.

Snow Creek Wall is located just south of Icicle Creek Canyon, and is visible from several points along Icicle Road as you drive into the canyon. It is reached via a 2-mile hike up the Snow Creek Trail, which begins from the parking lot across from *The Visor* overhang, approximately 4.3 miles up Icicle Road from the US 2 junction. The trail crosses Icicle Creek and an aqueduct before switchbacking up the opposite slope. Shortly after the switchbacks level off, the wall comes dramatically into view. At a point directly across from the cliff, where the trail passes some mossy cliffs, a side trail drops down to the creek and crosses via logs to gain the opposite slope, where a steep, dusty climb gains the base of the wall, directly below Two Trees Ledge. Hiking time to the wall is forty-five minutes to an hour for most parties. Start early to beat the heat and the crowds, particularly on sunny spring and autumn weekends.

Snow Creek Wall lies within the Alpine Lakes Wilderness, and permits are required for all use, including hiking and climbing. Self-issue day-use permits are available at the trailhead. If you plan on staying overnight, check with the forest service office in Leavenworth regarding permit availability.

In 1998 the forest service banned the use of fixed anchors in wilderness. If this ban survives, climbers will not be permitted to place bolts or fixed pitons at Snow Creek Wall.

During spring, particularly in May, Snow Creek Wall is infested with ticks. As elsewhere in Leavenworth, watch out for rattlesnakes, particularly during summer and fall months. Also, don't leave your pack and shoes unattended at the top of the wall; mountain goats are sometimes lurking nearby, and they will eat almost anything. As in other areas, but particularly at the Snow Creek trailhead, don't leave valuables in your car, visible or otherwise, as thefts are common here.

The routes are described from left to right. Most of the routes reaching the top of the wall, including variations along the way, are Grade III, meaning you should expect to be able to do one route in a day, allowing time to descend and hike out before dark, usually with time left to climb a few short routes in the Icicle on the way out. The descent for most routes is down the rocky gullies left of the wall, which at best involves scrambling down sandy ledges and gullies, and at worst involves rappelling once or twice. It is easy to lose the trail on the descent, and if you take the wrong gully down, you may find yourself down-climbing Class 5 rock. When in doubt, backtrack or rappel. In the dark the descent would be a nightmare, so allow yourself plenty of time to make the descent during daylight, and be sure you have a flashlight or headlamp.

1. Satellite (5.7) ★ On the left edge of the wall is an obvious wide crack. Climb the crack, then up discontinuous cracks (crux) to a right-facing corner. Pass through the

Snow Creek Wall

overhang and up knobby slabs to the top. Five pitches. Pro: to 2 inches.

2. Orbit (5.8 or 5.9) ★★★ One of the more popular routes on Snow Creek Wall. Begin directly beneath *Mary Jane Dihedral,* climbing a gully and chimney to a ledge at the base of the dihedral, then traversing an easy Class 5 ramp left to the base of a dihedral beneath a small roof. Climb the corner (or thin cracks just right) up to and then past the roof, then up the slab above to a ledge (5.8 mantle onto ledge). The route continues up the knobby slab, skirting the imposing roof via a knobby wall. Easier climbing continues to the top. A few runouts, but most of the climbing is not especially difficult. Pro: to 3 inches, including small wired nuts. (FFA: Ron Burgner, John Marts 1966)

2A. Blast Off (variation) (5.10a) ★ A dihedral crack left of the initial chimney joins *Orbit* near the end of the ramp. Pro: to 2 inches.

3. Mary Jane Dihedral (5.9) ★★ The obvious left-facing dihedral on the left side of the wall. Start as for *Orbit,* up the chimney to the ledge, then continue up into the dihedral, staying in the corner except when forced onto the face. Join *Orbit* at the roof and head for the top. Seven pitches. Pro: to 2 inches. (FA: Don McPherson, Ron Burgner, Jim Madsen 1966)

4. Galaxy (5.9) ★ A long route climbing the obvious brushy dihedral system in the middle of the wall. The route follows the gully nearly all the way to the top, linking cracks and corners along the way before finally traversing left under a roof at the top of the wall. Nine pitches, Grade IV; could take all day. Pro: to 3 inches. (FFA: Jim Madsen, Tom Hargis, Don McPherson, Dan Davis 1966)

5. Iconoclast (5.11b or 5.12b) ★★★ A long, fairly continuous route up the highest portion of the wall. Traverse in from *Galaxy* or start as for *Slingshot* to reach One Tree Ledge. Traverse left past a bolt to cracks and up a dogleg crack to a blocky ledge above the prominent triangular roof. Continue up the prominent left-leaning corner to a small tree (5.10c or 5.11a depending on how you do it), then traverse right and climb a runout slab past a bolt to Library Ledge. The proper finish is to climb a runout slab above the ledge (5.10d R), then either a 5.12a bolt ladder or a runout slab (5.11b R). Faced with this choice, most parties wisely finish via *Hyperspace* or *Outer Space.* Pro: to 3 inches. (FA: Mead Hargis, Tom Hargis to Library Ledge 1971; Pat McNerthney via 5.11b finish 1984; Jim Yoder, Bob Plum via bolt ladder finish 1985)

5A. Psychopath (variation)(5.11a) A shortcut on the far left end of One Tree Ledge, climbing a 5.11a thin crack. Pro: same as for *Iconoclast,* plus some thin nuts and cams.

6. Hyperspace (IV, 5.10d) ★★★ A wild finish to *Galaxy,* climbing the obvious overhanging crack and chimney system left of The Shield. A four-star route when linked with *Iconoclast.* Pro: to 4 inches. (FA: Jim Yoder, Neil Cannon, Kevin Buselmeier 1983)

7. Slingshot (5.10d) ★ A variation approach to *Iconoclast,* climbing through a roof using a tree as a catapult, or some such nonsense. Pro: to 3 inches.

8. Poodle with a Mohawk (5.11c) ★ A variation to the second pitch of *Iconoclast,* climbing the bolted face just right of the tree (crux), then past a triangular roof to rejoin that route at the blocky ledge. Pro: to 2 inches.

Snow Creek Wall

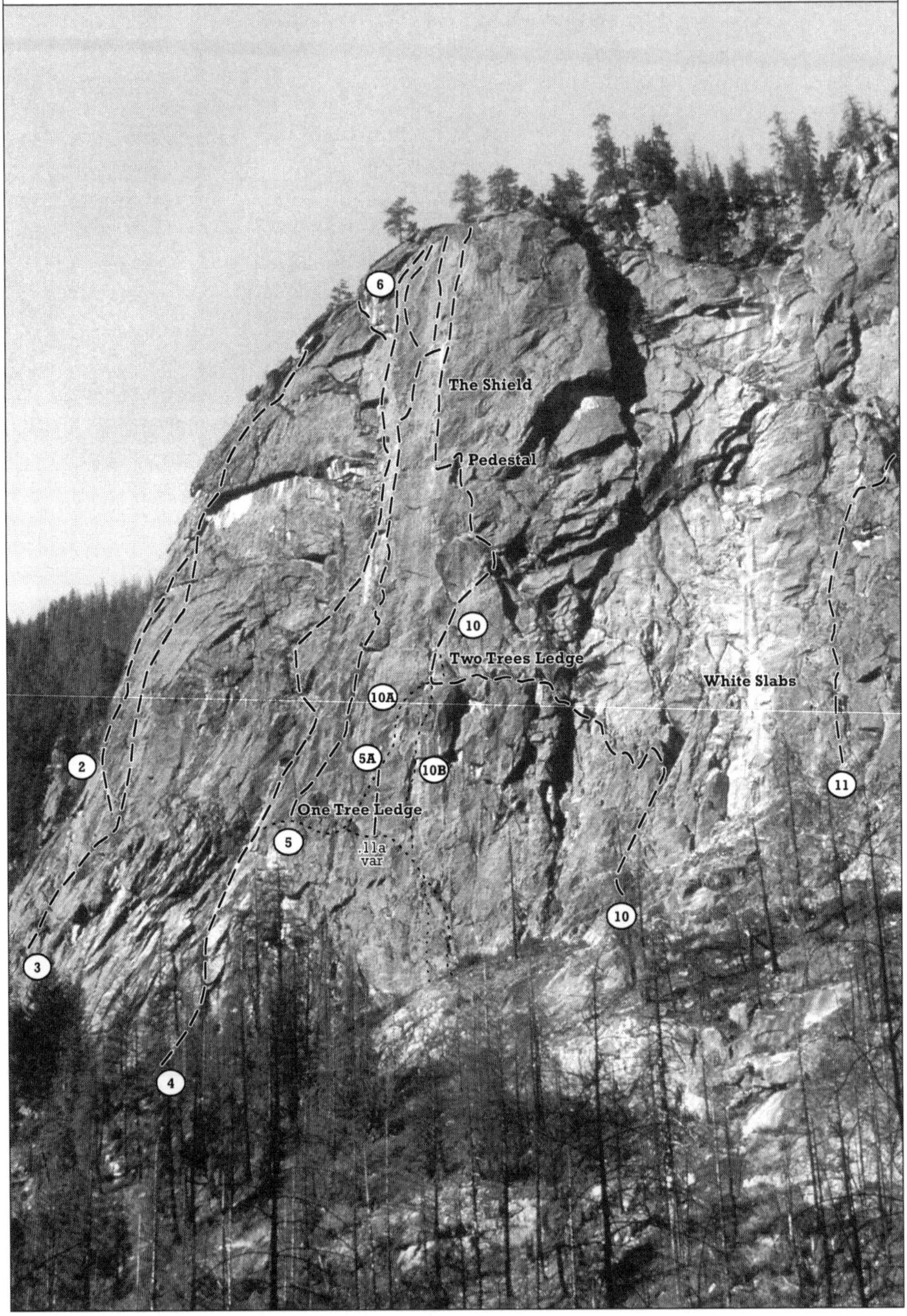

The Shield

Pedestal

Two Trees Ledge

White Slabs

One Tree Ledge

11a
var

9. Edge of Space (5.11c R) ★★★ A scary two-pitch route up the highest part of The Shield, climbing left from Library Ledge and up a sparsely bolted slab on the edge of the *Hyperspace* chimney. A thrilling finish to *Iconoclast*. Just don't fall over the edge. Pro: quickdraws. (FA: Pat McNerthney, David Rubine 1985)

10. Outer Space (III, 5.9) ★★★★ Considered by many to be the best route in Washington state. Although the lower pitches are nothing special, the upper crack pitches are simply spectacular! The route begins indirectly, in a dihedral just right of the massive dihedral right of The Shield area, then traverses across Class 4 ledges to Two Trees Ledge. From the left end of the ledge, climb up either of two short cracks (5.8 or 5.9) to a right-leading ramp and traverse cracks right and up (5.9) to a ledge. (A loose flake has been reported on the 5.9 traverse.) Continue up a knobby slab and corner to the top of a pedestal, then traverse down and left to the beginning of the crack pitches that lead to the top. Actually, the crack ends 15 feet short of the top; a short, knobby slab finishes things off. Seven pitches, or eight if you belay all the way across Two Trees Ledge, as you should. Pro: to 3 inches. (FA: Fred Beckey, Ron Niccoli 1960; FFA: Beckey, Steve Marts 1963)

10A. Remorse (variation start) (5.8) ★ A more direct start to *Outer Space* follows the first few pitches of the *Remorse* route to Two Trees Ledge. Find the first pitch of *RPM*, a dirty, water-streaked slab with two old bolts passed on the approach along the base of the wall. Just up from this is an indistinct slab/ramp leading up and leftward to the ledge above *RPM*'s bolts. Climb the ramp (5.6), then traverse the ledge farther left (5.8) to

the corner system that angles rightward (5.7) to the far left end of Two Trees Ledge.

10B. RPM (variation start) (5.10b) An even more direct variation start to *Outer Space*, climbing the second pitch of *RPM* (5.10b), climbing a corner and past a roof to reach Two Trees Ledge. This is a more popular start than the original route or *Remorse* variation. Pro: to 3 inches.

11. White Slabs (5.7) ★ Scramble to a tree right of the obvious water streaks in the white slab, then climb a long, easy pitch to the crux dihedral. Joins a long, left-trending ramp called *Country Club,* from where a rappel from a big tree just down the ramp is the best descent. Pro: to 2 inches.

12. Umbrella Tree (5.7) ★ A natural continuation of *White Slabs,* leading to the namesake Umbrella Tree. Most parties rappel from the tree, although the route continues to the top of the wall. Pro: to 3 inches.

13. Shark Attack (5.11b) ★ A bolted slab pitch leading to the top of Grand Arch. Begin via cracks just right of the start of *Country Club* to reach the crux slab. Pro: to 1.5 inches.

14. Grand Arch (5.10c) ★ The obvious arch right of *Country Club.* Begin down and right from *Shark Attack,* climbing cracks before traversing into the arch. Climb arch to *Shark Attack*'s rappel anchors. Pro: to 2 inches.

15. Easter Tower (5.8 or 5.10b) ★ Easter Tower is the leftmost of two prominent detached pillars on the right flank of Snow Creek Wall. It is approached via a blocky gully on the left. The main route begins from the notch and climbs around to the right face of the tower. The outside face route begins with a crack right of the approach gully, and climbs discontinuous

Snow Creek Wall

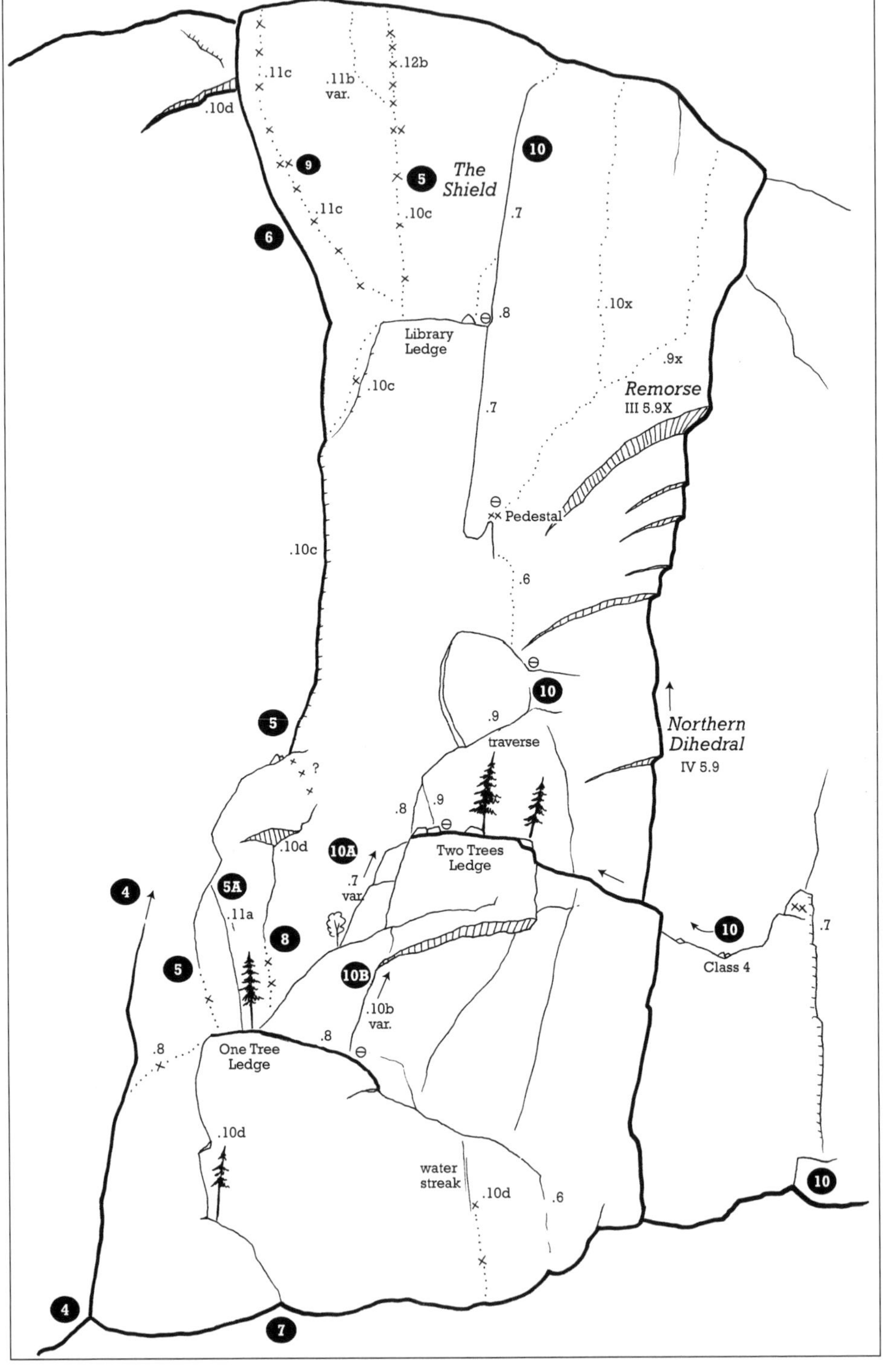

.11c
.10d
.11b
var.
.12b
The
Shield
9
5
10
6
.11c
.10c
.7
Library
Ledge
.8
.10x
.9x
Remorse
III 5.9X
.10c
.7
Pedestal
.10c
.6
5
10
?
Northern
Dihedral
IV 5.9
traverse
.9
.10d
.8
.9
4
Two Trees
Ledge
5A
10A
.7
var.
.11a
8
10
10B
5
.10b
var.
Class 4
.7
.8
.8
One Tree
Ledge
.10d
water
streak
.10d
.6
10
4
7

Snow Creek Wall

Nicola Masciandaro on *Outer Space* (5.9), Snow Creek Wall, Leavenworth

cracks on the left side of the tower. Pro: to 2.5 inches on each route.

16. Champagne (5.7) ★★ From the Easter Tower notch, climb cracks and knobs up and right to the top. Pro: to 2.5 inches.

17. Spring Fever (5.8) ★★ Just right of the Easter Tower notch, climb a crack system that joins *Champagne* at the first belay, then traverse right and climb a knobby wall just right of that route's second pitch. Pro: to 2 inches.

18. April Fool's Tower (5.8) ★ April Fool's Tower is the small pinnacle at the far right end of Snow Creek Wall. The standard route begins from the notch, which is best reached via a gully on the right. An easy ledge traverse on the right side of the tower (some loose rock) leads to an exposed ledge on the outside face, from where cracks lead up to the top. An inside corner crack from the notch is 5.11a. Rappel to the notch. Pro: to 2 inches. (FA: Dick Berge and party 1948)

19. Tarkus (5.9) ★ A crack line on the outside face of April Fool's Tower, climbing two pitches directly to the base of the standard route. Pro: to 3 inches.

Peshastin Pinnacles Vicinity Map

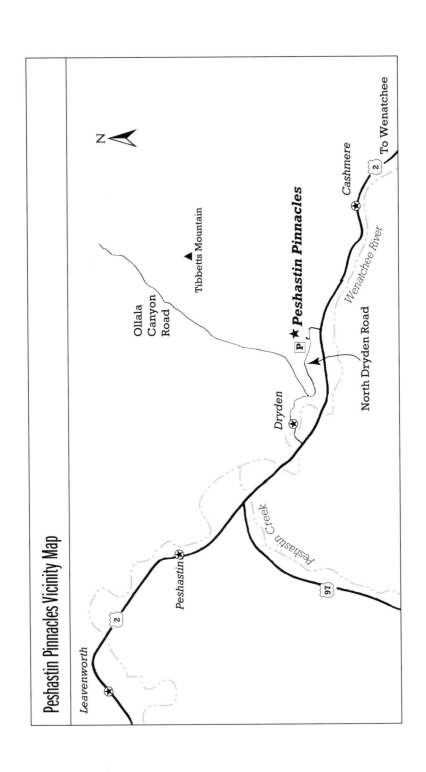

PESHASTIN PINNACLES

Peshastin Pinnacles are the several sandstone slabs and spires situated just northwest of the town of Cashmere, about fifteen minutes east from Leavenworth on U.S. Highway 2. The "Pinnacles" stand out from the otherwise rolling hills, so you shouldn't have any trouble spotting them. The rock here is Swauk sandstone, which at its best is solid enough and provides good friction climbing, but at its worst is a crumbly, decomposing mess that is all but unclimbable. The name is a misnomer, as the Pinnacles are really closer to Cashmere than to Peshastin, but the name Cashmere Crags was already taken. This area was closed to climbing in 1986, but finally reopened in 1992, and is now a state park. A new, big parking lot was graded, and eroding trails were rerouted and improved, alleviating access and conservation problems that plagued the area prior to its closure. Rebolting of several routes has improved safety.

Type of climbing: Peshastin Pinnacles has dozens of friction and crack routes ranging from easy Class 5 to 5.11. The routes are mostly one or two pitches in length. The Swauk sandstone offers fairly decent friction, although it is sometimes soft and crumbly.

Brief history of area: Climbers began visiting the Pinnacles in the late 1940s, and as usual, Fred Beckey and his gang get credit for most of the early first ascents. Some of their original bolts and ring pitons are still in use. The area was closed in 1986 due to the landowner's concerns about liability, and

climbing here remained in hiatus for five years. Eventually the state of Washington purchased the rocks and created a new state park. The upside of the area's newfound state park status is that the trails have been vastly improved, there is plenty of parking, there are toilets, and many routes have been rebolted to replace many rusty old 0.25-inch bolts. The downside is that the creation of a state park has brought tourists to the area, which sometimes makes the area quite crowded. Still, most agree that a crowded climbing area is better than a closed climbing area, and besides, the tourists pretty much stick to the trails.

Seasons and climate: The Pinnacles are situated about 15 miles east of Leavenworth, in the semiarid foothills of the eastern Cascade Range. The desertlike climate provides pleasant spring and fall climbing weather, but by summertime it gets much too hot here to climb except in the early morning and late afternoon. The usual climbing season is from early March through late October.

Because of the rain shadow effect of the Stuart Range, and the Pinnacles' easterly latitude, very little rain falls here, making this area a popular place to escape to when it starts raining in Leavenworth. If it's raining at Peshastin Pinnacles, your next best bet is Vantage, one hour's drive southeast from Wenatchee.

Precautions and regulations: Peshastin Pinnacles is a state park and is subject to rules,

Peshastin Pinnacles Approach Map

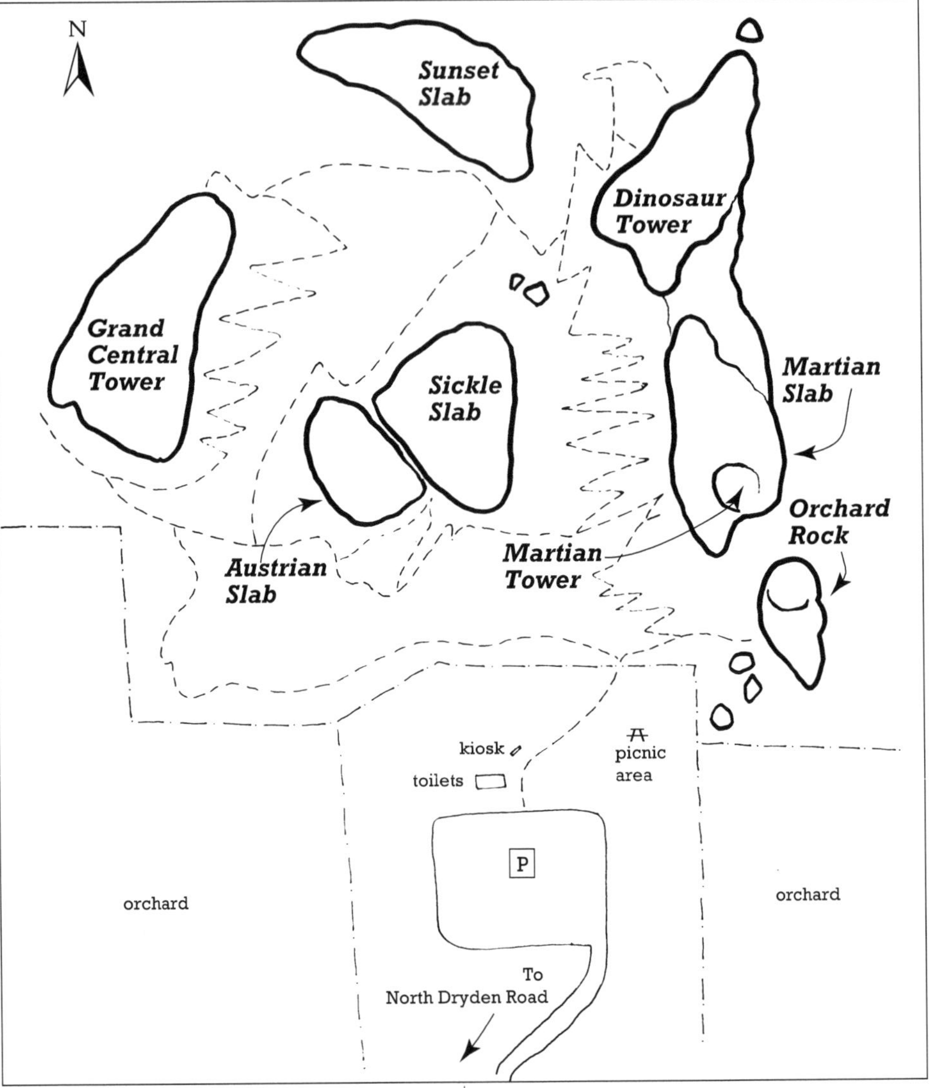

which are posted at the kiosk. Please follow the rules. Alcoholic beverages and smoking are not permitted inside the park. Pets must be leashed while inside the park. The park is open from dawn to dusk, although the gates are closed just before dusk (the time is posted on a sign). Climbers are required to be off the rocks a half-hour before closing time so make note of the time to avoid being locked in!). Also, entry and exit via the gate is mandatory; don't trespass in the surrounding orchards.

Although many of the old bolts have been replaced, beware of old 0.25-inch bolts. Some of these bolts were placed more than fifty years ago, and even those that aren't rusty and bent over are hardly trustworthy. Swauk sandstone is soft and erodes easily,

particularly around bolts. How reliable is a fifty-year-old, 0.25-inch bolt placed in decomposing sandstone? Not very. Feel free to replace old bolts, but in accordance with park rules, be sure to obtain permission in advance before you start drilling.

Be careful when climbing on or below decomposing rock, as it tends to break or crumble very easily. Even on the better routes, you might encounter a section of crumbly rock. Helmets are recommended, particularly on routes that climb on or below decomposing rock. Because of the decomposing nature of some rock, place gear carefully. When the rock is crumbly, deep placements are preferable, as shallow placements are more likely to blow out.

The new trails have pretty much eliminated concerns of erosion, but past damage continues to worsen, particularly along the base of some slabs, where the soil continues to wash away. Please stay on the trails as much as possible to avoid further erosion.

Rumor has it that there are rattlesnakes here, although no one has reported seeing one for years. Bats are frequently encountered in caves and cracks, so watch out. There was a big bees' nest in *The Gully* route on Orchard Rock once, so keep an eye out for stinging insects. Also be watchful for ticks in early season.

Gear and other considerations: The majority of routes are bolted slabs, requiring only quickdraws and a nut or two. On most crack routes, a comprehensive rack, including several nuts and cams in the 1- to 3-inch range on longer routes, should suffice. Double ropes are necessary to rappel off several of the formations.

Camping and accommodations: As at other Washington state parks, visitors to Peshastin Pinnacles are required to display a Discover Pass. Overnight camping is not permitted at the state park. If you aren't already camping near Leavenworth, there's a county park near

Doug Weaver on Washboard (5.10c), Dinosaur Tower, Peshastin Pinnacles.

Monitor, about 5 miles east of Cashmere, but you may need to make reservations there. The town of Cashmere has all accommodations, including grocery stores, motels, and fruit stands aplenty.

Emergency services: In case of emergency, dial 911. Hospitals are in Wenatchee and Leavenworth.

Other guidebooks: Kramar, Viktor. *Leavenworth Rock.* The fourth edition (2018) is the current guide to Leavenworth climbing areas.

ORCHARD ROCK

Orchard Rock is the tower just inside the entrance gate, on the right. It has two summits of sorts, separated by a wide chimney. The large cave on the west side is known as The Womb, and some of the routes in its vicinity are named accordingly. There are some small boulders on the west side that offer a few problems. A 5.10 bouldering traverse can be done around the base of the entire rock. The routes are described clockwise as you encounter them approaching from the trail. Anchors are in place atop each tower, although downclimbing is a feasible method of descent via several Class 4 and 5 scrambles.

Overuse of Orchard Rock has led to serious erosion at the base of the rock. Do your best to prevent additional erosion here and elsewhere in the park.

1. The Overhang (5.8) Pass the big overhang and climb the decomposing crack above. Pro: to 2.5 inches.

2. The Tunnel (5.6) ★ At the upper end of Orchard Rock is this unique route, climbing through a wind tunnel then up a wide crack to the summit. Pro: to 2.5 inches.

3. The Gully (5.0) The obvious wide chimney on the east face of Orchard Rock. Pro: to 1 inch.

4. Ass Crack (5.7) ★ The short overhanging crack left of *The Gully,* reached via a traverse left from midway up the gully, or directly (more difficult, not well protected). Pro: to 2 inches, and a long sling.

5. The Knobs (5.10a) ★ The obvious knobby face, leading to a decomposing crack system. A bold lead if the hangers are missing. Pro: to 2 inches, including quickdraws and wired nuts.

Orchard Rock—West Side

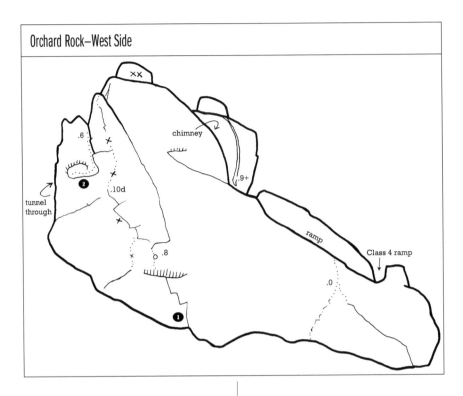

6. The Tubes (aka Tubal Ligation) (5.11a R) ★ The obvious wide, flaring cracks on the headwall left of *The Knobs*. Best toproped. Pro: to 4 inches or larger.

Orchard Rock—East Side

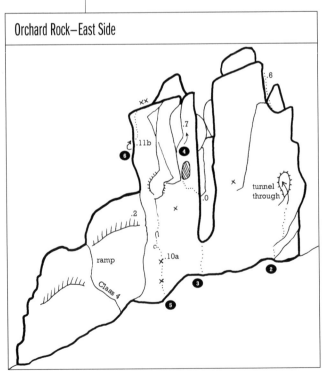

MARTIAN TOWER

Directly uphill from Orchard Rock is Martian Tower, a distinct summit at the lower end of the Martian Slab formation that has several routes leading to the top. Approach by hiking up the ridge via the most obvious trail, avoiding side trails if possible to prevent further erosion. The routes are described from right to left starting from *Catacombs.* Descend via a rappel from the notch down the east face, or continue up The Ridge and either rappel down the line of *Diagonal Direct* or continue traversing to the upper rappel anchors above *Grey Whale.*

7. Catacombs (5.7) ★ This route begins directly uphill from Orchard Rock, on the right side of the downhill face of Martian Tower. A short face crux climbs potholes into an odd chimney that leads to the summit. Rappel the route, or from anchors atop *Diagonal Direct.* Pro: to 2 inches.

8. Graham Cracker (5.10c) ★★ A direct start to *Catacombs,* climbing the bolted face on the left. Pro: to 2 inches; quickdraws.

9. Butter Brickle (5.8+) The big, sandy crack system just left of the arête left of *Graham Cracker.* Pro: to 4 inches.

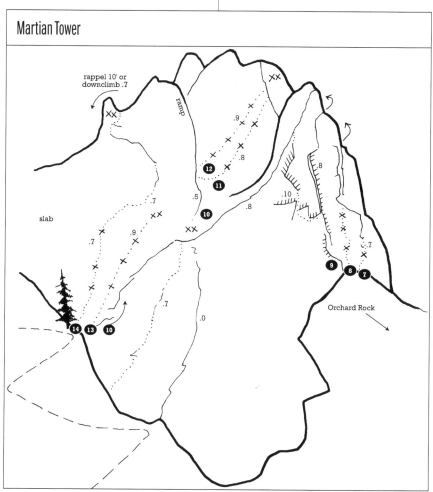

Martian Tower

MARTIAN SLAB

Martian Slab is the broad, gray slab visible directly above the parking lot. It has several popular bolt-protected friction routes. The long ramp of *Martian Diagonal* is the major feature of Martian Slab, and provides a convenient exit for most of the routes. Rappel anchors are located at the top of *Diagonal Direct* and at the upper left end of the formation, above *Grey Whale* (or you can downclimb 10 feet of 5.7 instead of rappelling). The routes are described from right to left as you ascend the slab from the base of *Martian Diagonal*.

10. Martian Diagonal (5.5) ★★ One of the most obvious and most popular routes in the area, climbing the long, left-leading ramp to the top of Martian Slab. The route has three variation starts. From the first anchors, climb a short crux wall, then cruise up the ramp

to the rappel anchors. Some runouts, but crux has bolt protection. Pro: to 1 inch. (FA: Dave Becksted, Fred Stanley 1948)

11. Diagonal Direct (5.8) ★ Bolt-protected grooves up the slab right of the second pitch of *Martian Diagonal*. Rappel from anchors. Pro: quickdraws.

12. Baseball Nut (5.9) ★★ The bolted slab just left of *Diagonal Direct*. Don't mistake it for either of two poorly protected slab routes farther left. Pro: quickdraws.

13. Nutty Buddy (5.9) ★ A bolted slab route squeezed in just left of the leftmost variation start of *Martian Diagonal*. Pro: quickdraws; small TCU.

14. Serpent (5.7 R) ★ A bold friction route climbing the slab about 20 feet left of the left-hand start of *Martian Diagonal*. Sporting runouts, with route-finding difficulty for

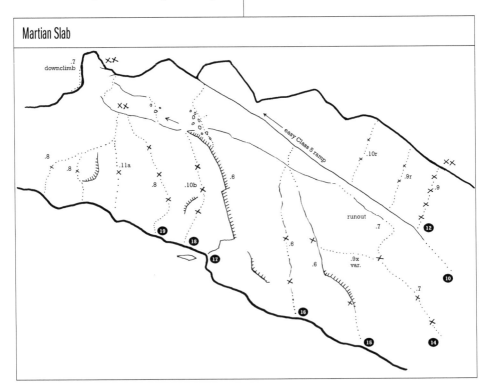

Martian Slab

those accustomed to linking up bolts. Pro: quickdraws; midsize cams.

15. Voyager One (5.6) ★ The *Voyager* routes begin about 40 feet uphill from the start of *Serpent. Voyager One* goes right, up a groove. Pro: quickdraws.

16. Voyager Two (5.6) ★ Go left up the sparsely bolted slab, passing a small cave. More runout than its neighbor. Pro: quickdraws.

17. Porpoise (5.6) This route climbs the slabby arête of the blocky dihedral just right of *Grey Whale,* then up potholes to the top. Pro: to 1 inch.

18. Harpoonist (5.10b) ★ A friction pitch squeezed in between *Porpoise* and *Grey Whale.* Pro: quickdraws.

19. Grey Whale (5.8) ★★★ An outstanding friction pitch up the wide, gray slab at the upper end of Martian Slab. Pro: quickdraws. (FA: Bill Sumner, Al Givler 1972)

DINOSAUR TOWER

At the ridge crest above Martian Slab sits Dinosaur Tower, a bulky formation that has several of the best and hardest friction routes at Peshastin Pinnacles. Most of the summit routes are sandy and of poor quality. The routes are listed from right to left from the base of the formation as you approach from Martian Slab. Rappel anchors are in place at various ledges, making descents possible from almost anywhere. A long rappel off the front of the tower is the standard descent from the summit, although two shorter rappels and scrambling off the back side are possible with one long rope.

20. Skyline (5.5) No topo. The easiest summit route on Dinosaur Tower. Climb a more-or-less obvious straight-in crack about 30 feet up from and left of the formation's nose (rightmost buttress, distinguished by a deep cave), then continue up the ridge to the summit. Pro: to 2.5 inches. (FKA: Fred Beckey, Dick Widrig 1948)

21. Potholes (5.8) ★ A two-pitch route beginning at the high point of the trail, the most popular route to the summit. Climb a bolted slab left up potholes (5.6+) to a sloping ledge. Most parties rappel from here, as the rock higher up is decomposing. If you continue, pass a steep headwall (crux) to reach cracks and chimneys leading to the top. Pro: quickdraws; slings; gear to 2 inches. (FFA: Fred Beckey, Ed Cooper 1960)

22. Potholes Direct (5.10a) ★★ At the base of the slab below Potholes Ledge is a small pine tree stump. Begin here and climb the slab and a short left-facing corner. A direct variation goes up the runout slab on the right (5.10c R; bring TCUs). Pro: quickdraws.

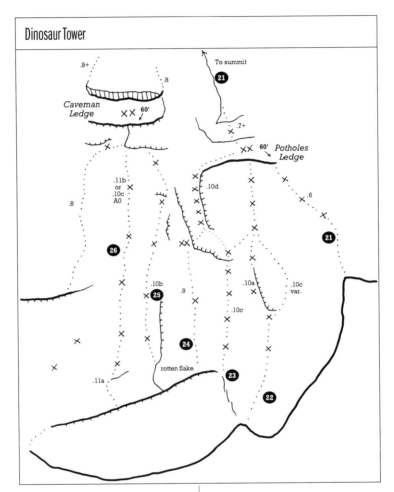

Dinosaur Tower

23. Washboard (5.10c) ★★★ One of Peshastin Pinnacles' finest friction test pieces. From the pine tree stump, climb left up semi-rotten flakes to the whitish, rippled slab. Above the crux, traverse right and climb the headwall to Potholes Ledge, or undercling left to finish via *Primate*. Pro: quickdraws. (FA: Pat Timson 1971)

24. Primate (5.10d) ★ Begin as for *Washboard*, but step left onto a ledge after 20 feet and climb a slab with one bolt to anchors at the base of a prominent left-facing corner (or climb *Washboard* and traverse over via a flake). Continue right and up a thin crack in the rounded dihedral, past several bolts, to Potholes Ledge. Pro: quickdraws. (FFA: Jim Madsen 1967)

25. Pebbles and Bam-Bam (5.10b) ★★ Start at the base of the obvious rotten flake and climb the slab up and left to Caveman Ledge. Pro: quickdraws. (FA: Jim Yoder, Lee Cunningham 1984)

26. Dr. Leakey (5.11b) ★★ A fine route climbing the blankest part of the slab directly to Caveman Ledge. The route is marred by a carved hold that can—and should—be avoided, if you can tell which hold it is, which is increasingly difficult as the slab erodes away. Pro: quickdraws.

SUNSET SLAB

Just downhill and west from Dinosaur Tower is Sunset Slab, which has several short, easy to moderate friction routes in the 5.5 to 5.8 range. Some of the routes climb to the top of the slab, but most parties wisely descend from anchors after one pitch, as the upper half of the slab is decomposing. Actually, the lower half of the slab is decomposing, too, and rock quality ranges from adequate to poor. Check those rappel anchors before trusting them.

27. Continuous Bullshit (5.6 or 5.9) ★ The rightmost route, friction climbing past several bolts. The route angles rightward after the first 30 feet and finishes via a decomposing gully. The route's rating depends on how you pass the first bolt. Pro: quickdraws.

28. Green Velvet (5.7) Directly above a prominent tree, follow a line of potholes and flakes to bolt anchors halfway up the slab, then up a groove to the gully. Pro: to 1 inch; TCUs.

29. National Velvet (5.6) ★★ The central route, beginning just left of the big bush. Friction past the bolts and exit via the gully. Pro: quickdraws.

30. Booby Vinton (5.5) ★ Another friction route just left of *National Velvet.* At the top, traverse off in either direction (toward Sunset Ledge if you want to avoid the gully). Pro: quickdraws.

31. Booby Trap (5.5) ★ A sparsely bolted slab just right of *Sunset,* leading directly to Sunset Ledge. Pro: quickdraws.

32. Sunset (5.6 R) The obvious right-leaning groove leading to the ledge on the left side of the slab. The route continues up a rotten crack, but nobody bothers. Pro: quickdraws; TCUs.

33. Sunrise (5.8 R) ★ A puzzling, poorly protected start passing a bulge leads to run-out friction. Pro: quickdraws.

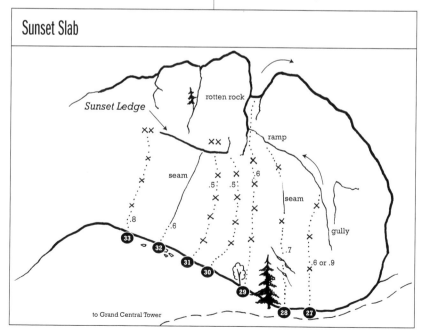

GRAND CENTRAL TOWER

Grand Central Tower is the highest of the Peshastin Pinnacles formations. Its west face rises some 100 meters from base to peak, offering several multipitch routes, mostly on rock in various stages of decomposition. The slab at the base of the west face has a few difficult, runout friction routes. The backside rises between 80 and 120 feet, and over-hangs, thus offering several short but strenuous routes, mostly up sandy cracks. Descend via rappel from various places on the tower.

34. Lightning Crack (5.8+ R) ★ A two-pitch route starting in the corner on the far left side of the west face, just right of Madsen's Buttress. Climb the ramp and corner crack past an overhang to the top of the buttress, then up a bolted slab to the lightning-bolt crack that leads you to a big ledge on the left shoulder of the tower. Some decomposing rock and scary runouts. There have been some long falls on this route, so don't approach it lightly. Double-rope rappel off the back, down the line of *Empire State*. Pro: to 2 inches. (FFA: Fred Beckey 1962)

35. West Face (5.8) ★ A three-pitch route leading to the summit of Grand Central Tower. Only the first pitch is worth climbing. Easy friction up the lower slab leads to a right-facing corner with too many bolts and a tricky friction traverse to reach the initial belay ledge. The route continues up a rotten face and chimney, then finishes via either a rotten crack directly to the top or a left traverse to join *Corkscrew*. Most parties wisely forego the summit and rappel as soon as possible. Pro: to 3 inches.

36. West Face Direct (5.10d X) The left-most of the three friction routes climbing the west face slab. Very runout, with scary, old 0.25-inch bolts. Best toproped. Pro: quick-draws; Screamers.

37. White Lightning (5.11a R/X) ★★ A direct friction route up the water streak in the middle of the west face slab. Usually toproped, for good reason. Pro: quickdraws; Screamers.

38. Scratch (5.10c X) Another hairy friction pitch, this one climbing the right side of the west face slab. Very runout, with scary, old 0.25-inch bolts. Best toproped. Pro: quick-draws; Screamers.

39. Nirvana Ridge (5.9) ★ A popular route climbing the buttress right of the west face. Has been retrobolted, but still has some sections of rotten rock. Pro: to 1 inch; quickdraws.

The following routes are located near the upper notch on the back side of Grand Central Tower.

40. Bomb Shelter (5.11a) The obvious overhanging crack high on the east face, just left of and downhill from *Vertigo*. A difficult hand traverse reaches the sandy crack. Most parties wisely rappel after one pitch, from dubious slings tied around a solution pocket. Said to be Washington's first 5.11, but assuredly not one of its best. Pro: to 2 inches. (FFA: Henry Barber or Don Madsen 1974)

41. Vertigo (5.8) ★ The corner crack directly above the upper notch. Climb the crack, traverse right around a corner, and climb the chimney to the upper notch. A direct finish (5.9) climbs the offwidth directly above the initial crack before traversing right into the chimney. Rappel from anchors, or from slings tied around the summit block. Pro: to 3 inches. (FFA: Fred Beckey, Charles Bell 1961)

Grand Central Slab

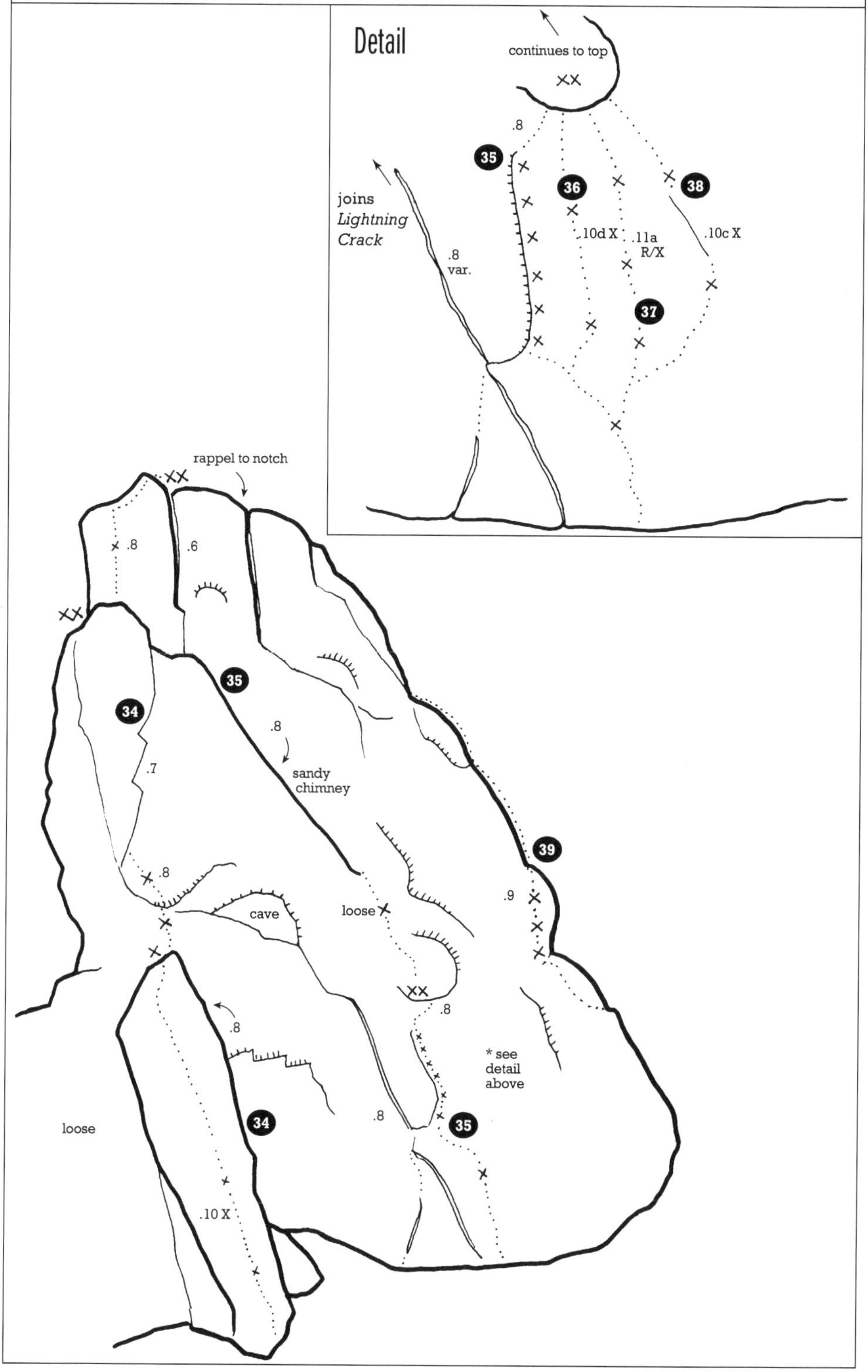

Detail

joins *Lightning Crack*

continues to top

××

.8

35

36

×

38

.10d X

.11a R/X

.10c X

.8 var.

37

rappel to notch

×× .8

.6

35

34

.7

.8

sandy chimney

.8

cave

loose ×

39

.9

loose

.8

×× .8

* see detail above

.8

34

.8

35

.10 X

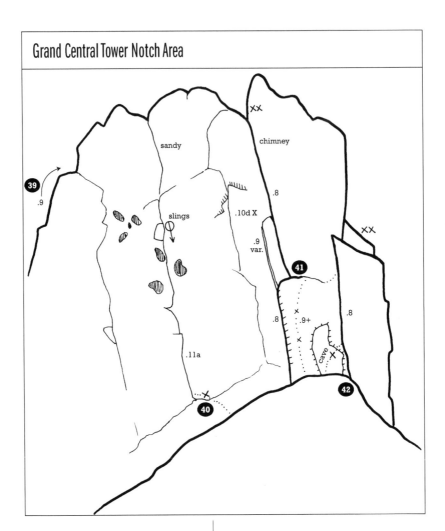

Grand Central Tower Notch Area

42. Empire State (5.8) A wide, sandy crack and chimney just right of the big cave down and right of *Vertigo*. Grunt up the crack directly from the base, or traverse across the cave. Pro: to 3 inches.

AUSTRIAN SLAB

Directly downhill from Dinosaur Tower is Austrian Slab. The lower half of this slab has several of the area's best friction routes, in the 5.7 to 5.10 range. The upper half of the slab is rotten. Most parties wisely scramble or rappel off from the ledge. The routes are listed from left to right. Please avoid further erosion by staying on the trail as much as possible.

43. Slender Thread (5.9 R) ★★ A friction pitch following a seam on the left side of the slab, above what's left of a pine tree that fell over due to climber-caused erosion. Twenty feet of sustained 5.9 moves reach the first bolt. Pro: quickdraws; an alert spotter.

44. Fakin' It (5.10a) ★★ A friction pitch starting from the base of the slab, just right of *Slender Thread*. Shares a first bolt with *Cajun Queen*. Mildly runout. Pro: quickdraws.

45. Cajun Queen (5.10b) ★★ The friction route heading up and right from the shared bolt. Runout on easier ground. Pro: quickdraws.

46. Austrian Slab (5.8) ★ The original route up Austrian Slab, climbing grooves and solution pockets just right of center, starting just right of a large fir tree. Somewhat runout at the start. Pro: quickdraws, plus gear to 1.5 inches, including nuts and small cams. (FA: Fred Beckey, Eric Bjornstad, Don Gordon 1952)

47. Slakin (5.8) ★ Solution pockets on the right side of the slab lead to a fun friction finish. Very runout to the first bolt, but relatively easy. A 5.9 R variation climbs the slab on the left. Pro: quickdraws.

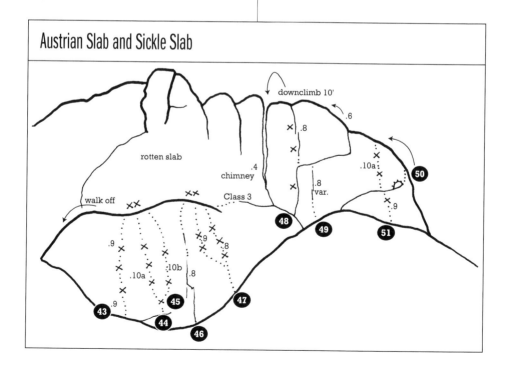

Austrian Slab and Sickle Slab

SICKLE SLAB

Just up and right from Austrian Slab is Sickle Slab, which is part of the same formation. It has several routes, the most obvious of which are the diagonal cracks of *Windward* and *Wind Cave*. The routes are listed from left to right. Descend via rappel, either a short rappel down the back or a long rappel down the front from the upper notch.

48. Windward Direct (5.8) ★★ Start as for *Windward,* but climb directly up the obvious grooves to the top. Pro: quickdraws; old bolts.

49. Windward (5.6) ★ Start at the high point of the trail from the base of the slab and climb the obvious groove, then traverse right along a narrow ledge, finishing left along the spiny ridge to the top. A direct start up a shallow groove just right (5.8) is not well protected. Pro: to 2 inches.

50. Wind Cave (5.8) ★ Traverse the obvious narrow ledge rightward past a small cave, then up the right-hand arête to the ridge, finishing via *Windward.* Pro: to 2 inches; bring some slings.

51. Testicle Fortitude (5.10a R) ★★ Find the first bolt on the slab just downhill from the start of *Wind Cave* and climb directly up from that bolt to the top of the slab, passing the wind cave on the left side. A bit runout. Pro: quickdraws; medium-size cams; a couple of wired nuts.

PINNACLES MISCELLANY

The boulders scattered on the plateau just below Dinosaur Tower are the remains of the Trigger Finger, once a 60-foot-high needle and a popular climb. The Trigger Finger fell over during the winter of 1979–1980, and only a 15-foot-high stump and a few scattered boulders remain. Vulture Slab, located just left from the base of Grand Central Tower, has several routes (5.6 to 5.8), but all feature decomposing rock, making them decidedly unpopular. Farther left from the base of Grand Central Tower is Donald Duck Rock, a small boulder with some entertaining routes; try it with no hands. Even farther left is Church Tower, with two 5.7 routes, both of which feature ancient bolts and decomposing rock. Church Tower may not be within the state park boundary.

SWAUK PINNACLES

On the north side of Blewett Pass, west of US 97, a half-hour drive from Leavenworth, is this "delightful area of sandstone spires," which offer a few decent routes. The area was reported in *Climbing* magazine, issue #114, and touted as an interim replacement for Peshastin Pinnacles. But, like Sandy Slab, although these routes gave Peshastin Pinnacles refugees something to climb while that area was closed, since the area has reopened only a few people have continued to climb here. There are reportedly about fifty routes up to 5.10 in difficulty, with room for more routes. For information about Swauk Pinnacles, refer to *Swauk Pinnacles: A Climbers' Guide* or *Climbing* #114.

FRENCHMAN COULEE (VANTAGE)

There are miles of rimrock lining the Columbia River and the hundreds of coulees, canyons, and gorges throughout central Washington. If the rock were solid, thousands of routes would surely have been climbed here. But the vast majority of the rock is flaky basalt, fit only as a scenic backdrop to desert lakes, rivers, and scablands. Fortunately, there are a few pockets of resistance, where solid basalt offers excellent climbing. One such area is Frenchman Coulee near Vantage, smack in the middle of the state. What's included here is just a sampling of the better routes. Since this chapter was initially prepared, route development has soared at Frenchman Coulee, so much so that this chapter may seem obsolete to those who make this a frequent destination. (Even the latest comprehensive guide to the area needed updating soon after its release.) Climbers disappointed with the route selection here should refer to the most recent guide or update for the area. This guide can keep you busy for a while, but there is a lot more to climb at the Coulee.

Type of climbing: Vantage climbing is typical of desert rimrock: mostly cracks between basalt columns, with a few face climbs up the columns and entablature. The routes are typically 60 to 100 feet in length, ending atop the columns or at anchors just below. Vantage also has some enjoyable sport climbs on the blocky entablature cliffs below the rimrock. The best rock is quite solid, but even on the best routes you should expect to encounter flaky rock and an occasional loose hold.

Brief history of area: The first climbers to visit Frenchman Coulee apparently came during the 1950s and 1960s, quietly climbed a few of the most obvious "practice" routes, and left with scarcely a clue of their passing except an occasional fixed pin or bolt anchor. It was not until the 1980s that the area was publicized, when a group of Spokane climbers "discovered" the columnar basalt and picked the ripest plums (which were probably climbed earlier by a rival group of Seattle climbers who didn't feel the area was worth much attention). By the late 1980s, most of the best crack routes had been climbed, and attention had turned to the arêtes and column faces, which yielded many more routes, some good, some not so good, some downright awful. Prior to publication of an updated guide in 1995, a flurry of new route activity produced several more routes, including sport routes on the previously uncharted entablature walls underlying the columns. Publication of a new guide in 1997 prompted another flurry of activity and the establishment of dozens of more routes. New route development continues unabated. Climbers most active in developing Vantage routes include Bob Buckley, Dane Burns, Matt Kerns, Kevin Kurtz, Mike Massey, Kevin Pogue, Leland Windham, Marlene Ford, and Jim Yoder, to name only a few.

Andy Fitz on *Throbbing Gristle* (5.9), Sunshine Wall, Frenchman Coulee

Frenchman Coulee Vicinity Map

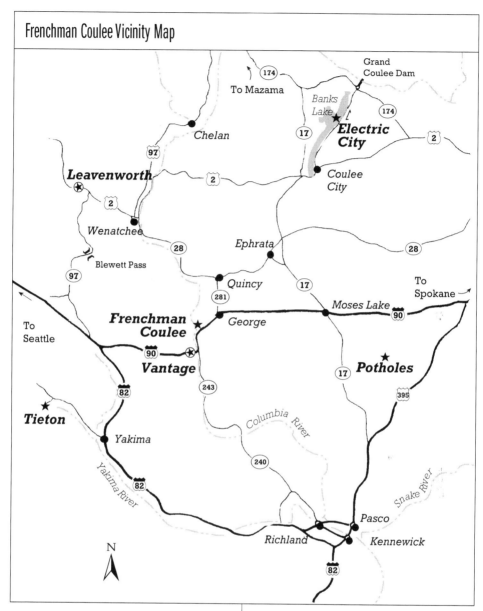

Seasons and climate: What makes Frenchman Coulee most popular is the weather. It is almost always climbable at Vantage, one of the driest areas of the state. Thus, climbers who would otherwise stay at home or head for the gym on rainy weekends can now sometimes spend a day or two cragging at the Coulee. It might be cold, and it might be windy, but it will probably be dry enough to climb.

Although weather is reliable here, from late spring to early fall it's too hot for most climbers. From June through September, temperatures regularly soar into the 90s and 100s. If you're climbing in the heat, drink plenty of water, protect yourself from harmful sun rays, and avoid overexerting yourself to avoid heatstroke. It gets a bit cold to climb in winter, although a few desperate climbers can be found here at all times of year. When it gets really cold, some nearby waterfalls offer ice climbing, if you're that desperate.

Precautions and regulations: The climbing area is within the North Columbia Basin Wildlife Area. Nearby areas, particularly the columns on the north rim of the coulee, are on private land. Accordingly, mind your manners, and above all, don't trespass across the coulee even if some of the rock over there does look enticing. Supposedly, because this is publicly administered land, power drilling may be illegal, although that doesn't seem to stop anyone. Actually, recent route development has created some concern, so climbers developing new routes are asked to keep it quiet and to camouflage the bolts and anchors to match the rock.

As is typical of desert rimrock areas, the rock is solid in places, but loose rock is the rule, as scree slopes below most of the cliffs attest. Much of the loose rock lies atop the columns, and there's lots of loose entablature above and below. Many of the routes are equipped with rappel anchors just below the top of the columns, and rappelling from the anchors is common practice. For safety reasons, except where the anchors are atop the columns, climbing to the top of the columns is ill advised. On most of the routes, loose

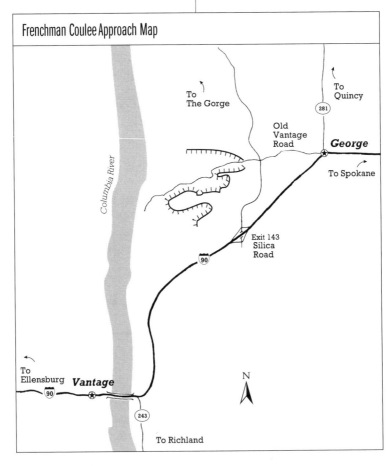

Frenchman Coulee Approach Map

To The Gorge

To Quincy

281

Old Vantage Road

George

To Spokane

Columbia River

Exit 143 Silica Road

90

N

To Ellensburg *Vantage*

90

243

To Richland

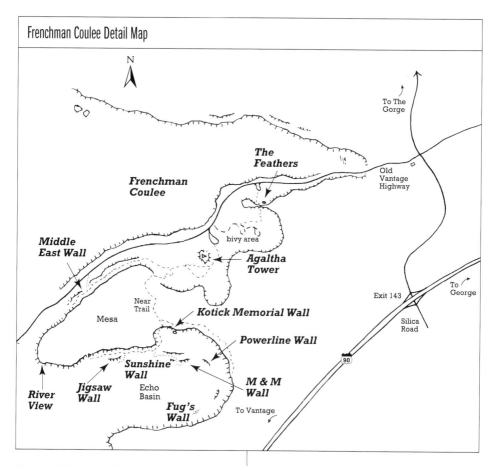

flakes and blocks will be encountered but can be avoided. On many routes, avoiding loose rock is impossible. Be careful when climbing bolted face routes, because some of the bolts appear to have been placed in blocks that could pull out under the weight of one too many leader falls. When climbing cracks, try to place gear on solid rock to avoid having a block blow out under the weight of a fall. Stranger things have happened; do your best to climb as safely as possible. There have been many accidents and at least one notable fatality here, so climb with great care for your own safety and the safety of those below you.

In this area, routes with unavoidable loose rock are generally given an R rating; routes with poor or no protection may get either an R or X. Do your best to avoid rockfall, and wear a helmet if you know what's good for you, particularly while belaying. While belaying, don't stand directly below the leader, as serious accidents have resulted from leaders pulling off loose rock and hitting their belayers—or landing on them! Don't try hiking up the scree to reach cliffs; as those who have tried it know, the scree here is dangerously prone to sliding. Also, some of these columns appear likely to topple with little provocation, so beware of routes climbing on, below, or behind detached columns. Spectators should stay out of harm's way, if possible. When pulling ropes after rappelling, get out of the way, because they can and have knocked off loose rock.

Beware of rattlesnakes, particularly in the shade, in caves, and near rocks. Your first reaction upon finding a rattler may be to kill it, but remember—you are in a wildlife area, and the snake lives here. If harassed sufficiently, rattlers will retreat, and if you do it right, you can steer them away from the routes. Thankfully, no one has reported finding a rattlesnake on a route here—yet. As with all wildlife in this area, please leave it alone.

Although this is not a state park, a Discover Pass is required to park at Frenchman Coulee.

Gear and other considerations: If you plan on climbing cracks, bring a wide selection of gear, from wired nuts to large cams. Most of Vantage's good cracks start out thin and end up wide, so you'll need a whole range of sizes, from 0.5 to 5 inches on some routes. Because many of the cracks are parallel sided and outward flaring, cams are recommended over chocks, although there are some nice tapering placements where chocks fit nicely. If you don't plan on climbing cracks, bring a bunch of quickdraws and a few wired nuts and TCUs up to 1 inch. There are plenty of all-bolt affairs on the columns in between the cracks, and some entertaining sport routes on the entablature cliffs. Descents from most routes can be accomplished with one rope. There are a few longer routes requiring double-rope rappels.

Camping and accommodations: Camping is permitted along the old highway on both sides of The Feathers and at the parking lot near Agaltha Tower, and also at the boat launch at road's end; but there is no running water, so if you camp here, bring plenty of water. There are presently no toilets in the area, so you'll have to do your best to use proper human waste disposal methods. A pit toilet has been suggested, but hasn't yet been installed. Campfires are discouraged because of the sparse desert vegetation and usually dry conditions. If you must have a fire, bring your own wood, don't make new fire rings, and keep an eye on it! If you cause a brushfire, you could be held liable for the cost of putting it out and any property damage that results from your negligence.

The nearest town is George, 5 miles east on I-90, which consists of a truck stop, restaurant, convenience store, and gas station. Vantage is less accommodating, but does have a motel.

Be warned that this area is used by folks attending concerts at The Gorge, and on concert days and nights the area is very overcrowded and unsanitary.

Emergency services: In case of emergency, dial 911. The nearest hospital is in Quincy, 20 miles north of George on WA 281.

Other guidebooks: Ford, Marlene, and Jim Yoder. *Frenchman Coulee.*

Finding the crags: To get there, take the Silica Road exit (exit 143) off I-90, about 7 miles northeast from Vantage and about 5 miles southwest from George, almost exactly in between Seattle and Spokane. Go north on Silica Road 0.7 mile, then turn left onto the old Vantage highway (not well marked, but it is the first paved left turn you come to), which descends along the south wall of Frenchman Coulee 1.2 miles to The Feathers parking area and another 0.2 mile to Agaltha Tower parking area.

THE FEATHERS

The Feathers is the first area you come to as you approach from I-90. The area is impossible to miss unless you're driving blindfolded (in which case you'll probably drive off the cliff on the north side of the road!). It is named for the basalt pillars said to "resemble feathers stuck in the ground," although the area also nearly resembles a row of teeth. An interesting feature here is Satan's Tower, a detached pillar on the northeast side. Trails lead up to the gap from both sides.

The Feathers has several short routes ranging from 5.4 to 5.10 in difficulty, and the better routes are almost always crowded. The face climbs here are mostly well-protected jug hauls, while the cracks are uniformly loose and not at all recommended. This area is very popular for toproping, and because of this you should be wary of any cold shuts still in place as anchors, which wear through quickly due to abrasion from climbers lowering off and toproping directly from the anchors instead of rappelling or toproping from quickdraws clipped into the cold shuts. As a rule, it's better to rappel than to lower from anchors anyway, but especially so here.

The Feathers North Side

The following several routes are located on the north side of The Feathers. Satan's Tower is the prominent freestanding column on the left. Its summit can be reached via a crumbly, unprotected 5.6 route from the notch, if you're desperate. Rappel from anchors instead of trying to downclimb the notch route.

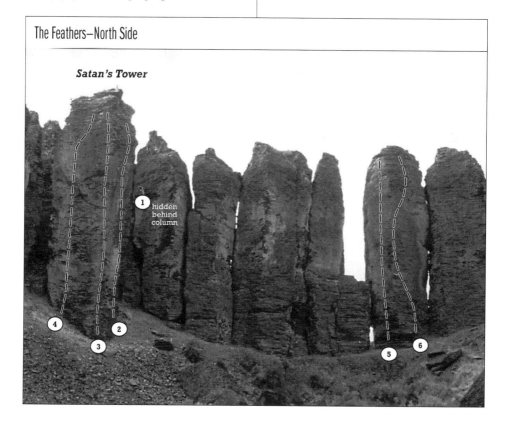

The Feathers–North Side

Satan's Tower

1 hidden behind column

1. Jesus Saves (5.8) ★ A short, bolted arête on the right side of Satan's Tower. The route is named for the prominent grafitto spray-painted on the rocks all over the place. Pro: quickdraws.

2. Blood Blister (5.10b) An unpopular sport route squeezed in between *Jesus Saves* and *Satan's Wagon*. Pro: quickdraws.

3. Satan's Wagon (5.10b) ★★ A popular sport route climbing the outside arête of Satan's Tower. Deceptively "easy." Pro: quickdraws.

4. Satan's Little Helper (5.8) ★★ A juggy face route on the left side of Satan's Tower. Pro: quickdraws.

5. Desert Shield (5.10a R) ★ The northern arête of the Medicine Man column, immediately right of the gap. The first bolt is way off the deck, which is too bad because otherwise it's a good route. Pro: quickdraws.

6. The Uprising (5.7) ★★★ A bolted face on the *Medicine Man* column, climbing what must be the most solid rock in the area—at least until the last few moves. Pro: quickdraws. (FA: Jeff Ball, Kevin Kurtz, Bob Buckley 1988)

7. The Beckey Route (5.7) ★ No topo. A flaky route climbing the face of the eighth column right of the gap. Pro: quickdraws.

The Feathers South Side

The following several routes are located on the south side of The Feathers. Approach by walking through the gap from the north side, or via the trail winding up from the bivouac area.

8. Medicine Man (5.10a) ★ The first sport route west of the gap, climbing a steep, juggy face. Pro: quickdraws. (FA: Dave Johnson, Mike Schwitter 1989)

The Feathers–South Side

9. So Funny I Forgot to Laugh (5.9) The bolted line just left of *Medicine Man*. May seem harder or easier than 5.9 depending on which holds broke off. Pro: quickdraws.

10. Don Coyote (5.8) ★ The first bolted route east of the gap. Loose holds, but still popular. Pro: quickdraws.

11. Dance of the Shaman (5.10b) ★ A tricky sport route on the second column east of the gap. If you fall off trying to clip the second bolt, you could deck! Pro: quickdraws.

12. Hardening of the Arteries (5.10b) No topo. A strenuous route up the column just left of *Ring Pin Crack*. Has loose rock and no anchors, but people still climb it. Go figure. Pro: quickdraws.

13. Ring Pin Crack (5.6) ★ The fourth crack east of the gap, and one of the earliest routes done at Frenchman Coulee. Regarded as the best crack in this area, not quite a ringing endorsement. Pro: to 2.5 inches. (FA: Gene Prater 1955)

14. Wind Walker (5.10b) No topo. A contrived face route squeezed in on the column just right of *Ring Pin Crack*. Pro: quickdraws.

15. Nightbird (5.10a) No topo. The bolted face to the right of *Wind Walker*. Strenuous, with loose rock. Pro: quickdraws.

Middle East Wall

Middle East Wall is the long, shady wall rising directly above the old highway about 0.5 mile west of The Feathers. It is mostly junk, but has one section of clean, solid rock featuring some of the best crack routes at Vantage.

To get there, park at Agaltha Tower and start up the Near Trail, skirting around Agaltha Tower and forking off right where the main trail begins climbing to the plateau

on the left. The low fork traverses a narrow, grassy shelf between cliff bands, and is steep in a few places, so watch your step or you could tumble down onto the highway. After about five minutes of traversing, you will reach the first of several routes. The routes are often approached directly from the road, up the first gully breaching the rotten lower cliff band. This approach is shorter and thus popular, but has caused irreparable erosion. The lower trail is marked No Hiking and should be considered closed. Please use the upper trail to keep climber-caused erosion to a minimum.

The routes are described from left to right as you approach along the upper trail. Descend from anchors. The upper entablature is much too loose to be climbed, unless you don't value your life or your belayer's life.

1. Pudding Time (5.11a) ★ No topo. A bolted route encountered as you approach along the upper trail. Starts just right of a blocky leaning pillar and just left of a bright yellow splotch of lichen. Pro: quickdraws.

2. Blinded by the Light (5.11b) ★ No topo. A bolted column encountered as you approach via the upper trail. Easily identified by the brown rock at the base of the column and the small roof right off the deck. Pro: quickdraws.

3. Aftershock (5.12a) ★ No topo. About 25 feet right of *Blinded by the Light* is this stemming test piece following a line of bolts between two shallow seams. Pro: quickdraws.

4. The Butcher of Baghdad (5.12a) ★ No topo. Another stemming and thin jamming test piece, climbing the bolted shallow corner just right of *Aftershock*. Pro: quickdraws.

5. Slim and Curvy (5.10a) ★★ No topo. About 100 feet right of and around the

corner from *Butcher of Baghdad* is this thinner twin of *Wide and Curvy*. Pro: to 2 inches.

6. Wide and Curvy (5.9) The distinctive offwidth crack immediately left of the *Creeping Death* column. Pro: to 4 inches.

7. Creeping Death (5.11b) ★ The bolted, flat-faced column just right of the curvy offwidth (the first bolted column right of *Butcher of Baghdad*). Pro: quickdraws.

8. Coup d'Etat (5.11b) No topo. The thin crack on the left side of the *Human Sacrifice* column. Pro: to 2 inches.

9. Human Sacrifice (5.10c) ★★★ The first bolted column right of *Creeping Death*,

starting with a 15-foot-long thin crack splitting a pillar. Protect the crack well so you don't deck if you fall off before clipping the first bolt. Pro: to 1 inch at the start, quickdraws the rest of the way. (FA: Bob Buckley, Kevin Kurtz 1989)

10. Coup de Grace (5.11b) ★ No topo. The crack on the right side of the *Human Sacrifice* column. Pro: to 1.5 inches.

11. Jihad (5.11a) ★ The second crack right of *Coup de Grace*. The initial thin crack ends halfway up the wall, from where you traverse right to another crack that leads to anchors. Pro: to 1.5 inches.

12. Desert Dessert (aka Jerusalem Ridge) (5.11a) ★ Connect the bolts up the outside face of The Minaret. Pro: quickdraws.

13. Savage Heart (5.10a) ★ The bolted column immediately right of The Minaret. Pro: quickdraws suffice, but a 2- to 3-inch cam is said to be useful near the top.

14. Sex Party (5.10b) ★★★ The hand crack immediately right of *Savage Heart,* one of the most popular routes on Middle East Wall. Most parties rappel from *Savage Heart's* anchors. Pro: to 2 inches. (FA: Dane Burns, J. Koopsen 1984)

15. Lingerie (5.11b) ★★ The thin crack just right of *Sex Party.* Thin Pro: to 1 inch.

16. The Elders (5.10c) ★ A crack up the right side of the short, yellow column about 20 feet right of *Sex Party.* Pro: to 3.5 inches.

Middle East Wall–Right Side

Matt Anderson on *Satan's Little Helper* (5.8), Satan's Tower, The Feathers, Vantage

SUNSHINE WALL

Sunshine Wall is, as its name implies, one of the sunnier spots at Frenchman Coulee. As the sunniest cliff in the area, it is the most popular, particularly in late fall, winter, and early spring, when it is much warmer than the north-facing cliffs. Sunshine Wall is the most developed of Frenchman Coulee's areas, and because of the combination of sun, development, and close proximity of the best routes, it is often very crowded. You may find yourself queuing up for routes, so be patient, and if your chosen route is occupied, climb something else while you wait.

Sunshine Wall isn't really in Frenchman Coulee, but rather on the north rim of Echo Basin, about a ten-minute hike from the Agaltha Tower parking area via the Near Trail. The best and fastest approach is via the Near Trail, which leads directly to a narrow, labyrinth-like chimney that deposits you at the far east end of the cliff. If you haven't done the approach before, you might miss the chimney, which is barely wide enough to accommodate one person. Traffic jams here are not uncommon, nor is it uncommon to find a rattlesnake enjoying the shade inside the chimney.

Helmets are recommended at Sunshine Wall, as loose rock is unavoidable on most of the routes. Due to daily freezing and thawing during the winter, yesterday's solid rock may well be tomorrow's scree. The rock on many of these routes is flaky, and holds can pull off without warning. Even the rock anchoring the bolts has been known to bust out under the weight of a leader fall, so climb—and belay—with caution. Belayers should stand off to one side, so as not to be in the direct fall path of loose rock, falling leaders, or both. Several notable accidents and a fatality have occurred at Sunshine Wall. Climb with great care.

The routes are listed from right to left as you approach along the base of the cliff from the chimney. Descend from anchors where they are in place; otherwise, top out and scramble back down the chimney.

Sunshine Wall Overview

Air Guitar Area

Stems and Seeds Area

Twin Cracks Area

Twin Cracks Area

The following several routes are located in the vicinity of Twin Cracks, the first good wall you come to as you traverse along the base of Sunshine Wall.

1. Ride 'Em Cowboy (5.9+) ★★ An unmistakable, wavy bolted arête on the right edge of the Twin Cracks wall, presently the first bolted route you come to as you hike down from the chimney. One of the more solid columns on Sunshine Wall. Pro: quickdraws.

2. Snooze, You Lose! (5.10d) A bolted column face. It's the second bolted column right of *Twin Cracks*. Flaky rock. Pro: quickdraws.

3. Easy Off (5.10c) The bolted column face immediately right of *Twin Cracks*. The name aptly describes the nature of the holds on this and other nearby routes. Has a photogenic finish when viewed from atop the columns. Pro: quickdraws.

4. Twin Cracks (aka Party in Your Pants) (5.8) ★★★ A popular route climbing the

Sunshine Wall–Twin Cracks Area

Tower fell over, no longer there

.10a

.10d

.9+

.10c

.8

5

1

4

3

2

obvious double cracks. Belay from a hidden bolt atop the columns, or from the anchors atop the column just right. Pro: to 2 inches; a #4.0 Friend is useful as a belay anchor. (FA: Fred Stanley 1960s)

5. Twin Towers (5.10a) ★ The detached pillar known variously as The Shaft, Herm's Tower, or Babylon Tower finally fell over, and with it two routes were lost. This route was soon climbed in the corner system vacated by the pillar. Pro: unknown.

6. A Midsummer Night's Dream (5.11a) ★ No topo. Presently the next bolted column left from *Twin Towers*. Pro: to 3.5 inches to get to the bolts, then quickdraws to the anchors.

Stems and Seeds Area

This is the next section of good rock as you traverse left along the base of Sunshine Wall, about 150 feet left from *Twin Towers*.

7. Mix It Up (5.11b) ★ No topo. A mixed route climbing a bolted corner to a thin crack. It's the first crack right of *Steel Grill*, if that helps. Pro: quickdraws, gear to 2 inches, cams.

8. Steel Grill (5.9) ★★ The widening crack immediately right of *Bob's Your Uncle*. Pro: to 4 inches; big hexes.

9. Bob's Your Uncle (5.11a) ★ A popular finger crack immediately right of *Stems and Seeds*. Some loose rock at the start. Pro: to 1.5 inches, mostly thin.

10. Stems and Seeds (5.11c) ★★★ A stemming test piece climbing the steep, wide corner, immediately obvious as you turn the corner below *Midsummer Night's Dream*. One of the best routes on Sunshine Wall. Pro: to 2 inches, mostly thin; wide pro recommended for belay anchors unless you exit early at *Hakuna Matata*'s anchors. (FA: Max Dufford 1986)

Sunshine Wall–Stems and Seeds Area

11. Hakuna Matata (5.10a) ★ The short, bolted column immediately left of *Stems and Seeds*. Pro: quickdraws.

12. Sinsemilla (5.10c) ★★ A narrower stemming corner about 25 feet left of *Stems and Seeds*. Pro: to 2 inches.

13. Justified Ancients of Mu Mu (5.9) No topo. The first bolted line right of *Throbbing Gristle,* ascending to anchors on a ledge, then continuing up and right to anchors higher up. Flaky rock. Pro: quickdraws.

14. Corner Pockets (5.10c) ★ No topo. The crack line intertwined with *Justified Ancients of Mu Mu.* Start up the loose-looking corner right of the *Mu Mu* bolts, then from the anchors continue up the crack just left. Pro: quickdraws for bolts; gear to 2 inches.

15. Throbbing Gristle (5.9) ★ A long, flaky arête about 40 feet left of *Sinsemilla.* Sustained and pumping. Pro: quickdraws.

16. Stokin' the Chicken (5.7) ★ The wide crack between the *Throbbing Gristle* and *Whipsaw* arêtes. Pro: to 3 inches.

17. Whipsaw (5.9) Presently the bolted arête left of *Throbbing Gristle,* and site of an occasional bolt war. If the bolts and hangers are in good shape, tick it off before they get chopped or mangled again. Pro: quickdraws.

18. Pony Keg (5.9 or 5.10a) ★ The widening crack just left of the *Whipsaw* arête. Pro: to 4 inches if you stop at the anchors, to 5 inches if you continue on to the top.

19. Air Guitar (5.10b) ★★ The very clean crack in a shallow corner, left of *Pony Keg.* Widens near the top. Pro: to 4 inches will suffice, to 5 inches if you've got any.

20. Crossing the Threshold (5.8) The inside column just right of the *Clip'Em or Skip'Em* arête. Pro: to 4 inches.

Sunshine Wall–Air Guitar Area

Sunshine Wall–George and Martha Area

21. Clip'Em or Skip'Em (5.9) No topo. The bolted arête just left of *Crossing the Threshold*. Pro: quickdraws.

22. Chemically Adjusted Reality (5.10d) ★ The second crack right of *Red M&Ms*. Some loose blocks. Pro: to 3 inches, mostly thin.

23. Red M&Ms (5.11d) ★★★ A stemming test piece up the shallow corner just right of *George and Martha*, ending at that route's anchors. It used to be a scary on-sight lead, but has been bolted for your convenience. Pro: quickdraws.

24. George and Martha (5.10a) ★★★ One of the best crack routes in the area, climbing the obvious crack left of *Red M&Ms* to the only visible bolts on this portion of the wall. The crack widens from fingers to fist to offwidth at the very top. Pro: to 5 inches, mostly 1.5 to 3 inches. (FKA: Karl Birkinkamp 1986)

25. Peaceful Warrior (5.6) The first line of bolts left of *George and Martha* protect this wide crack and contrived variations (to 5.10) up the arête. Pro: quickdraws.

Sunshine Wall–Narlux Area

Sunshine Wall–Boschido Area

26. Tangled Up in Blue (5.10a) ★ Double cracks climbing the big inside column just left of the bolted chimney. Pro: to 5 inches.

27. Narlux (5.11a) ★ The bolted arête left of the *Peaceful Warrior* chimney. Pro: quickdraws.

28. Seven Virgins and a Mule (5.6) ★ The big chimney about 40 feet left of *George and Martha.* Not bad as Vantage chimneys go. A crack in the chimney provides good protection. Pro: to 3 inches.

29. Steel Pulse (5.10b R) No topo. The bolted face just left of the *Seven Virgins* chimney. Has a dangerous runout between bolts high up. Flaky rock. Scary! Pro: quickdraws.

30. Never Forget Your Friends (5.10d) ★ Presently the second bolted pillar left of *Seven Virgins and a Mule,* visible above a lower flaky column. Pro: quickdraws, plus a #1.0 Friend to protect the crack at the top of the column.

31. Mr. Clean (5.11a) ★ The thin corner crack just left of the *Never Forget Your Friends* column. Starts down and left of the flaky column. Pro: to 1.5 inches.

32. Boschido (5.10c) ★ The long bolted column rising directly above the trail descending to Jigsaw Wall. One of the longest pitches up Sunshine Wall. Some flaky rock, just like all the other column routes at Vantage. Rappel from anchors on the left (west); be careful not to knock off loose rock, and to avoid getting your rope stuck. Pro: quickdraws.

JIGSAW WALL

The Jigsaw Wall is located directly downhill from the western gully, and is approached via a short trail down from the base of *Boschido*. The ledge is narrow and sloping in places, and a fall to the scree could be very gruesome, not to mention painful, so be careful. Stick clips are recommended for the first bolt of each route to minimize the risk of a fall on the opening moves. There are several sport routes in the 5.9 to 5.11 range on this cliff—all short, some better than others. Check the current edition of the local guide for route details.

FAT MAN'S WALL

Fat Man's Wall is located directly down and right from *Twin Cracks*. Approach via a short trail leading down from the base of *Twin Cracks*. There are several short, difficult sport routes rated 5.11 and up. If you can't tell which is which, ask somebody or just get on one and see how it goes. If all else fails, refer to the current Frenchman Coulee guide or Mountain Project.

THE M & M WALL

The M & M Wall is located just down and right from Fat Man's Wall. It has several short, popular sport routes, mostly on decent rock. The wall is named for Mike Massey and Matt Kerns, who developed nearly all the routes here. The routes are described from left to right as you encounter them on the approach.

1. Hang Over Hang (5.11c) ★ This is the leftmost route on the crag (or was at last check). Follow the bolts up the face, then pass an overhang to reach the anchors. Clipping the third bolt is difficult, and a fall could be nasty if you fell before making the clip. Pro: quickdraws.

2. Stemmin' M's (5.12a) ★★ A stemming test piece up the shallow corner right of *Hang Over Hang.* Pro: quickdraws.

3. High Five (5.8) ★★ A sport route just right of *Stemmin' M's,* climbing blocky face holds to pockets higher up. Pro: quickdraws.

4. Fifteen Minutes of Fame (5.11a) ★ The next sport route to the right. Can be made harder if you pass the first bolts on the left side. Pro: quickdraws.

5. The Pod (5.11b) ★ Another stemming route following the next bolt line to the right of *Fifteen Minutes of Fame,* passing a small roof. Pro: quickdraws.

6. Wide Load (5.11c) ★ Surmount a reddish pillar, then climb over the blocky overhang to the top. Pro: quickdraws; #0 TCU recommended.

7. The Golden Chillum (5.11a) ★ Just right of the *Wide Load* pillar is this bolted route passing a small, blocky roof. Pro: quickdraws.

8. Ridin' Sidesaddle (5.9) ★ The obvious blocky corner, with bolts in the blocks. More stable than it looks—you hope! Pro: quickdraws.

9. Cold Cut Combo (5.10c) ★ Climb double cracks above an initial overhang, passing a roof higher up. The route is easier since some doofus hammered out a new hold; it's 5.11a if you skip the offending bucket. Pro: quickdraws.

M & M Wall

POWERHOUSE WALL

An entablature wall located about 150 yards east of M & M Wall, featuring what are considered to be the best sport routes at Vantage. To get there, hike east across the shelf above Fat Man's Wall, then descend scree to the base of the wall. The routes are described from left to right.

1. King of the Ruins (5.12a) ★★★ The left-most sport route to date, passing the big roof, then connecting the bolts up the headwall.

2. House of Pain (5.11a) ★★★ Climb the steep wall just right of the roof. Two variations are possible, connecting bolts under the roof and then either joining *King of the*

Ruins (5.12a) or finishing at the *House of Pain* anchors (5.11b).

3. Pile Driver (5.11b) ★★★ Pass the initial roof, then pump it out to the anchors.

4. Death from Above (5.12a) ★★★ Pass the initial roofs, then go up the overhanging headwall.

5. Ask Matt Kerns (5.11d) ★★★ Skirt roofs on the left side and continue up the overhanging wall to anchors.

6. Take Hold of the Flame (5.11b) ★★★ Skirt the roofs on the right side, then pump it out up the headwall.

7. Violator (5.10d) ★★★ Yet another steep face climb. Easier than most at Powerhouse Wall, and thus quite popular.

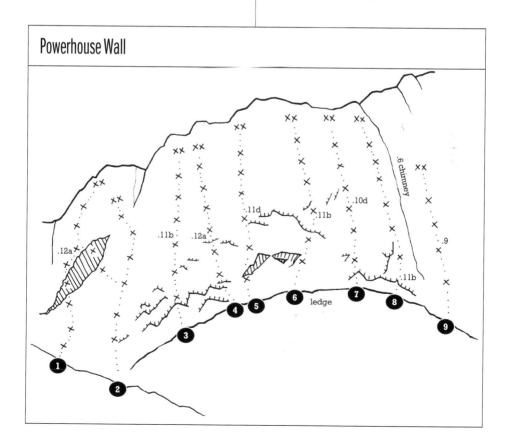

Powerhouse Wall

8. Ask Matt Kerns Again (5.11b) ★★ The next to last sport route on the right side of Powerhouse Wall.

9. Power Puff (5.9) ★★ Just right of the chimney on the right side of the wall. A bit runout.

FUG'S WALL

Fug's Wall is located on the south rim of Echo Basin, directly opposite Sunshine Wall. It is the least popular of the Frenchman Coulee areas, owing mostly to approach time and trouble, and also because the rock is not of the highest quality. Relatively few people climb here, so the routes overall are not as clean nor well protected as those at Sunshine Wall. Aside from that, Fug's Wall is about the same as the other areas. As always, watch out for loose rock and rattlesnakes. Also, plan your day to allow plenty of time to get back to the car before sundown. It's not that far, but the scrambling and hiking back over the mesa can be dangerous after dark.

Those interested in climbing Fug's Wall routes should consult *Vantage Rock* for route information and current restrictions.

Riverview Point

Riverview Point is located at the far west end of the mesa, about 0.5 mile west of Sunshine Wall. It has several good, short sport routes in the 5.7 to 5.11 range, with views of the Columbia River. To get there, drive Vantage Highway about a mile beyond The Feathers to the end of the mesa and a parking area on the northwest side of the road. Hike up the dirt road across the highway that leads into Echo Basin about 400 yards to where a trail leads left (north) up a broad gully. If you reach a right fork of the dirt road (at about 500 yards), you've gone too far. Hike up the gully to the rim, then traverse east across the mesa toward the cliffs. More routes lie along the rim as you continue east toward Sunshine Wall, as the wall transitions from Riverview Point to Riverview Park. Most of the routes in this area are listed on Mountain Project, which lacks good approach descriptions but you'll figure it out.

There are some good, short routes on the columns. The area is far from a destination area, but can provide a day or two's diversion if you're bored with Frenchman Coulee. The area was included in the 2009 edition of this guide, and is also covered in Rick La Belle's *Rock Climbs of Central Washington* guide. Refer to one of those guides for route information.

TIETON RIVER CANYON

The Tieton River Canyon is one of Washington's major cragging areas. With hundreds of routes, easy approaches, and reliable weather, one might think the area would be as popular as Leavenworth. Surprisingly, it isn't. However, with the development of so many good routes on high quality rock, the Tieton is far from the obscure area it once was.

Type of climbing: Although Tieton River is known mostly for its columns, the area has an abundance of sport climbs on its varied andesite cliffs. True, the majority of Tieton rock is columnar andesite, running slabby to vertical, with abundant cracks and edgy face climbs up to two pitches in length, ranging from easy Class 5 to 5.12. The columnar routes are typically cracks in corners between the columns, plus an occasional column face or arête. Face climbs are mostly bolt protected, although a few require intermittent gear placements in seams and cracks. On several cliffs, routes climb on solid rock above, below, or in between layers of flaky, loose, or rotten rock. Industrious cleaning has transformed several horrendous-looking walls into fairly decent sport crags. Otherwise blank-looking faces often feature thin edges and pockets, which have been well exploited by new-route pioneers. The Tieton has an abundance of excellent sport climbs, running the gamut from 5.7 to 5.12, with some projects destined to be 5.13 or harder.

Brief history of area: The Tieton was one of the last major Washington rock climbing areas to be developed, which seems surprising given the area's enormous wealth of good-quality rock. Prior to the mid-1980s, a small group of Yakima locals including Matt and Jamie Christensen, Matt Kerns, Tom Hargis, Kjell Swedin, and Paul Boving, to name a few, almost literally had the Tieton to themselves, and established several dozen routes, primarily crack climbs at Royal Columns and Moon Rocks, including most of the obvious classics. Of the group, Boving was particularly adept at boldly leading hard, thin cracks, and his ascents of some of the state's classic thin crack routes, including *Thin Fingers* (5.11a) at Index and *R.O.T.C.* (5.11c) at Midnight Rock, set him apart from his contemporaries of the era. Sadly, Boving's penchant for bold leading may have been his undoing; in 1977 Boving was killed in a fall from *Thin Fingers*. Although most of the close-knit group of Yakima climbers went on to impressive climbing careers, Boving's death stilled the waters of Tieton climbing for many years.

Although a few new routes were added each year during the late 1970s and early 1980s, it was not until the mid-1980s that new route development picked up in earnest. Andy Fitz and Ed Mosshart, two relatively inexperienced climbers at the time, met while bouldering near Yakima, and soon began exploring the Tieton. During the next

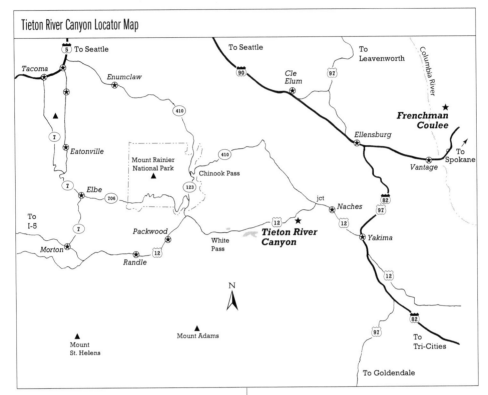

To Seattle

To Seattle

To
Leavenworth

Columbia River

Tacoma

Enumclaw

Cle
Elum

★ Frenchman
Coulee

Ellensburg

Eatonville

Mount Rainier
National Park

Chinook Pass

Vantage

To
Spokane

Elbe

To
I-5

Packwood

White
Pass

jct

Naches

★ *Tieton River
Canyon*

Yakima

Morton

Randle

N

To
Tri-Cities

Mount
St. Helens

Mount Adams

To Goldendale

decade, they would go on to develop several new cliffs and establish a vast majority of the new routes done in the Tieton from 1987 to the present. Spurred on by these newcomers, some of the old guard, including Matt Christensen and Matt Kerns, and others, including Norm Reid and Mark McGuire, stepped up the pace, and in all they nearly tripled the number of Tieton routes in only a few years.

As the quality of unclimbed crack lines diminished, new route development shifted away from the colonnades and onto the many steep entablature walls, which led to the establishment of dozens of good-quality sport routes throughout the Tieton River Canyon. Several cliffs under development are not included in this guide, but if you poke around a bit, you might come across a "secret" crag. Just don't be surprised if you find a bunch of people already climbing there.

Seasons and climate: The Tieton River lies on the semiarid eastern slope of the south Cascades, in a rain shadow created by Mount Rainier, which rises to an elevation of 14,411 feet only 60-odd miles due west. The landscape evokes the American West: ponderosa and western white pine forest, grassy buttes, scabby volcanic outcroppings, prickly pear cactus, free-range cattle, and diamondback rattlers. Although you can climb here almost year-round, the climbing season runs from early March through late October. It gets pretty cold during the winter months, although some of the crags get enough direct sunlight to provide fairly pleasant climbing conditions even in December and January. During the summer, temperatures regularly soar into the 90s. You can still climb comfortably on hot summer days by chasing the shade up the canyon from crag to crag, but

Tieton River Vicinity Map

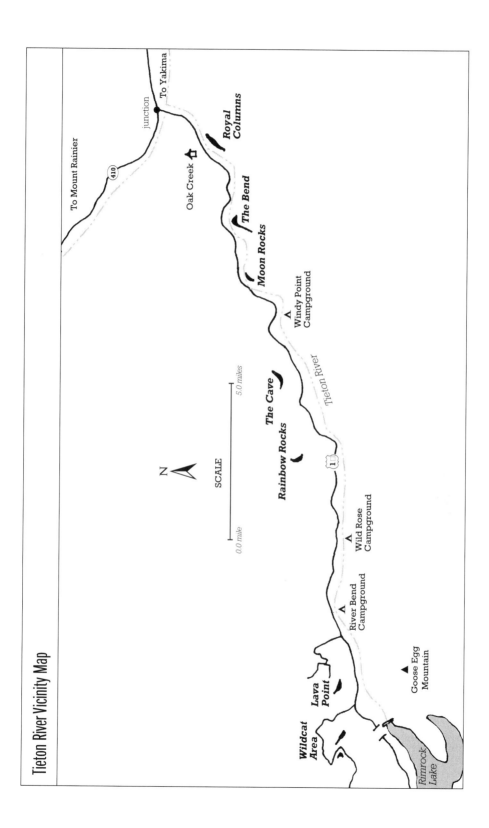

an afternoon siesta in the shade by the river is definitely recommended so you don't suffer heatstroke. On hot days, drink plenty of fluids to avoid dehydration.

Precautions and regulations: The Tieton crags are located on land administered by the Washington Department of Fish and Wildlife (DFW) and the Wenatchee National Forest, except Rainbow Rocks, which are located on private land. There are presently very few restrictions on climbing. Royal Columns, The Bend, and Moon Rocks are located within the Oak Creek Wildlife Recreation Area. There are seasonal nesting closures near the crags from February through June, but the crags themselves have not been closed in recent years. Other cliffs may be subject to raptor closures; check current closures before you climb. While the DFW hasn't greatly restricted climbing, climbers are encouraged to be on their best behavior in order to avoid any access problems in the future. Please stay on established trails to avoid unnecessary erosion, and don't litter, especially cigarette butts. Tossing a cigarette butt into the bushes or grass could ignite a fire, with disastrous consequences.

Rattlesnakes and ticks are abundant throughout the canyon. Rattlers are frequently encountered along the base of and atop the crags, usually in the early morning or late evening, but sometimes during midday on or around rocks. Ticks are everywhere during the spring, and even during the summer you should keep a close eye on yourself and your dog to make sure these nasty parasites haven't latched on.

Although most of the routes climb solid rock, there are layers above and below several of the crags that appear quite loose. Although there have been no known rockfall fatalities, there are a few columns and blocks poised above popular routes with no visible means of support. Helmets are recommended, particularly for belayers. Also, even the best routes have occasional loose holds, which can flake off while in use, so don't be surprised if you pull off a handhold or lever off a foothold.

Some areas of the Tieton are on free-range land, so if you are driving off the main highway, be careful not to hit a stray cow. Keep an eye out for deer and elk crossing the highway, during early morning and late evening hours especially.

Gear and other considerations: Most of the Tieton's routes are either cracks or sport climbs, so in general you either need a rack of nuts and cams or a rack of quickdraws. There are a few mixed routes requiring gear to supplement primarily bolt protection. On cracks, a rack ranging from small to midsize stoppers and a selection of cams will usually suffice. The cracks tend to flare inward in places, making protection sometimes difficult to place, especially if you're getting pumped—and you will be. Nuts often work better than cams in these places. Occasional horizontal fractures offer protection opportunities, so bring some wired nuts and TCUs for whenever the bolts look suspiciously far apart.

Chain anchors are in place atop most of the popular routes, and atop nearly all sport climbs. Double-bolt anchors are the norm, although there are some funky anchors here and there. It's a good idea to have a backup sling ready to replace any old, worn-out rappel slings you might encounter.

Camping and accommodations: There are several campgrounds in the Tieton River valley, but bivouacking is presently permitted pretty much anywhere in the canyon. If you can't find a riverside spot, drive up just about any side road until you find a flat spot. If there isn't already a fire pit, please don't make one. If you build a campfire, keep it small so embers don't get blown into the dry grass and brush, and make sure your fire is out cold before retiring. It would be very easy to start a grass fire, which would no doubt erupt into a full-on forest fire during the dry months of late summer and fall. Check for seasonal fire restrictions, common in late summer. Those bivouacking are encouraged to be on their best behavior, so this privilege is not taken away in the future.

There are several small stores along the highway, where you can grab a quick snack or drink. The nearest gas station, grocery store, and ATM is in Naches, about 17 miles east of Royal Columns. The city of Yakima, located 30 miles east of Royal Columns, has all accommodations. Public restrooms are located at the Oak Creek Wildlife Recreation Area offices directly across from Royal Columns. Water is available here and at campgrounds throughout the canyon.

Emergency services: In case of emergency, dial 911. The nearest hospital is in Yakima.

Guide services/local equipment suppliers: Svends Mountain Sports, Yakima; Gymnastics Plus, Yakima.

Other guidebooks: Ford, Marlene, and Jim Yoder. *Tieton River Rocks*. A new edition of the Ford/Yoder guide is reportedly in the works.

Finding the crags: If you are coming from the east side of the Cascades, follow whichever road leads you most directly to Yakima, then head west on US 12 to its junction with WA 410; take the left fork and continue up the Tieton River Canyon. If you

are coming from the west, there are several possibilities. From Seattle, the most direct way is probably to head east on I-90 to Ellensburg, then south on I-82 to Yakima, then west on US 12, staying left on US 12 at its junction with WA 410. From Tacoma, head over your choice of Chinook, Cayuse, or White Passes. During summer, it's faster to take WA 410 over Cayuse Pass and down WA 123, then over White Pass; during winter, I-90 and US 12 are the only options. From southwest Washington and the Portland/Vancouver area, head north on I-5, then east on US 12 and over White Pass.

Tieton River Canyon Mileage Chart

Point of Interest	From US 12/ Jct WA 410	Between Points
Royal Columns	2.1	—
The Bend	3.3	1.2
Moon Rocks	5.2	1.9
Windy Point Campground	8.0	2.8
The Cave	10.0	2.0
Trout Lodge	12.5	2.5
Willows Campground	15.2	2.7
Wild Rose Campground	15.7	0.5
River Bend Campground	16.9	1.2
Soup Creek Road	17.7	0.6
Wildcat Road	19.4	1.7
Westfall Rocks Tunnel	20.4	1.0
White Pass	34.0	13.6

ROYAL COLUMNS

Royal Columns is the first easily accessible columnar cliff band you encounter as you drive upriver on US 12 from its junction with WA 410. It is a long colonnade rising on the shoulder directly across the river from the Oak Creek Wildlife Recreation Area offices, about 2.1 miles from the WA 410 junction. Royal Columns offers typical columnar andesite climbing: lots of jamming and stemming in between the columns, and face climbing up the column faces and arêtes. The dozens of routes here are mostly under 100 feet long, with usually well-protected climbing on fairly sound, edgy rock, ranging from 5.3 to 5.12 in difficulty. An abundance of crack climbs in the easier grades makes Royal Columns a great novice and intermediate crag, although a good selection of 5.9 to 5.12 cracks and face climbs means experts will find plenty to do here as well. Royal Columns gets morning shade, making it a pleasant place to climb even during midsummer—until early afternoon anyway. On dry winter days, afternoon sun makes Royal Columns a relatively warm climbing venue.

Roadside parking is plentiful, although lack of shade means everything you leave in the car will get baked. Hike across the bridge and up the road to the right (not up the old climbers' trail leading straight up to the columns). Pass through a hinged gate (which keeps elk inside the fenced-in area so they don't rampage through the orchards farther down the valley in search of food during harsh winters) and follow the Tieton River Nature Trail a couple hundred yards to a well-marked climbers' trail forking off to the left, which switchbacks up the brushy slope to the base of the columns just right of the *Orange Sunshine* and *Thriller Pillar* area. The trail continues left along the base of the columns to *Inca Roads* and beyond.

The routes are described from right to left as you encounter them traversing along the base of the columns when approaching via the climbers' trail. Descend via rappel from various anchors atop the columns.

1. Paul Maul (5.10c) ★★ The crack immediately right of the *Morning After* column. Pro: to 2 inches.

2. Morning After (5.12a) ★★ The bolted column just right of where the trail reaches the rock, about 50 feet right of *Thriller Pillar*. A thin, technical test piece. Pro: quickdraws. (FA: Andy Fitz, Ed Mosshart 1989)

3. Jam Exam (5.9) ★ The crack immediately left of *Morning After*. Testy. Pro: to 3 inches.

4. Solar King (5.11a) ★★ The thin crack in between the *Morning After* and *Thriller Pillar* columns. Tricky thin pro at the start, which is the crux. Pro: to 3 inches, including a selection of small wireds and cams.

5. Cactus Love (5.9) ★ The first crack right of the *Thriller Pillar* column routes. Starts thin, widens, and passes a roof on the left side. Pro: to 2 inches.

6. Thriller Pillar (5.9) ★★ The bolted column just right of the *Orange Sunshine* thin crack. An edgy face route with a fun finish up big holds. Pro: quickdraws.

7. Orange Sunshine (5.10b) ★★ The finger crack splitting the flat orange wall just above where the trail meets the rock, immediately left of *Thriller Pillar*. Don't let the overhanging finish psych you out. Pro: to 1 inch. (FFA: Dale Farnham 1974)

8. Columns Holiday (5.10c) ★ The bolted column left of *Orange Sunshine*. Pro: quickdraws, small cam for start.

Royal Columns Approach Map

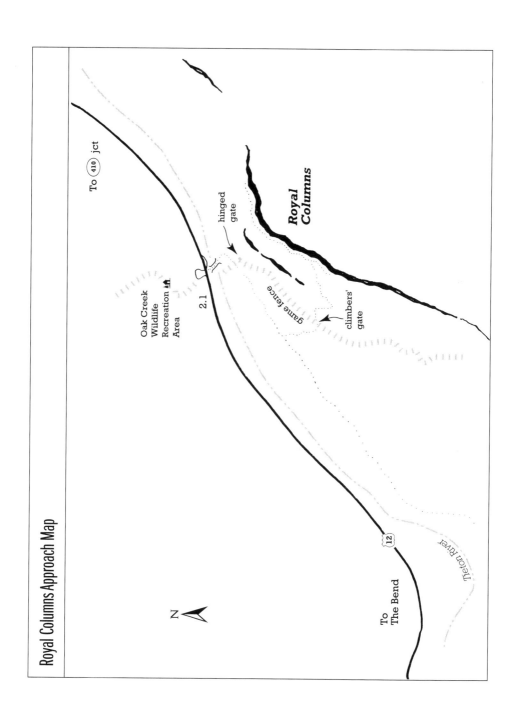

N

To 410 jct

hinged gate

Oak Creek Wildlife Recreation Area

2.1

game fence

climbers' gate

Royal Columns

12

To The Bend

Tieton River

9. Cross-Eyed and Painless (5.9) ★ The thinning crack just left of the *Columns Holiday* column. Pro: to 2 inches.

10. The Price of Complacency (5.11a) This route no longer exists; the column collapsed. I hope you weren't saving it for an on-sight attempt. A reminder that if you want to do something, you'd better get on it.

11. Stress Management (5.10a) Another popular route that disappeared when the column collapsed. There may be a new route or two behind the column; check the upcoming Yoder-Ford guide or Mountain Project for details.

12. Entrance Exam (5.6) Also no longer exists.

13. X Factor (5.7) ★ The crack immediately right of the more-obvious *Cutting Edge*. Pro: to 2 inches.

14. The Cutting Edge (5.7) ★ A distinctive route climbing a steep crack on the right side of a column, passing The Cleaver, a dangerous-looking flake hanging out near the top of the crack. Pass The Cleaver with care so it doesn't pull out. Pro: to 3 inches.

15. Dancing Madly Backwards (5.11a) ★ The column just left of *The Cutting Edge*, starting with a thin crack or bolted slab and ending atop the roof. Height dependent; may seem as hard as 5.11c. Pro: to 1 inch, including RPs for crack start, quickdraws.

16. Western Front (5.3) ★★ One of the best routes of its grade in the area, climbing the crack on the left side of the *Dancing Madly Backwards* column. Pro: to 3 inches.

Between *Western Front* and *Inca Roads* are numerous crack routes ranging in difficulty from 5.4 to 5.8. The best of these are included below, but feel free to try any old crack and see how it goes.

Royal Columns – Left Side

17. Thearetical (5.10a) ★ Just around the buttress from *Western Front* is this slabby, bolted arête. You might want to boulder up on the right to clip the first bolt. Pro: quickdraws.

18. Humble Pie (5.11a) ★★ An arête starting with a thin face crack, leading to an exposed finish over a roof. Pro: quickdraws; gear to 1 inch.

19. Slash (5.10b) ★ A hand crack to a 3-bolt face (crux), finishing up a fun flake. Pro: gear to 4 inches, quick draws.

20. First Blood (5.8) ★ A fist crack right of a slabby column, just right of the more obvious *Mush Maker*. Pro: to 4 inches.

21. Hard Last (5.10a/b) ★★ No topo. Climb the arete between First Blood and Mush Maker. Said to be really fun. Pro: quickdraws.

22. Mush Maker (5.7) ★★★ A great, long, straight-in hand crack. Pro: to 3 inches.

23. Little Known Wonder (5.7) ★★★ The facing corners just right of *Inca Roads*. Better than it looks; deserves more attention. Pro: to 3 inches.

24. Inca Roads (5.9) ★★★ A beautiful, steep finger and hand crack running up the right side of a column about 100 feet left of *Western Front*. Continuously difficult, with few rests, but good protection provided you don't plug up the best jams. Pro: to 3 inches will suffice, but a 5-inch cam might be useful at the start; lots of cams and midsize stoppers. (FA: Dale Farnham, Paul Boving 1974)

25. Imperial Master (5.11c) ★ The flaky column just left of *Inca Roads*. Sustained. Pro: quickdraws, optional piece to 1 inch for the top.

26. Ball and Chain (5.10a) ★ The "perfect" thin crack on the right side of the pillar immediately left of *Imperial Master*, starting with a bolted pillar. Pro: to 2 inches, include small nuts.

Beyond *Ball and Chain* are numerous easy to moderate routes (5.3 to 5.8). Most require protection from 0.5 inch to 3 or 4 inches. The best of these many routes are listed below, but by all means feel free to try some of the other routes.

27. Twin Cracks (5.6) ★ A set of double cracks leading up the right side of the protruding column about 75 feet left of *Inca Roads*. Pro: to 3 inches.

28. Journeyman Crack (5.9) ★ The obvious hand and fist crack splitting the wall left around the corner from *Twin Cracks*. Pro: to 3 inches.

29. Contraction Action (5.8) ★ A crack splitting blocky columns leads to a flaring chimney finish. Pro: to 3 inches.

30. Nimrod's Nemesis (5.5) ★ On the far left side, climb double cracks to a roof; continue left around the roof and up a crack to the top. Pro: to 3 inches.

THE BEND

Just over a mile upriver from Royal Columns is The Bend, another broad colonnade on the slope across the river from US 12. It has some of the longest routes at Tieton, and some of the area's best crack lines. Due to access difficulties and abundant vegetation, this crag was largely untouched until the late 1980s, when an easy approach across a suspension bridge was discovered by climbers who were willing to spend days unearthing the cracks. Prodigious cleaning revealed dozens of excellent crack routes, mostly in the 5.9 to 5.11 range. So proliferous are the crack lines at The Bend that the area was initially dubbed the Crack House (hence the many drug references in the route names). In addition to the cracks, a few of the columns have yielded face climbs, but cracks are what The Bend is really all about. The Bend has many long routes, up to two pitches, a few of which require double ropes for rappels. Some scrambling up blocky slabs is required to reach a few of the routes on the upper right side. The rock is less featured than at

Royal Columns, meaning that on cracks you will encounter more pure jamming and less edging. During the summer, The Bend is shady until early afternoon; after that you're wise to beat a retreat to a shady spot. Andy Fitz, Ed Mosshart, Matt Christensen, and Norm Reid were responsible for development of most routes at The Bend.

Park next to the Quonset hut beside the road, near the caretaker's house on the south side of the road (3.3 miles upriver from the WA 410 junction). Parking is limited; don't block the caretaker's driveway or the Quonset hut, and please don't block anyone else in. A trail begins through a gate left of the hut and leads west across the floodplain to a suspension bridge crossing the river. Once across the river, follow the trail downriver, toward the crag. A climbers' trail forks off to the right, cutting through the brush and heading up the slope, reaching the base of the columns about 30 feet right of *Community Project*.

The routes are described first from right to left as you encounter them on the

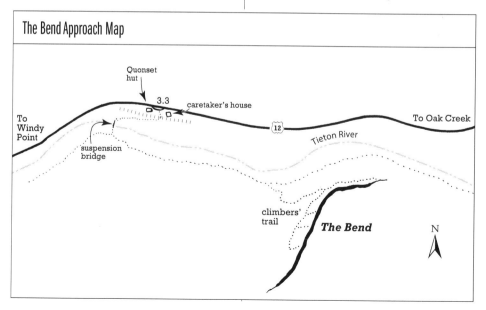

The Bend Approach Map

approach trail leading along the base of the formation from *Introductory Offer* to *Hot Botany,* then from left to right as they are encountered on the trail leading up from the base of the formation. Descend via rappel from anchors atop the columns unless there are no anchors, in which case be careful not to knock off loose rock while scrambling down the upper trail, which leads left and eventually outflanks the columns. If you venture above the cliff, watch out for snakes.

1. Introductory Offer (5.9) ★★ A widening crack beginning behind a cluster of gnarly oak trees just left of where the trail meets the rock, about 15 feet right of *Community Project.* Pro: to 2 inches.

2. Needles and Death (5.10c) ★ A continuation of *Introductory Offer,* climbing a thin crack just up and right, leading to the top of the cliff. Two pitches; the second pitch is short. Pro: to 2 inches.

3. Turning Point (5.12a) ★ The very thin crack in between *Community Project* and *Introductory Offer,* finishing at the latter's anchors. Pro: to 1 inch; small RPs. (FA: Norm Reid, Matt Christensen 1990)

4. Community Project (5.11d) ★★ A striking thin crack about 30 feet left of where the approach trail reaches the columns, about 15 feet left of two gnarly oaks at the toe of the formation. The crack gets thinner as it goes, and ends on blocky ledges about 50 feet up. Pro: to 2 inches, including

some thin wireds. (FA: Matt Christensen, Fliura Jirnova 1988)

5. Dancing Bear (5.10a) ★ The first good thin crack reached as you continue left from *Community Project,* easily identified by whitish rock on the upper part of the crack. Hardest at the start. Pro: to 3 inches, including some small wireds.

6. The Heartbreak of Psoriasis (5.10c) ★ A thin crack splitting a pillar just right of the more obvious *Winds of Change*; it also has some whitish rock higher up. Pro: to 2 inches.

The Bend–Right Side

The Bend—Winds of Change Area

7. Winds of Change (5.10d) ★★ A long pitch climbing a thin seam splitting the big pillar 10 feet left of *The Heartbreak of Psoriasis*. Pro: to 2 inches. (FA: Ed Mosshart, Andy Fitz 1988)

8. Living for the City (5.10c) ★ A thin crack just right of the leaning columns 25 feet left of *Winds of Change*, reaching anchors at a ledge 50 feet up. A short second pitch reaches anchors atop the wall. Pro: to 1 inch to the first anchors; to 3 inches for the rest.

9. Tongue and Cheek (5.10c) ★ Presently the first bolted column face you come to as you traverse left from *Community Project*, about 50 feet left of *Living for the City*. Pro: quickdraws.

10. Cherry Bomb (5.10a) ★★ The next bolted column face to the left. Pro: quickdraws; gear to 1.5 inches, including TCUs.

11. People, Places and Things (5.10) ★ A good thin crack. Pro: to 1.5 inches, including TCUs.

12. Farewell to Vegas (5.10d) ★ Face climb up a leaning column on the far left side. Pro: quickdraws; wired nuts.

13. Hot Botany (5.10b) ★ An obvious 50-foot-long thin crack on the extreme left side of the cliff, just left of the leaning column of *Farewell to Vegas*. May be dirty. Pro: to 2 inches, including thin wireds.

The following routes are reached by heading right from the base of the formation up the obvious climbers' trail. The routes

are described from left to right as they are encountered on the approach.

14. Local Knowledge (5.10b) ★★★ A two-pitch route starting from the base of the cliff about 30 feet right of *Introductory Offer.* The crux first pitch leads up a shallow dihedral to blocky ledges. From the belay, continue up an exposed crack splitting yellow-tinted columns. Pro: to 3 inches. (FA: Andy Fitz, Ed Mosshart 1988)

Approach the next several routes via the first side trail leading into the rock from the main trail ascending along the right flank of the formation. Slabby Class 4 scrambling leads to the base of the routes; be careful.

15. Seizure (5.10b) ★★ A long pitch climbing a striking steep crack on the left side of a column, passing two small roofs low down. Pro: to 4 inches.

16. MX (5.10a) ★ Another long pitch just right of *Seizure,* climbing a more continuous but less technical thin hand crack, also passing some roofs low down. Pro: to 3 inches.

17. Peace, Love and Rope (5.9) ★ The long corner crack immediately right of *MX.* Pro: to 3 inches.

18. Ed's Jam (5.8) ★★★ A long, enjoyable route climbing a continuous crack just left of the prominent orange dihedral visible as you approach the cliff. A few thin moves at the start lead to joyous hand jams up the long column crack. Enjoy! Pro: to 3 inches. (FKA: Ed Mosshart, Andy Fitz 1987)

Approach the following routes via the second side trail leading into the rock from the main trail up the right side of the formation.

19. Ninety-Meter Hill (5.10c) ★★ A thin crack leading up a corner that swoops down from above like a ski jump hill. A finger jamming and stemming test piece that gets steeper and steeper. May need cleaning. Pro: to 2 inches; lots of small wireds.

The Bend—Ed's Jam Area

The Bend—Right Side

The Bend–Tiers Roof

20. Intent to Deliver (5.10b) ★★★ An excellent route climbing a clean corner about 50 feet up and right from *Ninety-Meter Hill*. A tough move past a roof leads to stemming and thin finger jamming up the steepening corner. May need cleaning. Pro: to 2 inches, including RPs and small wireds. (FA: Andy Fitz, Matt Christensen 1989)

21. Cascade Curtain (5.9) ★ The second crack right of *Intent to Deliver*. A bolted slab leads to a roof; pass the roof and continue up the steepening hand crack to chain anchors. Pro: quickdraws; gear to 2.5 inches.

22. White Oak Massacre (5.10c) ★★ The first clean corner down and left from the *Tiers* roof. Pro: to 2 inches.

Approach the following routes via the third and final side trail leading into the rock from the main trail. The trail leads to a cluster of five oak trees, where a board has been wedged between some rocks and an oak tree directly below the obvious arête of *Tragically*

Hip and the bolted column of *House Rules*. The *Tiers* roof is the obvious double roof about 30 feet down and left from where the trail meets the rock.

23. Salmon Song (5.10a) ★★ A thin crack passing the *Tiers* roof on its left side and continuing up the left side of the column. Pro: to 2 inches.

24. Tiers (5.9) The right-hand crack through the distinctive tiered roof. Pro: to 4 inches.

25. Treatment Bound (5.10a) ★ A thin, right-facing corner crack on the right side of the column immediately right of the *Tiers* roof. Pro: to 2 inches.

26. Cruel Harvest (5.9) ★ These double thin cracks set in an inside column corner are just right of *Treatment Bound*. Pro: to 2 inches.

27. Pure Joy (5.10c) ★★ A thin crack splitting the column prow just right of *Cruel Harvest*. Start via *Reckoning*, then go left up

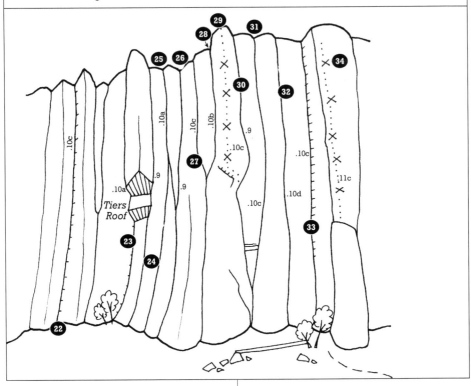

the crack. Pro: to 3 inches, including thin wireds. (FA: Andy Fitz, Ed Mosshart 1987)

28. Reckoning (5.10b) ★ The second thin crack right of *Cruel Harvest*, this one set in a shallow corner immediately left of the *House Rules* column. Not quite as joyous as *Pure Joy*, but still worthy. Pro: to 2 inches.

29. House Rules (5.10c) ★ The bolted column just right of *Reckoning*. A little runout. Pro: to 1 inch; quickdraws.

30. Hallowed Ground (5.9) ★★ The thin crack on the right side of the *House Rules* column, very obvious as you approach the rock via the uppermost trail. Pass a flaky-looking roof low down, then continue up the clean crack. Pro: to 1 inch.

31. Sugar Kicks (5.10c) ★ The thin crack immediately right of *Hallowed Ground*. Pro: to 2 inches.

32. Zero Tolerance (5.10d) ★ The next crack right of *Sugar Kicks*, immediately left of *Ambient Domain*; also thin and sustained. Pro: to 3 inches, but mostly below 1 inch.

33. Ambient Domain (5.10c) ★★ The steep corner crack immediately left of the *Tragically Hip* arête. Pro: to 2 inches.

34. Tragically Hip (5.11c) ★★ The steep arête right of *Ambient Domain*, easily located by the bolts. Pro: quickdraws.

MOON ROCKS

Another 2 miles upriver from The Bend is Moon Rocks, a small colonnade across the river from US 12 (5.2 miles upriver from the WA 410 junction). Although Moon Rocks is much smaller than Royal Columns and The Bend, it makes up for its diminutive stature with its uniformly excellent rock and difficult routes. Moon Rocks has about two dozen routes, almost entirely difficult cracks in the 5.10 and 5.11 range. The rock is less featured than at The Bend or Royal Columns, providing fewer edges and thus requiring better crack climbing technique on most routes. Matt Christensen, Andy Fitz, and Ed Mosshart developed many of the routes at Moon Rocks.

To get there, park in the big turnout about 0.1 mile downriver from the rocks and hike across a convenient bridge, then for a short distance up the trail to the rocks. The routes are listed from left to right. Descend by rappel where possible; double ropes are required for many rappels. Otherwise, scramble over the top and off to the left (east) side, being careful not to knock off loose rocks on those below you. (See Tieton River Canyon Vicinity Map on page 321.)

1. Internal Bliss (5.7) ★★ A unique route climbing up into a chimney and tunneling behind the columns nearly to the top of the cliff. Pro: to 2 inches. (FA: Matt Christensen 1986)

Moon Rocks

2. The Sun and the Moon (5.10b) ★ A bolted column face on the far left side, just left of an obvious leaning column (*Moon Struck Pillar*). Start up the left side of the column. Pro: quickdraws.

3. Moon Struck Pillar (5.10d) ★ A leaning column on the left side, with a few bolts. Pro: to 2 inches; quickdraws.

4. Middle Digit Destruction (5.11d) ★ A finish variation of *Moon Struck,* climbing the thin crack on the left from the top of the pillar. Pro: to 2 inches, mostly small wireds.

5. Moonstruck (5.10b) ★ The chimney/ corner system right of *Moon Struck Pillar,* leading to a thin crack finish. Pro: to 2 inches.

6. Comeback Crack (5.10c) ★★ From atop the *Blue Moon* pillar, follow the crack to the left. Pro: to 2 inches.

7. Blue Moon (5.11c) ★★ The bolted column immediately right of *Moon Struck Pillar*. Pro: quickdraws.

8. Bloody Knuckles (5.10c) ★ The crack on the right side of the *Blue Moon* pillar, beginning from the oak tree. From the top of the column, head up the right-hand crack. Pro: to 2 inches.

9. Lunar Rover (5.12a) ★★ A long, thin corner crack. Pro: to 1 inch.

10. Ages of You (5.11c R) ★ A continuous thin crack about 10 feet right of *Bloody Knuckles*. So pumping you'll have trouble hanging around to place gear. Flaring placements. Scary. Pro: to 2 inches.

11. Straight Talk (5.10a) ★ A prominent straight-in crack, also sustained but not quite as difficult as its neighbors. Pro: to 3 inches. (FA: Kjell Swedin, Ed Hart 1978)

12. Boving's Crack (5.11c) ★ A thin crack set between two facing corners. Long a Tieton test piece, latecomers discovered the route was only 5.10b if you stem out on the corners instead of jamming the vicious finger crack directly. Pro: to 3 inches either way. (FA: Paul Boving, Matt Christensen 1977)

13. Double Crack (5.6) ★ A double crack system on the far right side of the cliff. Not much to offer for the majority of climbers who visit this cliff, but some solace to those not up to the difficulties of most of the routes here. Pro: to 2 inches.

THE CAVE

About 5 miles upriver from Moon Rocks (10 miles upriver from the Highway 410 junction) is The Cave, one of the most popular areas in the Tieton. The Cave is located several hundred feet above the highway, and presents as a multilayered, yellowish cliff with a prominent row of short columns on the left side and a blocky, overhanging yellowish wall on the right. Hidden from view behind a grove of oak trees is an excellent short wall featuring numerous steep and overhanging sport routes. The Cave is one of the best sport crags in the Tieton, with a high concentration of short sport climbs ranging from 5.7 to 5.12. Most of the routes at The Cave were developed by Andy Fitz, Ed Mosshart, and Mark McGuire.

To get there, park on the river side of the road, along a short side road leading to a riverside bivy site. The trail begins directly

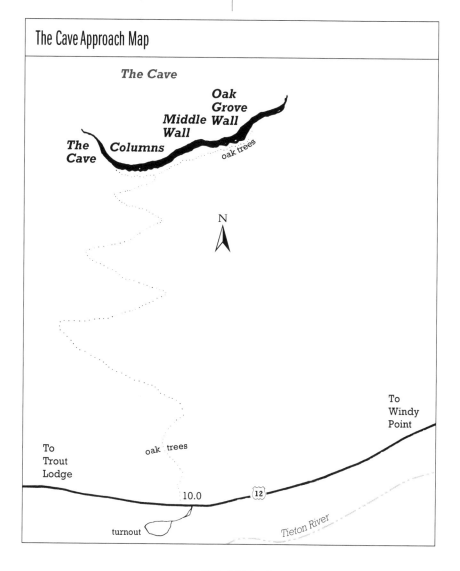

The Cave Approach Map

across the highway, passing through an oak grove, then switchbacking up the open slope via a well-defined trail. Please stay on the trail to avoid unnecessary erosion. The trail meets the crag below the left-hand columns, and traverses right along the base of the cliff past the middle wall to the oak grove on the far right side. The routes are listed from left to right. Descend via rappel from anchors atop each route.

The Columns (Mark's Wall)

The following routes are located on the columns low down on the left side of The Cave, visible as you approach from below. They are described from left to right. Descend from anchors atop the columns.

1. Arid Reaches (5.11b) ★ Presently the leftmost sport route on the columns, climbing a tan-colored, bolted column face. Pro: quickdraws.

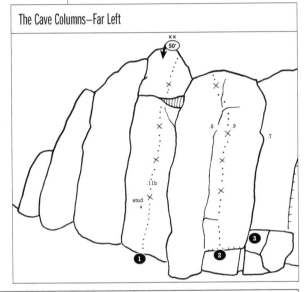

The Cave Columns—Far Left

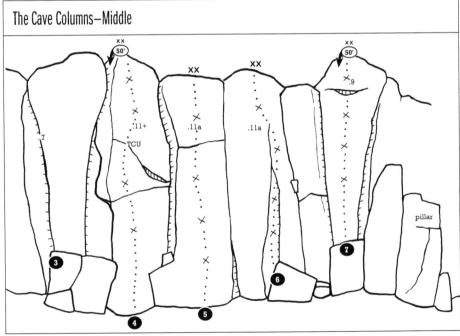

The Cave Columns—Middle

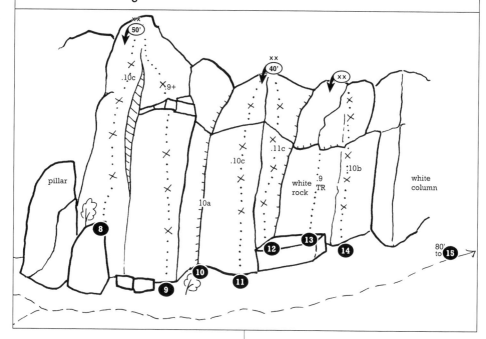

The Cave Columns–Right Side

2. Children of a Lesser Chaos (5.8) ★ The next to last sport route on the columns, climbing an obvious arête. The route is easier if you stay to the left, on the arête. Pro: quickdraws.

3. Flake Corner (5.7) ★ An obvious right-facing corner crack starting atop a block. The crack has a thin flake that would likely break under the weight of a leader fall, so protect it carefully. Pro: to 2 inches.

4. Cave Driller (5.11d R) ★ The bolted column face immediately right of the aforementioned corner crack. Pro: quickdraws, plus thin gear that might pull out if you fall at the crux.

5. Children of Chaos (5.11a) ★★ A sport route climbing a flat, brown column face immediately left of a nice-looking thin crack. Pro: quickdraws.

6. Childhood Injury (5.11a) ★ The next sport route to the right of *Children of Chaos*, climbing a right-facing corner, then up a column to anchors. Pro: quickdraws.

7. Age of Consent (5.9) ★ A sport route leading up a recessed column face directly up and left of the prominent pillars near the center of the columns, passing a small roof near the top. Pro: quickdraws.

8. Stone Embrace (5.10c) ★ A sport route climbing a narrow column face and arête immediately right of the pillars. Pro: quickdraws.

9. Cavewalk (5.10a) ★ A sport route climbing an orange column face about 15 feet right of *Stone Embrace* and ending at that route's anchors. Pro: quickdraws.

10. Thin Crack (5.10a) ★ A thin crack in the corner left of *Mark's Window*. Pro: to 1 inch.

11. Mark's Window (5.10c) ★★ A thin, edgy sport route just left around the arête from the flat boulder at the base of a prominent whitish column. Pro: quickdraws.

12. Bloodstone (5.11c) ★★ A thin, edgy sport route climbing the narrow, slightly overhanging, dark-red-stained face just around the arête to the right of *Mark's Window,* directly from the flat boulder. Pro: quickdraws.

13. Tumbling Blocks (5.9 TR) A face climb up the white column face leading directly up from the right side of the flat boulder. Not independent enough to be bolted, so toprope it after climbing *Frogs.*

14. Frogs (5.10b) ★ A pumpy face climb up the bolted arête starting just right of the flat boulder. Pro: quickdraws.

15. Where's the Cave? (5.9) ★ No topo. About 80 feet right of the *Frogs* arête is this blocky, lichen-spotted arête with five bolts. Pro: quickdraws.

Middle Wall

The following routes are located on the Middle Wall, a high, blocky, orange-tinted entablature cliff that is much more solid than it looks. The loose rock has been removed, but beware of loose blocks all the same. Despite its scary appearance, the several sport routes on the Middle Wall are quite popular, offering shady afternoon climbing if you don't mind sweating up the approach trail.

The routes are described from left to right as they are encountered on the approach. Descend from anchors. All but one of the routes are more than 80 feet long, so don't lower off unless you're sure both ends reach the ground.

16. Casting Stones (5.11b) ★★ The leftmost route on the middle wall, climbing a short, easy corner, then up the blocky face, connecting the bolts up and over a prominent roof. Pro: quickdraws.

17. Stones in the Pathway (5.11c) ★★ The next route to the right, starting up a short, bolted column face then up the very blocky wall, passing a roof high up to reach a short crack that leads to the anchors. Pro: quickdraws; a #1 Tech Friend and a couple of small TCUs (#0 and #1 if you have them) are recommended.

18. Middle Passage (5.11b) ★★ One of two routes starting via a short corner crack in the middle of the wall, leading to anchors 25 feet up (5.5 to here). From the anchors, follow the bolts leading slightly left and up to a prominent slot, then past a roof and up a thin crack to anchors atop the wall. Pro: quickdraws.

19. Abandonings (5.11b) ★★ Climb the 5.5 corner crack to the anchors, then follow the bolt line on the right, continuing directly up the blocky wall and passing a prominent prow on its right side, then skirting the big roof on the left side to anchors way up there. Pro: quickdraws.

20. Relics (5.11a) ★★ Start up a short, blocky corner with a single bolt, then follow the bolts angling right up the blocky wall to anchors just below the prominent roof. Pro: quickdraws.

21. Aboriginal Design (5.11b) ★★★ Start up a flaky brown wall immediately left of the petroglyphs and continue up and over the prominent large roof on the right. Pro: quickdraws. (FA: Andy Fitz 1992)

22. Mass Wasting (5.11d) ★★ The final route on the Middle Wall before you enter

The Cave–Middle Wall

the oak grove, just up and right from the petroglyphs. Pro: quickdraws.

Oak Wall

The following routes are located on the short, angular wall immediately right of the Middle Wall. This area is shaded by an oak grove growing beside the cliff, making it a pleasant place to climb even on hot summer days. The routes are described from left to right as they are encountered on the approach. Descend from anchors atop the columns.

23. Fallen Apples (5.11c) ★ The first sport route encountered as you enter the oak

grove, climbing a steep face immediately right of an arête before traversing slightly left and up a featured slab to anchors. Stick clip recommended. Pro: quickdraws.

24. Furball (5.11b) ★★ The second sport route from the left, starting atop a block and climbing a black-and-white-streaked wall past a short flake, then up the steep wall to anchors. Pro: quickdraws.

25. Elixir (5.12a) ★★ Just right of *Furball* is this steep sport route climbing up an orange-tinted wall right of a blunt arête. A stick clip is recommended. Pro: quickdraws.

26. Recreational Jugs (5.7) ★★★ A very angular, blocky, orange-streaked slab on the right side of the cliff. It feels very exposed

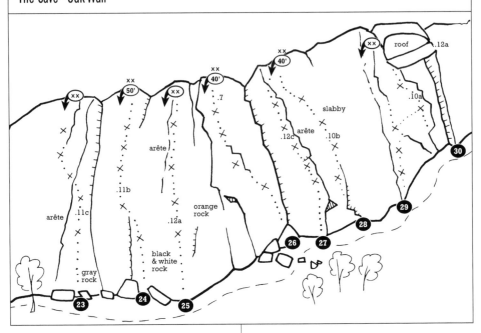

even though it's only 40 feet to the anchors. A fun route for a short 5.7 sport climb. Pro: quickdraws. (FA: Andy Fitz 1992)

27. Trigger Finger (5.12c) ★★ The very overhanging arête just right of *Recreational Jugs*. Thin, powerful face climbing. Pro: quickdraws. (FKA: Jens Klubberud 1996)

28. Caven Image (5.10b) ★★ The slabby face just right of the arête. Tricky, awkward climbing, but it's fun unless you fall off over the arête. Pro: quickdraws.

29. Nick Cave (5.10a) ★ A meandering route leading to anchors just left of the prominent roof on the far right side of Oak Wall. Pro: quickdraws.

30. Pop Goes the Tendon (5.12a) ★ A horizontal thin crack through a blocky roof on the far right side. Start via *Nick Cave*. The roof has no visible means of support, but it hasn't fallen on anybody yet. Pro: quickdraws; gear to 1 inch.

RAINBOW ROCKS

Rainbow Rocks is a small, colorful formation located up the hill from Trout Lodge, about 10.4 miles upriver from Royal Columns and 7 miles downriver from Wildcat Road (12.5 miles from the WA 410 junction). There are about a dozen routes here, in the 5.7 to 5.12 range, but only a few of which are worth the long approach.

Rainbow Rocks has the longest approach of all the Tieton River crags, and is best undertaken early in the day to avoid direct sun exposure. Park in the wide grade just down the highway from the Trout Lodge

Rainbow Rocks Approach Map

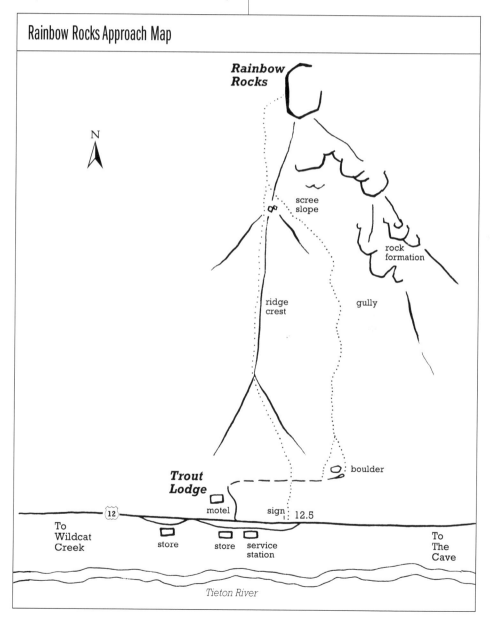

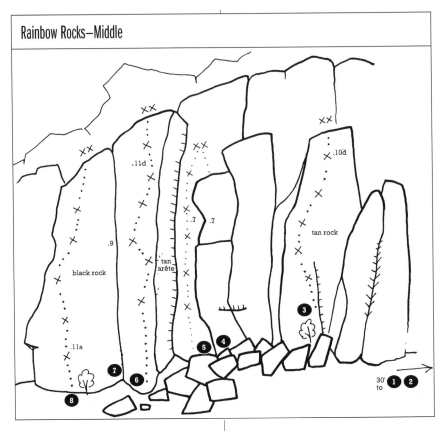

Rainbow Rocks—Middle

.11d

.9

black rock

tan arête

.11a

.10d

tan rock

.7 .7

7 **6** **5** **4** **3**

8

30'
to **1** **2**

service station. Cross the road and head up the hill just in front of the Entering Rimrock Retreat sign. About 100 feet uphill is a road grade. From here, you can hike up the grassy ridge, staying as near to the crest as possible, following game trails that get better as you get closer to the rock. Alternatively, go right about 150 feet to a large boulder just above the road, then head up the rocky gully just right of the boulder and follow the gully as far as possible uphill. Where the gully is impassable, follow game trails on the left, but parallel the gully as far as you can until it is possible to climb a scree slope to the ridge crest on the left, from where you can follow game trails and eventually a climbers' trail to Rainbow Rocks, which is too obvious to miss. The routes are located on the left (west) side, which gets full-on afternoon sun.

The routes are described from right to left as you approach them from below. Descend by rappel from anchors. Rainbow Rocks is on private land, so be on your best behavior.

1. Tortured Landscape (5.11b R) ★ No topo. Thin cracks leading up the right side of the *Angle of Refraction* column. Gets thinner and steeper at the top. Pro: to 1 inch, including RPs and TCUs.

2. Angle of Refraction (5.12b) ★★ No topo. On the right side of the cliff is a prominent column with a roof low down. Find the bolts on the left side of the column. Climb the left side and the headwall above. Pro: quickdraws; gear to 1 inch.

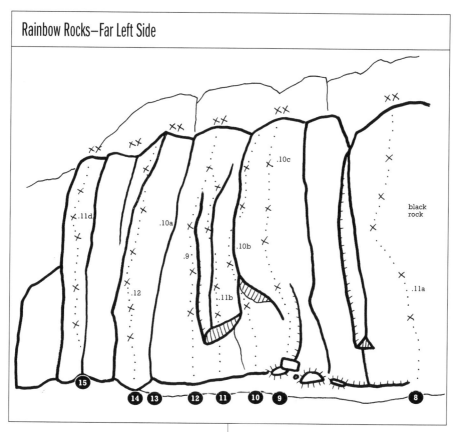

3. Chocolate Face (5.10c) ★ A sport route climbing a distinctive brownish wall directly above a maple shrub growing above the talus near the middle of the columns. Pro: quickdraws.

4. Crack Up (5.7) A blocky crack between *Chocolate Face* and *Ice Cream Girls*. Pro: to 2 inches.

5. Yummy Yummy (5.7) ★ A sport route squeezed in on the face just right of *Ice Cream Girls*. Pro: quickdraws.

6. Ice Cream Girls (5.11d) ★★★ An excellent sport route climbing a tan-colored pillar about 30 feet left of *Chocolate Face,* immediately right of *Boy Howdy*. This route alone is worth the hike up to Rainbow Rocks, but

just barely. The first bolt is 15 feet off the deck. Pro: quickdraws. (FA: Andy Fitz 1990)

7. Boy Howdy (5.9) ★★ A steep thin crack on the left side of the wall, immediately right of the very obvious section of black rock. Pro: to 1.5 inches. (FA: Matt Christensen, Andy Fitz 1989)

8. Black Celebration (5.11a) ★★ A sport route climbing the obvious section of black rock on the far left side of the columns. Boulder problem start. Pro: quickdraws. (FA: Andy Fitz 1989)

9. Donkey Song (fka Lunge or Plunge) (5.10c) ★ The first sport route left of *Black Celebration,* starting at a right-facing corner and traversing onto the column face above a big bulge. The first bolt is presently 20 feet up, but the route may be rebolted. Pro: quickdraws.

10. View from the Ridge (5.10b) ★ The bolted corner left of *Donkey Song*. Pro: quickdraws.

11. Backbone (5.11b) ★★ A bolted arête, starting with a difficult move past an overhang. Pro: quickdraws.

12. Fat Man (5.9) ★★ The bolted corner left of *Backbone*. Pro: quickdraws.

13. Trout Lodge Terror (5.10a) ★ The thin corner crack. Pro: to 2 inches.

14. Open Project (5.12) ★★ A striking, steep arête problem. Good luck!

15. Conceptual Edges (5.12a) ★★ A bolted pillar face on the far left side of the wall. Pro: quickdraws.

LAVA POINT

Lava Point is visible from the highway as the low rimrock band just up and right from the Wildcat Road turnoff. It has a few dozen quality sport routes on its steep, vesicular andesite, all steep or overhanging sport climbs in the 5.9 to 5.12 range. All routes here are bolt protected, although natural protection is possible in places on a few routes. The best of Lava Point climbing is on the Lava Wall, the name given to the rightmost section of the wall, which was the first of the Lava Point cliffs to be developed. The Dream Wall and Tick Wall are farther left, and have some quality routes that are shorter and easier on average than those at Lava Point.

To get to Lava Wall, turn up Soup Creek Road and follow it uphill, staying left at all

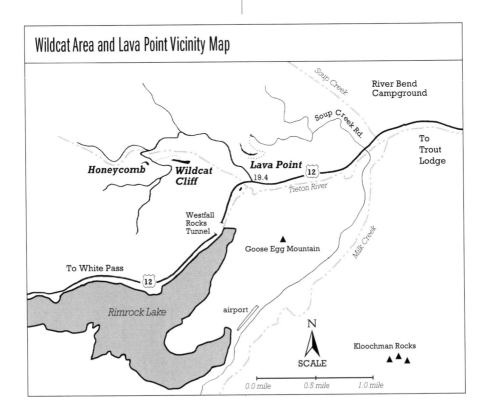

Wildcat Area and Lava Point Vicinity Map

Lava Point

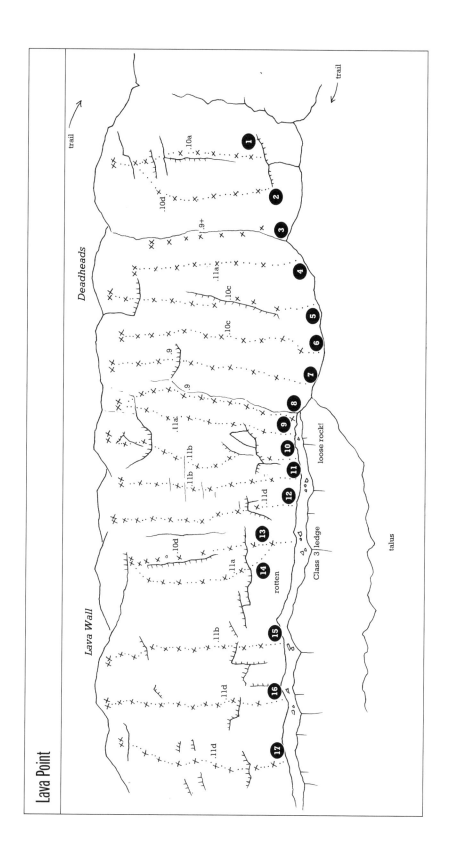

forks, until you reach road's end. Park here and walk south (downhill) toward the rim. When you reach the rim after about five minutes of hiking, stay left along the rim to the east edge of the cliff, where a trail switchbacks down to the base of the cliff. Please stay on the trail to avoid further erosion of the slope.

Afternoon sun exposure makes this a good morning and evening venue. Watch out for snakes in the talus below the cliff. This area is popular with hunters during hunting season, so avoid it near dawn and dusk, or at least wear bright-colored clothing or a flashing light of some sort, so you aren't mistaken for a deer or elk. Also, beware of free-range cattle and deer on the road, especially after dark.

The routes are described from right to left as you encounter them on the approach hike. Descend from anchors atop each route.

Deadheads

The rightmost section of Lava Wall is known as Deadheads Wall, or simply Deadheads. There are a few routes (5.9 to 5.10) on the initial buttress above the trail, but the best routes begin around the corner on the main wall.

1. B. Weir of the Dead (5.10a) ★ Mount the initial ledge, then climb the corner above. Pro: quickdraws.

2. Fit to Be Tie Dyed (5.10d) ★★ The next route to the left with a tricky face move crux. Finish at the B. Weir anchors. Pro: quickdraws.

3. Artificially Inseminated (5.9+) ★ The obvious corner. Pro: quickdraws.

4. Muted Reality (5.11a) ★ The steep, thin face left of the corner. Pro: quickdraws.

5. Saint of Circumstance (5.10c) ★★★ Face climb into a shallow corner, then pull over roofs at the top. Lots of vesicular pockets. Consider stick clipping the first bolt, or not. Pro: quickdraws.

Lava Wall

Left of the Deadheads area is a steep, multi-colored wall with several more sport routes. A Class 3 ledge traverse accesses these routes. There is quite a bit of loose rock on the ledge, and the first few moves on some of the routes have loose, blocky rock, so be careful. Consider stick clipping the first bolts on some routes for safety's sake.

6. Get a Job (5.10c) ★★ The first route encountered as you traverse the ledge. Starts about 15 feet left of *Saint of Circumstance*, passing a roof partway up. Pro: quickdraws.

7. Travalava (5.9) ★ Just left of *Get a Job*. A chossy start but gets better. Pro: quickdraws.

8. Scoria (5.9) ★ Climb a corner and over-bolted face to the *Windy Day* anchors. Pro: quickdraws.

9. Windy Day (5.11a) ★★ Start up the blocky wall right of *Altamont* and finish up vesicular pockets over a roof. Pro: quickdraws.

10. Altamont (5.11b) ★★ A steep, blank wall with a thin face crux leads to a roof finish. Pro: quickdraws.

11. Long Strange Clip (5.11b) ★★ A steep, black-streaked wall left of *Altamont,* with lots of horizontal edges. Pro: quickdraws.

12. Lavaland (5.11d) ★★ Power through the initial roof and mantel up to reach easier, enjoyable face climbing to the top. The initial roof can be avoided, but why? Pro: quickdraws.

13. Solid Froth (5.10d) ★★★ Face climb up the corner system left of *Lavaland*. Some rotten rock at the start, but the rest is brilliant. Pro: quickdraws.

14. Tim's Route (5.11a) ★★ Start at the first bolt on *Solid Froth*, then angle left over the roofs and up the steep face; finish at the *Solid Froth* anchors. Pro: quickdraws.

15. Vesicular Homicide (5.11b) ★★ The next route along the ledge, with some tricky climbing through the blocky middle section. Pro: quickdraws.

16. Igneous Journey (5.11c) ★★★ All vertical and overhanging climbing through the blocky roofs on the left end of Lava Wall. Pro: quickdraws.

17. Lahar (5.11d) ★★★ More vertical and overhanging climbing at the far left end of Lava Wall. Pro: quickdraws.

WILDCAT CREEK

Wildcat Creek is located high in the Tieton River Canyon. It has two developed crags, Wildcat Cliff and Honeycomb Buttress, both located within a few minutes of the highway, featuring a variety of routes in the 5.8 to 5.12 range. Not only is Wildcat's climbing enjoyable and unique, but so is the area's high-mountain ambience.

The crags are located 2.6 miles up Wildcat Road, which heads north from US 12 about 19.4 miles upriver from the WA 410 junction and 1 mile downriver from the

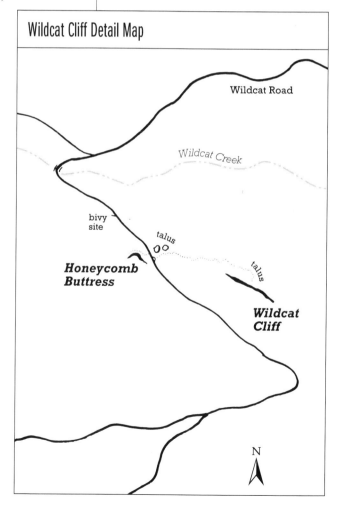

Wildcat Cliff Detail Map

Wildcat Road

Wildcat Creek

bivy site

talus

Honeycomb Buttress

talus

Wildcat Cliff

N

Westfall Rocks tunnel. Drive up the road, staying left at all junctions, until you arrive at Honeycomb Buttress, a big cliff of sideways columns that cannot be mistaken for anything else. Wildcat Cliff is a short hike downhill from the small turnout just across the road from Honeycomb. Road. Washouts may hinder your approach, but if you have to walk the last mile, it's still worth it assuming you don't mind fording a creek or two.

Higher elevation and strategic positioning make this one of the cooler areas in the Tieton. Both Wildcat Cliff and Honeycomb Buttress are partly or completely shady most of the day, even in midsummer.

Honeycomb Buttress (The Beehive)

Honeycomb Buttress is the big columnar buttress rising directly above Wildcat Road, a reddish stack of sideways columns with a grayish honeycomb slab on the upper right side. The lower routes are overhanging and very athletic, technical exercises; the upper routes are slopey, balancy test pieces. The lower routes catch the morning sun and afternoon shade; the upper routes get morning shade and afternoon sun. The routes are described from left to right as viewed from the road. Descend via rappel from anchors atop each route.

1. Land Down Under (5.11c) ★★★ The leftmost route on Honeycomb Buttress, climbing out from the talus and up the bulging wall to anchors. Very

sequential, occasionally awkward moves make this a difficult on-sight lead. The route continues to anchors near the top of the crag for those who aren't completely wasted after the initial difficulties. Pro: quickdraws. (FA: Mark McGuire 1990)

2. Anaphylactic Shock (5.12a) ★★★ The overhanging, leaning dihedral in the center of the crag. More sequential, powerful climbing, with a wild, go-for-it finish. Pro: quickdraws. (FA: Matt Christensen, Norm Reid, Mark McGuire 1990)

The Beehive

Note: The arête between *Land Down Under* and *Anaphylactic Shock* is reportedly a 5.13 toprope problem. It has been bolted and has probably been redpointed by now, but if not, it is an open project. Also, the arête and face to the right of *Anaphylactic Shock* is a project that will also be 5.13 when completed. Both routes are a bit contrived, but certainly difficult.

3. Honeycombs (5.11a) ★★★ The first sport route uphill from *Anaphylactic Shock.* An overhanging face traverse leads left, then right onto the namesake slab. Balancy friction leads to anchors. Pro: quickdraws. (FA: Andy Fitz, Matt Kerns 1988)

4. Fertile Ground (5.11b) ★★ Up and right from the start of *Honeycombs* is a short, blocky, columnar corner, where this route and *The Pollenator* begin. Climb up past two bolts, then traverse left and follow the left-hand bolt line up the slab, finishing just right of the final crux of *Honeycombs.* Pro: quickdraws.

5. The Pollenator (5.10d) ★ Begin as for *Fertile Ground,* but continue straight up the slab and finish via the obvious thin seam. Pro: quickdraws, gear to 1 inch.

6. Pinecone (5.11c) ★★ On the upper right side of the *Honeycombs* slab is this friction test piece, climbing a continuously difficult, well-scrubbed slab. Pro: quickdraws.

7. Taste of Honey (5.8) ★ A unique crack zigzagging up between the column ends on the upper right margin of the slab. Pro: to 1 inch; quickdraws.

Wildcat Cliff

Wildcat Cliff is a colonnade tucked into the hillside about a five-minute walk downhill from Honeycomb Buttress. The cliff is easily seen from across the canyon as you drive up Wildcat Road. It has several routes, ranging from 5.10 to 5.12, mostly climbing thin cracks between the columns. Although Wildcat Cliff is spectacular looking, it has some decomposing rock. Most of the routes are infrequently climbed and get a bit dirty, although with cleaning they are as good as any crack routes in the canyon—better, say some. Wildcat Cliff's higher elevation and shady disposition make it a cooler alternative

Wildcat Cliff

to the columnar crags downcanyon. Judging by the talus at the base of the crag and several hanging columns, rockfall is an occasional problem, although judging by the size of the rocks that seem prone to falling, a helmet would do you absolutely no good. Not that you shouldn't wear a helmet, but a ten-ton block isn't likely to just bounce off your helmet without doing any serious damage.

A short trail begins directly across the road from Honeycomb Buttress and skirts the talus slope on its right-hand side, then descends a rocky slope to the base of the cliff. The routes are listed from right to left as you encounter them on the approach. Descend via rappel from anchors atop the routes.

8. Ocelot (5.10d C2)

Twin thin cracks lead to a small roof (5.10d to here). Dirty clean aid climbing to the top of the columns. Pro: to 1 inch.

9. Keel Hauled (5.11d)

★★★ A long, bolted route up the right side of the cliff, about 70 feet right of *Wildcat Crack*. Pass the hanging column low down, then stem and jam your way to the anchors. Pro: quickdraws. (FFA: Matt Kerns 1996)

10. The Vulgar Streak

(5.11a) ★ The bolted column in the center of the cliff, just right of *Wildcat Crack*. Easily identified by the plentitude of bolts. The route is said to be

worthwhile, despite the decomposing rock. Pro: lots of quickdraws.

11. Wildcat Crack (5.10c) ★★★

The obvious thin crack in the center of the cliff. Steep, continuous, and airy, this is one of the better 5.10 thin crack routes in the Tieton. The rappel anchors suck, but they've held so far. Fortunately, so has the hanging column above the belay. Pro: to 1.5 inches, mostly smaller cams and stoppers. (FFA: Matt Christensen 1987)

12. Iron Oxide (5.11c)

A corner crack two columns left of *Wildcat Crack*. If cleaned, it's a three-star route. If not, watch out for dangerously loose rock near the top. Pro: to 2 inches.

Wildcat Cliff

13. Colonnade (5.11b) ★★ A continuous thin crack two cracks left of *Iron Oxide*. Gets dirty near the bottom. Pro: to 1 inch, mostly smaller cams and stoppers; quickdraws for bolts near the top. (FFA: Andy Fitz 1990)

14. Rhythm & Sorrow (5.11a) ★★ The long, left-facing corner around the corner to the left of *Colonnade*. Gets dirty. Pro: to 3 inches; RPs. (FA: Andy Fitz, Matt Kerns complete 1992)

15. Bohemian Mecca (5.11b R) ★★★ A thin crack up a shallow corner on the prow of a column two cracks to the left of *Rhythm & Sorrow*. An excellent climb with great position. Pro: to 1 inch; multiple RPs and wireds. (FA: Ed Mosshart, Andy Fitz 1990)

16. A Flake Worse Than Death (fka Deliverance) (5.10c) ★★ The corner system two cracks to the left of *Bohemian Mecca*. The "loose flake" mentioned in *Tieton Rock* was removed with one pull, and the upper part of the route has been retrobolted. Pro: to 3 inches; quickdraws.

17. Blue Highways (5.12a) ★★ A thin, bolted face climb leading up from the left end of a multicolumn ledge. Pro: quickdraws.

18. Turn to the Vices (5.11c) ★★ A two-pitch route starting with a 5.9 crack that widens to offwidth (face climb up the left column to avoid the offwidth) and finishing with a difficult, bolted stemming corner. Pro: to 3 inches; #1.0 Friend, quickdraws.

19. Casual Detachment (5.11b) ★★★ Start via the 5.9 crack of *Turn to the Vices,* then finish by bearhugging up this column, which is detached but reportedly solid. Pro: quickdraws. (FA: Andy Fitz, Mark McGuire 1990).

SOUTH FORK

The South Fork cliff is located high in Tieton River Canyon. It is a remote cliff with a definite high-mountain ambience, perched on a ridgeline with commanding views. It has two distinct aspects, the more typical columnar Main Wall, which features a mix of crack and face climbing, and the area's signature crag, Astral Wall, a blocky, overhanging sport wall.

Given its higher elevation, South Fork cliff is not accessible until the roads are snow free, by June of most years. The climbing season is typically from late June into November, and fall is the best season. In midsummer, the southern exposure means the walls can be insufferably hot, although they are fairly comfortable most days even if it's too hot to climb elsewhere.

A confusing network of dusty forest service roads makes driving directions to South Fork a little complicated. The most straightforward approach (though not the fastest) is to turn off of US 12 at Tieton Road, a loop road that skirts the southern shores of Rimrock and Clear Lakes. Follow Tieton Road several miles to FR 1000, a paved road, almost 6 miles to pavement's end, then turn right onto FR 750. Follow FR 750 just over 2 miles to a T intersection; take a left and continue 1.3 miles to FR 1204 (marked "Section 3 Lake"). Follow FR 1204 another 1.3 miles and take another left onto FR 755. Stay left at the fork at 0.7 mile and follow a short distance to another left fork. Make a choice here: continue on the main road to a large parking area, from where a boot path leads directly downhill, or take a left down a rugged logging spur 0.5 mile or so to a berm and park there (high-clearance vehicles only, limited parking, and tight turnaround). Hike west from there along the rim.

Whichever option you choose, follow the track along the top of the cliff about 10 minutes, then hike a rough trail down the gully behind Astral Wall, which comes out at the west end of the Hexagonal Satellites.

Like other areas of the Tieton, watch out for ticks and check current nesting closures.

Hexagonal Satellites

The Hexagonal Satellites are a pair of short buttresses at the far left end of the South Fork area, the first bolted walls passed as you approach, easily recognized by their hexagonal features. The routes tend to be a little dirty and mossy; they would improve with some cleaning and more use. Descend from anchors.

1. Ask Jim Yoder (5.9) ★ No topo. A short route climbing a mossy, sloping, staircase-like ramp right off the approach trail. Pro: quickdraws.

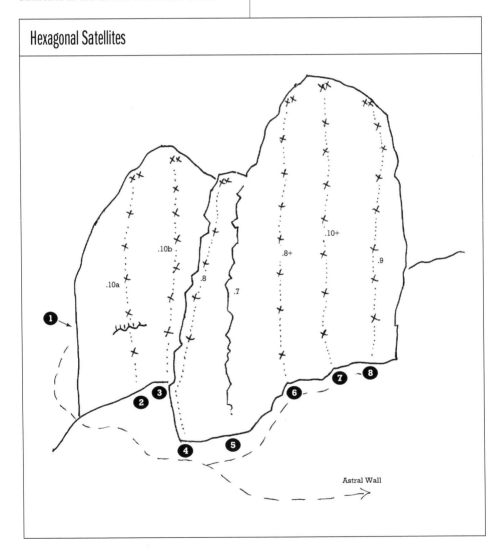

Hexagonal Satellites

Astral Wall

2. Ask Marlene Ford (5.10a) ★★ On the left side of the leftmost hexagonal wall, climb past a crooked horizontal crack and up the column ends above it. Pro: quickdraws.

3. Vultures (5.10b) ★★ More of the same column-end face climbing on the right side of the left wall. Pro: quickdraws.

4. Hexavalent (5.7+) ★ The left arête of the right wall, just left of the obvious hexagonal crack. Pro: quickdraws.

5. Hexagonal Crack (5.7) ★★ The obvious hexagonal crack on the left side of the right wall. Pro: gear to 2 inches.

6. Shade Grown (5.8+) ★ A bolted face route just left of the big fir tree. Gets better with cleaning. Pro: quickdraws.

7. Bough Beaten (5.10d) ★★ Ascend the wall directly behind the big fir tree. You'll get the name if the tree hasn't been pruned back recently. Pro: quickdraws.

8. Behind the Curtain (5.9) ★★ Face climb up to and then continue up the arête on the right edge of the right wall. Pro: quickdraws.

Astral Wall

Astral Wall is an impressive sport crag at the west end of the South Fork cliff. The routes are described from left to right, and are most easily identified by their location relative to the other routes, since they are all over-hanging face climbs connecting bolts up the tsunami-like wave of angular andesite col-umns. The rock is blocky but solid, though you should beware the occasional loose hold. Some known loose blocks have been marked with a white X, so avoid those. If you get off-route, you'll stray into some loose rock, so don't. Lower off or rappel from anchors atop each pitch. Some of the longer routes

require 16–18 quickdraws, and a double-rope rappel or two single-rope rappels.

1. Step on Up (5.10a) ★ No topo. A short, easily overlooked route on the "back" side of Astral Wall; the first route seen as you descend the approach gully (if you notice it). Pro: quickdraws.

2. West Arête (5.10a) ★★ The leftmost route on the front side of Astral Wall, a blocky romp up the slightly overhanging wall that never quite strays onto the arête, except maybe for a couple of moves at the top. Pro: quickdraws.

3. Thanks Andy (5.10b) ★★★ The route immediately right of *West Arête*, which ends much too soon. Pro: quickdraws.

4. Dusting from Heaven (5.11b) ★★★ This route starts just down and right from *Thanks Andy*. A steep hexagonal slab leads to power-ful, overhanging climbing. Can be done as a single long pitch or broken into two pitches (11b, 9). Pro: lots of quickdraws.

5. Astral Cloud (5.11a) ★★★ A steep hex-agonal slab just left of the approach ramp to *Milky Way* leads to powerful, overhanging climbing. Can also be done as a single long pitch or broken into two pitches (11a, 10c). Pro: quickdraws.

6. Milky Way (5.10+) ★★★ Scramble up the ramp/flake to a high first bolt, then pull up the spectacularly overhanging wall above. A single long pitch that can be broken into two 5.10d pitches that might feel like 5.11a to an on-sight leader doing the full pitch. Pro: quickdraws.

7. Mars Bar (5.11) ★★★★ Starts with thin edging up the hexagonal slab at the base of the wall past two bolts, then rears back to wildly overhanging, mostly on jugs, with

Astral Wall

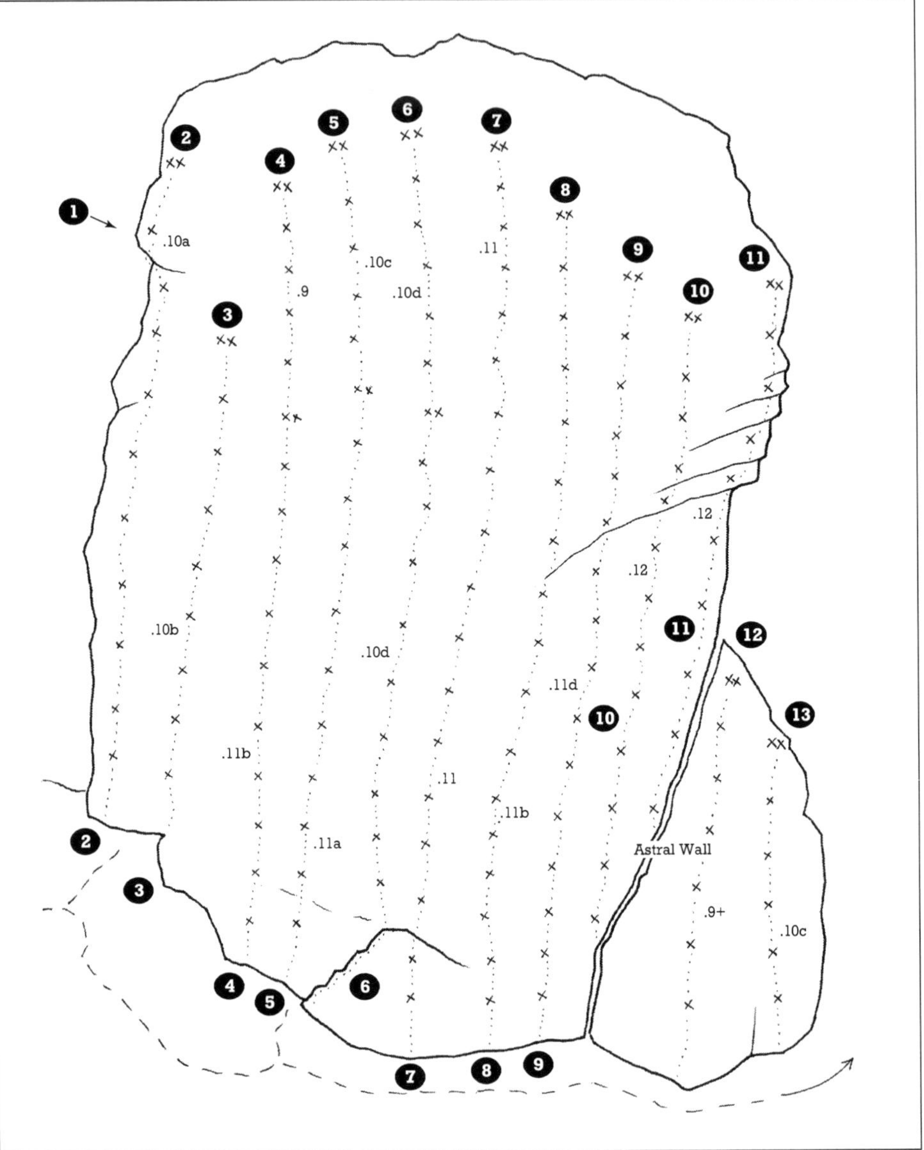

a crimpy crux coming near the top. Pro: quickdraws.

8. Snickered (5.11b) ★★★ Start up the right side of the hexagonal slab, aiming just right of a loose block marked with a white X,

then yard up the overhanging wall above. Pro: quickdraws.

9. Whitewashed (5.11d) ★★★★ "The best sport route in Washington," according to its description on Mountain Project, which also describes it as "hard, tenuous, sustained."

Athletic climbing through the overhang past several fixed draws leads to more of the same. Pro: quickdraws. (FA: Andy Fitz)

10. Project (5.12) ★★★ The farthest bolted line on the right that stays on Astral Wall proper, reportedly an uncompleted project. Pro: quickdraws.

11. Project (5.12) ★★ Another project on the farthest-right edge of Astral Wall, starting right of the crack separating Astral Wall proper from the Snack Attack buttress, then meeting the crack halfway up and launching up the headwall. Pro: quickdraws.

12. Snack Attack (5.9+) ★ The leftmost of the two bolted routes on the brownish buttress on the right margin of Astral Wall, ascending slabby columns to anchors. Pro: quickdraws.

13. Ask Matt Kerns (5.10c) ★★ An entertaining line just right of *Snack Attack*, ascending overhanging column ends. Pro: quickdraws. (FA: Matt Kerns)

Main Wall

Continue around the corner from Astral Wall and scramble up talus and brushy slopes to reach the Main Wall, a long wall of columnar andesite with several sport routes and a few traditional pitches. The rock is of fairly high quality and the routes are varied, with jamming, stemming, crimping, jugs, and everything in between, sometimes all in one pitch. This cliff has been in development since the 1990s, but still has much potential for new routes. Consult the *Tieton River Rocks* guide or Mountain Project for route information.

NORTH FORK

The North Fork cliff is located on the north side of same ridge as the South Fork cliff, but has a more remote aspect. It is higher in elevation, with a more difficult descent that involves hiking downhill about thirty minutes and, of course, a corresponding thirty-minute uphill hike at the end of the day. Since it is north-facing, it stays shady much of the day even in midsummer, but does get late afternoon sun, a curse during the summer months but a blessing on a crisp fall day. The cliff is under development, with a half-dozen high quality routes already done and more underway. Approach information and route details should be posted on Mountain Project by the time this edition is available. Some of the routes may also be included in the updated Tieton rock guide.

GOOSE EGG MOUNTAIN

A number of longer, semipopular routes have been developed on the south face of Goose Egg Mountain, a modest, craggy peak located just east of Rimrock Lake (see Wildcat Area and Lava Point Vicinity Map on page 348). The routes on Goose Egg Mountain are pretty much mixed sport and traditional rock climbing, with some loose, easy pitches on the lower-angled slabs at the base of the wall, then bolted pitches higher up. The rock quality is not high (and in some places downright poor) except on occasional pitches, and many parties climb only a few pitches and rappel rather than topping out, due to reportedly very loose rock higher up as well as descent difficulties. Climbers interested in Goose Egg Mountain's routes, including *Ride the Lightning* (III, 5.9), can refer to the *Tieton River Rocks* guide or Mountain Project for route details.

SPOKANE AREA

It's an old joke that "The best climbing in Spokane is in Idaho." The joke is just that: old. With the discovery and development of several high-quality sport climbing crags, Spokane and northeast Washington have evolved from a place where you might stop if you happened to be passing through to a destination worthy of a half-day's drive. Minnehaha, Dishman Rocks, Deep Creek, and Rocks of Sharon are either within or just outside of Spokane's city limits, and offer quick access to fun bouldering, toproping, and a variety of routes ranging from 5.0 to 5.13, while Tum Tum is only thirty-odd miles northwest of downtown, with a handful of moderate one- and two-pitch crack and slab routes and bouldering on old granite domes. Marcus and China Bend are about ninety minutes north of town, and offer a good selection of steep, high-end sport routes on quality limestone. Another fifty-plus routes have reportedly been developed on other limestone crags in the Metaline Falls area, and there is plenty of untouched rock in the region. If you haven't climbed in Spokane lately, you are missing out.

Type of climbing: Much Spokane-area climbing is on granite of varying quality, mostly very old Selkirk granite, which is clean and slabby at best, flaky and rotten at worst. At all of Spokane's granite areas, holds and flakes are prone to breaking, even on established routes, but overall the rock is solid. Deep Creek is an exception, featuring two dozen or more steep sport routes on frighteningly fractured basalt. Marcus and China Bend offer climbers reasonably solid limestone, with most routes going at 5.11 or harder. Metaline has a few routes in the 5.10 to 5.11 range, but mostly 5.12 and harder.

Brief history of area: Spokane climbing has a long, varied, and mostly unrecorded history. As at most other areas, climbing here did not begin in earnest until the 1950s, when local climbers used the cliffs of Minnehaha as a training ground for the real mountains. Aid climbing predominated until the 1960s, when John Roskelley and Chris Kopczynski "upset the established climbing community" by free climbing many of Spokane's aid lines and almost singlehandedly ushering in the 5.10 grade. The 1970s were, in turn, dominated by Thom Nephew and Ron Burgner, who brought 5.11 to Spokane and made their mark in other parts of Washington state. Nephew's free-solo ascent of *Don Quixote* in 1975 was particularly noteworthy. Dane Burns's discovery of Dishman Rocks in the early 1980s brought a new intensity to route development and ultimately ushered in the 5.12 grade. In the 1990s discovery and development of Deep Creek by Marty Bland, Bill Centinari, and Russ Schultz, and the establishment of an indoor gym, have pushed Spokane standards into the realm of 5.13. This has continued at Marcus and China Bend since their "discovery" in the mid-1990s, and at Metaline and other crags

Rick Rice toproping *Bat Crack* (5.9), Minnehaha, Spokane area

dotting the Inland Northeast since. For hard limestone sport climbing, the areas north of Spokane are the places to go in Washington.

Seasons and climate: Spokane gets relatively little rainfall, at least when compared with Seattle. A semiarid climate prevails, with grassy scablands and intermittent pine forests reminiscent of the Tieton River Canyon, much flatter but otherwise alike and subject to similar extremes in weather. While climbing is possible year-round in the Spokane area, spring and fall are the best seasons. Generally, it gets much too cold during the winter and much too hot during the summer for climbing. Locals flock to the rocks on sunny winter days, but if you plan on visiting, pick spring or fall for your trip.

Precautions and regulations: As previously mentioned, the rock at Minnehaha, Dishman, Rocks of Sharon, and Tum Tum is flaky granite, and holds sometimes break off without much provocation. The rock at Deep Creek is heavily fractured basalt, and helmets are highly recommended, particularly for belayers. Watch out for rattlesnakes and ticks at Pictograph Rocks, Marcus, and China Bend. Minnehaha and Dishman are

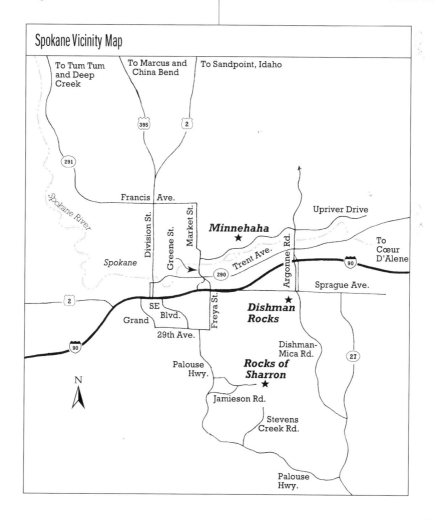

Spokane Vicinity Map

urban areas, subject to urban ills, including graffiti, litter, and broken glass. At Dishman in particular, you are advised to leave nothing of value in your car, since thefts have occurred in the past. Poison ivy grows everywhere at Marcus and China Bend and here and there at other areas.

Shortly after the first edition of this guide was published, a fence was installed along the property line at Dishman Rocks, barring access to several routes at the south end of the cliff. New route development is prohibited, which is just as well because the cliff is climbed out. Please contact Spokane County Parks, Recreation & Golf for current access information, (509) 625-6200.

Gear and other considerations: The Spokane area has about an equal number of traditional and sport routes, so bring a standard rack, with gear including wired nuts, stoppers, and cams and no more than a dozen quickdraws for the majority of the routes, except at Rocks of Sharon, Marcus, and China Bend, where twenty quickdraws may not be enough.

Camping and accommodations: Spokane has many accommodations, although you'd best stay at a motel or hotel, as campgrounds are not plentiful, especially within city limits. Riverside State Park (Bowl & Pitcher) has a small campground just a few minutes northwest of downtown Spokane, but it is usually full; make a reservation if you want to camp there. There are some other private campgrounds including a KOA nearby.

Emergency services: In the event of an emergency, dial 911. There are several hospitals in Spokane.

Other guidebooks: Bland, Marty. *Inland Northwest Rockclimbs*; Speaker, Jim. *Spokane Rock Climbs*; Loomis, Robert D. *A Guide to Rock Climbing in the Spokane Area*. 3rd ed. A small guide to Rocks of Sharon is also available from Mountain Gear.

Finding the crags: Spokane is located on the eastern edge of Washington state, about 280 miles east of Seattle on I-90. Spokane is Washington's second-largest city, and if you can't find it, you're in trouble. In eastern Washington, all roads lead to Spokane; at least, if you're headed in the right direction. Detailed directions to the individual areas are included where relevant.

MINNEHAHA

Spokane's most popular climbing area is Minnehaha, a small group of granitic boulders and cliffs at John H. Shields Park on the south slope of Beacon Hill, along the banks of the Spokane River just east of town. Minnehaha has several lead routes up to 80 feet in height, plus dozens of toprope and boulder problems. The area has long been used for practice by Spokane-area climbers, who often congregate here after school and work and on weekends.

The easiest way to get to Minnehaha is to take the Argonne Road exit (exit 287) off I-90 (about 6 miles east of downtown), then head north on Mullen Road. Mullen joins Argonne shortly; continue 1.7 miles north on Argonne to Upriver Drive. Turn left and continue another 2.3 miles to the park. The rocks are immediately obvious. An alternative route is to take the Altamont exit (exit 283A) and head east, paralleling the freeway to Thor Street. Turn left and follow Thor, which eventually becomes Greene Street; cross the river and take the first right, which

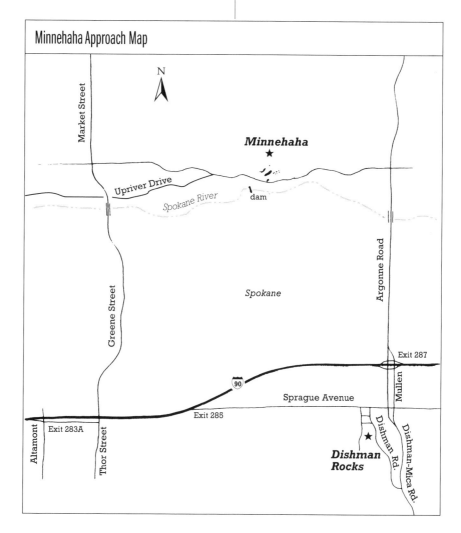

Minnehaha Approach Map

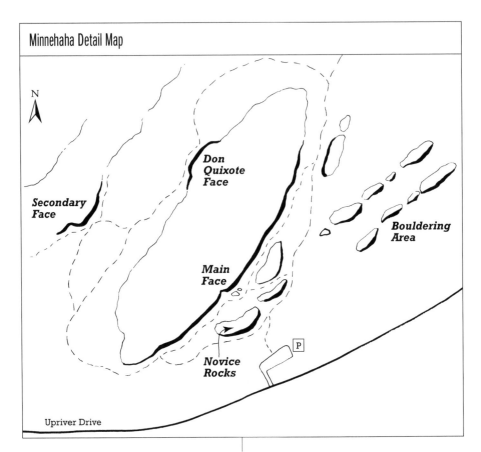

Minnehaha Detail Map

N

Don Quixote Face

Secondary Face

Bouldering Area

Main Face

Novice Rocks

P

Upriver Drive

---

curves down to Upriver Drive. Turn right onto Upriver Drive and continue almost 2 miles to the park.

Main Face

The Main Face is Minnehaha's largest and most obvious wall, rising to a height of 80 feet at its peak, and featuring most of the area's best lead routes (5.0 to 5.12) and some boulder and toprope problems. Descend by walking off to either side, or by scrambling down one of the easier routes.

1. Y Crack (5.4) ★ The obvious cracks on the lower left end of the main face. Traverse off to the left, or finish up a 5.6 crack past the left side of Coronation Roof. Pro: to 3 inches.

2. Heart Route (5.9) ★★ The first bolted face route right of *Y Crack*, joining that route after 30 feet or finishing via *Hot Licks*. Pro: quickdraws; gear to 1 inch.

3. Hot Licks (5.10d) ★ The second bolted face right of *Y Crack*, passing a short roof and finishing on the ledge beneath Coronation Roof. Pro: quickdraws; gear to 1 inch.

4. Main Crack (5.4) ★ The obvious offwidth crack on the left side of the main face. Pro: to 6 inches. A 5.7 toprope variation climbs the steep face immediately left of the crack.

5. Apprentice Route (5.6 R) ★ A meandering route climbing the cracks and ramps up the wall between *Main Crack* and *The Diagonal*, eventually skirting the paint-streaked upper roof. Pro: to 2 inches.

Minnehaha Main Face

6. The Diagonal (5.8) ★ The first crack system right of *Main Crack*. Face moves left of the initial roof lead to the crack proper. Runout at the start. Pro: to 2 inches.

7. Screaming Fingers (5.12a) ★ A face route in between *The Diagonal* and *The Dihedral*. The first bolt is at the lip of the roof 30 feet up. Pro: quickdraws; gear to 1 inch.

8. The Dihedral (5.9) ★ The obvious blocky, left-facing corner just left of center on the main wall. Pro: to 2 inches.

9. Bat Crack (5.9) ★ The clean crack on the slab right of *The Dihedral*. The crack ends 15 feet short of the top; face climb right to finish, or straight up (5.10a). Runout at the top. Pro: to 2 inches.

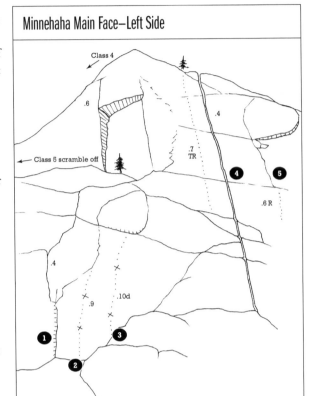

Minnehaha Main Face–Left Side

10. Love Bulge (5.10c) ★★ A sport route climbing past a small bulge and up the slab above to the upper ledge of *Ledges Route*. Pro: quickdraws.

11. Rusty (5.8) ★ Start via the right-facing roof crack (with the Rusty et al. graffiti at the base), then skirt around the left side of the *Smokey Overhang* roof and up the slab, finishing past *Mad Dog*'s final bolt. Pro: to 2 inches; quickdraws.

12. Southern Exposure (5.12a) ★ A bolted face climb directly over the left side of the *Smokey Overhang* roof. Start via *Rusty*. Pro: quickdraws; gear to 2 inches.

13. Smokey Overhang (5.10d) ★ The obvious right-slanting crack splitting its namesake roof. Start via *Rusty*, or directly (5.9 if you

jump for the holds at the lip of the roof, 5.11c if you don't). Pro: to 4 inches.

14. Strawberry Jam (5.10d R) ★ About 50 feet right of *Smokey Overhang* is this short crack passing the left side of an obvious overhang. Best toproped. Manky. Pro: to 2 inches, mostly smaller.

15. Jam Crack (5.8) ★★ A better crack passing the right side of the overhang, right of *Strawberry Jam*. Pro: to 2.5 inches.

16. Open Book (5.6) ★★ No topo. On the far right side of the main face is this blocky corner crack passing an overhang on its left side (or directly at 5.8). Pro: to 2 inches.

Minnehaha Main Face–Center and Minnehaha Main Face–Right Side

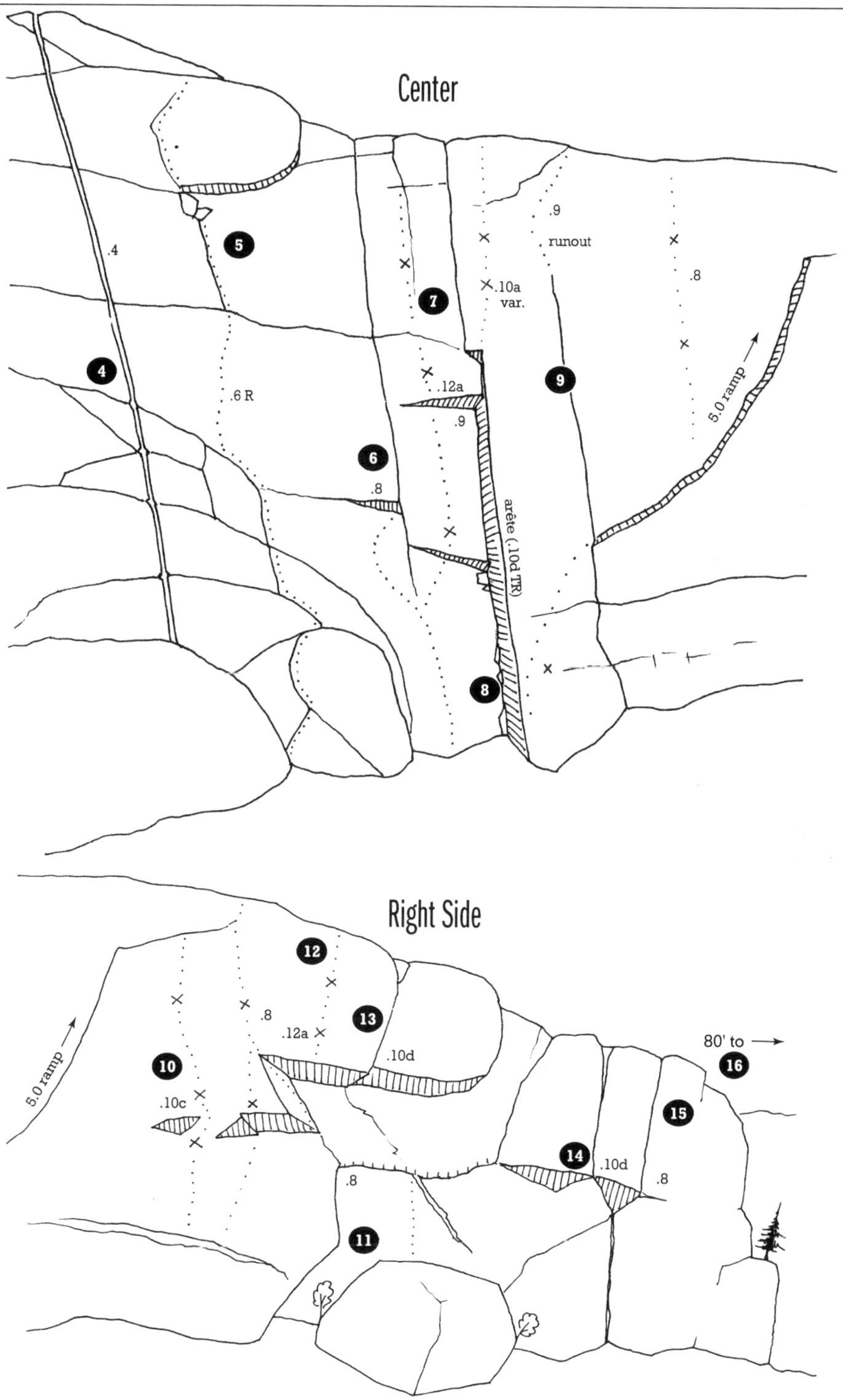

Center

.4

5

.6 R

4

.12a

.9

7

.10a
var.

.9
runout

.8

9

5.0 ramp

6

.8

arête (.10d TR)

8

Right Side

12

.8

13

.12a

.10d

10

.10c

5.0 ramp

80' to

16

15

14

.10d

.8

.8

11

Don Quixote Face

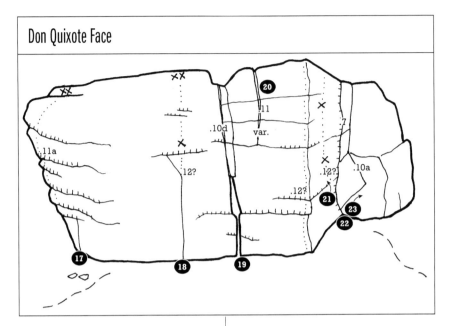

Don Quixote Face

On the back side of the main face is this 40-foot-high, blocky wall featuring several popular lead and toprope problems. Hike around either side of the main wall to get there.

17. The Rush-ins Are Coming (5.11a) A left-leading seam leads to overlapping flakes on the far left side. Usually toproped. Pro: to 2 inches.

18. Synchronicity (5.12+?) ★ An overhanging seam leads to a bolt 25 feet up, at the lip of an overhang. Pass the overhang and continue directly to the top. Reportedly unrepeated since a key hold broke off. If you try it, bring quickdraws and gear to 1 inch.

19. Don Quixote (5.10d) ★★ The obvious, blocky, double crack system in the middle of the wall. Pro: to 2.5 inches. (FFA: John Roskelley 1970s)

20. Delgato variation (5.11) ★ Halfway up the *Don Quixote* crack, traverse right 5 feet

and finish up the obvious wide, flaring crack. Pro: to 4 inches.

21. Romancing the Stone (5.12?) ★ The steep, bolted face immediately left of *Inside Corner*. More difficult since a key hold broke off. If you try it, bring quickdraws and a few pieces to 1.5 inches for the start.

22. Inside Corner (5.7) ★ The obvious corner crack on the right side of the Don Quixote face. Pro: to 3 inches.

23. Z Crack (5.10a) ★ A short, thin crack starting with a rightward zig and leftward zag. Pro: to 2 inches; TCUs.

Secondary Face

Behind the main face, across the hollow and about 100 feet west from the Don Quixote Face is this short wall, which has several popular lead and toprope problems.

24. The Hooker (5.11c) ★ On the left side of Secondary Face proper is this double seam passing a blocky roof. A variation (5.11d)

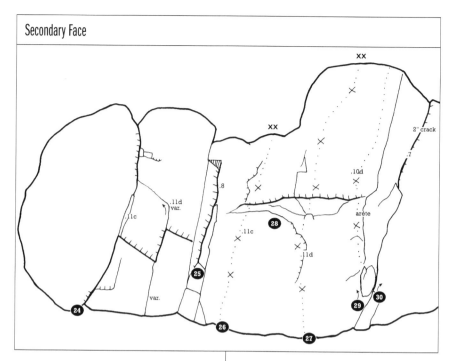

Secondary Face

climbs a thin crack on the right and traverses in at midheight. Pro: to 2 inches, mostly small stuff.

25. Black Corner (5.8) ★★ The obvious blocky, right-facing dihedral capped by a small roof. Pro: to 2 inches.

26. Lots of Nothing (5.11c) ★ A sport route immediately right of *Black Corner,* passing a roof to anchors 35 feet up. Pro: quickdraws.

27. Tea with the Queen (5.11d) ★ The second bolted face route right of *Black Corner,* climbing flaky rock past a roof and up the headwall. Pro: quickdraws.

28. Dave's Delicate Traverse variation (5.11c) ★ Link up *Tea with the Queen* and *Lots of Nothing* via a tenuous traverse.

29. The Prow (5.10d) ★ The obvious blocky arête immediately left of *Back Tree Crack.* Pro: quickdraws.

30. Back Tree Crack (5.7) ★ The obvious right-leaning crack on the right side. Pro: to 3 inches.

There are several new short sport routes on the cliffs above the mountain bike trails northeast from the east end of the Main Wall, some of which are worth the hike up there to explore. Beware of poison ivy!

Minnehaha Bouldering

Dozens of boulder and toprope problems have been established at Minnehaha, including lots of moderates and a few severe problems up to B2 (V7/8). Most of the popular problems are well chalked, making them easy to identify if not always easy to solve. Some of the best bouldering in the area is found on the rocks immediately right of the parking area, but there are good problems scattered throughout the park. Both current guides to Spokane climbing include extensive coverage of Minnehaha bouldering.

DISHMAN ROCKS

Dishman Rocks is a single, steep wall about 200 feet long and 50 to 80 feet high, featuring about twenty routes ranging from 5.8 to 5.12. The area is located at the fringe of the Dishman Hills Natural Area, just off of Sprague Avenue, about 6 miles east of downtown and just 1 mile south of I-5. The cliff's easy accessibility combined with its concentration of steep, hard routes has made it very popular, although Minnehaha remains Spokane's most popular climbing area.

Note: According to Spokane County Parks, climbing is not allowed inside the new fence. The rest of this cliff is said to be on private property. Please observe any posted regulations here.

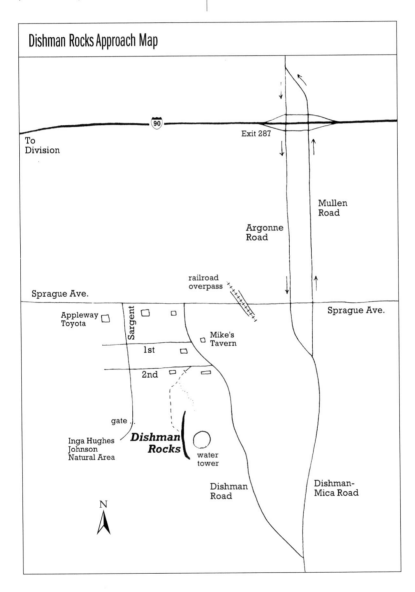

Dishman Rocks Approach Map

There has been considerable controversy here due to manufactured holds. This is not a pristine climbing area by any accounts, but efforts to turn this into an outdoor climbing gym have been sharply rebuffed by outspoken locals.

To reach the rocks, take the Argonne Road exit (exit 287) off I-90 and head south 1 mile to Sprague Avenue (or take exit 285 and follow Sprague for about 2 miles). Turn right onto Sprague and drive under the railroad bridge 0.2 mile to Dishman Road. Turn left, drive 2 blocks, then turn right onto Second and go about 50 yards to a side road on the left, leading up the hill toward a water tower. The road is blocked off, so park here and walk up the road about 50 yards to where a trail leads south into the ravine immediately right of the water tower. The wall is on the left, about 200 yards down the trail, directly below the water tower.

Although most of Dishman's routes are nice and clean, there is some mossy, dirty rock and several loose blocks and flakes, so climb with care. The cliff has been cleaned up a lot though, and most of the loose flakes (including the scary Klingon flake that was bolted in place to prevent it from falling off) have been removed. The routes are described from left to right. Descend from anchors where available.

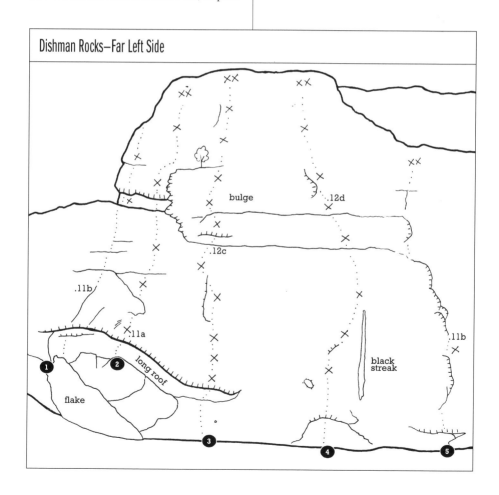

Dishman Rocks–Far Left Side

1. Raisins in Space (5.11b) ★ The leftmost route on the wall, starting up a big flake and passing a flaky roof to an obvious right-arching thin crack, then up the mossy headwall. Pro: to 3 inches; quickdraws.

2. All the People Are Watching (5.11a) ★ The sport route immediately right of *Raisins in Space*. Pass the initial flaky roof and connect the bolts up the flaky wall, past a roof, to chain anchors 80 feet up. Pro: quickdraws.

3. Metropolitician (5.12c) ★★ A sport route about 30 feet right of *A1 People,* climbing up a shallow, right-facing corner/groove, then passing a small roof and continuing up the headwall to anchors. Pro: quickdraws.

4. Return of the King (5.12d) A sport route about 20 feet right of *Metropolitician,* climbing the streaky wall left of a prominent black streak, then up the severely overhanging headwall to chain anchors. Pro: quickdraws.

5. Wings (5.11b) ★★ A series of right-facing flakes starting directly above a small cave. Cleaned up and fully bolted. Pro: quickdraws.

6. Rock Star (5.10a) ★ An easier version of *Wings,* which now has its own anchors. Pro: quickdraws.

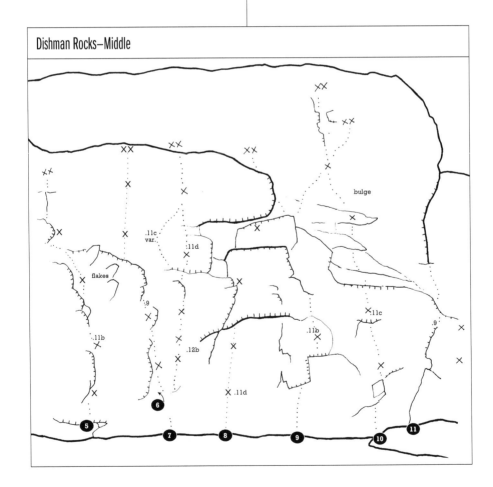

Dishman Rocks–Middle

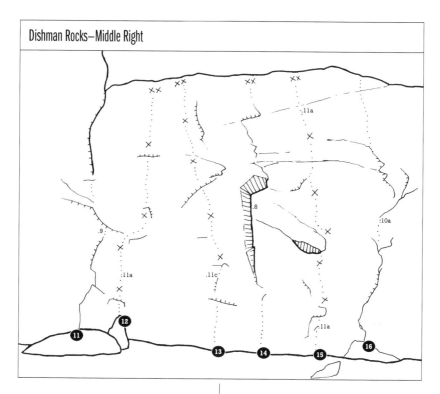

Dishman Rocks–Middle Right

7. Rock 106 (5.12b) ★★ Named for the "Rock 106" graffito that used to be here, the route is now a number grade harder since the Klingon flake came off. Thin, crimpy face climbing leads to burly undercling moves. Pro: quickdraws.

8. Klingon (5.11d) ★★ The formerly scary Klingon flake is gone, so now boulder up to the hanging flakes higher up and connect the bolts to the top. Pro: quickdraws.

9. Spock (5.11b) ★ About 20 feet right of Klingon is a bolt just above a small flake/roof. Climb up past the bolt to join *Klingon* briefly, then continue up the blocky, brownish headwall to anchors. Pro: quickdraws; gear to 2 inches.

10. Touch of Gray (5.11c) ★ A sport route about 10 feet right of *Spock*. Climb past a square flake to a bolt, then up and over a bulge to reach a sloping ledge. Some flaky

climbing leads to a bulging headwall finish. Pro: quickdraws.

11. Chicken Spread (5.9) ★ Start at a thin flake leading up and right about 10 feet right of *Touch of Gray*. Climb the flake and a right-facing corner to a ledge, then aim for the obvious right-facing corner leading to the top. Pro: to 2 inches. (FFA: Dane Burns 1980)

12. Digital Leadout (5.11a) ★★ A sport route starting directly behind the spike (a freestanding flake/block beside the wall), climbing up past two bolts, then angling right to a third bolt and up the headwall to anchors. Pro: quickdraws.

13. Firestone 500 (5.11c) ★★ About 30 feet right of the spike is an obvious right-facing dihedral. This sport route climbs the overhanging wall just left of the corner,

Dishman Rocks—Far Right Side

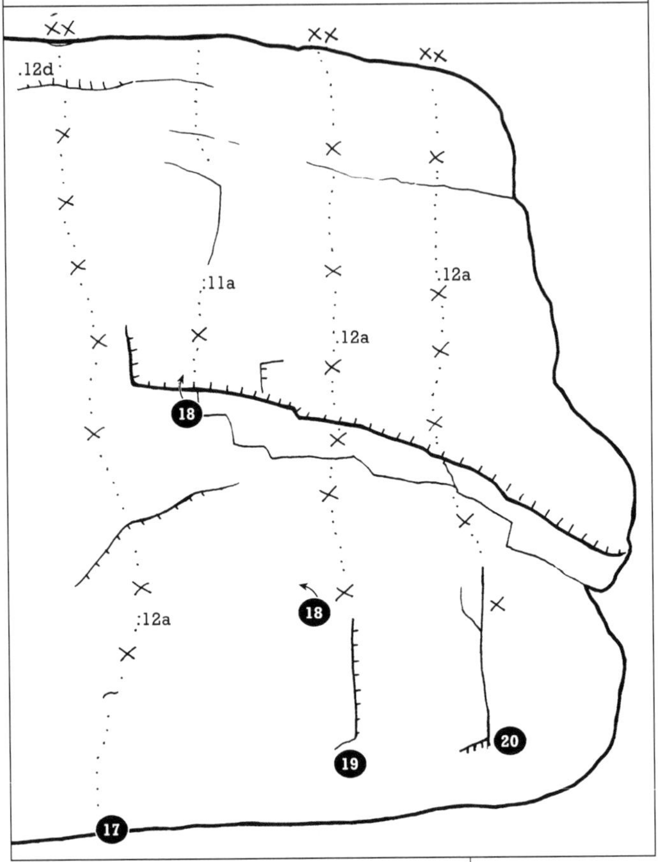

16. The Force (5.10a) ★
An obvious right-leaning
flake 20 feet right of
Grape Ape. Angle right to
some blocky flakes, then
left and up the mossy wall
above. Pro: to 2 inches.
(FFA: Dane Burns 1980)

**17. Dull Sickle (fka Hair
of the Dog)** (5.12d) ★★
The first sport route right
of *The Force,* climbing a
bolted, golden wall to
a ledge 30 feet up, then
skirting the blocky roofs
on the left and up to
anchors. Pro: quickdraws.

18. Free Installation
(5.11a) ★★ A fun sport
route about 20 feet right
of *Dull Sickle,* starting
up a left-facing flake to
a bolt 15 feet up, then
traversing left and passing
the blocky roof on the
left side and up the steep
headwall to anchors. Pro:
quickdraws.

19. Body Scarfer (5.12a) ★★ Start as for *Free
Installation,* but pass the blocky roofs directly.

20. Slave Labor (5.12a) ★★ The sport route
on the far right edge of the wall. Pro:
quickdraws.

trending left up the overhanging prow. Pro:
quickdraws.

14. Grape Ape (5.8) The obvious right-
facing corner leading past a blocky roof and
up the flaky, mossy wall above. Would be
better if it wasn't so dirty. Pro: to 1 inch.

15. Arms Shortage (5.11a) ★ The first sport
route right of *Grape Ape,* starting in a pit,
passing a small triangular roof about 15 feet
up, then skirting around an obvious blocky
overhang on the right side and finishing up
the mossy headwall. Pro: quickdraws.

ROCKS OF SHARON

Rocks of Sharon are a cluster of monolithic granitic boulders on a hilltop in the Dishman Hills Conservation Area just southeast of Spokane. The area has mostly short sport climbs, but has several multipitch and traditional routes as well. Long a popular hiking and wildlife viewing area used for practice by Spokane-area climbers, in recent years its popularity has increased due to completion of an improved trailhead and trail on the south side and development of several new, difficult sport routes. The routes are mostly good, but the rock isn't entirely trustworthy. Flakes and knobs have a tendency to break off, making bold runouts and free-soloing unwise, and climbers above you will probably knock something loose, so wear a helmet.

You can reach the climbing area several ways, all leading to Palouse Highway. From the west, take US 195 south to Hatch Road, then take a right (south) on Hangman Valley Road, which meanders to Palouse Highway soon enough. From the east, take WA 27 south to its junction with Palouse Highway. Neither of these routes is the shortest option, but for first-time visitors they are the easiest to follow. Either way, in a few miles, turn north up Stevens Creek Road and follow 2 miles to the parking area just short of road's end. This is a private road, so don't park except in the designated parking lot, and be respectful while hiking in and out. From the parking lot, hike up the road on the right 150 meters to a gated footpath that meanders up the hill, reaching the base of Big Rock in about 20 minutes.

The Rocks of Sharon area was acquired by Spokane County Parks in 2011. The Stevens Creek Road approach and trailhead parking area were completed in 2012 by the Conservation Futures Project. There is a portable toilet at the parking area. No camping, fires, hunting, or motorized vehicles are allowed in the Dishman Hills Conservation Area. In case of emergency, dial 911.

Big Rock

Big Rock, elevation 3,455 feet, is the largest of the Rocks of Sharon. Although it rises just 200 feet above its base, it seems to tower over the valley. Its north and west faces have several two-pitch routes up to 200 feet in length. The main trail from Stevens Creek Road leads directly below the east face of Big Rock. A dozen or so routes were established on the megalith in the 1960s and 1970s, but the mostly dirty, friable old traditional lines have been supplanted by sport routes installed in more recent years. Some of the bolts and anchors are camouflaged, so look carefully. The routes are described starting from the south face, where the trail reaches Big Rock, then around the rock in a counterclockwise direction. Descend by scrambling down the *Standard Route* or by lowering or rappeling from various chains and anchors.

South Buttress

As you reach the base of Big Rock on the approach hike, you encounter a slabby buttress with a log bench below and several bolted routes. There are also some dirty routes without bolts on the left side of this wall, but nobody ever climbs them, for good reason. Descend from anchors or slog to the summit and descend the *Standard Route*.

1. Grin and Barrett (5.8) No topo. The leftmost bolted slab pitch above the log bench at the toe of Big Rock. Pro: quickdraws.

2. Around the Horn (5.9) ★★ No topo. The middle bolted slab route, climbing a knobby

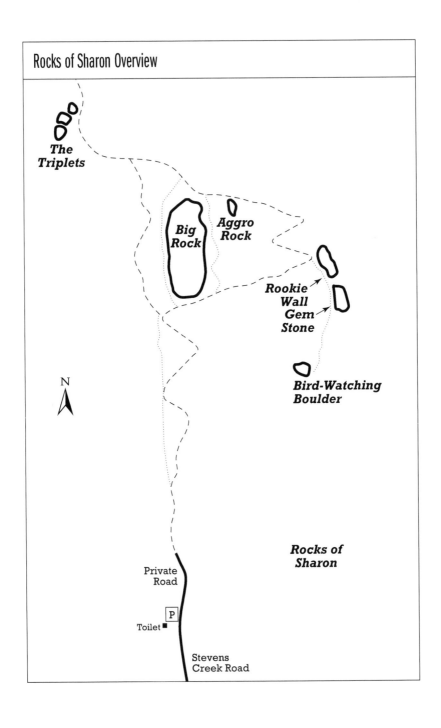

Rocks of Sharon Overview

The Triplets

Big Rock

Aggro Rock

Rookie Wall

Gem Stone

Bird-Watching Boulder

N

Rocks of Sharon

Private Road

P

Toilet ■

Stevens Creek Road

wall more directly up to the anchors shared with *Highland Malt*. Some runouts unless you tie off a knob or two. Pro: quickdraws; one or two slings.

3. Highland Malt (5.8) ★ No topo. The rightmost of the three slabby sport routes, leading up and right around a bulge. Pro: quickdraws.

4. Southern Comfort (5.5) ★ No topo. An easy route up the low-angle prow dividing the east and south faces. A second pitch (*Southern Comfort Straight Up*, 5.7) continues up the buttress above the first anchors. Pro: quickdraws.

East Face

The slabby East Face of Big Rock has a few good routes that would be better if they were cleaned up a little. There seem to be some new bolts on this face, but route details are unknown. Descend from anchors or rappel off. Downclimbing the *Standard Route* is an option, but not a great one.

5. Clean Sweep (5.9) ★ No topo. The obvious vertical crack in the middle of the east face. Thin to wide, steep to slightly overhanging. Ends at an anchor on the *Standard Route*. Like other cracks in this area, it could use a good cleaning. Pro: nuts and cams to 4 inches.

6. Standard Route (Class 4/5.0) No topo. The easy route to the top of Big Rock, following a ledge and ramp system that angles up from right to left, starting at a stump just left of the North Face chimney. Has some bolts associated with other routes, including two 5.7 sport routes that start up about 50 feet along the initial traverse and head up, one going left, the other going right. Some climbers scramble up and down this route

unroped, but it's loose and exposed in places. Non-climbers scramble up this route, too, and tend to kick loose rocks down on climbers below, so be careful if tourists are scrambling above you.

7. Northern Aggression (5.9) ★ No topo. The bolted face/buttress immediately right of the obvious North Face chimney. If you see a bunch of bolts running up the right side of a chimney, this is it. Pro: quickdraws.

8. They Call the Wind Mariah (5.10a R) ★ No topo. A two-pitch route, starting as for *Northern Aggression* to the first bolt, then traversing left across the chimney and onto the pillar face. A little runout getting to the second bolt; you wouldn't want to fall. Anchors atop the pillar; rappel here or continue up the second pitch. Pro: quickdraws; maybe a cam will fit in there somewhere.

West Face

At its highest point, the West Face of Big Rock rises 200 feet from base to top, providing some of the longest routes in the Spokane area. It was first climbed in 1966 with nothing but a few pitons for protection. Nobody climbs the old trad routes anymore; nearly everything worth climbing on this wall has been amply bolted. The rock ranges from fairly good to not so great; the good routes are steep and sporty, with solid holds where cleaning and traffic have removed most of the flaky, loose rock—although there are still knobs and flakes waiting to break off.

You can approach from below or above along the trail that parallels the base of the wall and a climbers' trail where the trail veers away from the wall. The routes are described from left to right as you descend along the trail. If approaching from below, start from

Big Rock West Face

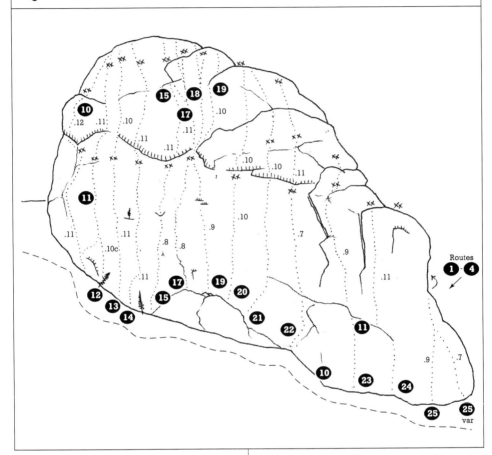

the bottom or turn the book upside down. The wall is in shade all morning, making for comfortable climbing even on hot summer days, although by afternoon it can be insufferably hot. It is common to lower or rappel from anchors rather than downclimbing the *Standard Route*. Because of the risk of rockfall from above, especially if climbers or hikers are above you, it's a good idea to wear a helmet.

9. Beautiful Disaster (5.11a) ★ About 50 feet down the climbers' trail from the "notch" is a small cave and roof just left of a leaning pine tree. This route climbs up to

and past a bulge left of the cave, then up slabby rock to anchors below the large roof. Pro: quickdraws. (FA: Todd Hamm)

10. Legends of the Fall (5.12 or A1+) ★ Climb the roof crack just left and above the *Beautiful Disaster* anchors. Rumored to have gone free at 5.12; otherwise it's A1+. Pro: cams to 2 inches; hooks if you're aiding. (FA: Bob Ordner, Rusty Baille 2003; FFA: unknown)

11. Dixie Crystals (5.11a) ★ A two-pitch sport route on the west face. The first pitch starts as for *Beautiful Disaster*, then traverses right above the cave/roof to join *.50 Caliber*

Barrett to anchors. There are some bolts between *Beautiful Disaster* and *Dixie Crystals*, another possible variation. The second pitch (crux) continues through the roof. Pro: quickdraws.

12. .50 Caliber Barrett (5.10c) ★★
A direct start to *Dixie Crystals*, starting directly behind the leaning pine tree. Although considered a variation start to *Dixie Crystals*, it is more direct and the better of the two lines. Pro: quickdraws. (FA: Eric Barrett, Bob Ordner)

13. Balanced Effect (5.11a) ★ About 12 feet right of the leaning pine tree, connect the bolts starting just left of a bush up a steep, reddish slab. A second pitch (easier) climbs through the apex of the roof system. Pro: quickdraws.

14. Iron Wolf (5.11b) ★ A three-pitch route starting about 15 feet right of the bush at the start of *Balanced Effect*. Connect the cold shuts up and past a gnarly right-facing flake, staying right of a small pine tree halfway up the slab. From the first-pitch anchors, continue up and over the roof and airy slab above to higher anchors, then finish up a short knobby pitch to the top. Pro: quickdraws.

15. Timeless Bond (5.11c) ★ This two-pitch route starts with a mantel on a slabby buttress just right of a pine tree, then climbs into and out of a U-shaped water-streaked dish. From the anchors, angle right to join other routes for a few bolts before striking out left above the roofs. Pro: quickdraws.

16. West Standard Route (5.8+ X) No topo. A historically significant route up the middle of the west face, first climbed by Chris Kopczynski and John Roskelley in

Big Rock–Upper West Face

1966. An attempted second ascent resulted in a fatal fall. The historical West Face route is largely ignored today because most everything has been bolted. If you want to climb it, just climb the easiest looking line up the middle of the face without clipping any of the bolts. Not recommended. Good luck!

17. Call of the Wild (5.11a) ★ From the ledge up and right of the *Timeless Bond* pine tree, climb up broken-looking rock to anchors, then continue up through the roofs, staying left when the option arrives. A difficult clip with bad fall potential at the roof (crux). Of course, you can avoid crashing into the roof here by not falling off. Pro: quickdraws. (FA: Rusty Baillie, Bob Ordner, Brad Gilbert)

18. White Fang (5.10c) ★★ A variation second pitch of *Call of the Wild*, following the line of bolts squeezed in between that route and *A Perfect Storm*. Pro: quickdraws.

19. A Perfect Storm (5.10b) ★★★ Another two-pitch sport route on the west face, considered perhaps the best route on Big Rock, all things considered. From the ledge up and right of the pine tree, start up a patch of whitish rock right of a small roof and connect the bolts to anchors in an alcove below the roofs. A second pitch (crux) continues to the top. Pro: quickdraws. (FA: Rusty Baillie, Bob Ordner)

20. Council of Elders (5.10c) ★★ Another two-pitch sport route starting atop a white flake just right of *A Perfect Storm*, then heading up flaky jugs through a reddish bulge to anchors past a roof. The second pitch starts with difficult stemming, then finishes up a right-leaning crack. Pro: quickdraws. (FA: Bob Loomis, Rusty Baillie, Bob Ordner)

21. The Thrill of Krell (5.10a) ★ A two-pitch sport route on the west face. Scramble or climb up to a ledge about 30 feet right of *Council of Elders*, then connect the bolts on the left, passing a prominent red flake and yellowish overhangs higher up. A short second pitch reaches the top. Pro: quickdraws.

22. The Issue (5.11b) ★ Yet another two-pitch sport route on the west face following the bolts up the scruffy looking wall between *Thrill of Krell* and the History Channel chimney (the leftmost of the two obvious chimneys). The first pitch is 5.7; the second pitch tackles the roof, which inspires most parties to stop at the first anchors. Pro: quickdraws; slings for rope drag.

23. Satori (5.9) ★★ A long sport pitch climbing the well-scrubbed face between the two chimneys on the lower West Face. Pro:

quickdraws, including a few longer ones for rope drag. (FA: Bob Ordner and Eric Barrett)

24. Bird Beak Bone (5.11) ★★ A sport route that climaxes on the arête on the right side of the Bottleneck Chimney (the rightmost of the two big chimneys). Pro: quickdraws.

25. B.O.B. (5.9) ★ Down and right from Bottleneck Chimney, climbing a flaky slab buttress past a ledge and up to anchors at the base of a short chimney. An alternate start climbs a lower slabby buttress (5.7). Pro: quickdraws.

Aggro Rock

This small formation is just east of the upper east face of Big Rock (a stone's throw away from the North Face chimney), with a handful of short bolted routes and an obvious crack on its overhanging west face. Stays in shade all morning.

1. Aggro Crack (5.9+) ★ The obvious left-slanting crack. Some gnarly old-school 5.9 awaits. Pro: gear to 3-4 inches depending on which guidebook you read, although the route is short enough you probably won't die either way.

2. The Unbearable Lightness of Being (5.11a) ★★ Connect the bolts up the wall closely left of the crack—so close, in fact, you could probably clip them to protect the crack if you weren't a staunch traditionalist. Pro: quickdraws.

3. Loud in the Morning (5.12a) ★★ You'd think somebody was probably dropping F-bombs on this short sport route up the middle of the wall, but it's named after the first ascentionist's dog. (Funny name for a dog.) Pro: quickdraws.

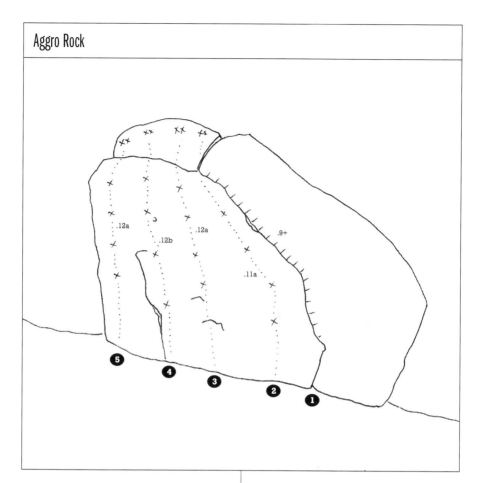

Aggro Rock

.12a

.12a

.9+

.12b

.11a

⑤

④

③

②

①

4. Hip Check (5.12b) ★★ The next short, bolted line to the left, starting at a sort of flake. Pro: quickdraws.

5. Forty-Foot Fred (5.12a) ★★ The leftmost sport route, which doesn't seem to actually be 40 feet long. Pro: quickdraws.

Rock #5

Rock #5 is the first formation you reach as you continue up the main (eastern) trail from the base of Big Rock. It has a couple of slabby bolted routes just off the trail, but the main attractions—the Rookie Wall and Gemstone Wall—are just down the faint climbers' trail.

Rookie Wall

This is the bulbous 50-foot-high rock formation on the downhill side of Rock #5 proper, the one with all the bolts on its overhanging southwest side. There are other routes on this formation, but these are the most visible and popular.

1. Special Sauce (5.12d) The leftmost and most difficult of the sport routes on the overhanging southeast side of the Rookie Wall. You may not see the bolts at first. Pro: quickdraws.

2. Visionary Spastic (5.12c) ★★ Start up the gully at the base of the wall, go left

Rookie Wall

to the first bolt, then connect the bolts up the overhanging wall to anchors. Pro: quickdraws.

3. Chronic Rookie (5.12a) ★★ An athletic climb up to and across the overhanging "chin" of the formation. Short but engaging. Pro: quickdraws.

4. Portly (5.11b) ★ A direct route up the steep wall just right of *Chronic Rookie*. Pro: quickdraws.

Gemstone Wall

Continue down the trail past Rookie Wall to this short wall with several overhanging sport routes. The routes range from 5.10 to 5.12 and get progressively more difficult as you move down the wall from left to right. If you start with the short 5.10c route on the

upper left and climb every pitch going left to right, finishing with these two routes on the far right, you'll have had a productive day.

5. Massive Attack (5.12c) ★★ No topo. On the lower right end of Gemstone Wall, climb the super-overhanging arête left of the *Super Fly* crack. Pro: quickdraws.

6. Super Fly (5.12a) ★★ Connect the bolts up the wall split by the obvious thin crack, only don't climb the crack. Pro: quickdraws.

Rock #6 (Bird-Watching Boulder)

Continuing down the trail from Gemstone Wall another 100 yards or so, you'll find this large boulder, which has several popular sport climbs and a decent crack. The routes are described from right to left as you

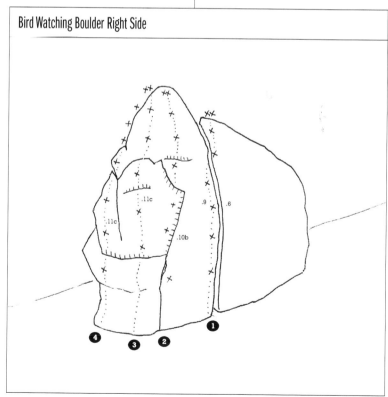

Bird Watching Boulder Right Side

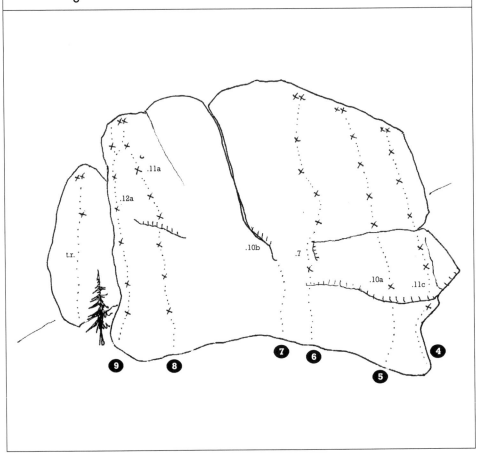

encounter them as you approach from above.

1. Early Bird Gets the Worm (5.6 or 5.9) ★ The rightmost bolted route on the boulder, following bolts up the wall left of a flaring offwidth crack. Easiest if you stay right of the bolts; harder if you climb the face staying left of the bolts. Pro: quickdraws.

2. The Vulture (5.10b) ★★ A tricky bolted thin crack/seam on the east face leads to fun face moves. Pro: quickdraws.

3. No Egrets (5.11c) ★★ Dyno and crimp your way past the protruding beak-like over-hang, then it's straightforward face climbing to the top. Pro: quickdraws.

4. Flipping the Bird (5.11c) ★ Thin face climbing through a rounded bulge/roof leads to easier climbing to the top. Pro: quickdraws.

5. Falcore (5.10a) ★ A face route left of the big roofs, with bouldery moves past a short overhang, then straightforward face climbing to the top. Pro: quickdraws.

6. Turkey Heads (5.7) ★★ A romp up big knobs right of the prominent left-leaning crack. Pro: quickdraws.

7. Spring Kitten (5.10b) ★ The left-leaning crack, a rare traditional offering. Pro: a few pieces of gear to 3 inches.

8. Subconscious Bird Watcher (5.11a) ★ Near the left edge of the wall left of the crack, slabby climbing leads to an overhang with an obvious hueco feature high up. Pro: quickdraws.

9. Snipe Hunt (5.12a) ★ The leftmost bolted line on the far left side of the boulder, starting behind a fir tree. Involves a dyno for a hold you can't see, followed by thin overhanging face climbing. Pro: quickdraws.

The Triplets

The Triplets are a cluster of three large boulders on the ridge crest just northwest of Big Rock. There are several worthy routes on the east side, in the 5.8 to 5.10 range, and a few routes on the west side that aren't as clean or popular. The rock on the "front" side is fairly clean and solid; some of the routes on the "back" side are a little scruffy.

1. Shelter from the Storm (5.9) ★★ The bolted right-leaning corner crack on the front side of South Triplet. Pro: quickdraws.

2. Deception Pass (5.10a) ★★ The left-leaning crack on the left side of the east side of Middle Triplet. Pro: gear to 3 inches.

4. Up Chuck the Boogie (5.11a) ★★ The middle bolted face climb on the front side of Middle Triplet. Pro: quickdraws.

5. Counter Transference (5.10a) ★★ The bolted arête on the right edge of Middle Triplet. More difficult if you refuse to stem across the chimney. Pro: quickdraws.

7. Legacy (5.10c) ★★ The obvious fist and offwidth crack just right of the chimney dividing the Middle and North Triplets. Pro: quickdraws; gear to 4 inches.

The Triplets

DEEP CREEK

Deep Creek is located about 10 miles north-west of downtown Spokane, on the banks of the Spokane River within Riverside State Park. The area features several hard, athletic sport routes on heavily fractured vertical to overhanging basalt. Some of the rock appears frighteningly loose, and some climbers won't climb at Deep Creek. However, the rock has held up for twenty years now, and it's still holding up. Despite its fractured rock, Deep Creek is popular among Spokane-area sport climbers, who insist the routes are safe and very enjoyable despite their sometimes scary appearance, and who bristle at any suggestion that the area is not totally awesome.

To get to Deep Creek from Spokane, take the Division Street exit (exit 281) off I-90 and follow Division north 4.3 miles to Francis Avenue. Take a left and follow Francis (now WA 291) west 3.2 miles to where it curves northward and down toward the Spokane River. Continue on WA 291 another 2 miles and take a left onto Seven Mile Road, which is followed 2.5 miles to the top of a

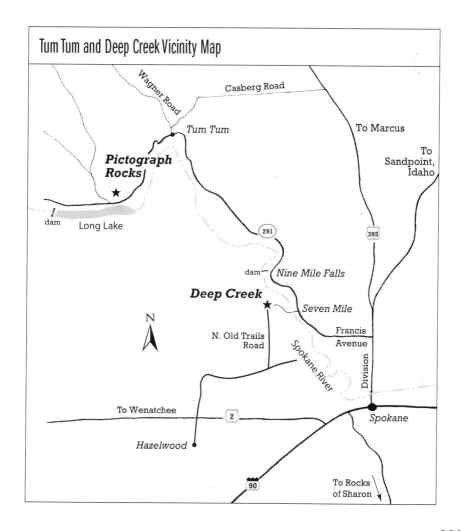

Tum Tum and Deep Creek Vicinity Map

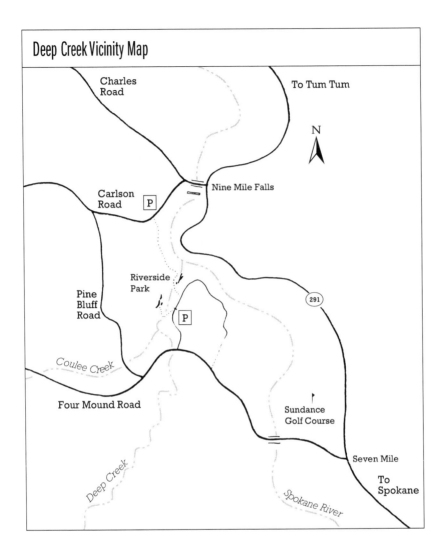

Deep Creek Vicinity Map

Charles Road

To Tum Tum

N

Carlson Road P

Nine Mile Falls

Riverside Park

Pine Bluff Road

P

291

Coulee Creek

Four Mound Road

Sundance Golf Course

Deep Creek

Seven Mile

To Spokane

Spokane River

hill, where a dirt road (State Park Drive) leads north another 0.3 mile to a gate. Park here. Riverside State Park opens at 8 a.m. and closes at dusk, which shouldn't be a problem since the crags are only five to fifteen minutes away.

Because of the very fractured rock, climbers at Deep Creek should be on guard against falling rock and cut ropes. Rockfall from non-climbers scrambling above the cliffs is probably a greater hazard than climber-caused rockfall. Helmets are advised,

especially for belayers. Those who are not climbing or belaying should stay well back from the cliffs. Although it hasn't happened yet, it seems possible that a bolt could pull out under the force of a leader fall—that is, the bolt and the chunks of basalt it's anchored to—which has happened at other basalt areas. Still, they've been climbing here for a long time and you'd hope by now all of the loose rock has broken off. The rock is knife-sharp in a few places, and care must be taken to avoid having your rope cut,

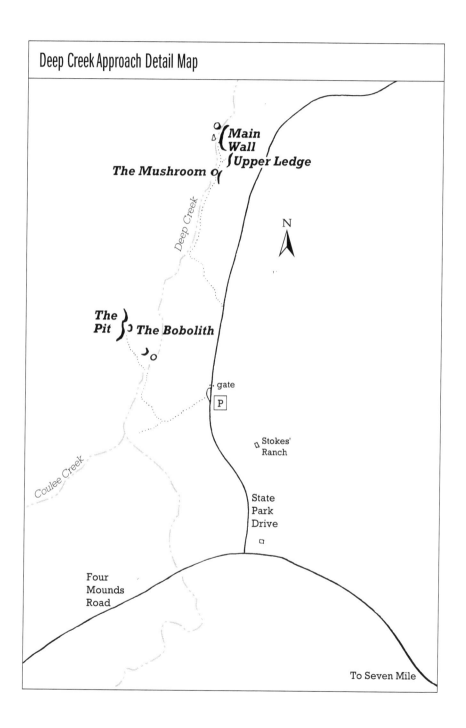

Deep Creek Approach Detail Map

Main
Wall
Upper Ledge

The Mushroom

Deep Creek

N

The
Pit }⌐ The Bobolith

gate
P

Stokes'
Ranch

State
Park
Drive

Coulee Creek

Four
Mounds
Road

To Seven Mile

especially on routes passing overhangs. Rappelling may be wiser than lowering off of some routes.

Deep Creek runs intermittently, particularly during winter and spring, at which time the routes are inaccessible. The canyon narrows near the creek's end, and although a deadly flash flood may seem unlikely, stranger things have happened.

Most of the routes at Deep Creek were developed by Bill Centinari, Marty Bland, and Russ Schultz.

The Pit

The Pit is the most accessible of Deep Creek's sport crags, and also the scariest looking. The area's name is apt, as it somewhat resembles a gravel pit. The rock here is very friable in places, and a few routes have glue-reinforced holds. Sharp edges have sliced through the mantle of at least one rope while toproping a route in this area, so exercise extreme caution when climbing in The Pit, no matter what anybody tells you.

To reach The Pit from the north gate, hike southwesterly down a road grade, then

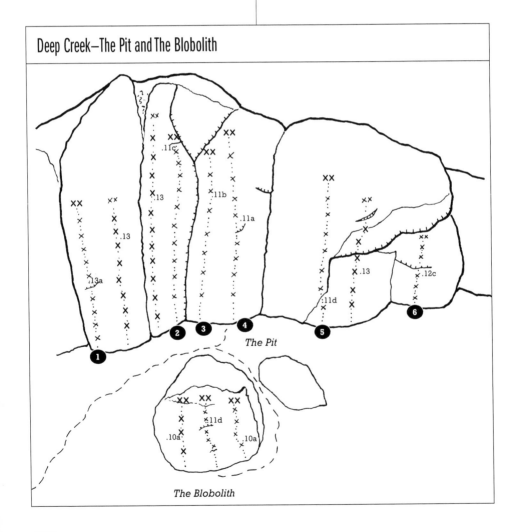

Deep Creek—The Pit and The Blobolith

The Pit

The Blobolith

down a short trail to the creek bed. Hike downstream until a big, round boulder comes into view, then head up a side trail, crossing a big scree slope to reach the base of the crag.

1. The Masochist (5.13a) ★★ On the far left side is this monstrosity, following the bolts past a bulge 30 feet up. Said to be a great route. Pro: quickdraws.

2. Fresh Produce (5.11c) ★ The first sport route right of the prominent Y dihedral in the middle of the crag. The last moves are the hardest. Pro: quickdraws.

3. Flogging a Dead Horse (5.11b) ★★ The first sport route right of the Y corner. Pro: quickdraws.

4. Pit Lizard (5.11a) ★ The second sport route right of the Y corner, passing a small roof midway up. Pro: quickdraws.

5. Eject (5.11d) ★★ A route climbing the "arête" and steep wall at the left edge of the monster roof on the right side of the crag. Pro: quickdraws.

6. Disco Athletic (aka Cord Saw) (5.12c) Presently the rightmost bolt line on the crag, passing a roof and ending at anchors just below the big roof. Sharp edges could cut through your rope on this route if you aren't careful! Pro: quickdraws.

The Blobolith

The Blobolith is the giant boulder directly in front of The Pit. It has three short routes on its downhill face, which seems fairly solid by comparison to the other crags in this area. Its routes are 5.10a,

5.11d, and 5.10a, respectively, from left to right.

Lower Creek Area

Deep Creek's original climbing area is located about 0.25-mile downstream from the gate. It has about eighteen sport routes in the 5.9 to 5.13 range. To get there, pass the gate and hike down the dirt road about 200 yards, then follow a trail leading left and down to the creek bed. Continue another 200 yards or so until you enter a narrow canyon, where you will encounter The Mushroom, an obvious bulging boulder right in the middle of the creek bed. The upper ledge and main wall are just beyond.

The Mushroom

This obvious blob of rock is encountered just upstream from the main wall. It has four routes, all starting on the west side from atop a flat boulder. The Mushroom's rock seems

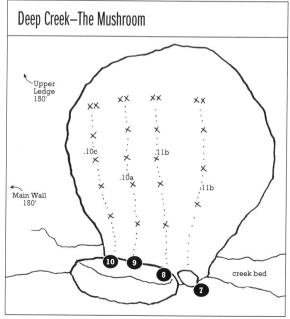

Deep Creek–The Mushroom

fairly solid by comparison to other cliffs at Deep Creek. Because it sits back from the canyon walls and is overhanging on all sides, The Mushroom has the lowest rockfall exposure of any crag at Deep Creek, and offers a good, relatively safe introduction to Deep Creek climbing.

7. Cancerous Mole (5.11b) ★ The rightmost sport route on The Mushroom. Pro: quickdraws.

8. Biopsy (5.11b) ★ The next sport route to the left. Pro: quickdraws.

9. Magical Mushroom (5.10a) ★ The second sport route from the left. Pro: quickdraws.

10. Giggler (5.10c) ★ The leftmost sport route on The Mushroom. Pro: quickdraws.

Upper Ledge

About 30 yards downcanyon from The Mushroom, and about 80 feet above the canyon wall, is the Upper Ledge, a small, fractured wall with a prominent Y crack on the left side. It has three established routes in the 5.10 to 5.12 range and a project destined for 5.13. A loose scramble up a blocky gully/ramp on the right side reaches the ledge. The routes are described from right to left as they are encountered on the approach.

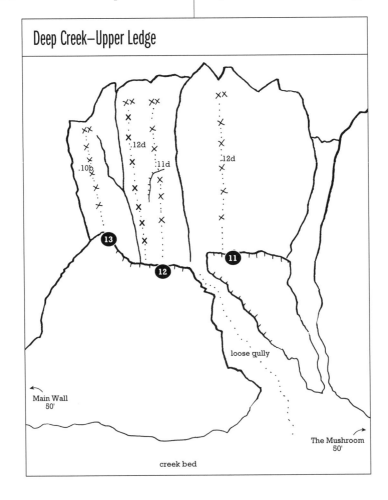

11. Body Tension (5.12d) The rightmost sport route on the upper ledge wall. Pro: quickdraws.

12. Ledgends on the Fall (5.11d) The next sport route to the left, climbing the bulging wall between the cracks in the middle of the upper ledge wall. Pro: quickdraws.

13. Nardo Head (5.10b) The leftmost sport route on the upper ledge wall, immediately left of the Y crack. Pro: quickdraws.

Main Wall

The Main Wall is located about 50 yards downstream from The Mushroom. It is a big, overhanging wall of fractured basalt rising directly out of the creek bed. The routes are described from right to left as they are approached from The Mushroom. The Main Wall is the most solid of all of Deep Creek's developed crags. The rock seems more solid on the left side; the upper right side of the wall has some very dubious rock. As at many sport crags, several of the routes are variations or link-ups of other routes. Several more routes are listed on Mountain Project. Also, a bouldering traverse of the base of the entire Main Wall is a popular endurance problem.

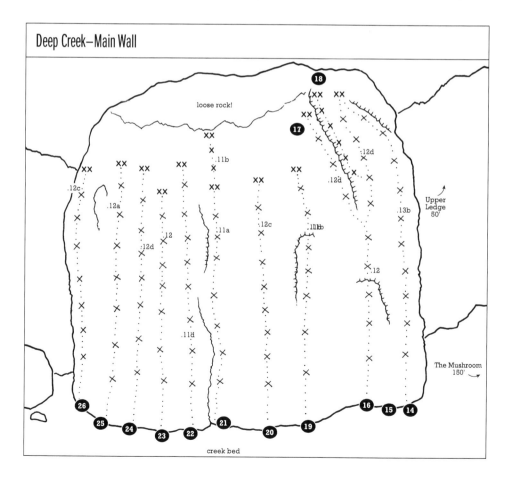

Deep Creek–Main Wall

14. Quiver (5.13b) The rightmost sport route on the main wall, angling left after 60 feet to finish at *Bitten*'s anchors. Pro: quickdraws.

15. Progressive Discipline (5.14b) Reported as the second route from the right end of the main wall. Pro: quickdraws. (FA: Mike Kennedy)

16. Bitten (5.12d) ★ The next sport route left of *Quiver,* passing an overhang to a no-hands rest, then up the headwall to anchors. A variation (*It's Like That* 5.13a) goes right from the third bolt staying right of the arête. Pro: quickdraws.

17. Left Bleeding (5.12d) From the no-hands rest above the roof on *Bitten*, angle left under the arch to anchors. Pro: quickdraws.

18. Russian Arete (5.13a) Climb the arête between *Bitten* and *Left Bleeding.*

19. Red Hair (5.11b) ★ The next sport route to the left, climbing into a right-facing alcove and passing a blocky overhang. The route was named after a rock fell and hit a climber in the head, lacerating his scalp. Pro: quickdraws.

20. Dumptruck (5.12b) ★ The sport route immediately right of *The Roach* crack. Pro: quickdraws.

21. The Roach (5.11a) The obvious left-leaning crack on the left side. Someone has added two bolts for a 5.11b extension. Pro: quickdraws.

22. Belly Rubber (5.12b) ★★ The sport route immediately left of the initial crack of *The Roach.* Pro: quickdraws.

23. Naked Man (5.12a) ★★ The second sport route left of *The Roach.* Pro: quickdraws.

24. 21 Run (5.12d) ★★ The third sport route left of *The Roach.* Pro: quickdraws.

25. Being Inferior (5.12a) ★★ The second sport route from the left edge of the main wall, passing the right side of a prominent small pillar visible as you stand below the route. Pro: quickdraws.

26. Mental Warfare (5.12c) ★★ The leftmost sport route on the main wall, passing the small pillar on the left side. Pro: quickdraws.

TUM TUM (PICTOGRAPH ROCKS)

Near the town of Tum Tum, on the shores of Long Lake, is the least popular of Spokane's rock climbing areas, Pictograph Rocks. The area features a few dozen routes, ranging from 5.0 to 5.12, on its several pinkish granite domes, and several good boulder problems. The climbing is decidedly slabby, with only a few steep cracks and faces. Neglected a decade ago, the area has no doubt seen some sport route development on its remaining few blank walls. For some reason, very few people climb here, which is just fine with those who do, who enjoy a solitude unknown to the denizens of Minnehaha and Dishman Rocks.

To get to Pictograph Rocks from Spokane, take the Division Street exit (exit 281) off I-90 and follow Division north 4.3 miles to Francis Avenue. Take a left and follow Frances (now WA 291) west 3.2 miles to where it curves north and down toward the Spokane River. Continue on WA 291 beyond Seven Mile and Nine Mile to the small lakeside town of Tum Tum, about 18 miles from Spokane. Pictograph Rocks is another 6.2 miles west of Tum Tum, along the shore of Long Lake.

Refer to the second edition of this guide or the current Spokane rock guide for route details.

MCCLELLAN ROCKS

Across the river from Tum Tum is this more recently developed area, which has several dozen routes on fairly solid granite. The area is fairly well documented on Mountain Project, including driving directions, access issues, overview map, and route descriptions. It features short, quality routes in the 5.6 to 5.12 range. If you are visiting Spokane, it is worth checking out.

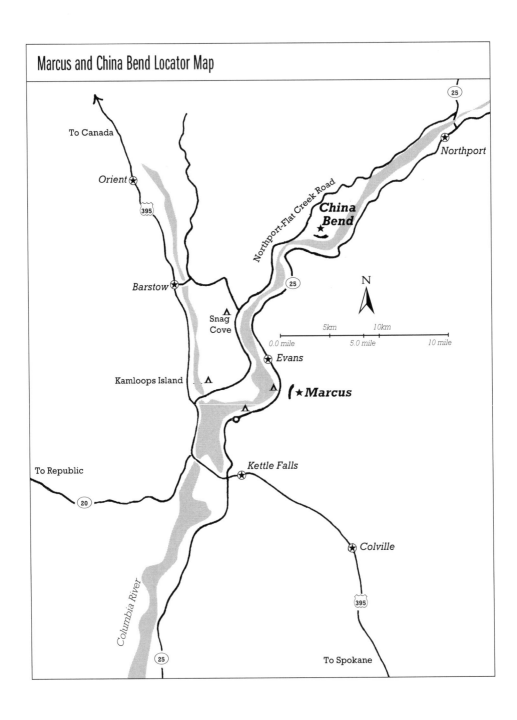

Marcus and China Bend Locator Map

To Canada

Orient ⊛

⬭395

Barstow ⊛

Snag
Cove ▲

Kamloops Island ▲

Northport-Flat Creek Road

China
Bend
★

⬭25

⊛ Evans

▲

▲ ⌒ ★Marcus

▲

⬭25 ⊛ Northport

N

5km   10km

0.0 mile   5.0 mile   10 mile

To Republic

⬭20

Kettle Falls
⊛

⊛ Colville

⬭395

Columbia River

⬭25

To Spokane

MARCUS AND CHINA BEND

Marcus and China Bend comprise the state's first developed limestone sport climbing. Lying along the banks of the Columbia River in the northeast corner of the state, about a ninety-minute drive north of Spokane, Marcus and China Bend are too distant from a majority of Washington's climbing population to have become popular, although Spokane climbers have taken to these areas with a vengeance, establishing over fifty new routes within the first two years of development. Given the quality and quantity of rock in this region, new route development should continue unabated for some time. Touted as "world-class" limestone by enthusiastic locals, the area offers something a bit different than most other Washington sport climbing venues. However, because of its remote location, the area is still known by reputation only to many Washington climbers.

Type of climbing: Marcus and China Bend offer typical limestone sport climbing—steep and steeper—in the 5.10 to 5.13 range, with some projects destined for 5.14 if anybody comes along who can pull them off. The cliffs of Marcus and China Bend have been prodigiously bolted, producing mostly high-end routes in the 5.11+ to 5.13 range, although there is potential for countless routes at easier grades, as well as future multipitch classics. Only the cost of stainless steel bolts has deterred development of dozens of easier sport routes here.

Brief history of area: Route development at Marcus and China Bend is basically the result of Spokane climbers becoming bored with the same old stuff at Minnehaha and Dishman, being unable to climb at Deep Creek during the winter and spring, and being tired of driving too far to find steep sport climbing. The first of the areas to be developed, Marcus, was discovered in 1994, with China Bend not far behind. A majority of the early routes at Marcus and China Bend were pioneered by Bill Centinari, Russ Schultz, and Marty Bland. Development continues, although not quite as feverishly here since the discovery of the Metaline walls farther east. There are no doubt dozens of new routes at Marcus and China Bend and other limestone cliffs in the area not included here. The area awaits publication of a new comprehensive guidebook.

Seasons and climate: Autumn is the best season for climbing at Marcus and China Bend, although climbing in winter and spring is sometimes pleasant. The Marcus wall faces west, making it a shady morning-hours venue on warm days. China Bend's south-facing cliffs are often warm enough for climbing even on cold winter days, but are impossibly hot by late spring.

Precautions and regulations: The routes are generally well cleaned of loose rock, but there are a few routes that climb past loose-looking flakes and blocks. As always, helmets are recommended, at least for belayers (dropped quickdraws hurt, too). Poison ivy runs riot along the base of these cliffs; long pants are recommended for the approach hike, and do what you can to keep your pack and gear up off the poison ivy at the base of the cliffs. As at other eastern Washington venues, beware of rattlesnakes, ticks, and stinging insects. If you drive up at night, watch out for deer on the highways. Bears and cougars are hereabouts as well.

Nesting eagles have been reported on the Marcus wall. Please do not disturb eagles or falcons, or their nests, should you happen to encounter either.

Gear and other considerations: All you need to climb at Marcus and China Bend is a rack of quickdraws and a rope (or two). On average, routes here have ten to fourteen bolts, plus anchors, and there is at least one pitch requiring twenty quickdraws! Some long draws will be useful on routes passing roofs, of which there are many. A 60-meter rope is recommended so you can lower off some of the longer pitches. Double-rope rappels are rare, but are noted where recommended. Some routes have multiple anchors to facilitate lowering off with a single rope. Be sure your rope will get you safely to the ground before you lower off. Insist that your belayer tie in before lowering you off of a longer route. Before starting up a route here, always know how many ropes are required for the descent!

Camping and accommodations: There is a bivouac site just up the road from the Marcus wall trail; take the right fork to the road's end. There are several riverside campsites at China Bend. There are also several US Forest Service campgrounds in the vicinity. Evans Campground is within walking distance of the Marcus wall. It is reported that bivouacking is no longer allowed at China Bend and forest service campgrounds must be used.

If you just want to wash up or use the toilet, stop at any of the forest service campgrounds in the vicinity. The Chevron station in Kettle Falls offers public showers and laundry facilities. If Kettle Falls doesn't have what you need in the way of supplies, Colville is just another 3 miles down the highway.

Emergency services: In case of emergency, dial 911. There is a hospital in Colville, about 3 miles south of Kettle Falls on US 395, and a medical clinic in Northport, about 15 miles northeast from the climbing areas. Forest service rangers and campground hosts have phones and radios in case you need to summon emergency assistance.

Other guidebooks: Bland, Marty. *Inland Northwest Rock Climbs*; "Steepness in Spokane: Modern sport climbing comes to eastern Washington" by Marty Bland, *Rock & Ice* #84, March/April 1998.

Finding the crags: Marcus and China Bend are located near the town of Kettle Falls, which is about ninety minutes north from Spokane on US 395. Driving directions to the individual crags are given beginning from the US 395/WA 25 junction just west of Kettle Falls.

To get to the Marcus wall from Kettle Falls, turn right onto WA 25 and follow just over 5 miles to the town of Marcus, then continue another 3.2 miles past the Marcus General Store to a dirt road on the right, across the highway from a cluster of houses. If you miss it, turn around at the Evans Campground entrance and backtrack 0.75 mile to the road. Drive up the primitive road to where it forks and turn around, then drive back about 100 yards and look for a moss-covered boulder on the left. About 30 feet downroad from the boulder is a fir tree with a length of climbing rope tied around its trunk. The trail begins here.

To get to China Bend, continue 6 miles north from Kettle Falls on US 395, crossing the Columbia River, and turn right onto Northport-Flat Creek Road (signs point to Kamloops Island Campground). Follow Northport-Flat Creek Road 15.2 miles to China Bend Road. Turn right and follow this primitive road down to the north bank of the Columbia River, where the cliffs come into striking view. At 1.1 miles from the turnoff is a side road leading down to the river's edge. Turn around and park here. A trail begins just up and across the road.

MARCUS

Marcus is a small limestone cliff located just east of Evans Campground, about 4 miles northeast of the town of Marcus. It has about thirty routes and a few wild-looking projects. The rock ranges in quality from good to really bad, with the majority of better routes being found on the left side of the wall and in the vicinity of the big cave on the right side.

Find a place to park near the big, moss-covered boulder without blocking the road (no easy feat), then locate the large fir tree with the length of climbing rope tied around it. The trail begins at this tree and

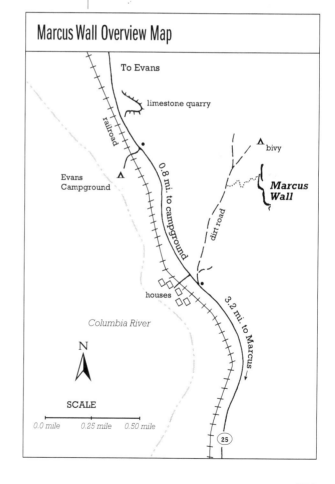

Marcus Wall Overview Map

To Evans

limestone quarry

railroad

bivy

Evans Campground

0.8 mi. to campground

Marcus Wall

dirt road

3.2 mi. to Marcus

houses

Columbia River

N

SCALE

0.0 mile   0.25 mile   0.50 mile

25

switchbacks up scree and forested slopes to the wall. The trail meets the cliff just below the *Citizen Kaned* route. The routes are described from left to right, which is approximately how they are encountered as you approach via the trail. Most of the anchors are less than 25 meters up, but some are over 30 meters high. Make sure your rope is long enough to safely lower you off.

Poison ivy is the main problem at Marcus, although it isn't as bad as the poison ivy at China Bend. Snakes are infrequently encountered at this crag, but stinging insects can be a problem. Do not disturb nesting eagles if you encounter them.

The Ledge

The following several routes begin from a broad ledge on the far left side of the cliff. Approach the ledge via a steep slab. An old rope is presently fixed here to aid you up the slab. If not, expect fairly easy Class 5 slab climbing, which would be awkward to

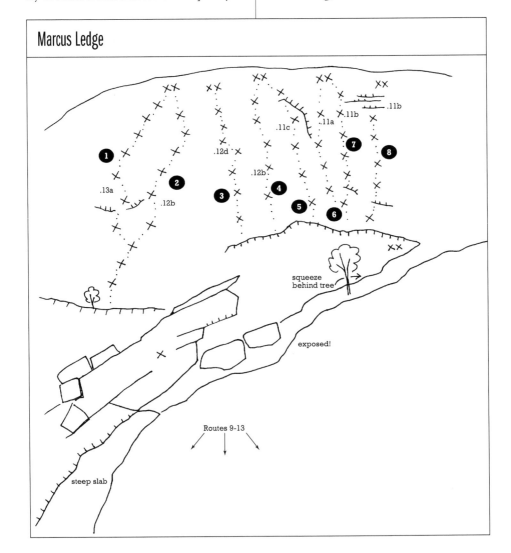

Marcus Ledge

descend. Either way, be careful, especially when descending or if the slab is wet. Once on the ledge, climb over or skirt around some big blocks to reach the routes. The ledge is exposed in places. Where anchor bolts are in place, use them for safety's sake.

1. The Grimace (5.13a) ★★ The leftmost route on the ledge. Traverse left across the blocky ledge to the base of the route. Shares the first three bolts of *Sport of Spew*, then angles left over a crux bulge and up the sustained headwall. Pro: quickdraws.

2. Sport of Spew (5.12b) ★★ Start as for *The Grimace*, but continue right and up to shared anchors. Not quite as steep as *The Grimace*. Pro: quickdraws.

3. All Spew, No Do (aka Boo Hoo Marty) (5.12d) This route begins from the narrow ledge just up and right from the fixed rope anchor. To get there, traverse the big ledge right, squeezing past a bush, then traverse the narrow ledge left to the start of the route. Pro: quickdraws.

4. Spewing for Sponsorship (5.12b) The next route to the right of *All Spew*. More of the same. Shares anchors with *Roughrider*. Pro: quickdraws.

5. Roughrider (5.11c) Climb straight up the wall and past a left-facing arch and roof. Pro: quickdraws.

6. True Value (5.11a) The third route from the right, following welded shuts up and right of the arch. Shares anchors with *The Groper*. Pro: quickdraws.

7. The Groper (5.11b) The second route from the right, following more welded shuts up the sustained wall. Pro: quickdraws.

8. Peeping Tom (5.11b) The rightmost of the ledge routes, passing some small overlapping roofs at the top. Pro: quickdraws.

Left Side

The following several routes climb the steep wall at the base of the cliff on its far left side, where the trail meets the wall. These routes are mostly overhanging, and offer some of Marcus wall's better sport climbing.

9. The Hanging Man (5.12d) The leftmost route, skirting around a bulging roof and angling right up the headwall to anchors shared with *Citizen Kaned*. Harder since a hold broke. Pro: quickdraws.

10. Citizen Kaned (5.12c) ★★ The route directly above the trail, climbing past an apex in the bulging roof and up the overhanging headwall. Pro: quickdraws.

11. Gaston Chamber (13b/c) ★★ A severe route passing the roof at its steepest spot and continuing up the headwall, with a final strenuous move over a left-leaning arch. Shares anchors with *Walk the Plank*. Pro: quickdraws.

12. Walk the Plank (5.12c) ★★ Start just left of the arête on the right side of the roof. Surmount the arête and continue up the steep headwall, past a final roof to anchors. Pro: quickdraws.

13. Nose Evulsion (5.11d) About 50 feet right of *Walk the Plank,* just right of an impressive cave, is a large flake at the base of the wall. This route starts atop the flake and climbs the slabby wall above. Hopefully you won't mistake it for the 5.13 project on the left. Pro: quickdraws.

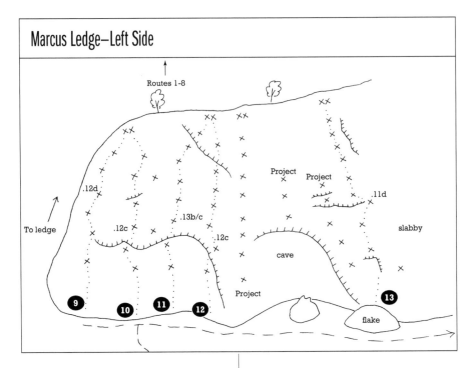

Marcus Ledge–Left Side

Routes 1-8

Project
Project

.12d

.11d

To ledge   .12c

.13b/c

.12c

slabby

cave

Project

flake

9 **10** **11** **12** **13**

14. Ask Russ Schultz (5.12a) About 70 feet right of *Nose Evulsion* is a scary-looking line up the left side of a monstrous arête. Said to be better than it looks. Pro: quickdraws.

15. Satori (5.11b) A scary-looking route climbing the orange-tinted wall just up and right from *Ask Russ Schultz*. Flaky, blocky rock. Said to be worse than it looks. Pro: quickdraws.

16. Stinking Pile (5.11b) The route just right of *Satori*, climbing an uninspiring wall to anchors below an ugly bush. The name says it all. Pro: quickdraws.

The Cave

On the right flank of the Marcus wall is a big cave that features a plethora of bolts but so far only two established routes, which are really only the short versions of longer problems that nobody has so far been able to

pull off. Consult the locals for current status before stealing somebody's project.

17. Natural Born Puller (5.13a) ★ The leftmost line in the cave. Scramble up choss to the first bolt, then angle out to the lip and pull your way up to the ninth bolt. The anchor bolts are staggered, and to claim a legitimate redpoint you have to clip both without hanging. Good luck! Pro: quickdraws.

18. Black Ops (5.13c) ★ The next bolt line right of *Natural Born Puller,* following big holds up out of the back of the cave and across the roof as far as you can go. Finish it if you can. Pro: quickdraws.

19. The Last Great Outlaw (5.14a) Start right of *Black Ops* up a route called *Short Bus* (5.12b), then continue up the cave to join and finish via *Black Ops*. Good luck! Pro: quickdraws. (FA: Brian Raymon)

Marcus–The Cave

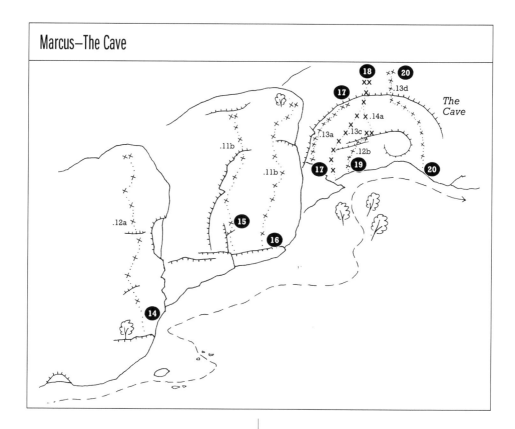

20. Banned for Life (5.13d) ★ The bolt line up the right edge of the cave, leading up and over the lip. Pro: quickdraws.

Right Side

The following routes climb the walls right of the cave. The rock on this section of the cliff gets worse as you move farther right. A couple of the pitches are long, so make sure your rope is long enough before you start lowering off.

20. Freeloader (5.12d) ★ This is the second bolted line right of the cave, starting from the top of an eroded ledge and climbing past a roof and up the gently overhanging headwall. Sustained climbing. A bit runout. Pro: quickdraws.

Free Schultz variation (5.12d) ★★ A better variation of *Freeloader,* angling left from the route's sixth bolt to finish via the steep project just left. Pro: quickdraws.

21. Abuse Your Illusion (5.12d R) The next bolted line, starting about 15 feet right of *Freeloader,* directly above two horizontal tufas. From the fourth bolt, angle left and up a short corner to a ramp, then straight up the gently overhanging headwall, passing a final small roof. Ankle-breaker falls possible in a couple of places. Pro: quickdraws.

22. The Blow of Choss (5.11b) ★ A long pitch, starting as for *Abuse Your Illusion,* but continuing straight up. Above the ramp, angle right around the prominent left-facing corner to anchors. The first route done at

Marcus—Right Side

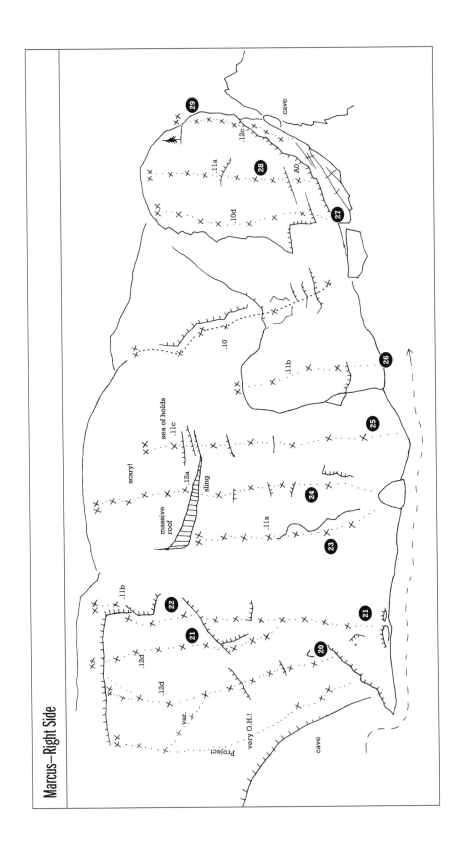

Marcus, and one of the most popular since it was retrobolted. Pro: quickdraws.

23. Son of Sam (5.11a) A short route climbing past a curvy, left-facing flake and ending at anchors just below the left edge of a massive roof. Pro: quickdraws.

24. Safety Sam (5.12a) Climb the blocky face up to the roof, clip the fixed sling, then crank it up and over the roof and up the headwall. Has bad fall potential above the roof. Pro: quickdraws.

25. Tumor Boy (5.11c) ★ Climb up to and past the roof on its far right side. Lots of little holds to perplex you as you pass the roofs. Pro: quickdraws.

26. Ozmosis (5.11b) A short route on a short pillar on the right side of the cliff. Pro: quickdraws.

27. Techweenie (5.10d) The leftmost of three routes on the fractured buttress at the far right end of the wall, ascending a blocky arête up the slab. Pro: quickdraws.

28. Bad Betty (5.11a A0) The next route to the right, starting with an aid move to get past the roof. Pro: quickdraws.

29. Trails of the Ripped (5.12c) The rightmost route on the cliff. Very contrived. Be careful not to fall off and whack your head on the chimney. Pro: quickdraws.

CHINA BEND

China Bend is a big bend in the Columbia River about 8 miles upriver from Marcus. Looming above the river to the north is a series of impressive limestone cliffs. One of these has so far been partially developed, offering about two dozen steep, difficult sport routes on mostly good-quality limestone. The cliff is said to be reminiscent of Sinks Canyon, only on a much smaller scale. The area has quite a bit of potential for new routes, especially routes in the 5.9 to 5.11 range, which have so far been neglected by the hardcore route setters.

After descending the side road to the campsite at the river's edge, park in the shade of three pine trees (or nearby if this spot is taken, but don't block the road). A hard-to-follow trail leads up to the right side of the cliff, starting just 30 feet up the road from the turnout. The trail becomes easier to follow about halfway up the slope. The routes are described from right to left as you encounter them on the approach. Watch out for poison ivy and rattlesnakes on the approach hike and along the base of the cliff. Dive-bombing swallows may startle you at first, but you'll get used to them.

There are some very long routes at China Bend, so don't assume you can just lower off on a single rope from the anchors. Many of these routes can be descended by lowering to intermediate anchors, untying and rethreading the rope, then lowering the rest of the way, or by rappelling from double ropes. Sixty-meter ropes are recommended at China Bend.

Raptor nesting area!: The entire China Bend area is closed annually due to golden eagles nesting on the cliffs. Closure notices are usually posted but could be missed, so climbers planning to visit this area **must** check current restrictions and respect

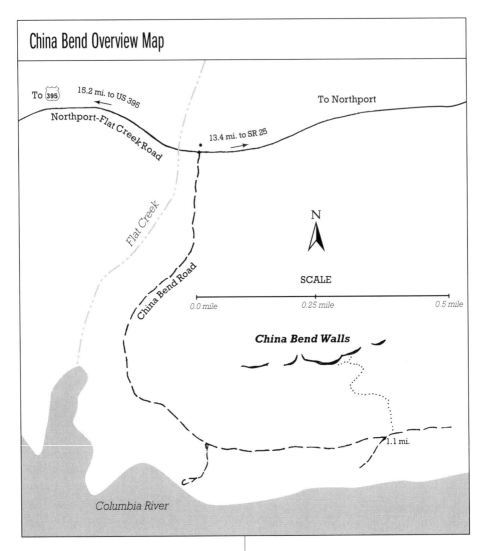

China Bend Overview Map

To (395)   15.2 mi. to US 395 ←

Northport-Flat Creek Road

To Northport

13.4 mi. to SR 25 →

Flat Creek

China Bend Road

N

SCALE

0.0 mile   0.25 mile   0.5 mile

China Bend Walls

1.1 mi.

Columbia River

---

any closures or risk the entire area being closed to climbing.

Right Side

The wall on the far right side of China Bend's main crag features a large, long roof system that so far has not been fully developed. A number of projects reported in the first edition of this guide have been completed. Refer to Marty Bland's *Inland Northwest Rock Climbs* for route details.

1. Hypnotic (5.12c A0) The obvious route beginning from the lowest point of the brushy ramp. Pull up on the first bolt to get established. A little dirty. Pro: quickdraws.

2. Sprint (5.12c) ★ The bolted line directly above *Hypnotic*, climbing past low roofs and up the bulging headwall. To get there, scramble up the brushy ramp to the top of the cliff and rappel in from anchors. Pro: quickdraws.

China Bend—Right Side

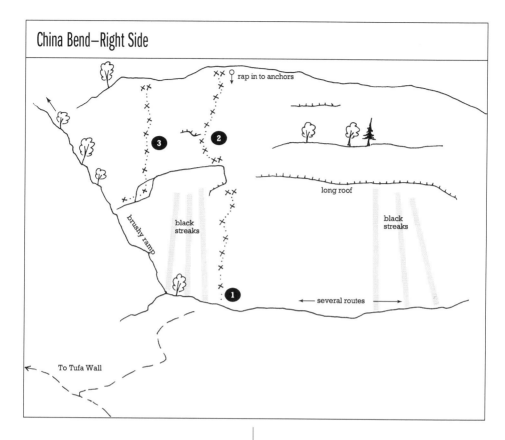

rap in to anchors

long roof

black streaks

black streaks

brushy ramp

black streaks

several routes

To Tufa Wall

3. Route 3 (5.10d) ★ The right-angling line about 40 feet left of *Sprint,* climbing tan-colored rock. Approach via the brushy ramp. Pro: quickdraws.

Tufa Wall

The so-called Tufa Wall is the steep central wall of China Bend's main crag, named because of the plethora of tufas on the lower half of the wall. It is a prototype limestone wall, gently overhanging with a plethora of pockets, big and small, and one project that looks futuristically hard. There are several long routes here, up to 100 feet in length. Double-rope rappels are recommended.

4. Where's My Hero (5.11b) ★ The right-most route on the main wall, ascending the left side of a big, right-leaning arch. Pro: quickdraws.

5. Prearranged Illness (5.11b) ★ From the right edge of the blocky ledge on the far right side of the cliff, ascend the bolt line between the arête and the intrusion of jagged gray rock. Pro: quickdraws.

6. Pork Sausage (5.11a) ★★ This route climbs up the obvious jagged, gray-colored dike. It was the first route completed at China Bend, and remains one of its most popular. Pro: quickdraws.

7. Blue Chunks (5.12b) ★★ Ascend straight up from the bush on the ledge and climb the steep wall just left of the jagged dike. Pro: quickdraws.

China Bend—Tufa Wall

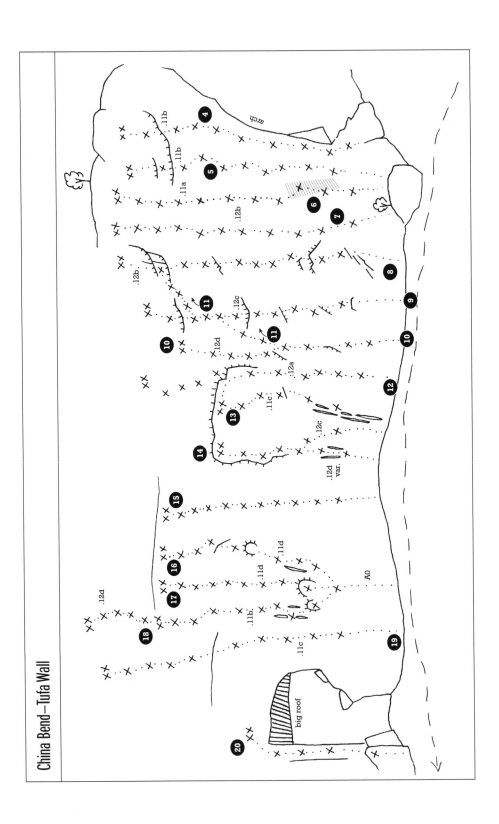

8. Pot Sticker (5.12b) ★★ Just left of the ledge, climb up to and past a small, angular roof, then continue up to and over a steep bulge. Pro: quickdraws.

9. Lesser of Two Evils (5.12c) ★ Climb the steep wall about 20 feet left of *Pot Sticker,* straight up to and over a high roof. Pro: quickdraws.

10. Spillway (5.12d) Start just right of the obvious black streak and ascend the blocky wall to anchors just left of the small roof of *Lesser of Two Evils.* Pro: quickdraws.

11. Traversing the Bullshit (5.12c) ★★★ A linkup angling right from the fourth bolt of *Spillway,* then again from the ninth bolt of *Lesser of Two Evils,* to finish at the *Pot Stick-er*'s anchors. Said to be one of the best routes at China Bend. Pro: quickdraws.

12. Grady the Great (5.12a) ★ The bail-out version of a longer project, starting just left of the first obvious black streak left of *Spill-way.* Climb up to a left-facing arch, then angle left to the anchors of *A River Runs Through It.* Pro: quickdraws.

13. A River Runs Through It (5.11c) ★★ Ascend the many black-streaked tufas and the steep wall above to the anchors below the roof. Often wet, hence the name. Pro: quickdraws.

14. Divine (5.12c) ★ Just left of the many black-streaked tufas is this short pitch climbing up to and along a right-facing flake, leading to anchors at the left end of the long roof. Pro: quickdraws.

Divine Intervention variation (5.12d) ★ A harder variation start to *Divine,* climbing up the thin white tufas just left of the easier version. Pro: quickdraws.

15. Project (5.14?) ★★★ A direct line up the gently overhanging, nearly featureless

wall about 30 feet left of *Divine.* An over-optimistic local with an aesthetic eye bolted this line first. It looks wicked hard, and is predicted to be 5.14, if ever redpointed.

16. Tufa the Price of One (5.11d A0) The rightmost of three routes beginning via a rope ladder. Yard up the knotted rope to the first bolt, then free climb right and up to anchors below a long roof. Pro: quickdraws.

17. Moo Burger (5.11d A0) The middle route starting via the rope ladder. From the first bolt, climb straight up past a bulge and up the headwall to anchors below a long roof. Pro: quickdraws.

18. Bigwig Bill (5.12d A0) The leftmost of the routes starting via the rope ladder. From the first bolt, find the bolts hidden in the big pockets on the left and cruise on up the wall. The short version of this route is 5.11b, and is a popular warm-up. Pro: quickdraws.

19. Neo-Pagan Hillbilly Bash (5.11c) ★ The leftmost route on the Tufa Wall, climbing a gently overhanging bulge. Pro: quickdraws.

Left Side

The following several routes climb the steep, blocky wall on the left side of China Bend's main crag. A big, triangular roof is the most prominent feature here. Some of the routes are well over 100 feet long, thus requiring double-rope rappels or lowering partway and rethreading your rope through lower anchors. Watch out for dive-bombing swallows, and for poison ivy!

20. Dancing with the Refrigerator (5.11a) A unique line climbing the obvious rib left of the large triangular roof. Can't be mistaken for anything else. Kind of scary. Pro: quickdraws.

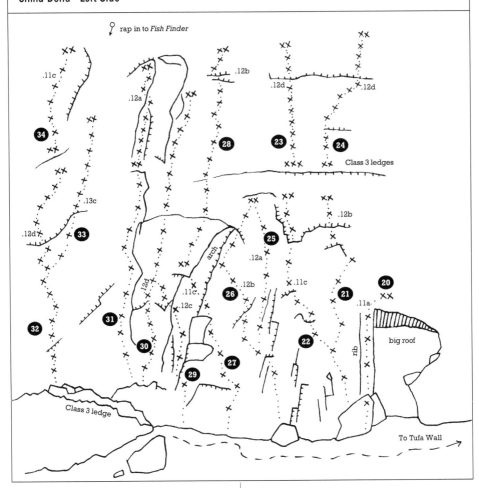

21. Gateway (5.12b) ★ The first route left of *Dancing with the Refrigerator*, following a line of welded shuts past a roof. Pro: quickdraws.

22. The Sporting Guy (5.11c) ★ Start as for *Gateway*, but stray left from the second bolt to a left-facing corner and up to anchors. Hard-to-clip anchors. Pro: quickdraws.

23. Way Out on the Way Out (5.12d) ★★ An airy continuation of *The Sporting Guy*. From the *Sporting Guy* anchors, pull up on bolts (A0) to clip the upper route's anchors.

Alternatively, approach via the brushy ramp and Class 3 ledge. Pro: quickdraws.

24. Shut Out (5.12d) ★ The route just right of *Way Out*, starting from anchors on the ledge. Again, either climb *The Sporting Guy* and aid up to the ledge, or scramble up the brushy ramp and across the exposed ledge. Pro: quickdraws.

25. Primer (5.12a) Start atop the block 15 feet right of *Psycho Trucker*. Climb up and left, past a blocky corner and roof, then head straight up the blocky wall above to anchors below a small roof. Pro: quickdraws.

26. Won Ton (5.12b) ★ Start as for *Primer,* but climb left from the second bolt and ascend into the apex of the big arch and up to anchors shared with *Primer.* Pro: quickdraws.

27. Psycho Trucker (5.11c) Ascend precarious-looking flakes and ledges left into the corner below the big, right-leaning arch, then left across the overhanging arête to anchors on the ledge just above. Pro: quickdraws.

28. Running with Scissors (5.12b) ★★ A continuation of *Psycho Trucker.* Connect the many bolts up the steep wall capped by overhangs. Can be done in one long pitch from the ground, but with unavoidable rope drag. Pro: quickdraws.

29. Poacher (5.12c R) A variation start to *The Game Warden,* starting at the base of the big, right-leaning arch and angling left around the overhanging arête and past a V-shaped roof. If you blow the clip at the third bolt, expect a trip to the hospital. Pro: quickdraws.

30. The Game Warden (5.12d) ★★★ A better alternative to *Poacher,* climbing directly up the blocky, overhanging buttress and continuing up the right side of the big arête above. One of the best routes on the crag. Pro: quickdraws.

31. Adventure People (5.12a) A long line starting up the curving flake and corner on the left side of the *Game Warden* buttress and finishing up the leftmost of the big arêtes above. Can be split into two pitches, although the lower anchors were placed to facilitate lowering off. Pro: quickdraws.

32. Evil Betty (5.12d) ★ Presently the leftmost route on the main wall, climbing a steep, orange-tinted wall about 30 feet left of *Adventure People.* The route starts on a blocky ledge about 30 feet off the ground; your belayer should be anchored, if possible. Climb up and left, passing a bulge to anchors that are higher than it appears from below. To descend, either double-rope rappel or lower to a set of lower anchors and rethread your rope. A 60-meter rope is recommended. Pro: quickdraws.

33. The Big Thrutch (5.13c) ★ From the sixth bolt of *Evil Betty,* angle right and up the bolts. Reported as a project in Marty Bland's mini-guide, it is rumored to have been completed. Confirm, though, before you steal somebody's project. Pro: quickdraws.

34. Fish Finder (5.11c) ★ A continuation of *Evil Betty.* If a 5.12d approach isn't your bag, approach by scrambling up the brushy ramp on the far right side of the cliff and rappelling in from the top of the cliff. Apparently, this requires two rappels. Said to be more trouble than it's worth. Pro: quickdraws.

Far Left Buttress

There are three routes on the prominent buttress about 100 yards left from the base of *The Game Warden* route, reached via a brushy traverse below the cliff. These three routes, in the 5.11a-b range, are said to be good climbs but not quite worth the hassle of bushwhacking over to them. For details about these routes, refer to the *Rock & Ice* mini-guide. There is said to be, and looks to be, much potential for new route development on this side of the cliff.

METALINE

The towns of Metaline and Metaline Falls are located in the far northeast corner of Washington state, in limestone country. This area has an amazing abundance of largely unexplored limestone. Development so far has been limited mostly to Washington Rock, the main formation visible above the bridge leading into Metaline Falls. The routes are mostly one-pitch bolted sport routes in the 5.11 to 5.13 range. Climbers interested in exploring this area should refer to Marty Bland's *Inland Northwest Rock Climbs* (see Appendix).

BANKS LAKE

Steamboat Rock, a massive basalt butte rising 800 feet above Banks Lake, was used as a landmark by Native Americans and pioneers. While climbing on Steamboat Rock isn't anything to get excited about, there is a wealth of granitic rock at Banks Lake (and some great winter ice climbing), which has made this area a very popular desert venue.

Type of climbing: The routes are a mix of cracks (some of which need cleaning) and bolted sport routes on mostly solid desert granodiorite, including some traditional leads and multipitch routes, ranging from 5.4 to 5.13, the majority of which can be approached more traditionally (i.e., via land). You don't need a boat to climb here, but if you have a canoe or small boat, you can enjoy the novelty of boat climbing without incurring the expense of renting.

Brief history of area: The area was for many years known only by word of mouth. An article in the June 1987 issue of *Climbing* magazine revealed the "New American Genre" of "boat climbing," that is, approaching routes from the water on the many granite domes sticking up from Banks Lake. At the time, a reported thirty-five routes had been established, nearly all of them requiring a boat or canoe. Since then, many more routes were developed on the larger land-based formations, and the area now has more than 160 routes, most of which are nowhere near the water.

Seasons and climate: It can be insufferably hot here during the summer months, and bitterly cold during the winter months (hence the popularity of this area with ice climbers). The best seasons are late winter/early spring and late fall/early winter.

Precautions and regulations: Although the rock is mostly solid, there is loose rock on some formations, particularly higher up on Highway Rock and in Northrup Canyon. Some of the sport routes inexplicably lack top anchors, and some of the older bolts may be in need of replacement. If you are boat climbing in a canoe, beware of the wakes of passing pleasure boats, which have the potential to swamp you. Also beware of rattlesnakes (which are abundant in this area), ticks, bees, wasps, hornets, and poison ivy, especially on the approach to Highway Rock, and at the base of many of the routes, and especially in spring and through the summer. On some routes, the primary difficulty is managing your rope to keep it out of the poison ivy.

Most of the climbing areas in the Northrup Canyon area are in a Natural Area Preserve (NAP), which is off-limits to all forms of recreation. To find out what is within the NAP, contact the state park ranger station. There are plenty of routes at Highway Rock, Steamboat Rock State Park, the golf course, "camp crag," and on the lake to keep climbers busy without invading the NAP. Accessing the golf course crags

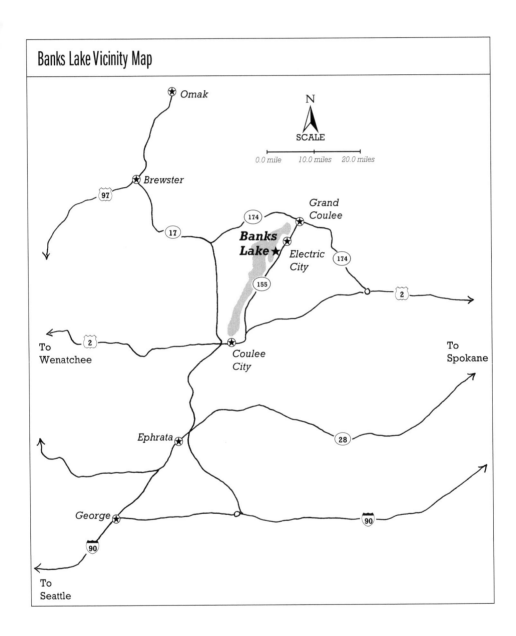

Banks Lake Vicinity Map

Omak

N

SCALE

0.0 mile   10.0 miles   20.0 miles

Brewster

97

17

Grand
Coulee

174

**Banks
Lake** ★

Electric
City

174

155

2

2

To
Wenatchee

Coulee
City

To
Spokane

Ephrata

28

George

90

90

To
Seattle

Banks Lake Detail Map

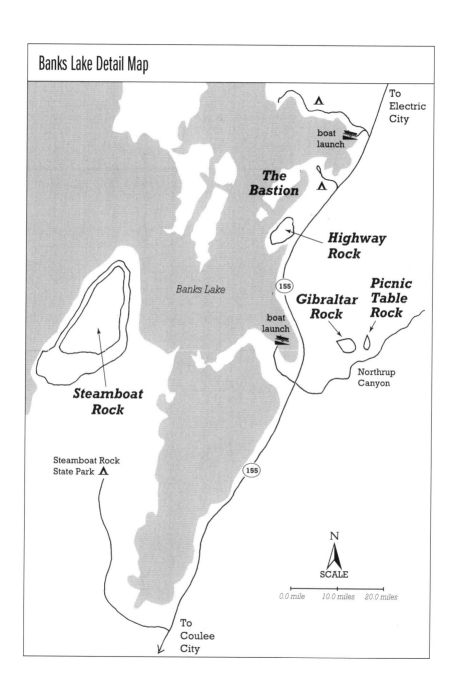

To
Electric
City

boat
launch

The
Bastion

Highway
Rock

Picnic
Table
Rock

Banks Lake

(155)

Gibraltar
Rock

boat
launch

Steamboat
Rock

Northrup
Canyon

Steamboat Rock
State Park

(155)

N

SCALE

0.0 mile   10.0 miles   20.0 miles

To
Coulee
City

requires crossing private property; be polite and keep a low profile, please.

Gear and other considerations: There is a good mix of trad and sport climbs at Banks Lake. If you're a trad climber, bring a comprehensive rack. If you're a sport climber, bring quick draws. Some reported sport routes have camouflaged bolts that can be difficult to spot from below. Some sport routes don't have anchors, so bring some gear just in case. There's enough loose rock to justify wearing a helmet here even if you usually don't. Deep-water soloing is popular on several cliffs, but be sure your landing is clear of watercraft, swimmers, and submerged rocks before you commit.

Camping and accommodations: Overnight camping is available at Steamboat Rock State Park and at other more primitive campsites in the vicinity (Jones Bay Campground just north of Big Rock is the closest). Call Steamboat Rock State Park for information about camping fees and reservations, and about boat launch fees (see Appendix). Basic services are available in Electric City, including food and lodging.

Emergency services: In case of emergency, flag down a passing boat, dial 911, or contact the state park rangers for assistance. The nearest hospital is in Grand Coulee; there is also a hospital in Coulee City.

Other guidebooks: Although many Banks Lake climbers of old would have preferred that the area not be published in a guidebook, there are now at least three guidebooks to the area, so the "secret" is definitely out. David Whitelaw's *Weekend Rock Washington* reveals a dozen or so routes in the 5.7 to 5.10 range, including some of the classic boat routes and a few on Highway Rock, as well as the beta on

getting there, camping, what kind of boat you need, and so on. *Inland Northwest Rock Climbs* (Bland) and *Rock Climbs of Central Washington* (LaBelle) provide more complete route information. You could probably get along without a guidebook and just explore the area—climb the routes that look feasible; talk to other climbers (if you see any); paddle around to the domes and climb, toprope, and boulder; do some deep-water soloing; and jump in the lake—having an adventure like climbers used to do back in the day, before guidebooks "ruined the place."

Finding the crags: Banks Lake is located between Coulee City and Electric City (not far south of Grand Coulee Dam) on WA 155, under two hours from Spokane or Wenatchee via US 2. You can't miss Highway Rock, and the turnoff to Gibraltar Rock is easy to spot.

Highway Rock

Highway Rock (aka Roadside Rock) is the big granitic dome west of the highway. You can't miss it. It has routes ranging from short to full-pitch sport climbs and multipitch face, crack, and slab routes on all sides. The south, north, and east sides of the rock are accessible by land; the west side can be approached by land during low water, or by canoe for those who want to go to the trouble. Routes are described as you approach from the parking area, the big turnout directly east of rock and moving clockwise around the east and west faces. Most of the routes (even many of the cracks) are bolted with anchors; lower or rappel as you deem appropriate or scramble off the top. A popular outing is to work clockwise around the rock from the highway face to the lakeside, eventually linking pitches up the west-side buttresses to the

Roadside Rock–Southeast Face

top, then scrambling down from the top. Be watchful for poison ivy at the base of the routes, especially on the highway side, ticks, and rattlesnakes.

1. Rolling Blackout (5.12a) ★ The approach trail reaches the rock at the toe of a buttress. Just a few steps up and right is this bolted line up an overhanging wall and roof above. Clip your way past the roof and up the slab above. There are two variation starts, one that traverses right across a blocky ledge, the other attacking the overhangs more directly. Pro: quickdraws. (FA: Marty Bland)

2. Black Roofs (5.11?) About 30 feet up the trail from the base of the wall are two bolt lines through the low, blackish overhangs. Pull past the overhangs, then climb the steep slab above. Rating uncertain, not sure if these are projects or completed routes. They aren't tagged, so give them a try. Pro: quickdraws.

3. Downtown (5.10a or 5.6 A0) ★ A two-pitch slab route up the ramp below and right of the prominent red roofs. Traverse across big blocks and flakes to gain the corner (bolts: one guide reports a 5.10a move, or pull on the bolt to make the route 5.6 A0, but could go at 5.6), then angle out onto the easy but airy ramp and up. Best to rappel down *Washington Pass*. Pro: quickdraws.

4. Tom Thumb's Blues (aka Red Roof Inn) (5.10b) ★★ Start up the slab as for *Downtown*, then follow bolts straight up toward the roofs. The route angles right, following a line of weakness through the intimidating overhangs. Pro: quickdraws.

5. Washington Pass (5.8) ★ The blocky crack and dihedral system directly right of the bolted *Short Circuit* arête. Originally reported as a trad route, it appears to have substantially, if not fully, bolted. A second

pitch is reported at about the same grade, which can be continued to the top of Highway Rock. Otherwise, rappel the route. Pro: quickdraws; possibly also gear to 4 inches.

6. Short Circuit (5.12c) ★★ The steep, long, bolted face climb leading up the prow left of the *Washington Pass* dihedral. Had draws in place as of fall 2018. The crux comes 20 feet below the anchors. Don't blow it! Pro: quickdraws. (FA: Marty Bland)

7. Playing God (5.10b) ★ The dihedral left of *Short Circuit*, bolted as an approach pitch for the next route, although it can also be used to approach the other routes starting from the ledge. Pro: quickdraws.

8. Marty Bland's Ego (5.12a) ★★ A bolted face pitch leading directly from the anchors of *Playing God* to the *Short Circuit* anchors. Pro: quickdraws.

9. Even Better Than the Real Thing (5.9) ★ A bolted dihedral left of *Playing God*; an easier way to reach the big ledge. Pro: quickdraws.

10. Traditional Values (5.8) ★ The obvious crack splitting the wall above the terrace. Not to be confused with the chimney in the corner, which can also be climbed. Pro: gear to 4 inches.

11. Banks Lake Marathon (5.10c) ★★ A three-pitch linkup of 5.10c pitches starting with the bolted face left of *Even Better Than the Real Thing*, then the bolted face left of *Traditional Values* (called *Land of a Thousand Stances*), and finally the bolted pitch leading right and up corners from the *Thousand Stances* anchors to the top. Pro: quickdraws.

12. Brownout (5.11c) ★★ A steep sport route through a roof and up the juggy buttress/arête to the right of the obvious black streak. Pro: quickdraws. (FA: Marty Bland)

13. Blackout (5.12a) ★ Connect the bolts up the prominent black streak. Pro: quickdraws.

14. Teenage Criminal (5.11c) ★ A bolted route between the black streak and right-facing flake. Scramble up a brushy ramp to reach the bolts, or rappel in from above to avoid the choss. Pro: quickdraws.

15. Young Lions (5.11c) ★★ The first bolted route past the choss as you continue left on the approach. Starts about 20 feet right of *Red Arête* via a left-facing flake, then goes up a bolted crack. Pro: quickdraws. (FA: Vince LaBelle)

16. Flower Power (5.11a) ★★ The bolted face just right of *Red Arête*. Pro: quickdraws.

17. Bono (aka Red Arête) (5.8+) ★★★ The nice rust-colored arête just right of the big offwidth; one of the most popular routes at Banks Lake. Pro: quickdraws.

18. Allergic Reaction (5.12a) ★ A bolted line starting up the gaping offwidth left of *Red Arête*, then squeezed up the overhanging face and arête to the anchors. Pro: quickdraws. (FA: Vince LaBelle)

19. The Edge (5.8) ★★ The bolted route up the right side of the slab to the left of *Allergic Reaction*. Pro: quickdraws.

20. Reflecting Depths Imbibe (5.8) ★★ The leftmost of two bolted routes on the rust-colored slab on the south side of the rock. Pro: quickdraws. (FA: Leland Wyndham)

The following routes are located above the *Red Arête*, either on the approach to or starting from the large terrace below the upper headwalls area. Approach via the gully and slabs on the left. A scrambling route can be ferreted out to reach the terrace and other headwall routes.

21. Renaldo (5.7) ★ Scramble up the gully left of the *Red Arête* formation to the base of this bolted slab pitch, which provides access to the big terrace below the upper headwall. Pro: quickdraws.

22. White Crystal (5.12c) ★★★ A steep line up a quartz dike and seam on the right side of the headwall above the terrace. Pro: quickdraws.

23. Secrets and Liebacks (5.9) ★★ Layback up the crack in the corner. An easier traverse pitch can be used to exit below the crux second pitch. Pro: quickdraws.

Southwest Buttress

The following routes are located on the Southwest Buttress of Highway Rock, which forms the left skyline of the formation as viewed from the highway as you approach from the south. Approach from the south side, hiking past the *Red Arête* area and over the ridge, then either scrambling down a brushy gully to the base of the wall at lake level and climbing one of the routes on Aqualine Wall, or by going up and over ledges.

24. Supprehension (5.9+) ★ To reach this and the next two routes, hike down the obvious gully to the lakeshore, then traverse north until you are stopped by a blocky granite wall rising straight out of the lake. This is the first (rightmost) of the three bolted lines on this wall, with some interesting, varied climbing. If you fall on the first few moves, you'll probably end up wet. If you fall higher up, you could drag your belayer into the lake. Pro: quickdraws.

25. Prophylactic Crowbar (5.9) ★ The middle bolted route climbing up and past a gray dike. The middle anchor may consist of just one bolt, so it may be best to combine

Roadside Rock–South Side

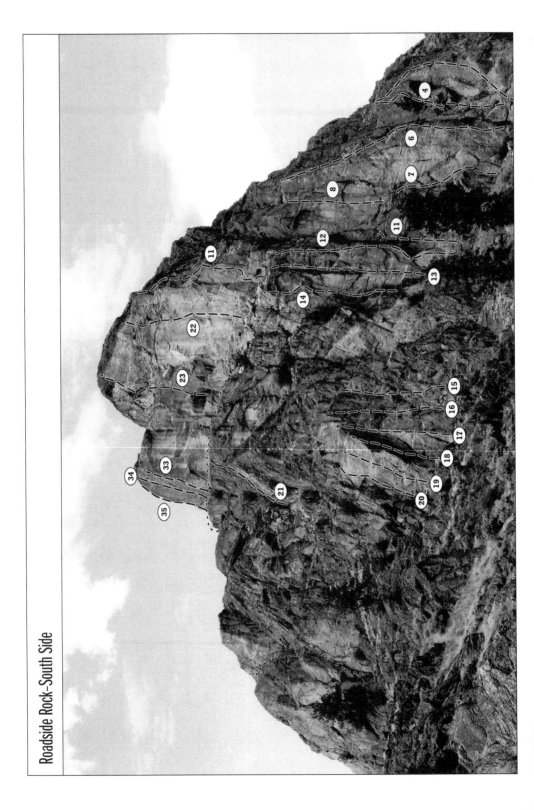

in one pitch. Descend from anchors or continue to the top. Pro: quickdraws.

26. Aqualine (5.9) ★★ The leftmost bolted line up the blocky arête, with a second pitch up the left edge of the headwall. This route is pictured on the cover of the local guide, so it's popular. When the water level of the lake is high, it's trickier to traverse to the start of the route. Pro: quickdraws.

There are several routes on the slabby buttress just above and left of the Aqualine Wall. They are often approached by climbing one of the 5.9 sport routes directly from the lake, as the gully approach is the easiest access to climbing and provides for a convenient, quality multipitch experience with a walk-off descent. Alternatively, scramble in however you can manage it, or rappel from anchors at the top of the buttress.

27. Hello Dalai (5.10a) ★ Not shown. Scramble 30 feet up the gully directly above the Aqualine Wall until you find bolts on the right. Connect the bolts for a long pitch or two short pitches up the buttress above. Pro: quickdraws.

28. Creamsicle Buttress (5.8) ★★ From the top of the Aqualine Wall, traverse left on ledges about 50 feet to the base of a clean, bolted slab. Some easy climbing leads to the first bolt, then connect the bolts as they meander left and up to join *Danton* just below its anchors. Or do the direct finish (5.10b), which follows bolts more directly up the slab. Pro: quickdraws.

29. Danton (5.8+) ★★ Continue left past the start of *Creamsicle Buttress* to the base of the big arête/corner system in the middle of the *Creamsicle Buttress*. Climb up the left side of a bolted flake then go right, making a dirty traverse to a short corner and anchors. Rope drag can be a problem on this pitch. Continue up the scruffy dihedral crack above. Other variations to this route are reported at 5.8 to 5.10 in difficulty. Pro: quickdraws; gear to 2 inches.

30. Lafayette Arête (5.11a) ★ Start as for *Danton* but cut left at the top of the flake and head up the obvious rounded arête. Pro: quickdraws.

31. Robespierre (5.10a) ★★ This sport route starts near the lone pine tree on the ledge left of *Lafayette Arête*, climbing up to and past a downward-pointing flake to anchors midway up the wall. There's rumor of a second pitch through the headwall above. Pro: quickdraws.

32. Marat (5.10d) ★ Left of *Robespierre*, climb flakes angling left, then up to anchors halfway up the wall. Descend from the anchors or continue up a second (crux) pitch that skirts the headwall on the left. Pro: quickdraws.

From the top of *Creamsicle Buttress* you can scramble up easier rock to the base of the headwall, which has three good routes, then traverse over to *Airy but Easy* or *Rashomon* to reach the summit. These routes can also be reached by scrambling up the gully and ledges left and up from *Red Arête*.

33. Calanques (5.10a) ★★ The rightmost bolted line on the right edge/arête of the headwall. Pro: quickdraws.

34. Money (5.10c) ★★ The middle bolted line on the headwall, closely left of *Calanques*. Pro: quickdraws.

35. Whatever It Costs You (5.12a) ★★ The leftmost bolted line, climbing the highest, steepest section of the headwall. Thin but fun. Pro: quickdraws.

The following routes climb the distinct buttress forming the prow of the summit

Roadside Rock–West Face

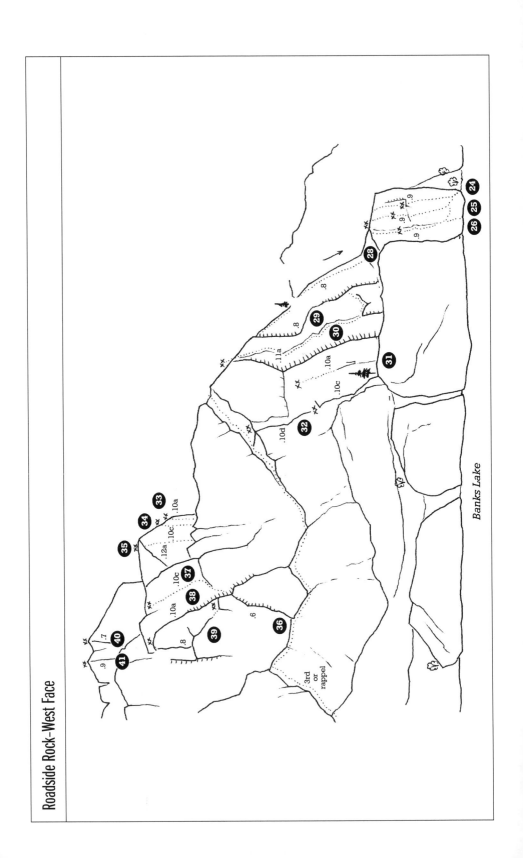

Banks Lake

Roadside Rock–Upper East Face

formation, culminating in two fantastically positioned arête climbs on the summit block. The base of the buttress can be approached by scrambling via ledges across the top of *Creamsicle Buttress*, or via another more devious scrambling approach.

36. Kurosawa (5.6) From the base of the buttress below the *Rashomon* arête, climb the bolted ramp/corner up and right to a ledge left of a dihedral. Pro: quickdraws.

37. Throne of Blood (5.10c) ★ From just below the *Kurosawa* anchors, continue right across the dihedral and up a ramp, then directly up the slabby wall above. Pro: quickdraws.

38. Yojimbo (5.10a) ★ A logical second pitch of *Kurosawa* that seems to have its own name. Continue up the bolted corner/crack system directly above the first anchors to the ledge below the start of *Rashomon*. Pro: quickdraws.

39. Seven Samurai (5.8) ★ Another second pitch option to *Kurosawa*, angling left from the anchors up the slab and cracks to anchors shared with *Yojimbo*. Pro: quickdraws.

40. Airy but Easy (5.7) ★★ An airy romp up a low-angle arête on the west face of the summit block. To get there, either climb up the *Kurosawa* buttress, link pitches up from *Aqualine* and *Creamsicle Buttress*, or scramble in from above *Red Arête*. Follow bolts up the slabby rock, staying right when two bolt lines diverge. Pro: quickdraws.

41. Rashomon (5.9) ★★★ The striking, airy, photogenic arête on the left, a proud finish to your Highway Rock west face linkup. Pro: quickdraws.

Circling back around to the highway side of Highway Rock, the following routes are located on the steep wall visible from the

parking area about 100 meters right (north) of the roadside wall as viewed from the parking area. Approach via a brushy trail that forks right after crossing the swamp. The routes are described from left to right as you pass them while approaching from the parking area. Descend from anchors.

42. Boo Ya to Babylon (5.10c) ★ A bolted crack leads up to and around the left side of a prominent hanging flake. Pro: quickdraws.

43. Unnamed (5.9) ★ Climb up to, then up the left-facing dihedral below the big flake. Pro: all gear to anchors.

44. Rock the Casbah (5.9) ★ Connect bolts up the steep face immediately right of the flake. Pro: quickdraws.

45. Mr. Newton (5.11b) ★★ The leftmost of a trio of bolted routes climbing a brownish face visible from the parking area. Each climb ends at one of the closely spaced anchors at the top of the cliff. Pro: quickdraws.

46. Eccentricity (5.12a) ★★ The middle bolted line, passing a roof at mid-height. Pro: quickdraws.

47. Electric Shitty (5.12b) ★★ The rightmost bolted line, angling left onto a brown face. Pro: quickdraws.

The Bastion

The Bastion is a weathered, slabby granite cliff rising out of the lake on the southwest tip of the craggy peninsula jutting out west of Roadside Rock. It has several of Banks Lake's most popular canoe routes, including the area classic, *Bassomatic*, which gets most of the traffic. Anchors are in place atop most of the routes, allowing one to lead and lower back into the canoe. Since the routes are

The Bastion

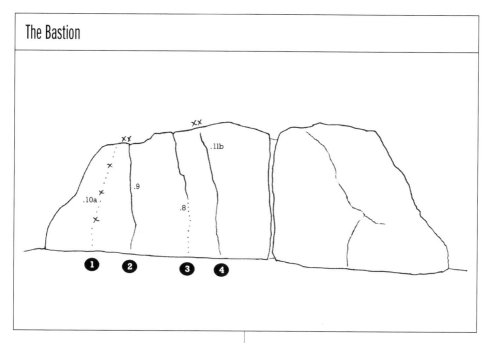

above water, they are popular with the deep-water solo crowd, although they aren't quite steep enough to guarantee you won't hit the slab on the way down.

1. Hook Line & Sinker (5.10a) ★ A steep, partly bolted face route on the left side of the main wall. Pro: quickdraws; nuts and cams to 2.5 inches.

2. Bassomatic (5.9) ★★ The must-do route at Banks Lake—a thin crack on the left side of the wall. Pro: to 3 inches. (FA: Chris Greyell, David Whitelaw 1984)

3. Half-Bassed (5.8) ★ A crack in the middle of the wall, with a bouldery start. Pro: to 3 inches.

4. Perfect Basser (5.11b) ★ A thin crack on the right side of the wall route that starts hard and gets harder. Pro: to 2 inches.

Tent and Awning Rock

The Tent and Awning formations lie on the east side of the island directly west of the campground. The routes are short, but if you already have a canoe, add them to your voyage. *After the Gold Rush* (the obvious bolted wall, 5.10c ★★★) is the best line on the crag, but the arête and overhanging face to the right have been climbed and are popular with deep-water soloists. Descend from anchors or take the plunge.

Golf Course Wall

The Golf Course Wall is a small, slabby buttress with some of the best rock at Banks Lake, but sadly only a few routes. Several other short cliffs in the area have developed routes. To approach, take the golf course/airport road west from WA 155, then turn left on Kruk Road. Continue just over a mile past the last fairway until you see Golf Course Wall on the right. A primitive road leads from an old sheep pen to the base of the rock. This is private property, so be respectful.

1. Right Side (5.10a) ★ No topo. A bolted line up the slabby face on the right. Looks harder than it is. Pro: quickdraws.

2. Center Crack (5.11a) ★★ No topo. The superb thin crack and face route splitting the dome. Although the route follows a crack, there's a lot of thin face climbing. Pro: mostly thin nuts and cams to 1 inch; a couple of pieces up to 3 inches.

3. Left Arête (5.10a) ★ No topo. A bolted line up the slabby face on the left. Descend from anchors atop the route. Pro: mostly nuts and cams to 2 inches, plus a 3- and 4-inch cam.

Gibraltar Rocks

The Gibraltar Rocks are about 1 mile south of Roadside Rock on WA 155, up Northrup Canyon Road. There are two Gibraltar Rocks (Gibraltar Rock proper and Picnic Table Rock), with a dozen or so decent routes in the 5.6 to 5.12 range on steep, mostly decent granodiorite or basalt, although the main attraction is *Dr. Ceuse*, which climbs a bold arête on the edge of a large column on the west face of Picnic Table Rock. Most climbers park at the "equestrian area," the first left turn past the private driveway, although it is reserved for the horsey set. If it's in use, park at the start of the hiking trail a little farther down the road. Climb only in the established areas, as the area west of the equestrian area is private property. A parks pass is required to park in this area.

Gibraltar Rock

Gibraltar Rock is the big granite monolith that grabs your attention as you drive up Northrup Canyon Road. It has a handful of good routes and some decent bouldering. Stay on the south and east sides of the rock to avoid trespassing onto private property. Beware of poison ivy, which runs riot in late spring and summer along the base of the wall and in gullies on the descent.

1. Southwest Arête (5.8-5.9) A two-pitch route up the slabby cracks on the left skyline arête. Several variations possible. Walk off the back. Pro: quickdraws.

2. Flight from Urushiol (5.11b) ★ A sport route up the dihedral on the left edge of the main wall of Gibraltar Rock. Quality technical stemming. By now there may be a second pitch. Pro: quickdraws.

3. Night in Tunisia (5.12c) ★ Start up the slight corner in the middle of the overhanging wall, then face climb to the anchors. Pro: quickdraws.

4. How Homer Got His Groove Back (5.10b) ★★ The most popular route on the wall, climbing the steep slab with thin, technical moves that keep you engaged all the way to the anchors. Pro: quickdraws. (FA: Vince La Belle)

5. Fusion (5.12b) ★★ A three-pitch route up the prow of the formation. The first pitch (5.12a) is popular, and most climbers lower from the first anchors. Another hard (crux) pitch follows, then an easier pitch to the top. Pro: quickdraws.

6. Don't Beta Me (5.10a) ★ A right-leaning bolted flake and corner system. Since the anchors are so far to the right of the start of the route, it isn't easy to lower to clean the

Gibraltar Rock

Picnic Table Rock

pitch. A second should follow and lower off. Pro: quickdraws.

7. Baptism by Whipper (5.12c) ★ Around the corner from *Don't Beta Me* is this seriously overhanging route. Pro: quickdraws.

Picnic Table Rock

This formation is immediately east of Gibraltar Rock. It has several routes, but the only route that's on anybody's tick list is *Dr. Ceuse*. The approach to the routes on the right side of the cliff involves traversing around the left side of the giant boulder below the wall, then tunneling upward. Alternatively, a 5.6 bolted route leads up from behind the chimney to a ledge that gains access to these routes. A couple of other easier routes (5.4 to 5.7) are on the slabby wall behind the boulder. There are also a few trad routes at the left end of the formation.

1. Tower to the People (5.10b) ★ Climb the left edge of the pillar / face, then up a crack to anchors. Pro: quickdraws.

2. The Marriage of Figaro (5.12b) ★ A pumping sport route up the buttress left of the overhangs. Pro: quickdraws.

3. Macho Plastic Bullshit (5.13a) ★ Another bolted route through the roofs. Pro: quickdraws.

4. Project (5.13?) ★ A bolted line through the roofiest section of the roofs. Had fixed draws in fall 2018 Uncertain whether it's a project or completed route. Looks hard. Pro: quickdraws.

5. Cato and Beatrice (5.11c) ★ The bolted face left of the *Dr. Ceuse* pillar. Pro: quickdraws.

6. Dr. Ceuse (5.10a) ★★★ Easily the best and most popular route on the cliff. Start up *Jugoslavia*, then finish up the arête on the right side of the colorful pillar. Pro: quickdraws.

7. Jugoslavia (5.9) ★ The steep bolted corner left of the chimney. Has a reported loose block that could be dangerous. Pro: quickdraws.

8. Earnest Stemmingway (5.6) ★ Stem your way up the bolted chimney. Pro: quickdraws.

9. The Pit and the Pendulum (5.10a) ★ Climb the bolted arête right of the chimney. Pro: quickdraws.

10. The Second Joy of My Life (5.8) ★ A sport pitch on the slab right of the chimney. It's something to do while you wait your turn on *Dr. Ceuse*. Pro: quickdraws.

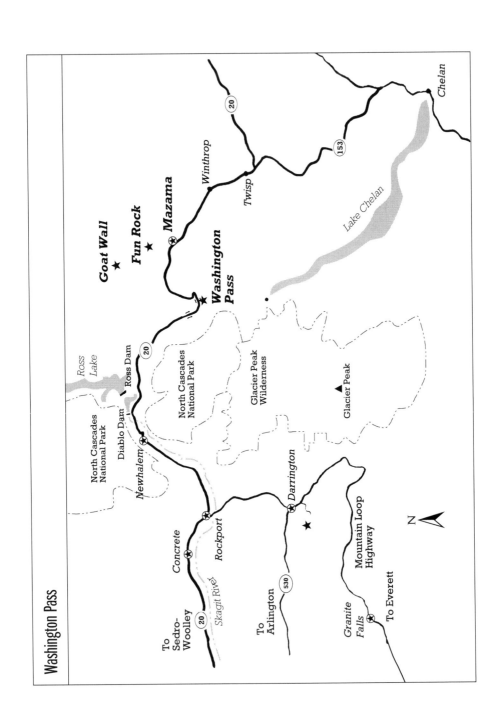

Washington Pass

There is little doubt that the routes on Liberty Bell and the Early Winters Spires include some of the best alpine rock climbs in North America. However, because these are mountain routes, subject to mountain weather, with snow and ice on approaches and descents—and sometimes on the routes themselves—a more serious level of commitment is needed. Therefore, this area lies at the fringe of the intended scope of this guide. This is, after all, a guide to rock climbs, not mountain climbs. Nevertheless, this area is included here because its roadside location and unparalleled high-mountain ambience combine to lure many rock climbers from the safety of their lowland crags for some great alpine rock climbing.

Type of climbing: The routes included in this section are all located on the Liberty Bell massif, consisting of the namesake Liberty Bell Mountain (7,720 feet), and continuing south along a jagged crest including Concord Tower (7,560 feet) and Lexington Tower (7,560 feet), and the more pronounced North (7,760 feet) and South (7,807 feet) Early Winters Spires. This cluster of granite peaks offers an impressive assortment of alpine rock climbs, from the easier classic *Beckey Route* (II, 5.6) to the extremes of *Liberty Crack* (V, 5.13a or 5.10b A3). The routes are on clean, mostly solid granite, from three to a dozen pitches long, with reasonably short approaches and reasonably uncomplicated descents.

While most of the attention received by the Liberty Bell group is focused on the impressive east face of Liberty Bell, be assured that there are worthy routes on the other peaks, too, including several nearby peaks and walls that are not included in this guide. Still, it would be a fair estimate that most of the traffic is on *Liberty Crack* and the *Beckey Route,* and for good reason.

Brief history of area: Early ascents of many of these routes were made without the benefit of a trans-Cascade highway. If not for the close proximity of WA 20 and the establishment of North Cascades National Park, this area definitely would not have been included in this guide. As it is, many fine alpine rock routes in the North Cascades and elsewhere are excluded from this guide simply because they are too far from a road.

Lack of easy access did not stop early pioneers from visiting the Liberty Bell massif. In 1937 Kenneth Adam, Raffi Bedayn, and Kenneth Davis summited South Early Winters Spire via the nontechnical *Southwest Couloir* route. History has it that they intended to climb Liberty Bell, but made the mistake of climbing the highest summit of the group instead. The honor of being the first to summit Liberty Bell went to none other than Fred Beckey, who with partners Jerry O'Neil and Charles Welsh made the ascent in 1946. Beckey, one of the most prodigious new-route pioneers in Cascade

A climber on *West Face* (5.9), North Early Winters Spire, Washington Pass FOREST WOODWARD

alpine climbing history, went on to establish many more firsts in the Washington Pass area.

The area's most famous route, *Liberty Crack,* was first climbed by Steve Marts, Don McPherson, and Fred Stanley in 1965. *Liberty Crack,* the *Beckey Route* on Liberty Bell, and the *South Arête* on South Early Winters Spire (also established by Beckey along with brother Helmy in 1942), were firmly established as area classics long before the North Cascades Highway opened in 1972. After that seminal event, the floodgates opened and many new routes were climbed, although until the late 1980s, climbing at Washington Pass remained largely within the realm of alpinism. Since then, with the freeing of several classic lines and the establishment of several new and equally classic free routes on the Liberty Bell massif and other granite peaks nearby, Washington Pass has evolved into what is widely considered the best of the Pacific Northwest's alpine rock venues.

Seasons and climate: Climbing is possible from May through October most years. Winter ascents are also possible, but approaches are complicated by closure of the North Cascades Highway during winter. For rock climbing, the best season is late June through September, with autumn being the preferred season and, alas, the most crowded. During early season, snow and ice must be dealt with on approaches and descents—and occasionally on the routes, too.

Precautions and regulations: Unlike most of the other areas included in this guide, the Liberty Bell routes are mountain routes, subject to mountain weather and other objective hazards not ordinarily encountered at lowland cragging areas. Many routes include sections of snow or ice on the approaches, and sometimes on the routes. Most descents involve rappelling and downclimbing gullies filled with snow and loose rock. Although the rock is mostly solid, there are plenty of loose flakes and blocks, and a few sections of rotten rock. Loose rock should be expected on most routes, and helmets are highly recommended.

Weather is the biggest variable. Rain, snow, wind, lightning, surprise storms—expect them all, and be prepared. Rain gear is a must on any climb here, and if you aren't certain of your speed on a given route—particularly the longer routes—be prepared for a bivouac. Many a party has been forced into an unplanned bivouac because they overestimated their speed and ability. And while a cold night out on a ledge without food or water will certainly be memorable, take heed if it doesn't sound like your kind of fun.

Also, if you are spending the night below the cliffs prior to your climb, bring insect repellent, especially during the summer months, when the mosquitos and biting flies are at their peak voracity.

Gear and other considerations: A standard multipitch rack should suffice for most of the routes. Bring a comprehensive selection of nuts, TCUs, and cams up to 3 or 4 inches for most routes, and lots of slings to help reduce rope drag, which should be expected on all routes. A few routes involve aid climbing on or free climbing past bolt ladders, so bring plenty of quickdraws. Double ropes are required for all rappelling descents.

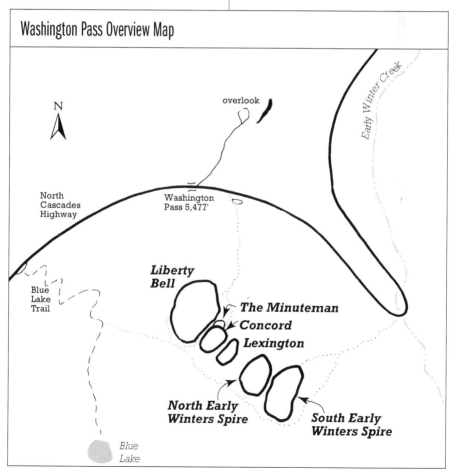

Washington Pass Overview Map

Camping and accommodations: Since the Washington Pass area is part of North Cascades National Park, camping is allowed only in designated campgrounds. Most climbers drive to Mazama, only 20 miles east, and either camp out at Early Winters Campground or bivouac somewhere in the vicinity. The nearest store is in Mazama. The nearest gas station is in Winthrop. Refer to the Mazama chapter for details about camping and accommodations.

Emergency services: In case of emergency, dial 911. The nearest phone is in Mazama, 20 miles east on WA 20. Packing a cellular phone along might be a good idea, just in case.

Guide services/local equipment suppliers: Mazama Mountaineering in Mazama (see Appendix).

Other guidebooks: This guide offers only a brief overview of some of the more accessible and popular routes in this area. Washington Pass is high, mountainous terrain, not a local crag. Climbers visiting this area are urged to consult other guidebooks and online sources prior to climbing here, where you will find up-to-date weather and snow conditions, trip reports, gear recommendations, detailed route descriptions and topos, loose rock warnings, and photos that can help you approach, locate, and follow your destination route. These sources include the following:

Mountain Project Washington Pass Rock Climbing page (good route information, photos, trip reports)

Supertopo Washington Pass page (more good route information, photos, trip reports)

Nicholson, Ian. *Washington Pass Climbing.* Supertopo 2012.

Herrington, Blake. *Cascades Rock: 160 Best Multipitch Climbs of All Grades.* 2016.

Finding the crags: If you are coming from eastern Washington, head for Wenatchee or Okanogan. From Wenatchee, head north on US 97 to Chelan and continue north to Pateros, then northeast on WA 153, then north on WA 20 through Twisp and Winthrop, all the way past Mazama and up to Washington Pass. From Okanogan, head west on WA 20 all the way to Washington Pass. If you are coming from western Washington, follow I-5 to WA 20, then head east along the North Cascades Highway over Rainy Pass to Washington Pass.

Approaching the routes is fairly straightforward. The east face routes are best approached directly from the Washington Pass overlook turnoff, where a crude trail ascends across from the pullout. However, it is very difficult to approach the Early Winters Spires this way, due to an obstructing buttress. The west face routes are approached via Blue Lake Trail, which begins from a turnout just west of Washington Pass. A climbers' trail breaks off from the main trail where the trail bends east toward the lake. The east faces of Early Winters Spires may be approached via a trail leading south from a sharp bend in the highway just east of Washington Pass. Trail improvements were completed in 2018, and the old climbers' trail was rerouted in a few places to avoid further erosion and degredation of the alpine wilderness setting, so please stay on the new trail.

Washington Pass Overview

LIBERTY BELL

Liberty Bell Mountain is the northernmost summit of the Liberty Bell massif, an impressive, bell-shaped shaft with a striking 1,200-foot east face. There is no easy way to the top, and that, combined with access problems prior to 1972 (when the highway was completed), and the fact that Liberty Bell is not the highest peak of the group, probably account for the fact that Liberty Bell was not climbed until 1946, when Fred Beckey, Jerry O'Neil, and Charles Welsh made the ascent. The original route is the fastest and thus the most popular route on Liberty Bell.

While each of Liberty Bell's faces has yielded routes, some free climbs included, its impressive east face has four direct, distinct Grade V climbs, including the classic of all classics, *Liberty Crack*. Liberty Bell has generally sound rock, and most routes follow distinct crack systems. Route-finding is usually not a problem.

The routes are listed from right to left, starting from the south notch and circling clockwise around the mountain. To descend, scramble back down to the notch between the west summit spur and the true summit, then downclimb as far as seems feasible (you may want to rappel from a tree or belay if the going seems a bit risky). Eventually you should find rappel anchors, from which a 150-foot rappel reaches the notch (or two 75-foot rappels if you forgot to bring two

ropes). Beware of jamming your ropes on the last rappel.

1. The Beckey Route (II, 5.6) ★★ The original summit route, and still the most popular route up Liberty Bell. Fred Beckey describes this as "400 feet of distinctly sporting climbing." The route begins some distance up the west gully, traversing left across a ledge system to a chimney. Climb Class 5 chimneys and continue up slabs, past a small roof and up a clean crack to the summit shoulder and up easier slabs to the top. The usual descent is via rappels directly to the notch. Pro: to 4 inches. (FA: Fred Beckey, Jerry O'Neil, Charles Welsh 1946)

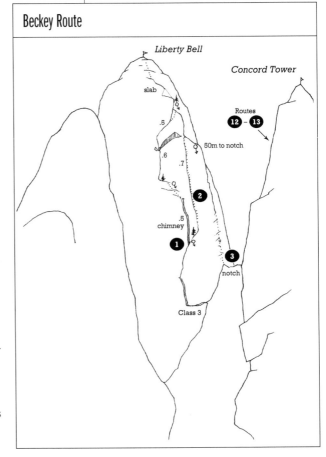

Beckey Route

Liberty Bell

Concord Tower

slab

Routes

12 – 13

.5

.6

50m to notch

.7

2

.5
chimney

1

3

notch

Class 3

2. Rapple Grapple (II, 5.8) ★★ After one pitch of the *Beckey Route,* traverse right on the ledge and ascend a corner system to the top of the buttress, rejoining *Beckey Route* to the summit. A direct first pitch is 5.8, in case the *Beckey Route* is clogged up. Pro: to 3.5 inches.

3. Overexposed (aka Notch Route) (II, 5.8) ★ Ascend directly from the notch following corners and cracks. Make note of rappel anchors on the way up, as this is the line of descent. Pro: to 3 inches.

4. Independence (V, 5.12a) ★★ A formerly imposing big wall aid route on the far right side of the east face of Liberty Bell that has been climbed free. The original free ascent climbed a variation, but the following year the original line was also freed with the addition of a couple of bolts. A detailed history of the route and its pioneering free ascents, as well as pitch-by-pitch detail, can be found on Mountain Project. Pro: duplicate rack to 4 inches; multiple wireds, TCUs and cams from 0.5 to 2.5 inches; slings to avoid rope drag. (FA: Alex Bertulis, Don McPherson 1966; FFA: Steve Risse, Keith Hertel 1991)

5. Live Free or Die™ (IV, 5.12) ★★★. A mostly 5.11 route up the wall between *Independence* and *Thin Red Line,* touted as "an excellent (V5+) boulder problem halfway up the east face of Liberty Bell." The boulder problem (a sideways downclimb dyno, or so it is described) is three pitches up the wall; do the dyno or pendulum past it and

Liberty Bell—West Face

Liberty Bell

Concord Tower

Liberty Bell–East Face, Right Side

Lexington Tower

Concord Tower

Hercan Roofs

M&M Ledge

Liberty Crack

Minutemen descent route

5

6

10   7   4

Liberty Bell—East Face, Left Side

Medusa's Roof

Hercan Roofs

M&M Ledge

4

8

11   10   9   7

6   5   4

Liberty Bell

Concord Tower

Medusa's Roof

Hercan Roof

.7

.7

8

C1

C1

Well Hung Roof

.11b

.11d

Barber Pole III, 5.9

The Minuteman

.10

.10

.10

.10

.10

.10b

C3

C2

.12a

.11c

C3

.11c

.11d

C2

.10d

Lithuanian Lip

.11d

.11b

.12a

.11b

.10a

.6

.10

.10d

.11

8

10

Class 4

11

9

7

4

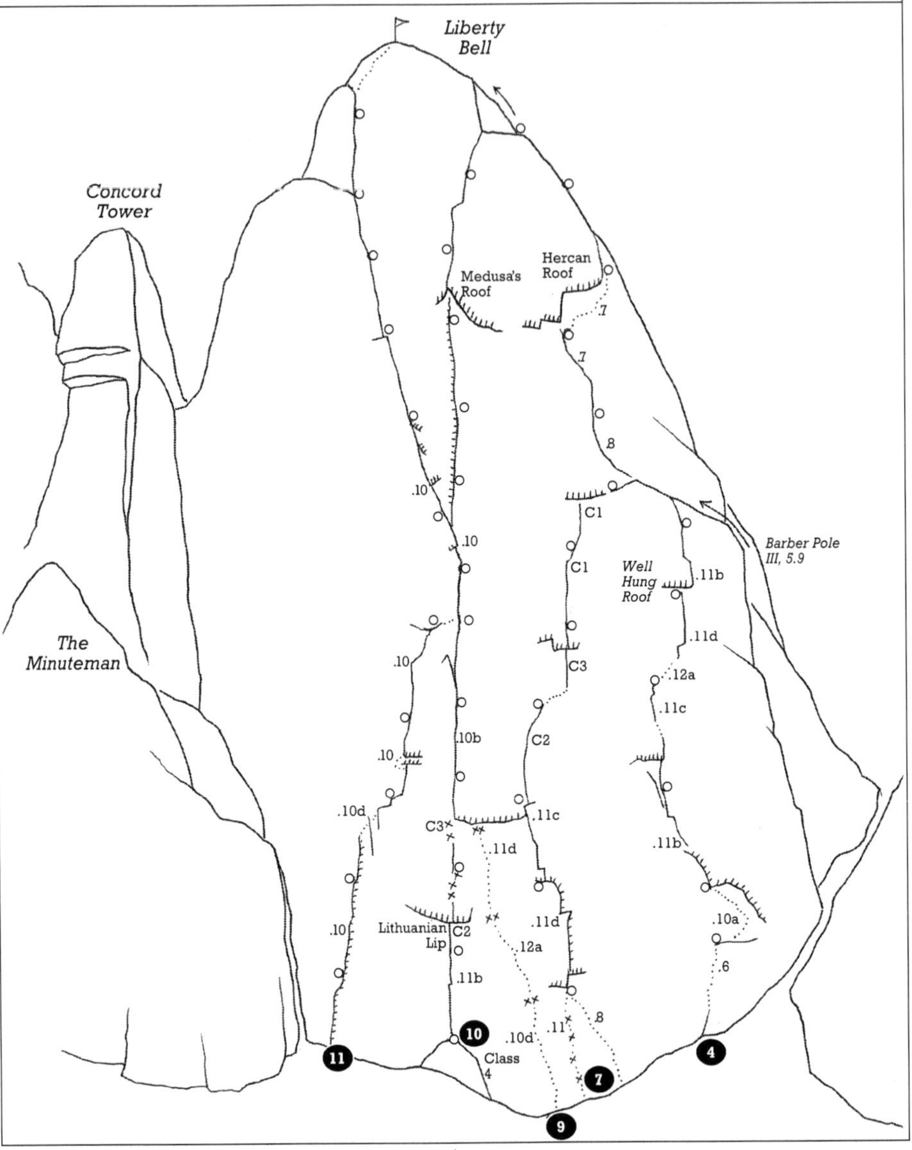

continue up four more 5.10–5.11 pitches to reach M&M Ledge and join *Thin Red Line* to the top. A blow-by-blow description is on Mountain Project. Pro: standard rack to 4 inches, plus doubles tips to #.5 cams, small wires, slings, and quickdraws. (FA: Nathan Hadley, Blake Herrington 2017)

6. Liberty and Injustice for All (IV, 5.12a)

★★★ A variation start to *Thin Red Line*, starting about 30 feet right of that route, following bolted face and thin crack climbing that sounds exceptional. Pitch-by-pitch detail can be found on Mountain Project. Pro:

quickdraws; small cams (TCUs and C3s); wired nuts. (FA: Mikey Schaefer 2014)

7. Thin Red Line (V, 5.12 or 5.9 C3) ★★
One of Washington's classic big aid routes, it is also among the state's best long free routes. This long, technical route climbs the east face of Liberty Bell just right of *Liberty Crack,* following cracks and corners up the blank-looking wall. The entire route goes clean (C3); with pins it is A2+, and now a version of the route goes free at 5.12. Refer to Mountain Project (route description and topo) or one of the Washington Pass guides for explicit details. Pro: for the aid route, double rack to 3.5 inches, including double sets of stoppers, aid nuts, HB brass nut set, small cam hooks, talon, large hook recommended by clean ascent party; bring some pitons just in case. For the free route, cams and nuts to 2 inches, double on the .5- to .75-inch cams; quickdraws. (FA: Jim Madsen, Kim Schmitz 1967; FFA: Mikey Schaefer 2008)

8. A Slave to Liberty (V, 5.13-) ★★★. A remarkable free route up the face between *Liberty Crack* and *Thin Red Line.* Start up the first three pitches of *Freedom or Death,* then continue upward. A detailed topo and route description is available on Mountain Project or refer to one of the current area guides. Pro: to 3 inches, mostly small to 2 inches. (FA: Mikey Schaefer 2016)

9. Freedom or Death (5.12a) ★★★ A free variation start to *Liberty Crack,* climbing the steep wall between *Thin Red Line* and the Lithuanian Lip, joining *Liberty Crack* on pitch four, bypassing all of that route's aid. Touted as a more reasonable free version of the route. The first pitch (5.10d) climbs flakes left of the 5.11a variation start to *Thin Red Line* to anchors. The second pitch (5.12a) climbs the "enduro slab" in a single

60-meter pitch or two shorter pitches to the long roof connecting *Liberty Crack* and *Thin Red Line.* From there, traverse left to join *Liberty Crack.* Pro: to 2 inches; quickdraws and slings. (FA: Eli Helmuth 1996)

10. Liberty Crack (V, 5.10b C3 or 5.13b) ★★★★ This route, climbing a continuous crack system splitting the east face of Liberty Bell Mountain, is considered one of North America's classic alpine rock climbs. The line is easy to see as you approach from below. Locate the Lithuanian Lip and start climbing. Route-finding shouldn't be a problem; just

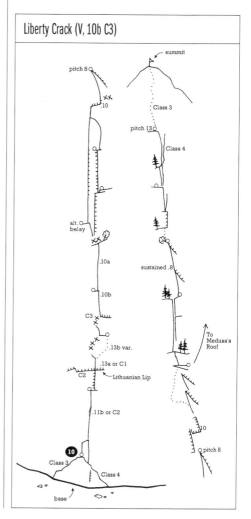

Liberty Crack (V, 10b C3)

follow everybody else up the crack and corner system, which leads pretty much all the way to the summit. The route has been done free (the current free version is rated 5.13b and skirts the bolt ladder below and right), but the climb is 5.10b C3 for most climbers, with only a few clean aid sections on the second and third pitches below and above the Lithuanian Lip. Also, this route made one guidebook's list of unrecommended routes due to old bolts and fixed pins, so be wary of old gear and back it up. Pro: standard rack with doubles in finger sizes; include hooks if aiding. (FA: Steve Marts, Don McPherson, Fred Stanley 1965; FCA: Mark Gallison, Dave Seman, Steve Swenson 1974; FFA: Brooke Sandahl 1991)

11. Freedom Rider (V, 5.10d) ★ The first entirely free breach of Liberty Bell's east face, following the obvious dihedral system left of *Liberty Crack.* After six pitches up the dihedral, the route joins *Liberty Crack* to that route's ninth belay, then climbs the crack and chimney system leading up through Medusa's Roof. Surprisingly, the roof goes free at 5.8. Not as popular what with all of the higher-quality free routes on this wall. Pro: to 4 inches, with lots of cams. (FA: Bryan Burdo, Steve Risse 1988)

CONCORD TOWER

Concord Tower is the sharp peak directly south of Liberty Bell. It is about as high as its twin, Lexington Tower (7,560 feet), but appears higher from some vantages. Descents are best made down the *North Face* rappel route to the Liberty Bell–Concord notch.

12. Patriot Crack (5.8) ★ No topo. The cracks in the middle of the north face of Concord Tower lead straight up from the notch. Not the easiest or most popular route, and has some precarious blocks, but it's an option if the other routes are slammed. Pro: to 4 inches.

13. North Face (II, 5.6) ★★ No topo. The most often climbed summit route on Concord Tower, primarily due to its proximity to the *Beckey Route.* From the Liberty Bell–Concord notch, climb a short, direct crack to a ledge. Traverse right, then up left-trending cracks to the base of the summit block. Finish via a ramp and crack on the left (5.6), or a crack and arête on the right (5.7). Two double-rope rappels down the route reach the notch. Pro: to 4 inches. (FA: Fred Beckey, John Parrott 1956)

14. Cave Route (II, 5.7+) ★★ Begin about 50 feet down the gully from the notch and traverse right across a ledge to a traversing flake. Climb the flake (crux) to a tree, then climb up and left to the namesake cave. Exit the cave and continue up a long slab crack, then easier rock to the top. Pro: to 4 inches. (FA: Ron Burgner, Don McPherson 1968)

THE MINUTEMAN

The Minuteman is a small spire on the east face of Concord Tower. It has one reported route.

15. East Face (III, 5.10b) ★★★ See photo on page 437. Start at the far left toe of the Minuteman formation and climb slabby rock for two pitches past 5.8 overhangs. Angle right across easier rock (some loose) to the base of the upper buttress. Ascend the obvious crack (crux, 5.10b or C1) to a ledge below a roof; pass the roof and continue up the shield via a brilliant crack (5.8). Easier rock leads to the summit. Rappel and downclimb off the back toward the Liberty Bell–Concord gully, then rappel down the gully. Late season is best to avoid snow on the approach and snow patches on the descent. Pro: to 3 inches, mostly small to 2 inches.

LEXINGTON TOWER

Lexington Tower is the next summit southward along the Liberty Bell massif. Routes ascend from either notch, but the best routes are on the tower's east face. Bad rock on the upper east face encourages many climbers to descend without summiting. The standard descent is a walk-off (may need to rappel once or twice) down a loose gully system from the southern base of the summit block. The first gully directly along the base is the wrong gully; take the next gully to the left and downclimb loose rock. Scramble down from the notch toward the west side of the Liberty Bell group until you pick up a climbers' trail.

16. East Face (IV, 5.9 R) ★★ An obvious wide crack line up the east face of Lexington Tower. Begin up the slabs just left of the Lexington–Minuteman gully, climb a corner and traverse ledges left; or start on the far left, some distance up the southeast gully and traverse ledges right. From the left end of the ledges, climb slabs from ledge to ledge, following the easiest or most protectable line (5.8; some runouts). Continue up more of the same, staying on the left side of the face, aiming for the base of the big, left-facing dihedral. Climb the dihedral to a ledge that leads to a higher dihedral, which leads to the first roof (5.8 undercling), then up another dihedral to the gaping chimney right of the major roof. Move right onto the face and traverse a ledge to a flake (5.9). Continue up the widening flake (more 5.9) to an easier chimney (some unprotected climbing). More wide cracks follow, and the route eases to the top. A bit more wide crack and chimney climbing than many modern rock climbers are willing to subject themselves to, but still a fine alpine rock route. Like on other routes on the east side, be wary of old gear

Lexington Tower

false summit

chimney

Concord Tower

class 4

16

class 3

17

and loose rock. Pro: to 3 inches. (FA: Steve Marts, Don McPherson 1966; FFA: Paul Boving and partner 1970s)

17. Tooth and Claw (5.12a) ★ A difficult free route climbing the buttress right of the *East Face* route on Lexington Tower. This route, established on lead from the ground up, has some impressive climbing. The crux slab involves friction and thin-edge face climbing. The route has some unavoidable runouts and rope drag problems, and the last two pitches are reportedly frighteningly loose, which compels many climbers to rappel after six pitches. Pro: to 3 inches; quickdraws; lots of runners. (FA: Steve Risse, Dave Tower 1989)

NORTH EARLY WINTERS SPIRE

This is the northernmost of the impressive twin spires rising at the south end of the Liberty Bell massif. North Early Winters Spire (NEWS) has a couple of excellent, long, free routes that are among the best routes in the area.

To descend from North Early Winters Spire, downclimb south and west from the summit. Multiple rappels lead to the notch between the Early Winters Spires, then scramble and rappel down the couloir to the giant chockstone. A rappel from atop a giant chockstone leads to more downclimbing. When in doubt, rappel.

18. Northwest Corner (aka Boving-Pollack)
(III, 5.9) ★★★ A fine route climbing an impressive dihedral on the left side of the west face. Start via the obvious chimney on the left side of the wall (5.8) and continue up tree-infested ledges to a higher ledge at the base of a pillar. Climb the left side of the pillar, then continue up a left-facing, wide flake/crack system to the summit. Pro: to 4 or 5 inches. (FA: Paul Boving, Steve Pollack 1976)

19. West Face (aka Beckey-Becksted) (III, 5.11a or 5.10a A1) ★★★★ An obvious line up exposed cracks splitting the broad west face. Start via the chimney as for *Northwest Corner*, and continue to the ledge at the base of the pillar. Climb the right side of the pillar, then up cracks and flakes. Traverse right under an exposed flake / arch to gain the upper crack system. A thin crack (crux) and left face traverse lead to a brilliant 5.10 hand crack. A rightward face traverse high up gains the exit crack. Pro: to 4 inches; mostly below 2 inches. (FA: Fred Beckey, Dave Becksted 1965; FFA: Steve Risse, Dave Tower 1985)

20. Labor Pains (III, 5.11a) ★★ A steep, burly route up the right side of the west face of NEWS, climbing up to, then around, the big roofs on the left. The cracks in the middle of the north face of Concord Tower. Not the easiest or most popular route, and has some precarious blocks, but it's an option if the other routes are slammed. Start up the *Chockstone Route*, then angle left to the base of a shallow corner—the first crux—with a wide finish. Pitch four skirts the big roofs on the left and is described as "fierce," but eases up. Pro: standard rack to 4 inches, mostly smaller. (FA: Steve Risse, Donna McBain 1988)

North Early Winters Spire

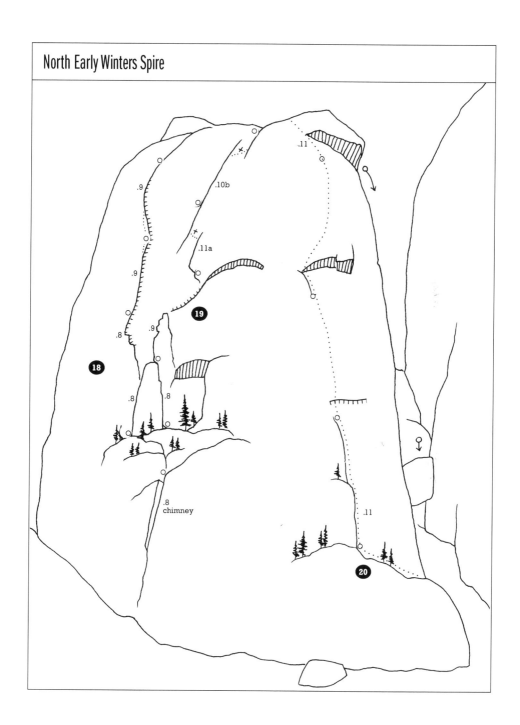

SOUTH EARLY WINTERS SPIRE

South Early Winters Spire, situated at the south end of the Liberty Bell massif, is the highest and most impressive summit in the area. Its south face and east buttress are equally impressive, and offer several difficult routes. The first-ascent party mistook South Early Winters Spire for Liberty Bell, an understandable mistake since it is the highest of the group at 7,807 feet. Descents may be made via downclimbing and rappelling the *Southwest Couloir* route, which has loose rock and snow in early season, and just loose rock in late season. Many climbers prefer descending the *South Arête* route, which is mostly Class 3 and 4 with a few short steps that must be rappelled or downclimbed, although that route is often crowded, leading to delays.

21. Northwest Face (III, 5.11a) ★★ A fine route climbing a continuous crack line directly through the overhangs on the steep Northwest Face. The route is most easily located as the only feasible-looking crack line up the imposing Northwest Face.

Climb a left-facing corner, then continue up the thin crack past a small roof (crux). Easier cracks and corners lead right and up to the big ledge below the Boving Roofs. Jam and layback around the roofs (5.10c), then continue up easier cracks to the top of the Dolphin. Continue as for *Southwest Rib* to the top. Alternative finishes include the 5.10 chimney of *West Face* on the left or via *Southwest Rib* on the right. Pro: to 3 inches. (FFA: Paul Boving, Matt Kerns 1977)

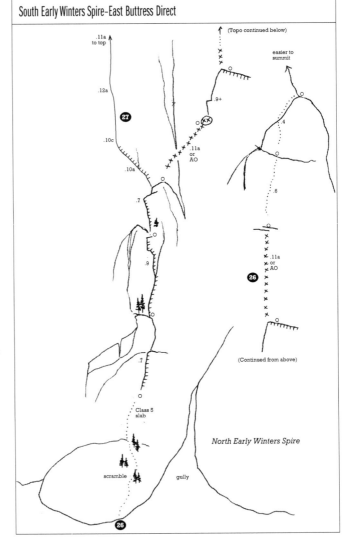

South Early Winters Spire-East Buttress Direct

South Early Winters Spire-East Side

false summit

26

.11 bolt ladder or aid

27

.12a

rod

.11 bolt ladder or aid

North Early Winters Spire

24

25

26

South Early Winters Spire—West Side

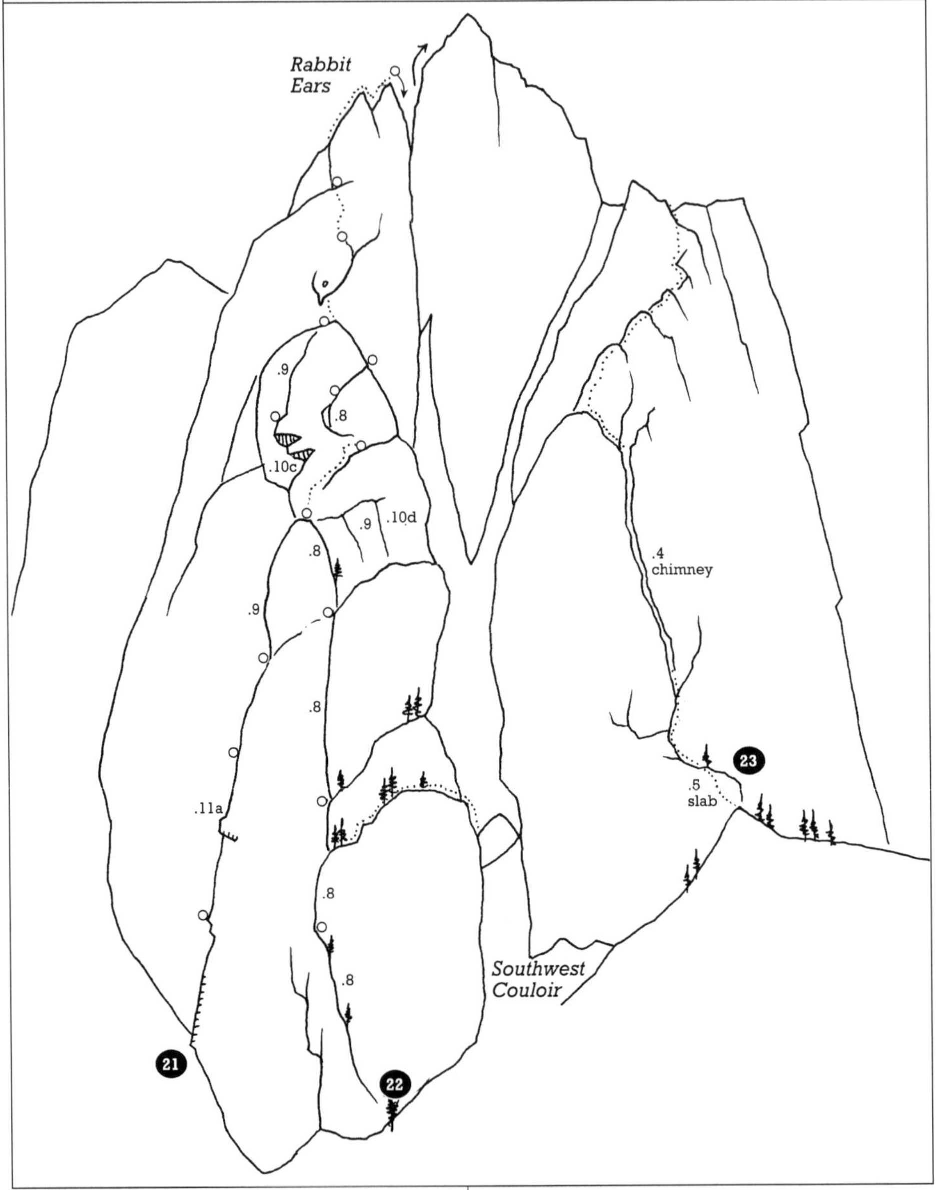

22. Southwest Rib (II, 5.8) ★★★ A popular crack route on the buttress left of the Southwest Couloir. Two starts are possible. A direct start begins from the big, split-tipped larch tree standing alone at the base of the wall, from where a scramble up slabs leads to two 5.8 crack pitches that gain a ledge below a third 5.8 crack. Another approach is to ascend the couloir past the chockstone, then traverse left on tree-grown ledges, downclimbing several steep steps to reach the base of the third pitch. Continue up the superb 5.8 crack pitch, then a second shorter crack or one of the 5.9 or 5.10d variations up the headwall just right, until directly below the Boving Roofs. Traverse right and up on slabby rock, from where slabby climbing rightward leads to a headwall right of the roofs. Continue via the famed Bear Hug pitch; layback up to the parallel wide cracks (5.8), after which easier ramps lead right and up to the top of the Dolphin. From there, slabs and cracks lead over the Rabbit Ears to the summit. Pro: to 4 inches will suffice, including two #4 Camalots for the Bear Hug pitch. (FA: Don Anderson, Larry Scott 1964)

23. South Arête (III, 5.5) ★★★ The pronounced spur immediately right of the Southwest Couloir. One of the more popular routes on South Early Winters Spire, a modestly difficult, airy romp that makes a great introduction to alpine rock. Hike up to the ridge crest, then start up a clean slab below a gnarled tree just right of the arête proper to enter a chimney system. Climb the chimney and blocky ridge crest above, then on up to the summit. Mostly Class 3 and 4, with a few short, steep walls and an exposed slab/hand traverse higher up. Referred to as a scrambling route by some, but has a few Class 5 sections. Unfortunately, this route can be overcrowded, making it difficult for climbers ascending and descending. Descending the Southwest Couloir is an option, although it is loose, blocky, and may involve exposed climbing on snow or ice depending on the season and time of day. Pro: to 3 inches. (FA: Fred and Helmy Beckey 1942)

24. The Passenger (IV, 5.12a) ★★★ A seven-pitch route up the southeast face of South Early Winters Spire, regarded as one of the highest quality alpine rock routes in the area. Approach from the base of the *South Arête*, scrambling (Class 3-ish; wear your rock shoes). Follow the base until forced away from the wall down a gully and across broken rock, aiming for the big roof on the left side of the face. A ledge leads to a corner below the roof. The first pitch climbs up to and around the roof on the left. Continue up cracks (including a stellar finger crack on pitch 3), then angle left across a slab to the crux (5.12 boulder problem), before cutting back right to a crack system that continues to the top. A loose block has been reported in the awkward chimney at the end of pitch four. Not as many bolts as *The Hitchhiker*, giving it a more serious, committing, alpine flavor. Don't let the boulder problem crux stop you from enjoying an otherwise stellar crack route; pull past it to make the route 5.11c A0. Longer pitches can be broken up with intermediate belays. Descend the *South Arête*. Pro: standard rack plus double sizes 2-3 inches; slings for rope drag.

25. The Hitchhiker (IV, 5.11b) ★★★ Twin of *The Passenger*, closely paralleling it on the right. This is mostly bolted, making it more of a sport route with some trad climbing mixed in, but just as high quality. Approach as for *The Passenger*, but start farther right in a left-facing, thin, bolted corner crack. From here, route-finding is not difficult; just keep following the bolts and obvious crack systems. Critics of the route claim it is overbolted, but don't let that stop you—just bring more quickdraws than you might think you need. Descend the *South Arête*. Pro: many quickdraws; standard rack to 4 inches; a double rack has been suggested but some think it's too much. (FA: Bryan Burdo, Scott Johnson 2007)

26. East Buttress Direct (IV, 5.11a or 5.9+ A0) ★★★ An imposing route up the striking

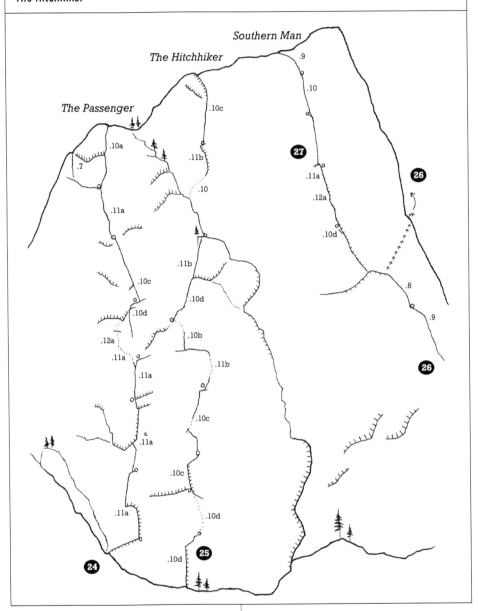

Southern Man

The Hitchhiker

The Passenger

.9

.10

.10c

27

26

.11a

.12a

.11b

.10a

.7

.10d

.11a

.8

.9

.10

.11b

.10d

.10c

.10d

.10b

26

.12a

.11a

.11a

.11b

.10c

.11a

.10c

.11a

.10d

.10d

24

25

east buttress of South Early Winters Spire, which surprisingly goes free at a fairly moderate grade. Climb slabs from the toe of the buttress to a dihedral system, easily identified by a large block high up. Pass the block on the left side to reach a ledge, then follow a bolt ladder right (5.11a or A0), crossing the ridge crest, where another bolt ladder (also 5.11a or A0) and crack systems continue to the top. If you aid the bolt ladders, it's 5.9+

Andy Hanneman on *The Hitchhiker* (5.11), South Early Winters Spire, Washington Pass

MARK GUNLOGSON/MOUNTAIN MADNESS

A0. Pro: to 4 inches; lots of quickdraws.
(FA: Fred Beckey, Doug Leen 1968)

27. The Southern Man (IV, 5.12a) ★★★ A
variation finish to *East Buttress Direct*, going
left at the bolt ladder and climbing a continuous, steep corner/crack system up the
headwall. The first pitch off the bolt ladder is
nondescript 5.10 climbing, but once on the
headwall pitches it's pretty much straight up
to the top. Mostly thin, sustained climbing
with some cruxes up to 5.11+. There are
no set belays or anchors, and in general the
route is a serious traditional alpine rock outing. Pro: same as for *East Buttress Direct*, plus
multiple thin and finger-size nuts and cams.

NEWHALEM

Climbers driving up WA 20 toward Washington Pass have no doubt noticed the
many steep cliffs in the vicinity of the town
of Newhalem and along the Skagit River
Gorge. There has been quite a bit of development on a few of the gneiss cliffs here,
although access problems have limited route
development. There are currently about two
dozen sport routes in the 5.9 to 5.13 range
and twice as many boulder problems in the
area—and potential for many, many more
routes. An online guide to routes on Ryan's
Wall, one of the developed cliffs, is available on Mountain Project. There are several
more areas under development, but access
issues have not been fully resolved so they
are not included in this guide.

MAZAMA

Mazama is a quiet mountain town located just off WA 20, tucked into the upper reaches of the Methow River Valley about 20 miles east of Washington Pass. Thanks to the development of a few roadside crags, Mazama is also one of the newest sport climbing destinations in Washington, although as a destination it is usually visited by climbers rained off their routes at Washington Pass. Mazama has abundant unclimbed rock, and will no doubt continue to be developed by sport climbers as areas closer to Seattle and Spokane are climbed out.

Type of climbing: Mazama's rocks offer several dozen sport routes and a few traditional routes, mostly in the 5.8 to 5.11 range. The area is similar to Little Si and Exit 38, featuring Rhino rock at its finest (well, sort of). In addition to its dozens of sport routes, there is some good bouldering in the area.

Brief history of area: As with the other Rhino rock areas, Mazama's crags were developed almost entirely by Bryan Burdo. Of the fifty-six routes reported in *North Cascades Rock*, Burdo takes credit for all but four. Although the earliest routes were led in traditional style, the nature of the rock lent itself to rappel bolting, which has resulted in a variety of accessible sport climbs. Several new areas have been developed since the last edition of this guide, including several multi-pitch lines on Goat Wall and sport crags such as the Matrix and Prospector Crags.

Seasons and climate: The Methow's climate is similar to Leavenworth, in that the area lies just east of the Cascades, within a rain shadow, meaning it's often dry here when it's raining on the west side of the Cascades. The Methow River Valley is best known for its winter recreation opportunities, primarily cross-country skiing, and from November through February rock climbing is pretty much out. The rocks face southwest, and you might be able to climb a few routes on the sunniest of winter days, but the best climbing season is May through October. An easy indicator: When the North Cascades Highway is open, it's rock climbing season at Mazama.

For weather information, call The Mazama Store at (509) 996-2855.

Precautions and regulations: Aside from the usual eastern Washington critters (ticks, yellow jackets, and rattlesnakes), there's little to worry about at Mazama. If you need something to worry about, consider that grizzly bears are making a comeback in the North Cascades, and that cougars, known mostly for pouncing on pets and children, have attacked at least one stray climber. You're not likely to encounter any of these wild creatures at the cragging area. Watch out for deer, though; herds that migrate through the Methow Valley are a major hazard, and if you are driving before dawn or after dusk, slow down and keep a sharp eye out.

Mazama Vicinity Map

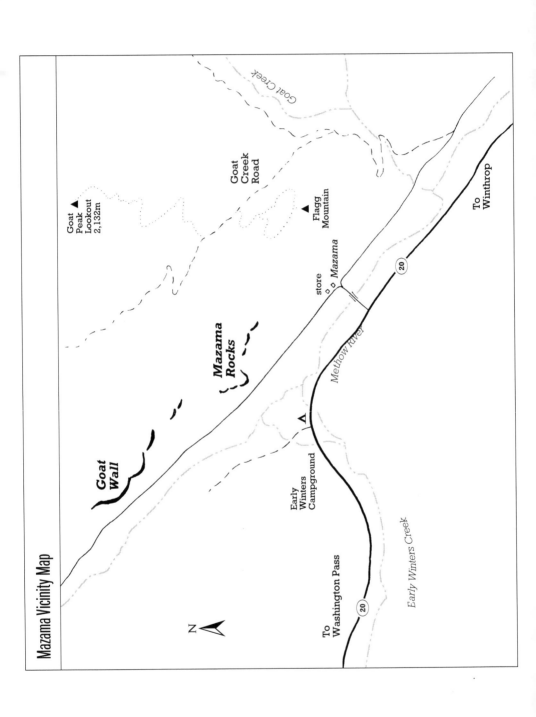

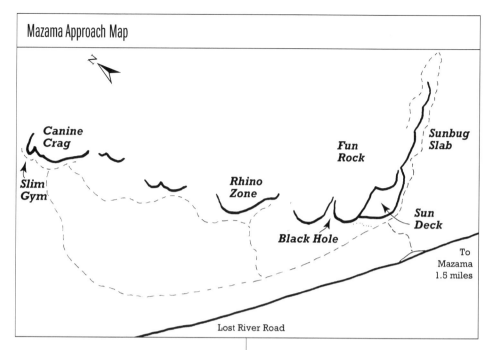

Mazama Approach Map

Canine Crag

Slim Gym

Rhino Zone

Fun Rock

Sunbug Slab

Black Hole

Sun Deck

To Mazama 1.5 miles

Lost River Road

Actually, loose rock is the major concern at Mazama. Although most of the routes are well cleaned, some still have loose holds. Helmets are recommended, especially for belayers. Venturing above the anchors is not recommended, due to very loose rock atop several crags.

Access to the rocks is across private property. Granted, it's only a stone's throw from the road to the rocks, but that airspace—and the land beneath it—is privately owned. The owner presently permits access to the rocks, but owners change, and so do their minds, so to ensure continued access climbers must be on their best behavior.

Parking can be a problem here, especially on spring and summer weekends. There is no parking area near the crags, so parking alongside the road must suffice. Do your best to find a spot where you can get your car completely off the paved road and at least 5 feet back from driveway entrances. There are no toilets, so please try to go where no man or woman has gone before,

well away from the rocks, and don't leave a mess for others to find. The best option is to just hold it until you can get to a bathroom only a few minutes down the road.

Gear and other considerations: Most of Mazama's routes are sport routes, so if all you remembered to bring was a rack of quickdraws, you'll have plenty to keep you busy. Very few routes require gear, and for those that do you should bring a small but varied selection including wired nuts and cams up to 3 inches. Most of the routes top out at chain anchors 80 feet up or less, so a 50-meter rope will suffice for nearly all routes. Helmets are recommended, particularly for belayers, since the rock is not entirely trustworthy on most routes.

Camping and accommodations: There are several campgrounds in the vicinity of Mazama, but climbers usually bivouac. Private property along the Lost River Road makes bivouacking there a bad idea, but if you continue far enough up the road, or head up Goat Creek Road a bit, you'll no doubt find a decent bivy site. Please keep a low profile and mind your manners, so we may continue to enjoy no-fee camping in this area.

Mazama has a few amenities. Mazama Store, which is passed as you turn up Lost River Road toward the crags, offers groceries, clothes, books, and hot soup and coffee. Mazama Mountaineering, two doors down from the store, has gear and offers guiding and instruction. North Cascades Basecamp, a family-style inn located just up Lost River Road from the rocks, makes a great base camp for a climbing weekend. The nearest "big town" is Winthrop, 14 miles south on Highway 20.

Emergency services: In case of emergency, dial 911.

Other guidebooks: Bryan Burdo's guide, *Mazama Rock: A Vertical Paradise* (2008), is out of print, but may be reprinted or updated by 2019. Burdo's *North Cascades Rock*. A new Burdo guide to Mazama that will include dozens of new routes is reported to be in the works. There is also a mini-guide to the Matrix (Gabe Grayum, Bryan Burdo, Matrix & Europa) available through Goat's Beard Mountain Supplies.

Finding the crags: If you are coming from eastern Washington, head for Wenatchee or Okanogan. From Wenatchee, head north on US 97 to Chelan and continue north to Pateros, then head northeast on WA 153. Follow WA 20 through Twisp and Winthrop, along the Methow River all the way to Mazama. From Okanogan, head west on WA 20 to Mazama. If you are coming from western Washington, follow I-5 to WA 20, then head east along the North Cascades Highway over Rainy Pass and Washington Pass and down into the Methow Valley to Mazama, which is 0.5 mile off the highway. Once in town, take a left onto Lost River Road and continue 1.5 miles to the rocks, which are more than obvious. A short trail leads up to the toe of Fun Rock.

FUN ROCK

Fun Rock is the first roadside crag you come to as you drive northwest from Mazama, 1.5 miles past the Mazama Store, and about 100 feet off the road on the right. It presently has several dozen bolted routes, many of which are not included here. It has been suggested that Fun Rock is overbolted, which it may be, but it still has some fun routes. A short trail leads from the road to the base of Fun Rock; from there trails lead in both directions along the base of the crag. The routes are listed from the toe of Fun Rock, first right, then left as you encounter them when approaching via the trail. Most routes have descent anchors at the top.

Sunbug Slab Area

The slabby right side of the crag is known as Sunbug Slab. Approach via the right-hand fork, along the base of the slabs. You can either rappel, lower off, or walk off the routes on the far right side of Fun Rock.

1. Pygmalion (5.8) The first route encountered as you hike up the trail toward Sunbug Slab, skirting left around the double roofs at the toe of Fun Rock, then climbing a slab to anchors atop the roofs. Blocky, but solid enough. Pro: quickdraws.

2. Steppenruf (5.10b) ★ Turn the double roofs on the right side, starting just left of a chimney, and finish up a slab to anchors. Pro: quickdraws.

3. Drive-By Nose Job (5.8) ★ The slabby arête just up and right from the roofs. Start via the route of your choice to get to the Sun Deck, then traverse 10 feet right on polished rock, under the roof, then up the groove just right of the arête. Pro: quickdraws.

4. Unnamed (5.10d) ★ A clean, edgy slab pitch immediately right of the chimney right of *Steppenruf*. Finish at the anchors below *Nose Job,* or continue up that route to its anchors. Pro: quickdraws.

5. Snakefingers (5.10a) ★ A widening crack about 15 feet right of the chimney, passing a bolt then continuing up the blocky crack to anchors. Pro: to 2 inches.

6. Cream (5.9) ★ A slabby, two-pitch venture beginning about 30 feet right of the aforementioned cracks. The first pitch climbs an edgy, bolted slab curving left to a sloping shelf and anchors (5.7), from where you can continue up the more difficult headwall to the top. Pro: quickdraws.

7. Plethora (5.10b) ★★ A very popular sport route up the left edge of Sunbug Slab, starting from a ledge. The rock is flaky at the start, and the first bolt is far enough off the deck that if a hold broke you could pull your belayer off the ledge, so stick clip or forego a belay to the first bolt, even though it's easy. Pro: quickdraws.

8. Gridlock (5.10c) ★ The next sport route right of *Plethora,* with a mildly runout finish up the steep, blocky headwall. The first bolt is 20 feet up; it's easy getting there, but the rock on the lower part of the slab is flaky, so climb carefully. A 5.10d variation angles left near the top. Pro: quickdraws.

9. Boltergeist (5.8) ★ A blocky face pitch between the so-called "cracks" on the right side of Sunbug Slab, about 30 feet right of *Gridlock.* Much better than it looks. Pro: quickdraws.

10. Bolterheist (5.7) ★ The rightmost bolted route on Fun Rock, climbing a blocky wall. Much better than it looks. Pro: quickdraws.

Fun Rock

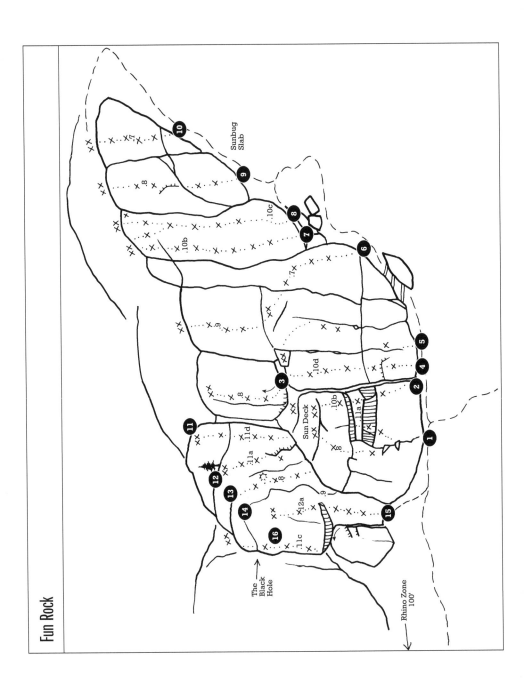

Sun Deck Area

The Sun Deck is the low-angled slab in the center of the formation, so named because of its full-on sun exposure. An easy Class 5 crack leads up to the Sun Deck on the left to access the routes on the slab, a few of which are of surprisingly good quality.

11. Hillbilly Surprise (5.11d) ★ Immediately left of the anchors below the *Nose Job* arête is this pockmarked, bolted slab leading past a horizontal crack and up a bulging headwall. Pro: quickdraws.

12. Fractured Fairy Tales (5.11a) ★ About 10 feet down and left of *Hillbilly Surprise* is this bolted thin crack starting just left of a left-facing corner and continuing up a clean slab to the top. Pro: quickdraws.

13. Unnamed (5.8) ★ A bolted slab pitch passing the left side of a small, shallow cave and leading to a stubby pine tree about 50 feet above. Pro: quickdraws.

14. Crack of the Bat (5.9) ★ The obvious curvy crack system on the prow left of the Sun Deck. Flared and overhanging at the start, slabby after that. Pro: to 3 inches.

15. Arapilesian Dog (5.12a) ★★★ The obvious sport route on the left side of Fun Rock, climbing white- and orange-streaked rock up a bulging headwall, passing five bolts. One of the hardest routes on Fun Rock, and generally regarded as the best hard sport route at Mazama. Pro: quickdraws.

16. They Might Be Giants (5.11c) ★ The leftmost arête of Fun Rock. Approach via a scree gully leading to the Black Hole (a narrow gully on the far left side of Fun Rock), about 75 feet up from the trail. Pro: quickdraws.

THE RHINO ZONE

As you hike left along the trail past Fun Rock, you enter the Rhino Zone, which is really just a small crag with a few routes, most of which are very short. This crag is partially shaded in the afternoon.

17. Rhinovirus (5.10b) ★ This route begins up a right-leading ramp, then angles left across a short, steep wall to a sloping ledge and up the blocky wall above. Rope drag might be a problem if you don't bring some long slings. Pro: quickdraws.

18. Rhinoplasty (5.10d) ★★ The arête left of the *Sticks and Stones* crack (5.10a) leads past a roof to anchors. Pro: quickdraws.

The Rhino Zone

CANINE CRAG

At the far left end of the Mazama rocks is Canine Crag, featuring a monstrous roof dubbed "The Woof," which serves as an umbrella for a few routes. Canine Crag presently has fifteen reported routes in the 5.8 to 5.12 range, with several upper-end ventures and very little in the moderate grades. The routes all get lots of stars in *North Cascades Rock,* but at first glance they look flaky and loose. More than one route on Canine Crag has glue-reinforced holds, which should not surprise you once you've seen it. Because of loose rock, it is recommended that you don't venture above the anchors; at the very least, you'd probably knock something off and hit your belayer.

The slab routes below the big roof are 5.8 and 5.9, and are almost always dry. The routes turning the roof range from 5.12a

to 5.12d, but are marred (or improved, depending on how you feel about this issue) by glue-reinforced holds. The routes are described from right to left as they are encountered on the approach. Descend from anchors.

19. Margin of Air (5.12a) ★ The rightmost route on Canine Crag, climbing up slabby rock to anchors below the big roof (5.8 to here), then up the right edge of the roof to anchors. Pro: quickdraws.

20. Animal Control (5.12b) ★ The next route to the left, climbing up slabs to anchors below the roof (5.9 to here), then right out the roof following a crack to anchors at the right edge of the lip. Pro: quickdraws.

21. Out of Control (5.12c) ★ A direct finish variation of *Animal Control,* cranking straight up and over the roof. Popular because it's

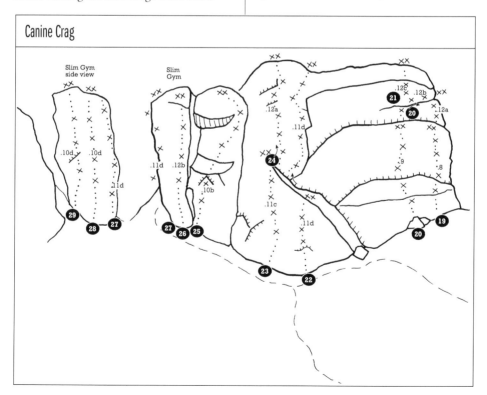

the hardest route in the area so far, and because it appears on the cover of *North Cascades Rock.* Pro: quickdraws.

22. Bigwig (5.11d) ★★ The central route on Canine Crag, climbing the blocky arête left of The Woof. It looks like choss and has flaky rock, but is highly regarded by Mazama devotees. Pro: quickdraws; long slings to reduce rope drag.

23. Doggy Stylee (5.11c) ★ A steep sport route climbing the lower wall, about 20 feet left of *Bigwig,* leading to anchors 40 feet up. Pro: quickdraws.

24. Down Boy (5.12a) ★ A continuation of *Doggy Stylee,* leading up a steep face left of the arête. Pro: quickdraws.

25. Simon Says (5.10b) ★ A weird-looking route climbing a colorful, blocky slab just right of the Slim Gym pillar and angling right around a bulging roof to anchors. Pro: quickdraws.

At the far left end of Canine Crag is the Slim Gym, a big fin of relatively solid rock featuring a short handful of recommended sport routes in the hard 5.10 to 5.12 range.

26. Beefcake Pantyhose (5.12b) ★ The rightmost arête of the Slim Gym, immediately left of *Simon Says.* Pro: quickdraws.

27. Yello (5.11d) ★ The obvious yellow-orange lichen-streaked arête on the left side of the Slim Gym. Stick clipping the second bolt is recommended. Pro: quickdraws.

28. Everyday Nirvana (5.10d) ★★ The first sport route left and up the gully from the *Yello* arête. Considered the best route on the Slim Gym. Pro: quickdraws.

29. Hatful of Heaven (5.10d) ★ The second sport route left and up the gully from the *Yello* arête. Pro: quickdraws.

GOAT WALL

Goat Wall is the huge, slabby buttress rising off in the distance from Mazama, about a mile up Methow Valley from Fun Rock. Like some of the metavolcanic walls near North Bend, Goat Wall has friable rock in abundance, but there are quite a few routes here now, up to sixteen pitches in length, at grades from 5.9 to 5.11. Goat Wall has become a modestly popular objective for those looking for a bit more exposure than can be found at Fun Rock, and especially for climbers escaping from bad weather at Washington Pass. A few of the better quality routes are included here. The topos included here are fairly simple, but route information and topos can be downloaded fairly easily by anyone familiar with the term Google, and a review of online photos will help you spot key features on the approach. The Mazama climbing shop has detailed topos available as well, so do your homework so you don't get lost up there.

A 60-meter rope and a 12 to 16 quickdraws will suffice for most routes, but a 70-meter rope is recommended since some routes are set up for longer single-rope rappels. Bring some alpine draws and long slings to help reduce rope drag or to tie off trees for belays in a few places. Helmets are highly recommended, especially if there are climbers or goats above you, as the rock is loose in places and handfuls can and do pull off or get kicked off. Each route has solid rappel anchors, and although a single rope will get you down most routes, double ropes will expedite rappel descents. There have been several rappelling fatalities on Goat Wall; be sure to tie knots in the ends of your ropes and double-check your rappel setup. Tandem rappels are ill advised; you might save time, but you also might get killed. Since these are long routes, be prepared for

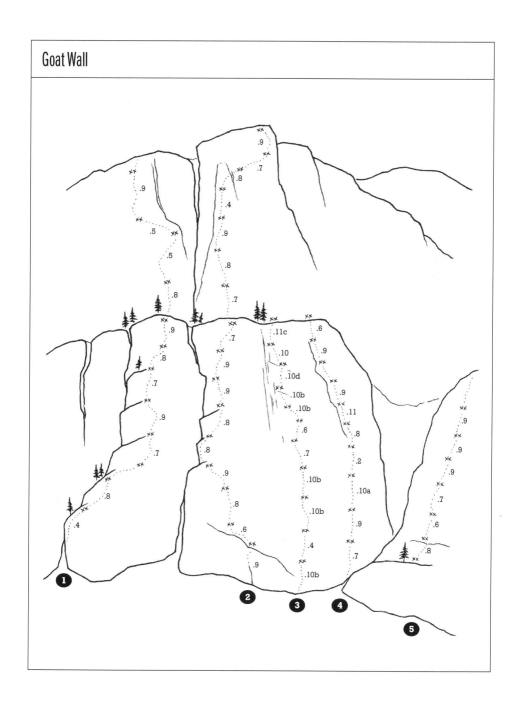

Goat Wall

weather changes and don't start up too late in the day. Hiking off the backside is an option, made easier if you have a shuttle car waiting for you.

1. Prime Rib of Goat (III, 5.9) ★ A popular

eleven-pitch 5.8+ sport route on the left side of Goat Wall. Drive Lost River Road north from Mazama 3.1 miles to the swimming hole parking area. Hike 100 meters up the road to the approach trail, then climb the trail and talus slopes, angling left to the foot of a buttress just south of Goat Creek. Start up the buttress, following the bolts, occasionally belaying from a tree, sometimes moving a belay. Most parties rappel; for some reason there are a lot of rappelling accidents on this route, so be careful! Rated 5.9 in some guides but considered "soft" for the grade. Pro: quickdraws.

2. Flyboys (IV, 5.9) ★★ A sixteen-pitch 5.9

sport route up the middle section of Goat Wall. From the swimming hole parking area, hike south on the road for about 200 feet to the approach trail, which trends left toward the wall. A talus gully with cairns leads to the base of the route. The route starts in a blocky V-slot next to a large dead tree. From there, as one climber put it, "Follow the trail of 275 shiny bolts to the top!" Route-finding is not a problem. Rappel via anchors parallel to the route, taking care not to knock rocks loose on climbers below. Pro: quickdraws.

3. Restless Natives (III, 5.11c) ★★ A ten-

pitch sport route up the prominent white streak in the middle of the wall. Approach as for *Flyboys*, but trend right on the approach trail as you near the wall, angling up talus to a large tree near the base of the water streaks. Route-finding is easy; just clip your way up the wall, which is composed of limestone-like lime-silicate rock. The first eight pitches make for a popular 5.10b route; the last two pitches are 5.10d and 5.11c respectively, unless you yard on bolts to get past the hard parts. Pro: quickdraws.

4. Sisyphus (III, 5.11a) ★★ A ten-pitch 5.11a

sport route up the Goat Wall. The approach trail starts 2.9 miles from Mazama, just right of a road sign indicating curves ahead. Go left at double cairns and aim for a lone ponderosa pine tree visible at the base of the wall. Skirt around cliffs to the left and scramble right up the ramp until you see a fixed rope that marks the start of the route. Mostly 5.8 to 5.10, slabby to steep, with a crux sixth pitch reported by some as "soft" 5.11a, and some scrambling sections. Rappel from anchors. Pro: quickdraws.

5. Methow Inspiration Route (II, 5.9) ★

The original Goat Wall route, climbing five pitches up the slabby buttress right of the *Restless Natives* wall. Approach via a climbers' trail that starts 2.9 miles up the road from the Mazama turnoff. The route starts from a shelf with a prominent fir tree. Scramble up to the tree then find the anchor bolt just up from the tree and start climbing, connecting the bolts up the wall. The final two pitches are hardest. On the last pitch, stay right of the chossy gully, which is easy but nightmarishly loose. Has cleaned up nicely, and is considered better and a little more representative of the 5.9 grade than *Prime Rib*. Rappel the route. Pro: quickdraws.

PROSPECTOR CRAGS

Prospector Crags is a cliff band located northwest of Goat Wall. It has some of the best rock in the Mazama area, featuring sharply featured climbing on the blocky, square-cut, lime-silicate rock. The walls are south-facing, making them warm on cool days and insufferably hot on hot days. To get there, follow Lost River Road to where it turns to gravel; cross the river and continue up the gravel road through a series of curves, after which you should see the cliffs on the right. Park at a turnout on the south shoulder just past the clearing where you see the cliffs, then find the approach trail marked by a cairn. If there is a sign-in box, please sign in. If you don't have or can't get a copy of the Mazama Rock guide, several routes in the 5.7 to 5.11 range are described in detail on Mountain Project.

THE MATRIX & EUROPA

The Matrix and Europa are new Mazama crags. The Matrix is located about 1.5 miles south of Mazama, and has more than sixty developed sport routes (and a few trad routes) in the 5.6 to 5.11 range. Europa is a crag on Goat Wall between *Prime Rib of Goat* and *Fire Wall*, which has more than forty reported routes up to 5.12 in difficulty. A guidebook to the Matrix and Europa is available from Goat's Beard Mountain Supplies. Some route information is available on Mountain Project.

Greg Collum on *Kite Flying Blind* (5.11b), The Country, Index Lower Town Wall

LARRY KEMP COLLECTION

BIBLIOGRAPHY AND SELECTED REFERENCES

(Most current or recommended "best" local guidebook denoted by "★".)

Beckey, Fred. *Cascade Alpine Guide*. Seattle: The Mountaineers, 1996.

———. *Darrington & Index Rock Climbing Guide*. Seattle: The Mountaineers, 1976.

Bland, Marty. ★ *Inland Northwest Rock Climbs*. Spokane, 2001.

Boyle, Dale. *Swauk Pinnacles: A climbers' guide*. Bremerton: Sandstone Press, 1996.

Brooks, Don, and Rich Carlstad. *Index and Leavenworth*. Mount Vernon: Signpost Publications, 1976.

Brooks, Don, and David Whitelaw. *Washington Rock*. Seattle: The Mountaineers, 1982.

Bruce, Garth. *Exit 32 Rock Climbing Guide*. North Bend: Free Solo Publishing, 2003.

———. *Exit 38 Rock Climbing Guide,* 2nd ed. North Bend: Free Solo Publishing, 2006.

Burdo, Bryan. *Exit 32: North Bend Rock*. Seattle: Technorigine Productions, 1992.

———. *Exit 38: A Guide to North Bend Sport Climbing (including North Fork)*. Seattle: Rhinotopia Productions, 1996.

———. *North Cascades Rock*. Seattle: Rhinotopia Productions, 1996.

———. "North Fork, Little Si and Deception Crags." *Rock & Ice Magazine,* no. 62 (1994).

Burns, Dane, and Bob Loomis. *Minnehaha Guide to Selected Routes*. 1980.

Christensen, Matt, and Holli Christensen. *Tieton Rock*. Yakima: The Wilderness Athlete, 1989.

Climbing magazine. Issue #54 ("Basecamp" report on Leavenworth); Issue #63 ("Basecamp" report on Leavenworth); Issue #65 ("Basecamp" reports on Leavenworth, Index); Issue #84 ("Basecamp" reports on Index, Leavenworth; Leavenworth article); Issue #88 ("Basecamp" reports on Index, Leavenworth); Issue #90 (Index Town Walls article); Issue #92 (Icicle Creek Canyon article); Issue #93 ("Basecamp" reports on Index, Leavenworth); Issue #98 ("Basecamp" reports on Index, Snoqualmie Pass); Issue #102 ("Basecamp" articles on Inland Northwest areas including Spokane and Vantage and "Boat Climbing" article including Banks Lake); Issue #108 ("Basecamp" report on Index); Issue #110 ("Basecamp" reports on Tieton River Canyon, Index, Spokane); Issue #114 ("Basecamp" report on Swauk Pinnacles); Issue #117 ("Basecamp" reports on Index, Vantage); Issue #121 ("Basecamp" report on Index); Issue #122 (Basecamp report on Tieton River Canyon); Issue #128 (Index update by Larry Kemp); Issue #129 (mention of reported FFA of *Liberty Crack* route); Issue #144 (North Cascades article by Fletcher Taylor).

Cramer, Darryl. *Sky Valley Rock*. Seattle: Sky Valley Press, 2000.

Cummins, Clint. *Index Town Wall Climbing Guide*. Self-published, 1994.

Eminger, John, and John Kittle. *The Washington Desert.* Serac International Press, 1991.

Ford, Marlene, and Jim Yoder. ★ *Frenchman Coulee.* Eatonville: HomePress Publishers, 2008.

———. *Frenchman Coulee: A Rock Climber's Guide.* Puyallup: HomePress Publishers, 1997.

———. *Rock Climber's Guide to Fossil Rock.* Tacoma: HomePress, 1994. Updated version 1996.

———. ★ *Tieton River Rocks.* Eatonville: HomePress Publishers, 2004.

_____. ★ *Rock Climber's Guide to Fossil Rock.* Puyallup: HomePress, 1996.

Henrie, Jason. *A Rock Climber's Guide to Bellingham Rock!* Self-published, 1997.

Henson, Aaron; Robert Order; Eric Barrett; Jon Jonckers. ★ *Climbing the Rocks of Sharon.* Spokane: Mountain Gear, 2012.

Herrington, Blake. ★ *Cascades Rock: 160 Best Multipitch Climbs of All Grades.* 2016.

Hicks, Kurt. ★ *Snoqualmie Rock.* North Bend: Obvious Gully Press, 2018.

Kloke, Dallas. ★ *Rockin' on the Rock! A Guide to Mount Erie Rock Climbing,* 2nd ed. Anacortes: Premier Graphics, 2013.

Kramar, Viktor. ★ *Leavenworth Rock,* 4th ed. Self-published, 2018.

La Belle, Rick. ★ *Rock Climbs of Central Washington.* Spokane Valley: Mountain Gear, Inc., 2006.

Loomis, Robert D. *A Guide to Rock Climbing in the Spokane Area,* 3rd ed. Self-published, 1990.

Mountain (magazine). Issue #117 ("Ten Best Crags" article including Index Lower Town Wall); Issue #125 (Index Town Wall Review article by Larry Kemp).

Nelson, Jim, and Peter Potterfield. *Selected Climbs of the Cascade Range.* Seattle: The Mountaineers, 1994.

Nicholson, Ian. ★ *Washington Pass Climbing.* Supertopo, 2012.

Olson, Tim J. ★ *Portland Rock Climbs: To the Edge and Beyond,* 4th ed. Portland: Tim J. Olson, 2016.

———. Beacon Rock Topographic Resource Map. Portland: http://www.portlandrockclimbs .com/gorge-rock-climbs/beacon-rock.htm.

Perkins, Matt. ★ Darrington rock climbing website. http://www.mattsea.com/darr.

Rock & Ice (Magazine). Issue #33 ("Route of the Month" article about *Outer Space,* Snow Creek Wall); Issue #62 ("Mini-Guide" to North Bend Areas by Bryan Burdo); Issue #67 ("Classics" article by Vance Atkins about *On Line,* Static Point); Issue #71 ("Hard Cracks" article reference to *City Park,* Index).

Skagit Mountain Rescue Unit. *Climbing Guide to Mount Erie.* Self-published, 1995.

Smoot, Jeff. *Rock Climbing Washington,* 2nd ed. FalconGuides; 2009.

Smoot, Jeff, and Darryl Cramer. *Index Town Walls: A Guide to Rock Climbs including Stevens Pass.* Seattle: Sky Valley Publications, 1985.

Speaker, Jim. *Spokane Rock Climbs.* Spokane: Stone Publishing and Graphic Design, 1996.

Stanley, Matt. *Vantage Rock.* Ellensburg: AdVantage Press, 1995.

Van Biene, Matty, and Chris Kalman. ★ *The Index Town Walls: A Guide to Washington's Finest Crag.* Boulder: Sharp End Publishing, 2017.

Washington Mountain Alliance. *Traveler's Guide, Puget Sound.* Seattle: Washington Mountain Alliance, 1999.

Whitelaw, David. *Weekend Rock.* Seattle: The Mountaineers, 2005.

———. *Private Dancer.* Alaska: Tundra Press, 1985.

Workman, Brandon. *Skagit Valley Crags: A Climber's Guide.* Self-published, 2013.

APPENDIX

LAND MANAGERS

This is not a complete list of all land management agencies governing Washington rock climbing areas. Some of these agencies do not manage any nearby climbing areas but may provide valuable information, including current weather, road, trail, and access information. Current land manager contact information for all Washington climbing areas can be found on the Washington Climbers Coalition website at washingtonclimbers.org.

FOREST SERVICE AND NATIONAL PARK OFFICES

Colville National Forest

(Marcus and China Bend)
Colville Ranger District
765 South Main St.
Colville, WA 99114
(509) 684-7000

Mt. Baker Ranger District

(Mount Baker Rocks)
810 WA 20
Sedro Woolley, WA 98284
(360) 856-5700

Mt. Baker-Snoqualmie National Forest

(Darrington Areas)
Darrington Ranger District
1405 Emmens St.
Darrington, WA 98241
(360) 436-1155

Mt. Baker-Snoqualmie National Forest

(Index and Stevens Pass Areas)
Skykomish Ranger District
74920 NE Stevens Pass Hwy.
Skykomish, WA 98288
(360) 677-2414

Mt. Baker-Snoqualmie National Forest

(North Bend Areas)
North Bend Ranger District
902 SE North Bend Way, Building 1
North Bend, WA 98045
(425) 888-1421

North Cascades National Park

(Washington Pass Areas)
Headquarters Information Office
810 WA 20
Sedro Woolley, WA 98284
(360) 854-7200 or 7246

Wilderness Information Center

(360) 856-1934

Okanogan-Wenatchee National Forest

(Washington Pass Areas)
Methow Valley Ranger District
24 West Chewuch
Winthrop, WA 98862
(509) 996-4000

Okanogan-Wenatchee National Forest

(Leavenworth Areas)
Leavenworth Ranger District
600 Sherbourne
Leavenworth, WA 98826
(509) 548-2550

Okanogan-Wenatchee National Forest

(Tieton Areas)
Naches Ranger District
12037 WA 12
Naches, WA 98937
(509) 653-1401

WASHINGTON STATE PARKS
General Information Center

(360) 902-8844

Camping reservations: (888) 226-7688

infocent@parks.wa.gov

Beacon Rock State Park

(Beacon Rock)

34841 WA 14

Skamania, WA 98648

(509) 427-8265

Iron Horse State Park

(Exit 38)

150 Lake Easton State Park Rd.

North Bend, WA 98045

(509) 626-2230

Larrabee State Park

(Bellingham Area)

245 Chuckanut Dr.

Bellingham, WA 98226

(360) 676-2093

Riverside State Park

(Deep Creek)

4427 North Aubrey L. White Pkwy.

Spokane, WA 99205

(509) 456-3964

or

9711 West Charles

Nine Mile Falls, WA 99026

(509) 465-5064

Steamboat Rock State Park

(Banks Lake)

51052 WA 155

Electric City, WA 99123

(509) 633-1304

Wallace Falls State Park

(Index Town Walls–Local)

14503 Wallace Lake Rd.

Gold Bar, WA 98251

(360) 793-0420

Wenatchee Confluence State Park

(Peshastin Pinnacles)

333 Olds Station Rd.

Wenatchee, WA 98801-5938

(509) 664-6373

OTHER JURISDICTIONS
Wenberg County Park

(Index Town Walls–Regional)

15430 East Lake Goodwin Rd.

Stanwood, WA 98292

(360) 652-7417

Bureau of Land Management

Spokane District Office

1103 N. Fancher Rd.

Spokane, WA 99212-1275

(509) 536-1200

City of Anacortes Parks & Recreation

(Mount Erie)

Sixth & Q Streets

P.O. Box 547

Anacortes, WA 98221-0547

(360) 293-1918

Columbia Basin Wildlife Area

(Frenchman Coulee)

Road 3 NW

Quincy, WA 98848

(509) 765-6641

Washington Department of Natural Resources

(Tum Tum and Dishman)

Northeast Region Office

225 S. Silke Rd.

Colville, WA 99114

(509) 684-7474

Hutchinson Irrigation District No. 16

(Dishman)

618 N. Sargent Rd.

Spokane, WA 99212

(509) 926-4634

Mount Si Natural Resources Conservation Area
(Little Si)
Department of Natural Resources
South Puget Sound Region
950 Farman Ave. North
Enumclaw, WA 98022-9282
(206) 375-3558

Oak Creek Wildlife Area
(Lower Tieton Areas)
16601 WA 12
Naches, WA 98937
(509) 653-2390

Spokane County Parks & Recreation
(Minnehaha)
404 N. Havana St.
Spokane, WA 99202
(509) 456-4730

Washington Department of Natural Resources
Northwest Region
(Samish Wall and Julia's Outcrop)
919 N. Township St.
Sedro Woolley, WA 98284-9384
(360) 856-3500

PERMIT REQUIREMENTS

For current information regarding trailhead parking passes and other permit requirements for public lands included in this guide, or to obtain passes and permits, consult the following references:

Forest Service Recreation Pass website
https://www.fs.fed.us/main/r6/passes-permits

https://www.fs.fed.us/visit/passes-permits/recreation-fees-passes

https://www.fs.fed.us/visit/passes-permits

Washington Department of Fish and Wildlife Vehicle Use Permit website
https://wdfw.wa.gov/licensing/discoverpass

North Cascades National Park Backcountry Permit website
https://www.nps.gov/noca/planyourvisit/permits.htm

Washington State Parks
https://parks.state.wa.us/204/Passes-permits

INDEX

ABOUT THE AUTHOR

Jeff Smoot is a climber, hiker, author, and lawyer based in Seattle, Washington. He is the author of five other FalconGuides, including *Backpacking Washington's Alpine Lakes Wilderness, Hiking Washington's Alpine Lakes Wilderness, Adventure Guide to Mount Rainier, Climbing the Cascade Volcanoes,* and *Climbing Washington's Mountains.*